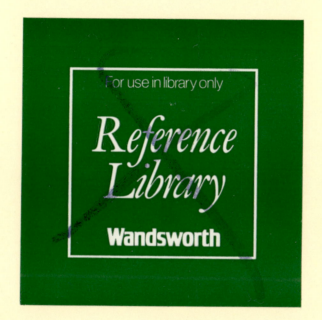

MEN OF VALOUR

MEN OF VALOUR

The Third Volume of the History of
The VIII King's Royal Irish Hussars

1927-1958

by

OLIVIA FITZROY

With a foreword by
H.R.H. THE DUKE OF EDINBURGH
Colonel of the Regiment

LIVERPOOL
1961

© OLIVIA FITZROY 1961

Made and Printed in Great Britain by
C. Tinling & Co. Ltd., Liverpool, London and Prescot

This book
is dedicated to
the
208 officers and men
of the
VIII King's Royal Irish Hussars
who gave up their lives in the
Second World War 1939–1945
and
Korea 1950–1951

'Arm yourselves, and be ye men of valour, and be in readiness for the conflict: for it is better for us to perish in battle than to look upon the outrage of our nation and our altars'

Antiphon for the Trinity-tide Magnificat

This third volume of the long history of the 8th King's Royal Irish Hussars opens in the winter of 1927 with the Regiment joining the British Army of the Rhine taking up quarters in a German Cavalry Barracks at Wiesbaden.   It ends with the 8th Hussars marching off the Parade Ground of another German Barracks thirty-one years later.

For three reasons only this volume is the most important in the whole history.   First, it covers the change from a horsed Cavalry Regiment to Motor Reconnaissance and eventually to Tanks. The conversion from horses to tanks was the most revolutionary change in land warfare since the invention of gun powder and probably the greatest strain the Regiment has had to bear.

Secondly, this story covers three utterly different and most recent campaigns the world has known.   The open spaces and great advances and retreats in North Africa, the invasion of Europe and the final battles in Germany and then, six years later, the bitter fighting in Korea.

Lastly, it tells of the amalgamation of the 8th King's Royal Irish Hussars with the 4th Queen's Own Hussars.

That is the end of this story but it is not the end of the Regiment because within a few minutes of it marching off the Parade Ground at Hohne on the 24th October, 1958 I watched it march on again, merged with the 4th Hussars, as The Queen's Royal Irish Hussars. The partnership is now complete and the new Regiment has more than succeeded in upholding the history and traditions of the 4th and 8th Hussars.

I know that all who read this book will recognize in it the real strength and value of the regimental system.   I also know that everyone connected with the 8th Hussars both in the past and in the future will have every reason to feel proud of this great Regiment.

28th June, 1960.

PREFACE

I STARTED to write this book many years ago with no clear conception of the work that lay before me. No clear conception of either the amount of work and length of time it would involve or of the kind of people I was writing about. It did not take more than the first few pages before they emerged, officers and men, as a united, dedicated company, whose own personal accounts of various major actions had to be carefully pruned lest their sense of humour should seem too ribald. They were men of whom I knew nothing and to whom I became, through diaries and letters personally attached. I even married one. Throughout the writing of the History their personalities emerged truly as men of valour of whom I was more than proud to write.

The many inaccuracies and inadequacies must be put down both to my own lack of knowledge of military affairs, and also to the fact that, if the book is ever to be published at all, at some stage there has to be an end to checking and correcting and re-writing. Another difficulty was the length of time that had elapsed since some of the events took place.

It would be impossible to mention by name all those who have helped both intentionally and otherwise with this History. There are the authors of the Regimental and Squadron War Diaries which were kept up with remarkable zest and vigour even in the midst of battle. There are the authors of other Regimental and war-time histories, published previously to this one, which have enabled me to get a better picture of the many facets of war and at varying levels of command, ranging downwards from the most famous war-leader of our times, Sir Winston Churchill. Then there are the individual members of the Regiment who willingly gave advice on every matter of detail, most of which I would never have been able to check myself. They never failed to give both constructive and quite often distructive criticism, not always appreciated at the time but never-the-less always valid.

Those to whom I am especially grateful are firstly Air Marshal Sir John Baldwin for his endless help on every subject and constant reminders to hurry the book along. Without his generosity and co-operation there could not even have been a start made to this History. To the following also I am most grateful:—

Mr. L. R. Bradley of the Imperial War Museum who gave every possible assistance in the finding and prompt despatch of photographs from the enormous collection there.

Major R. P. G. Dill for the loan of photographs and for endless unrewarding research and work on the appendices, especially the Roll of Officers, a truly vital part of the History.

Mr. Arthur Dundas for his patience and the great trouble he took over the maps, which, no sooner had he completed them than he was asked to re-draw them.

Brigadier C. Goulburn, D.S.O., for the loan of his diaries and for valuable information and corrections, up to the time of going to press.

Major C. Hedley for the loan of back numbers of Cross-belts and his help over the period 1927-39.

Miss H. Howell for endless patience in typing and re-typing a finally almost illegible manuscript.

Mr. W. Humphries of C. Tinling and Co. Ltd. for his help and advice, and whole-hearted co-operation.

Lieut.-Colonel P. H. Huth, D.S.O., M.C., for his diaries and the prompt despatch of photographs of armaments.

Major C. J. G. Meade for the loan of precious papers and photographs.

Captain P. C. Ormrod, M.C., for photographs and first-hand advice about the Korean Campaign.

Mrs. J. Stewart for her help with that most tedious job, the Index.

And lastly I must thank G. V. B. who has uncomplainingly checked proofs, given advice, chosen photographs, and in fact taken over the whole of the publishing side, and without whose constant encouragement and help I could never have finished this History.

Gyrn,   OLIVIA FITZROY
September 1960.

CONTENTS

LIST OF ILLUSTRATIONS

LIST OF MAPS

MAPS IN TEXT

BATTLE HONOURS

Major Battle Honours

LESWARREE	HINDOOSTAN	ALMA
BALAKLAVA	INKERMAN	SEVASTOPOL
CENTRAL INDIA	AFGHANISTAN, 1879–80	SOUTH AFRICA, 1900–02

THE GREAT WAR 1914–1918

Major Battle Honours

GIVENCHY, 1914
SOMME, 1916–18
CAMBRAI, 1917–18
BAPAUME, 1918
ROSIERES
AMIENS
ALBERT, 1918
BEAUREVOIR
PURSUIT TO MONS
FRANCE AND FLANDERS, 1914–18

Engagements—separate actions

Bazentin
Flers-Courcelette
St. Quentin
Hindenburg Line
St. Quentin Canal

THE SECOND WORLD WAR 1939–1945

Major Battle Honours

NORTH AFRICA, 1940–42
BUQ BUQ
SIDI REZEGH, 1941
GAZALA
EL ALAMEIN
NORTH-WEST EUROPE, 1944–45
VILLERS BOCAGE
THE LOWER MAAS
THE ROER
THE RHINE

Engagements—separate actions

Egyptian Frontier, 1940
Sidi Barrani
Relief of Tobruk
Bir el Igela
Mersa Matruh
Alam el Halfa
Mont Pinçon
Dives Crossing
Nederrijn
Best

KOREAN CAMPAIGN 1950–1951

Major Battle Honours

KOREA, 1950–51
IMJIN

Engagements—separate actions

Seoul
Hill 327
Kowang-san

PART ONE

1927–1939

BETWEEN THE WARS

(a) Weisbaden, 1927-1929

THIS is a story of thirty years. Thirty years soldiering in war and in peace, thirty years in which the Regiment saw greater changes in the art of fighting than in all the two hundred and sixty-three years since it was first raised.

Since the day to day record of peace-time soldiering is mercifully uneventful and makes somewhat dull reading for those who were not there at the time, the story of the thirteen years from the end of the last Regimental history will not be given in too great detail. Not that they must be thought of as in any way unimportant. Without the training and discipline and above all the upholding of the spirit and traditions of the Regiment during those years it could never have played its part in the desperate struggles ahead. There was more to contend with too than just training and discipline. There was the change-over from horses to tanks, via Light Cars. To any Regiment this change would obviously be a very hard one but to one that was so basically Light Cavalry in deeds and in spirit the change-over might have caused a serious stumbling-block to efficiency. The story of that change and of its results came later. This one starts at Weisbaden in 1926.

* * *

In Europe at this time, midway between the two wars, there was a truer feeling of peace than at any time before or since. The Treaty of Locarno had been signed and although no occupying army is ever very popular in the country it possesses, the Army of the Rhine was to have a shorter stay than originally designed and therefore was on a more friendly footing with the German people. All through the time of the 8th Hussars occupation, however, the German army was being secretly built up to a far greater strength than that allowed in the Treaty of Versailles. And not only the Army but the Navy also and a shadow Air Force camouflaged under a lawful civilian one. By now, too, Hitler had already been two years released from Landsberg prison where he had written *Mein Kampf*, and was becoming a figure of sinister power to Hindenberg and his General Staff.

* * *

After three years in York the 8th Hussars under the command of Lieut.-Colonel A. Currell, left on November 20th for Weisbaden and took their place there as part of the British Army of the Rhine. They were quartered in old German Cavalry Barracks on the outskirts of the town, which proved to be a pleasant enough place, famous as a spa and for the Opera House and Gardens. There were steamers too on the river that ran trips to Coblenz, Koln and particularly Ausmanhausen of the red wine, a race-course at Erbenhiem and, except for the hard winters, the climate was good.

The Regiment was respected in the town, especially as their forerunners had been French Colonial Troops of which the military-minded Germans could hardly approve. The Garrison church parade became something that crowds turned out to see and soon an article in the local paper commented with amazement and admiration on the manners of the British troops.

The most important event of 1926 from the Regimental point of view was the reduction of the twelve Cavalry Regiments at home by one squadron. The 8th Hussars now consisted of Headquarters Wing, a machine-gun squadron of four troops of two guns each and 'A' and 'B' Sabre Squadrons. Old 'A' Squadron was broken up and 'D' and 'C' became 'A' and 'B'. All Hotchkiss guns were withdrawn and Squadron Headquarters were reorganised.

In May the Regiment provided an escort for General Guillament, General Officer Commander in Chief the Allied Armies of Occupation, on the occasion of his first official visit to the new G.O.C.-in-C., British Army of the Rhine, and the following appeared in Army Orders:

"The impression made by the squadron of the 8th K.R.I. Hussars which formed the escort on May 1st was exceedingly good. The accuracy and dignity with which the escort moved upheld the traditions of British Cavalry, the men were well turned-out and the horses showed the best results of good horse-management."

All through the spring and summer of 1927 the Regiment was present at parades and inspections. In September they went to Furfield to take part in Brigade and Divisional training with the 1st Rhine Brigade. The mud and rain there reminded them of Flanders. Apart from these military matters they had a successful season in racing and polo and won the Inter-Allied Team Jumping at the Rhine Army Horse Show. Lieutenants J. W. Phillips and C. E. R. Duff joined the Regiment, both of whom were to become well-known not only on the polo ground but later in the Desert Campaigns.

★   ★   ★

This was the first year that German pilots were being trained in Russia in spite of Hitler's denunciation of Communism. In exchange, arms were secretly being sent there by Germany.

★   ★   ★

In June 1928 Lieut.-Colonel Currell left and was succeeded by Lieut.-Colonel H. L. Jones, D.S.O. of the 5th Inniskilling Dragoon Guards. He was already known to the Regiment from earlier days in Egypt and in India. Major Decimus Pope became second-in-command in place of Lieut.-Colonel Blakiston Houston.

That year the first whiff of petrol stole through the stables. In August half the machine-gun squadron was mechanised and given six-wheeled lorries, and crews were sent to Aldershot for training in preparation for the manoeuvres in September.

This exercise with the French Cavalry Division was the first occasion in peacetime at which a British Regiment had taken part in a foreign country's manoeuvres. The 8th Hussars were attached to the Dragoon Brigade, 18th and 19th Dragoons under Colonel Meyer. Each of the French regiments were divided into self-contained halves consisting of two squadrons each that could be sent out on independent missions under their own commanders.

The 8th Hussars arrived safely at Birkenfeld Neubruche on September 2nd. Major

L. W. D. Wathen marched his squadron into billets at Walhausen while the rest of the Regiment stopped at Gonnesweiler. They had to dine on iron rations that night as the lorry column, averaging a steady 4 m.p.h., did not arrive until nearly midnight.

Next day the Regiment changed billets and on September 5th marched forty-seven miles and had reveille at one o'clock next morning. Their role that day was 'decouverte' and they were supposed to go ahead to find not a point of resistance but a line. They quickly realised that the main object was to cover as much ground as possible and achieved in one day a march of eighty miles. Several things about our men amazed the French, apart from this marathon. One was that at the finish of a day's march the horses were all fit and none had to be sent back, while out of the five hundred French horses there were always at least three hundred casualties. At the end of the day the Frenchmen would leave their horses outside the café while they refreshed themselves inside. Our horses were rubbed down before anything else and the result was a hundred per cent fitness all through the exercise.

Another thing that surprised our allies was the fact that the Commanding Officer could give his orders to the Squadron Leaders verbally and that very soon afterwards they were carried out. The French on the other hand had to have everything written down and were lucky if after an hour or so anything happened. Neither could they understand the silence with which the Regiment turned out after dawn reveille. They would have wakened the village but the 8th Hussars won the nickname of 'The Silent Cavaliers'.

In spite of coming under the orders of a French Commanding Officer who frankly admitted that he had no idea what was happening, and in spite of bombardments that never took place and a gay luncheon party for officers and N.C.O.s in the middle of the exercise, it was successfully completed and General Partonneaux sent a message of congratulations and thanks to everyone taking part. Not so the German press who protested angrily against "This affront to the spirit of Locarno" and had to have it explained that the arrangement was made so that the 8th Hussars should not be deprived of their annual exercises.

However, instructive though the manoeuvres may have been, they did not inspire those taking part with any feeling of over-confidence when, ten years later and encased in armour, they took sides in earnest with their old allies.

As well as normal training the Regiment found time to make a name for themselves on the polo ground, although but a small one compared with the lustrous one ahead. However, they won sixteen trophies that season with a team that already included G. P. Kilkelly, J. C. Vernon-Miller, C. E. R. Duff and J. W. Phillips, and which was eventually to carry all before it.

That winter of 1928-29 was the coldest for seventy years. The Rhine was frozen from bank to bank and a carnival was held on the ice. Several people walked right across, following the route that Napoleon's army had taken on the march to Moscow. This 'Ice-Age' lasted for at least two months. Horses were confined to their stables for a fortnight and sentries were not allowed to be on duty for more than half an hour and were given coke braziers on their beats.

★   ★   ★

At home in May 1929 there was a General Election resulting in a Socialist Government under Ramsey MacDonald. Later that same year in America came the Wall Street crash followed, not unnaturally, by enormous unemployment there and in Britain as well. This came at a time when Germany was building up her resources with every means at her disposal and with all the furious energy of her hardworking people. But unemployment struck her too and out of the ensuing chaos rose Hitler, ever more menacing and powerful.

★ ★ ★

The year 1929, a singularly uneventful one, saw the Regiment in October embarking for England. By now the machine-gun squadron was entirely mechanised and was savouring for the first time the ease of travelling without horses and their attendant equipment.

Although there may have been a few regrets on leaving Germany, most people were only too glad to be going away from a country which, as *The Times* said: "Offers little professionally and nothing socially." The Regiment left Weisbaden on October 4th with a send-off from the C.-in-C., a party of French officers and a detachment of French Cavalry trumpeters who marched the length of the train sounding a fanfare. The Regiment was greeted at Aldershot by more fanfares, this time from the 11th Hussars, who also, with the 14th/20th Hussars, lent a hand with the baggage.

(b) Aldershot, 1929-1932

FOR their three-year stay in Aldershot the Regiment found themselves quartered in the Beaumont Barracks, typical old Cavalry Barracks with the men's rooms over the stables and the married quarters within the barrack boundaries. They were brigaded at first with their old friends, the 11th and 14th/20th Hussars and later with the 7th Hussars and 5th Inniskilling Dragoon Guards. They had brought with them the horses originally taken over from the Kings Dragoon Guards on the Rhine. Although on the whole they were very old there were some grand old performers amongst them. Lieutenant C. Goulburn joined that year.

As the Regiment became settled in they were able to turn their attention to things other than training. Polo, of course, came high up on the list, but for the first two years of their stay at Aldershot they did not get really into their stride. Show-jumping was another field in which they did well with F. R. W. How and D. S. Cripps winning most of the events they entered for. How also went to America and Canada in 1931 as a member of the British Army Team and was second in the King's Cup at the International Horse Show. Racing too became more and more popular with Tweseldown Race Course conveniently close. By 1932 officers were riding as far afield as Towcester, Wincanton, Taunton Vale and Sheriton and also at Sandown, but without any conspicuous success there. As much hunting as possible was also crammed in, between various more essential duties, and Wathen was huntsman to the Aldershot Drag in 1931-32, with Phillips and Dunne as his first and second whips.

Early in 1930 the machine-gun squadron received new guns and Carden Lloyd carriers. There was a certain amount of trouble with these at first, but eventually they were mastered and by August demonstrations were given to O.T.C.'s.

In June for the first time the Regiment sent a squadron to the Aldershot Tatoo. Under Wathen a hundred men from 'A' Squadron and a hundred from the 14th/20th

Hussars represented the British and French Cavalry at Dettingen and also took part in Light Cavalry evolutions of 1759.

September saw the Regiment en route for Salisbury Plain. They rode in two days to Windmill Hill where they formed part of the 1st Cavalry Division. The weather was so bad that the horse lines equalled the mud and filth of the war and a fortnight seemed much too long.

Also in September occurred the death of the Colonel, Sir Bryan Mahon, who had served with the Regiment from 1883 to 1921. He was the reliever of Mafeking and, so the story goes, being without a cipher, heliographed his message to Baden-Powell who commanded the garrison and wanted to know the relievers strength: "Numbers Naval and Military Club multiplied by 10 (94 Piccadilly x 10). Guns number of sons in Ward family (6). Supplies O.C. 9th Lancers (Little)."

Another Regimental death in May the next year was that of Colonel F. W. Mussenden who had commanded the Regiment from 1914-1917 and whose father had been the Colonel from 1896-1910. He was a very famous horseman and also a most distinguished soldier. A third obituary notice was that of Lieut.-Colonel Sir Harry Malet whose family had had three consecutive generations in the Regiment. The same year Brigadier John Van der Byl was made Colonel-in-Chief, which appointment he held for the next eighteen years until 1948. This must surely be a record.

★   ★   ★

Yet another General Election took place in 1931 resulting again in a Socialist victory with Ramsey MacDonald at its head. And at the end of the year another power began to be felt in the world. Japan, equally hit by the current of unemployment and with a vast rise in population, felt a need to expand. China, as usual, being the nearest and most convenient stepping stone, was invaded and in 1932 the Japanese annexed Manchuria and reached the Great Wall of China, asserting for the first time the power that was later to force America into war.

★   ★   ★

The year of 1931 seems to have been singularly uneventful for the Regiment, the highlight of training being the capture of the bridges over the Basingstoke Canal. Although they were gradually becoming more mechanised there were still headaches over remounts and saddlery. Both 'A' and 'B' Squadron provided troops for the Aldershot Tattoo which, although less decorative this year being modern cavalry drill, was entered into with the same vigour.

★   ★   ★

In 1932 Britain was not only disarming but allowing Germany to rearm, and arguing with the few faint voices that protested that equality between nations was the only thing that mattered. Although the state of Germany's arms were unknown the pacifist leanings of the British Government were such that even if they had been aware of it, and even if they had taken notice of what Hitler had already written in black and white for all the world to read, they would have done nothing about it.

★   ★   ★

Lieut.-Colonel Decimus Pope, M.C., took over command of the Regiment on April 3rd, 1932. He had been with them since 1910, served through the war with them and continuously ever since. Sir Edward Malet joined that year, the 4th generation of his family, as did Lieutenants W. G. Lowther and P. H. V. de Clermont, both of whom were later to command.

'C' Squadron was re-formed in April under Captain F. R. W. How with men and horses from 'A' and 'B'. The Regiment now consisted of Regimental Headquarters comprising: one administration troop, one band troop, one machine-gun troop (on pack), one signal and Austin scout troop and three sabre squadrons of three troops each.

The training in 1932 was memorable chiefly for a highly successful charge in the Miles Hill area and for a forty-one mile march home on a wet dark night from a week-end in Cowdray Park. A detachment of a hundred men took part in the Lord Mayor's Show as did the band, mounted and in full dress. The day was remembered for the early start, the slippery ride and two large meals with the Life Guards. At the Aldershot Tattoo the Regiment provided about eighty-five men for the Pageant of the Empire with costumes even more colourful than those of two years before. At the Small Arms Meeting they carried off the Aldershot Command Cavalry Cup and the Hemingway Cup. In Birmingham Sergeant-Major Charles Dawes, a ninety-seven year old veteran of Crimea and the Indian Mutiny died. He had survived the horrors of the hospital at Scutari and, as he said, owed his life to Florence Nightingale.

On October 4th, on a fine day in that rather uncertain summer, the Regiment marched to Hounslow. Troop movements nowadays are undertaken with immense troop carriers, the rattle of tanks, scout cars sent on ahead, wireless communication and convoys. It seems impossible that only thirty years ago the 8th Hussars moved from Aldershot to Hounslow with over four hundred horses.

★   ★   ★

Abroad, events were slowly but surely moving towards their ultimate end. In January 1933 Hitler became Chancellor of Germany and in April the German Army was officially expanded beyond the hundred thousand mark. There was a plan of Ramsey MacDonald's afoot to equalise the French and German armies, although luckily the French insisted that they should postpone the destruction of their heavy armaments for four years. Hitler, by now all-powerful and uncaring, withdrew from the League of Nations and the Disarmament Conference, making clear his disdain for both. Japan also left the League of Nations this year, already showing an affinity with her future colleague. Meanwhile, in Britain, all talk was of disarmament and equality between the nations, for the British, those most magnanimous of victors, could or would not credit their vanquished with motives and actions less praiseworthy than their own.

(c) Hounslow, 1933

THE year that the Regiment spent at Hounslow was chiefly a year of preparation for the next move, to Egypt, but it was not a popular move from anyone's point of view. However, Balaclava was celebrated as usual, this time with a banquet. One wonders how the guests felt on returning home having partaken of the "Hot Plumb Puddings" that figured on the menu. The dictionary's definition of 'plumb' is a ball of lead. A hot one must have been as indigestible as the shot and shell that swept down the Valley of Death.

From Hounslow the Regiment attended various functions in London. A squadron under Captain D. S. Cripps was present at the funeral of Field Marshal Sir William Robertson, another under Major J. P. Robinson enhanced the Lord Mayor's Show. On that particular occasion the troops had to march to London and the day, a rainy one, which began at 5 a.m., did not end until after midnight. In May a contingent went to Olympia to perform an exceptionally good Trick Ride at the Royal Tournament there under Lieutenant J. C. Vernon-Miller, and later at other places. Lieutenant J. R. Cairnes won the Army Racquets Championship, Lieutenant J. D. Harbord on 'Jimmy' won the Open Jumping at Islington and Lieutenant Phillips won the Grafton Lightweight Race on 'Perspective'.

In June there was a memorable Reunion and Farewell Dinner given by the Regiment and the Old Comrades Association at Aldershot and attended by some three hundred members, past and present.

In August the Regiment was ordered to send a squadron as Divisional Cavalry to the 2nd Division on Salisbury Plain. Owing to an insufficiency of trained men in any one squadron a composite squadron was formed and set off on the 29th under Major T. G. Watson for Fargo Camp.

Although departure for the Middle East was imminent there was yet another Divisional Exercise to be undertaken. Again a composite squadron left Hounslow, this time for Pangbourne. The object of this exercise was to practise swimming the horses across a river, and so a suitable stretch of the Thames was chosen. Although in theory when a horse is swimming the rider should hold its mane or tail, this becomes impossible when the mane is hogged and the tail docked. In the end the horses had to be launched off on their own and, as the weather was perfect, everyone, except perhaps the horses, enjoyed themselves. On the last day, there was a demonstration in front of various Generals and it was found possible to get the whole squadron and machine-guns across and established in forty-five minutes.

There were few regrets at leaving Hounslow. It had been a hard year in some respects as, with the closing down of the Cavalry Depot, the Regiment itself had to handle the training of the innumerable recruits who replaced many of the seven year men who did not have sufficient time left for it to be worth while their accompanying the Regiment abroad. Some of the most eager to get overseas were the Polo Team. There were sixty-six Australian ponies, procured by Major P. E. F. Chirnside from the Ashton brothers, waiting for them in Cairo in the care of Vernon-Miller, and although most of these were untrained there was going to be a good deal of fun and hard work ahead for everyone concerned. This was the result of Lieut.-Colonel Pope's far-sighted policy. He had managed to raise the money to obtain these ponies and was prepared to help young officers to buy them over a period of time. It was a policy that was to be well worth while.

With these prospects ahead the Regiment sailed on December 19th 1933 for Cairo.

(d) Cairo, 1934-1936

CHRISTMAS of that year was spent at sea and the Regiment arrived at the Main Barracks, Abassia on New Year's Eve. They were expecting to remain there for three years and then go on to India. Although they carried on as usual with training, with the thought of that move in mind polo became of first importance. There were the sixty-six untrained ponies to be schooled, which, at the end of three years, should be just about ready to sweep the polo grounds of India, however high the standard there. When the Commanding Officer was asked desparingly by one conscientious young officer: "Which is the most important, sir, soldiering or polo?" he replied: "At the moment, polo."

* * *

In Europe the landslide had started. To the man in the street, happenings abroad seemed, as they always seem to these islanders, too remote to be their concern. They could never be involved. It could never happen here. Hitler already had three million storm troops and the Munich Putsch was the consequence, with five thousand bullet-ridden corpses in the streets. It could never happen here. Dollfuss was assassinated in the Chancellery in Vienna and King Alexander of Yugoslavia in Marseilles, and Laval stepped on to the scene. Russia joined the League of Nations and at the end of the year Italy sent the first bullets over the border into Abyssinia, which event took the world's eyes off Germany. She was thus able to continue her preparations for martial dominance and at the end of the year Laval granted her the Saar with all its coal mines.

* * *

On arrival in Egypt the Regiment took over the horses of the 14th/20th Hussars, and occupied the same barracks as in 1922.

An advance party left on February 5th for the training camp under the Pyramids at Mena and the rest of the Regiment followed on the 14th. They took part then in Command Manoeuvres in the desert round Bir Victoria, Bir Hooker and Khataba, at one moment the horses being watered by air. In spite of fifty-mile marches there were no sore backs in the horse-lines, a remarkable feat in the heat and dust and sand.

In June the Regiment attended the King's Birthday Parade at Gezira and from then until 1935 nothing spectacular happened, although life was pleasant enough and the polo ponies already showed an improvement.

In the early spring of 1935 the Regiment went to the Brigade Camp at Beni Yusef for a fortnight. That year St. Patrick's day was spent in the desert near Helwan, an uncongenial place, but although the shamrock failed to arrive by air there were the usual number of sore heads next morning.

The War Office having announced that they would reopen the question of past battle honours for various Regiments, a certain amount of research was undertaken, and in June the following claims were sent in: Spain 1705-12; Barcelona 1705-6; St. Estevan 1706; Valencia 1706; Almanara 1710; Saragossa 1710; Flanders 1794-95; Farakhabad 1804; Ofzulghan 1805 and Nepal 1814. The Regiment, although it had served in Spain from 1705-12, had no earlier honours than Leswarree in 1803.

In spite of almost continuous training in the desert the Regiment was able to win 3rd place in the Egypt Command Sports Championship and entered in every contest, a feat of which they were justly proud. Polo was equally successful and Lieut.-Colonel Pope's policy was beginning to show results. However, already the threat of mechanisation was approaching, and as it did, the promise of India faded. In September the thin edge of the wedge was felt and, a Light Car Recce Regiment being wanted for the Lybian desert, the Regiment was chosen and a composite Squadron was sent to Helmieh for training on Ford V8's with the 11th Hussars.

★ ★ ★

1935 saw Italy becoming increasingly aggressive. Agreements were signed by her with France (or for France read Laval), and strips of land changed hands in Lybia and Somaliland. It was revealed officially too that there was a German Air Force, that it was a far greater one than Britain's and expanding fast, faster than we could keep up with even if we had tried. Italy became more menacing towards Abyssinia. Germany brought back conscription and began increasing her fleet, especially the U-boats, and built Scharnhorst and Gneisnau and laid down the Bismarck and Tirpitz, while Britain, France and America, bound by their agreements, were unable to build anything half that size. The first steps in the art of Radar were being taken. Italy poured more troops into Abyssinia and sanctions were applied, thus throwing her into Germany's arms at a time when Germany was altogether too strong on her own. At the General Election the Conservatives were returned on a 'Peace at any Price' basis.

★ ★ ★

On November 11th the last mounted parade was held near Coombe Hill. It was a sad yet magnificent sight. There can have been few present who, although perhaps they realised the necessity of keeping up with the rest of the Army, did not feel that their particular brand of soldiering was at an end. And that mechanisation would have very little to offer in exchange. There was also the difficulty of adapting men who were first class horsemen into mechanics, a totally different type, and far more difficult for the older men than the young. It is unnecessary to point out, in view of what happened four years later, how well this was carried out, how unspectacularly and how efficiently by both officers and men.

On this Armistice Day 1935, the Regiment was drawn up before the G.O.C.-in-C., Lieut.-General Sir George Weir. The three squadrons and the mounted band were on parade. After inspection the Regiment trotted past, wheeled and then galloped past, for the last time in its two hundred and forty-two years of soldiering, perhaps a fitting place to do it, here in the desert, whose shifting sands have known so many different kinds of war and which, when the dust subsides and the wind blows over, look exactly as they have looked for thousands of years. Perhaps the least popular aspect of the change-over was the introduction for the first time of compulsory physical training.

On the 21st the faithful 'old hairies' were handed over to the Royal Dragoons who were on their way from India to England. It was sad to see them go, especially as some of them were young horses, newly trained. However, there was little time for regrets and on November 26th 'C' Squadron was sent to the 11th Hussars for training.

The Regiment was to be equipped with 15 cwt. and 30 cwt. Ford V8's after the vehicles had been modified in the Ordnance Workshops. Also the Vickers Machine-

Gun on which some training had already been carried out was dropped in favour of the Vickers Berthier Light Automatic. Even then this equipment must have seemed very slight in the event of war, especially after the lecture on November 30th on the Italian Tank Corps.

To the 11th Hussars, who took on the whole Regiment during the end of 1935 and 1936 and trained them in driving, maintenance and generally eased the difficult change-over, the 8th Hussars were especially grateful. However, much of the success that resulted from this mechanisation was due to the unflagging and excellent work of Major J. P. Robinson who both organised the Regiment and liaised with the 11th Hussars.

On December 18th 'C' Squadron under Robinson was sent back to the dust-storms of Mersa Matruh as part of the newly formed Mobile Force. On one of the reconnaissance parties into the desert a lorry overturned, killing two men, Sergeant Winters and Trooper Dawson. That year also Colonel Charles Duff, who had commanded the regiment in 1901, died, as did Mr. Pamplin who had been the untiring Secretary to the Old Comrades Association for many years.

By the time 'C' Squadron was operational in the desert, there were enough trained men in the Regiment capable of instructing the rest of the troops in the barracks at Abassia, where the barrack square was turned into an enormous garage. A black spot was Christmas when the turkeys were all sent to Sidi Barrani instead of to that particular part of the desert where the Regiment was stationed. However, a very small pig that 'C' Squadron took with them to Mersa Matruh to fatten for Christmas, returned with them three months later, carried in a litter and wearing a scarf of regimental colours and sun glasses. When the time had come for its slaughter no one could bear to kill it and it became the Squadron mascot.

*   *   *

At home in 1936 Radio Location Stations, as they were then known, were being set up along the south coast. Hitler proposed a twenty-five year peace pact of a de-militarised zone, non-aggression and limited air forces, and two hours later marched into the Rhineland, announcing that he had no further territorial claims. Later in the summer Spain was plunged into Civil War with Franco, the army and the church opposing the Communists. In spite of the agreed policy of non-intervention, Italy and Germany on one side and Russia on the other, supported their own parties. This same year saw the abdication of King Edward VIII.

*   *   *

In January 1936 a troop of Royal Signals joined the 8th Hussars as part of a mechanised regiment. They were to be known as 'H' Troop, Cavalry Division Signals. Also that month the rest of the Regiment, minus 'B' Squadron who was waiting for vehicles, joined 'C' Squadron at Mersa Matruh.

In February 'A' Squadron was sent on a reconnaissance to Siwa Oasis. This strange place, which although actually built in a depression, rises up out of the desert some hundred and fifty miles west of Cairo, built on the ruins of age-old houses. The Squadron, who, mechanised, reached it in two days along one of the few possible routes, was amazed by the sight of its abruptly rising cliffs, the river that gushes out of the sand and then in again and the desolate sand seas where the lorries got bogged. There was also a ruined temple, visited by Alexander the Great and a circular pool known as

Cleopatra's Bath. The Squadron swam there too, and returned after ten days to the sand-storms at Mersa.

On the 3rd April, Lieut.-Colonel Pope handed over the Regiment to Lieut.-Colonel F. Thornton of the 16th/5th Lancers who at once became an 8th Hussar through and through. Lieut.-Colonel Pope had commanded during one of the most critical moments of the Regiment's history, its change-over from horses to cars. He must have been proud to see things already working smoothly before he left, and shortly after the Regiment returned to Cairo the G.O.C.-in-C. said of them: "I think the whole-hearted way in which this regiment adapted itself to mechanisation, which must have been a wrench to many, reflects the greatest credit on all ranks."

(e) Palestine, 1936

AT the end of June the Regiment had orders to go to Palestine to help in suppressing the disturbances between the Arabs and the Jews, and three days later they left Cairo by road, their first operation as a mechanised force.

'B' Squadron, under Major T. B. A. Evans-Lombe, was the first to leave as advance party. They crossed the Suez Canal at Tel el Kebir, bivouacked for the night of June 26th at Bir Hassana and, in spite of overturning one car, arrived on time in Jerusalem. Once there it fell to them to lay out the camp and start pitching tents on a ploughed field next to the barracks occupied by the Cameron Highlanders. Although over-crowded it became quite comfortable, shower-baths were laid on and a very necessary wire fence put up. The rest of the Regiment arrived at Balaclava Camp on the 28th, also having overturned a lorry, and feeling slightly insulted at having been provided with an escort of armoured cars and an aeroplane in case they were ambushed in the hilly country round Beersheba, and could not deal with it on their own. As it happened there was no trouble at all.

Before two days had passed the Regiment had settled in to a way of life that was to become monotonous in the extreme. Major Robinson and 'C' Squadron were the first out on road reconnaissance near Khar Ras. A telephone pole was across the road with wires attached to boulders on either side. Although a shot was fired at the column it was not returned. Yet another road block in the shape of a pile of stones was found half a kilometre east of Bir Nizah and again the column was fired on, this time from the shelter of an olive grove. 'C' Squadron retaliated but there were no casualties and they returned, christened, to Jerusalem.

Next day the Regiment was inspected by the High Commissioner for Palestine, His Excellency, General Sir Arthur Grenfell Wanchope, and for the next three nights they were out on patrol. On the 5th they took part in a big operation in which all available troops were to make a drive through the hills north of Jerusalem to try and round up the roving armed bands. On the way to their position the advance guard was fired on by a party of about eight men, one of whom was killed in the return fire. After being out for two nights they were ordered back to camp, encountering a good deal of sniping on the way. Although they claimed six killed and four wounded the Regiment felt they could have done much better had they had more local knowledge. Their only guide consisted of a civil police corporal who did not know the area.

And so it went on. Life settled into a routine, broken occasionally by the strangeness of seeing places and people, read about so often in the Bible, now an actuality. Reconnaissance to Jericho. 'Bethlehem Municipal Council' on a notice board. Daggers found in a search for arms. Snipers in orange groves.

Nearly every night the telephone wires from Jerusalem to the country were cut. It became the Regiment's job to provide escorts for the Post Office parties repairing them. Another job was the patrolling of the railway lines under whose sleepers the Arabs were very fond of putting bombs. On July 23rd Lieutenant Duff stopped and searched two Arabs riding donkeys. They found an automatic pistol and nineteen rounds of ammunition hidden in a basket of fruit. A troop of 'C' Squadron accompanied by a police inspector and a police dog went to 7 K Post where the Jericho wires had been cut. The dog picked up spoor and led them over the hills to the village of Abudis where he stopped in the courtyard of the Mudir (the village hall). The Muktar was found and he and nine others were taken back to Jerusalem as hostages. On escorting the High Commissioner from Jaffa to Jerusalem, His Excellency's chauffeur drove so fast that he arrived in Jaffa some time before the escort.

Since the beginning of the troubles no troops had been permanently stationed in the southern part of Palestine except for a small guard on the railway and aerodrome at Gaza. Both these were important; the railway and telegraph line was the main link of communication with Egypt; the aerodrome was an essential link in communications to India and the East. Towards the middle of July it became a nightly occurrence for the telephone wires to be cut and the railway damaged. The authorities also feared that the Bedouin tribes, who frequent that part of Palestine, were becoming discontented. The Regiment was therefore sent down to try and keep the country quiet. First a squadron went to Beersheba, a few days later Regimental Headquarters and another squadron were sent to Gaza where they joined up with a platoon of the Cheshire Regiment and one of the Royal Scots Fusiliers. The third squadron had to stay in Jerusalem and with the three thus distributed they were able to ring the changes and avoid the monotony of being too long in one place. At Beersheba the troops were billeted in the school as the children were on strike.

All through August the patrolling and escorting of post office parties continued. Patrols were fired on and there were mines buried in the sandy tracks along which the cars had to pass. Luckily only one man was hurt, Trooper May, who was wounded in the backside, although Major Chirnside's car was blown up. North of Beersheba there was no road in the area ordered to be patrolled, so the squadron concerned made one. There was evidence of digging round the old Turkish shell-dumps and the Muktar and inhabitants of nearby villages were rounded up to remove suspicious objects found lying about which might have been bombs but turned out to be tyre-puncturing gadgets. Snipers at Ali Muntar broke the outer glass of the searchlight attached to the Regiment. Fire was returned when a 'B' Squadron patrol was sniped at and the police reported a woman wounded as a result. The troop leader visited the place and found it was impossible for her to have been hit by fire from his troop. Footprints were followed and lost. A patrol fired on four Arabs crawling through an orchard towards the telephone wires. A troop of 'C' Squadron found two Cameron Highlanders badly wounded when a concealed shell exploded. A mounted Arab on being asked to dismount refused to do so and bolted. With Air Force co-operation he was traced to a village which was searched but nothing found. The only retaliation was to demolish the houses of those known to be disloyal, a job that no one liked.

Recreation during this time was of a very low standard. A seven o'clock curfew existed in Jerusalem which prevented any evening amusements. Bathing was dangerous and apart from Jerusalem there was no electricity for working the cinema. However, eventually it was made possible for leave parties to be sent to Cairo which greatly cheered things up. In September Lieut.-General Dill took over command of the British Forces in Palestine and Transjorden from Air Vice-Marshal Peirse.

Early in September, owing to a deterioration of the situation in the north, 'C' Squadron was sent up to protect a Jewish colony at Hadera, a few miles south of Haifa. This meant that they had to be replaced in Jerusalem by 'A' Squadron from Gaza, leaving only 'B' Squadron in the south. They had therefore to leave Beersheba even though they were reinforced by four armoured cars because protection of the railway and telegraph was the primary job. Thus the Regiment became very scattered, each squadron being separated by sixty miles, although 'A' and 'B' changed places during the middle of September.

It was while 'A' Squadron was at Gaza that Lance Corporal Mellor was mentioned in despatches for good work while on patrol. His section was lying up by the railway and caught ten Arabs about to blow up the line. If it had not been such bad country with so many cactus hedges and sunken roads his troop might well have caught the remainder.

'C' Squadron up at Hadera had to send a troop to Zikhron for two weeks to reinforce the garrison there. They spent a night on the beach at Caesarea, co-operating with a cruiser from Haifa in an attempt to catch some arms' smugglers.

Towards the end of September the 1st Division from home started to arrive which meant a redistribution of units already in the country, and 'B' and 'C' Squadrons returned to the Regiment at Gaza. After the reuniting of the three squadrons their task remained much the same. They were still responsible for the whole southern part of Palestine and in addition an area in the north which contained some Jewish colonies.

On October 11th a message was received from the 2nd Infantry Brigade: "The Arab Committee has ordered followers to stop rebellion unconditionally." It had seemed a petty kind of war but peacetime in Gaza was even worse as the usual amenities of life were practically non-existent. Rumours of an early return to Cairo filtered through but nothing definite was heard and arrangements had to be made to stay on through the cold weather. Rain was expected and the ploughed-field camp would become uninhabitable. Billets had to be found, luckily there were some quite good schools to be had, if rather too near the native dwellings. The officers were lodged in a girls' school; the girls, who were on strike, wisely deciding to remain so. A complicated change-over of squadrons and billets had just been accomplished when the order came to return to Cairo.

Exactly a year after their last mounted parade the 8th Hussars returned to Abassia. At a farewell parade the Corps Commander, General Dill, said: "If I want any more troops back in Palestine, you will be one of the first regiments I shall ask for," a compliment they felt at the time might almost have been dispensed with. The Commanding Officer wrote wistfully that they "had had just a taste of real war." He need not have worried, they were to have their fill of it before long.

Back in Abassia they found the 12th Lancers in possession of the barracks but managed to squeeze in with them for a fortnight, it was worth anything to be in civilisation again. It helped, too, to know that the Commander 1st Division British Forces in Palestine, Major-General Armitage, had said: "It is thanks to the energy and efficiency of your Regiment that the Gaza-Beersheba area has remained comparatively

quiet during the troubles. The cheerful spirit in which your officers and men have
carried on in conditions of great discomfort has been an example to all units."

Evidently they had not done too badly.

(f) Cairo Again, 1937-1939

POLO, which started late that season owing to the troubles in Palestine, at last got into
its stride. Lieutenants Vernon-Miller and Lowther played in the winning England team
against Ireland in the International Match in January. They won also their match
against the 7th Hussars, the Subaltern's Cup and the Open Cup, although they lost the
last big tournament, the King's Cup. Other names worthy of mention in the sporting
field are those of Lance Corporal Jim Pavior, captain of the football team and also in the
cricket eleven, and Trooper Sharman who became Inter-Services Featherweight
Boxing Champion.

After the excitements of the Palestine campaign nothing of much interest seemed to
happen during the next year.

★ ★ ★

At home Baldwin retired and his place was taken by Neville Chamberlain. The
German Army was spending ever more millions on re-armament while Britain, although
by now aware that something should be done about it, was hopelessly left behind.
Hitler was shouting for more living space and made the appropriate plans, and also the
statements that he was resolved to unite all Germans living inside or out of the borders
of Germany. Not only were the plans made to invade Austria but also Czechoslovakia.
On the other hand, however, Stalin became aware of growing Nazism in the Russian
Army and in January the purge began during which nearly five thousand officers were
liquidated. Stalin did not believe in half-measures and showed beyond doubt his opinion
of the Axis.

★ ★ ★

In the desert, 'B' Squadron under Major Evans Lombe had a trip out to Maghra
Oasis, a small salt lake in the desert, and another to St. Anthony's Monastry south of
Wadi Araba. In February the Regiment took part in the Cavalry Brigade Exercises,
driving over very rough country some two hundred and fifty miles from Cairo. It
was the hardest time they had had since exchanging horses for cars, but the vehicles
stood up to the test fairly well and the Brigade Commander was pleased. The Colonel
of the Regiment, Brigadier Van der Byl, paid a visit in February.

In May the Regiment took part in the Coronation Day parades of King George VI
both in England and Cairo. At home there was a mounted section on horses belonging
to the 4th/7th Royal Dragoon Guards, but in Egypt in the grounds of the Gezira
Sporting Club the Regiment used cars for the first time in a ceremonial parade.

The hot weather season was mostly spent in listening to lectures and discussions and
in October the Commanding Officer and several officers and non-commissioned officers

Wiesbaden, 1928.

General Partoneaux, Lieut.-Colonel Jones and General Guillaumat, September, 1928 (page 5).

The Last Parade at Aldershot, October 4th, 1932 (page 8).

Lieut.-Colonel D. Pope, Commanding Officer, leading the Regiment into Hounslow Barracks, October 4th, 1932 (page 8).

A Regimental escort party in the Sinai Desert on their way to Palestine, June, 1936.

An Arab suspect is arrested, Palestine, 1936.

The coastal area of Palestine, 1936.

The Station-master's house at Beersheba was taken over as the Squadron Headquarters and attacked on several occasions by the Arabs. It is here being bravely defended by the officers in their night attire (page 14).

flew over the desert to the Siwa Oasis in aeroplanes belonging to 216 Squadron, Royal Air Force.

Major Chirnside, Captains H. C. Hope-Murray and How and Lieutenant de Clermont all left the Regiment this year and Lieut.-Colonel Thornton, Major Robinson, Captain J. D. Harbord and Lieutenants Lowther, J. W. Hackett and W. V. H. Nelson were mentioned in despatches for work in Palestine. After a bad start in polo when no one seemed able to get into form, thus losing the Inter-Regimental Cup, they eventually carried off the King's Dragoon Guards Cup, the Grenadier Guards' Cup, Inter-Regimental Handicap, the Subalterns' Cup, the Open Cup and the King's Cup, with Duff, Vernon-Miller, Lowther, Kilkelly, Nelson, J. C. Pringle, D. R. W. G. Charlton, Goulburn, J. A. Comyn and P. D. Sandbach playing. Major Kilkelly and Captain Harbord also won the army doubles at tennis.

Training started again in December with the three squadrons going out in turn to recce different areas, and in the new year combining for a regimental exercise and in February for a cavalry brigade exercise. The Regiment had by now become proficient enough in cars to be congratulated by the Brigade Commander, Brigadier Friend, on the excellence of performance and high standard reached and improvement of tactical work since last year.

★ ★ ★

The drums all over Europe were beginning to beat. In February 1938 Anthony Eden resigned his post as Foreign Secretary, unable any longer to carry out a policy so alien to his own principles. The Germans marched into Austria a month later and took the country for their own. In September Chamberlain flew to Munich to try and reason with a madman and as a result of this the French Army was partly mobilised as was the British Fleet. The German generals were against war but Hitler's will was to override that of everyone connected with him. Czechoslovakia was in the melting pot and the events that concerned their country were decided without the knowledge of the Czechs. Chamberlain flew for a third time to Munich and returned with the historic slip of paper. Sudetenland was handed over to the Germans without a blow being struck and Hitler told the world that he had no further territorial claims in Europe.

In spite of this promise and the hopes that there would be no war in our time, rearmament began at last to go ahead. Britain was hopelessly ill-equipped in all three services, and in defence, and by this time German military strength was immeasurably more than ours and increasing every hour.

★ ★ ★

In spite of the mounting tension in the air the Regiment had an uneventful year. It was certain now that they were not going to India but they were already looking forward to an early return to England. Rumours circulated too, about a change-over from cars to tanks, but when and what sort were not specified. In June two matters of interest stand out in the Regimental Diary, apart from the King's Birthday Parade. One is an order announcing that water bottles will be hung upside down and the corks removed, and the other is an extract from a private letter from the Inspector-General of Cavalry: "I was simply delighted to see that very good report you got from the Mechanical Inspector. It is the best I have ever read of any cavalry regiment on their maintenance and I offer you my very best congratulations."

B

Their hard training and their determination that "whatever they should be called called upon to do, that thing they would do to their utmost," was beginning to pay. 'B' Squadron won the reliability test in the desert at the end of manoeuvres, getting 100 per cent. (no faults) out of the twenty teams entered.

Soon it became clear that if there was war with Germany her ally Italy would join in on her side. There were large numbers of troops massing not only in Cyrenaica but on the Sudanese and British East African frontiers as well. To counteract this menace on September 17th the 8th Hussars, together with the 7th and 11th Hussars; H.Q. Cairo Cavalry Brigade and Signals; 3rd Regiment, Royal Horse Artillery; 1st Royal Tank Regiment; 5 Company, Royal Army Service Corps and 2nd/3rd Field Ambulance were sent to Mersa Matruh where, under Brigadier H. E. Russell, they formed the Matruh Mobile Force, the precursor of the 7th Armoured Division.

The force was based and leaguered inside Matruh Fortress, its object being to support the garrison there, part British-part Egyptian, by operating in the area of Charing Cross.

Their equipment was pathetic. The 8th Hussars had Ford 15 cwt. pick-ups mounting Vickers-Berthier machine-guns. The 7th Hussars had an assortment of light tanks, Marks III and VIB. The Royal Tank Regiment was slightly better equipped having left England in March with all the light tanks available there, but by now these had very little track mileage left and the new tracks did not fit. The 11th Hussars had First World War Rolls Royce Armoured Cars and a few Morris Light Armoured Cars, and the Royal Horse Artillery had 3·7 Howitzers towed by dragons or towing tractors. Such was the force, supported in the air by 208 Army Co-operation Squadron with Lysanders, 80 Fighter Squadron with Gladiators and 45 Bomber Squadron with Harts that opposed Mussolini's modern army.

Luckily the time was not yet ripe. The force returned to Cairo in October to be welded into a Mobile Division by Major-General P. C. S. Hobart, and months of training followed. That same autumn Lieut.-Colonel Thornton was promoted to full Colonel and then to Brigadier commanding the 2nd Cavalry Brigade. He left the Regiment for Palestine and his place was taken by Lieut.-Colonel T. G. Watson who had been second-in-command. On December 14th an order was received and with it the New Peace Establishment for a Cavalry Light Tank Regiment on which the Regiment was to be reorganised. If uniformity in Cavalry had not been wanted they would have almost certainly remained a Light Car Regiment, as of their kind they were unique and on manoeuvres their loss would be greatly felt.

That same year the Regiment was allied (forewarning of war?) to the 6th Duke of Connaughts Royal Canadian Hussars and the 8th (Indi) Light Horse Regiment of Australia, both regiments with fine fighting records, the Canadians having fought in France throughout the First World War and collected more battle honours than any other Canadian regiment, while the Australians fought in Gallipoli.

In this, their last polo season, the Regiment won more cups than ever before. As usual they were off to a slow start but once they got into their stride there was no stopping them. They carried off the July Tournament (Alexandria), Public Schools' Cup (Old Etonians), Junior Championship, Inter-Regimental, Subalterns' Cup, Open Cup and the King's Cup. The players were the same with the addition of P. H. Huth, G. W. G. Threlfall, Phillips and N. G. F. Dunne and with Duff and Charlton not playing as the first had left to instruct at Sandhurst and the second to join the Transjordan Frontier Force.

January 1939 started with an announcement that showed at any rate it was still peace-time, that of stating that officers would only be entitled to an issue of one Government charger. Undeterred by this the Regiment hurried on training with its latest form of equipment, light tanks. These were the cast-offs of the 7th Hussars and the 6th Battalion, Royal Tank Regiment, and consisted of eleven Mark III's with a ·303 machine-gun and seven Mark VIB's with both a ·5 and ·303 machine-gun. On February 2nd at Abbasia they held the last quarter guard in mounted dress.

★   ★   ★

In March 1939 Germany invaded Czechoslovakia. Seeing the way the wind really blew and that Poland would be next on the list, Britain undertook to support her in the event of any attack.

★   ★   ★

The whole of March saw the Regiment in the Western Desert. The new Division moved to Gerawla for its first exercises. None too soon either. On April 7th, Good Friday, the Italians invaded Albania.

On the day following Easter Monday, the 11th, all troops were mobilised, on the 15th the Regiment was ordered to Mersa Matruh. Regimental Headquarters and the two light car squadrons left the next day, leaving behind 'A' Squadron who were still being reorganised with light tanks, and arrived on the 17th. This time it was a six-week stay, patrolling the wire with reconnaissances as far as Siwa and Sollum on the Western Frontier, enlivened one week-end by a visit from two ships of the Navy who enjoyed themselves so much that they collided with each other on the way home to Alexandria. The Regiment stayed at Mersa until the 25th May, when they returned to Cairo. All personnel in April had been transferred to the Royal Armoured Corps.

★   ★   ★

At home, following Italy's attack on Albania, conscription was introduced, which, however, produced very little in the way of a trained army in those days before National Service. It also led to an alliance between Britain, France and Russia, guaranteeing protection to the countries most likely to be next on the German list. They, however, being almost more terrified of Russia than Germany were in no position to ask for aid. At the same time Russia was secretly negotiating with Germany, who assured her she had no claims to Russian territory. Molotov became Foreign Commissar and Russia leant more and more towards her Nazi enemies. In June Belgium declared her neutrality.

★   ★   ★

In July, General Sir Archibald Wavell became Commander-in-Chief, Middle East. Under him General Sir Henry Maitland Wilson commanded the British troops in Egypt. The most imminent danger there was the presence of the Italian Army on Egypt's western frontier. This was estimated to consist of nine Divisions alone in Tripolitania and another five in Cyrenaica, in whole a force of some 215,000 men.

Across the frontier from this enormous strength was the 7th Armoured Division, the Infantry Brigade in Mersa Matruh and the newly-arrived 4th Indian Division. The 6th Australian Division, and the New Zealand Division were to arrive soon afterwards and, although splendid troops, they were as yet unused to desert conditions.

This force was even less strong than it sounded. The 8th Hussars had not yet finished training with their light tanks and the 4th Indian Division was short of a brigade. Equipment and motor transport was practically negligible and artillery of all kinds was desperately short, especially anti-tank guns. Under these conditions it was impossible, in the event of war, for General Wavell to plan an offensive, and a strong forward screen of troops carrying out offensive patrols was as much as he could contemplate for the present.

★   ★   ★

In August Russia and Germany secretly signed a Non-Agression Pact while in the middle, on Russia's part, of negotiating with Britain. This had the effect not of frightening Britain but of strengthening her resolve to fight at last. Reserves were called up, defences manned, the Dominions were informed of these measures. The drums in Britain were now beating the call to arms.

★   ★   ★

In the desert the Mobile Division was being reorganised and by August the situation was much improved. Although their equipment was about the same, the 11th Hussars had at least received some more Morris Armoured Cars and the 6th Battalion The Royal Tank Regiment had A-9 Cruiser tanks. However, the greatest improvement was in morale and training, in confidence in themselves, in their commanders and in their comrades.

PART TWO

1939-1941

I.

DESERT WARFARE

(a) Preparing for Battle, 1939

AT the end of that uneasy August in 1939 the 8th Hussars were sent once more as a precautionary measure to Mersa Matruh. It is as well, at the beginning of this story of some of the most confusing campaigns in history, to obtain a clear picture of how the Middle East Command was formed, of the principle characters and of the forces that took part.

Chief player on this stage was General Sir Archibald Wavell, Commander-in-Chief, Middle East, which included command of the troops in Palestine, the Sudan and Cyprus. Under him General Sir Henry Maitland Wilson commanded the British troops in Egypt. These consisted of the Mobile Division, an Infantry Brigade and the 4th Indian Division, newly arrived. The Mobile Division was commanded by Major-General P. C. S. Hobart, who had created it, and it was made up of:

Light Armoured Brigade—Brigadier H. E. Russell
   7th Hussars (light tanks)
   8th Hussars (obsolescent two-man tanks and Ford pick-ups)
   11th Hussars (Rolls and Morris armoured cars)

Heavy Armoured Brigade—Lieut.-Colonel H. R. B. Watkins
   1st Btn. Royal Tank Regiment (old light tanks)
   6th Btn. Royal Tank Regiment (old light medium tanks)

Pivot Group—Lieut.-Colonel W. H. B. Mirrlees
   3rd Regt. Royal Horse Artillery (25 pdrs. and 37 mm. anti-tank guns)
   'F' Battery, R.H.A. (25 pdrs.)
   1st Btn. Kings Royal Rifle Corps (motor btn.)

Both the Division and the Brigades were to change their names later, as they were to change their Commanders, and the regiments were to be reshuffled and increased. But that is how they stood in August, 1939.

The tanks used in the desert battles were the following:

The 'Infantry' tank, heavy, slow and strongly armoured, designed to accompany and support the infantry.

The 'cruiser' tank, fast, better gunned but with lighter armour. It had a highly mobile fighting rôle.

The 'light' tank, fast with thin armour and only machine-guns for armament, and meant to be used for recce.

On the other side of the rusty wire that marked the frontier of Egypt and Cyrenaica lay the pride of the Italian Army under Marshal Graziani. He had a force of some six divisions, masses of artillery and about two hundred tanks, as well as nine more divisions waiting in Tripolitania, a total of about 215,000 men. In August, 1939 all that Wavell could have pitted against him was the Mobile Division and about one third of the 4th

Indian Division, keeping in reserve some eight infantry battalions and four artillery regiments to hold the Suez Canal and Alexandria.

All the same the Mobile Division was a very different one from the force that had been sent so often to Mersa Matruh in the past. Although their equipment was much the same they were now welded together into a fighting machine, strong in morale and training and full of confidence.

Thus, on August 25th, the 8th Hussars left Cairo for Mersa Matruh once more, stopping for the night at a village called el Alamein. The tanks of 'A' Squadron made the journey by rail but the rest of the Regiment travelled by road, a road they already knew well and were soon to know a great deal better.

They found themselves bivouacked with the rest of the Light Armoured Brigade at a place some two miles south of the Sidi Barrani-Siwa road junction, later to become famous under the name of Charing Cross.

"The European situation on August 26th," states the War Diary, "was very indefinite." Though by now the Regiment was used to the threat of war, this time it really did seem more than a threat, and at the camp all necessary precautions in case of attack by Italy were taken. Vehicles were dispersed and altogether the Regiment covered nearly a square mile. These first days were spent in endeavouring to dig slit trenches, which in ground seventy-five per cent. solid rock was an exhausting procedure and took the men five days. An added discomfort was the fact that everyone had to carry gas-masks and wear eye-shields. Shortage of water, too, put baths out of the question, but luckily the sea at Mersa Matruh was only eight miles away. It was difficult to realise, whilst lying in the crystal-clear water there with a cloudless sky above, that war was but a matter of days, and anything more incongruous than a gas-mask and a pair of eye-shields under such conditions was hard to imagine.

On September 1st at dawn Germany attacked Poland, and on September 3rd Great Britain declared war. Although Italy had not yet shown her hand there was not much doubt that she would come in soon, and in that case British domination of Egypt and the Mediterranean was vital. The army in the desert began to take on a new importance.

News in the desert was scarce and rumours throve, each one more wild than the last. The Mobile Division started a daily news sheet *The Gerawla Gossip* (subsequently *The Bagush Bugle*) which brought events into perspective. After the declaration of war the men were able to hear the evening news broadcast from England on the No. 11 wireless sets.

Although tents had been issued most people preferred to sleep in the open under the stars, in spite of the threat of scorpions, snakes and poisonous spiders. Five days after arriving at Matruh, troop training began.

The Regiment was at this time in a half-and-half state, being partly equipped with tracked and partly with wheeled vehicles which was most unsatisfactory, as far as training was concerned.

On the 13th the Regiment was paraded for a visit from King Farouk of Egypt and on the 19th Major-General The Hon. P. G. Scarlett, M.C. inspected troop cars of 'C' Squadron. There was as yet no fighting anywhere on land, although at sea the enemy had started laying mines at harbour entrances. In France all was quiet, each army waiting behind immense fortifications for the other to strike the first blow.

Training went on, in the desert, much the same as in peace-time. Regimental and Brigade exercises were carried out. The Regiment practised replenishing with petrol, oil and water and 'B' Echelon (the administrative section) was able to carry out a complete replenishment in three-quarters of an hour. Methods of evacuating wounded during an action were tried out and operations at night included the formations of leaguers. The R.A.F. dropped practice bombs, the signallers tested their communications, mock-enemy camps were located and shadowed. The Regiment became daily more skilled in their rôle of a Light Armoured Reconnaisance Regiment.

It was during October that the A-9 cruiser tanks appeared on the desert scene and ten reached the 6th Royal Tanks in the Heavy Armoured Brigade.

On October 13th came an inspiring message from His Majesty King George VI to the Army: "In all its long and glorious history, the British Army has never been called upon to take the field for a cause more just than that which is ours to-day; it has never entered a campaign in which the issues were greater or more vital to our race, and, indeed, of all civilisation. I know well that you realise what is at stake, and that, in the struggle which lies ahead, every man in my armies will play his part with gallantry and devotion. It is my earnest prayer that God will have you in His keeping and grant success to your arms. GEORGE R.I."

Training continued all through October and November. On November 9th all that the War Diary recorded was "A seething sandstorm all morning and afternoon," followed, on the 20th by "the heaviest downpour of all times coupled with a fierce gale." This proved too much for the tents, and for the ground. Everyone was soaked and all the transport embedded in a quagmire. The tanks proved their worth and hauled out everything, and the dripping troops were evacuated to Mersa Matruh. Rations were scarce too as all the R.A.S.C. vehicles also sank in the mud, and had to be rescued by tanks.

By the 12th the Regiment had moved out to a new camp site, but the next day came news of a return to Cairo which was received with some relief. By the end of the month they were back at Helmieh and stationed in the old 11th Hussar lines. These lay on the northern edge of Cairo between the town and the desert in a camp that was entirely surrounded by wire. Although the chief reason for their return had been to bring the Regiment up to full tank strength they had to wait until the end of April before this was accomplished.

Major-General Hobart, who had created the Division, left in December and his place was taken by Major-General Michael O'Moore Creagh. The Heavy Armoured Brigade then became the 4th Armoured Brigade under Brigadier J. A. L. Caunter, the Light became the 7th under Brigadier H. E. Russell and the Pivot Group became the Support Group first under Brigadier E. S. B. Williams and then Brigadier W. H. E. Gott.

All through the new year training had continued and by the end of April the Regiment was at last fully equipped. 'A' and 'B' Squadrons had Mark VI tanks armed with a ·303 and a ·50 machine-gun and 'C' Squadron, minus one troop, had Mark III's with one ·303 machine-gun. Regimental Headquarters Squadron consisted of four Mark VI's and a Bofors Anti-Tank troop. It was then decided that 'C' Squadron should have two troops of Mark VI's and two of the new A-9 cruiser tanks. These were armed with a 2 pdr. gun, a Besa and a power traverse and were much slower, weighing nearly thirteen tons and with a speed of eighteen miles per hour. However, before this could take place a scheme for full mobilisation as a field unit was ordered. At a practice mobilisation parade on May 6th, attended by Major-General O'Moore Creagh and Brigadier H. E. Russell, six Italian bombers flew low on their way to land at Almaya.

By now the situation in Egypt was becoming tense. Relations with Italy were strained and the news from Europe increasingly bad. After the invasion of Norway and Denmark, Germany suddenly and swiftly overran the Low Countries and then fell on France. The French, with few exceptions, proved men of straw, and the Panzer Divisions swept all before them. The French Army collapsed and Britain with a single Tank

Brigade, stood alone. On the last days of the month came the surrender of the Belgian Army and the miracle of Dunkirk. By the beginning of June an invasion of Britain seemed only a matter of time.

The fall of France had far-reaching results. The French military commanders in North Africa and Syria threw in their lot with their government and capitulated. Thus without a blow all the French Armies laid down their arms and General Wavell's Command stood alone on the frontiers of Egypt, Somaliland, Kenya and the Sudan.

On May 14th the newly-named 7th Armoured Division moved up to Gerawla less the 7th Armoured Brigade which remained in Abassia as the 8th Hussars had not yet equipped and trained more than one squadron. The regiments of the Armoured Brigades had been reshuffled and the 7th now consisted of the 8th Hussars and the 1st Royal Tanks while the 4th Armoured Brigade was made up of the 7th Hussars and 6th Royal Tanks.

The 11th Hussars, now Divisional Troops, with the Support Group were already at Mersa Matruh, with one troop on the frontier at Sollum.

The 7th Armoured Division was now the main part of the Western Desert Force, the only other troops there being the Cairo Infantry Brigade garrisoning Matruh and a small air force. The stage was now set, the actors in their places, and if their parts had been learnt a trifle quickly, they still waited eagerly for the curtain to go up.

They had not long to wait.

On June 11th Italy, judging the time was ripe, declared war on Britain and France. Three days later, on the other side of Europe, Russia, having subdued Finland, then invaded Lithuania, Latvia and Estonia and shortly afterwards two provinces of Roumania.

It was, of course, only Italy's action that immediately affected the troops in the Western Desert. The 11th Hussars and the Support Group moved up to the frontier wire and immediately went into action, capturing Sidi Omar before the occupants knew war had been declared. Three days later Fort Capuzzo was taken and the prisoners started to roll in. The rest of the Division, less the Regiment, moved up to the frontier on the 12th and a period of intense patrol activity began. Fort Maddalena followed Capuzzo, an Italian general was taken prisoner and nearly four thousand square miles of territory in Libya was regularly patrolled. All this threw a tremendous strain on the troops and vehicles involved. Enemy aircraft flew over constantly and almost without interruption. The frontier itself was one hundred and twenty miles from the railhead at Mersa Matruh and supply was becoming more of a problem every day.

At the end of June the 7th Armoured Brigade relieved the 4th near Sidi Suleiman. At this time the tactical plan was to stop an enemy advance at Mersa Matruh, and here the main force was positioned, with the 7th and 11th Hussars and a company of the Kings Royal Rifle Corps forward to give warning of an advance.

On July 8th the 8th Hussars received orders to move immediately from Helmieh, where they were still equipping, to the Western Desert. Accordingly the Regiment was reorganised. R.H.Q. Squadron had five light tanks, 'A' and 'B' Squadrons each had fifteen light tanks and 'C' Squadron seven cruisers and eight light tanks. They moved out to war on July 13th, less 'C' Squadron who were still re-equipping at Abassia. In their place came a squadron of cruiser tanks from the 1st Royal Tank Regiment.

At this time the Regiment was commanded by Lieut.-Colonel T. G. Watson who had been in command since 1938. Major G. Kilkelly was second-in-command, Major H. C. Elton had R.H.Q. Squadron, Captain J. D. Harbord had 'A' Squadron, Major D. S. Cripps had 'B', and Major Hayes commanded the cruisers of the Royal Tank Regiment.

There must have been many mixed feelings that day as the Regiment went to war for the first time. Those of 'C' Squadron who were being left behind and of the others who were now to prove their months of training. In this the 8th Hussars were luckier than most as they had been in Egypt since 1933 and were well accustomed to the climate. They were now to experience three years of desert warfare and all that it involved. The endless vista of the sandy coastal plain that stretched between the escarpment and the sea for three hundred miles from Alexandria, where it is thirty miles wide, to Sollum where it is only a few hundred yards. The escarpment itself, in places six hundred feet high, and south, beyond it, the real desert, that unknown, untracked expanse of rocks and shifting sand, of wells, of scrub and hills, depressions and ridges, where navigation was always by compass. They would experience great heat by day and extreme cold at night, they would suffer the Khamseen, that stifling, choking dust storm. They would endure the shortage of water, the monotony of bully beef and biscuits, the desert sores, the fever, the lack of sleep, and the strain of continually being on the alert. They would be under fire for the first time for most of them, and though perhaps to begin with it would be very like just another exercise, it would be an exercise with no appointed end, where at times each man would be alone and at times have enormous responsibility thrust upon him.

It was to be a journey that would not end in Africa but would continue across France and the Low Countries until at last it ended in the ruins of Berlin.

(b) The First Action, July 1940

ON their arrival at Mersa Matruh on July 14th the Regiment went at first into the dispersal area on the Matruh-Barrani road and later in the afternoon moved to the bivouac area, near Wadi el Halazin. On the 16th they moved to Bir el Hamarin at night, moving again the next night to a leaguer south-west of Sollum. They arrived at one in the morning of the 18th and at 4 a.m. they heard that the Italians would probably attack Sollum. This attack, however, did not materialise, and at 9 a.m. they had their first visit from enemy aircraft. On the 17th Captain C. Goulburn was appointed to Brigade Headquarters as Brigade Major.

The Regiment was now at the frontier and on the 19th Lieut.-Colonel Watson, Major Hayes, and Captain Harbord, Lieutenants Comyn and H. H. Firth accompanied patrols of the 7th Hussars into enemy territory as they were to take over this job.

The purpose of these tank patrols across the frontier was mainly to harass the Italians without becoming heavily involved with them, in order to give them the impression that opposing them was a large and strong force. In fact it was a very weak one, equipped with obsolete tanks, and playing for time, hoping the Italians would not invade Egypt until they were more prepared.

The tactics employed by the 7th Armoured Division were to keep one Armoured Brigade forward on the wire and the other in reserve. The forward brigade pushed artillery and tanks through the gaps in the wire some five miles or so over the frontier every morning before first light and withdrew them every evening after dark.

Harbord and 'A' Squadron, who were to have the honour of this first patrol, moved up to the frontier under cover of darkness and leaguered on the Egyptian side of the wire, that four hundred mile, five-foot high, rusty barbed-wire fence that the Italians had put up and which served to indicate the frontier rather than prove an obstruction.

At 4.30 next morning 'A' Squadron crossed the wire and moved off in the half-light. They set up Squadron Headquarters some ten kilometres north-west of Fort Capuzzo which had been evacuated as tactically unimportant and promptly retaken by the Italians. Various recce patrols were sent out, and 2nd Lieutenant J. Hooper's troop came under fire but there were no casualties. In the evening the Squadron withdrew to the leaguer east of the wire, leaving patrols on the frontier. At nine that night the attached cruiser squadron arrived to take over the patrols next day.

One of the main objectives was to harass the roads from Fort Capuzzo to Bardia and Sidi Aziez, along which the garrison's supplies had to come. As soon as the tank squadrons reported anything moving along it the guns of the supporting troop of Royal Horse Artillery opened up. Early in the morning of July 22nd, in spite of bad visibility, 'A' Squadron reported forty enemy lorries moving towards Capuzzo from Bardia. The fire of the attached troop of Royal Horse Artillery was accurate enough to make the convoy turn back and to cause some casualties. In the afternoon Captain Dunne went out with a troop and was able to identify to what regiments the dead Italians had belonged. The same afternoon while Lieutenant J. N. A. Baldwin was bringing up transport he was attacked by low-flying aircraft, but apart from a loss of twelve and a half precious gallons of water there were no casualties.

On July 23rd 'B' Squadron reported that four anti-tank guns had been sited on the Capuzzo-Sidi Azeiz road a few miles from Sidi Azeiz. Another patrol was sent out to verify this and, as it approached the place, found a convoy of about thirty lorries protected by ten light tanks. As the whole Regiment was supporting this day's patrol Lieut.-Colonel Watson ordered the Royal Tank Squadron of cruisers to attack. They advanced with the enemy tanks withdrawing towards Azeiz and managed to score hits on some of the lorries. As they drew closer they came under machine-gun fire from dug-outs and also fire from anti-tank guns in a building south of the road. A shell burst under one of the cruisers and one man was slightly wounded. The Squadron then wheeled to the north, firing broadside, and withdrew, the damaged cruiser limping home under its own steam.

This was a busy day. After this skirmish a Gloster Gladiator pilot baled out about two miles away and the Commanding Officer and Comyn rescued him on a tank.

At 7.30 p.m. day patrols were withdrawn and 'B' Squadron was responsible for those during the night. 2nd Lieutenant P. Earle went out well into enemy territory towards Bardia and reached an enemy observation post. The very useful result of this was a haul of Italian maps and an Italian code.

The skirmishing continued. Patrols were sent out daily, and by night, and reported more anti-tank guns and the fact that tanks were being used more frequently for the protection of the convoys. The Italians were getting respectful. They shelled Regimental Headquarters for some hours on July 24th and twenty-seven light tanks were reported to be approaching but the attack came to nothing.

An annoying feature of these patrols were the mirages, which meant that most of the work had to be done before nine in the morning and after five at night. Another entry says desperately: "Tormented by flies."

There was nothing of special interest to be recorded for the rest of July except for the establishment of an observation post at Bir Beda on the 29th. The officer on duty there had to arrive before dawn and leave under cover of darkness so it was no easy job. But in August the enemy decided to show their claws.

Just after midnight on August 1st two enemy columns were reported moving towards the frontier along the tracks to Sidi Omar and Musaid. The Italian invasion of Egypt had been expected for months and this might be it. Although the place was south of the 8th Hussars' area, a patrol from 'A' Squadron was sent out and the rest of the Regiment concentrated for action. Nothing came of this excitement but by August 4th it was established that about two hundred and fifty Italian vehicles were massed at Gabr Saleh, midway between the two tracks and about thirty miles west of the wire. This was the area patrolled by the 11th Hussars, and the Royal Tank Cruiser Squadron attached to the 8th was ordered to Bir Sheferzen to support them.

The next day, August 5th, saw the Regiment's first tank battle. Cripps with 'B' Squadron and with a troop from 'D' Battery, 3rd Royal Horse Artillery armed with Bofors 37 mm. anti-tank guns under his command, were patrolling as usual round the Azeiz-Capuzzo road. At about 10 a.m. a force of approximately thirty Italian M11 medium tanks appeared to the north, approaching rapidly and bearing down towards 'B' Squadron. These were different tanks from any that had been seen before, the usual kind, the C.V.3, were more a cross between a British carrier and a scout car. These M.11's were equipped with 37 mm. guns and were thus more powerfully armed than our tanks, although they did not have an all-round traverse. Later it transpired that both M11's and M13's were used.

Meanwhile Cripps immediately moved forward to a better position from which to engage the enemy, at the same time ordering forward the troops of Bofors. At that moment the enemy opened fire. Unfortunately the troop officer, Captain Brian Stewart, was just then otherwise engaged some little way from his troop and before he could get back to his guns the troop sergeant was wounded. The driver of one of the portées decided to evacuate him on the portée back to the Regimental Aid Post, some five miles away. As he dashed off in a cloud of dust the other three portées thought the troop had been ordered out of action. They made off and pursued the first gun back towards the wire. Captain Stewart gave chase in his truck but could not overtake them until they had gone a mile. He immediately brought them back in time to get into action against the enemy.[1]

In the meantime Cripps was left to engage the advancing enemy alone. His machine-gun fire rattled off the Italian armour with no effect and he ordered his squadron to withdraw. Two of his tanks were knocked out, one with a track breakage and one by a hit. The crews had baled out and one crew was rescued by Cripps himself, while the other just failed to reach Lieutenant Threlfall before they were surrounded by three enemy tanks.

Cripps found himself withdrawing in close company with the leading Italians who were still advancing and were by now only eighty yards away. This running fight continued for some three miles, and luckily for 'B' Squadron the Italians kept firmly closed down, thus limiting traverse and perhaps accounting for their indifferent shooting.

Meanwhile the Bofors had engaged six enemy tanks that had become separated from the rest of the party and were moving south. Firing from their trucks at six to eight hundred yards the gunners stopped all six tanks but eventually had to withdraw owing to very heavy machine-gun fire from which they had no protection.

In the meantime Lieut.-Colonel Watson had ordered 'A' Squadron to advance in support of 'B' and to sweep round to the left, engaging the enemy from the west. His

[1] Captain Stewart had a very gallant record in the war. He was finally blown up and killed on a mine in Normandy while commanding the Anti-Tank Regiment of the 7th Armoured Division, Norfolk Yeomanry.

third squadron, the Royal Tanks cruisers, were still at Bir Sheferzen with the 11th Hussars. This move was successful and the threat of 'A' Squadron approaching caused the enemy to break contact and withdraw, with 'A' Squadron getting some very long shots at a party retreating towards Azeiz.

When all was over the enemy were left dominating the high ground between Bir Beder and Hagfet el Charruba which had previously been ours. Of the 8th Hussar casualties, two men were presumed prisoners of war and one who had not been seen to leave the knocked-out tank, presumed killed. These were the Regiment's first casualties and from the skirmish they had gained one wounded enemy motor-bicyclist. For his conduct in this action Major Cripps was awarded the Regiment's first D.S.O. of the war.

Early next morning 'A' and 'B' Squadrons moved out on patrol. Night patrols had reported everything quiet. There was no sign of the enemy on the ridge he had taken the day before and no activity anywhere. The Squadrons re-occupied the ground and found that the Italians had not attempted to consolidate their position and probably their only object on the previous day had been to keep the tanks occupied while they moved reinforcements into Fort Capuzzo and Sidi Azeiz. 'B' Squadron found two tracks shed by the tanks that had been hit, and that had now been removed by the Italians along with their own two casualties. These and a quantity of bloodstained green shirts and field dressings were all that were left to show that an action had been fought there the day before.

During the day Regimental Headquarters and the Bofors Troop moved to Bir Hafid and the Cruiser Squadron returned from the 11th Hussars, who reported that the force at Gabr Saleh was still there but quiet. 'B' Squadron, returning from patrol, reported the triangle Bir Sleman-Azeiz-Capuzzo clear of the enemy, and for the next few days the only event of any note was the visit of the "Kumangetit" car with comforts.

(c) In the Desert, August 1940

ON August 10th at about 10 a.m. 'A' Squadron, patrolling to the west, reported forty medium enemy tanks advancing from Sidi Azeiz. The patrol, which was fired on as the enemy tanks approached, maintained contact and withdrew. On approaching Hagfet el Charruba the enemy turned south towards where the Regiment was lying. Immediately the Bofors Troop was sent out to the west to try and engage their flank but the enemy changed direction and finally disappeared in a northerly direction.

Next day, the 11th, Vernon-Miller with 'C' Squadron put in a welcome appearance and took over the cruiser tanks.

Then on the 14th came the orders to withdraw slowly by night towards Bir el Kenayis in the Taref Mountains south of Mersa Matruh. This was part of General Wavell's plan to withdraw the 7th Armoured Brigade from the frontier. All their vehicles, which had been worn out months ago, were by now on their last legs. There were no spare parts nor any reserves with which to replace them. The Italian advance was expected at any moment and Wavell did not want to meet it with half his armour out of commission. They must have some time for maintenance and refitting.

So, slowly and with no hurry, the Regiment, less 'C' Squadron left the wire after dark, travelling for four hours the first night. Next night, after a wonderful day with no flies, they moved seventy kilometres to Bir Khamsa and the next night to Bir Qatrani. Here they were allowed to use as much water as they liked, an unheard of thing in those days, and were visited by Lieut.-Colonel Robinson, an 8th Hussar officer on loan to the British Military Mission to Egypt.

On the 18th they were joined by 'C' Squadron and the Regimental doctor, Captain Windsor, R.A.M.C. left. He was replaced by Lieutenant J. B. Heycock who was to remain with them throughout all the campaigns that followed.

On the 20th at half-past ten at night they left for Bir Kenayis which lies on the track running from Matruh to the Siwa Oasis. The Regimental area was some ten kilometres north-east of Bir Kenayis itself and here they settled down, with plenty of water, to the all-important job of maintenance.

They had several important visitors and events. On the 25th the Rev. A. V. Kingston, padre of 7th Armoured Division, arrived with comforts from Alexandria. On the 26th the Regiment was visited by Prince Ismail Daoud, commanding the Egyptian Mechanised Brigade, and on the 29th Major Kilkelly arrived with the leave party, and took a poor view of immediately having to dig a slit trench. On September 6th two officers, while bathing in Matruh Harbour, found themselves watching an air raid in steel helmets and birthday suits. The G.O.C., Major-General O'Moore Creagh visited the Regiment later in the month as did General Maitland Wilson. On the 11th they were on six hours notice owing to movement along the wire, and on the 13th came the long awaited Italian advance.

It came as a surprise to no one and went very much according to plan. The great Italian Army of ten Divisions crossed the wire, one column making for Sofafi via the top of the escarpment while the other rumbled slowly down Halfaya Pass to Sollum and along the coast, harried by the guns of the Royal Horse Artillery. When they came to Sidi Barrani they stopped, much to everyone's surprise, and dug themselves in. The Regiment moved south, and were sent with all available tanks, twenty-three light and five cruisers, to do large "figure of eights" all over the sand in order to make as many tracks as possible and so confuse enemy Recce aircraft. Dummy tanks made of canvas and wood were also erected at night with the same idea in mind. These two-day manoeuvres showed that the Regiment's vehicles were still far from "desert worthy". The tanks all boiled over and eight had to be evacuated as unsafe. This was no surprise to the Regiment who knew well how old and worn-out they were.

However, these capers had the desired effect. The Italians showed no enthusiasm for venturing any further. They dug themselves firmly in and surrounded themselves with barbed wire, this only eighty miles short of Mersa Matruh, the British key position and the start of the metalled road to Alexandria. They had had some 3,500 casualties as against the British 150 which perhaps had something to do with it.

R.S.M. C. F. Hedley now took over the duties of Quarter-Master, a position he was to occupy, on and off, for the next twelve years. Also at this time while Lieutenant J. Weston Simons, taking over Liaison Officer from Lieutenant J. W. Gwyn, was trying to contact Headquarters Support Group, commanded by Brigadier Gott, on the Sidi Barrani-Bir Enba track at night, he motored into an Italian column. Luckily both sides were equally astonished and in the ensuing chaos he got away. After a gruelling journey he found that the message he was carrying had arrived some hours earlier by wireless.

On the night of the 17th-18th the Regiment moved back to their camp at Bir Kenayis where they remained with one exception for about a month. At the end of

September Lieutenant J. N. A. Baldwin returned from Brigade as Regimental Transport Officer and the Regiment was visited by the War Correspondent of an American paper and one from the News Chronicle.

(d) The Maktila Raid, October 1940

OCTOBER, 1940 was the month of the ill-starred Maktila Raid. The early part of the month was uneventful and the Regiment was still refitting at Bir Kenayis, just west of Mersa. There had been little activity on the frontier, and such as it was had been carried out by the 11th Hussars and the 'Jock' [1] Columns. However on the 19th all Squadron Leaders were suddenly called to a conference where they were told that Higher Command had decided that the Italian Camp at Maktila, occupied by the 1st Libyan Division, had to be attacked and destroyed. The 2nd Cameron Highlanders and the 8th Hussars had been chosen to carry this out. The Maktila Camp was situated about three miles east of Sidi Barrani, between the main coastal road and the sea. It was in fact the most easterly point the Italians on their own ever reached. The armoured cars of the 11th Hussars had the camp under constant observation but were not taking any part in the raid.

The next day, the 20th, the Squadron Leaders were summoned to a conference held by Brigadier Gott of the Support Group, who was in command of the raid. It was a long and dusty drive to Brigadier Gott's Headquarters, thirty miles in fact, and so dusty that he failed to recognise two of the Squadron Leaders although he knew them well. Two days later at 6.30 a.m. the Regiment set off on the approach march, 'B' Squadron in the lead followed by 'A', 'C' and Regimental Headquarters at one hour intervals. This much was uneventful except that they had to pass a newly-arrived Indian Brigade who were reputed not to be very good at tank recognition. However, apart from regarding the Regiment with a great deal of interest they took no notice. In the evening after travelling thirty-seven miles they halted some two miles south-west of Bir Hashim and brewed up. The petrol lorries which had travelled with them came round and all tanks were filled up. The Commanding Officer and Squadron Leaders had a last recce of enemy positions. After this, final briefing was held and the whole plan explained to everyone. Up to this moment everything in connection with this operation had been regarded as Top Secret and nobody in the Regiment below the rank of Squadron Leader knew anything about it at all. The move from Bir Kenayis had been regarded as a routine relief of the armoured regiment holding the front line.

The plan was for the 8th Hussars and the Camerons in lorries to move up to the assembly position after dark. The Camerons would then dismount and advance to the starting line on foot. On crossing this line they were to make a frontal attack on the camp with a smaller attack coming in along the sea-shore, on the left flank of the camp. 'B' Squadron was to be in direct support of the frontal attack with 'A' Squadron on their left and 'C' Squadron in reserve. By the time the plan had been explained to everyone

[1] A 'Jock' Column was a small, mobile, self-supporting force consisting of detachments of tanks, infantry and artillery which operated at long range behind and around the enemy positions. They were inspired by Brigadier Jock Campbell, V.C., who later, as Major-General Campbell, was killed in a motor accident shortly after taking over command of the 7th Armoured Division.

Subalterns' Cup, 1939. W. V. H. Nelson, P. H. Huth, W. G. Lowther and J. C. Pringle (page 17).

Polo at the Gezira Sporting Club, 1939.

Open Cup, 1939. Capt. J. C. Vernon-Miller, Capt. C. Goulburn, Lieut. J. C. Pringle, Major G. Kilkelly.

The Riding School at Abbassia, Cairo, 1939.
Lieutenants J. N. A. Baldwin, J. F. Weston Simons, J. W. Gwyn, J. A. Comyn and W. V. H. Nelson.

An 'Order' group for an exercise at Cairo at the beginning of the war.
Lieut.-Colonel Watson, Captains J. C. Vernon-Miller and N. G. F. Dunne, Lieutenants J. F. Weston Simons,
J. N. A. Baldwin, J. A. Comyn and R. E. McDonnell.

8th Hussars lined up in the barracks, Abbassia, at the beginning of the war. Regimental Headquarters tanks are on the right.

Lieut. Newman, Capt. Nelson, 2nd Lieut. McLintoch and two crew men and their Christmas dinner, 1940. The pudding consisted of Army biscuits, prunes, marmalade and rum (page 40).

The answer to the German Panzers. Capt. J. W. Gwyn and the crew of his Honey having an early-morning 'brew-up', November, 1941 (page 51).

The same tank as above, camouflaged for Operation 'Crusader'. This picture was taken on the approach-march to Sidi Rezegh where the Germans were encountered for the first time, November, 1941 (page 52).

it was nearly dark and time to move off. This rather difficult night march was accomplished without a hitch and everyone was in position in plenty of time. So far the Italians did not seem to have any idea that an attack was about to be launched. It is interesting to note, here, that this was the first occasion on which tanks were used in a properly planned night attack by any Army. Previously the difficulties involved had always been regarded as too great.

One o'clock in the morning of the 23rd.

Zero hour and the Commanding Officer's birthday. Everyone ready for this first action by night, a little tensed, tank crews in position, the infantry in their appointed places. Pitch dark and rather cold. Visions of the Italian garrison snug in bed.

Then, at one minute to zero, every single gun in the Italian camp opened fire. The noise was shattering and, being so totally unexpected, the more frightening. In spite of this the Camerons attacked gallantly but had no chance against a garrison dug-in, well-equipped and alert. The night was brilliant with flashes and the rattle of machine-gun fire. 'B' Squadron were unable to help, apart from long-range supporting fire, as they could not close in owing to minefields which were known to exist but whose exact location had not been determined. The only part of the attack which had any success was the party that worked its way along the shore and got round the defences by wading. But even they could not achieve much owing to the failure of the main attack.

Much later on, 6.30 a.m. to be exact, signals came through that the Camerons were out of touch with the enemy. 'B' Squadron were able to go to their rescue and picked up numbers of men who had got lost and were still in danger from gun-fire. 'A' Squadron could take no part until well after dawn, then they too helped pick up lost Camerons. While doing this 'A' Squadron were sharply engaged by an Italian armoured force of some twenty strong which had emerged from Camp Tummar East. Fighting this small action was somewhat complicated owing to the numbers of Camerons inside the tanks as well as the normal crew. Both Lieut.-Colonel Watson and an 11th Hussar armoured car who arrived just as this action finished were surprised and embarrassed to find their vehicles immediately filled to overflowing with Cameron Highlanders.

At 1.45 a.m. the order to withdraw came through and, all Camerons being picked up, the Regiment started on their return journey to Bir Kenayis. What was described by one taking part as "an abortive attack" was over.

It was very strongly felt by everyone that this attack had been compromised. In fact they heard later that three days before the Squadron Leaders' conference the whole operation was being discussed openly in Cairo. The only thing to be said for it was that there were no casualties and at least experience had been gained.

The rest of October passed without incident. All Squadrons started training and on the 30th they were visited by Major-General Clark, G.O.C. Cavalry Division, Palestine.

On the 17th November the Regiment were ordered to relieve the 3rd Hussars on the frontier and were moved up to the Bir Enba area to keep open the gap between the Sofafi groups of armed camps and Nibeiwa. This gap was to play a vital part in the campaign ahead when the two Armoured Brigades passed through it in December in their drive to cut off Sidi Barrani from the west.

'B' Squadron took over forward patrols, linking up with the 11th Hussars patrol covering the whole area from Nibeiwa to Rabia. 'A' Squadron kept the area east of Nibeiwa under observation from Hileqat. On the 21st the 3rd Hussars returned and the Regiment moved to Bir Abd el Razig.

The Italians periodically sallied out from Nibeiwa and every morning indulged in a

C

shelling 'hate'. It was during one of these sallies, when 'A' Squadron was in the line, that the news was received from Brigade of a telegram from England bearing the glad tidings that 2nd Lieutenant Hooper's wife had had a baby. This was relayed to 'A' Squadron at a moment when Captain Dunne had his hands very full indeed. The rear link operator poked his head out of the tank and shouted: "Mr. Hooper's had a baby!" which brought forth the reply: "Well, he's damn clever, so shall I in a minute!"

It was during one of the bad days that Dunne caught a stray shot from an air battle between Gladiators and C.R.42's, wounding him in the hand, and he became the first wounded casualty in the Regiment.

The Regiment had under command at this time 'Rocket' Troop, Royal Horse Artillery, one Company Kings Royal Rifle Corps for night patrols and local guards, and various squadrons in turn of the Central India Horse. The latter were put on hills and then shelled, to give them experience.

This was a time of perfect weather, cloudless skies by day and cold fresh nights. Just before the Regiment left the Enba area Captain C. E. R. Duff arrived from England to take over 'A' Squadron from Dunne who retired to Cairo with a bad attack of desert sores on his hands. Captain J. W. Phillips also arrived from the Desert Air Force and became second-in-command of the same squadron. 2nd Lieutenant D. C. Ricardo joined 'B' Squadron.

On the last day of November the 1st Royal Tank Regiment arrived to take over from the Regiment who went back in reserve to the Bir el Munin area, eighteen miles north-west of Bir el Kenayis.

(e) The Battle of Buq Buq, December 1940

THESE months of September, October, November, were, for those in charge, a period of waiting as well as of preparation. The Mediterranean was by now more or less closed and the eagerly awaited supplies had to come round by the Cape. All the same an offensive was planned for December. In the meantime there was much harrying and patrolling of the new frontier, mostly by the famous 'Jock' Columns which were formed in September. The 3rd Hussars arrived from England and the 7th Armoured Brigade, under Brigadier H. E. Russell, now consisted of the 3rd Hussars with light tanks (less one squadron), with one squadron 2nd Royal Tanks; the 8th Hussars; the 1st Royal Tanks; and one Battery 1st Regiment Royal Horse Artillery. The tank strength of the 4th Armoured Brigade was similarly doubled and two regiments of Royal Horse Artillery also joined the Division.

By the time the December offensive materialised, the Western Desert Forces had been reinforced by the 7th Royal Tanks with Matildas, the first Infantry tanks to be seen in the Middle East.

At the beginning of December the Italian Army was spread over a wide front. Rather than maintain a continuous defended line they had dug themselves in to a series of camps that could not even support one another and the gaps between were tempting. The forces opposing the Desert Rats were approximately 75,000 troops and a hundred and twenty tanks against the 7th Armoured Division and the 4th Indian Division, less than a third in numbers, and with two hundred and seventy-five tanks, mostly obsolete. As far as was known the enemy had 7,500 troops at Maktila and Sidi Barrani, 2,500 at Nibeiwa and 7,000 at both the Tummar Camps and Sofafi.

General Wavell's plan was for both Divisions to concentrate in the Bir Enba area, then, while the 7th Armoured Division protected the south and west flanks, the Indians were to strike north for Sidi Barrani. Meanwhile the garrison force at Mersa Matruh would make feint attacks at Maktila. This was a plan intended to cover a campaign of a few days. In point of fact it lasted for two months.

By December 6th all was ready. On the 7th the Regiment received the warning order to move west next day at 6 a.m. On the 8th the whole desert was on the move, a most inspiring sight. A dust storm kept the Italian air force on the ground and they had no idea of what was going on a few miles away across the sand. The news was then broken to the troops that this was the real thing at last. The Regiment spent all of D-Day on the top of the escarpment at Ghot el Washka, and at dusk moved on.

At Brigade Headquarters that night a tired Colonel, who had been writing Movement Control Orders all day, was heard to remark:

"They won't be much use. The Cavalry never read them, the Gunners make their own arrangements and the Infantry can't understand them."

Half an hour later Regimental Headquarters was charged by a battery of 25 pounders and an unholy mix-up ensued. Their explanation was that they were moving to ——— and had made their own arrangements, and in spite of all the Commanding Officer could shout and curse they still kept moving. As all major moves at this time were done on bearings with the sun compass by day and the prismatic by night, any deviation of course could cause chaos. After a further half-hour an Indian column tried to get across the Regiment's line of move. A voice from the leading pick-up shouted:

"Where the hell is the Enba track? I've read the army map reference and I'm lost."

He was informed coldly that the track was to the north and that he was heading south, and there was another splendid mix-up of vehicles.

The Regiment slept that first night round their tanks, and anyone waking at midnight could have heard and seen all hell let loose round the Nibeiwa camps before the 4th Indian Division went in to attack.

All next day, the 9th, the Regiment with the rest of the 7th Armoured Brigade lay in reserve at Ghot Shalludi between Piccadilly and Bir Enba. All that disturbed them was a machine-gun attack on Regimental Headquarters and 'B' Squadron by a Hurricane with British markings. But the news was good and prisoners were pouring back. The Regiment was right on its toes and straining at the leash. Comyn handed over Signals Officer to Baldwin and took over a troop of 'C' Squadron, and the night was spent in Regimental leaguer.

Meanwhile the main attack was going well. The 4th Indian Division swept through Nibeiwa Camp and went on to attack the camps at Tummar. The 7th Armoured Division's task was to cut off the Italians in Sidi Barrani, and the 4th Armoured Brigade drove forward over the main coast road west of Barrani and by the evening the town had fallen. The Tummar Camps were taken too, and on the 10th the 7th Armoured Brigade was ordered to secure Buq Buq.

The Regiment's part in this attack was to threaten the southern flank of the enemy and make an attack on the camps at Sofafi and Rabia. Accordingly they moved from leaguer at 8.30 a.m., in independent order of march. At Bir Thalata there was a Squadron Leaders' conference and they then moved off to recce the area round Bir Habata. On reaching Hagfet ikda Ramadan they were told that they were to return that night and not to make their way up to the top of the escarpment to outflank Sofafi, but that 'A'

Squadron was to send a patrol to Qabr el Mahdi to find out the strength and defences of the camp at Rabia. The object of this operation was more of a demonstration or 'holding' attack, intended to pin down the garrison at Rabia and prevent them from sending reinforcements to the camps being attacked from the north.

After going some four miles a thick sandstorm enveloped them and navigation was by guess and by God. 'A' Squadron was in the lead with 'C' on right flank guard and 'B' in reserve. After the estimated distance to the camp had been covered and there was still no sign of the enemy, Comyn and his troop were ordered north to try and locate them.

The sandstorm was so thick that the troops had to go in very close indeed, even when they had located the camp, to make certain of details. One tank broke down and one broke a track pin so Comyn went in alone. The storm lifted and he found himself right under the enemy guns. In a few moments he received a direct hit which killed his driver and blew him straight out of the turret, knocking him unconscious. The two other tanks managed to withdraw, but Comyn was taken prisoner. Two days later when the Regiment captured the Italian Field Hospital at Sofafi an Italian priest told them that he was all right but that his crew, Troopers Bishop and Powell, had both been killed. Bishop's parents and family had been killed two weeks before in the raid on Coventry.

Months later Comyn wrote from the Prisoner of War camp: "I am responsible for it but I hope you remember the weather. I could see nothing with that dust storm until going up close and Charlie (Duff) wanted definite information."

That night, after a patrol by Lieutenant Scott of 'B' Squadron towards Bir Habata, the Regiment returned at midnight by the same route to their former positions.

Meanwhile to the north the 7th Armoured Brigade had taken Buq Buq, the Italians having evacuated it and departed for Sollum. However a force of almost Divisional strength was reported to have taken up position a few miles west of Buq Buq among the sand dunes and mud flats. They were being watched by the armoured cars of the 11th Hussars.

At 5 a.m. there was a Squadron Leaders' conference and orders were given for the Brigade to move up to the enemy in the sand dunes. The Regiment moved off an hour later, 'B' Squadron leading, followed by Regimental Headquarters, 'A' Squadron and 'C' Squadron, with a total strength of thirty tanks. They went by Wadi el Shaludi, Wadi el Kabsh and Abar Mideiwir el Arad where they halted and filled up with petrol. It was a hot unpleasant journey and the going very bad over 'camel humps' varying from three inches to two feet in height and formed by blown sand accumulating round bunches of camel grass.[1]

However the Regiment had several miles of this objectionable ground to cover going north. After about five miles they caught the first glimpse they had had for weeks of the sea. The day was very hot, too, for the time of year and made even more unpleasant by the fact that the bully beef for lunch had turned into a congealing mass of grease.

At Aba Mideiwir a troop of 25 pounders from A/E Battery, 1st Royal Horse Artillery under Captain Armitage, came under command.

At midday Brigadier Gatehouse arrived with the news that the Brigade objective was clear and that the 3rd Hussars had reached the coast and turned west, but that the

[1] They were a common feature of this part of the desert within ten miles of the sea. Further south there was very little vegetation except in the "Ghots" which were depressions where rain water collected on rare occasions and bushes and camel grass grew.

11th Hussars had met with opposition near Alam Idris. The Regiment was ordered to go to their assistance at once.

At half-past two they reached Alam Idris and Lieut.-Colonel Watson went forward to confer with the Commanding Officer of the 11th Hussars, Lieut.-Colonel J. F. B. Combe, D.S.O., while the enemy lurked in the sand dunes, north of Ilwet el Na'as.

Threlfall and 'B' Squadron were sent west along the Sollum road to support an 11th Hussar patrol who had captured some lorries, while 'C' Squadron remained in reserve. The Regiment moved up to just south of Ilwel el Na'as where 'A' Squadron, with only three tanks, stayed to guard the 11th Hussars' prisoners.

At just about this time there was a tremendous barrage to the right front and the leading squadron reported heavy gun fire to the east and about a mile ahead. They had been previously told that a Battalion of Blackshirt Infantry supported by two batteries of guns were holding the line of the Sidi Barrani-Sollum road in order to keep the escape route from Sidi Barrani open. They had been ordered to overrun that line at all costs and the leading squadron was practically up to it.

Suddenly the Regiment was ordered to halt and orders started pouring in over the air. The information was that the 3rd Hussars on their right had got across the Barrani-Sollum road and turned west on to the salt pans. A battery of enemy guns had been drawn up facing west, and as each tank in turn stuck in the marsh they brewed them up, with the result that the whole leading squadron was out of action, together with part of their Regimental Headquarters.

Duff with 'A' Squadron in the lead, pushed on over the road to a small hill. Lieut.-Colonel Watson took his Regimental Headquarters to the south of the hill under cover from the enemy, 'B' Squadron and Threlfall were put on left flank guard while 'C' and Vernon-Miller came up to Regimental Headquarters. Lieut.-Colonel Watson and Brigadier Russell of the 7th Armoured Brigade then rushed the top of the hill together.

West were the tanks of the 3rd Hussars, on fire some seven hundred yards away. To the north, drawn up on the edge of the salt pans, was a battery of 75 mms. facing the hill, with transport and dozens of little men in black hurrying about. The guns then came into action against the Regiment and shells started landing in 'C' Squadron, so that Vernon-Miller withdrew about four hundred yards, and got cursed by the Commanding Officer.

A plan was immediately made for the 25 pounders of the attached Artillery battery to shell the enemy for four minutes while 'C' Squadron charged them on the forward edge of the dunes. When 'C' had got to within five hundred yards they were to cease fire, and 'B' were to follow-up if necessary.

The 25 pounders carried out their job nobly and as always were most accurate. 'C' Squadron came round either side of the hills, guns blazing, Squadron Headquarters and the cruiser tanks in the centre and the Mark VIs on either flank. The Italians opened up and the guns, which until recently had been facing west and firing on the 3rd Hussars, were hastily brought to bear on 'C' Squadron.

However, an action that looked like developing into a second Balaclava, soon stopped. Nelson in a cruiser hit a lorry which was drawn up just behind the gun line with his third shot. (They fired on the move in those days.) This proved to be full of ammunition which blew up with the most terrifying crash. It was too much for the Italians, and before they had recovered 'C' Squadron was on to the gun line, and up went everything white that could be produced.

Sidi Barrani was now properly sealed off. The 7th Armoured Brigade was over the road and the 11th Hussars with their cars started pushing west.

'B' Squadron was sent up to help 'C' with the prisoners who were now pouring in from all sides. It transpired that they had captured a complete Field Regiment with all its transport. This, without loss of one man to the Regiment, was entirely done by the dash and speed at which the attack was put in and carried out.

As evening came on one of the cruisers was detached to pull out an 11th Hussars armoured car which had got stuck in the salt pans. Vernon-Miller objected strongly, "a gross misuse of equipment," and with good cause, as the tank itself became stuck in the sand and is probably there to this day. They never got a replacement and it would have been invaluable later.

Regimental Headquarters, two 'A' Squadron tanks, A/E Troop and Blackburn Troop, 3rd Royal Horse Artillery leaguered that night near Ilwet el Halfa while 'B' and 'C' Squadrons guarded the prisoners. Cripps brought in the Colonel of the Italian Gunner Regiment on the back of his tank. The old man was in tears, cursing the war and Mussolini. He was still wearing an M.C. given to him in the last war. On searching the enemy baggage some maps of Tobruk were found with the overprint of what appeared to be defences inserted on them. These were sent back to Brigade at once, and they proved later to be completely accurate in every detail and were used with great success by all troops assaulting Tobruk.

That night Brigade asked how many prisoners had been captured and Threlfall on the 'B' Squadron rear link replied: "One acre of officers and two and a half of other ranks!" In fact there were 14,000.

The R.A.F. paid them a visit later at 9 o'clock that night and dropped a stick of bombs right across the mass of prisoners guarded by 'C' Squadron. The result was appalling and amongst the casualties was Trooper Westcott killed, as well as several wounded. They were lucky, however, not to suffer more as they had no cover at all and could only try to disappear into the sand.

While the afternoon's fighting was going on, the Support Group was dealing with the Italians at Sofafi, and the 4th Armoured Brigade were preparing to pursue along the escarpment and into Cyrenaica.

The next day, the 12th, was spent in getting rid of the vast amounts of prisoners, and on the 13th the whole Regiment went south and climbed the escarpment west of Sofafi. It was at the Italian First Aid Post at Rabia that they heard about Comyn, and they were hopeful of catching up the Italians and recapturing him, but were unlucky, and leaguered that night some five miles south of Halfaya Pass.

That evening the 4th Armoured Brigade advanced and at dawn crossed the frontier and were soon not twenty miles from Bardia.

On the 14th at 6.30 a.m. the Regiment pushed west towards Sidi Omar, 'B' Squadron to take over the rôle of protecting Gap 40 in the frontier wire that faced Capuzzo and north-east to the Musaid area, and 'C' Squadron to Gap 45 which overlooked Sidi Omar itself. Captain Armitage's troop of Bofors of the Royal Horse Artillery accompanied them, and as soon as they discovered Sidi Omar was in enemy hands, Lieut.-Colonel Watson decided to attack the fort under a tremendous barrage from the guns. However, as Armitage had not got the ammunition they had to sit and look at it while the guns "managed to put down two rounds per gun at breakfast, lunch and tea, about 10 at night and again at one in the morning, just to annoy. It certainly annoyed us if not the Italians."

However a 'B' Squadron patrol, north of Gap 40, managed to pick off a lorry, one out of four, and the rest withdrew.

Squadrons that night leaguered in their own areas with patrols out.

(f) Bardia and Tobruk Encircled, December 1940-January 1941

THEN ensued a short interval while the 7th Armoured Division waited for the 6th New Zealand Division to come up for the assault on Bardia. Many nice things were said about their successes so far, the Prime Minister, Mr. Churchill, announced that Buq Buq and Sidi Barrani were victories of the first order. Indeed it was the first victory gained by the Army in the war and very welcome at that moment of depression. Britain and the Commonwealth still stood alone facing invasion, and the blitz was shattering the homes of the men in the desert.

In August there had been an irritating campaign in Somaliland against the Italians, which ended in the only British defeat at Italian hands on record. In September was the abortive Dakar expedition and in October, Italy had invaded Greece. General Wavell had had to send some of his precious troops and aircraft there, in vain as it happened. November saw the beginning of Lend-Lease from America, but to balance this was the ever-mounting toll of shipping taken by U-boats, a toll that was to increase steadily. Then in December came a victory over the Italians in Abyssinia and at the same time, the Western Desert Forces pushed them back from the Egyptian frontier.

Although the victory was only over the Italians, no one knew in those days quite what unsubstantial enemies they were. Anyway their equipment could have hardly been worse than that of the Western Desert Force who were crying out for new tanks, and spares for almost everything. It is so difficult from the spot to take a broad view of war, if in fact possible. Events are not neatly tabulated and in order. To the Middle East Forces it seemed unbelievable that Britain would not send them more troops, more tanks, more guns. But Britain herself was, single handed, facing an invasion and could ill spare anything that could be turned to her own defence. Also at this moment the risk of sending anything by the Mediterranean was great and the alternative Cape route took so long as to be hardly worth using as anything sent that way might arrive too late.

After the action in the salt pans the Regiment were on patrol again every day from dawn, leaguering each night in a different place. They were visited regularly at about midday by an enormous 'circus' of Italian Savoias and CR 42s, cruising about and trying to cause mischief. Sometimes a lone Hurricane would dive at them out of the sun, get one and dash off before the CR 42s had time to retaliate.

The 4th Armoured Brigade under Brigadier Caunter went through their lines one day to try and cut the road from Bardia to Tobruk by out-flanking the still-held Capuzzo and Sidi Azeiz, and at night Threlfall took the 4th Armoured Brigade Echelon through the wire to join them, no mean feat navigating at night through unknown enemy territory.

After their period of watching, the Regiment handed over to the 4th Armoured Brigade who succeeded in capturing Sidi Omar on the 16th. Meanwhile they had an appalling night march to the west of Sidi Azeiz, under the full moon to start with and then in pitch darkness. It was a distance of some forty miles on two 'legs' or bearings, to a Bir. "When we had done our distance," the navigator wrote, "we stopped, but not at a Bir, in fact at a dip in the desert with no signs of any well. I got soundly cursed, but the Colonel decided to stop and try to find out where we were at first light. It turned out that the Bir was only fifty yards away over the top of a rise. I was truly pleased with myself, but everyone else said that I should have looked that night and not been so vague!"

However the Regiment crossed the Azeiz-Barrani track (the Trigh Capuzzo) on the 20th and the leading squadron halted, overlooking the road from Bardia to Tobruk, some five miles west of Bardia. They were to stop the enemy using the road and to support the 11th Hussars who had already reached it. 'B' and 'C' Squadrons leaguered either side of the track at Gabr Bzeu, and Regimental Headquarters, the Battery of Anti-Aircraft Guns and the Troop of Anti-Tank Guns at Hagfet el Carmus. However, the next day 'B' Squadron moved north of the escarpment as it was found to be impassable at night except by road or at small points which could not be found in the dark.

Here they remained till after Christmas, resting and doing maintenance. On Christmas Eve they were visited by Major-General O'Moore Creagh, G.O.C. 7th Armoured Division and on Boxing Day by a CR 42 which flew out of the sun and machine-gunned Regimental Headquarters, but with no casualties.

Regimental Headquarters were close to a Bir and they made themselves as comfortable as possible. Wireless news from England regaled them day and night with descriptions of the delicious Christmas dinner that Wavell's gallant Army was going to get. As the fare had been bully, biscuits, bacon, jam, marg. and tea with a bully stew at night every day since the campaign had started, they looked forward to the promised treat and it was the main topic of conversation.

Christmas Day came and with it some dried fruit, less bully than usual and no rum. How they cursed. They often wondered who had all the dinners.

At about this time Nelson developed his famous recipe for porage, one crushed biscuit at night left to soak in water until breakfast time, then heated up. Followed by tinned bacon this was considered the height of luxury. Cigarettes were a great problem too at this time. The issue was a brand called 'R.A.F.' which rightly had a Spitfire on the outside. The manufacturer was at last put in prison as they were found to be made of the sweepings from cinemas, but even after this was made public they were still issued. Woodbines came up occasionally and these were highly prized and kept to be used as an after-dinner smoke.

On the 30th the 6th Royal Tanks arrived to take over and the Regiment prepared to move west.

On New Year's Eve they moved up the road towards Tobruk in order to delay an enemy force operating from Tobruk and trying to relieve Bardia. Their route lay parallel to the escarpment and south of the road. Regimental Headquarters leaguered at Bir el Hamsa with 'C' Squadron at Sghifet el Charregh as a protective screen. Blackburn's Troop of 3rd Royal Horse Artillery Anti-Tank Guns and one Troop 151st Anti-Aircraft Regiment, R.A., under Lieutenant Hope, leaguered with 'B' Squadron, while the other Anti-Aircraft Troop protected the unarmoured vehicles of Regimental Headquarters.

It was a memorable New Year's Eve. Bitterly cold and with no rations. Everyone went to bed cold and hungry and nobody was full of joy.

At about this time, January 1941, Lieutenant R. E. McDonnell joined the Regiment from Cairo. He was attached to Division and was the first 8th Hussar officer to be killed when, on February 7th he was struck in the legs by a blast from an aerial mine at Benghazi and died of wounds.

After the Regiment had been in the ghot for some forty-eight hours an old Arab arrived, and by means of signs indicated that an aeroplane had force-landed about three miles to the north. Simons who was the Intelligence Officer, well over six feet, wrote:

"We immediately set off, Colonel Watson and Major Kilkelly in the Dingo and myself as the keen Intelligence Officer in a 15 cwt. Just after we had reached the Bardia-Tobruk road a figure sprang out of a bush on the verge and the Dingo halted. It was an Italian who, with a flourish, whipped his ceremonial dirk from its scabbard to present to the Colonel. The latter though he was about to be stabbed and nearly fell off the back of the Scout Car. However, when all had quietened down, we proceeded with our new prisoner as the guide. On finally arriving at the aeroplane we discovered that none of us were armed, but on finding that three of the crew had broken legs and the only one on his feet was the very small and insignificant Captain of the aircraft, we all felt braver and approached. The aircraft was a Savoia shot down by a Hurricane. With a view to getting the rations Colonel Watson climbed in the plane, leaving me to interrogate the small Captain and get the wounded on to my 15 cwt.

"I was full of information about getting prisoners to talk so I started to try the gentleman in English—no result—I shouted—no result—in French—no result—then a mixture of Latin and French—at last some understanding! I racked my brain for something to talk about and remembered Amalfi which I had visited before the war.

" 'Ah! Almalfi! ! Magnifico! ! !' came from the little man, who was so overcome that he stood on his toes and kissed me on both cheeks. At that very moment the Colonel and Major Kilkelly looked out of the aeroplane—the language! However we got them back safely and away to Brigade, who I trust had more success than I did."

It was while the Regiment were at Bir el Hamsa that they watched a thrilling ground-air battle between the attached Bofors troop and some CR 42's. The Regiment were tucked into the side of the cliffs and the Bofors were camouflaged in the middle of the ghot. The CR 42's saw them but not the Bofors, who gave a terrific display. They only shot one down, but winged several.

On January 1st the Western Desert Force was renamed 13th Corps. On the 3rd the Australians attacked Bardia and on the 5th it fell. The 7th Armoured Brigade was moved west to what was later called Knightsbridge and from there to Acroma, patrols cutting the road west of Tobruk. The 4th Armoured Brigade followed to the area north-west of el Adem, and the Support Group took over near Acroma, establishing itself, as at Bardia, astride the coast road. The 7th Armoured Brigade then moved west to Gazala, south of the escarpment, the 11th Hussars patrolling to the Gebel Akhdar and Mechili, which latter place was still in enemy hands.

From the 1st to the 5th of January the Regiment remained at Bir el Hamsa watching Tobruk, with patrols from 'B' Squadron out along the Bardia-Tobruk road. After staying there a week the maps of the Tobruk defences arrived, the very same that the Regiment had captured at Buq Buq. On the 5th came the order to move to el Adem airfield that night. At lunch time a patrol of the 7th Hussars came to take over 'B' Squadron's duties on the road as the 4th Armoured Brigade were going to cover the approach of the Australian Brigade up the road from Bardia.

At 4 o'clock Regimental Headquarters and 'C' Squadron left, going by Bir el Chewazi over Trigh Capuzzo to the Tobruk road where they met the Echelon and leaguered for the night. 'B' Squadron followed at 6 p.m., having waited for the 7th Hussars. The object of this move was to stop the enemy using el Adem airfield, while the 3rd Hussars consolidated the road from Tobruk to el Adem and kept the Tobruk-Derna road under observation.

Regimental Headquarters took up day positions north of the aerodrome and 'B' Squadron was ordered to push patrols up the el Adem-Tobruk road and the Sidi Han-Han-Mdannar track, while the other two squadrons lay in reserve. By night they withdrew to a position east of the main buildings.

On the 6th, while approaching the airfield, one light tank of 'C' Squadron was blown up on a Thermos bomb.

The days consisted purely of patrols probing into the defences of Tobruk in order to verify the map and pin-point the gun positions. One patrol on the 8th led by 2nd Lieutenant Jermyn Scott was heavily shelled but obtained valuable information. The aerodrome itself was full of the skeletons of aircraft and the officers' mess still had the billiard table and balls. In spite of the cloth being torn the Regiment had some excellent games during their stay. When off duty they all had baths which were most welcome as no one had seen so much water for three months and had hardly washed their hands, let alone bathed, for two.

It was extremely cold at this time and a biting wind from the south blew for most of the day.

Whilst on the aerodrome the Christmas hamper sent by the wives in Cairo arrived. It had started off filled with good things from the shops there but by the time it arrived it was nearly empty which was a great disappointment. No one had had any luxuries since the start of the campaign as the Naafi was at Derna, where it remained until after the battle of Beda Fomm and the capture of Benghazi.

By this time the Echelon was beginning to feel its age. It had been with the Regiment with a few exceptions since mechanization. It was decided that the time had come when it could no longer be depended upon, despite the tender attentions of Captain Sir E. W. St. Lo. Malet, the Technical Adjutant.

The 3rd Hussars passed through the Regiment on their way north to Acroma, and thus Tobruk was surrounded. When this was completed the Regiment received orders to hand over their sector and push west along Trigh Capuzzo once more. That night, the 8th, two men of the Anti-Aircraft Regiment and Trooper Morgan were killed by Thermos bombs, and three men were wounded.

On the 9th at 4 p.m. the move began and the Regiment finally halted at six hours later in a shallow Ghot "lately vacated by the Italians judging by the extraordinary smell!" Next day, the 10th, 'B' Squadron put a patrol astride the Trigh, 'C' Squadron went due west and the thinskins east, while the 3rd Hussars were north at Gazala and the 1st Royal Tanks in reserve. Here the Regiment remained, for about a week, acting as flank guard to the assault forces.

(g) El Mechili, January 1941

REST and maintenance and recce were the order of the day, the shortage of wheeled vehicles being so great that the Regiment were forced to use fitters' lorries on recce. But as they had twenty-four light and five cruiser tanks they did not expect to be relieved.

However on the 17th orders arrived by Captain de Courpelay, Liaison Officer, that the Regiment were to hand over fifteen of their light and their five cruiser tanks to the 3rd Hussars and nine light to the 1st Royal Tanks and to go back either to Cairo or Alexandria on the 19th.

All units of the 4th and 7th Armoured Brigades were very short of tanks by this time, due to mechanical breakdowns and the long distances they had travelled. There were no reserves in Ordnance Field Parks or even back in the Delta. It became necessary therefore to send one Armoured Regiment in each Brigade back to Egypt, and from the 7th Armoured Brigade the 8th Hussars were selected and from the 4th, the 6th Royal Tanks.

However, in the end a composite Squadron, 'A', was formed under Duff, of ten Mark VI Vickers tanks from 'A' Squadron, two from 'C', two from Regimental Headquarters and five cruisers from 'C' under Nelson. Lowther was second-in-command and Charles and Simons Troop Leaders with Sergeants McDonald and Clarke. Sergeant Kirkham was on rear link. This Squadron joined the 3rd Hussars and the remainder of the Regiment handed over their tanks to the 7th Hussars and 6th Royal Tanks.

The 3rd Hussars were now composed of the new composite 'A' Squadron from the 8th, one Squadron 3rd Hussars in Mark VI Vickers and one Squadron 2nd Royal Tanks in A13 Cruisers, the whole being under the command of Lieut.-Colonel W. Petherick, 3rd Hussars, making up, with the 7th Hussars and the 2nd Royal Tanks, the 4th Armoured Brigade.

On the same day, the 19th, Major R. F. W. How with three troops manned by 'B' Squadron crews joined the 7th Hussars south-west of Tobruk, one troop going to each of their squadrons.

Duff and 'A' Squadron left the Regimental leaguer at dawn on the 19th and moved along Trigh Enver Bei for about thirty miles. One troop was on patrol eight miles west along the track as local protection for a party of Royal Engineers who were preparing an advanced landing ground.

They came under command of the 3rd Hussars in the afternoon and joined their leaguer at the track junction. Nelson and the five cruisers, went to the 3rd Hussars cruiser squadron and two of their Regimental Headquarters Squadron joined Duff. One troop was put on standing patrol two miles west of the leaguer.

At dawn they moved out to the previous day's positions and in the afternoon met the R.A.F. recceing their landing ground. That night they returned to the same leaguer and next day, the 21st, the attack on Tobruk began.

While the Squadron was on patrol that day near an old airstrip suddenly out of the sky at about fifty feet came twelve German Junkers Troop Carriers, the first time the squat black crosses of the Luftwaffe had been seen in the Western Desert. They circled round like gigantic eagles and at first everyone was so astonished that nobody opened fire. Then everyone let loose with everything they had, and several definite hits were obtained as they could see the shots from the machine-guns pouring into the fuselages.

Nelson rejoined the Squadron that day as second-in-command.

They moved out at dawn again on the 22nd and the news of success at Tobruk came through. As soon as it was plain that the attack was going to succeed the 4th Armoured Brigade was sent off at once to el Mechili. The code word for advance came through to the Squadron at 2 p.m. and they moved forward to be level with the leading 3rd Hussar squadron, south of Trigh Enver Bei.

At 3.30 the 3rd Hussars moved with 'A' Squadron in the lead. The going was good to Segnali and they leaguered after thirty-four miles, just after dark, but were not able to replenish.

"The first night," wrote Simons, "we got into real 'Tiger' country, an amazing change after the camel scrub of the desert. I can well remember halting below a gigantic granite pinnacle which struck a note of magnificent glory when it was caught by the blood red of the setting sun. It was this night that suddenly a black cat appeared in my troop. No one knew how it arrived and as it refused to leave me all the troopers thought it an excellent omen."

'B' Squadron with the 7th Hussars were also on the move and did the hundred miles to el Mechili in thirty hours.

'A' Squadron moved off at four next morning. It was pitch dark, no moon, and the track was very poor. At dawn they halted having covered eight miles in an hour and a half. At half-past eight they were off again, moving due west and the going became worse. Four miles south of Baltet el Ramla the Regiment turned north-west for Ghot el Gafsa.

'A' Squadron was ordered to take up position east of Ghot el Gafsa and to recce the gap between the north-west corner of Baltet el Ramla and the south end of Wadi Belater. Mechili was visible about eight miles to the north and a troop was sent forward to recce the gap. The little fort looked like a picture from one of P. C. Wren's books, white with four watch towers and a flag staff over the main door which was closed. Behind and to the west was a high hill covered with lorries and about two troops of 75 mm.'s; to the north was a long low hill extending round to the east with two more troops of 75 mm.'s, about two troops of M11 Italian tanks and a lot of men in black shirts running about. In all the garrison appeared to be a Brigade group of Infantry with a Field Battery and a squadron of tanks attached. The country south of the fort was completely open with a landing ground to the south west. This flat stretch extended for about 1,600 yards and ended at a Sugar Loaf Hill.

The Regiment halted to the west, the idea being to cut the escape to Benghazi while the 3rd Hussars squadron pushed north to cut the track. 'A' Squadron's troop went east to probe the area of the fort. As soon as they reached the north-west corner of the airstrip they came under fire from the guns on the high hill, so they retired, but on arrival back were immediately ordered to make their way back to the 'B' Echelon and bring up the petrol at first light.

The Squadron, meanwhile, leaguered near Gasfsa and moved out again at dawn on the 24th to a point a mile and a half north of the leaguer. At about 9.30 enemy M13's were reported coming out of Mechili and the Squadron was ordered forward on the left flank of the cruiser squadron, but no attack developed.

However enemy vehicles, tanks and guns were concentrating to the north-west and there seemed to be a possibility of a get-away to the west which was only guarded by a weak light squadron. 'A' Squadron was then moved up to a position behind that squadron astride the two tracks running west from Mechili.

Sergeant Kirkham's troop was sent north about two miles to recce a route up the ridge and to observe any movement through the hills. He found a way up on the second attempt but was unable to see into the deep wadis that ran to the north.

At about 1.30, just as the squadron was brewing up and just as Captain Crowther arrived bringing the much needed petrol, three M13's and five lorries appeared out of the hills to their rear, about half a mile to the west. The Squadron was ordered to check this party and after a rapid move a few long-range shots were exchanged and the enemy withdrew into the hills.

'A' Squadron was then recalled to Regimental Headquarters at about 3.30 p.m. after being partially refilled with petrol. Captain Crowther replaced Nelson on the rear link and Nelson took over Sergeant Kirkham's troop.

Simons and the petrol had meanwhile reached Sugar Loaf Hill in time to see the cruiser squadron of 2nd Royal Tanks, under command of the 3rd Hussars, in action with Italian tanks who had apparently motored down from their hill to do battle. About four of the cruisers had run out of petrol but the Italians were driven off and the tanks refuelled with the petrol he had brought up.

At five o'clock the Regiment moved due east and found excellent going after crossing the north edge of Baltet el Hamba. They leaguered that night south-east of Sugar Loaf Hill.

That same day, the 24th, 'B' Squadron with the 7th Hussars had been in action with fifteen M13 tanks and some guns near Mechili. The two cruisers that came into action checked the enemy advance so that the 2nd Royal Tanks were able to put in a successful counter attack, and there were no 8th Hussar casualties.

On the 25th, 'A' Squadron moved out at dawn with orders to refuel as soon as the 'B' Echelon appeared. They were then to probe in towards Mechili from the south and to guard the left flank of the Royal Horse Artillery who were coming up to shell the enemy positions from the east. The 'B' Echelon arrived at breakfast time and the squadron got rations and petrol together.

'A' Squadron Headquarters and Simons' troop moved forward as soon as possible and the remaining troops followed when they were ready. They pushed north and got near to the south Bir before coming under shellfire from the guns just north of the fort when they withdrew about a hundred yards and watched.

At about ten o'clock a party of men climbed out of the trenches by the fort and started moving south. The Royal Horse Artillery troop were asked to stand by for counter battery fire on any guns that opened up. Simons advanced to the area of the north Bir, firing with his guns at the men. After about two minutes the fire from the guns that had opened up behind Mechili became too accurate and he withdrew.

Meanwhile Nelson was pushing forward into the hills but was spotted and shelled by guns on the ridge.

On arrival back at his patrol position Simons found that he had burst a rubber hose connection in his tank and lost most of the water. Corporal Friel and his fitters were ordered to repair the damage, and while they were doing so Major Duff came up on the air with the information that Brigadier J. A. L. Caunter, commanding the 4th Armoured Brigade, had requested him to send in an officer under a white flag to demand the fort to surrender. Major Duff refused as he said he would not commit an officer to fight under a white flag, but if Simons volunteered he would send him in as an armed patrol to get as close as possible. "As a cheerful start he said he considered that I should be written off to a sandy grave!" The Brigadier still maintained the fort would surrender and ordered Major Duff to send in the officer with or without the offending flag.

Sergeant McDonald's troop was then sent to reinforce Simons and came under his command. The latter was ordered (1) to advance under cover of a dust storm that was then blowing to discover the nature and extent of the anti-tank ditch shown by the air photos and (2) to draw fire from the enemy guns when the dust cleared to enable our O.P.'s to spot their positions.

A Royal Horse Artillery spotter, Captain Cook, in a 15 cwt. truck was put under command to provide counter battery and defensive fire. He was to follow two hundred yards behind and if he saw Simons in trouble he was to cease counter battery fire and put down a smoke screen just west of the fort. Sergeant McDonald's two tanks were on the right flank and if they found the trench or anti-tank ditch shallow enough to cross all tanks were to give covering fire while Simons would make for the fort.

There was a two-minute concentration on the enemy gun positions behind the fort and then off they went.

Simons wrote: "I passed the north Bir, all guns of the Troop firing at the transport, and as I came up to the shallow trench I ordered all guns on to the fort, hoping to rattle up the occupants, if any!

"The trench turned out to be only three feet deep and though I went over the bridge it proved no obstacle. The dust was now lifting. Just as we got there the enemy opened up on my right flank tanks (Sergeant McDonald's) with 75-mm.s so I ordered them to retire. Sergeant Glew started to get into the bad ground on my left so I ordered him to change over and come fifty yards to my right. So far nothing had fired at us as they were still firing at my right pair of tanks, and the Fort itself was silent.

"Just as I reached the edge of the left anti-tank ditch with Sergeant Glew coming up on my right, the Fort opened up with a blaze of small arms fire which rattled on the outside of my tank like hailstones, and, owing to the quality of the armour, small bits chipped off inside. At the same time all the guns switched on to Sergeant Glew and myself, landing some fifty yards to our rear. This was a cat and mouse game as they realised we would have to turn back into their fire. On both sides of the Fort were Breda anti-aircraft guns of about 40-mm. calibre mounted on lorries. These also opened on to us but at first they fired high.

"I really got very frightened indeed. I ordered Sergeant Glew to retire and opened fire on the anti-aircraft guns, turning in a left circle myself so as to keep the engine as a protection for my driver. Sergeant Glew's driver, Trooper Rees, turned right and promptly got hit in the stomach with a 50-mm.

"I saw Sergeant Glew baling out and at that moment there was a sickening jerk and my right front sprocket was removed. I ordered my crew to bale out and, as they got clear, ripped a petrol lead in the turret to fire the tank. I reported the troop out of action and got the Very pistol to fire the petrol. At that moment another shell struck the tank, blowing me off the turret, and setting it on fire, so I joined the crew sheltering in the lee of the tank.

"The Artillery were terrific, and Cook, as soon as he saw me out of action, brought down the smoke. We had about two hundred yards to go on our feet to the 15 cwt. and when I looked back at the Fort I saw a platoon of black shirts with fixed bayonets scramble out of the trenches to chase and take us prisoners.

"The Ities started bursting shrapnel about twenty yards to our rear and about ten yards up in the air as we ran for the 15 cwt. It made a red hot sizzling noise and made me more frightened than ever. Sergeant Glew was running about fifty yards to my east.

"My two chaps were grand. I cursed them with every word I could lay my tongue to and we finally made the truck, to find Cook on the top of the Bir firing with his rifle at the Ities who were now some hundred yards behind.

"We all climbed on, and off we went, zig-zagging as hard as we could, looking like an Egyptian taxi, the three R.H.A. and five of my troop hanging on for grim death.

"As we started the Ities stopped firing, as the smoke and the blazing tank had done their bit and they could not see us."

This patrol gained valuable information and for their part in the action Captain Cook and Lieutenant Simons were awarded the M.C. and Sergeant Glew was Mentioned in Dispatches.

The next day they moved out again at dawn. A thick mist prevented them from taking up their positions as on the day before. Some CR 42's came over and they were fired on, one being brought down. Nelson was on the same western patrol and had orders to go further north to try and get up into the hills. On his way out he located the enemy machine, shot down earlier in the day, some seven miles west of Squadron Headquarters. He went on a foray after it, well north of Mechili, and Major Duff thought he was in the bag since he got out of wireless touch. However he only went to look for the clock in the plane, an explanation that was not well received. 'A' Squadron leaguered that night at dusk.

It must be remembered that the all-important left flank was open and that night the Italians pushed off to Benghazi.

On the 27th 'A' Squadron moved out at dawn as usual. As the light improved Captain Lowther saw that there were no enemy on the ridge above the Fort. This was reported and the squadron was ordered to investigate. Nelson was sent in between the ridge and the Fort with Lieutenant F. R. Charles as flank guard on the west. Simons was ordered to come in towards the Fort from the south-east when he saw the leading troops reaching the high ground.

The whole Fort was deserted and Simons was able to find his burnt-out tank and bury his dead driver.

'A' Squadron was ordered to push on eight miles west and started forward with two troops up. As Charles was emerging from a deep wadi his tank struck a 'Coffin' mine, blowing off his driver's legs. "The poor chap died before we could do anything. He was a very gallant chap and kept apologising for being such a nuisance."

That night they had a gazelle shoot, got two and leaguered just south of the big hill on the edge of the air strip.

Next day the Regiment pushed north at dawn, passing to the east of Mechili which was not yet clear of mines. 'A' Squadron, now consisting of only five tanks, was in reserve. After going some five miles it poured with rain, the first they had seen for months. It was a strange feeling. They were in a country now of enormous Wadis and very green, a complete change from the flat desert.

At midday, having covered about fifteen miles astride the Giovanni Berta track, the leading troop of 3rd Hussars reported four M13's hull down to the front. The Regiment deployed for action and the cruiser squadron was sent up under covering fire from the Artillery. On arrival and after much back-chat on the wireless it was found that the tanks were four camels grazing!

After breakfast on the 29th 'A' Squadron handed over their remaining tanks to the 3rd Hussar relief crews, climbed on to Corporal Friel's 15 cwt. and a three-ton lorry and set sail for Cairo. They picked up rations at Tobruk and an Australian A.P.M. on the quay threatened to lock up Nelson for stealing water. This so enraged him that he threatened to knock the Australian into the harbour. However they got their water and had an enormous brew that night above Bardia. Some of 'A' Squadron returned to Mena by lorry, some by boat from Tobruk and some by 15 cwt. trucks all the way by road.

"We made Alexandria the next night," wrote Simons, "where we were de-loused and had a wonderful meal of oysters and champagne to celebrate Duff's birthday. Next day we reached Cairo and went on leave."

(*h*) *Back to Cairo, February-October 1941*

FOR the next ten months the Regiment were relatively out of the war. They were months of very necessary refitting and training, but back in the desert the Army swept on. General Wavell took a bold decision and sent the 4th Armoured Brigade on swiftly across a hundred and fifty miles of desert to cut off the retreating Italian Army before it could reach Benghazi. When it was discovered that they were already leaving that town the Brigade struck south-west in order to trap more Italians. It was a nightmare journey, the going impossible, the maps non-existent and most of the vehicles on their last legs. However it was accomplished and on February 7th the Italian Army was defeated at Beda Fomm and the whole of Cyrenaica was in British hands.

It was to be a short-lived triumph, but for the moment it was complete. The 7th Armoured Division had defeated an Army nearly ten times their size. They had marched seven hundred miles and had all the time been short of equipment, transport and supplies.

However General Wavell was now told not to advance beyond Cyrenaica but to send all the troops he could spare to Greece, which was on the verge of being invaded by the Germans. It was hard to spare any troops, harder still when it was obvious it was but a matter of time before the Germans arrived in North Africa. Their Air Force had already put in an appearance there.

By this time there had been changes in high command. When the crisis in Greece arose General Wilson went to command in that country and Lieut.-General O'Connor became commander of the British troops in Egypt. Lieut-General P. Neame, V.C. became Commander of 13 Corps and C.-in-C. Cyrenaica.

Back in Cairo the Regiment, although they had taken no part in the fighting, had not been wasting their time. By February 5th they were established at Mena, in the Jubbulpore Lines. On the 8th twelve other ranks were attached to C.M.P. for traffic duties on the roads from Cairo to Alexandria and Port Said. In fact on the 11th the whole Regiment, which consisted of 'B' and Headquarters Squadrons under Major Howe and 'A' and 'C' under Major Duff, was sent to Sidi Bishr by Alexandria for local duties such as guarding prisoners and so on, while Regimental Headquarters remained at Mena.

On the 24th the Commander, 7th Armoured Division, Major-General O'Moore Creagh sent the following message to the Regiment:

"The enemy resistance in Cyrenaica has been finally overcome. 7th Armoured Division have had a large share in the achievement of this success. They have been in contact with the enemy since the outbreak of war (with Italy), and after nearly eight months have won an outstanding victory. I congratulate all ranks on their endurance and fine fighting spirit. Your skill, energy and courage, have alone made the victory possible."

In March the two composite squadrons returned from Alexandria and the whole Regiment was in the Kirkee Lines, Mena. They at last drew forty-five light tanks and seven cruisers but after they had had them a few days they had to be handed over to the Australian Division at Helwan. On St. Patrick's Day the long-awaited Christmas dinners appeared and with them a message of good wishes from the Chief of the Imperial General Staff, Sir John Dill who was in Egypt with the Foreign Secretary, Mr. Anthony Eden. Shortly afterwards, Major C. Duff and 'A' and 'C' Squadrons left for Maadi to guard the ammunition dumps in the Tura Caves for a week.

The rest of the Regiment in parties of six in charge of an N.C.O. were sent to man Hotchkiss machine-guns on the transports sailing between Greece and Egypt.

Eleven new officers and fifty-three other ranks joined the Regiment in March and courses in Driving, Maintenance and Gunnery were attended at the R.A.C. Base Depot. Captain J. D. Harbord left to become Brigade Transport Officer and Major D. S. Cripps, Lieutenant C. F. Hedley, S.S.M. Harrold, Sergeant McMasters and Corporal Clarke were all mentioned in the C.-in-C.'s dispatches.

The Regiment became General Headquarters reserve in May, to be used on internal security duties, and gradually the Hotchkiss parties returned. For a short time they were in the 4th Armoured Brigade under Brigadier J. A. L. Caunter, and later Brigadier A. H. Gatehouse, and later became part of 1st Armoured Brigade Group under Brigadier H. V. S. Charrington.

On May 17th, Lieut.-Colonel T. G. Watson (after twenty-seven years with the Regiment) was appointed to Army Headquarters, India, and Major D. S. Cripps was promoted Lieut.-Colonel and given command.

At the beginning of February the Afrika Korps was formed in Tripoli and consisted of the 5th Light and 15th Panzer Divisions under General Erwin Rommel. On March 1st Germany invaded Bulgaria and advanced on Jugo-Slavia, and on the 31st Rommel advanced from Tripolitania. The 15th Panzer Division had only just arrived and was not in action but he had under command the 5th Light Division and the Italian Divisions, Ariete and Brescia. By April 3rd his headquarters were at Agedabia and the British were withdrawing. The troops facing him were newly-arrived and inexperienced, mounted in the worn-out tanks of the 7th Armoured Division, with spare tracks that did not fit and transport lorries in the same sorry state. Some regiments even had captured Italian tanks. There was no Intelligence organisation across the frontier as that had been the department of the French, now non-existent. The seasoned desert troops were back in Egypt, re-fitting and resting after nearly a year's fighting. Wavell's plan had to be one of defensive retreat to Benghazi.

Lieut.-General Neame had not long been in command when he was forced to retreat to a new line from Derna to Mechili. The Germans were close behind, there was a certain amount of confusion and in it and in the darkness, Lieut.-General Neame, Lieut.-General O'Connor and Brigadier Combe were all captured.

The German advance was so swift that all available troops of the 7th Armoured Division were scraped together in Cairo and sent forward. By April 13th Tobruk was surrounded and the enemy were close to Sollum.

Even so Rommel had not yet got his 15th Panzer Division in action. It was essential therefore to seize any opportunity for a counter-attack before he did, but the 7th Armoured Division was still not re-equipped. Precious tanks had been sunk in convoy through the Mediterranean and what with the slowness of repair to old tanks, and the training of the crews of the new, an offensive was not possible until June.

However, the possession of Halfaya Pass and Capuzzo were essential to any future attack and although by May 14th the 7th Armoured Divisional Headquarters were back at el Hamman, only thirty-five miles west of Alexandria, on the 15th an attack to relieve Tobruk was launched and enemy positions at Capuzzo and Halfaya Pass were taken. But by the 27th Rommel had counter-attacked and driven the Coldstream Guards from their foothold on the pass, leaving him in a commanding position, facing east.

Elsewhere in Europe plenty had been happening. The new year had opened with an even more furious blitzing of ports and docks and especially London, in spite of improved Radar defences. The German Air Force was concentrating on the Mediterranean too, operating from Sicily, and the siege of Malta began. In the Atlantic U-boats were hunting in wolf packs and sinking more merchant shipping than ever. Yugo-Slavia had rebelled against German rule and as a reprisal had suffered 'Operation Punishment', which left, after three days, over 17,000 people dead in the streets of Belgrade. The British Navy had had a victory over the Italian Fleet at Cape Matapan at the end of March, but the collapse of Yugo-Slavia in April had opened the back door on Greece and through it poured the Germans. Greece surrendered on April 24th and the

D

evacuation of the British troops, ill-spared by General Wavell from the desert, began. At the same time fighting broke out in Iraq so that Wavell had not only three major fronts to contend with, but also Syria on the verge of war and Crete to reinforce. When the time came the few troops there fought desperately for ten days, but they were over-whelmed by paratroops, used for the first time and with great loss, and by 1,280 air-craft, flying in from Greece, as opposed to the British twenty-six. Meanwhile Hess had landed in Scotland, starting a flood of rumours that have never died down, and while the Battle of Crete was at its height, the German battleship Bismarck and her attendant Prinz Eugen slipped from their hideout in Bergen to raid the Atlantic. After three days shadowing and the loss of the Hood, she was sunk in the cold seas off Greenland. By the end of May almost all the surviving troops were out of Crete and General Wavell was planning his next offensive.

The Regiment stayed on at Mena, still without tanks. In June they started Hotchkiss gun and bayonet training and were organised into a mobile column in 15 cwt. trucks armed with Hotchkiss guns, crowbars, Molotov bombs and so on. This was with a view to the possibility of a paratroop landing, a possibility not to be ignored after the disaster of Crete. On June 15th out in the desert, Operation 'Battleaxe' began.

The purpose of this operation was to drive the enemy back west of Tobruk, but after a hard-fought three-day battle the reverse happened and our troops were pushed back again to Buq Buq and Sofafi. Although this was a minor operation it had a tre-mendous bearing on later battles in the desert. It was the first full-scale battle against the German armour, and it showed the Germans that to their 88-mm. gun we not only had no answer, (the 2-pounder mounted on our tanks was about as much use as a pea-shooter and the artillery's 25-pounder had no armour protection), but neither had we any tanks capable of competing with theirs. Most of ours were the five-mile-an-hour, heavily armoured 'I' tanks while the rest were cruisers, having amongst them the faster, unreliable 'Crusaders'. The 88-mms. could knock out a British tank at 2,000 yards while we had to close to six or eight hundred yards before becoming effective.

For three days the battle surged round Capuzzo and Sollum and Halfaya. It was at Sollum that a battery of 88-mm. anti-aircraft guns, commanded by a German officer, were brought to bear on the 'I' tanks which were knocked out one after another, suc-cessfully stopping the attack. The Germans never forgot this and soon after used their 88-mm. guns as anti-tank weapons with devastating effect, improving on their methods of propelling them until eventually they had them mounted on their tanks.

After exceptionally heavy and exhausting fighting, when Rommel brought up ever more and more tanks from Tobruk to fling into the battle, and while half of our two hundred were made casualties, General Wavell was forced to break off the engagement. Although the losses were enormous, casualties had been slight and enough damage had been inflicted on the Germans to hinder their advance for another five months. All the same very few tanks were recovered as the enemy were left in possession of the field.

After the battle the Support Group and the 11th Hussars were left near Sofafi with the Guards Brigade under command at Buq Buq. The rest of the Division withdrew south of Matruh, the 4th Armoured Brigade returning to the Delta to re-equip. 'Jock' Columns continued their rôle of harassing the enemy who were building defences from Sidi Omar to Halfaya. As long as Tobruk was in our hands they had only sixty miles range. On June 21st General Wavell was given the post of Commander-in-Chief in India and his place in the Middle East was taken by General Sir Claude Auchinleck. Lieut.-General Sir Alan Cunningham took over the Army of the Nile, soon to be renamed the Eighth Army.

The next day, June 22nd, Germany invaded Russia, and Rommel had therefore to take second place. He, like us, was suffering from the difficulties of being supplied by sea. During the summer his 5th Light Division became the 21st Panzer and as well he formed a 90th Light Division, infantry with strong artillery support. By November he had three German Divisions and six Italian.

Apart from the forays of the 'Jock' Columns the summer was quiet. Each side was preparing for what lay ahead. The Regiment continued their training at Mena, but not until the beginning of August were there indications that American tank equipment would soon be available. Tank drivers courses were started and Gunnery courses on American Browning machine guns. Squadrons were told to practise night driving and night navigation. By the 7th they had drawn thirty-two Chevrolet four-wheel-drive lorries and soon each squadron received one American M3 Light tank. These were at first called Honeys and later known as General Stuarts, and mounted a 37-mm. gun and a Browning ·300. They arrived complete, even to the wireless, and it was decided to name each one after a famous race-horse.

All through August tanks were arriving as well as lorries and Ford Utilities. Three American sergeants and Major Kornog of the American Army also visited the Regiment to help with the teething troubles of the new vehicles, and Captain Nelson took a party of tanks to the Gebel el Kashab area to try out various experimental devices for the recognition of ground troops by the air arm. On the 21st, 2nd Lieutenant E. Mc C. Hector and Lance Corporal Carpenter were killed in accident during a night navigation exercise. On the 26th Captain, the Right Honourable Oliver Lyttleton, the Minister of State, paid an unofficial visit to the Regiment and the next day 'C' Squadron was filmed by the Army Film Unit. At the end of the month the Regiment could boast thirty-six tanks.

Training continued throughout September and during battle practise north of Mena Camp they were visited by General Sir Claude Auchinleck.

The next day a United States Army Officer, Lieutenant Garrett Fonda and two N.C.O.'s were attached to the Regiment as observers and advisors, and on October 1st the Regiment paraded at full strength in the new tanks. On the 7th the advance party under Major How left for the Western Desert.

II.

THE BATTLES FOR SIDI REZEGH

(a) Prelude to Action, October-November 1941

AFTER long months of frustration and waiting the 8th Hussars were at last on the move. The road party under Major Duff left Mena on the 8th, staying the night at Amariya. The tanks, less 'B' Squadron, travelled by train from Giza to Maholofa under Major Vernon-Miller. By the 10th all the Regiment had assembled and were fitting 'sun-shields' to their tanks at the Delivery Squadron on the Matruh-Siwa track. These were superstructures which covered the whole tank and were designed to make it look like a lorry. "It fell apart in theory when one pulled a string but in practise it required crowbars and a lot of very bad language! However the idea was excellent and it foxed the Hun." Early on the 12th they left for Allam Abu Hileqat and had a successful trip apart from one of 'A' Squadron tanks catching fire and having to be abandoned. The stony ground was thought to have played havoc with the rubber tracks and this started what has been since described as a 'groundless flap' about the track situation.

Early in September Major-General O'Moore Creagh returned to the United King-dom and handed over his command to Major-General W. H. Gott. The 4th Armoured Brigade was now commanded by Brigadier A. H. Gatehouse, the 7th by Brigadier G. M. O. Davy and the Support Group by Brigadier Jock Campbell.

Major-General W. H. Gott visited the Regiment on the 14th October and expressed his pleasure at seeing them again in the Western Desert.

The sun shields were removed on the 17th when the Regiment began two days of squadron training. A fierce Khamseen ruined the first day and there was more track trouble. Captain J. C. Pringle rejoined the Regiment here from the West African Fron-tier Force and went to 'B' Squadron.

The seriousness of the track situation was thought to be such that training was interrupted and the Brigade Commander flew to Cairo to see the Tank Advisory Board. Captain Nelson was ordered to report to the 8th Army to take up a G 3 appointment.

The flight to Cairo produced results. On the 25th R.A.S.C. transporters arrived and the tanks were lifted back to the Kenayis area. One tank with 2nd Lieutenant G. McCulloch left by road to test the tracks. The new tracks arrived and were fitted and on the 31st the Regiment left for Minaar Ziwar el Bahari to join the Brigade.

The Regiment now formed part of the 4th Armoured Brigade, and together with the 3rd and 5th Royal Tanks, were equipped with Honeys. Training for these three regiments started near Bir Kenayis and at the end of October they joined the rest of the Division in the forward area. The 4th Armoured Brigade now consisted of the 8th Hussars, 3rd and 5th Royal Tanks, 2nd Regiment, Royal Horse Artillery and the 2nd Scots Guards. In the 7th Armoured Brigade, the 7th Hussars and the 2nd and 6th Royal

Tanks had the unsatisfactory Crusaders and a few of the old cruisers, while the 11th Hussars who joined them had new Humber armoured cars. The 7th Armoured Division now consisted of the 4th and 7th Armoured Brigades, Support Group and Divisional Troops, and the 22nd Armoured Brigade which had arrived ahead of the 1st Armoured Division.

The Brigade, less the 3rd Royal Tanks who were replacing a regiment from the 7th Armoured Brigade in the forward area, moved south to the west of Bir Hilw on the Siwa track which had been chosen as suitable for training. On the 2nd, 2nd Lieutenant McCulloch arrived in his tank which had now done eleven hundred miles without undue damage to the tracks, thus exploding the track-myth. A two-day Brigade scheme then took place, and on the 6th the Regiment replaced the 3rd Royal Tanks near Sofafi and came under the command of the 7th Armoured Brigade.

During the week they were there all leave from the Western Desert was cancelled. On the 14th their own Brigade joined them in the forward area and they came back under command. The final preparations were made and completed. There was an eve-of-battle feeling in the air.

On the 17th Major Phillips, Captain Gwyn and Lieutenant R. H. Ames with five other ranks were sent to the Left out of Battle Camp at the railhead, which had by now been extended fifty miles west of Mersa. Two days extra rations were drawn for the Regiment, and in the evening Lieutenant J. Robertson with a party under Major Uniacke, 5th Royal Tanks, slipped through the line to dump petrol over the frontier for 'topping up' the next day.

This column consisted of representatives from the 8th Hussars, the 3rd and 5th Royal Tanks, a platoon from the 2nd Scots Guards, two troops of Northumberland Hussars Anti-Tank guns, 122 Light Anti-Aircraft Battery, a detail of 3rd Field Squadron, Royal Engineers and 5 Company, R.A.S.C. Petrol Lorries. They moved forward in open formation until darkness fell, and then closed up while two officers walked in front, navigating. Gap 70 was reached by about 1 a.m. and the wire was cut by the Royal Engineers. There they slept until dawn when they moved forward again, and left the petrol in three dumps, one for each regiment. The dumps too were marked with enemy signs so that in the event of air reconnaisance they would not be bombed.

Elsewhere things had been happening during the last five months and not only in Europe. In June a campaign had been undertaken in Syria against Vichy France which ended successfully in July. Russia was experiencing the Luftwaffe and demanding that we should start a Second Front and give them all possible aid in the form of war materials and supplies. At the end of July Japan occupied Indo-China, thus moving into a more favourable position for a possible attack on Malaya or the Philippines. At the beginning of August Churchill and Roosevelt, although America was not yet in the war, met at sea to discuss the Atlantic Charter. Russia meanwhile, although receiving all the assistance we could possibly send her, remained unhelpful, ungrateful and hostile, but we fell in with their Second Front wishes to the extent of embarking on a campaign in Persia to occupy the essential oil-fields. It was successful and over quickly, the Persians had no chance against both Russia and Britain but German agents were at work there and had to be eliminated.

In September the Australian Government demanded the relief of their troops who were garrisoning beleaguered Tobruk. In spite of it being both difficult and dangerous to move them, the government insisted, and it was carried out on the moonless nights of October.

Although Mr. Churchill continued to press for an early advance in the desert General

Auckinleck insisted that his army there was not yet ready to meet Rommel's panzers, and it was not until November 18th that Operation 'Crusader' was launched, an operation during which the tide of battle flowed in our favour, ebbed and then flowed again.

(b) First Clash with the Germans, November 1941

Now at last the months of training and waiting were at an end. Now at last the plans so carefully laid so long before were to materialise, the guns, the tanks and the men to be put to the test. D-Day for Operation 'Crusader' was November 18th. The plan was this, to recapture Cyrenaica destroying in the process the enemy's armour, and if all went well, to take Tripolitania.

The Eighth Army under General Cunningham was divided into two corps, 13, mainly infantry, under General Godwin Austen, and 30, consisting of the 7th Armoured Division, the 1st South African Division and the 22nd Guards Brigade, under Lieut.- General Sir Willoughby Norrie. These two corps were to attack west and north towards Tobruk, whose garrison at a given signal, would break out and try to join up. 13 Corps was to engage the enemy defences from Halfaya to Sidi Omar and then reach Tobruk, while 30 Corps was to sweep across the desert flank, searching for Rommel's armour, engaging it and it was hoped, destroying it.

This time no hint of the advance leaked out. It was a complete surprise. Rommel was even in Rome when, on November 18th, in driving rain, the Eighth Army struck.

The task of the 7th Armoured Division was to advance towards the airfields at el Adem and Sidi Rezegh and at 6 a.m. they drove forward through the wire north of Maddalena. Sir Winston Churchill has written that the sense of drama is missing from most modern battles owing to the wide spaces they cover and the length of time they take, and that that is most true of desert battles. However, dawn on November 18th 1941 must surely be an exception, for as the sun rose and the sky lightened and the tanks of the Regiment rumbled forward, southwards and as far as the eye could see were the tanks of the Armoured Brigades in perfect formation, with tossing pennants lit by the blood red sunrise. It was indeed a stirring sight and the whole desert seemed activated by some gigantic Battle Fleet deployed for action.

The Regiment moved off at 5.30 a.m. They crossed the wire and refuelled success- fully from the advance dump. It was an altogether successful day. They cast off their lorry top disguises and had breakfast. Then they turned north-westerly, crossed the Trigh el Abd and leaguered in battle formation near Gabr Taieb el Essem after a march of some seventy-five miles.

Next day, the 19th, was a day of continuous fighting. On the left the 22nd Armoured Brigade was engaged against the Italians at el Gubi. In the middle the 7th fought all morning and by the evening had taken Sidi Rezegh airfield, complete with nineteen aircraft. The 4th on the right had met Rommel's Panzers and fought desperately until it was too dark to see any more.

At first light on the 19th the Regiment moved forward into battle positions, 'C' Squadron commanded by Major Vernon-Miller on the right, 'B' Squadron commanded by Major Sandbach on the left and 'A' Squadron commanded by Major Duff in reserve near Gabr Taieb el Essem, 40 miles west of Sheferzen. The Brigade was disposed with the Regiment on the left, the 5th Royal Tanks on the right with the 3rd Royal Tanks in reserve.

Almost immediately an enemy column of some sixty vehicles was reported about sixty miles to the north and moving in a westerly direction. However nothing came of this and the column disappeared north, leaving armoured cars in observation.

The Regiment halted after some five miles just south of a long, low ridge, had breakfast, did maintenance, had lunch.

During the morning the enemy armoured cars were increasingly active, probing for a gap in the British armoured car screen as they moved south in an attempt to reach the wire.

Reports came in that there were a number of tanks in the vicinity and also that about a hundred tanks were moving south-west, about twelve miles north.

The Regiment and the 5th Royal Tanks were ordered to meet this attack on the track between Sidi Azeiz and Gabr Saleh. Actually, as it happened, the German force had turned due south and the full force of the attack developed on the position held by the Regiment.

Just as the tank crews were finishing a lunch-time 'brew' the first and only warning of an impending attack came through, sent in by 2nd Lieutenant T. M. Mills whose troop was the 'B' Squadron standing patrol. Apparently the Kings Dragoon Guards Armoured cars had reported a large German force of between seventy and a hundred Mk. III tanks, armed with 50-mm. guns supported by Mk. IV's armed with 75-mm.'s lorried infantry and guns which had found a gap in the screen and were making straight for the Regiment. At the same time a squadron of Messerschmitts started dive bombing to show the German force their position.

The Regiment was drawn up in extended order over about a mile and a half, 'C' Squadron left flank, 'B' Squadron right flank, with 'A' in reserve just behind Regimental Headquarters. All were in visual touch on a front of 2,000 yards. This was at four o'clock.

The enemy force advanced in compact formation from the north, Mk. III's on both flanks, Mk. IV's and guns in the middle, and when they came to within 1,500 yards of the Regiment's position they opened out and began to fire. Their shooting was very accurate and a number of the Honeys were laid out before the enemy came within effective range of their guns. As the maximum range with the 37-mm. was six hundred yards, 'B' and 'C' Squadrons had to wait for the Germans to close, which they were not keen to do, remaining at about 700 yards until the later stages of the battle when they tried to break through on the left which was held by the 5th Royal Tanks. Early on a number of German tanks began working round the left flank, beyond 'C' Squadron, making things extremely unpleasant. Major Vernon-Miller's tank was hit in the driving sprocket and became immobile. He had just time to get through to his second-in-command, Captain Lowther, to say that he was out of action when another shell damaged the wireless. By this time several of 'C' Squadron tanks had been knocked out but Lowther managed to withdraw the remainder, still fighting, slowly but surely without getting completely encircled before dusk.

It was now 'A' Squadron's turn, and they came out of reserve and closed to within five hundred yards of the Germans. Again the all-round superiority of the enemy tanks was established; not only did they have better telescopes and larger-calibre guns, but their tanks were far more heavily armoured and the British shells were seen "bouncing off their noses, a most depressing sight." One by one the 'A' Squadron tanks started brewing up, but in spite of this the battle was fiercely contested until dark, and this very gallant stand by the Regiment, heavily out-numbered though they were, prevented the enemy from breaking through our line.

At 4.30 a welcome troop of Northumberland Hussars arrived with their 2-pdr. anti-tank guns and, just as it seemed that the Regiment would be overrun by pure weight of numbers, the Royal Horse Artillery Battery under command of Major Livingstone-Learmouth, M.C., arrived, ventre à terre, and brought down all the fire they could and with tremendous effect.

Throughout the whole battle one lone tank with Brigade H.Q. markings on it had been careering in and out of the Squadrons, loosing off its guns in all directions and obviously having a wonderful time. They found out later that this tank had been stolen from Brigade by the 'Neutral' U.S. Army, and the crew were the driver, Major Kornog; Commander, a U.S. Ordnance Captain; and Gunner, a "God-damned Subaltern!"

The Germans never attempted to come any closer than about seven hundred yards except in the later stages of the battle when they tried to break through on the left flank, which was being held by the 5th Royal Tanks.

The battle raged fiercely until dark and even then it was not quite over.

Just after last light Simons picked up Mr. Jordan and Lieutenant N. A. St. G. Gibbes and with about two others they had some success in cutting off the German stragglers who were limping home on their left flank. If they saw a tank on the move they went up to about fifty yards and then fired Very lights over its head. If it was a German they opened fire, and accounted for about four or five in this manner. They finally got back to the Regiment at 10 o'clock and learnt the appalling casualties they had suffered.

The casualties were indeed fearful. The Regiment had lost twenty tanks for about twenty of the enemy. There is no doubt that had these come in closer they could have accounted for more but they could not do better against the long range German guns.

As darkness fell the Regiment withdrew into leaguer near Gabr Meliha, a few hundred yards from Brigade and the 3rd Royal Tanks. The Germans themselves leaguered some two miles to the north and recovered their damaged tanks under cover of darkness.

When the noise and the confusion subsided and when the roll was called, Major Vernon-Miller, Lieutenant Charles and 2nd Lieutenant McCulloch were all missing. Presently Sergeant Willetts arrived and said that Vernon-Miller was lying severely wounded by his tank several miles away and that Corporal Preston, also wounded, was trying to walk back towards the leaguer. The medical officer, Captain J. B. Heycock, decided to go and look for them.

He set off in his armoured car with a tank for protection. They went to a burning tank about a mile away and then made off on a compass bearing to where they thought the other tanks should be.

It was pitch dark. They stopped after half a mile and S.S.M. Hunter went on on foot while everyone shouted out Corporal Preston's name. Unbelievably they got an answer and found Corporal Preston collapsed on the ground. He was put in the Doctor's car but all he was able to tell them was that Vernon-Miller was a prisoner of the Germans, which in fact was not correct.

They went on for another half mile or so and did another foot patrol but they heard tanks moving about only a short distance away. Captain Heycock called up the Regiment telling them there were tanks ahead and giving his bearing and asking whether he should continue. He was told to return, which he did, bringing the wounded corporal with him. Afterwards they found that it was lucky they had not gone on as they would have almost certainly been taken prisoner too.

Meanwhile during the afternoon Major Vernon-Miller's tank had been hit again several times as the enemy closed, so the crew abandoned it and lay low. As soon as it started to get dark the crew tried to carry Vernon-Miller, who was badly wounded in the leg, but found he was too heavy. He therefore gave them the compass and sent them off to where he thought Regimental Headquarters would be, Lance-Corporal Broadfield remaining with him.

"We had an extraordinary night with burning tanks of both sides all round and the enemy all around us. Next morning a German Observation Post established itself nearby, nobody appeared very interested in us and by then I wasn't taking much interest in anything myself. Later on in the morning the Germans began withdrawing and some of our own tanks went by us and we were eventually picked up by one of our Staff cars about 12 noon."

(c) Second Clash with the Germans, November 1941

NOVEMBER 20th dawned. The 7th Armoured Brigade were by now insecurely established on Sidi Rezegh airfield where they were joined by the Support Group, while the 5th South African Brigade hurried to reinforce them. The Germans were still in possession on the western edge of the escarpment, entrenched behind anti-tank guns and determined to stay there. Sidi Rezegh was vital to them, as, apart from the airfield the high ridge to the north dominated the Trigh Capuzzo and overlooked Tobruk. Rommel, who had been hanging about near Sidi Omar expecting an attack there, had therefore to rush his Panzer Gruppe Afrika back to meet this threat which had crept round behind him. All that stood between him and the airfield was the 4th Armoured Brigade, so the 22nd, who had been entangled with the Italian Ariete Division at el Gubi, was about-turned to assist them. They, however, were up against refuelling difficulties and were consequently very much delayed. In Tobruk the code word to break out next morning had been received by the 70th Division and the Polish Brigade.

At first light patrols moved off and at about 8 a.m. saw a large force of tanks a mile ahead, going north. This might have been the expected 22nd Armoured Brigade so they went on to investigate.

After about half a mile they were seen to be in six lines of about ten tanks each. The British did not usually move like this so the patrol warned the Regiment and started to close for further investigation. Suddenly about two hundred yards away appeared a further ten tanks in line ahead, the flank guards. These were Mk. III's with their crews standing on the back, enjoying the morning air.

"They saw me at the same time as I saw them, but luckily they all got in their tanks before opening fire, thus giving me time to about turn and report the matter. I came back flat out and before they started firing I was a good six hundred yards away, zig-zagging and chucking up dust. Their fire was very wild and they missed badly."

Meantime the 5th Royal Tanks reported that they were engaging fifty-one enemy tanks and asked for reserves to be sent up. The 3rd Royal Tanks were ordered up and the Regiment, who had meanwhile advanced a short distance from their leaguer area, halted in extended order, coming under long range fire from 75-mm. guns. The Royal Horse Artillery came straight into action and brought down a devastating fire on the massed formation of enemy tanks. Then the Regiment moved into position, ready to engage the tanks that they had fought the day before. However the 3rd Royal Tanks took over while they came into reserve, taking the opportunity to have breakfast.

At 8 a.m. the 3rd Royal Tanks reported that they were engaging thirty-two tanks who were working round their left flank. The Regiment were ordered to move to their left but this was immediately countermanded and they were sent to support the 5th Royal Tanks, who were being forced to withdraw. They moved up and fought for about three quarters of an hour when the enemy withdrew north, and the Armoured Cars took over and shadowed the force.

Ammunition by this time was very short and orders had been received not to waste a single round. The enemy must have been in the same state for as soon as they were out of range they stopped and began to replenish, and could easily be seen walking about between tanks, discussing plans and studying maps, a moment when quick liaison with the Royal Air Force would have proved its worth.

It was soon clear that the enemy had decided to withdraw and the column of tanks and lorries moved off north-east. By 10 a.m. they were two and a half miles from the forward patrols.

By now Brigade had received a report from the 7th Armoured Division that the 15th and 21st Panzer Divisions had joined together and that an attack from them could be expected at about midday. The 22nd Armoured Brigade, which had been sent for from Gubi, was still having refuelling difficulties and could not be expected for some time.

Brigade then took up battle positions near Bir bu Meliha, just south of a long hill, the Regiment right flank, Brigade Headquarters centre, and the 5th Royal Tanks left. The 3rd Royal Tanks were sent out to investigate.

However, the attack did not materialise when it was expected and most of the tank crews managed to 'brew up' and have lunch.

At about 3.30 the 3rd Royal Tanks reported the enemy on their north-west flank, a similar force to that on the previous day but not the same unit. Again the attack was preceded by the Luftwaffe with machine-guns, giving their tanks a line to aim for. The 3rd Royal Tanks withdrew across Brigade positions, hotly pursued by German Mk. III's and IV's. As they got level with Brigade Headquarters the whole line moved up to the crest of the hill and found the enemy only three hundred yards away and broadside on.

This was the signal for all hell to be let loose. Both sides opened up with everything they had and the noise was tremendous. Vast clouds of dust completely obscured the battlefield, through which it was impossible to see the enemy. Squadrons became hopelessly mixed up and until darkness fell both sides remained locked in combat, a far fiercer struggle than that of the previous day.

The Regiment were able to put in some good shooting, and in many cases they got into advantageous hull down positions. There was no doubt that they did great damage to the enemy, who came in much closer than he had the day before. During this action Major Dunne was wounded.

As darkness fell the Germans withdrew north and a Regimental leaguer was formed a short distance back from the battlefield. This had no sooner been formed than orders came from Brigade and they had to 'upsticks' and join the Brigade leaguer some distance away. It must have been after midnight before anyone got a chance of sleep and it had been a tedious night march. It was well after midnight too before 'B' Echelon reached the leaguer area.

All that night the desert was astir with parties from both sides, trying to get back to their own units. There were false alarms and scares as supply columns moved up. There was not much rest for the weary troops.

It was hardly long enough to be called a night. A very short distance from where Brigade was leaguered the two Panzer Divisions spent the night. Rommel, having by now realised that this was no raid but a major attack, ordered them to move as early as possible against the forces with the precarious handhold at Sidi Rezegh. At four in the morning of November 21st enemy tanks were heard withdrawing north and the patrols at first light reported that they had folded their tents and slipped away.

(d) The Last of 'A' Squadron, November 1941

THE 22nd Armoured Brigade had joined the 4th during the night and the order of the day was "to attack and relentlessly pursue the enemy."

At dawn on the 21st the Brigade pushed north towards Bir bu Meliha over the battlefield of the previous night. It was a terrible sight. Bodies, tanks, guns and lorries lay smashed and still smouldering, while over all hung the heavy smell of decomposing flesh. As they went along they picked up some prisoners, magnificent specimens excellently turned out and very full of themselves.

The Regiment were in reserve to start with, 'A' Squadron with four depleted troops and 'B' and 'C' with about two troops each. For the first time since their approach march the ground allowed them to make a good advance.

At 7 a.m. an enemy column of about four hundred vehicles was reported moving south-west and the 3rd and 5th Royal Tanks were ordered to attack on the left flank, while the 22nd Armoured Brigade engaged the head. As usual the Artillery did great work against the enemy column which all the time edged further westwards. Unfortunately they drew away because Brigade had to stop and refuel, while the 22nd Armoured Brigade seemed to vanish away to the west.

Replenishing took place at Bir bu Meliha and the tank crews were able to snatch a quick 'brew up'. At 1.30 they moved off once more, the Regiment in the lead this time, thrusting on towards Sidi Rezegh where the Support Group and the 7th Armoured Division were very hard pressed.

They pushed on over increasingly bad going, 'A' Squadron on the left, 'B' on the right, Regimental Headquarters, and 'C' in reserve. A mist came down, slowly growing thicker, and in it an enemy column was reported somewhere ahead. Captain Threlfall, whose tank had been knocked out the day before, rejoined with a fresh tank and definite information about the enemy column, now about four or five miles in front.

At about 2 p.m. Lieutenants H. C. Carver and J. D. Derouet were detached to the left flank to try and link up with the 22nd Armoured Brigade, and just as they achieved it Threlfall came through on the air with the information that a large German 'soft' echelon, unguarded by tanks or guns, was moving west, parallel with them.

Both squadrons were ordered to right wheel, 'B' to get behind the enemy and shoot them up and 'A' to attack them in the flank. The Artillery were to bring down fire as they went in to the attack.

'B' Squadron went in first for a quick 'mosquito' attack and met the first tragedy, the ground. The guns of the Artillery got stuck, 'B' Squadron was slowed up and all this caused by the rain making the sand sticky. They encountered an unexpected hail of anti-tank fire, but luckily had no casualties although at least two tanks were hit.

Then it was the turn of 'A' Squadron. They could only muster Squadron Headquarters and two troops under Lieutenants Simons and Gibbes as the other two had not yet returned from their recce in the west. The six of them went in in line abreast in much the same way as their predecessors had at Balaclava. To get within effective range they had to close to at least six hundred yards, and at that range their armour was no defence at all against the 4-pounder and 75-mm. German guns, which were effective at 2,000 yards. 'A' Squadron closed to five hundred yards and opened fire, hitting several lorries that burnt well and catching a lot of men on their feet with the Brownings. They got in to two hundred, moving at about 15 m.p.h. and Duff gave the order to close right in. But the enemy were fully prepared. They let fly very accurately with at least six high-calibre anti-tank guns, which at this close range, were murder.

Simons was the first to be hit, the shell setting off his ammunition and killing his crew. Then all the rest of the tanks but Duff's were knocked out and three brewed up at once. It was decided not to send in 'C' Squadron and the Regiment withdrew, leaving the shattered remains of 'A' Squadron on the field. The surviving Germans went off after about twenty minutes.

Both Simons' legs were broken and he was badly burnt, but at the second attempt he managed to climb out and lie beside his tank. He was the only survivor of his Troop. He then discovered that both Troops were out of action. The S.S.M., Mr. Jordan, was killed, Gibbes had a broken leg, one of his crew was blinded and one had a broken leg. Sergeant Kirkham, Gibbes' Troop Sergeant, was unwounded.

"Then followed a nightmare of a night. At about midnight a large German force moved just south of us and Sergeant Kirkham went out and sat in a camel thorn bush counting the vehicles as they passed."

The Regiment by now was in leaguer near Bir Reghem with the rest of Brigade. 'B' Squadron was last in as they had lost touch during the attack and had had difficulty in finding where they were. Also Lieutenant D. C. Ricardo had rounded up a party of stragglers from the enemy column and taken them prisoner. 'B' Echelon had had a long march following Brigade all day and was now leaguered some five miles behind them. "The position," states Brigade War Diary, "was generally obscure."

Meanwhile on the airfield at Sidi Rezegh the battle had raged all day. Towards it converged two friendly and two enemy forces, 13 Corps and the New Zealanders driving west and north from the frontier towards Bardia and Tobruk, and the Tobruk Garrison battling with the Italian Trento Division in the north. From the south and south-east came Rommel's Panzers and the remains of the Ariete Division with the 4th and 22nd Armoured Divisions determined to engage them in battle before they reached the airfield. By evening riflemen of the Support Group with tanks and artillery had taken the northern and southern escarpments and were dug in there having suffered very heavy losses. To the south the 7th Armoured Brigade had been attacked by the Afrika Korps, with the result that the 7th Hussars and 2nd Royal Tanks had been practically wiped out. The 5th South African Brigade, on its way to join in, had been kept back out of the scrum, and the 70th Division from Tobruk had not yet advanced far enough to be of any help to the troops on the airfield. Against this the Indians had surrounded Sidi Omar and the New Zealanders were up to Bardia and had cut the enemies' communications to the frontier.

Night fell on the desert and everyone there knew that the dawn would bring a day bloodier and more desperate than the one before.

(e) The Disastrous Day, November 1941

ON the sand beside the burning tanks the survivors of 'A' Squadron lay waiting through the long night. Simons wrote:

"In the morning two 15 cwts. from 2nd Royal Horse Artillery motored up and informed me they were lost so I showed them where we were and sent them packing to get up ambulances.

"Just after they left a German motor-cyclist arrived, also lost, so we took him prisoner and felt rather pleased with ourselves as a result.

"Then Heycock arrived with the ambulances and fixed us up. He was very rude about my tourniquet which I had made with my hunting horn. This got lost in the hurry to get us off and Sergeant Kirkham picked it up later. I had had two tanks shot under me carrying it and he had seven in the succeeding days."

November 22nd was a disastrous day.

It began well enough. Brigade orders were to attack at first light the enemy who were supposed to be in leaguer near by. However, early morning patrols reported him gone and at about 10.30 a.m. the advance of the previous day was continued towards Sidi Rezegh.

On the march the Regiment was right flank guard to Brigade, with 'B' on the right, 'C' on the left and 'A' in reserve. They advanced to Carmuset Nbeidat and moved up to the escarpment. Below them 'B' Squadron could see a quantity of enemy transport to the north and east along the Trigh Capuzzo. They also reported what appeared to be fifty armoured vehicles approaching the escarpment about eight miles away. Brigadier Stirling then came up from Brigade to make a personal reconnaissance but apparently saw nothing of sufficient importance to warrant further investigation. The unidentified vehicles were assumed to be New Zealanders.

At 1.20 Brigade was ordered to move up on to Sidi Rezegh airfield as a heavy enemy attack against the 7th and 22nd Armoured Brigades was being launched. The Regiment were in reserve and stayed with Brigade Headquarters on the high ground to the east, and had a magnificent view of the battle on the airfield below. It looked like the Royal Tournament at Olympia with burning aeroplanes, tanks and lorries as far as the eye could see.

Down there, on the airfield, it was all dust and smoke and confusion. It was impossible to see clearly what was going on. The enemy appeared to be on the north-west edge with the Support Group and the 22nd Armoured Brigade to the south. It was decided to attack the airfield with the 5th Royal Tanks on the right and the 3rd Royal Tanks on the left. They were told to work round to the south but the attack was considerably hindered by the dust and heavy shell fire and the complete lack of information as to what was actually happening. Even when the 3rd Royal Tanks managed to contact the 22nd Armoured Brigade they still could not find out what was going on.

By 4.30 p.m. the order had to be given to withdraw. What was left of the Armoured Brigades and the Support Group retired, fighting to the last, and with the German infantry very close behind. Just before dark the enemy put down smoke to cover an infantry attack on the Support Group and though it was held off for some time by the 3rd and 5th Royal Tanks, when darkness fell Sidi Rezegh airfield was once more in German hands.

At about 5 p.m. the Regiment, still with Brigade Headquarters, came under fire from the east. The 25-pounders replied, firing over open sights at the anti-tank gun crews on the escarpment. Suddenly, as they watched, the enemy began shelling accurately and heavily. The Regiment turned west but were met by concentrated fire from enemy tanks that had crept round their flank.

It was impossible in the dark to see who was firing at them and the only targets they had were the gun flashes and tracers of the enemy shells. The battle lasted until after dark and Brigade then stopped and formed into a close leaguer with the tanks of the Regiment and the anti-tank guns of the Northumberland Hussars round the edge. It was clear that they were either surrounded or being attacked by their own forces by mistake.

With the idea of bringing in the Brigadier who had been observing the battle at Sidi Rezegh, Brigadier Stirling, second-in-command, 4th Armoured Brigade, fired three Very lights. The next thing that happened was that about thirty tanks and a lot of infantry carriers appeared just outside the leaguer and brilliant Very lights were fired by them, lighting up the whole scene.

It was still thought that they might be friendly as the rest of the Brigade tanks were expected. All the same everyone got ready with all available small arms, but the order was given not to fire. The Commander of the leading vehicle asked in English who they were and the information was given to him.

Captain Heycock, the medical officer, takes up the tale.

"Suddenly," he wrote, "I heard German words being shouted and our men shouting: 'They're Jerry tanks!' The Brigadier immediately had a message sent to warn the Brigade tanks not to come into the leaguer as the enemy were there.

"Everyone then rushed to their vehicles, German tanks came up fast on the outside of the leaguer and put up flares which lit everything like day. Sparks then began to fly, machine-gun, tommy-gun and tank shells poured into the leaguer from all sides and German soldiers rushed in firing Tommy-guns.

"A splendid fight was put up but we could not get away, the whole area was full of Germans."

Lorries and tanks were blazing but in spite of being both outnumbered and taken by surprise the Regiment fought desperately and it was not until after three-quarters of an hour's fighting at close quarters that the enemy had completely overcome resistance. Everyone was rounded up by Germans with Tommy-guns and all those who had got into their tanks were attacked with grenades if they did not at once surrender.

Captain Heycock continued: "A German with a Tommy-gun forced me to put up my hands. We were then put in a long line with our hands up and impudent Nazis went through my pockets taking my compass and other things from me. They then sorted us out into Officers, Sergeants and men. I told an officer that I was a doctor and was going to see to the wounded. I then proceeded under escort and collected all the wounded together, searching vehicles etc. Colonel Cripps called over to me to say that Major Duff was wounded. I examined him and found he was suffering from a severe abdominal wound. I got all the wounded and Major Duff together, lying for warmth round a burning vehicle.

"I then saw a senior German officer and told him I was going to stay with the wounded and that he must get us to hospital at once. He said we could go with their transport later. I spoke to Lieutenant Huntingdon and the Colonel and Lieutenant Derouet and Lieutenant R. S. Roffey. They were put in a car and driven off very soon afterwards. They appeared in good heart.

"I was left with the wounded. We were in the centre of about a Regiment of Infantry and tanks were leaguered all round us.[1] All through the night Very lights were put up in the leaguer and their repair and transport vehicles were hard at work. I got my wounded blankets and tarpaulins and bully beef and biscuits and water from our tanks. We were given an armed guard of four men all night.

"I was interrogated during the night and after he drew a blank the interrogator searched me. Luckily searching revealed nothing. In the morning I went on insisting that they took us to hospital and they continued procrastinating. I then became extremely angry and told them I should report the lot of them to the Red Cross and I would not stand for such scandalous delay. By this time I had drawn a large crowd round me and I picked out a more senior man wearing the Iron Cross and I repeated all this to him and I was extremely angry.

"This did something. They brought my wounded some black bread and coffee and cheese and I got them to clean out the captured A.C.V. to use as an ambulance after they had said there was no available vehicle. Shortly before this their tanks left in a southerly direction. I counted a hundred and fifty and two large cars. We were left with the Regiment of Infantry possessing anti-tank guns. They were practising driving the captured American tanks.

"Two of the very seriously wounded had died by this time. A German ambulance suddenly appeared and I got them to put the remaining four seriously wounded into it and I got into the A.C.V. with the four walking wounded. Their Sergeant Major got into the driving seat and we were just about off when suddenly heavy 2-pounder fire was directed on to us, followed by machine-gun fire. The A.C.V. got a direct hit but there were luckily no casualties and I got the wounded out. I saw a white flag lying on the ground, presumably from the ransacked A.C.V. I stood up and waved it towards our tanks about a thousand yards away.

"A Nazi then stuck a revolver in my back. I told him in German that he could not shoot me as I was a doctor and he did not. The machine-gun bullets from our tanks made him lie down. I bundled the walking wounded into the ambulance and got into the cab to drive off but could not make it work. I saw the German driver standing near so I went up to him and told him in German that we were both in the Red Cross and that he must drive us off. I pushed him into the cab with his orderly and we started off.

"We met a New Zealand carrier and warned them of German anti-tank guns, and they directed us to their headquarters where I handed over my patients and the two prisoners. I could not get back to the 8th Hussars as they said the line of communication was cut, so I stopped and helped their Field Ambulance."

Out of the Regiment only six tanks had escaped from the leaguer, including those of Major P. O. Sandbach, Captain Threlfall, Lieutenants Ricardo and T. M. Mills and Sergeant Brown. Lieut.-Colonel Waller in command of the Northumberland Hussars escaped in a Staff car and from Brigade only Captain Stibbs and Lieutenant Attenborough got away.

After driving south for some eight miles the four first mentioned tanks halted for the night and, for the rest of it, vigilant guard was kept by the officers.

[1] They were in fact the 15th Panzer Division.

They had spent the night near Sidi Mohammed el Abeied and the first people they encountered next morning was a South African patrol. Shortly after they had appeared tanks were seen and Sandbach went to investigate. They turned out to be a party of the 5th Royal Tanks who were able to tell this tiny company, which now comprised the 8th Hussars, a certain amount about the general situation.

30 Corps had had such tremendous losses the day before on the airfield that the only thing for them left to do was to withdraw back into the desert to reform near Gabr Saleh, while the 5th South African and the remains of the 22nd Armoured Brigades held a defensive position along the southern escarpment below Sidi Rezegh. As by now the Germans had more tanks left than we had, they were able to single out and hunt down the small groups of our armour, and the battles on the 23rd were more confused and isolated than those of the day before.

The four 8th Hussar tanks were by now practically out of petrol and were greatly relieved when Lieutenant N. D. A. Hall with the thinskins turned up about midday. Also during the morning the remaining two tanks appeared having had an engagement with two German staff cars.

They amused themselves during the afternoon by chasing a party of enemy transport but gave up the chase when almost in reach of them in order to attack another column. This was presumably the enemy as a German staff car drove towards them from it. It was thought just possible that the column might contain the prisoners taken in the leaguer but it turned out to be a New Zealand column which fired on them with 25-pounders over open sights, but fortunately their fire was inaccurate.

Shortly after this episode they contacted Brigadier Davy who appointed the four tanks commanded by Sandbach, Threlfall, Ricardo and Mills to be his personal body-guard. In that rôle they had some good shooting against a party of German tanks in the evening and accounted for, for certain, one German Mk. IV and had direct hits on several others.

During this action a fine-looking mallard flew over quite low just in front of the tanks. He no doubt enjoyed the spectacle of men shooting at one another instead of at him.

All that day the fighting had raged round the South Africans and the 22nd Armoured Brigade on the edge of the airfield. Three times during the morning they flung back attacks, but in the afternoon came enemy reinforcements with more than a hundred tanks supported by lorried infantry and guns. These descended like an avalanche and, though they lost fifty tanks, succeeded in practically wiping out both brigades, and the South Africans ceased to exist as a fighting formation. Now almost all that was left, with the Support Group and the 7th Armoured Brigade crippled by the fighting on the previous days, was the 4th, and that at only half strength. What was left of the 7th and 22nd Brigades leaguered that night south of the airfield, with the 4th Brigade south-east and the Support Group at Gabr Saleh. The Division had borne for the last four days the whole weight of Rommel's armour, defying it unflinchingly with inferior weapons, save those of courage and determination. Of these last they had plenty and they would continue to need all that they had.

(*f*) In the German Advance, November 1941

ON the 23rd while the 8th Hussars' four tanks were with Brigadier Davy, their 'B' Echelon had a well-earned rest near Gabr Fatma. In the morning Lieutenant P. H. Wagstaffe was sent off with a party consisting of Lieutenant G. Fonda, U.S. Army, and Amt/Q.M.S. Patman, R.A.O.C. with three cars and drivers to recover two tanks that were thought to be repairable.

They found the tanks and discovered that one belonged to the 5th Royal Tanks and had the tracks off while the other was one of their own with a broken front sprocket and track. After about three hours' work and when one tank was almost ready to tow, the unwelcome figure of a Sapper officer appeared, wanting to blow them both up. He was asked whether he would not rather blow up instead some 'dead' German tanks that were close by and leave the others alone but the incident had put doubts into their minds. Was the position still static or had it become fluid? They decided to call up 'B' Echelon only to find that they had gone off on a bearing and were strength three.

However, they were ready to move, and with their own tank towing the other minus its tracks, they ground off. Almost immediately they met a Squadron of the 11th Hussars who told them that a large German column was heading towards them. Again they tried to contact 'B' Echelon, but with no success, so they decided to climb to some higher ground in the hopes of being able to see something.

They moved at a snail's pace as the towed tank sank deeply into the sand. At last they arrived at a Trig. point and decided it was Point 189. While they were there a 'Jock' Column of 25-pounders turned up. They were convinced on the other hand that the enemy were behind them, and heading for the wire.

They were also joined by Brigadier Davy's car which, under an officer of the 7th Hussars, had been trying to rescue some cruisers. The car had been attacked and a sergeant in it was badly wounded. The Trig. point had now become a general meeting place and it was decided to disperse. Wagstaffe's party hoped to travel with the 'Jock' Column but it was too fast for them.

They travelled south-east for some five miles and just before dusk were attacked by six Messerschmidt 109's. They kept going for as long as they could but the attack was too persistent and they stopped at some convenient slit trenches. As many people as possible crowded into the tanks as the aircraft would not give up and seemed to be convinced that they must be very important. Sergeant Hall, driving Lieutenant Fonda's truck, was killed in the attack.

Eventually they found 'B' Echelon of the Support Group who took over the body of Sergeant Hall. They had more or less run out of petrol too but were able to replenish now. Dusk was falling and there was firing from all sides but the north, so they turned north with the Support Group and leaguered somewhere between Gabr Saleh and Sheferzen.

All through the night there was continual firing and a great deal of activity. It turned out, on investigation, to be German columns taking up some sort of battle positions. It seemed extremely likely that the Gemans were going to attack somebody at dawn so they slipped away while it was still dark on the morning of the 24th, driving in a diamond formation, Fonda and Wagstaffe navigating from the Dodge. The plan was to go south and try to join Brigade by turning eastwards.

E

Although the first part of the battle for Sidi Rezegh was over the fighting was by no means at an end. Realising that the armour of 30 Corps was so badly shattered that it could hardly be expected to constitute any menace to him, and knowing that 13 Corps was still some way away, Rommel decided on a daring plan, to sweep forward down the Trigh el Abd to the Egyptian frontier and then to turn north and cut the communications of 13 Corps. If this manoeuvre was successful then there was no reason why he should not carry on right into Egypt and beyond to the Suez Canal. A glittering prize indeed. The only fly in the ointment was the unlikely possibility of the survivors of 30 Corps rallying enough to cut his own communications, but from the battering they had taken it seemed hardly likely.

So on November 24th the German advance began. The main column came south from Sidi Rezegh and then joined the others moving east down the Trigh el Abd, alongside Wagstaffe who was looking for Brigade.

After travelling carefully for about five miles, dawn broke over the little party of cars and with it came the unpleasant sight of about fifty German tanks and a large amount of transport that were travelling parallel to them. As the cars were not able to reply to the recognition signals a patrol came out to investigate, but they managed to cut across the front of the column. Unfortunately they ran into the back of another column which was being attacked by the Royal Air Force. At that moment a heavy early morning mist descended, and although they were able to pass fairly freely amongst the new column, they were unable to get out of it, and in the confusion lost Q.M.S. Patman and Wagstaffe's car. It was interesting to see that the Germans had a lot of small guns, pulled by anything from a 3-tonner to a Ford 8 cwt.

By about midday on the 24th Fonda and Wagstaffe imagined they must have come through the column. They must also have travelled a long way with it in the mist as they now found themselves close to the wire. They planned to try and reach Maddalena and find out what was happening, and came to within six miles of it to find German tanks, motor cyclists and lorries refuelling there. These did not take any notice of them while they approached "but fired a little as we went away and sent cars after us."

The party halted and 'brewed up' whilst another plan was thought up. This time they decided to go further south before trying to get through the wire and reach Maddalena. They managed this without much difficulty having picked up some German petrol which was a great asset. They found the other cars there before them, a great relief as during their passage through the German column there had been a considerable amount of firing.

(g) Searching for the Regiment, November 1941

ALL that day the four tanks of the Regiment continued in their rôle of bodyguard to Brigadier Davy. During the morning they travelled to Gott el Moheta with Brigade where they were replenished. There was a tremendous amount of movement all over the desert, columns were reported everywhere and many of them were friendly. No longer could anyone tell by the direction in which a column was moving whether it was friend or foe.

After replenishing, Sandbach's small force went on with Brigade towards Bir el

Hamarin. When they were a short distance south-east of it and at about 4 p.m. Sandbach reported seeing a column of about 2,000 enemy vehicles moving south. The four tanks were sent off at once to attack this vast force from the east while Brigade came in from another direction.

A running fight then took place and continued for about sixteen miles. Darkness fell and the Regiment went on fighting by moonlight. They chased some Italian ME 13's which fought a running rearguard action at the tail of the column.

In the meantime Brigade had received orders from Division to move at once to Aghierat Scedida but of this Sandbach knew nothing. Luckily 2nd Lieutenant V. A. Buist, the Liaison Officer, had kept in contact and was able to keep them informed. They began to run out of petrol but again were lucky in running into the leaguer of the Kings Dragoon Guards who were able to let them have some.

Then they marched practically due south for some twenty-four miles, the small column of five tanks and a dingo passing right through the German columns. They could see the enemy leaguer lights to their right and left and also a number of their own vehicles which were still burning as a result of ground and air attacks. However, they were not stopped and eventually finished up near Aghierat Scedida.

In the meantime the stay of the 'B' Echelon near Fatma had been rudely interrupted. At about midday they came under shell-fire and left hastily in a south-easterly direction. The Regimental Echelon got separated from Brigade Echelon and halted at Point 187 where they managed to make wireless contact with Brigade, who were ten miles to the north. As there was a large enemy column between both parties it was thought better not to try to join up.

At 3 p.m. they were joined by a convoy of fifty Royal Army Service Corps lorries and the 3rd Royal Tank's Echelon. At about 4.30 they were again attacked by enemy tanks and guns, so they moved eight miles to the south and halted once more. Here they were attacked by ten Messerschmitt 110's but suffered no casualties.

After this they moved to join the Divisional Axis four miles further south and leaguered there for the night. They were joined by Lieutenant B. T. Attenborough and two Brigade Headquarters tanks which had managed to escape from the leaguer on the night of the 22nd, and later by stragglers from almost every unit in the 8th Army.

Everyone not on guard that night slept at his post and piquets were set out on all sides. Throughout the night the rumbling of tanks was heard and Very lights were seen to the north, south and west. It appeared as if a battle was raging to the north-east as there were gun flashes all night from that direction.

That same day, the 24th, Lieutenant C. F. Hedley, the Quarter-Master, left the Echelon with a replenishing party consisting of three ammunition, four petrol, one water and one ration lorry to try and find the remaining tanks of the Regiment. Considering the confusion that reigned in the desert at that moment with no one quite sure what was happening it was not surprising that it took him a long time.

He left at 11 a.m. and reached the arranged rendezvous only to find that the tanks had been sent off after an enemy column. On his return to Berraneb, Hedley was told that the main Echelon had been attacked and was being pursued by enemy tanks. He left again at dusk meaning to catch up with Brigade and replenish them, but at 1 a.m. he still had not found them. Enemy columns were by now reported between him and Brigade and he was ordered to leaguer for the night. German leaguer lights were going up on all sides and it felt horribly like being surrounded. In spite of a hard day everyone 'stood to' until dawn, and Tommy-guns were very much in evidence.

At first light on the 25th they left for their meeting place, but again were disappointed as when they reached it at 9 a.m. they found that Sandbach and his tanks had not been back that night. While they were waiting there a large number of lorries filled with infantry were seen approaching from the north-west and the replenishing party thought they were in the bag. However, they turned out to be the much-battered South Africans from Sidi Rezegh who were heading for a point nearby to reorganise. Late at night they contacted Brigade again and, none of their own tanks being in leaguer, they replenished anybody within sight. And then had a few hours welcome rest.

On the 26th they "tagged along behind Brigade" again, hoping to hear where they could obtain fresh supplies of all kinds. Then over the air came a message, telling them to investigate some vehicles on their right flank that had apparently been abandoned. Hedley went off in his utility with the Brigade 'B' Echelon Commander and R.Q.M.S. O'Malley and found nearly forty German and British vehicles, the British evidently having been captured and used by the enemy. For the most part they were bogged and there was one Honey tank, holed in the turret, and with them a badly wounded officer and an N.C.O. of the 3rd Royal Tanks, together with six German lorry drivers.

The Brigade Medical Officer, who had followed in an ambulance, was attending to the wounded when four armoured cars hove into sight from the north and halted on a ridge about five hundred yards away. Hedley wrote: "I identified them as British and took no further notice. I instructed O'Malley to go back to the replenishing party three miles away and bring up a lorry to take away the prisoners. Immediately the car began to move the armoured cars opened up with machine-gun fire, effectively stopping the car, fortunately without injury to the occupants. The M.O. waved his red cross flag and firing ceased. Thought we were in the bag again and didn't give much for my identification of armoured cars, but they were ours. They couldn't see us as we were attending to the wounded on the ground but they could see the German drivers and thought they were attempting a getaway. Rather shaking."

Later that morning they had a grand stand view of 25-pounders effectively silencing an enemy H.E. battery unpleasantly close. They then did a thirty mile trip to refill and heard that Sandbach was in the vicinity but did not see him.

Next day, the 27th, they left Morley to replenish Brigade, but the going was so very bad that they did not reach Brigade Headquarters until ten that night. Here they eventually met Sandbach, having by then replenished almost everybody in the desert but the ones they had originally set out to find. They had previously met Captain Baldwin with the main part of the Echelon near Taieb el Essem and had picked up Lieutenant Hooper near Morley. Later they were dive-bombed by twenty Stukas and Messerschmitts near Berraneb but, although Brigade had a car written off, no one was hurt.

(h) Reduced to a Squadron, November 1941

OPERATION 'CRUSADER' now entered into its second phase. The 8th Hussars also. They, with the exception of Sandbach and his four tanks, had had all their tanks knocked out and the task now was to reform the Regiment. Major Phillips, commanding Head-quarters Squadron, and a few others who had been extra regimentally employed, formed the nucleus of the new Regiment, a Regiment which although it had been overwhelmed and practically wiped out, carried on fighting without a pause with all the tanks at its command. The feeling of those who remained, knowing that their comrades had been taken off to untold years in prison, may well be imagined. But they never flagged and what was left of the Regiment went on, fighting.

November 25th. As it became light the small party of five tanks and the dingo, who had spent the night watching the German leaguer lights on either side and the flames from their own burning vehicles, were able to see enemy columns on the move, heading north. At the same time they saw, three or four miles to the south-east, a large leaguer. This turned out to be a more than welcome R.A.S.C. centre which provided them with rations and water.

They then went on to Advanced Divisional Headquarters, arriving at ten, and found about thirty-two Honeys and a number of reinforcements waiting to man them. Although he must by this time have been exhausted and in need of a rest, Sandbach started immediately on the task of organising them into a composite force, complete with the 'B' Echelon commanded by Doctors McMillen and Heycock, the latter having returned after his short stay with the enemy.

Meanwhile 'B' Echelon, which with the various other vehicles and convoys that had joined them now formed a column of some five hundred vehicles, moved east along the Divisional Axis under command of Major Strange, 3rd Royal Tanks. The wire was crossed at 1.30 p.m. and the Echelon stopped near the Eighth Army Headquarters. Here they replenished, having collected in a few stragglers belonging to them and disposed of various others that had become attached.

All that day scattered but successful fighting continued, from Taieb el Essem to Sheferzen. Damaged and bogged tanks were recovered and to the north the New Zealanders struggled forward, taking Zaapan and, in the evening, Belhamed. The troops in Tobruk were still forcing their way out and the Indians in Sidi Omar repulsed all attacks and reduced the 21st Panzer Division to ten tanks. The 4th Armoured Brigade, having supported the 1st South African Brigade at Taieb el Essem all day, watched the enemy withdraw to the north-east in the evening but were unable to pursue him as the men by now were so exhausted after eight days hard fighting that the drivers kept falling asleep. So they leaguered a few miles south near the dump area.

Next morning, the 26th, the newly formed force under Sandbach with Threlfall as second-in-command moved out to join Brigade. There were two squadrons, one 8th Hussar, which was joined by Lieutenant Barrass of the Royal Tank Regiment, and the other composed almost entirely of Royal Tank Regiment personnel and commanded by Captain Joly. They joined the 4th Armoured Brigade at Bir Berraneb, where they found everyone suffering from a new problem, that of the shortage of wireless sets. By now most of these in existence had flat batteries, which made any move or manoeuvre just that much more difficult.

After leaguering for the night at Bir Berraneb the new force split up, Sandbach keeping sixteen tanks and part of 'B' Echelon, while the rest were divided between the 3rd and 5th Royal Tanks.

Meantime 'B' Echelon (whose activities were described earlier in the chapter), was still in search of its Regiment. With great difficulty they got permission to recross the wire and march west. They leaguered near Point 168 and came into wireless contact with the Regiment at Bir Berraneb. Then, having replenished from the South African Division, they pushed on, but when they arrived at Bir Berraneb all they could find was a German leaguer. By now their batteries were flat too so that they could not get in touch with their Regiment and had to leaguer on their own for the night.

Elsewhere the day went well and by nightfall the New Zealanders recaptured Sidi

Rezegh. Rommel, returning from his raid, found his way back along the Trigh Capuzzo barred by the rear of the New Zealander Division.

At dawn on the 27th the 8th Hussars sent out patrols but they returned with nothing to report. Everyone was able to take advantage of this brief respite and find time to shave, for the first time since the battle started. It was a pleasant morning too, but it did not last, and soon the desert was swept by wind and rain.

Neither did the pause last. By one o'clock a message came in that a very large column was moving west. This turned out to be made up of something between 1,500 and 2,000 lorries, protected by tanks and anti-tank guns and was part of Rommel's army hurrying home along the Trigh Capuzzo.

The 4th Armoured Brigade was ordered to attack and they advanced north-east with the squadron under Major Sandbach in the lead. Meanwhile the 22nd Armoured Brigade also came forward, and while they attacked the head, the 4th engaged the southern flank of the enemy force.

A long fierce fight then began. The Regiment managed to split the enemy column and engaged one section which appeared to have no protection with it. They got in close enough to use machine-gun fire and one German officer gave himself up with a lorry and six men.

2nd Lieutenant Mills was then left in observation of this column, which before long collected itself and moved off west. The remainder of Major Sandbach's force went to the assistance of the 3rd Royal Tanks who were grappling with enemy tanks that had become separated from the rest of the column.

The battle was fiercely contested and raged until dusk. The Regiment had two tanks knocked out, those commanded by Major Sandbach and Sergeant Clark, but there were no casualties and both crews were picked up. Sandbach was commanding Threlfall's tank at the time and it unfortunately had on it large and valuable stocks of rum and whisky!

As darkness fell the action was broken off and the Regiment rallied and moved back with Brigade into leaguer about three miles south.

As leaguer was being formed a staff car was reported by Trooper Dovison to be moving about in a suspicious manner just outside. Lieutenant Ricardo went out with Dovison and they succeeded in capturing a German who was armed with a Tommy-gun but his companion escaped in the staff car.

During the day Captain Baldwin and 'B' Echelon eventually met Hedley and the replenishing party at Taieb el Essem. Here they remained and had the doubtful pleasure of watching Corps Headquarters being bombed at Gabr Sceidida.

The combined fighting of the 4th and 22nd Brigades this day seemed to have stopped the Germans from attacking the rear of the New Zealanders, precariously lodged at Sidi Rezegh and who had at last joined up with the 70th Division, breaking out of Tobruk. This however did not last long. A German counter-attack broke through and separated them, leaving the 4th New Zealand Brigade more hard pressed than ever as one of its battalions had by now joined the 70th. Supplies were running short but after dark a column escorted by the 8th Hussars got through to them with much needed food and ammunition.

(i) A Desperate Enemy, November 1941

ON the morning of the 28th the Regiment, with the 4th Armoured Brigade, was ordered north-west to help the 22nd Armoured Brigade near Bir Reghem. It was not long before a large enemy column was sighted moving west along the Trigh Capuzzo. This was at once engaged and a two-hour battle with a force of some seventy German tanks resulted. The 4th Armoured Brigade could now muster sixty tanks and the 22nd only thirty. The attack pressed hardest on the junction between the two Brigades and eventually a gap was formed. The Regiment, however, in their part of the battle, fought well and successfully, with splendid artillery co-operation. "This," says their War Diary "was a successful action which definitely finished in our favour."

Lieutenant Barrass, attached to Sandbach's force, put up a particularly stout show when two tanks in his troop were knocked out and set alight. With the assistance of Corporal Lightfoot of the Royal Tank Regiment he succeeded in rescueing a badly wounded man, and for this he was granted the immediate award of the M.C.

At midday a message was received from Major-General Gott, the Divisional Commander, congratulating the Regiment on what they had been able to do so far and saying that though they had already been fighting for a longer period than men were usually called upon to endure, they would be expected to fight one more battle, after which they would be rested.

Heartened, they moved on, the Regiment leading the Brigade, with the rôle of contacting the enemy and then withdrawing into reserve. Needless to say this did not happen.

The Germans were encountered just south of Sidi Rezegh and immediately both sides became locked in battle. The Regiment came into action again as the Germans tried to break through on the left flank, and they were called up from reserve to prevent this. It was a long and grimly fought battle, the Regiment getting in some good shooting, but the Germans were desperate to break through this barrier across their line of retreat. During the battle the Regiment were replenished by a tank which came up from Brigade laden with cases of ammunition, a courageous performance. Practically all their tanks had fired more than two hundred 37-mm. rounds during the day. As night fell the battle was broken off, and the Regiment leaguered with Brigade some distance south near Charrubet ez Zchemat.

Although at the end of this action neither side had given ground, the British tanks had been continually outclassed by the Germans, who mounted guns of superior calibre and range and whose rear was protected by the unequalled 88-mm. anti-tank gun. It says much for the gallantry of the crews of the Honeys and Crusaders that they were able to inflict the many casualties they did.

(j) Beating up the Italians, November 1941

ON November 29th, after a brief engagement from which the enemy withdrew, the 4th Armoured Brigade heard that the Germans were massing on Sidi Rezegh airfield and preparing to attack the New Zealanders at el Duda, although later patrols reported the airfield clear.

At 1.30 p.m. Brigade was ordered to advance to the 400 Grid so that they could counter-attack any threat to our own troops on the north of the airfield. They advanced, north-west, the Regiment once again in the lead, over the Sidi Rezegh battlefield. It was a hideous sight. The advance patrols went just over the escarpment and were fired on by anti-tank guns, one tank commanded by Corporal Morris being knocked out. Sergeant Bennett put up a fine show in rescuing the crew. Lieutenant Ricardo's troop then disappeared and were missing for the rest of the day, but turned up again in the evening having joined up with the 5th Royal Tanks on the left.

At the same time as an enemy column was seen moving along the Trigh Capuzzo to the west, orders were received by Brigade to help the infantry who were in trouble at Point 175.

A new course was set but owing to a wireless set being left on "send", thus making wireless communication impossible, as well as a strong enemy attack coming in from the west, Brigade had to fight where they were as the attack had developed on their tail and they had to guard their guns.

At dusk the engagement ceased, and the sadly depleted Brigade moved south and leaguered in the same place as they had the night before.

The Regimental 'B' Echelon had remained at Taieb el Essem for the last two days, and on the 29th were dive-bombed at eight in the morning, midday and at four. Four men were wounded and four lorries burnt out, but there were no more casualties.

As a result of this day's fighting the New Zealanders had been protected from the main force of the German tanks, and, although hard pressed, had advanced a little and even captured General Ravenstein of the 21st Panzer Division. But both the 4th and 22nd Armoured Brigades had lost so many tanks that they could no longer operate as two separate formations, but were amalgamated as the 4th Armoured Brigade under Brigadier Gatehouse.

Again a squadron of 8th Hussars, led by Major Phillips, escorted a large supply column up to the New Zealanders under cover of darkness, and reached them at dawn with no loss.

On the 30th, while the new 4th Armoured Brigade Headquarters was reorganising, the 8th Hussars with the other regiments moved north of Bir Reghem where they encountered the Italian Arriete Division. They moved into a good hull down position and had a magnificent shoot while the 3rd Royal Tanks on their left managed to work round the enemies' flank and press home the attack. "It was most invigorating to beat up the Italians in this fashion," says the War Diary, "and they ultimately took refuge in flight leaving nineteen of their tanks behind."

However, during the battle Lieutenant R. H. Ames was wounded and his tank knocked out, as were those of Captain Threlfall and Lieutenant Barrass, but all three were recovered.

After this the day was quiet and Brigade moved two miles south to leaguer.

Meanwhile the 'B' Echelon, still at Taieb el Essem, was bombed again at exactly the same times in the morning. Three lorries were lost, but there were no casualties. However the Royal Air Force were waiting for the four o'clock raid and accounted for no less than twenty-four dive bombers, much to the joy and uplift to morale of the 'B' Echelon. One British plane made a forced landing in the leaguer area and the pilot was unhurt.

(k) Last Fight on the Airfield, December 1941

BY now the New Zealanders at Sidi Rezegh who had been hanging on by their eyelids and repelling attacks from both front and rear could hold on no longer. The 1st South African Brigade had not been able to reach them in time owing to the continual worrying of strong forces of enemy tanks against their own weak tank escort, enfeebled by days of fighting against superior forces.

The first thing the Regiment heard on the morning of December 1st was that the New Zealanders on Sidi Rezegh airfield had been overrun by German tanks and that they were to counter-attack and do what they could to get the survivors out.

The Brigade advanced, led as usual by the Regiment in their rôle of drawing the enemies' fire. They moved forward over the airfield with Captain J. W. Gwyn and 2nd Lieutenant T. M. Mills doing advance guard with their troops. The field was covered with German and Italian planes but was otherwise deserted, and they reached the escarpment beyond under heavy shell-fire from the high ground to the south-west.

During the advance it was clear that the enemy was subjecting the New Zealand leaguer, which was on the plain beyond the escarpment, to a merciless artillery barrage.

As they got to the escarpment the leading tanks of the Regiment could see below them the New Zealand leaguer with practically every vehicle ablaze. Away to the left, stretching towards Tobruk, lay the German Army.

They descended the escarpment on to the plain below and came themselves under a barrage of fire of all kinds, including anti-tank fire from the north and north-west. Sandbach formed his force up into line and they swept down, guns blazing, into the New Zealand leaguer.

As they came on they could see the New Zealanders sheltering in slit trenches. Many of them, thinking this new force was German and that therefore they were hopelessly overwhelmed, came out with their hands up. When they realised who it was many of them fixed bayonets and formed up behind the tanks, wishing to attack the enemy positions, in the circumstances a very courageous action.

It was during this action in the leaguer that the Regiment suffered a grievous loss in the death of Major Sandbach. His tank was put out of action by shots fired from a captured 'I' tank, manned by the enemy. As he baled out, he was hit by a burst of machine-gun fire, and fell, fatally wounded. This very fine soldier died two days later in a German Hospital at el Adem.

The remainder of the Regiment then rallied under Captain Threlfall on the east of the leaguer where they came under heavy shell-fire. The New Zealanders had by now decided to withdraw eastwards and the Regiment, with Brigade, formed up in front of and to the north of them to protect them, coming again under a hail of shell-fire from north, east and west.

During this shelling Sergeant Jones's tank was hit and no trace of him was ever found. 2nd Lieutenant Ricardo too was wounded in the neck by shrapnel.

On reaching the pass up the escarpment the New Zealanders were heavily shelled from the south and south-east and withdrew rapidly and in some disorder northwards. German tanks now came into the attack from the south and south-west and all units of the 4th Armoured Brigade were ordered to move to the top of the escarpment at once and take up a position on the ridge near the block house. Then, when nearly surrounded, they went south, fast, and got out safely. But Sidi Rezegh had changed hands.

They leaguered that night near Bir Berraneb with the rest of the 4th Armoured Brigade, while 'B' Echelon moved up from Taieb el Essem having lost two more vehicles in the midday raid. 2nd Lieutenant Mills' tank was so damaged at the airfield that he had to take it back to the Light Recovery Section next morning.

This action completed for the Regiment twelve days of almost continual fighting without rest. In practically every operation the Regiment and latterly Sandbach's Squadron had led the advance and had made first contact with the enemy. For this honour they had suffered accordingly, but not without recognition from the units they fought beside. Although in the newspapers at home the New Zealanders and South Africans were mentioned in the reports of the battle, no one was allowed to know that the Regiment had even been in action, much less fought so gallantly. But a letter received by Major Phillips from Lieut.-Colonel Bolton of the 2nd Royal Horse Artillery said briefly all that needed saying.

Lieut.-Colonel L. Bolton,
2nd Regt. R.H.A., M.E.F.
22 December, 1941.

Dear Jumbo,

This is not merely a letter from me to you, but from my Regiment to yours.

I would like you to know how bitterly sorry we all are at your heavy losses. I hope that the world will get to know that, far from being in vain, the 8th Hussars chiefly, together with the 3rd and 5th Royal Tank Regiments, stood between the British Empire and perhaps defeat, for eight days.

They were simply magnificent from the first engagement when they took the brunt of the attack till the end when there were so few left.

Gerry Hulbart of ours died in damned fine company.

Yours,
Lyndon Bolton.

(l) End of Operation 'Crusader', December 1941

THERE is a limit to what men and units of men can stand, in both mental and physical exhaustion. It is a characteristic of the British soldier never to admit to this state and thus to perform prodigious feats of endurance that normally no man could contemplate. It was this quality that enabled the fragments of 30 Corps to go on fighting on the battle-scarred sand between Sidi Rezegh and Bir Gobi where the new goal was the track to el Adem. It was this quality that enabled the 8th Hussars, scarred as the sand and shocked by the death of Major Sandbach whose conduct over the last few days had been such an inspiration to them all, to rally again under Major Phillips. Once more they had been reduced from a squadron to a mere handful, but, after three days of essential rest and maintenance, where a wash and shave were of outstanding importance, they were back in action, this time as a squadron attached to the 3rd Royal Tank Regiment.

In such a small and family Regiment as the 8th Hussars the losses both in those killed and those taken prisoner would have severely shaken their morale had they not possessed the same spirit that carried them down the Valley of Death, and back. Even so, too much cannot be asked of any man, and they were not alone in suffering from the effects of war. What was left of the New Zealand Division had to be sent back to refit, and almost the only forces the 7th Armoured Division could muster were 'Jock' Columns and a pitifully weak force of tanks. Luckily Rommel's Army was in much the same state and the first few days of December were spent by both sides in trying to rescue the hundreds of abandoned vehicles and guns. Rommel had left garrisons at Bardia and Halfaya but these he had to write off. Tobruk itself was becoming too much of a problem to invest any longer. And so his retreat began.

By December 7th, after five days spent without even seeing the enemy, the Regiment were in action again. At eight in the morning they became engaged with a German force of some forty tanks south-west of el Gubi. The enemy position was screened by their formidable anti-tank guns which held up the attack, although the Artillery put in some effective shelling. However, after fighting all day, the result was five enemy tanks burnt out, eight probables and twenty-seven definitely hit. An anti-tank gun and much transport was put out of action and the remaining tanks were forced back behind a strong anti-tank screen with their artillery position on the ridge. During this action the Regiment suffered no casualties and leaguered that night with Brigade near the battle area.

Next day, the 8th, was spent by the Regiment patrolling round el Gubi, the enemy having withdrawn north-westerly. Although the 4th Armoured Brigade was in action all day attacking the new position on a high ridge on the Trigh el Abd, about ten miles from el Gubi, the Regiment did not take part.

However, on the 9th they were pursuing Rommel once more. He had withdrawn north-west during the night and they marched fast after him to Bir Hatiet Genadel and from there north to Bir Bellefaa. By noon they were in contact with a defensive position on a ridge, strongly defended by tanks, anti-tank guns and artillery, a few miles south and south-east of Knightsbridge, the track junction twenty miles west of el Adem.

The 4th Armoured Brigade immediately went into action and attacked the ridge on both flanks. The 5th Royal Tanks were able to get round on to the high ground on the escarpment north west of Bir Bellefaa, from which position they commanded the ground north and south-west of them.

At four o'clock twenty enemy tanks were seen advancing down the valley from the west. These were strongly engaged from the north-east by the 3rd Royal Tanks, with whom the Regiment was fighting, and by the 5th Royal Tanks from the north. The battle which followed was intense, but it was at too long a range for any tanks to be claimed as definitely destroyed. As darkness fell the action was broken off and the night march to the leaguer was made the more tiring by the many slit trenches everywhere and the presence of supply and ammunition dumps.

And this, as far as the Regiment was concerned, was the end of Operation 'Crusader'. After several days rest and maintenance they started on their long journey back to Cairo. They crossed the wire on December 15th and on the 17th spent the whole day resting and cleaning themselves up. They paraded at midday for an address by Major Phillips when he read out various letters of congratulation.

On the 19th they reached Beni Yusef Camp and parties began proceeding on leave. On the 27th they were joined by the rest of the 4th Armoured Brigade and on the 31st a memorial service for the Regiment was held in Cairo Cathedral.

The desert where so much fighting had taken place was quiet for the moment. The

Eighth Army had chased Rommel back to el Agheila and Agedabia, and Benghazi became ours on Christmas Eve. Leaving the 1st Armoured Division and the 22nd Armoured Brigade in charge, the 7th Armoured Division returned to Cairo to prepare for what was coming. What that would be it was only too easy to imagine. Rommel had no taste for being driven out of Cyrenaica and, when he too had licked his wounds and rested awhile, would with his Afrika Korps engage once more in bloody battle.

III.

FROM BIR HACHEIM TO ALAMEIN

(a) Refit in Cairo, December 1941-March 1942

DECEMBER 1941 is a good moment to pause and take stock of what was happening in the rest of the world. Events there had been sweeping forward and great changes had taken place.

The defeat of Rommel in the desert was to have serious consequences. Hitler, realising at last how important was the North African campaign and if it succeeded what a hold he would have over Britain, transferred on December 5th a whole Air Corps from Russia to Sicily and North Africa. In the months that followed the Luftwaffe were to be supreme in the air, not only in the desert but over the vital supply route through the Mediterranean.

As if this was not enough the British Navy, which played an essential part in the desert war, was itself to suffer terrible losses. In November the Ark Royal and the Barham were sunk, followed in December by the loss of the battleship Queen Elizabeth and the Valiant, sunk in Alexandria harbour by Italian human torpedoes. The cruiser Neptune and the destroyer Khandahar were lost on new minefields off Tripoli, thus facilitating the running of German and Italian convoys to supply Rommel's troops. Soon the Mediterranean was virtually denied to British convoys, and even those sent from the east lost more than half their ships before reaching half-starved Malta. Then came an event the results of which were first to detract from the desert campaigns and finally to aid them. Pearl Harbour.

On December 7th, without warning, the Japanese attacked the American Fleet. On the 8th Britain declared war on Japan and on the 10th the Repulse and the Prince of Wales were sunk by Japanese torpedoes off Singapore. On the 11th Germany declared war on America, and at last that nation of unlimited resources was in action with Britain against the Axis. For a second time in the space of twenty five years history was slowly but surely repeating itself when, earlier in December, Britian had had reluctantly to declare war on Finland, Roumania and Hungary as Russia, fighting the Germans along an enormous front in hideous winter conditions, was a great and valued ally.

A new theatre now opened in the Far East demanding men and guns and ships and aircraft. The forces that could have been sent to General Auckinleck were diverted, and many already in the desert were pushed on eastwards, some to be made prisoner of war on arrival at Singapore. One other factor weighed against the Eighth Army, the amazing power of recovery that Rommel possessed. Twenty-one days after he had been for all intents and purposes soundly beaten and forced to retire as far as el Agheila with only a remnant of his Afrika Korps, he emerged as deadly as ever, giving his few troops the orders to follow him as far and as fast as they could.

By then the British forces at the front were weak, inexperienced and widely dispersed. The 7th Armoured Division who might have held him, was back in Cairo having handed over to the 1st Armoured Division, newly arrived out east. And they, by February 1st, had lost a hundred of their hundred and fifty tanks and had been driven back to the Gazala-Bir Hacheim line. December's fighting was all to do again.

At home it seemed all-important that the Eighth Army should attack as soon as possible, chiefly as a means of saving Malta who was being bombed out of existence. General Auchinleck was equally decided that there should at least be some chance of success for his troops, before they were engaged in battle, and eventually a date for an offensive was fixed for not later than the middle of June. Meanwhile Rommel was receiving reinforcements of tanks by convoys that came through the Mediterranean unscathed, and increasing his strength every moment, while the Eighth Army supplies had to run the gauntlet of the U-boats and come round by the Cape. But Malta's plight was desperate and she must be saved, even at the risk of losing Egypt.

This then was the position in the desert in January 1942. General Auchinleck was still Commander-in-Chief. The Eighth Army was commanded by Lieut.-General N. M. Ritchie and, at the front, consisted of the Guards Brigade and the 1st Armoured Division under Lieut.-General H. Lumsden. Major-General Gott had left the 7th Armoured Division, back in Cairo, and now commanded 13 Corps of which the Division was part, his place being taken by Major-General Campbell late of the Support Group (renamed the Motor Brigade and under Brigadier Renton). Tragically, a few weeks after Major-General Campbell had taken over and only a few days after receiving the V.C. that he won at Sidi Rezegh, he was killed in a motor accident and his place was taken by Major-General Messervy.

Of the fighting back to the Gazala line the 7th Armoured Division saw nothing, although they were to see plenty later on. During January, February and March the 8th Hussars were concentrating on regaining their normal fighting efficiency at the Beni Yusef camp back on the outskirts of Cairo.

At the end of December, Major Harbord, Captain Nelson and Captain P. K. Earle all rejoined the Regiment from their various appointments with the 7th Armoured Brigade, Eighth Army Headquarters and the R.A.C. Base Depot. On January 1st the actual strength of the Regiment was fourteen officers and two hundred and ninety men but all through the month officers and men were rejoining. Major Sir E. Malet, Captain J. T. Wright, Captain H. H. Firth and Lieutenant Ames came from hospital. There were many new arrivals too, 2nd Lieutenants F. L. Coleman, W. Gimblett, L. F. Carter, M. C. Walker, J. D. Elliott and G. D. T. Taylor. Units took over guard duties at the Citadel, the Hospital and with the Royal Air Force. On January 12th they were visited by Major-General Gott and, on the 19th, being up to strength once more, Regimental training was started.

On February 8th the Regiment was reorganised as an Armoured Car Regiment on orders from General Headquarters, Middle East, and accordingly all training was changed. Sixteen armoured cars were drawn and they quickly adapted themselves to this new form of warfare. Not for long however. By February 17th they handed their cars over to the 6th South African Armoured Cars and turned back into an Armoured Regiment once more. Next day it was decided that 'C' Squadron should have light tanks and 'A' and 'B' heavy, and on the 28th they drew the first of their new equipment, four of the new Grant tanks, mounting a 75-mm. gun, and four Stuarts or Honeys, of which the latter they knew well from Operation 'Crusader'.

At the end of the month, too, Lieut.-Colonel G. Kilkelly rejoined the Regiment from the Transjordan Frontier Force and took over command. It had been a struggle to get back but he had been determined to do it, especially after a visit to them in January. He wrote back to Brigadier-General Vander Byl, the Colonel.

"You will no doubt have heard from different sources how well the Regiment did, and also the knock they took. Nevertheless I have found all those who have come out of the line in tremendous form. They have the means of getting back to full fighting strength and all squadrons and 'A' are intact again. Their keenness and cheerfulness are quite astounding. This applies to all ranks, officers and men. It would make you the proudest man in the world if you could see them. I visited the wounded, they are rather scattered but their one idea is to get back. Blandford (Vernon-Miller) who lost a leg is trying to find out when he can get a new leg, and how long it will take to walk without a limp so that he can be passed 'A' and get back to the Regiment. He is doing very well now but he was very weak through being left in the desert for twenty hours before he could get any real attention. Punch (Dunne) and all young officers are doing well, although John (Simons) will take a long time as both his legs are badly broken, but they will be saved. Everyone I saw was full of praise for the magnificent work of the Regiment. It is difficult to give you much more information as I cannot mention names or details of the battles. Dick (Cripps) was a first-rate commander and Charlie (Duff) and Peter (Sandbach) did tremendous work before they were killed. They all tell me they knocked out more German tanks than their own and are thirsting to get at them again."

At the beginning of March, Sergeant P. Willets, L/Sergeant W. Broadfield and Trooper Dovison were granted the immediate award of the Military Medal. The Regiment was still being brought up to strength and 2nd Lieutenants W. G. Lockhart, J. A. C. Ladenburg, G. V. Bates and D. S. Scott were posted, as were a hundred and forty-five N.C.O.'s and men. By the 21st the Regiment had started field firing and came back under command of the 7th Armoured Division. On the 24th the D.M.T., Major-General Harding and Major-General Messervy visited 'C' Squadron to watch the field firing, and on the 26th the Regiment came under direct command of G.H.Q. Middle East Forces. They were visited by the Governor, His Excellency Sir Miles Lampson on the 28th, and, at the end of the month, possessed a total of twenty Stuart tanks and twenty-four Grants.

(*b*) *Forward Area Again, April 1942*

TRAINING went on during April until the 8th. By now the Regiment had reached their customary state of keenness and efficiency and were ready to play their part in the desert once more. With their new General Grant tanks they felt that they at last had a new fighting vehicle with which they could compete on equal, or nearly equal, terms with the German Mark III's and IV's. Though with the limited traverse of their 75-mm. guns, which suffered the additional disadvantage of being mounted in the hull of the tank, there were some members of the Regiment who had their doubts. The 7th Armoured Division was concentrating near Sidi Azeiz for training, and on April 8th Captain Huth and Lieutenant Robertson left Beni Yusef at first light with the advance party to join the 4th Armoured Brigade. During the next two days the Regimental tanks were loaded on to flats at Giza Station, and on the morning of the 10th they left for the desert. Captain

Fitzherbert, who was acting as A.D.C. to Sir Miles Lampson, came to the Station to see them off and to represent the British Ambassador.

Next day the road party left under Major Sir E. Malet, and on the 12th the first train started unloading soon after midnight at the railhead at Capuzzo. An extract from the War Diary reads: "The second train arrived at the railhead about three hours later and some bombs and flares were dropped during the unloading but no damage was done. In fact they speeded it up and the flares helped to light things up as it was a dark night."

By 5.30 a.m. all was completed and the Regiment was in leaguer some seven or eight miles from the railhead. Later in the morning 'sun-shields' were put on the Grant tanks and the Regiment moved to Gabr el Meduar for lunch, by which time a very unpleasant sandstorm had blown up.

Later in the day they moved to Got el Maraa which had been vacated by the Headquarters of the 7th Armoured Division an hour earlier. It was a very pleasant place and carpeted with grass and flowers.

On April 13th Captain Baldwin, the Adjutant, and Lieutenant Hedley, Q.M.S., arrived in advance of the road party and by 5.30 that evening the Regiment was complete. Orders were received next day to join Brigade on the 15th, and this was done after a scheme carried out in conjunction with the 1st Battalion Kings Royal Rifle Corps during which 'C' Squadron played the most active part as the Grant tanks all had their sun-shields fitted. On arrival in their new leaguer area the Regiment was greeted by Captain Hooper from Brigade who brought with him the new Codes which were to play an important though trying part in the subsequent training.

For the rest of April the Regiment carried out intensive Brigade schemes and battle practice. The heat throughout was intense and most unpleasant, especially for the tank crews, and to add to the general complication of life, in all training the somewhat impracticable new coding systems had to be used in every wireless communication which resulted more often than not in much misunderstanding and consequent loss of temper! At midday on the 25th orders were received from Brigade to move as soon as possible and by 1 p.m. the Regiment was advancing westwards. They leaguered that night some thirty miles on, in a salt pan at Giof el Baar in which place they were to remain for just over a month, carrying on with Brigade training and a certain amount of cricket and football, and enduring the miseries of the Khamseen which blew fiercely from the south.

After May 11th, with Brigade training finished, the Regiment was told that they were likely to be in for a period of waiting, during which they should carry on with Squadron and Regimental training and also take advantage of all opportunities for bathing and recreation. Accordingly parties went daily to Jerboa Bay to bathe, some went on leave to Cairo and others to the Eighth Army Rest Camp.

On May 15th Lieutenant Ladenburg went on a four days recce with the King's Dragoon Guards and the South African Armoured Cars, and on the 18th the Colonel of the Free French Brigade at Bir Hacheim came to lunch. This was the beginning of two days almost intolerable Khamseen. The combination of intense dry heat and thirst were a great trial to everyone. On top of this came the news of a possible attack by the Germans from the north during the full moon, and Brigade accordingly moved to a position further north. As the Regiment had been on the north flank of Brigade they stayed where they were, and the 3rd and 5th Royal Tanks with Brigade Headquarters moved north so that the Regiment was now in a position to the south of Brigade Headquarters.

For the next five days the Regiment stood to for half an hour at dawn and dusk in

An 'A' Squadron 'O' Group before the ill-fated leaguer, November, 1941 (page 61). *From left to right:* Major Sandbach, Lieut. Pringle, 2nd Lieut. H. C. Carver, Rev. F. Hone, Lieut. J. Weston Simons, Major C. R. Duff, Capt. Dunne, Sgt.-Major Jordan.

Portee 2-pounder anti-tank guns firing in the desert.

Recovering a broken-down Crusader with a tank transporter, June, 1942. When the big ones start to drop close, the recovery crew flatten themselves on the ground.

Halfaya Pass, June, 1942.

A typical water point in the desert, where lorries and camels alike load up with supplies.

Another feature of watering in the desert. At this particular hole, a Roman cistern, water was hauled up in tins by means of a windlass.

'A' Squadron in pursuit across Cyrenaica after the Battle of Alamein, December, 1942. Major Harbord commanding, and Capt. Harari, second-in-command, whose Honey tank was blown up on a mine. A day or two later Major Harbord was killed (page 124).

Lieut.-General I. P. Hughes, G.O.C.-in-C. Cyprus, inspecting 8th Hussars and their armoured cars, February, 1943 (page 132).

case of a German attack. Otherwise life went on very much the same with bathing and leave parties, Regimental training and a recce, carried out by the Commanding Officer and Squadron Leaders with the Brigade Commander round el Adem.

Events elsewhere in these first four months of the new year had been advancing with lightning speed, and all in the wrong direction. The Japanese had swept through Malaya towards Singapore, which, defenceless from the land, had surrendered in February together with 100,000 troops. The German battleships Scharnhorst and Gneisnau with the cruiser Prinz Eugen slipped from their hideout in Brest, ran the gauntlet of the Channel and went to ground in their home ports. The Tirpitz had earlier taken refuge in Trondheim Fiord. The U-boats in the Atlantic were becoming more and more daring and sinking an enormous amount of shipping, seventy-one merchantmen being lost in February alone. They lurked in the Caribbean and the Gulf of Mexico and ranged from the Cape of Good Hope to the Indian Ocean and Brazil.

March provided a small gleam in all this darkness, although a bloodstained one, in the shape of the successful Commando raid on St. Nazaire. That was the only bright spot however. In the same month the Dutch East Indies surrendered, Burma was overrun by the Japanese who, in April, from their enormous fleet, attacked Ceylon. By May, Burma was lost and the Congress elements in India under Gandhi were demanding that the British should leave, as without them there they imagined the Japanese would never invade.

In the Pacific the Americans were fighting doggedly, and by degrees successfully, round the romantically-named islands in the Coral Sea. In May an expedition landed on Madagascar to secure it for the Allies before, in the event of Ceylon being captured, the Japanese could grab it. It was a long campaign and not successfully won until November when the Vichy-French Governor-General surrendered. All this time both American and Russia were imploring Britain to send more convoys through the Arctic Seas to Russia. Apart from the fact that all material was desperately wanted by the British forces, they sent what they could ill spare, losing many ships, not only merchantmen but naval ships as well, sunk by torpedo, shadowed by aircraft based in Norway and threatened by the Tirpitz, Scheer and Hipper. There seemed to be nothing but disaster facing, whichever way one turned, even in the desert where Rommel, so safely pinned down behind his minefields at el Agheila, had swept out and east to pin us down behind ours.

(c) The Battle of Bir Hacheim, May 1942

(1) THE REGIMENT

AT the end of May Rommel and the Afrika Korps were held up on a line from Gazala on the coast to Bir Hacheim, forty miles south in the desert. Between these two positions stretched a belt of minefields and behind them were a series of 'boxes', surrounded by wire and mines, constituting self-contained and impregnable fortresses. Rommel's main objective was Tobruk, and to get there he had either to break through the minefields and destroy the 'boxes' or else skirt round the southern end of the line by Bir Hacheim and then push north. It was this latter plan that he chose to follow. Opposing him on this corner was the 7th Armoured Division and the 4th Armoured Brigade in particular.

The 7th Armoured Division at this time had under command the 4th Armoured, the 7th Motor, the 1st Free French, the 29th Indian Infantry and the 3rd Indian Motor Brigades. The 4th Armoured Brigade, commanded by Brigadier G. W. Richards, consisted of the 1st Regiment Royal Horse Artillery, the 8th Hussars, the 3rd and 5th Royal Tanks and the 1st Battalion Kings Royal Rifle Corps.

The Brigade was situated in a position about fifteen miles east of Bir Hacheim and seven miles north of Retma with part of the 7th Motor Brigade, under Brigadier Renton, operating as 'Jock' Columns near Segnali and Tengeder, a hundred or so miles to the west. The remainder of the Brigade were preparing the position at Retma.

On the afternoon of May 26th Rommel began to move eastwards, pushing out strong advance guards of tanks which were harassed by the 7th Motor Brigade who withdrew before him towards Retma. During the night he was watched and reported on by patrols of the 4th South African Armoured Cars.

Meanwhile the Regiment in their positions east of Bir Hacheim had as yet received no indication that anything out of the ordinary was going to happen in the near future. Bathing and leave parties continued and tanks went off in twos to be overhauled. Two Squadron Leaders were away from the Regiment at this time, Major Harbord of 'A' Squadron who was instructing the 4th Hussars at Cowley Camp, Mena, in the use of Grant and Honey tanks and whose place was taken by Captain Nelson, and Major Sir E. Malet who had handed over Headquarters Squadron to Lieutenant Robertson. Squadrons had fitted up miniature ranges, and training in sighting and ranging was carried out with Tommy-guns mounted on the 75-mm. barrels. The Regiment was comfortably dug in and, as 2nd Lieutenant G. D. T. Taylor of 'B' Squadron wrote: "Its camouflage from the air might not have been perfect, but it was well concealed from generals driving past on the Divisional Axis, so except from numerous recce's of prepared battle positions in all directions, life was fairly peaceful."

Squadron sports were being organised too, always a mixed blessing, but there were obstacle races in plenty ahead without the need for arranging a course.

The evening of the 26th May brought with it the first appearance, a long way to the west, of German Very lights, seen so often the previous winter, and it looked as though the report by British Intelligence of a possible attack was going to come true.

At 3.30 a.m. on the 27th May the 4th Armoured Brigade rang up to say that there was forward enemy movement and that the Regiment must be ready to move within fifteen minutes of first light. All Squadrons were informed by 4.30, but with the dawn there was no further information. There was time to risk a quick 'brew up', and at 6.30 one troop at a time went to the Cookhouse. By 7 a.m. Brigade came through again to say that a large enemy column had overrun the 3rd Indian Motor Brigade about eight miles to the south-west and that they might be moving towards the 8th Hussar position in the Giof el Baar. Lieut.-Colonel Kilkelly therefore ordered a patrol of light tanks from 'C' Squadron to recce to the south. They met the 'B' Echelon of the Indian Brigade, who had no news of anything untoward. At this juncture the Regiment were still expecting to take up their northern battle positions, and imagined that any movement to the south must be in the nature of a demonstration or a feint, as the attack was expected through the minefields north of Gazala.

At about 7.20 however Brigade sent through the code word 'Majority' which meant 'Move to southern battle position,' followed by an order to move to the Start Point which was immediately east of the leaguer area. It was while the Regiment was moving to this position that 'C' Squadron reported enemy tanks about 4,000 yards to the south, advancing north-east. These were on a ridge on the Regiment's left flank and consisted of a large column of Mk. III and IV tanks, closely supported by anti-tank guns.

The Regiment formed line and prepared for action, and 'C' Squadron was the first to engage. Major Hackett, in command, had his tank knocked out in the first few minutes and was himself badly burned. However he mounted another tank and continued to command his squadron.

Meanwhile 'A' and 'B' Squadrons had formed up on the left and right of 'C' and were immediately involved in the battle. The first shot fired by Nelson in command of 'A' scored a direct hit on an 88-mm. anti-tank gun, but being on the southern flank of the Regiment, his squadron bore the brunt of the enemy attack and came under a merciless hail of fire from 88-mms. and Mk. III and IV tanks. Captain Huth wrote:

"We all opened up at once as the whole column appeared to do a right wheel and advanced directly on to us.

"Fighting lasted about fifteen minutes by which time all our tanks except two had been hit and put out of action. We had hit many enemy tanks but at the time I could not estimate enemy losses, although I saw three or four go up in flames.

"My own tank had been penetrated by an 88-mm. after I had fired only two shots with the 75-mm., and the driver, Lance-Corporal Dixon, and the 75-mm. gunner, Trooper Prescott, were killed immediately. The 37-mm. also having been hit, we baled out and two more of the crew were killed. I then managed to get on to the back of 2nd Lieutenant Coleman's tank. By this time the Squadron was retiring, firing at the same time, being completely outnumbered.

"By the end of fifteen minutes Captain Nelson had been wounded and of the three Troop Leaders, David Elliott had been killed, Nigel Gibbes wounded and died within an hour and Francis Coleman also wounded. There were about twelve wounded and twelve killed among the other ranks of the Squadron."

Finally the only two tanks left from 'A' Squadron were No. 1 Troop Sergeant, Sergeant Morris, in 'Arctic Star', who evacuated Lieutenant Gibbes, and Lieutenant Ames, the navigator's light tank. He backed up the wadi, firing and picking up some of the baled-out crews on the way. They were dumped at the top and he then, with Lieutenant Hall, engaged a Mk. III tank which was offering a good broadside target. Later Hall was forced to abandon his tank with a broken track and Ames picked him up with 2nd Lieutenant Taylor and some eight or ten men and took them out of the battle.

'B' Squadron, although not so heavily engaged, was having its own difficulties. 2nd Lieutenant Taylor who previously was running the Squadron sports, takes up the tale.

"At 7.10 'C' Squadron reported two enemy Mk. III's approaching their leaguer. At 7.15 'B' Squadron crossed the Sports ground or mud flats and formed line to engage about fifty enemy tanks. Breakfasts had been thrown away and the Tommy-gun strapped on to the Squadron Leader's tank for the Miniature Range was hurriedly pulled off. 7.15 to 7.45 was a period not to be forgotten. Grant tanks lost their tracks and bogey wheels. German tanks were left blazing but they were being reinforced by the 8th Tank Regiment or the Death's Head Hussars, at least a hundred and fifty tanks strong. 'A' Squadron who were lined across the Giof el Baar facing south had been severely dealt with by German 88-mm. and other anti-tank guns, but no anti-tank guns had yet engaged 'B' Squadron, who were on their right rear, facing south-west. However most tanks in 'B' had by this time either their guns jammed, tracks off or were short of ammunition, so when the order came to withdraw east up the hill only one tank commanded by Sergeant Morgan was able to get out. The remainder fought it out until forced to evacuate their tanks, and about twenty-four crews, led by Major Threlfall and Captain Gwyn did various items of the Squadron Sports across the mud flats and up the hill, including the obstacle race with H.E. from Mk. IV tanks in place of camouflage nets. For some reason the Germans did not machine-gun these crews and all by various routes got back to safety. Major Threlfall and Captain Gwyn were picked up by the Regimental Liaison officer after a three mile point over fair country, and were able to put the Brigade Commander more or less in the picture. Lieutenant Hall, Lieutenant Taylor and other crews were picked up by Captain Ames in the 'A' Squadron Honey. Nine tanks went into action that morning, two being under overhaul, and eight were left on the battlefield. These were probably too badly damaged to be recovered by the Germans and most of them were collected or destroyed by our own recovery sections a few days later."

By now 'A' and 'B' Squadrons, heavily out-numbered, had fought themselves to a standstill. 'C' Squadron continued to fight on, and taking up a flank position knocked out at least ten German Mk. III's and IV's, bringing the total of enemy losses to thirty tanks knocked out or destroyed. A number of German Mk. III's infiltrated and found their way round the flanks, so that Regimental Headquarters were engaged. They had by now withdrawn to the high ground to the east, hoping to rally the Regiment here, but it was impossible as 'A' and 'B' had but three Grant tanks left between them, although 'C' Squadron turned up later.

Lieut.-Colonel Kilkelly succeeded in knocking out a Mk. IV which went up in flames at a distance of thirty yards, but the squadron lost all its tanks. The armour of the Grants withstood the anti-tank fire of the German tanks but was pierced by the ground weapons, 88-mms. and 20/28-mms., and many were immobilised by damaged tracks. Major Phillips, the second-in-command, and 2nd Lieutenant D. Gimblett, Signals Officer were taken prisoner, and, although some crews found their way back on foot, a party with the Adjutant, Captain Baldwin, were machine-gunned and killed.

It was a gallant fight. The Regiment had destroyed thirty out of the hundred or more German tanks and had gone on fighting until they were overwhelmed. Owing to the rapidity of the advance and the fact that no adequate warning was received by the Regiment (although the advance of this column had been accurately reported throughout the night by the Divisional Armoured Car Regiments to Divisional Headquarters. For some reason, never explained even to this day, these reports were never taken seriously), the enemy had been able to make a surprise attack and to engage and destroy the Regiment before any support or artillery could be brought up.

Some of those taken prisoner managed to escape, as will be recorded later, like most of the 'B' Echelon and the thinskins. But the Regiment had suffered many casualties, chiefly from 'A' Squadron who lost all their officers. However, heavy though their losses were they were not alone in this respect. Divisional Headquarters too, was overrun, and the whole of the 4th Armoured Brigade fought desperately all day.

(2) 'B' ECHELON

Meanwhile 'B' Echelon commanded by Captain Earle was also having difficulties. At 7.15 on that same morning of May 27th, armoured cars reported that two columns of the enemy were some three miles away, one passing north and one east. At 8 a.m. the Echelon moved east, with many stops and starts owing to other transport. However at

9 a.m. they were approached by a small car with an English-speaking officer of unknown identity inside it. He told Earle to halt and proceed south-east, which he refused to do, but on discovering that the officer was a German he halted the Echelon. Captain Earle wrote later:

"I was then told to dismount and, together with the Quarter-Master, Lieutenant Hedley, was made to put my hands up. By this time armoured cars and an anti-tank trailer-drawn gun were round the front of us. We managed to get rid of all codes by burning and burying them, and also to send through by wireless to Brigade 'B' Echelon Headquarters our position, circumstances and the strength of the enemy.

"Meantime Lieutenants Walker, Lockhart and Captain Alcock R.A.O.C., came up to the head of the column to see what was the matter, not realising the position, and were made to put up their hands. Walker and Lockhart managed to wander off as the opportunity occurred, jumped on to a 15 cwt. and headed north. They were headed off by German armoured cars and forced south, but by making their way through gaps eventually got away south-east, although they covered some ten miles before getting clear. Two days later they made their way back to 'B' Echelon west of el Adem, collecting two stray 'B' Squadron vehicles on the way.

"Scott in the meantime quickly summed up the position and moved off south-east with all his vehicles. He managed to get clean away and via Bir Berraneb and Capuzzo returned to the Echelon four days later east of el Adem. His action and judgement were creditable.

"Ladenburg's action is best described in his own account to me, and will follow.

"The enemy meanwhile had taken over all the vehicles nearby and made the drivers, etc. prisoners. They put their own men on the lorries and drove them off south-east to join their main column, which was now appearing. Hedley, Alcock and all the prisoners were also dispatched.

"While all this was going on a 15 cwt. driven by an Indian pulled up. In it was a wounded British officer and an Indian officer. I got permission to attend to the British officer and in so doing missed being included in the party containing the prisoners and captured vehicles, which had been sent to join the German columns. When we did finally join them we found that all the other prisoners had been sent back. Our party was therefore forced to accompany the columns. I myself was placed in a staff car with two German officers. I estimated that the German column consisted of some 2,000 vehicles, all told. We went east as far as Bir el Gubi and then turned north and proceeded to the first escarpment between Sidi Rezegh and el Adem. Opposition was negligible and our speed of progress unbelievably swift. The head of the column consisted of a mass of guns of all sorts, together with lorried infantry.

"The escarpment was reached at about 4 p.m. Below us lay several hundred British vehicles completely unaware of our existence. Fortunately the Germans opened fire from the top and gave enough warning for a very large number to get away. Had they gone quietly down I'm sure they could have captured practically the lot. At the bottom of the escarpment we came across a badly wounded British officer. I was given permission to attend to him and in so doing got away from my escort who went on ahead.

"At about 6 p.m. I came on some more prisoners and joined up with them, and half an hour later we were shelled by 25-pounders for ten minutes or so. At 7.30 p.m. the shelling started in earnest and the Germans withdrew their softer stuff up the escarpment again. The shelling became very heavy and a lot of men and a few officer prisoners made off with the enemy. About twelve officers and a hundred men remained, and for two hours we lay low while the battle raged. Fortunately we had few casualties. British tanks joined in at about 10.15 p.m. and added to our misery by firing at us with their 37-mm. and machine-guns.

"The Germans made three attempts to make us fall back to their lines, but they had the wind up pretty well and disliked standing up and arguing with us. Eventually they all withdrew up the escarpment as darkness fell, leaving us behind. When it was quite dark we set off north-west towards Tobruk, but after a couple of miles ran into the 4th Armoured Brigade, moving east. The following morning I rejoined the unit and then Brigade 'B' Echelon, when during the next few days more than fifty per cent. of our vehicles were collected together.

"Until the Regiment was withdrawn no further untoward events took place other than the usual fortunes of war such as bombing, machine-gunning and so on. Supplies became disorganised and on one day we spent thirteen hours obtaining rations from the R.A.S.C. The average time spent in getting up to the Regiment from leaguer was five hours."

Lieutenant Ladenburg, who had been at the other end of 'B' Echelon column that morning, saw the Germans capture Earle and Hedley. He wrote:

"As it seemed impossible to open fire on the Germans for fear of killing you and Charlie, I ran over to Sergeant Garrod and told him to lead his line of vehicles after me, as we were going to try and make a break for it. On returning to my own vehicle which was less than a hundred yards away and was alongside the S.Q.M.S.'s 3-tonner, I noticed Garrod already being taken prisoner so I shouted to Newman to get moving and follow me. I shouted the same thing to several vehicles on my way through the halted column but as I had no driver I could not see whether they had got their lorries moving or not.

"Having drawn off about a mile I stopped and found there were only three vehicles following me. As there didn't seem to be much activity in the halted column and I could still see the main crowd gathered round you and Charlie I returned to the scene, picked up a few men who had already had their lorries taken away from them and, with the encouraging aid of their shouts this time I was able to draw out of the column almost the complete L.A.D. and a few other vehicles. When I reached the other three who were still waiting for me (or perhaps they had already moved off on their own, I really cannot remember now) we were about twenty-five vehicles in all.

"As Sergeant-Major Patman had much the fastest car I told him to get ahead in a north-easterly direction to act as scout, and the rest of us followed on. After going about a mile Patman stopped and we followed suit. I found we were being fired on by small arms. The majority of the men went to ground and just then a Royal Artillery officer came up with us. We decided between us the best direction to move on, having regard to the fact that about a regiment of enemy tanks was approaching from the south, about two miles away, and that the small arms fire had apparently come from two or three armoured cars to our north-west—I don't know whether these were enemy or our own.

"As the Artillery officer and myself started to move I shouted to Patman to follow on. After going less than a mile I told the man on my left to make sure the other vehicles were following me. To my amazement he said they were far behind and going far more south than us, in other words they were heading straight for the enemy tanks.

"It only remains to say that we got through and they did not and I have no reason to offer why Patman failed to follow us. By then it was too late to try and chase after him again."

The thinskins, under command of Lieutenant Robertson and S.S.M. Spooner, succeeded in getting away intact from the morning's hold-up, which was, in the circumstances, a creditable performance. They withdrew north-east and joined Brigade 'B' Echelon at Bir el Chelb, and then went east with them to Abiar el Mgaier where they were joined by what was left of Regimental Headquarters and various personnel from the Sabre Squadrons.

Captain Wagstaffe took over the Adjutancy on this day.

(3) ESCAPE STORIES OF SOME WHO WERE TAKEN PRISONER

However, May 27th was not yet quite played out. When Captain Ames and Sergeant Morris, the sole survivors of 'A' Squadron had withdrawn, the remainder of the crews were taken prisoner with the exception of fifteen men gathered together by Huth.

"We then," he wrote, "got the wounded into a wadi and did what we could for them. More German vehicles passed through our area and relieved us of our arms except for some Tommy-guns which we managed to hide.

"The enemy, although they treated us very well, and in fact gave me some bandages, seemed so intent on pushing on to el Adem and so certain that we could not escape that they did not bother much about us.

"Having collected what food and water and arms that we could, and got the wounded together, and having then burnt four of the tanks to prevent them falling into enemy hands, I ordered the remainder of the unwounded men to scatter out and hide until dusk.

"At dusk we collected together and walked back to el Gubi, that is myself and ten men. Of the other five two had been captured that afternoon whilst three were left behind to look after the wounded. After walking all night and passing through two enemy leaguers we covered about sixteen miles and were picked up at dawn on the 28th by some South African Armoured Cars."

There is still one story belonging to this memorable day, that of the capture and escape of Major Phillips.

"As far as I know," he wrote, "mine was the only tank moving in Regimental Headquarters, both the Colonel's and the Intelligence Officer's tanks having been knocked out. Even my tank was not moving well and we could only crawl along with the stuff pattering on the outside. When there were sounds as if a blacksmith with a very large hammer was hitting the outside we wondered how long we could keep it out. Eventually one of the tracks was knocked off and my driver wounded so we had to dismount. We lay on the ground hoping the Germans would pass us by, but unfortunately whoever knocked us out had been watching because within a few minutes a lorry drove up and we were taken prisoner.

"My wounded driver, after I had shouted to the Germans that he couldn't stand up, put up his hands. He was well treated and actually freed when a short time afterwards a German field station was captured by us.

"I spent the rest of that day with a German field gun team on the back of a British lorry which was used for towing the gun. Incidentally the gun was of Russian make and about 75-mm. calibre. It went into action several times that day. It was part of a column moving east and the column was engaged on numerous occasions by 25-pounders. Very interesting it is seeing it from the other end.

"I made one or two tentative efforts to escape whenever the gun team dismounted to go into action but I was too well watched for any to be successful. I had hoped that the team would pack up after firing and forget that I was lying on the ground.

"That night was a disappointment to me as the German sentries round the leaguer were very wide awake. They appeared to call out to each other every quarter of an hour something like 'It is a fine night. All's well. Are you awake Number Two?' Number Two would answer 'Yes,' and pass the call on to Number Three and so on round the leaguer. I should add that it was a period of full moon and to anyone who knows the Western Desert that means it was as light as day.

"The next day an attempt at a short interrogation took place. I was searched but not very thoroughly. I let them find my diary and a private letter in the breast pocket of my overalls and then I started producing toilet paper out of all my other pockets, rather like a conjurer, with the result that their I.O. said, 'O.K.', or words to that effect. He little realised that I still had my wallet and some paper on which I had been making notes about his formation.

"Another officer (R.A.S.C.) and myself were separated from the remainder of the prisoners and put in a lorry under the guard of a sentry with a Tommy-gun. This lorry was one of a supply column moving west. The column had hardly started when it was attacked by R.A.F. Hurri-bombers who bombed and machine-gunned, scoring several direct hits. I managed to persuade our driver to edge out to a flank and drive on the outside of the column as opposed to the middle of it, pointing out that the bombs would be much more likely to fall in the centre than on the flanks of the column and that I had a marked objection to being hit by my own planes. However there was more in it than fear of our bombers as we had decided there was a very good chance of driving off with the lorry as our guard seemed fairly confident of us. Sure enough we didn't have long to wait. At a halt the sentry wandered off to talk to a friend, leaving his tommy-gun on the seat. Almost too good to be true the driver left his seat and went about 30 yards away to get a light. We both said, 'Now!' The R.A.S.C. officer jumped into the driver's seat and tried to start the engine. There was an agonising moment when the self-starter purred but the engine did not start. A second time he pressed. This time success and the engine roared into life. Meanwhile I had been standing beside the lorry in a suggestive attitude, watching. As soon as I heard the engine firing I leapt aboard only to be greeted by the words, 'I can't get into gear!' In his excitement he had over-revved the engine. Naturally there was a cry from our guard and driver who came rushing back. We had to pretend it was a joke, very much on us. I could have wept as we had a very good chance of escaping, being right on the flank of the column, and with any luck could have been well away before anything happened.

"The guard and driver didn't appear to do much about it, hoping I think that no one had seen the incident which would have got them into hot water for leaving us alone. However another man with a large pistol came and sat in the back of the lorry with us for the rest of the day. That night we were on the move most of the time and too well guarded to try anything.

"The next day we left our lorry and were herded with a lot of other prisoners on to another vehicle. I felt rather depressed as our chances didn't look too good and we were getting further west along the German line of communication. Very much further would have meant that walking was out of the question, especially as I had only just left hospital after a bout of fever and didn't feel too strong.

"However we halted and stayed in the same place all day and had the doubtful pleasure of again being smartened up by the Hurri-bombers. They were very good and luckily did not come too close to our lorry.

"That evening the Italians appeared with a large column of prisoners and we were handed over to them. I was quite sorry to leave the Germans. They had treated me well, sharing their rations with me and giving me blankets at night. One knew with the Italians one would get little, as generally they hadn't enough themselves. However they produced a barrel of water and we, the officers, about twenty of us I suppose, had to arrange the distribution.

"While we were doing this the shelling started and an attack was launched against our captors. This caused great excitement especially as the Germans started retiring. No lorries were available and we were herded all together and ordered to march south along the edge of a minefield. You may be sure we marched slowly much to the annoyance of the Italians. An Italian armoured car which was escorting us fired a few bursts over our heads to try and speed things up. An N.C.O. next to me was hit. We all stopped and made a great fuss, telling the Italians exactly what we though of them.

"In the confusion and the half-light I spotted a gap in the wire, nipped through and walked on with the column of prisoners on my left. The only trouble was that some well-meaning people shouted: 'Oi! Come back, you're in a minefield! It's dangerous!' I informed them in a loud whisper that I was prepared to risk the mines. Actually it was an English minefield sown with anti-tank mines so I was fairly confident it would require more than my weight to detonate them. After walking a short way I came to some bushes and lay down and let the rest of the party go by. I felt horribly conspicuous as I was only about 15 yards from the wire and the bushes were only about 18 inches high.

"I covered myself with a blanket and hoped for the best. The attack petered out about this time and there was continuous traffic up and down the wire. It was bright moonlight now so I still could not move. I ate biscuits and dried apricots, which I had found in our mess lorry which had also been captured, to pass the time.

"About 1 or 2 a.m. the traffic ceased and I decided to start. Through the wire again I went and started moving east. I had to crawl on my hands and knees between six groups of German vehicles. They were not very close but the moon was brilliant.

"Eventually, I considered it safe to walk normally which I did until dawn. There is little cover in the desert and I knew I had not gone nearly far enough as I could hear German voices ordering vehicles to start up. Luckily I found a deep slit trench and decided to lie up there during the day and push on again the next night. I pulled my blanket over me and placed a steel helmet, which I had picked up, over my head, hoping that if anyone came along they would take me for a corpse. I think it worked, for shortly after I had made myself comfortable I heard a car drive up and then go away again. You can imagine my feelings.

"I had been lucky. I had my pockets full of dried apricots but I had found two full water-bottles and a book by Conan Doyle in a burnt-out vehicle. With the aid of these I managed to pass several hours of the morning, but as the sun got higher it became unbearably hot and I had to discard my blanket and my disguise of being a corpse.

"During the first part of the morning it sounded as if a battle was going on quite close to me but by about 2 p.m. the sounds died down. I peered out and saw several men moving east. They looked English so I hailed them and found they were, like myself, escaped prisoners and that they had not seen anyone for some time. They had escaped the previous evening when the lorry they were travelling in blew up in trying to move west through a minefield.

"We all moved east together until it got too hot and we decided to rest in the shade of a broken-down lorry until the cool of the evening. In the evening we pushed on again and saw some vehicles coming towards us. Thank goodness they turned out to be a South African armoured car patrol. I asked to be taken to the nearest Headquarters as I had some very useful information about the enemy and his morale. By coincidence the first Headquarters we came to was my own Armoured Brigade where I spent the night, and the following day rejoined the Regiment."

(d) 'C' Squadron with the 3rd Royal Tanks, May 1942

THERE had been savage fighting along the whole front of the 7th Armoured Division on May 27th. Not only did the 8th Hussars lose relatively all their tanks but so did the 3rd Royal Tanks. The 3rd Indian Motor Brigade east of Bir Hacheim had been overrun and the Germans pushed on from there to oust the Riflemen from the Box at Retma. The whole Division was fighting from Bir Hacheim to el Gubi and in the midst of the confusion Divisional Headquarters was overrun. They managed to bring out a few vehicles but until they got sorted out, 30 Corps Headquarters took over.

As night fell on May 27th the 29th Indian Brigade and the survivors of the 7th Motor Brigade arrived at el Gubi. The 4th Armoured Brigade was a few miles south-east of el Adem and had, at a price, kept the 90th Light Division from its goal. The 3rd Indian Motor Brigade had relatively ceased to exist but the Free French still hung on in their box at Bir Hacheim.

May 28th saw none of the savage fighting of the previous day. Both sides had to patch themselves up if they were to continue at all, although Rommel had intended pushing straight on.

Lieut.-Colonel Kilkelly and Major Threlfall left in the morning for Capuzzo with a party to draw a fresh supply of tanks. They were able to find enough to bring 'C' Squadron up to strength, who were reinforced so as to make a complete squadron ready for operation under command of the 3rd Royal Tanks on the next day.

Huth, who after his escape had been taken by the South African Armoured Cars to the 3rd Indian Motor Brigade, had left his men there and had been loaned two 15 cwt. trucks with Indian drivers and an Indian Medical Orderly. He wrote:

"We drove off back to the wadi where I had left the wounded. There was a German encampment about a mile away, but I reckoned to get the wounded on to my vehicles and away before the Germans noticed me.

"As I drove up to the head of the wadi I found a German with a Tommy-gun guarding the wounded, but he put his hands up immediately. I was then about to descend into the wadi and take away the wounded when Captain Nelson shouted to me to go at once.

"I then noticed a German tank about a hundred yards away, and the crew preparing to mount. Realising I had got myself into an awkward corner I mounted at once and drove off at top speed. Trooper Paul who was only slightly wounded had managed to scramble on to one of the cars, but I had no time to collect the rest. The tank fired about half a dozen rounds at me at very close range before I got over the hill, but by jinking I avoided being hit.

"About three days later I went back to the scene of our engagement with the padre, the enemy having been driven off, in order to bury our dead.

"Of our nine tanks which had been knocked out, four had been burnt by us, two blown up by the Huns and the other three we saw being recovered by our own Recovery Sections.

"We went over to where the German leaguer had been established after our action of the morning of May 27th and counted twenty-seven German tanks abandoned. There was also one German 88-mm. burnt out with two dead beside it, but apart from these two dead we saw no others. The Germans had apparently established a Tank Recovery and repair park here and had been forced to leave the area at short notice as kit lay all over the place.

"About June 5th whilst at the Tank Delivery Regiment near el Adem I was questioned by General Ritchie and told him what I had seen. He informed me that no less than thirty-six German tanks had been blown up by our R.E.s in the area of Giof el Baar. How many the Regiment had accounted for and how many had been brought in from other actions I cannot say for certain, but I think the majority had been almost certainly accounted for by the Regiment."

During the day of the 28th the 29th Indian Brigade came up to el Adem, where in the evening the 4th Armoured Brigade attacked their opponents of the day before, the 90th Light Division, and they succeeded in driving back a force who were trying to reach the escarpment south of Sidi Rezegh airfield.

Rommel was by now behind the minefields although unable to get north to Tobruk and Acroma. He was finding it increasingly difficult to bring up supplies and was trying to drive a gap back through the minefield to establish a line of communication. Most of the fighting on the 29th took place round the Knightsbridge box which was held by the Guards Brigade.

'C' Squadron, 8th Hussars, now came under command of the 3rd Royal Tanks. Major Hackett had to be evacuated as a result of the burns he had received in the battle on the 27th and the squadron was taken over by Captain Firth, 2nd Lieutenant A. F. McClintock being second-in-command. The troop leaders were 2nd Lieutenant L. F. Carter, 2nd Lieutenant Thurston of the 7th Hussars, 2nd Lieutenant Twiss of the Royal Tank Regiment and Sergeants Atkins and Knill.

'C' Squadron, who was with the 3rd Royal Tanks on the right of Brigade, moved from a position about three miles north-west of el Adem to intercept an enemy column which had been reported moving north-east near Bir el Harmat. However, thanks to a sandstorm, visibility was about ten yards and although battle positions were taken up it was impossible to see anything.

In the evening yet another attempt was made to get in touch with an enemy column to the south-east, but this time darkness fell before the squadron could make contact.

At dawn on May 30th the 3rd Royal Tanks were ordered to advance to a position about ten miles south-east of their leaguer area, while 'C' Squadron was ordered to reconnoitre towards Harmat as it was suspected that the enemy had established himself there.

Sure enough the Panzers were encountered about two miles east of Harmat and reports came in from the forward patrols of nine Mk. IV tanks and some anti-tank guns.

'C' Squadron lost no time in coming to grips with this force. 2nd Lieutenant Thurston, whose troop was protecting General Headquarters, had his tank knocked out and was himself severely wounded in the head. 2nd Lieutenant Carter, whose troop had been one of the forward patrols, succeeded in rescuing him and towing his tank out of the action, a very courageous act carried out under heavy fire.

Then the 5th Royal Tanks came up and preparations were made to engage this enemy force. 'C' Squadron was again sent out on a recce to the south. After covering about three miles the enemy was found in strength, and two troops under 2nd Lieutenant Twiss and Sergeant Atkins were sent off to investigate some enemy vehicles to the south of Harmat. They returned with three German prisoners having shot up seven enemy lorries.

That night a leaguer was formed four miles east of Harmat with patrols out to the west.

On May 31st 'C' Squadron with the 3rd Royal Tanks advanced to a point on the Trigh Bir Hacheim north of Bir el Harmat, and patrols were sent out to the north-east.

The day was principally taken up with an artillery duel, and the enemy appeared to withdraw under the terrific barrage. That night 'C' Squadron withdrew a mile east to leaguer, 2nd Lieutenant Carter's troop being sent out as a night patrol to Bir el Harmat. During the night, as always happened so near the front line, the leaguer was straffed by enemy aircraft.

The tank situation was causing grave concern. The 8th Hussars and 3rd Royal Tanks could between them only muster nine Grants and twenty-four light tanks. The 5th Royal Tanks were not much better off and Brigade Headquarters had three of each. Although the 4th Royal Tanks, who had been attached to Brigade, had thirty-six, they were 'I' tanks and very much slower than Grants or light.

By now almost the only serious opposition to Rommel on this southern sector of the line was from 150th Brigade Box, which stood directly in the middle of the lane he had cut back through the minefields, and the Free French who were still holding out at Bir Hacheim. The fighting round 150th Brigade Box was intense, added to which the Royal Air Force were continually bombing the area, which came to be known as 'The Cauldron'. However by midday on June 1st, when the defenders of the Box were running short of ammunition, they were overpowered and Rommel now had a clear run through the minefields. Severe fighting in this area still continued however, and the Free French clung on for a few more days.

On June 1st at dawn 'C' Squadron, still with the 3rd Royal Tanks, returned to their position of the day before, and enemy tanks to the north-west were kept under observation. At about 11 a.m. they were relieved by the 4th Royal Tanks and moved back into reserve on the Trigh el Abd. Their new position however came under shell fire, so they withdrew a mile to the east, where they were joined by 2nd Lieutenant Bates with a troop of Honeys.

That afternoon a battle position was taken up at Nadaret el Ghesceuasc to meet a threatened enemy attack from Harmat but nothing came of it and a comparatively quiet night was spent in the same area.

The next day, June 2nd, the German 90th Light Division was sent down to concentrate on the Free French at Bir Hacheim. The 21st Panzer Division to the north was trying to cut off the 1st South African and the 50th Divisions who were still holding their original positions on the line from Gazala to Alam Hamza.

At dawn on June 2nd the 4th Armoured Brigade heard that an enemy attack was coming in on Knightsbridge from Harmat and the west-north-west. Brigade was ordered to Point 187 and the 3rd Royal Tanks advanced with 'C' Squadron, 8th Hussars, doing left flank guard.

As they arrived at their destination, enemy tanks and anti-tank guns were reported at Eluet el Tamar to the east, and orders were received to advance two miles north of this position. However as they did so the enemy withdrew and a terrific sandstorm came up. 'C' Squadron then received orders to advance to Point 166 on the western flank of the 3rd Royal Tanks, an order easier said than done. Visibility was by now practically nil and the only chance of contacting the enemy was to make frequent halts to switch off engines and listen.

The storm became so dense that when they reached the escarpment on which Point 166 was situated the tank commanders dismounted and led their tanks on foot. Two troops under Lieutenant Bates and Sergeant Atkins were then sent off to recce to the west-south-west, and almost immediately they reported nine Mk. IV's and four anti-tank guns to their west. That they had surprised the enemy was evident too, as they were standing about, unconcerned.

The remaining Grants of the combined Regiments came up as quickly as possible, but unfortunately not unobserved, and a fierce battle ensued. 'C' Squadron lost two tanks knocked out, with 2nd Lieutenant Carter wounded and missing. Bates succeeded in rescuing 2nd Lieutenant Twiss, who was badly wounded, and two other men. It was impossible in the dust and smoke to estimate the number of enemy tanks knocked out but there was no doubt that a great deal of damage was done. That night the Squadron withdrew into leaguer on the Trigh Bir Hacheim.

It had been a hard day for the whole Brigade, and by nightfall 'C' Squadron and the 3rd Royal Tanks were the only effective fighting force left, the 5th Royal Tanks having but one Grant and two light tanks to their name.

On this same day the remainder of 'B' Squadron and Regimental Headquarters withdrew to Bardia, where they were given the job of guarding a pumping station as well as coastal defence. The town and the harbour by this time were both more or less flattened, but all the same their short stay was enjoyed by everyone, it enabled them to clean themselves up for one thing.

June 3rd dawned on a diminished 'C' Squadron. All they could muster were three troops of two tanks each, commanded by Bates and Sergeants Atkins and Knill. The battle of the Cauldron was still raging. At first light the Squadron was ordered to recce to the west, but very little was seen. However a concentration of seventy enemy tanks was reported south of Eluet el Tamar, facing north. 'C' Squadron took up battle positions and remained in observation until nightfall, but the attack never materialised, and they eventually withdrew into leaguer about a mile to the north.

Meanwhile the survivors of the Regiment at Bardia received orders to go to the Tank Delivery Squadron at el Duda and there make up a Grant Squadron.

This composite squadron was commanded by Major Harbord with Captain Huth, second-in-command, and three troops under 2nd Lieutenant Taylor and Sergeants Barnett and Wilmshurst, while 2nd Lieutenant Scott commanded 'B' Echelon. They left Bardia in the afternoon and arrived at el Duda that evening, taking over nine Grants from the 9th Lancers and the protection of the Tank Delivery Squadron for the night.

Dawn on the 4th June saw 'C' Squadron again taking up their position on the Tamar Ridge, but at 9 a.m. the area was taken over by the 1st Royal Tanks, and 'C' Squadron were sent to make a demonstration near Bir Hatieza about six miles to the west.

'C' Squadron was again in the advance positions to the west and south-west owing to the high standard of reporting on the enemy which had been reached by Troop Leaders during the campaign.

As a result of these reports the Royal Air Force were able to bomb a large column of enemy mechanized transport. Sergeant Atkin's troop was engaged by two Mk. IV's and an anti-tank gun which closed to within a thousand yards and then withdrew, having only inflicted superficial damage.

Leaguer that night was formed at Bir el Taaleb.

Meanwhile the composite 'A' and 'B' Squadron at el Duda was having problems of its own. A message was received which would have meant splitting up the Squadron amongst various regiments in various Brigades. Major Harbord went to 30 Corps to remonstrate and obtained a guarantee that the Squadron could carry on intact. During his absence the tanks taken over on the previous evening were recalled and others had to be drawn. These were in a deplorable state. Most were minus internal communication and W/T sets, while the guns in some cases were so rusty that they would not work at all. Rations were missing and the general cleanliness had to be seen to be believed. Three days hard work at least were necessary before they were fit for war.

However before the last tank had been drawn imperative orders were sent by 30 Corps to the effect that the Squadron would have to leave immediately and report to the 1st Armoured Division.

A vain attempt was made to delay the start in order to get the tanks into a more fit condition, but to no avail. Two more messages were received from 30 Corps stating that no excuse for delay would be accepted, so the Squadron had no alternative but to take to the field as they were.

On June 5th the struggle for Bir Hacheim was still going on, and in the Cauldron the 10th Indian Infantry Brigade, although fighting, were surrounded. 'C' Squadron however had a quiet day, being in reserve until about 6 p.m. when they went forward to support the 1st Royal Tanks who were grappling with the enemy near Bir el Taaleb. However they were not called on and leaguered in that area.

Major Harbord's Composite Squadron at el Duda moved at 8 a.m. to join the 1st Armoured Division. After some delay while maps, codes, tracings of minefields and orders were collected, the Squadron eventually joined the Bays in the 2nd Armoured Brigade during the afternoon. The greatest trouble they experienced was in tuning in either to the Bays or to Brigade owing to the condition of their W/T sets, and they could only receive orders by liaison. Eventually a set was persuaded to work and orders came through to form line on the right of the Bays opposite Bir el Aslagh where an attack was expected.

It did not, however, develop, and after an attack by Stukas they moved off just before dark in the direction of the Knightsbridge Box. At nightfall they hit the edge of a minefield and moved on west round it in double line ahead. They halted that night on the west of the Knightsbridge Box and moved on at first light on June 6th to the neighbourhood of the blockhouse north-west of Bir Bellefaa. Already four tanks had fallen out through mechanical trouble.

At 10 a.m. on June 6th the Composite Squadron moved due east to an unnamed Bir just east of the blockhouse with the intention of attacking Bir Bellafaa. Again the plan came to nothing and they retraced their steps. They then moved in a south-westerly direction to the escarpment and on reaching the top had a shoot at enemy tanks at 2,000 yards, hitting several and with no damage to themselves. An attempt at a further move forward was stopped by enemy anti-tank guns in well concealed positions.

The Squadron remained there for the rest of the day with an occasional shoot at targets as they appeared, and at dark withdrew into night leaguer under the escarpment.

In the meantime Captain Firth in command of 'C' Squadron had handed over his remaining tanks, one to the 3rd Royal Tanks, and the other two troops commanded by Bates and Sergeant Atkins to the 5th Royal Tanks. Next day, June 7th, 'C' Squadron personnel under Captain Firth joined Regimental Headquarters at Bardia and remained with them until June 23rd when they joined the 7th Motor Brigade.

(e) The Composite Squadron with the Bays and the 4th County of London Yeomanry, June 1942

MAJOR HARBORD's Squadron with the Bays stood to at 4.30 a.m. on June 7th and again took up their position of the previous day on the escarpment. However once there they came under fairly accurate H.E. fire and at 3.30 p.m. were ordered to withdraw north-east of Rigel. As soon as they reached their destination they were ordered to about face and to take up a fire position on the ridge to the south, the enemy having promptly occupied the ridge they had left an hour before.

That evening they were bombed by planes that were thought to be ten Kittihawks, belonging to the R.A.F., and at dusk withdrew into night leaguer.

For the next three days they remained in the same place, and this short respite enabled them to put in some essential maintenance on their tanks and even to send away one at a time for overhaul.

During this time the attacks on the Free French Box at Bir Hacheim grew more and more violent, both from the air and with great pressure from tanks, artillery and infantry. The moment was drawing near when the French could hold out no longer, and, on the night of the 10th/11th, the French, who had fought with the utmost gallantry, managed to break out with the main part of their force.

Also on the 10th the Bays left to join the 4th Armoured Brigade and their place was taken by a squadron of the 4th Hussars, commanded by Major Knight. In the afternoon of the 11th, Major Harbord's Squadron moved to join the 4th County of London Yeomanry, commanded by Lieut.-Colonel Arkwright, and were given a troop from the 3rd County of London Yeomanry to bring the Squadron strength up to eleven Grant tanks. Soon after joining, information came through that three enemy columns consisting of twenty-five, thirty-six and twenty-seven tanks respectively were south, moving east. The 4th County of London Yeomanry together with the 8th Hussars Squadron then moved south-east for nine miles and formed line on the right of the 4th Armoured Brigade, two miles north-east of Naduret el Ghescaeusc. However the enemy did not attack and the Squadron moved into a closer formation when darkness fell.

Rommel, without the Bir Hacheim Box to hinder him, could now sweep forward. Although he himself had lost many tanks he had his screen of formidable anti-tank guns behind him, whereas the British had their tanks alone, and precious few Grants at that. Rommel advanced on the 11th with the 90th Light, the 15th Panzer and the Italian Trieste Divisions, leaving the 21st Panzer and the Ariete Divisions to continue fighting in the Cauldron. By nightfall he was within five miles of the positions at el Adem. Next day, the 12th, the 90th Light had reached el Adem and were over the Trigh Capuzzo.

The retreat to el Alamein began. At first it was fiercely contested for every step of the way and the idea of giving up the Gazala line was hardly contemplated. But gradually positions were surrounded, precious and slightly damaged tanks had to be abandoned and the surging mass of armour, dust and men rolled slowly eastwards over the desert.

What remained of the 8th Hussars fought on doggedly although attacked from every side. On June 12th the composite 'A' and 'B' Squadron was standing to at 8 a.m. and returned to the previous night's position at Naduret el Ghescaeusc. At 8 a.m. large columns of the enemy, headed by tanks, moved across their front as if directed on Sidi Rezegh. At three o'clock they moved north-north-east to engage an enemy reported to be moving northwards, and had a shoot at opportunity targets until 7 p.m. when the enemy appeared to be forming up for an attack. This took place at 10 p.m., and from then until dark a tank battle raged. At nightfall only six out of the eleven Grants were left to withdraw into leaguer, but only one man, Trooper Edwards, had been killed, while others had received minor injuries.

That night by the light of the blazing tanks, three of which were German, the 4th County of London Yeomanry 'B' Echelon came up and evacuated the wounded.

All that day the defenders of the Knightsbridge Box were heavily engaged, supported by the 4th Armoured Brigade. By the 13th the fighting had moved north and was concentrated against Rigel Ridge, held by the Scots Guards. Both the 4th and 22nd Armoured Brigades were flung in to support them and were able to hold some of the enemy back, at a cost of twenty-five tanks against an enemy loss of eleven.

The Composite Squadron fought all that day. They stood to at 4 a.m. on the 13th and, facing south, they extended to the west. However a large number of enemy tanks attacked them from the rear so that they had to face both north and south and, at 7.30 a.m., had to begin to withdraw westwards, conforming with the Bays on their left.

An hour later they halted between the blockhouse and Bir Bellefaa and at 9.45 again withdrew to the high ground near the blockhouse which Lieut.-Colonel Arkwright of the 4th County of London Yeomanry ordered them to hold at all costs.

"Colonel Arkwright was brilliant," wrote Major Harbord. "Although at this time the situation looked precarious he inspired everyone with immense confidence."

At 10.30 a.m. to their relief 'I' tanks were seen to the south, but they did not appear to be too effective. The Squadron made a slight move forward 'more for morale's sake than anything else'.

At 11.45 more 'I' tanks arrived to the north and the enemy fire, which up until now had been intense, died down. Now only three Grants remained, three having had their guns knocked out.

All day the battle raged. By 10.15 that night fire became more intense and it continued until darkness fell, when the Squadron withdrew half a mile west into night leaguer. Only two of the tanks reached it as the third had withdrawn earlier to replenish. Orders were received that night from Lieut.-Colonel Arkwright that they were to move next morning at 4 a.m. to Acroma.

That same night, that of the 13th/14th, the Knightsbridge Box was evacuated. With the loss of that position it became clear that the Gazala line could no longer be held. The problem now was how to extricate the 50th and 1st South African Divisions who were still holding out in the north-west.

The first attack on June 14th on the 8th Hussars Squadron began at 1.10 a.m. The leaguer was attacked in force and many of the vehicles were hit, whilst the rest scattered. The few remaining tanks belonging to the 4th County of London Yeomanry were gathered in by means of Very lights, but only one tank of Major Harbord's Squadron remained and that was only fit for another five miles. It's engine had been holed and it was leaking oil badly.

Just before first light the 4th County of London Yeomanry and what remained of the 8th Hussar Squadron moved north to Acroma. Here they joined up with their 'B' Echelons, the 8th Hussars' having attached itself to that of the 4th County of London

Regimental Headquarters at Benghazi, 1943 (page 136)

H.M. King George VI visiting the Regiment at West Tofts, Norfolk, February 24th, 1944. Accompanied by Lieut.-Colonel Goulburn, he is talking to Major Huth, commanding 'C' Squadron (page 139).

Officers of the Regiment at Bognor Regis, D-Day, May 7th, 1944.

Back row, left to right: M. Jephson, †H. R. D. Pegler, †D. S. Scott, †P. F. de May, R. P. G. Dill, †J. G. M. Young, J. L. Lombard, †R. H. Anstey, †M. M. Browne, †. K. R. McClurg, F. D. C. Barnes.

Second row: P. G. Hartwright, M. Payne, G. L. Atkinson-Willes, Gadsby, Evans, D. Rampf, Dickinson, †A. L. Preston, †H. L. Talbot-Hervey, †S. E. Apthorp, D. J. Mossop.

Third row: W. St. C. Tisdall, A. Newman, M. Walker, C. J. G. Mea, F. Hone (Padre), J. Haycock (M.O.), W. Best (R.E.M.E.), A. V. Case, P. McClintock, G. R. C. A. Kirkham, †A. B. Brodie, D. F. Carver.

Seated: Capt. J. Robertson, Capt. R. H. Anes, Major J. W. Gwyn, †Major G. W. G. Threlfall, Major J. W. Phillips, Lieut.-Col. C. Goulburn, Major N. G. F. Dunne, Major P. H. Huth, Capt. H. H. Firth, Capt. J. Ladenburg, Capt. A. Hepburn (page 140).

† Denotes those killed in action in the European Campaign.

The Warrant Officers and Sergeants of the 8th Hussars at Bognor before D-Day, June, 1944. Owing to the length of time that has elapsed since this photograph was taken it has been impossible to trace more than a few names and so it was thought better not to include any.

A Cromwell tank disembarking from an **LST** at Le Hamel near Arromanche, June, 1944 (page 146).

A destroyed German Tiger tank in the ruins of Villers Bocage, June, 1944.

Yeomanry. After one or two minor complications the 'A' and 'B' Echelons of the Composite Squadron joined forces and moved together to Bardia.

Although by now all their tanks had been written off, the only casualties to personnel were one complete crew missing, one man killed and one wounded.

On June 15th Major Harbord's Squadron joined the rest of the Regiment at Bardia. Orders were received later that day to move to Misheifa, which task was accomplished by the 16th, two days before the installations at Bardia were destroyed and the place abandoned. Then, until June 21st the Regiment had a period of comparative rest while they waited to be re-equipped with tanks, meanwhile carrying out some essential maintenance on the thinskin vehicles.

The tide of war swept on. Although they had inflicted heavy casualties on the German tanks the British Armoured Brigades had desperately few left themselves. On the night of the 17th el Adem was evacuated and on the 21st Tobruk was in German hands. It was left to the Eighth Army to struggle bitterly and doggedly back to the defended positions at el Alamein, and there to hope that they could at last hold Rommel's panzers in check.

It was a confused retreat in the sense that squadrons, companies, and units straggled east independently, hoping that they would eventually catch up with the rest of their regiment, battalion, or brigade. No two men had the same tale to tell, some of the time they seemed to be travelling almost as part of the Afrika Korps. That so many did reach the el Alamein line says much for their resource and ability to navigate.

(f) With 'C' Squadron to Alamein, June 1942

ON June 22nd, after five days spent at Bir Abu Misheifa, the Regiment moved to Bir Enba, ten miles to the north-west, and there 'C' Squadron obtained a full squadron of Honey tanks. These are described in the War Diary as 'a very sorry lot' and were in a really bad state. However after a good day's maintenance and some improvisations by M/Sergeant Friel they were just about fit to go into action, although there were very few W/T sets and hardly a tank with inter-com. Orders were then received that the Squadron was now under the command of the 7th Motor Brigade Group and was to join them on the following day. The rest of the Regiment, consisting of Regimental Headquarters and the composite 'A' and 'B' Squadron under Major Threlfall, remained at Bir Enba for another day and then moved to Fuka where the Tank Delivery Regiment was situated. For the moment it is best to leave them there and follow the fortunes of 'C' Squadron.

The 7th Motor Brigade was at this time commanded by Brigadier J. M. L. Renton, and consisted of the 4th Royal Horse Artillery, the 9th Kings Royal Rifle Corps and the 2nd and 9th Rifle Brigades.

'C' Squadron was commanded by Major Hackett with Captain Firth, second-in-command, Captain Ames spare Captain and four troops under 2nd Lieutenants Ladenburg and Scott and Sergeants Atkins and Melsom. 'B' Echelon was commanded by 2nd Lieutenant McClintock who had the doctor, Captain Heycock, and the padre, Captain Hone, with him.

Before joining the 7th Motor Brigade, Major Hackett moved the squadron on

G

June 23rd to the 4th Armoured Brigade Workshops, who were about seven miles south of Bir Thalata, so that they could inspect and carry out a few minor repairs on the tanks. It was there that they saw their Commanding Officer, Lieut.-Colonel G. Kilkelly for the last time before he was captured at the breakout from Gerawla, from where he was killed in a prisoner of war camp as a result of R.A.F. bombing

As at this time the enemy was advancing with considerable speed, the Squadron and the workshops were ordered by Headquarters, 7th Armoured Division, to withdraw that night, under cover of darkness, to a position some twenty miles east.

The rôle of the 7th Motor Brigade at this stage was to protect the southern flank of the Eighth Army during the withdrawal to Alamein, and accordingly the Brigade was formed into three columns 'June', 'July' and 'August'.

The next day, June 24th, the Squadron moved south to Bir Washket el Arnab at about midday and joined 'July' Column commanded by Lieut.-Colonel Christopher, R.H.A. The column consisted of the 8th Hussars' 'C' Squadron, some armoured cars, anti-tank guns, 25-pounders and a motor battalion and was completely mobile.

The enemy was by now approaching Bir Thalata and 'C' Squadron was ordered to reconnoitre to the north and north-west towards the Bir. During the afternoon contact was made with the enemy near Thalata but the Squadron did not become involved.

That night they were ordered to move independently of the Column along their northern flank to Bir el Bul, about forty kilometres east-north-east. On arrival patrols were sent out to contact the rest of the Column but without success, and 'C' Squadron went into close leaguer on its own. Apparently the rest of the Column had got off course and there was considerable danger of it being split up.

From the Very lights that night it was obvious that the enemy was exceedingly close and moving in around the Squadron's flanks, particularly to the north-west.

At first light on the 25th leaguer was broken and patrols sent out. Major Hackett went off in search of the rest of the Column but no sign was found of them nor sound heard.

At about 7 a.m. a column of obviously British vehicles and guns approached 'C' Squadron from the west. Thinking these were probably part of the 'July' Column a troop was sent off under Sergeant Melsom to investigate.

However as he drew near to the doubtful column his troop was fired on by anti-tank guns, fortunately without effect, and he withdrew. The column turned out to be a German one with previously captured British vehicles and equipment.

"At this stage," wrote Major Firth, the second-in-command, "one experienced a feeling of extreme loneliness. One could see no sign whatsoever of any of our own troops and we were without our supporting arms. It was learnt afterwards that our own troops had already withdrawn to the Siwa track and we were in fact completely alone."

The time had come, Major Hackett decided, to pull out, and he ordered 'C' Squadron back towards Bir Kenayis, the scene of their earlier training. They moved back in box formation with the 'B' Echelon in the centre, and travelled fifty kilometres in an easterly direction, pursued most of the way by enemy armoured vehicles, before they contacted their own troops.

As it was becoming very difficult to recognise the enemy owing to the use they were making of captured British vehicles, 'C' Squadron approached some British armoured cars near Bir Kenayis waving a large flag. They found 'July' Column had taken up a position just to the south, and the Squadron was sent out on a patrol to the west. There they reported enemy concentrations to the west and north-west which were successfully shelled by the gunners.

That night they all moved about thirty kilometres east, to 'conform' as the War Diary put it 'to the general withdrawal'.

The situation was indeed serious. On the same day that 'C' Squadron was moving alone across the desert, General Ritchie had handed over command of the Eighth Army to General Auchinleck. He, well aware of the seriousness of the situation and, having lost precious troops when Tobruk fell, decided against shutting any up to defend Mersa Matruh, from which Rommel was but forty miles, and to hold the line at el Alamein.

By the morning of June 26th it was known by Major Hackett and 'C' Squadron that their withdrawal during the night had been followed up by the Germans, and patrols, at first light, reported a concentration of enemy transport in a depression a few miles to the west.

These enemy vehicles appeared to have very little immediate protection and Major Hackett decided to attack them at once. Quickly rallying the Squadron, he said simply: "Follow me," and off they went, making use of the ground to get a covered approach.

This was one heartening incident at that depressing time. 'C' Squadron was able to get right in amongst the enemy transport and created considerable havoc there, in addition to knocking out one 50-mm. anti-tank gun, which unfortunately it was impossible to bring out. Although Sergeant Melsom lost his tank in the engagement no casualties were suffered.

That night the Column withdrew to the el Buweib area on the Khalder track.

The enemy were still forging ahead. By the evening of the 26th they had swept through the 29th Indian Brigade and next morning surrounded the 2nd New Zealand Division, twenty-five miles south of Mersa Matruh. The New Zealanders, however, broke out during the night and managed to re-assemble near el Alamein, the destination of all other Eighth Army units. The force acting as rear guard in this long and difficult action was the 7th Motor Brigade, of which 'C' Squadron of the 8th Hussars was part.

'C' Squadron heard during the night of June 26th/27th that the enemy in the north had penetrated almost as far as Fuka (through the position held by the 29th Indian Brigade) and they were ordered to withdraw immediately to the area Point 129, south of Fuka, about 65 kilometres away. Accordingly they broke off contact with the enemy and, after an uneventful journey, arrived at their destination at about 3 p.m.

There, however, great difficulty was experienced in telling friend from foe, so mingled had the two armies become. 'C' Squadron eventually made contact with some friends to the north, who were holding the escarpment to the west of Fuka, and being heavily engaged by the enemy. The attack however was beaten off and they leaguered about two miles south of Point 189 that night.

But on the morning of June 28th, the enemy, held along the escarpment west of Fuka, started to feel around the Squadron's southern flank towards them, and at about 11 a.m. a tank battle developed between the Panzers and 'C' Squadron, assisted by a Squadron of the Queen's Bays to their immediate north. It was fought at extreme range in rather open country and 'C' Squadron suffered no casualties, although their anti-tank guns 'brewed' one enemy tank.

The battle died down during the heat of the day, but towards evening, and with the sunset behind him, the enemy attacked in strength, and 'C' Squadron was forced to withdraw. However their 25-pounders took a good toll of German transport and left many vehicles blazing.

Morning saw the Column again withdrawing. Information had come through that the enemy in the north had once again penetrated and they were reported as being near Bir umm Habib, about forty miles to the east, moving south-east.

'C' Squadron received orders to withdraw to Niswet abdel Mawla to avoid being cut off, but a violent sandstorm made visibility very bad. However they moved fourteen kilometres south and then east to Mawla, a pathetically reduced party with only five tanks as runners, and three of these towing non-runners. One of the difficulties of working with a Column was that they did not cater for tanks, and had no transporters or equipment for carrying out repairs.

It was during this time that Captain Ames was badly injured in the thigh due to a tow-rope snapping, and he had to travel in the ambulance.

On reaching Mawla, enemy A.F.V.'s and transport were encountered to the east and this opportunity was taken full advantage of by the gunners. It also became apparent that by this infiltration of enemy, the line of withdrawal was more than precarious. The Column was in fact surrounded.

The Brigadier commanding the 7th Motor Brigade, Viscount Garmoyle, decided that the only chance they had of reaching the Alamein line was to make a break-out under cover of darkness. They planned to move five miles west, ten north and then due east until they met their own troops. However the move did not come off and, during the night, the Squadron had to abandon the three broken-down tanks. They also had to ensure that they were made useless before being left, a difficult task as strict silence was enforced.

June 30th. "This," writes Major Firth, "was an extremely fortunate day for our column."

At first light it was decided to move six miles south and then try to make south-east, for the area north of Gebel Kalakh. By doing this the Column passed right through a position in which the enemy had leaguered that night, only a couple of miles away. For some unknown reason they had moved north just before first light and had thereby left a gap through which the British column was able to travel, and eventually join up with their friends.

As the Squadron passed through the Deir el Qattara they met Captain Gwyn, wearing an Australian hat. He had hitch-hiked back from Garawla on the coast, where the rest of the Regiment had broken out, and was now with the New Zealanders in their box in the Alamein Line. He was able to give 'C' Squadron news of the Regiment too, something which they had not had since June 22nd.

Although the Column had managed to slip through the German position, the enemy was hot on their heels, and shortly after they reached their goal, put in a big attack. This was held however, mainly by the New Zealanders, who were in fine form after their break out south of Mersa Matruh a few days earlier.

'C' Squadron was now put under command of the 1st Armoured Division and went to the 7th Motor Brigade Headquarters before joining them. They arrived at Qaret el Himeimet at first light on July 1st and were ordered by Headquarters, 7th Armoured Division, to join and assist 'August' Column, who were on Ruweisat Ridge, before joining the 1st Armoured Division. This meant a march of fifty kilometres as they had to go by Alam Halfa.

On arriving at their destination they found a heavy tank battle in progress, just south of Ruweisat Ridge. However 'C' Squadron was not involved but was directed to recce on the northern flank with 'August' Column.

On July 2nd 'August' Column was withdrawn south-east to re-organise, and 'C' Squadron was ordered to collect their 'B' Echelon from the 7th Motor Brigade and report to the 1st Armoured Division who were nine miles south-east of Alamein. This meant another long march, and the Squadron did not arrive until after dark.

Next morning, July 3rd, more orders were received, this time from the 1st Armoured Division. These said that in view of the small number of tanks left in the Squadron they were to move back to Amyria and refit as quickly as possible at the Tank Delivery Regiment there.

The Squadron duly arrived there in fine fettle at about 6 p.m., and were accommodated in the leave and transit camp. They handed over what tanks they had left and settled down to enjoy thankfully twelve days away from the front.

The long but swift withdrawal to the Alamein Line had been an anxious time for them all, for various reasons. Firstly, they did not know what had happened to the rest of the Regiment, and secondly, they suffered from extreme fatigue from continually patrolling or fighting by day and withdrawing by night. There were the difficulties of supply and replacements, too; the absence of facilities for recovery and repair; the scarcity of information and the lack of contact with the flanks due to the great distances covered, all of which added to the normal anxiety of fighting a very long rear-guard action.

During this trying period the Squadron was inspired and given great confidence throughout by their Squadron Leader, Major Hackett.

(g) The Break-out from Garawla, June 1942

HAVING followed the fortunes of 'C' Squadron during the withdrawal to Alamein, it is now necessary to return to the Regiment which had been ordered to report from Bir Abu Misheifa to the Tank Delivery Regiment at Fuka. They arrived there on June 25th, and Lieut.-Colonel Kilkelly decided to form what was left of his tank crews into a Regimental Headquarters and one Composite Squadron of Honey tanks. On arrival there were found to be no Honeys available at all, and the Squadron spent what was described as a rather disturbed night there, being heavily bombed.

However, by the 26th, with still no Honeys available, the Regiment drew twenty Crusaders on trailers and took them up to Garawla on the coast road just east of Matruh. It was there arranged that they should be exchanged for twenty Honeys previously issued to the 4th County of London Yeomanry and after a certain amount of delay, owing to a time lag with the orders, Lieut.-Colonel Arkwright arrived at about 6 p.m. with the Honeys. This was an excellent arrangement as the 8th Hussars had little experience of Crusaders, whereas the 4th County of London Yeomanry knew all about Crusaders but nothing about Honeys.

The delay was to prove unfortunate as the Regiment had to remain for the night in the areas, where it was difficult to disperse. This resulted in yet another heavy and accurate bombing attack, causing about a dozen casualties, Corporal Forrester being killed together with Captain Rees of the Yorkshire Light Infantry.

Crews had to be reorganised and trouble was experienced with No. 19 wireless sets which were new to the Regiment, all of which made it impossible to move out to the 1st Armoured Division Rear Headquarters near Bir el Qai'm that night.

It was decided to send Major J. W. Phillips on for orders and move the Composite

Squadron at first light. However he was not able to return as the enemy cut the track from Bir el Qai'm to Garawla during the night 26th/27th.

At 6 a.m. on the morning of the 27th the Regiment moved out to join the 1st Armoured Division. The Composite Squadron consisted of Major G. W. G. Threlfall in command, Captain P. H. Huth, second-in-command, Captain J. W. Gwyn spare Captain and Lieutenant N. D. A. Hall, 2nd Lieutenant G. V. Bates and Sergeant Wilmshurst, Troop Leaders.

The Regiment set out with Major Threlfall's Squadron in the lead, followed by Regimental Headquarters and with 'B' Echelon commanded by Captain P. C. Earle bringing up the rear. The route was south, following the Qara telephone wires. On reaching the top of the first escarpment, Threlfall's tank was engaged at long range by anti-tank fire and had a track shot off. Huth, who was in the next tank, led the remainder of the Squadron to the cover of some wadis close at hand, and Threlfall and his crew made their way back to him on foot.

It was impractical, with the Squadron as yet unorganised and with no proper W/T communication, to try and fight their way out. It was also evident that the Germans had pushed a strong column of tanks, artillery and anti-tank guns through the Charing Cross minefields the previous night and had cut the track between Garawla and Bir el Qai'm. These were however engaged by 25-pounders of the 50th (Northumbrian) Division and the Squadron rallied under the escarpment and withdrew back to an area about two miles east of Garawla.

Lieut.-Colonel Kilkelly then went to 10 Corps Headquarters and reported that his Regiment was cut off from the 1st Armoured Division Headquarters, and the Regiment came under the command of 10 Corps.

On June 28th, Major Sir Edward Malet, with the non-essential thinskin vehicles and one tank which was a crock, was sent down the Matruh road to Daba, and they must have been some of the last vehicles to get through before the road was cut. The remainder of the Regiment prepared for a siege, and the situation looked pretty grim.

A patrol under Sergeant Wilmshurst was sent up on to the escarpment to the east of the Qara telephone wires, and, whilst placing this patrol, Threlfall managed to persuade a Crusader tank bound for the 1st Armoured Division not to continue its crusade straight into the enemy positions. This tank joined the Regiment and later proved to be of the greatest assistance.

That afternoon, Lieut.-Colonel Kilkelly was sent for by the Officer Commanding 50th (Northumbrian) Division and was told that the Matruh-Garawla garrison was going to break out and beat up the German leaguers south of the Matruh escarpment that night. It was finally decided that the Regiment's rôle should be to make good the start line just south of the escarpment, and reconnoitre the next escarpment to pin-point the enemy positions. The Regiment should then rally and guard the flanks of the 50th (Northumbrian) Division when they withdrew to Garawla before the dawn.

Three patrols under Lieutenants Hall, Bates and Sergeant Wilmshurst moved out at 7 p.m. to go up the escarpment by different routes. The start line was reported clear by 10 p.m. and the enemy was located on the next escarpment soon after. Squadron Headquarters and one troop in reserve moved to the top of the escarpment, the Commanding Officer remaining with Divisional Headquarters. The raiding parties then passed through the patrols, which were withdrawn.

Soon afterwards Lieutenant W. G. Lockhart appeared with the thinskins and all vehicles were topped up in case the order came to break out of the Matruh Box.

However nothing further materialised, except for a grand firework display and a considerable amount of bombing from about 2.30 a.m. until dawn.

Huth as Liaison Officer was kept busy with his dingo as the wireless communication was still difficult.

It was evident from the explosions in the German positions that the 50th (Northumbrian) Division was giving them a very uncomfortable night, and had in fact penetrated right through their leaguer positions.

The order then came through to withdraw back to Garawla, and the Composite Squadron joined Lieut.-Colonel Kilkelly and Regimental Headquarters there just before dawn on the 29th. They went back down the track to the place where they had changed over tanks two days before. The traffic congestion was terrific but luckily there was no bombing to add to the confusion.

A good position in a deep wadi was found for the 'B' Echelon and the tanks were dispersed to the east on some level ground, which was a good place for taking up battle positions facing east and south should the Germans break through.

(h) Rendezvous el Alamein, June 1942

IT was by now the morning of June 29th, and a lull in the activity gave everyone a chance of having breakfast. However, during it, General Holmes, commanding 50th Division, drove up and ordered a troop to be sent down the Mersa road towards Bagush to reconnoitre enemy positions which were astride the road about ten kilometres to the east. Four medium guns and their observers, with one recce troop, would then shell the Germans and if possible drive them off the road.

Three Troop under Lieutenant Hall was detailed for this job, and made contact with the enemy in considerable force just east of Qasaba aerodrome. Huth assisted him in the dingo and the Commanding Officer went with his tank to Corps Headquarters. The Germans were seen to be looting the dump at Sidi Haneish siding and, as a result of this patrol, effective fire from the artillery was brought down on them for most of the day. The Germans however did not withdraw from their positions although a good deal of movement was observed.

The rest of the day was spent in artillery duels, not with any great effect from the German end, although from the position of Corps Headquarters at Qasaba it looked as if they should have been able to wipe it out with ease.

Bates and Sergeant Southworth were sent that afternoon either to recover or destroy Threlfall's tank, lost the previous morning, and after much discussion on the wireless it was decided to destroy it, after the tank had been towed under cover.

Mr. O'Malley had failed that morning to get through to Matruh with his replenishing party as the road was under shell-fire. However he had been able to draw water at Garawla, and the Squadron was well off for rations. There was plenty of Octane petrol too in the wadi where the 'B' Echelon was lying up, and what could not be carried was destroyed.

At about 5.30 that evening Lieut.-Colonel Kilkelly arrived with the news that the Matruh-Garawla force was going to break out that night in small parties and rally at Fuka. Lieutenant Hall's patrol was withdrawn and a conference was held to decide on a plan of action. During this conference and before any orders could be given, the news came through that an Indian Battalion south-east of the Squadron on the escarpment had been overrun. The Squadron immediately manned their tanks and took up as good a battle position as was available, preparatory to a break through by German tanks.

One Troop under Bates patrolled south on to the escarpment by the route taken by Squadron Headquarters the previous night.

Huth went off in the dingo to collect the three petrol lorries to accompany 'A' Echelon in the event of the Squadron having to fight its way out.

Lieutenant V. A. Buist, who was acting as Liaison Officer, was at Corps Headquarters in his tank.

The Squadron remained in their position until sunset. Nothing had yet materialised except for a few overs from 50-mm. shells that pitched very close, and Bates returned to report that the escarpment was free of the enemy.

At 11.15 p.m., no further orders having been received, Lieut.-Colonel Kilkelly gave the order to break out, the rendezvous being el Alamein.

The W/T was still giving trouble, so a close formation of three lines of tanks was chosen, with Huth navigating from his dingo.

The moon, which was full, was rising by the time the escarpment was cleared, and a south-south-westerly course was taken for about five miles which brought them to where the Qara track rose over a small escarpment. No leaguer lights had been put up in this area which seemed to indicate there was no enemy about, so the course was altered to south-east for about a mile and a half along the foot of the escarpment.

The Squadron then changed direction and headed south until, on rising over the escarpment, they found themselves passing between two large enemy leaguers about a mile apart.

"Fire was not opened on us at once," wrote Threlfall, "and it appeared that we might get through without any trouble, but we were soon to find out that this was far from the case. All hell was let loose from both flanks and the next three miles was a flat-out hunt on a roaring scent. It was a miracle that anything could live under such a barrage of fire, tracer shell-bursts and gun flashes lighted the tanks up as bright as day and speed was our only chance of reaching safety."

When at last the southern flank of the German Leaguer was reached and an armoured car had been shaken off, a halt was called. Of the eighteen tanks, three lorries and the dingo which had started the hunt, only six Honeys commanded by Threlfall, Hall and Bates, Sergeant Barnett, Corporals Woodford and Wells, the Crusader commanded by Captain P. H. Wagstaffe and Captain Huth in his dingo rallied. After about five minutes the order to advance slowly south-east was given in the hopes that stragglers would hear the noise of their tracks, then speed was increased.

The next six or seven miles were uneventful until a track was reached and a small leaguer observed on the right flank. This was successfully avoided but a few minutes later the dingo went up in smoke.

Threlfall's tank was then hit twice almost simultaneously, the force of the second explosion practically turning it over. The next tank to go was Bates', which went up in flames, but thanks to Wagstaffe, Sergeant Barnett and Corporal Wells, who halted about half a mile further on, the crews of the two tanks were picked up.

The force was once more split up and the situation did not look too healthy.

The last trouble had obviously been a minefield covered by fire, and the whole countryside looked hostile. South was the order and south they went, until at 2.30 a.m. on June 30th, they had covered forty-two miles from Garawla. Several German leaguers had been passed and Corporal Well's tank had run out of petrol and been smashed up. From the track marks in the sand it looked as if they were well south of the German advance and a conference was held. As there were no enemy in sight, it was decided to bed down for the night, syphon the petrol into the Crusader from the Honey in the morning and ration the water to a quarter of a gallon per man per day. They reckoned they had water for ten days after the Crusader had run out of petrol.

With these disturbing thoughts to sleep on, an officer watch was posted and the remainder of the party bedded down.

(*i*) 'B' Echelon's Escape, June 1942

MEANWHILE the 'B' Echelon had been having adventures of their own. With an escort of Honeys they also had attempted to break out as soon as it was dark. Perhaps that attempt is best told in the words of Lance-Corporal E. W. Cook who was one of the few to get through.

"There had been a tense feeling all that day, the 29th June, for on that Sabbath day we meant by the Grace of God to break out of the box so cunningly closed by Jerry.

"As the long day drew to a close, the Echelon, with its escort of Honey tanks, formed line facing south. Whilst the sun was still a ball of fire on the horizon came the welcome order, 'Brew up.' A few heavy curses went up as one or two Stukas interrupted the performing of that sacred ritual.

"Darkness! Everyone waiting the order to move. Slowly the long line of vehicles moved forward as the moon grew stronger and brighter. Into no-man's land we crept— no smoking—no talking—one thought only in everyone's mind—shall we make it? Then, as we learnt afterwards, Mersa went up in a welter of flame and smoke, to every-body's dismay. With the moon on our left, Mersa alight on our right and bomber flares right ahead, every vehicle stood out in its own stark outline.

"Vague figures around us told us our listening posts had been active, but still we drifted on. Suddenly the air was rent with the drumming noise of machine-gun fire, tracers whistled across our front, the worst had happened and enemy infantry had cut the Echelon.

"The leading vehicles stood no chance in that hail of lead and, it must be assumed, were captured en-bloc, but the remaining few whipped around and headed back from whence they had started. Impossible to get them together again, in the melée the vehicles split up and again some must have taken the wrong way out and no more was heard of them.

"Two at least, being the water lorry and the 'Fitter's Ferry' (of which we shall hear more) intended to follow an Indian Brigade in a mad dash by road, but met up with three more stragglers headed by Mr. O'Malley in a 15 cwt. Morris, one 15 cwt. Ford, one Ford utility and a Chev. 3-tonner, which was soon out of the race, the crew scrambling aboard the 'Ferry'. Managing to maintain contact, the four vehicles raced along.

"Then, in the moonlight, a Jerry column swung into view and at that precise moment the water lorry swung out on a sharp rise, failed to maintain speed and the utility found it impossible to avoid a collision. This event happened with startling suddenness, the 'Ferry' behind clearing the locked vehicles with inches to spare being superbly handled by its driver, Sergeant Southworth. One man with great presence of mind managed to hang on to the 'Ferry' as it crashed by. With only two vehicles left things were not too bright.

"Ten minutes after this Mr. O'Malley's Morris was scuppered by a riddled petrol tank and, stopping, we picked up Mr. O'Malley and his driver.

"With the above-named directing and myself acting as observer by standing up in the Morris we raced on, heedless of trenches, camel humps or rocks.

"On our left, i.e. westward at that time, a terrific tank and artillery battle was in progress. To our right rear a similar 'event' was also taking place, and like shadows in the moonlight, the enemy supply and support columns weaved round us.

"Again that ghastly rattling broke out as the 'Ferry' was gunned, and the cough of a quick-firing pom-pom kept us alert and tense. (We learnt afterwards that our petrol tank was hit and our off-side near tyre ripped during that little incident.) Gradually the main enemy echelons were left behind and the outflung patrols were an immediate danger. We crossed an aerodrome and were at once shelled by what appeared to be a 2-pounder or probably heavier gun, firing high-explosive. Happily we came through unscathed and raced on.

"Suddenly—'Armoured Car to our left!'—After a pause—'Eight wheeler!'—I reported. And again 'Armoured Car (eight wheeler) to our right!' 'Half left' the driver was told and screaming at top speed we apparently dumbfounded them by tearing between the two deadly-looking armoured cars. (Here I must give praise to that sturdy, speedy, tough ugly-duckling of the desert, the Morris 15 cwt.)

"To see that same little 'bug', as it was called, outstrip those speedy Jerry cars was grand and in fact nothing we approached that night, be it armoured car, lorry or Staff car, stood an earthly when the Morris took the bit between her teeth and decided to go.

"The night wore on, the worst danger seemed over when 'Phut', the 'Ferry' stalled and stopped. That riddled tank had let us down. But, listen! Away on our left was heard a familiar sound. Tanks and lorries were moving. Not an English column, oh no, but the clank-clank of Jerry assault tanks, Mks. III and IV, and the soft purr of revving lorries. Crouching behind the 'Ferry' we hoped for the best, blessing the deep clinging mist that surrounded us. The time was then 3 a.m. and as our little band, ten strong, set out walking in a south-easterly direction, we knew we could cover at least ten miles before first light.

"Came the dawn and, wet, footsore but still safe, we huddled into a few shallow slit-trenches to await whatever the day might bring. Suddenly, away on the distant ridge, transport was seen moving. Cautiously in twos, about half a mile apart, we approached the convoy. Thank God it was friendly, and we piled on the lorries of a Sikh Indian Division. Our troubles seemed over, and for some they were. What happened to three of us, including myself, is yet another story, but even we at last found our unit after days of thirst and hunger."

(j) The Composite Squadron Reaches Alamein, June-July 1942

BACK with the Composite Squadron, which consisted of one Crusader and one Honey without any petrol, the officers kept watch through all of what was left of the night of the 29th/30th June. At 3.15 a.m. while Threlfall was on guard they were stalked by a Staff car which moved round them for some time. This was rather unnerving as they particularly wanted to be left in peace to get themselves organised on to the Crusader, which had the longer range, and abandon the solitary Honey. However nothing materialised from the prowling car and they decided it must have been a friend.

Reveille was at 5 a.m. and, whilst the Honey was being evacuated and essential pieces of guns and engine removed, a thick fog came down. Vehicles were heard moving close by and these were stalked on foot but not identified.

At about 6 a.m. the Squadron set off east with a bit of south in it. "Rather a comic party," wrote Threlfall, "the Crusader now carrying a complement of twenty and all the food and water we could salvage."

When the fog eventually lifted the desert was found to be covered with refugees, all heading east and hoping to face the enemy once more behind the el Alamein defences. A medium gun was the first to be met, but it would not play, so the Crusader party gave up trying to persuade it to join them and left it well alone. They felt it would be a poor end to be knocked out by a gun in the same situation as themselves.

Three trucks were equally suspicious of their identity, but Bates walked over with his hands up. They turned out to be Indians from Matruh with Major Searle, R.A.M.C. in command. Six Punjabis on foot were then picked up, and by midday the party consisted of approximately forty vehicles including two Bofors guns, one 25-pounder and about a dozen Bren-gun carriers. Major Threlfall commanded this heterogeneous force, Major Searle acting as interpreter.

The route taken was south-east, with the intention of hitting the Qattara Depression at Qareb el Tarfaza, which was in fact reached at 1.30 p.m. when a halt was called. Only one enemy column had been seen to the north, but it had taken no notice of them as they had given it a wide berth.

By now the Crusader was nearly out of petrol but luckily an R.A.S.C. lorry in the column was found to be carrying petrol, and eighty gallons were exchanged for about half a dozen cans of beer.

On they went until about 3 p.m. when they found a friendly Royal Air Force wireless station. They reckoned by this that they must be nearly home and, as the heat was appalling, they halted for two hours.

A conference was then held and they decided to push on again as far as possible as the Indians were very short of petrol and rations. The Crusader now brought up the rear ready to tow anyone who ran out of petrol.

Except for one amusing incident when what appeared to be a hostile 25-pounder towed by a lorry put its trail down and looked aggressive, terrifying the whole Column, nothing else of note occurred. "Actually this gun was one from the Column which had got separated and took us to be an enemy force. We had the ammunition, he the gun."

By sending a signal from a Royal Air Force post, 500 gallons of petrol was sent to a post five miles north-east of Nagb el Dweis, where the Column spent the night of the 30th June/1st July. The petrol was of the utmost assistance as the enemy was pushing on as hard as they could for el Alamein.

Lieutenant Hall, Corporal Woodford and their crews were also found at this post, having run out of petrol and been picked up. Sergeant Southworth and Corporal Fry rolled in also.

On the morning of July 1st there was news of an enemy column approaching. The Crusader here parted company with the Indians, and continued, with a party of twenty-two on board, and reached Burg el Arab by 5 p.m. Here they met Major Sir Edward Malet and his party of lorries which had left Garawla some two days before.

Thus, for the Composite Squadron, ended a midnight steeplechase over a course worthy of any country, with a point of nearly 250 miles. Other members of the Regiment turned up here too, after long and adventurous marches and many days of hunger and thirst. Regimental Headquarters had suffered a somewhat similar fate to the Composite Squadron. On reaching the top of the escarpment above Garawla, on the night of the break-out, they ran into German leaguers, and all the tanks were either knocked out or broke down. It was here that Lieut.-Colonel Kilkelly and the other members of Regimental Headquarters were taken prisoner. Captain Gwyn and his crew crawled from their tank after losing a track between the first two German leaguers on the night of the 29th, hid in a slit trench and then walked south until picked up. Captain Huth walked for four hours south-east after being blown up in his dingo on the landmines and was also picked up. Sergeant Wilmshurst and Trooper Bateman got back after their tank fell into a pit at the bottom of the first escarpment out of Garawla. Corporal Wizard, although hit four times, got his tank back to el Alamein after collecting petrol on the way. Corporal McBride and crew turned back at the first enemy leaguer and found an easier way further east, destroyed their tank after running out of petrol and got a lift back. Sergeant Southworth, Corporal Witmore and the crew of his lorry arrived back at Abbassia after a very long journey on foot and many days of hunger and thirst. The Doctor's 15 cwt., driven by Trooper Van-der-Sloot, came back after having made contact with a convoy of ambulances. This was the only 'B' vehicle which had been with the fighting echelon to survive the break-out and rejoin the Regiment.

All 8th Hussar details (less 'C' Squadron, which was still intact at Amyria with the Tank Delivery Regiment under command of the 1st Armoured Division) were ordered to report back to the Armoured Corps Base Depot at Abbassia.

IV.

THE BATTLES OF ALAM HALFA AND ALAMEIN

(a) The Regiment less 'C' Squadron moves to Alexandria, July 1942

THIS then was the position in the desert at the end of June. The Eighth Army, under the direct command of General Auchinleck, stood at bay along a line bounded on its northern flank by the Mediterranean and on its southern by the impassable Qattra Depression. For the first time therefore there was no question of being outflanked by Rommel, which had happened every time so far along the battle-scarred road from el Agheila. Although the line was thirty-five miles long, it was only fifty miles from Alexandria which, although at a first glance seemed a calamity, had the advantage of needing a very short line of communication for supply and re-inforcement, as opposed to the miles of desert that Rommel had to cover.

There was no question, right from the beginning, of the Eighth Army playing a purely defensive rôle. However, owing to lack of reinforcements they could not do more than hold their own at first, but already the 8th Armoured Division had arrived and were being equipped with American Sherman Tanks and the 44th (Home Counties) and 51st (Highland) Division were expected shortly.

Rommel himself was in a scarcely better state. He had twelve tanks left when he arrived at the Alamein defences and a long and vulnerable supply line behind him across the desert. A desert he was to re-cross before very long.

At the end of June Lieut.-Colonel Goulburn arrived in Cairo from India where he had been instructing at the Quetta Staff College, to become second-in-command of the Regiment. He was met by a series of alarming stories. Individual members of the Regiment, who had taken part in the break-out from Gerawla and who had become separated from what remained of the Regiment, believed that they were the only survivors. In actual fact, during the next few days, more and more officers and men reported back to the Base Depot, Abbassia, and the state of the Regiment could then be assessed. Regimental Headquarters and the Composite Squadron, de-horsed in the break-out from Garawla, had lost their commanding officer, Lieut.-Colonel Kilkelly, Captain Earl, Lieutenant Lockhart, 2nd Lieutenant Buist and a number of tank crews. 'C' Squadron, under Major Hackett, with its squadron 'B' Echelon, was intact at Amyria and still under command of the 1st Armoured Division. The Regimental 'B' Echelon under Major Sir Edward Malet, which had been ordered out of Garawla before it was cut off, was more or less complete.

In the absence of the Commanding Officer, for it was not known until later that Lieut.-Colonel Kilkelly was a prisoner of war, Lieut.-Colonel Goulburn assumed command of the Regiment, this being confirmed by General Headquarters a day or two later. He made it quite clear to all concerned that the Regiment was still in being. On

July 2nd maintenance was carried out on the twenty-seven 'B' vehicles which had reported back under Malet. On July 4th Lieut.-Colonel Goulburn organised the Regiment into a small Regimental Headquarters, with Major Phillips as his second-in-command, Captain Wagstaffe as Adjutant and Lieutenant Hall as Technical Adjutant, and one Squadron, 'A', under command of Major Harbord, with Captain Huth, second-in-command, Lieutenants Adams and Bates, troop leaders, and a hundred and thirty-two other ranks. Other officers who had been extra regimentally employed, including Captain M. Harari, rejoined the Regiment, and on July 6th individual training was started. On that day, too, Lieut.-Colonel Goulburn gave a 'pep' talk to all ranks.

On July 8th the Regiment was ordered to move to the Khatatba road junction on the Cairo-Alexandria road, where the Reinforcement Squadron of the Tank Delivery Regiment was located. Here they came under command of the 1st Armoured Brigade. Lieutenants J. E. Chapman and A. R. Newman, who had previously served in the Regiment as Sergeant and Lance Corporal respectively, rejoined here. On the following day Lieut.-Colonel Goulburn visited 'C' Squadron at Amyria and found them in good heart.

On July 12th, Lieut.-Colonel Goulburn attended a conference at the Headquarters of the 1st Armoured Brigade, under Brigadier G. Todd, at Amyria and was ordered to find one Squadron to come under command of the 4th Hussars. The 4th Hussars, which in common with other Regiments had suffered heavy casualties, was then to be called the 4/8th Hussars. For this task, Lieut.-Colonel Goulburn selected Major Hackett and 'C' Squadron, which, as already explained, was at Amyria and intact, although temporarily without tanks. The story of this Squadron will follow in the next chapter.

On July 13th, the Regiment, consisting of Regimental Headquarters and 'A' Squadron, moved to the comparative luxury of the tented reinforcement camp at Khatatba, and the Commanding Officer visited Major-General McCreery (Major-General Armoured Fighting Vehicles) at General Headquarters, Cairo, to find out the proposed future rôle of the Regiment. He was informed that, for the time being, they were to act as reinforcement to the 4/8th Hussars, and that they were to draw their complement of Stuart tanks from the Tank Delivery Regiment at once.

The next ten days were spent in Khatatba, drawing tanks and carrying out training. On July 25th the Regiment was ordered to move to Ikingi Maryut where they leaguered alongside Headquarters, 1st Armoured Brigade, on the shores of Lake Maryut, and Lieutenants A. V. Case and J. N. Lombard joined. During the next four weeks, troop and squadron training was carried out actively, while some reinforcement tank crews, obtained after much opposition on the part of General Headquarters, joined the Regiment from the Reinforcement Squadron. Some tank Commanders were selected by the Commanding Officer from the Base Depot, Abbassia, with the assistance of Major de Courpalay, 8th Hussars. By this time 'A' Squadron had become semi-operational and, on August 25th, they were ordered to go forward with the rôle of protection on Main Headquarters, Eighth Army, from ground or sea attack. Eighth Army Headquarters was set up at Burg el Arab between the road and the sea, and 'A' Squadron, which was moved on transporters, leaguered half a mile from the Headquarters, immediately south of the road. Permission was granted to the Squadron to continue training, provided one troop remained in leaguer at immediate call, and a Squadron Liaison officer stayed at Army Headquarters. Full advantage was taken of this arrangement even to the extent of carrying out gunnery practice.

Regimental Headquarters and Headquarters Squadron remained at Maryut in the rôle of anti-paratroop defence until this task was taken over by the Free French. On August 31st they were ordered to move to Sidi Bishr Camp on the eastern edge of Alexandria. We will leave them there and continue the story of 'C' Squadron.

(b) 'C' Squadron as part of the 4/8th Hussars, July 1942

'C' SQUADRON under Major Hackett was last described as coming under command of the 4th Hussars on July 12th. Although a composite regiment, to be known thereafter as 4/8th Hussars, was thus formed, it must be clearly understood that the 8th Hussars, consisting of the Regiment less two Squadrons, remained in being throughout this time. At no time were they in suspended animation.

On July 14th, 'C' Squadron joined the 4th Hussars, moving up on transporters with a full complement of sixteen Stuart tanks. The Squadron was made up of Major J. W. Hackett, Squadron Leader, Captain H. H. Firth, second-in-command, Lieutenant Newman, 2nd Lieutenants J. H. G. Ladenburg, D. S. Scott and Bates, troop leaders, and 2nd Lieutenant A. F. McClintock, 'B' Echelon. The 4th Hussars under Lieut-Colonel Shepherd, D.S.O., were at Hammam and formed part of the newly organised 4th Light Armoured Brigade under Brigadier W. G. Carr, D.S.O. The Brigade consisted of the 4/8th Hussars, light tanks; 11th Hussars, armoured cars; 12th Lancers, armoured cars; one battery the 3rd Royal Horse Artillery, 25-pounders, and one company the 9th Rifle Brigade, motorised infantry. The primary rôle of the Brigade was deep reconnaissance, with a secondary rôle of the follow up of any successful break-through by the Eighth Army. The Brigade itself was under command of the 7th Armoured Division, under Major-General J. M. L. Renton, whose area comprised the southern end of the front.

July was not an active month for the Division, or in fact for any of the Eighth Army, although there was a good deal of skirmishing round Tel el Aisa and Ruweisat Ridge. Both sides had more or less fought themselves to a standstill and, apart from tentative probings on the part of their mobile columns, were content to rest and refit and prepare for what lay ahead. The Eighth Army lay watchful and aggressive behind its front line of wire and minefields. It was desperately hot and a perpetual horde of flies covered food and men alike. Throughout the hours of daylight they were on every bite that was eaten, in cups of tea, on scratches and sores; they tormented, disgusted and brought sickness with them.

July 16th to 20th was spent in training by 'C' Squadron, which had also been christened Eight Squadron and on July 21st the 4th Light Armoured Brigade was reorganised on the basis of one squadron of light tanks to one regiment of armoured cars. 'C' Squadron joined the 12th Lancers, commanded by Lieut.-Colonel G. Kidston, M.C., the group containing also one troop of 'J' Battery, Royal Horse Artillery, 25-pounders, and one platoon the 9th Rifle Brigade, and on July 22nd the group moved west to the Munassib Depression.

On July 24th the Squadron carried out a ground reconnaissance into the Qattara Depression to test the going, and two days later a reconnaissance of the Abu Dweis pass was made. This entailed advancing westwards through the Depression and then north-wards up the pass in the escarpment which marked the northern limit of the Depression.

The top of the pass was found blocked by a minefield and covered by artillery. Fortunately the enemy were caught unawares, and the tanks were able to withdraw down the steep, narrow and winding pass without casualties.

On the night of July 27th, the whole 4th Armoured Brigade moved north under cover of darkness to support an attack by the Eighth Army in the northern sector. The Brigade was not employed, however, and returned on the following night to their original area, with the exception of the 12th Lancer Group, including 'C' Squadron, which occupied an area immediately west of Qaret Himeimat.

The following day Major Hackett, whose award of the D.S.O. had just come through, and who had been suffering for some days from malaria, was evacuated to the Delta. Captain Firth took over command of the Squadron with Lieutenant Ladenburg as second-in-command.

Two further reconnaissances of the Qattara Depression found that the enemy had established guns in emplacements at various points along the top of the escarpment, proving that the continual activity of Eight Squadron in the Depression had made him nervous of his southern flank.

On August 1st the 12th Lancer Group was broken up and 'C' Squadron rejoined the 4th Hussars three miles south of Munassib. An air reconnaissance report of the movement of an enemy unit southwards towards the Abu Dweis pass caused some excitement that day. 'C' Squadron was ordered to ambush the column if it descended the pass into the Depression. Two troops under Lieutenant Newman occupied suitable positions, but by last light the enemy had not shown up and they were withdrawn.

August 1942. A fateful month for the Eighth Army and, through them, for the world. A month of little activity, of much training, of many changes, culminating in a battle, the first of a sequence that led from the fiercely-contested ridges round el Alamein to the white walls of Tunis.

Elsewhere in the world there were no outstanding happenings in August. During July the events of most note were the stopping of the deadly Russian convoys (twenty-three out of thirty-four ships had been sunk in the convoy PQ 17 owing to pack ice keeping them on a too southerly route); the first introduction of 'window' in a raid over Hamburg; the surge forward of the Germans in Russia all along the line and the planning of 'Torch', as the landings in North Africa were to be called.

In August events moved slowly forward. There were some setbacks too, the tragic Malta convoys from one of which only five ships reached harbour out of fourteen, and the heavy casualties of the Dieppe Raid. But one event warmed the cockles of the Eighth Army's heart. Mr. Churchill visited them in the Desert and as a result of that visit brought about changes that were to have far-reaching consequences.

Chief of the changes in the Eighth Army were those in the higher command. On August 8th General Alexander became Commander-in-Chief, the Near East, relieving General Auchinleck. Lieut.-General Gott took over the Eighth Army from Lieut.-General Ritchie but was almost at once killed as a result of an air crash, and he in turn was succeeded by General Montgomery.

On August 6th Major Hackett returned to the Squadron, and on August 10th Captain Gwyn came up to take over second-in-command. During this period, the 4/8th Hussars moved a few miles westwards to protect the engineers and infantry who were strengthening the southern sector of the front by laying new minefields. This sector was regarded by Army Headquarters as the weakest part of the el Alamein line and the most likely flank of any enemy attack. In fact, the 4th Armoured Brigade, which was far from being heavily armoured, and unlikely to be able to beat off any major attack, was now given the rôle, in the event of this attack materialising, of withdrawing slowly towards Samaret Gaballa and harassing and delaying the enemy as much as possible. Some training, including gunnery practice, was organised with this task in view. Sickness in the form of mild dysentry and desert sores was taking its toll, but the situation was eased by Lieut.-Colonel Goulburn sending up from Regimental Headquarters sufficient tank crews to man one complete troop. This permitted one troop of 'C' Squadron to go to the Delta on leave, in rotation. 2nd Lieutenants Case and W. St. L. Tisdall also came up for a turn with the Squadron.

On August 14th, Captain Gwyn commanding two troops led by 2nd Lieutenant J. N. Lombard and Sergeant Melsom, carried out a very valuable reconnaissance of enemy gun positions in the Taqa Plateau. Heavily engaged by gun-fire, he located a gap in the defences which he penetrated with great skill, making full use of the ground. He then turned south and worked his way back without losing any tanks. His information on gun positions and minefields was most useful.

On August 16th, another valuable and gallant reconnaissance was carried out by Lieutenant Ladenburg commanding two troops, under Lieutenant Bates and Sergeant Knill and accompanied by a gunner-observer in a Stuart tank who had a call on one sniping 25-pounder located well forward. The object of the reconnaissance was to locate a suspected enemy minefield between the escarpment of the Qattara Depression and the Taqa Plateau, and to continue advancing westwards, if possible, to pin-point enemy positions as far as the 86 Easting grid line. At about midday the patrol arrived on the high ground where they were accurately engaged by high explosive fire from unseen guns. They took cover in a nearby wadi from whence a dismounted party from the tanks climbed up the west side of the wadi. From here they could see some enemy on their feet, and the latter were effectively engaged by the sniping 25-pounder. The patrol then advanced in a north-westerly direction, emerging from the wadi in single file. Bates, who was in the lead, was engaged by three enemy anti-tank guns as he crossed some open ground. His troop took cover behind a ridge and Bates himself carried out a reconnaissance on foot, locating an enemy minefield, wired on both sides. Unfortunately the gunner-observer had remained in his original position and could not see the anti-tank guns and engage them. Bates, subsequently, led his troop back across the open ground without sustaining any casualties, and the whole patrol withdrew eastwards. This was a skilful and daring reconnaissance which brought back valuable information without losing a tank.

Throughout this period, when 'C' Squadron was under command of the 4th Hussars, Lieut.-Colonel Goulburn visited the Squadron on a number of occasions. The Squadron was visited, too by the Divisional, Corps and Army Commanders. This was the first but by no means the last visit of the latter, General Montgomery. He spoke to the Regiment as one who was master of the situation, and was able to give them a clear picture of the part they were to play in the forthcoming battles. These forecasts, which subsequently in the battle of Alam Halfa proved to be remarkably correct, gave the Regiment a confidence in him which remained as an inspiration to them until victory came in Europe.

A change of command occurred in the 4/8th Hussars which had its repercussions upon 'C' Squadron. Lieut.-Colonel Shepherd was posted as second-in-command of the 27th Armoured Brigade and Major Kidd, 4th Hussars, took over the Regiment, with Major Hackett, 8th Hussars, as his second-in-command. Thereupon Captain Gwyn became Squadron Leader, with Ladenburg, second-in-command, and Bates, Lombard, Tisdall, and Sergeant Knill troop leaders.

H

Towards the end of August, and with a growing moon, more and more information pointed to an early attack by the enemy, and all indications were that it would fall upon the southern sector. To counter this attack General Montgomery had reorganised his forces to form a new reserve formation, 10 Corps, which was given the rôle of holding, as a lay-back position, the important Alam Halfa ridge. This ridge ran north-east, south-west, several miles to the rear of the Alamein Line, which was held by 13 and 30 Corps, a truly Imperial force including the 9th Australian Division north on the coast, the 1st South African Division, the 5th Indian Division and the 2nd New Zealand Division. Between the last two ran the Ruweisat Ridge, east and west, and behind the New Zealanders lay Alam Halfa, held by 10 Corps with the 10th Armoured Division at its southern foot and the 44th Infantry Division entrenched upon its crest. South of the New Zealanders and facing the main German thrust was the 7th Armoured Division. If the enemy penetrated the Alamein defences in the southern sector, his subsequent progress would depend on securing the Alam Halfa ridge. If it remained in our hands, it would serve either as a base from which to block the enemy's progress to the north towards Ruweisat Ridge, and the backbone of the Army's defences in the central sectors, or alternatively to cut the axis of any hostile thrust attempting to strike east or north-east towards the Nile. Facing our defences the Axis forces under Field Marshal Rommel comprised five German divisions, the 15th and 21st Panzer Divisions, the 90th Light Division, the 164th Infantry Division, the Rameke division of parachutists, and nine Italian divisions including the Ariete and Littorio Armoured Divisions.

General Montgomery had banked on Rommel following the plan of attack that he subsequently did follow, and had gone to enormous trouble to make sure that he did this, such as the planting of maps with the bad going marked as good. His plan then was to lure the German armour through the minefields to the south, withdrawing before it into the soft sand below Alam Halfa and under the guns of the 44th Division.

This was precisely what Rommel did. He made two feint attacks, one in the north which was brushed aside by the Australians, and one against the Indians which succeeded temporarily but later in the day was thrown back. But the main attack came in the south in this, his last desperate attempt to reach Egypt and the Nile.

(c) The Battle of Alam Halfa, September 1942

JUST after midnight on August 30th 'C' Squadron saw the Very lights of the expected enemy attack go up. From the forward positions it was possible to see, by the bright moonlight, masses of enemy vehicles forming up behind the westerly minefields. Rommel's attack began with two simultaneous thrusts, a holding attack in the centre which was held after some initial success; and the main thrust, as expected, in the south. Bates' troop was sent forward to support the 1/60th Rifle Brigade anti-tank guns which were covering our minefields. At the same time bombs fell among the Squadron 'B' Echelon, killing Troopers Emblem and Janney, and severely wounding Lance Corporal Hunt and Troopers Wilson and Chapman. At 5.15 a.m. on the 31st, the 1/60th Rifle Brigade began their withdrawal in accordance with orders not to get pinned to the ground, and the rest of 'C' Squadron moved up to protect their anti-tank guns which had been left to the last moment. Large masses of enemy vehicles could be seen formed up on the far side of the minefield while the enemy engineers were busy clearing gaps, and not long afterwards the leading enemy tanks were through, closely followed by the infantry. At about 9 a.m., Lieut.-Colonel Goulburn turned up unexpectedly on a routine visit to the Squadron. He had met the 1/60th Rifle Brigade and learnt of the enemy attack. Shortly afterwards the Squadron was dive-bombed by four enemy aircraft and the two anti-tank guns of the 1/60th Rifle Brigade, 6-pounder portées, were knocked out, their crews being killed or wounded. One portée was set on fire and, while the ammunition was exploding, Lieut.-Colonel Goulburn extracted one of the crew who had lost both his legs. Fortunately no casualties had been sustained by the Squadron, and after some long range and ineffective shooting, they were ordered to withdraw, keeping contact with the advancing enemy who were still pouring through gaps in the minefields. Contact was maintained all through the day until 4 p.m. when the enemy easterly advance appeared to change to a north-easterly direction, and the Squadron was ordered to withdraw further eastwards to leaguer at el Wesheika near Gaballa, which, after a long and very slow march, they reached late at night. Lieut.-Colonel Goulburn in the meantime had left the Squadron during the afternoon, and calling first upon Brigadier Carr at Headquarters, 4th Light Armoured Brigade at Gaballa, he resumed his journey to Headquarters Eighth Army where he had a personal interview with General Montgomery that night, and was able to confirm the north-easterly direction of the enemy thrust line which was the General's main pre-occupation. He acted thus as a useful liaison officer and was complimented by the General on the clear picture he presented.

On September 1st the 4/8th Hussars moved off from their leaguer before dawn and, after a long march first eastwards and then southwards, reached Munqar Afram in the Qattara depression. 'C' Squadron was immediately sent off to reconnoitre an ascent up the escarpment between Qaret Somara and Qor el Laban, and to locate, if possible, the enemy's right flank. No contact was made with the enemy, which added further confirmation to the rumour that the whole of the enemy's force had swung north-eastwards. In fact the enemy had advanced towards the Alam Halfa ridge and had met the 10th Armoured Division in their carefully reconnoitred battle position on ground of their own choosing. The Italians had come to grief under the guns of the 2nd New Zealand Division and twice during the day Rommel's Panzers went in to the attack, only to be repulsed with heavy casualties in the sand below Alam Halfa. There they settled down and awaited attack.

By first light on September 2nd the remainder of the 4/8th Hussars had joined 'C' Squadron, and were ordered to find the enemy southern flank and to mount harassing attacks against it. The Regiment, with 'C' Squadron leading, advanced to Humar, from where large numbers of enemy transport vehicles could be seen near Gaballa. Lieut.-Colonel Kidd ordered the two 4th Hussar Squadrons to attack, holding 'C' Squadron in reserve. Both squadrons advanced rapidly and, taking advantage of the surprise created, drove in among the enemy transport, destroying some fifty vehicles and killing or wounding approximately two hundred men. This was a most successful attack and resulted in no loss among our own tanks and very few casualties. During the afternoon 'C' Squadron remained in observation near Humar, and rejoined the Regiment at last light to leaguer in the Depression.

In the meantime, the Axis forces proved reluctant to resume the offensive against the 10th Armoured Division. It was not General Montgomery's policy to attack, however tempting the target, and they were plainly disconcerted by their failure to draw his armour from its prepared position. Rommel, unable to bring up supplies was finding the administrative situation difficult, and furthermore, the Desert Air Force was causing great damage and confusion.

'C' Squadron was ordered to return to Humar on September 3rd and to carry out a harassing attack similar to that of the previous day, but further to the west, should a suitable target present itself. Moving in a north-westerly direction, they came under anti-tank gun-fire, and, as all elements of a surprise attack had been lost, they were recalled. They had collected some useful information, however, of gun positions, and of the fact that the ground between Humar and Qaret Himeimat was held by the enemy. That night the Regiment did not return to the Depression but leaguered on top of the escarpment between Somara and Gaballa.

Further north, in the area of the main attack, first light reports that day indicated that the enemy had withdrawn from contact and moved south and slightly westwards. General Montgomery therefore ordered 13 Corps to attack that night in a southerly direction to close the minefield gaps through which the enemy attack had come. Air reconnaissance that afternoon reported large enemy columns moving west from the minefield area.

At first light on September 4th 'C' Squadron was back at Humar with a similar harassing rôle. Advancing towards Himeimat they engaged by fire some enemy transport at long range. At this moment twenty enemy tanks were seen on the top of the escarpment moving towards the Squadron, a danger which compelled Major Gwyn to withdraw before they became cut off. Captain Ladenburg's tank was hit three times but not knocked out. Later in the day Lieut.-Colonel Kidd ordered all three squadrons to attack enemy transport north of Deir el Risw. But just as they were moving off, seventeen enemy Mk. III's advanced down the escarpment towards Humar. A defensive plan was made quickly to protect the 25-pounders which were operating in support of the Regiment. The enemy halted at a range of about two thousand yards and engaged the Regiment with both high explosive and machine-gun fire. This, however, was outside the range of the Stuart tanks, and at dusk the enemy withdrew.

In the north, the attack by the New Zealand Division of 13 Corps to close the gap in the minefields was met with a fierce reaction. Bitter fighting took place and the enemy launched heavy and repeated counter-attacks to repel this attempt to bottle him. He was not cut off, but was forced slowly and relentlessly back throughout the day, leaving the desert littered with his wrecked vehicles and tanks.

The 4/8th Hussars, ordered to operate again in the Himeimat area on September 5th, found no targets and the day was uneventful.

In the main battle area the enemy counter-attack to keep open his line of withdrawal continued, while his main forces continued moving westwards through the minefields.

The 7th Armoured Division continued their pursuit throughout the 6th. There was nothing in the nature of a triumphal surge forward, General Montgomery made it clear that they should drive the enemy so far and no further, in his opinion they were neither equipped nor at the moment trained for more.

Meanwhile 'C' Squadron carried on as before. At first light they were back at Humar, but on this morning there was a heavy mist and visibility was practically nil. A fair indication that there were no enemy about, however, was provided by a herd of gazelle grazing peacefully close by. The surprise therefore was all the greater, when the mist lifted, and a German 8-wheel armoured car, two 4-wheelers and a British 6-pounder portée were seen two thousand yards to the west.

The enemy seemed unaware of the presence of the Squadron, but the ground allowed no chance of approaching them unseen, and almost as soon as the Squadron began to advance they made off west at speed towards their own defended area.

At 11 a.m. Major Gwyn was ordered to reach the gap in the Taqa Plateau, and was given two 6-pounders in support. The Squadron moved westwards through the Qattara Depression, every tank carrying extra petrol which was to be dumped in a suitable place. Leaving Captain Ladenburg in command of half the Squadron, the additional petrol and two 6-pounders to form a reserve, Gwyn continued his advance westwards with the two remaining troops under Bates and Lombard, climbed the escarpment by one of the passes and advanced across the Taqa Plateau. In the meantime Ladenburg had spotted three enemy 50-mm. anti-tank guns moving westwards along the top of the escarpment with the intention of cutting off Gwyn's withdrawal down the pass. Gwyn, informed of this fact, continued his advance towards his objective until Bates, in the leading troop, was engaged by a concealed anti-tank gun only two hundred yards from the Taqa gap. A direct hit was sustained on his tank which, however, was not disabled. Having obtained the required information that the gap was held, Gwyn was faced with the problem of withdrawing, with the knowledge that the pass behind him was now denied to him. Continuing therefore in an even further westerly direction, and under enemy fire for most of the way, he skilfully led his troop down the escarpment by a previously unknown route and regained the depression.

Meanwhile Ladenburg's party below was shooting with machine-guns at the enemy on the other pass, but the range was too great and results could not be observed. The whole Squadron returned at last light and it was reported later that the enemy had moved a number of tanks up.

Meanwhile in the area of the main enemy withdrawal, fighting continued between the two minefield belts, and it was clear that they meant to retain their foothold here and were prepared to fight for it.

'C' Squadron was out again at first light on September 7th in observation. In the afternoon, combined with one of the 4th Hussar Squadrons and under command of Major Archer, 4th Hussars, they were ordered to advance north towards Himeimat. They were held up, however, by an enemy force estimated at about twelve Mk. III and Italian tanks and, after an exchange of fire, the two Squadrons were ordered to withdraw.

On this day General Montgomery called off the battle, leaving the enemy in possession of the western edge of our original minefields. The victory of Alam Halfa had a profound effect on the morale of the Eighth Army, and the troops entered into the preparation for the decisive battle that was to come with tremendous enthusiasm. This battle of Alam Halfa was a vital action, because, had it been lost, Egypt might well have been lost as well. In winning it the way was paved for success at el Alamein and the subsequent advance to Tunisia.

On 11th September, the 4/8th Hussars went into reserve north-east of Gaballa, and Lieut.-Colonel Goulburn ordered 'A' Squadron, under Major Harbord, which throughout this time had continued in their rôle of protection of Eighth Army Headquarters, to relieve 'C' Squadron. 'C' Squadron, with the exception of Captain Gwyn and twenty-five other ranks who were transferred to 'A' Squadron, were withdrawn to Burg el Arab, and all personnel were sent on leave.

The period spent by 'A' Squadron at Headquarters Eighth Army near Burg el Arab from 25th August to 11th September had been of the greatest value to them. Reinforcements had not been easy to come by, and the Squadron had had to accept fifty men who had never been in tanks before. But under the skilled hand of Major Harbord the

Squadron had now become a team, and the Commanding Officer deemed them sufficiently battle-worthy to take over from 'C' who were in need of a rest.

At the end of September, Brigadier Carr, strongly supported by Lieut.-Colonel Goulburn, recommended to the Commander, 7th Armoured Division that Regimental Headquarters, 8th Hussars should take over from Regimental Headquarters, 4th Hussars. His request, however, was refused on the grounds that the 4th Hussars element in the Regiment so outweighed that of the 8th Hussars, that a 4th Hussar officer should command it. Regimental Headquarters, 8th Hussars was condemned, therefore, to the frustrating and inactive rôle of remaining in Sidi Bishr Camp with 'C' Squadron at Burg el Arab, and 'A' Squadron under command 4th Hussars in the forward area.

While the Eighth Army were preparing actively for the coming offensive, the 4/8th Hussars, still a part of the 4th Light Armoured Brigade in the 7th Armoured Division remained in the southern sector sharing in the lull in operations which followed the victory of Alam Halfa.

During this time, however, active preparations were being carried out for the coming offensive of the Eighth Army, to be known as the Battle of Alamein. A carefully-arranged cover plan was organised in order to mislead the enemy about the direction of the main thrusts and the date of our readiness to attack. The basis of 'visual deception' was the preservation of a constant density of vehicles throughout the zone of operations so that the enemy would be denied the inferences made from the changes disclosed in day to day air photography. By means of the construction of a large number of dummy lorries, this collection of vehicles required for the assault in the northern sector was established as early as October 1st. Meanwhile, active measures were employed to cause the enemy to believe that the main blow would be delivered in the south where the 7th Armoured Division was located. A dummy pipeline and dummy dumps were constructed in that area.

In broad outline, General Montgomery's plan was, firstly, to penetrate the mine-field belts and blow a hole in the enemy positions; then to destroy methodically the enemy infantry divisions holding their defensive positions. Those positions were forward, between and behind minefields, and were from four to six miles in depth. For success, the method depended on holding off the enemy's armour while the methodical destruction or 'crumbling' was carried out. To do this, it would be necessary to position our own armour beyond the area of the 'crumbling' operations, on ground of its own choosing, in order to hold off the enemy tanks.

General Montgomery's orders provided for three simultaneous attacks. The main thrust by Lieut.-General Leese's 30 Corps had the task of forcing two corridors through the enemy's minefields. Lieut.-General Lumsden's 10 Corps was to pass through one of these corridors and hold off the enemy armour from interfering with 30 Corps' 'crumbling' operations. The rôle of Lieut.-General Horrocks' 13 Corps was primarily to mislead the enemy into believing that our main thrust was being delivered in the south, and to contain enemy forces there, particularly the 21st Panzer Division. The 7th Armoured Division was available for this operation, but was to be kept intact for a break-through northwards towards Daba if all went well. The Corps Commander was faced, therefore, with the difficulty of two conflicting tasks. He planned to penetrate the minefield immediately north of Himeimat with the 44th Division and then to pass through his two armoured brigades, the 4th Light Armoured Brigade and the 22nd Armoured Brigade, to establish bridgeheads beyond.

Now once more the Eighth Army was to be given the chance of proving itself against the lately victorious Germans. This time they had new tanks, new troops and a new Commander. The Afrika Korps was heavily armed too, but it lacked one vital thing. "Rommel," it has been said, "*was* the Afrika Korps"[1] and on the October 23rd Rommel was in Germany, ill.

(*d*) 'A' Squadron and the Battle of Alamein, October 1942

'A' SQUADRON, described in the 4/8th Hussars as Eight Squadron like their predecessor 'C' Squadron, spent the day of October 22nd south-west of the Alam Halfa ridge. After dark they formed up with the rest of the regiment, and with the 1/60th Rifle Brigade and 'M' Battery, 3rd Royal Horse Artillery in four columns facing west. This was the eve of no ordinary battle. The planning, the training and the waiting of the last few months were the prelude to a turning of the tide. A tide which was to flow in favour of the Allies, and which, overwhelming all those who stood in its path, would carry them forward slowly but surely to victory. At 9.40 p.m. the battle opened with a barrage from one thousand guns which could be heard very clearly by the rest of the 8th Hussars, fifty miles away in Alexandria. The column marched forward by shaded lamps through previously prepared gaps in our own minefields. They then halted until 3.30 a.m. on October 23rd.

The two enemy minefields had been given the code names 'January' and 'February', the latter being the most westerly one. Shortly before dawn 'January' had been penetrated by the 44th Division and the 22nd Armoured Brigade had been passed through. It was clear that the penetration of 'February' would no longer be possible under cover of darkness, and that in daylight it would be a very costly operation. It was decided therefore to resume the attack that night. 'A' Squadron, still on our own side of the enemy minefields, was employed throughout the day in forming a protective flank north of the main axis of advance. As soon as it was dark they formed up again on the axis with the rest of the 4th Light Armoured Brigade, now commanded by Brigadier M. Roddick who had taken over from Brigadier Carr just before the battle, and advanced westwards to within three quarters of a mile of 'January' minefield. Here they halted for some hours as it appeared that 'February' had not yet been penetrated.

At 3.30 a.m., on the 24th, the advance was resumed and the Squadron passed through 'January'. Before they were clear of the gap, however, they were ordered to halt and close up. While doing so they came under heavy enemy fire. Sergeant Major Kirkham's tank received a direct hit which broke a track. Corporal Howard's tank also had a track blown off, and a third tank was blown up on a mine. Major Harbord was ordered to withdraw his Squadron back to the east side of 'January'. They spent the rest of the day again forming a defensive screen on the north flank of the Division.

In the minefield area, during the night of the 23rd/24th, the 131st (Queens) Brigade was put under command of the Division and secured a bridgehead west of the second enemy minefield, 'February'. But they quickly became pinned to the ground by enemy fire, and efforts to clear a lane for the armour proved slow and costly. Eventually two

[1] *Rommel* by Desmond Young.

regiments of the 22nd Armoured Brigade moved forward to pass through the gap, but immediately began to lose tanks from both anti-tank fire, and scattered mines. In view of the instructions which the Divisional Commander, Lieut.-General Sir John Harding, had received, he had no alternative but to abandon further attempts to move the armour through.

During the afternoon of October 25th the 4/8th Hussars in company with the 60th Rifles and one battery, the Royal Horse Artillery were ordered to advance north-west-wards in support of operations by the 50th Division on the right. The objectives were some pockets of enemy resistance on the east side of their minefields. The force moved off in two columns, led on the right by 'A' Squadron and on the left by 'A' Squadron, 4th Hussars. They had not gone far when 'A' Squadron was engaged by concealed enemy 88-mm. anti-tank guns and quickly lost five tanks. Almost simultaneously 'A' Squadron, 4th Hussars, ran into an unsuspected minefield losing all their tanks except two. The force was then ordered to withdraw. This was an unfortunate affair. Personnel casualties within the Squadron, however, were light, Trooper Bellantyne being killed and Corporals Emery and Scrugham wounded.

It was on this day that 13 Corps was ordered not to press the attack in the southern sector.

On the 26th 'A' Squadron was given the remaining two tanks of 'A' Squadron, 4th Hussars, and Major Harbord sent his de-horsed crews with 2nd Lieutenants R. P. G. Dill and P. Dale Smith back to the Tank Reinforcement Squadron. The 4/8th Hussars were now ordered to remain in observation of the ground northwards towards 50th Division. They carried out this rôle until the afternoon of the 27th, when they were ordered to move back into reserve at Qaret el Humar. Here they leaguered for the night.

The 4/8th Hussars spent the 28th and 29th October in reserve at Qaret el Humar. 13 Corps had now been ordered to go on the defensive and stage no further major opera-tions. They were to prolong the enemy's anxiety, however, by means of patrols and artillery action. Despite their failure to form a bridgehead west of the enemy minefields with their armour, they had fulfilled their primary rôle, which was to contain the 21st Panzer Division in the south until October 26th, and had inflicted heavy casualties on the enemy in the area between his two mine belts. Rommel by now had returned to take command but, unfortunately, for him, too late. General Stumme, who had been in command, had died of a heart attack twenty-four hours after the Eighth Army assault began. The 15th Panzer Division in the north flung in attack after attack, especially at Kidney Ridge, but could gain no ground and lost many tanks.

On October 30th, Captain Firth arrived to take over second-in-command of the Squadron from Captain Gwyn. It will be remembered that he had been commanding 'C' Squadron for a time before its relief by 'A' Squadron.

Three tanks sent forward by 'C' Squadron from Bourg el Arab arrived to reinforce 'A' Squadron.

That night Captain Harari carried out on foot a reconnaissance of the fifteen Stuart tanks lost on the 25th by 'A' Squadron, 4th Hussars and 'A' Squadron. He was ordered to remove the paybooks of the dead crews and any maps which he could find. The derelict tanks covered an area of approximately one square mile and were more or less evenly scattered about.

"As the moon was nearly full," wrote Captain Harari, "and a party of men would have been clearly visible, I preferred to leave the patrol halted before reaching the task area, and advanced with Corporal Lister of the East Yorks, to examine the furthest tanks, instructing Corporal Winch to inspect the near ones. Everything that might have been of value to the enemy was removed, and the frequencies altered on the wireless sets. I was unable to visit the foremost tank, however, as it was patrolled by an enemy listening post, though I crawled to within seventy yards of it. Corporal Lister remained in the shadow of a tank, a little further back.

"I was presumably seen or heard as I was challenged and several flares went up accompanied by a burst of machine-gun fire. After lying low for half an hour I decided to return and reached the East Yorks lines at 3 a.m. My activities were much hampered by enemy patrols and a vehicle which kept moving about nearby. The moon, which had risen at nine, made everything but the slowest movement difficult. I saw no sign of the East Yorks patrol on my way back, though they apparently waited for me until 04.30."

The 4/8th Hussars continued to be held in reserve until November 3rd, in the area of Qaret el Humar, and efforts by 'A' Squadron to recover some of the fifteen Stuart tanks occupied most of their time. On the night of October 31st/November 1st, Harari, in company with a patrol of the 1st King's Royal Rifle Corps, carried out another reconnaissance, and selected four tanks as a first attempt at salvage. He removed the wireless sets from two others. Moving about by night in a minefield area was a dangerous job, and Harari's work showed great credit. On the morning of November 1st, he guided two Infantry tanks, Mk. II, towards the Stuarts. But one of them ran over a mine and the attempt at recovery had to be abandoned owing to enemy shelling. Later that day Major J. D. Harbord and S.S.M. Kirkham took advantage of a quiet moment when a small enemy party advanced with a white flag to request a two-hour truce period on the following day to bury their dead. They went forward to look at the tanks and make a plan for recovery on the following day. After dark on the 2nd, Harbord, Harari, S.S.M. Kirkham, Sergeant Fry and Lance Corporal Winch conducted four Scammel recovery vehicles to the forward positions of the Royal West Kents. They were unable to start operations, however, until after midnight owing to a local attack planned by the infantry for 10 p.m. The Scammels, however, succeeded in recovering only one tank before dawn, and, as the Squadron was ordered to move on the afternoon of the 3rd, no further attempts were possible.

No attempt will be made to describe the main thrust by 30 Corps in the northern sector. Sufficient to say that the battle had been raging for a week before 10 Corps, containing most of our armour, could be passed through into the open country behind the enemy position, bring Rommel's panzers to battle, and get astride his lines of communication. In the meantime, General Montgomery had re-grouped his forces, which included the movement north on October 31st of the 7th Armoured Division, less the 4th Light Armoured Brigade which was to follow later. The 7th Armoured Division went into Army reserve fifteen miles east of el Alamein, awaiting the opportunity to exploit the break-through which was expected shortly.

At midday on November 3rd, the 4/8th Hussars, with the remainder of the 4th Light Armoured Brigade, moved north to join the Division east of el Alamein. That evening Lieut.-Colonel Goulburn and Major Huth arrived up from Regimental Headquarters to visit them. The War Diary mentions that "the Colonel brought some eggs, the first we had had for many weeks." He stayed the night in the Squadron leaguer and noted with pride that all ranks were straining at the leash for orders to advance and exploit the victory which, by now, had been fully confirmed. The last enemy anti-tank screen had been forced back and everywhere Rommel's forces were in full retreat.

(e) The Pursuit from Alamein, November 1942

AT 6 a.m. on November 4th the Squadron received orders to advance westwards. A word here might explain General Montgomery's plan for the pursuit. His intention was to cut the coast road at the bottlenecks of Fuka and Matruh. 10 Corps (consisting of the 1st and 7th Armoured and 2nd New Zealand Divisions) were to lead the chase. Meanwhile, to the south of the breakout area, 13 Corps formed mobile columns which raced westwards to round up the Italians, four of whose Divisions had been left by the Germans without transport and with very little food and water. The 4th Light Armoured Brigade found themselves under command of the 2nd New Zealand Division, and were directed upon Fuka which they reached that night, only to find the tail of the enemy was clear of its already.

'A' Squadron made no contact with the enemy that day, and on the 5th, after by-passing Daba to their north, and with their Squadron leading the 4/8th Hussars, they made rapid progress, contacting one small enemy column consisting of anti-tank guns and two Italian tanks. The Squadron moved two up, Four Troop (Lieutenant J. G. M. Young) right and One Troop (Lieutenant J. E. Chapman) left. During their night leaguer they were shot up by small arms fire, coming from what was believed to be a small enemy party trying to rejoin its unit. One petrol lorry was set on fire in the leaguer.

Moving on at first light on the 6th the Squadron, still leading the 4/8th Hussars, was directed upon Mersa Matruh. Very soon they made contact with a group of fourteen Panzers, German Mk. III's and IV's. 'M' battery, Royal Horse Artillery, came into action and the enemy withdrew. Soon after continuing the advance, Major Harbord was ordered to attack a small column of Italian transport which was seen to be moving parallel with them to the south. Major Harbord wheeled Two and Three Troops into line and raced at the enemy. Out came the white flags and the enemy surrendered. One and Four Troops, in the meantime, gave chase to some more vehicles and captured three lorries and three Opel staff cars. The total of prisoners was one hundred and thirty, of which seventy-five were Germans from the Rameke Parachute Brigade, and the remainder Italians. They were in a very bad state, both physically and mentally. "The Italians showed evident pleasure at being captured" says the Squadron War diary. The advance then continued, and the whole brigade leaguered together that night.

November 7th was a most unfortunate day for the pursuit forces. Heavy rain had started before dawn, and very soon every wheeled vehicle was bogged down, as were some of the tanks. Supply lorries were not able to move up to deliver petrol to the tanks, and little or no progress was made. Meanwhile Rommel's defeated forces were hurrying westwards on the one and only metalled road. The enemy made good use of this respite of some twenty-four hours.

'A' Squadron made better progress than some, but the Squadron War Diary described the day as follows: "A new day, and what a day! Rain had started during the night but we moved off at first light and had covered about six miles when orders came through to move south for about two miles, make the telegraph wires and follow them to where they intersected the Siwa track. This was all right, but the ground by this time was like a mud bath and it was still raining. By 4 p.m. all the wheeled vehicles had become bogged, and by the time the tanks neared the wires there were six bogged. Captain Harari's, Lieutenant Dill's and Lieutenant Chapman's were in mud up to the drivers' seats. Water was everywhere, and Corporal Pickergill's tank was a complete write-off. However, by 6 p.m. the Squadron was again complete after a hard day's digging, although three tanks did not come into leaguer until last light."

In the early hours of that morning the carefully planned Operation 'Torch' came into being, and British and American troops were landed on beaches in Morocco and Algeria. Rommel now had to turn about to face an attack from the west as well as the east, and still the relentless pursuit by the Eighth Army continued.

The Squadron continued the advance to Bir el Himla under the same terrible conditions on the 8th and 9th of November. There was much digging out of vehicles, and the continual towing was a great strain on the tanks, two of which had to be left behind as a result. Progress was slow and no contact was made with the enemy. At last light on November 9th leaguer was formed on the Kalder track.

"Our hardest day yet," the War Diary calls November 10th. "We broke leaguer at first light, making for the Charing Cross-Siwa road, which we all knew so well. We had our first "brew-up" at the old camp area by the fig tree on the road, and then made a fast run to Kilo 107. West of Sidi Barrani we met an anti-tank gun which quickly withdrew. The whole road from Mersa Matruh to west of Sidi Barrani was littered with burnt-out or disabled enemy tanks and wheeled vehicles, clear evidence of the destructive action of our Desert Air Force. A beautiful sight! At Kilo 120 we came under fire from a number of guns which, however, were silenced by 'M' battery. We then received orders to cut off some enemy transport on the road. We left the road and headed south-west at top speed. On reaching the landing ground at Kilo 130, at last light, we found it well defended by anti-tank guns. Permission to attack was not given."

The Squadron moved out of leaguer at first light on the 11th with orders to cut the road at Buq Buq. However, due south of Sidi Barrani heavy opposition was encountered and there was a delay of over an hour before they came into sight of the road and the tail of the enemy column. "And here a frustrating event overtook us," states the War Diary. "Our tanks began to run out of petrol and we had the galling experience of watching two 88-mm. guns escape westwards along the road and come into action far beyond our effective range. Here four more anti-tank guns joined them and we came under heavy and accurate fire. It was three hours before 'M' battery could silence them, and the advance towards Sollum continue."

The Squadron got to within one mile of Sollum but were then ordered to turn back and to come into Regimental leaguer below the Halfaya pass, having covered one hundred miles that day.

At 5.45 a.m. on November 12th the Squadron was ordered to carry out a reconnaissance of Sollum. An hour later they entered the village and found it deserted. They were then recalled to the foot of the Halfaya pass, where they refilled with petrol and had the pleasure of watching seven hundred prisoners being escorted eastwards. They then ascended the pass themselves and joined the Regiment on the top of the escarpment. Lieutenant Newman's tank could not make the grade and had to be left behind. The advance continued by Fort Capuzzo and Sidi Azeiz, familiar landmarks, and leaguer was formed at half past three. Lieutenant D. Dale Smith and Corporal Winch rejoined the Squadron unexpectedly that night in a jeep. The Squadron strength was then ten tanks.

The advance continued throughout the 13th but no contact was made. The 4th Light Armoured Brigade came under command of the 7th Armoured Division on this day.

On November 14th the 4/8th Hussars moved off at 6 a.m. following a track along the top of the escarpment. After a mid-day halt the Squadron took over the lead, descended the escarpment and reached the main road from Tobruk to Tmimi at Kilo 122. Some miles further west they were held up by fire and mines, where the road runs down an escarpment. After attempting to find a way round they were recalled to leaguer with the Regiment, at Kilo 115. That night it was decided that two more tanks were mechanically unfit to continue the advance. "Like the ten little nigger boys" says the Squadron War Diary, "then there were eight." The Squadron was reorganised into Squadron Headquarters and two troops commanded by Lieutenants Chapman and Young. Captain Firth was evacuated sick.

A Flying Column was organised on the 15th for the advance which was to continue towards Martuba. The composition was as follows: Headquarters, 4th Light Armoured Brigade (Brigadier M. G. Roddick); 'A' Squadron, 8th Hussars; one troop of Grant tanks of Royal Scots Greys; two troops of Armoured Cars; two troops Royal Horse Artillery (25 pounders); two troops of anti-tank guns; one company of the 60th Rifles, and one section of Royal Engineers.

'A' Squadron took the lead, and all went well until reaching Kilo 100 on the Via Balba where Lieutenant Chapman's tank was blown up on a mine. The crew suffered only superficial wounds, and S.S.M. Kirkham assumed command of the troop. The bridge at Tmimi, reputed by three natives as mined, caused some delay before the sapper section had cleared it. At Kilo 74, Captain Harari's tank, which was fourth in the order of march, hit a mine without causing casualties to the crew. "And then there were six." The Column reached Zt. Umm er Rzem at 4 p.m. and leaguered at Kilo 35. An enemy petrol dump containing two thousand jerry cans was found close to the road, but unfortunately the petrol was Grade III and not suitable for the tanks.

There was little rest for a Flying Column, and Martuba was reached by midday on the 16th. The five airfields to the south of the village were littered with damaged enemy aircraft. The Squadron then took the lead and reached Giovanni Berta by 5.30 p.m. to be told by the natives that the enemy had left two hours earlier. They captured five prisoners that afternoon. Leaguer was formed on the west side of the village, but they had little sleep since heavy rain began to fall from 11 p.m. onwards.

Rain fell for the whole of the next day, and the Column remained in Giovanni Berta, billets being found for as many men as possible. A further two tanks, those of Lieutenant Young and Sergeant Barnett, M.M., had to be evacuated as mechanically unfit for further operation. "And then there were four." "The only bright spot in an otherwise totally gloomy day," says the War Diary, "was the arrival of rations—the first for four days."

November 18th was a day which will be remembered by all those who knew that gallant and honourable officer, Major Harbord. The Column left Giovanni Berta with 'A' Squadron still leading. At about midday, S.S.M. Kirkham, in the leading tank, was warned by two natives that a party of Germans were laying mines on the road at the village of Slonta. Major Harbord ordered the advance to continue, when a party of men some 800 yards away, was seen to run from the road into the old fort of Slonta which stood on some high ground two hundred yards on the north side of the road. The leading tank, on rounding a corner, met with a road block, so Major Harbord took the lead, turned left off the road, and gave the order to form battle line. Knowing that the fort was occupied, he himself took the right hand and most dangerous flank. Captain Harari was in the centre and Sergeant Kirkham on the left. The fourth tank, having no wireless, was kept in the rear. Two anti-tanks guns then opened fire on the tanks, one from the fort and the other, a 20-mm., from about ten yards from the right of the road.

Major Harbord advanced, but his guns jammed and he decided to overrun the gun by the road. The road here was on an embankment and, on descending the bank, his tank cast a track. Being under direct fire he gave the order to bale out, but he himself did not abandon his tank. Manning the anti-aircraft gun from a position on top of his tank, he engaged the enemy and provided covering fire for his crew. While firing the gun he was wounded in the leg by a 20-mm. cannon shell, but he carried on firing until a second and then a third cannon shell killed him outright. But for this gallant action it is doubtful whether his crew would have escaped with their lives. Trooper R. Weir, Major Harbord's driver, who baled out through the front of the tank, found himself faced by a German, armed with a light machine-gun. He rushed forward and struck the man with his fist. After a brief struggle the German broke loose and ran back to his party who were now abandoning their position.

While all this was going on, Captain Harari's tank was fired on from about seventy-five yards range by another anti-tank gun which had remained concealed up till then, and the driver was wounded and unable to carry on. Sergeant Kirkham, who had seen the flash of the gun, immediately outflanked it to the left. The German crew abandoned it and made good their escape. The gun, which was captured intact by Kirkham, proved to be a 48-mm.

By this spirited and gallant action, no delay had been imposed on the Column. The enemy had been disturbed before he had had time to lay the mines, and their rearguard had been destroyed or put to flight. The Column passed through 'A' Squadron who were left to bury their Squadron Leader in a grave on the high ground, to the east of the Slonta Mosque. Having marked it with a cross, Captain Harari took over command of what was left of the Squadron and continued the advance. They caught up the Column before it leaguered for the night.

From the 19th to the 24th November the advance continued, but the Squadron did not come into contact again with the enemy. On the 19th they reached Marua after a very wet day. On the 20th four tanks (three Grants and one Stuart) of the Royal Scots Greys joined the Squadron and came under their command. They reached Barce that evening after being held up by demolitions on the Barce escarpment. They remained in Barce throughout the 21st while Sappers repaired demolitions on the Tocra pass. On the 22nd they found themselves leading the Column again. Ten miles beyond the Tocra pass one of the Royal Scots Greys' tanks was blown up on a mine and Captain Heycock, the Medical Officer, who had been with the Squadron throughout the pursuit, also ran over a mine, and transferred himself into a three-tonner. They entered Benghazi at 1.45 p.m. The 23rd was spent in Benghazi, carrying out maintenance and doing a run round the town for some Newsreel photographers who had appeared on the scene. "We had run out of drinking water," says the Squadron War Diary, "but were lucky to find some Italian bottled mineral water in one of the buildings." The last remaining 'A' Squadron Stuart had to be left in Benghazi as mechanically unfit. On the 24th the advance continued and the Squadron reached Magrun at 3 p.m. Their tank strength by now had been reduced to three Royal Scots Greys' tanks under command, two Grants and one Stuart. This was the furthest point of the Squadron advance for, at 5.30 p.m., Captain Harari received orders to hand over the two Royal Scots Grey Grants to the Artillery, as observer tanks, and return to the Regiment in Alexandria. The remaining Royal Scots Grey Stuart was to be handed in at Msus, and the personnel of the Squadron were to travel in the Squadron 'B' echelon.

The long march east began on the afternoon of the 25th. It was sad, after having travelled so far and nursed the tanks so carefully, to have to go home while the pursuit and the glory lay ahead. But with no replacement tanks available, little more could be done by the Squadron. It was not the first time that the Regiment had had all their tanks shot from under them, or had had them die honourably from old age and over-work. So let glory and excitement go to the others still fortunate enough to be in the chase. The Squadron had paid a heavy price to travel as far as they had.

By nightfall on the 25th they had reached a point twenty miles west of Msus, and, the Royal Scots Grey Stuart, having run into an old anti-tank ditch, had to be left behind.

On reaching Msus by 8.30 a.m. on 26th, Captain Harari arranged with the R.A.O.C. there to recover the abandoned Stuart. They learnt there that the Squadron B 2 echelon was at Mrasses. So they directed their course there and picked up the echelon for the rest of the march.

On the 27th they reached a point twenty miles west of Bir Hacheim; on the 28th they were ten miles east of el Adem; and on the 29th they crossed the frontier into Egypt near Capuzzo, descended the escarpment at Halfaya Pass and leaguered for the night twenty miles east of Sollum. Throughout this period the replenishment of water, rations and petrol had been a chancy affair, but their requests had been met everywhere with kindness and understanding.

By nightfall on the 30th they reached el Daaba, and after an early start on 1st December, drove into Sidi Bishr camp that evening where Regimental Headquarters was awaiting them. "This was the closing," says the Squadron War Diary, "of a very happy but rough three months." It was also a day of reunion. It was the first time the Regiment had been together since mid-June!

(f) Regimental Headquarters at Sidi Bishr, September–December 1942

REGIMENTAL HEADQUARTERS was last heard of moving into Sidi Bishr Camp on August 31st. In the two previous chapters we have read, first of 'C' Squadron under command of the 4th Hussars from 12th July to 11th September, and then of 'A' Squadron in the same rôle from 12th September to 24th December. Throughout this entire period, Regimental Headquarters always had either the one or the other Squadron under command. Although the composite regiment 4/8th Hussars was in existence during this time, the 8th Hussars was still an operational unit and never lost its identity. Frustrating as it was for Lieut.-Colonel Goulburn and Regimental Headquarters to be out of the battle themselves, the former had the satisfaction of knowing that he had overcome the inclination of General Headquarters Middle East to place the Regiment in suspended animation after the heavy casualties it had sustained at the end of June. By the rapid reorganisation of Regimental Headquarters and a second fighting Squadron ('C' Squadron was always intact and battle worthy) at the beginning of July, the Commanding Officer had proved that he had a force which could be useful to the Eighth Army, immediately, in the rôle of local protection troops for Army Headquarters.

Back at Sidi Bishr camp throughout September and October Regimental Head-quarters enjoyed the luxury of a tented camp, sea bathing and the 'flesh-pots' of Alexandria. Early in July, at the time of the battle of Alam Halfa, trouble was expected from the crews of the two French battleships which were bottled up in Alexandria harbour. It was believed that the Admiral and his sailors were very pro-axis. And if Rommel was to break through at Alam Halfa it was feared that the sailors, some four thousand in strength, would attempt to take over the town. Plans were made accordingly, by the Garrison Commander, to deal with the situation by means of the hotch-potch of British troops stationed in camps, base units and workshops in and around Alexandria. Regimental Headquarters and Headquarters Squadron had their task to play in this plan which, however, never materialised. A further anti-parachute task was given to them, which entailed various reconnaissances and plans to move to vital targets. On October 26th all 'left-out-of-battle' personnel from the 7th and 10th Armoured Divisions arrived at Sidi Bishr. They came under command of Lieut.-Colonel Goulburn, and Regimental Headquarters with its small Headquarters Squadron, and had the task of administering the Camp. This kept the Regimental 'Q' branch very busy. On November 10th, Headquarters 24th Armoured Brigade arrived in Sidi Bishr camp, and command of the camp passed from Lieut.-Colonel Goulburn to the Brigade Commander.

Soon after this, 'C' Squadron, who had been at Bourg el Arab, de-horsed since handing over to 'A' Squadron, rejoined the Regiment in Sidi Bishr.

On November 16th Lieut.-Colonel Goulburn received instructions from Headquarters Armoured Fighting Vehicles, General Headquarters, Cairo, to send 8th Hussar personnel on Armoured Car Courses at the Royal Armoured Corps Base Depot in Abbassia. This was the first indication that the Regiment was to be converted into an Armoured Car Regiment, and it resulted in the rapid journey of the Commanding Officer up to Cairo to find out what it meant.

On December 2nd, the day after the arrival of 'A' Squadron in Sidi Bishr, Lieut.-Colonel Goulburn was informed by Headquarters, Middle East Forces, that the 8th Hussars were to be sent to Cyprus. On the following day he attended a conference at General Headquarters where the Deputy Adjutant General informed him that certain units were to be broken up and that the Regiment was to receive reinforcements from one of them, the 2nd Royal Gloucester Hussars. This was good news since the 2nd Royal Gloucester Hussars was a fine regiment.

On December 11th, four Marmon Harrington Armoured Cars were issued to the Regiment for training purposes, and Lieut.-Colonel Goulburn was informed that one complete squadron, strength about a hundred and forty officers and other ranks of the 2nd Royal Gloucester Hussars, was to be posted to the Regiment. On the following day he reorganised the Regiment into three squadrons, reforming 'B' Squadron which had been in suspended animation since the end of June. Major Gwyn was given command of the squadron. Shortly after this Major Threlfall and Captain J. Robertson returned to the Regiment from the Jnior Staff School and the R.A.C. Base Depot respectively.

On December 19th Regimental Headquarters, 'B' and 'C' Squadrons moved by train to Port Said, while 'A' Squadron was left behind at Sidi Bishr to follow later with the 2nd Royal Gloucester Hussars personnel who had not yet been posted. After spending Christmas Day in the Transit Camp at Port Said, the Regiment, less 'A' Squadron, embarked on s.s. Fouadieh for Cyprus, where they arrived two days later. They disembarked at Famagusta and moved by motor-transport to Kondea, a village on the Famagusta-Nicosia road, seventeen miles from the former. Here the men were accommodated in huts and the officers in billets, in comparative peace after the dust and clatter of the desert war, which, without them, was to continue for another five months.

PART THREE

1943-1944

I. CYPRUS

January-June 1943

NOW began for the Regiment some six months of quiet for rest and reinforcement amongst the hills and Crusader castles of Cyprus. By January 19th, 1943, 'A' Squadron had joined the rest of the Regiment in their billets at Kondea; the first time since May 26th, 1942, that the whole Regiment had been together.

The first impressions of Cyprus after years spent in the heat and dust of the desert, was of green country and cool rain. It was an almost English climate, at any rate as far as the winter was concerned. In March torrential rain flooded the low-lying countryside, but in the spring the foothills were a mass of wild flowers and cherry, while the plains below were covered with orange blossom. There were fresh vegetables of every kind and plenty of Commandaria, the local red wine, and cheap brandy, while sherry was only 1/6d. a bottle. In those days, too, the peasants, 80 per cent. Greek and 20 per cent. Turkish, were friendly in spite even then of an embryo Enosis or Union with Greece.

Cyprus itself consists of a central coastal plain which stretches right across the island, with steep hills to the east and high mountains to the west. The highest of these is Mount Olympus, 6,403 feet, which rises at a place called Troodos, the district of the Summer Hotels. All except one of these had been taken over by the Army for hospitals.

At first the Regiment was stationed in stone and mud built huts at Kondea on the plain, with the addition of a few requisitioned houses on the outskirts of the village. Squadrons were split up into squadron billets and on the whole everyone was very comfortable. They came under the command of Brigadier Moffat, Headquarters 20th Indian Infantry Brigade of the 1st Indian Division, commanded by Major-General Blaxland. This Division was part of 25 Corps, commanded by Lieut.-General Hughes. The Garrison of Cyprus was all Indian except for the 8th Hussars, Armoured Cars; 4th Hussars, Tanks; the 97th Field Regiment, R.A., the Kent Yeomanry and an Infantry Battalion at Famagusta.

During the first three weeks of January the Regiment was allotted thirteen Bren-gun Carriers, an assortment of trucks and lorries and forty-five old Marmion Harrington armoured cars. Few people had ever seen one before, let alone driven one, and training was soon in full swing. At first there were one or two nasty moments as it was far from easy to drive these big vehicles on the narrow, twisty and in some cases very hilly island roads. However, it was a good training area, as suitable ground could be found for almost any kind of exercise.

Sport was organised too, although handicapped by a shortage of playing fields. However, a means was soon found to keep everyone fit. Anyone who was not playing in a game was transported to the foot of the eastern hills where they were put out and told that they would be picked up on the other side of the hills. They had no alternative but to climb the hills or walk about fifteen miles back to camp. In fact, most people enjoyed the climb though it was very rough-going with a good deal of scrub growth on both slopes, and right on the top the ruins of the crusader castle of St. Hilarion. The view from here was magnificent, and looking east one could see, on a clear day, the coast of Turkey. Below, the town of Kyrenia was just able to fit itself in between the foot of the hills and the sea, and west one could look right across the plain to the foothills of the western mountains, with Mount Olympus, still snow-capped even in late summer, in the background.

Swimming was not as good as might have been expected as all the best places were mined. However, several rocky pools were found, and on one occasion 'B' Squadron thought they had spotted a promising-looking cove, but on approaching to investigate they were halted, and routed, by a wicked-looking unexploded bomb.

In off-duty hours there was plenty of amusement to be found. There was an other-ranks leave centre in Famagusta, which was the main port of the island. There were a variety of places of entertainment in Nicosia, the capital; dances were organised, in particular on St. Patrick's Day; a restaurant-cum-club opened in Kondea called the 'St. Patrick's Arms'; the Regiment organised a dance band and there were Squadron week-end camps at the sea.

The usual assortment of pets appeared also; to mention only two, Major Gwyn's pig, Pamela, who was looked after by a venerable old gentleman who spoke no known language but answered to the name of Tiki-tiki; and 'B' Squadron's Famagusta cabaret girl whom they kept just outside the Squadron Leader's office.

Football was played against the 4th Hussars stationed at Kokkini Trimithia and the British Infantry Battalion at Famagusta. The padre, Captain Frank Hone, held services in the Greek Orthodox Church in Kondea with the Regimental Choir and band. Voluntary attendance was 60 per cent. of the Regiment, and as a result of all the training, recreation and general fitness, very high morale was developed in the men.

The general strategy of the troops in the island was defence against invasion. In this event they were to withdraw to the hills into 'keeps', which were strong points already constructed and stocked with food and ammunition. As there was only one Indian Division and a few Corps troops on the island, they were far too few to defend all the beaches. Local labour was employed in building airfields.

For the Regiment, January passed quietly. The only event worth mentioning was on the 30th when they were ordered to send two armoured car patrols along the coastal roads between Famagusta and Boghaz and Famagusta and Larnaca. An enemy submarine was reported to be shelling Cape Andreas, or 'Panhandle' as the most easterly tip of the island was called. Two troops were sent out from 'A' and 'B' Squadrons, but nothing was seen, nor by the 'C' Squadron troop sent out the next day.

A Corps Commander's inspection that was to be held on February 1st was cancelled as Mr. Churchill put in an unexpected appearance on the island after his conference in Turkey. However, it took place on the 13th and General Hughes showed a keen interest in the Regiment.

On February 6th, the signal was received that Trooper Weir had been awarded an immediate D.C.M. for his conduct in the action when Major Harbord was killed, and on March 26th S.S.M. Atkins and Lance-Corporal Scrugham were awarded the M.M.

March came in with a roar and for part of the month rain and floods made movement impossible, but at the end of the month the rain eased off.

The Corps Exercises started on April 5th with 'Tiger', the move to and occupation of battle positions in the event of enemy invasion, and was followed on the 8th by 'Tough', which lasted for thirteen days.

'Tough' took place on the western hills of the island and the Regiment moved to an assembly area where they were uncomfortable to say the least, as there was torrential rain for two days and not much cover. However, everybody made the best of it and it might have been worse. 'We had a certain amount of difficulty during this period,' wrote Major N. G. F. Dunne, who arrived from the mainland on D-Day plus one. 'All the signal operators were Indians who spoke very little English, and if anyone rang up about anything it was more than likely that the only reply he could get would be 'Teeka', which was both unhelpful and infuriating."

However, when the operation started the weather cleared and everybody enjoyed themselves. Major Gwyn, who was riding a motor-bicycle up a mountain road to see how the battle was going, was ditched by an Indian-driven carrier and had to lie pinned under his machine until rescued by some Infantry about three quarters of an hour later. Fortunately, he was not hurt.

The Cyprus Defence Force, who were on the opposite side, were commanded by a British Officer. During the course of the Operation they had the misfortune to meet face to face a joint force of enthusiastic 8th Hussars and even more enthusiastic Ghurkas. This was too much for them so they took to the hills, losing in the meantime, their Colonel. He gave himself up to 'B' Squadron two days later, tired, dirty and hungry, and with a broken ankle. 'B' Squadron took the liberty of sending him home straight away to have a bath and a meal. In spite of all this, and the fact that all the troops on the island were involved, there was not one claim for compensation or damage made by the local population.

April was further enlivened on the 24th, three days after the end of 'Tough' and when the Regiment was back at Kondea, by a demonstration by Paratroops from Egypt, on the coast east of Larnaca. They were commanded by Brigadier Hackett, late of 'C' Squadron. The whole Regiment turned out to see this, and the 'fly in' was most impressive. The gallant Brigadier jumped first but the effect was rather spoilt as he landed in a tree and had to be rescued.

It was some time during the beginning of May when the next incident of note occurred. A Commando raid on Cyprus had been laid on by the Special Service (Boat Squadron) from Antelat in Palestine, the idea being to practise both the Commandos in a sea-borne crossing and the Cyprus Defence Force in repelling an invasion, which at that time was still a possibility.

The plan was to drop a party of paratroops somewhere in the centre of the island who were to set up a wireless station for the main paradrop which was to take place later. Owing to bad weather, the exercise was postponed. The Commanding Officer of the Special Service Squadron, however, decided to take his wireless party across to Cyprus by sea; and acting on his own authority, he hired a 'kyke' (the local name for a sailing ship) crewed by Greeks. Unable to land on the pre-arranged open beach on the south coast of the island, he ordered the Greek skipper to make land just north of Famagusta where more shelter would be found. The Greek skipper, however, sailed into the port of Famagusta at 2 a.m., thereby breaking all orders that no shipping should enter ports by night. The coastal defence gunners of the Royal Artillery, suddenly waking up to see a large sailing ship in the port entrance which they claimed as moving, although it had been anchored for the last two hours, fired one round across its bows. According to the version given by the Gunners at the subsequent Court of Inquiry, the ship continued to move. A second shot was fired which brought down the mast. They then rushed to their motor-boat and, after an hour's delay in trying to get it to start, they boarded the 'kyke' and arrested the crew, none of whom could speak a word of English. Suspicious signs of military equipment were found on board and the alarm was given than an invasion party had landed. This was true, since the enthusiastic Commando party had rowed themselves ashore long before the existence of the 'kyke' had been discovered.

Early that morning an S.O.S. was received by the Regiment from a Senior Staff Officer saying that Nicosia was about to be invaded and the assistance of the 8th Hussars was required at once. 'B' Squadron had just come in from a two-day exercise, but as both the other Squadrons were out they were detailed for the job. Nobody quite knew whether this was a real invasion or an imaginary one, so to be on the safe side it was taken seriously.

The orders were that the miniature metre-gauge train, which ran from Famagusta to Nicosia and then on to the foot of the western moutains and on which the invaders were travelling, had to be intercepted at all costs before it reached Nicosia. 'B' Squadron started without delay, and it is unlikely that the armoured cars had ever travelled so quickly before. The second-in-command of the Squadron, Captain Robertson, had been in Nicosia on duty and was on his way back when he met the Squadron who were in such a hurry that he wisely left the road. Nobody had time to stop and tell him what was happening, so he was convinced that this was the real invasion.

The Squadron managed to intercept the train just outside Nicosia, and attacked it on foot, covered by the guns of the cars. The dismounted attackers were led by Sergeant Brooker and, armed with Thompson sub-machine-guns, rifles and bayonets, they boarded the train and captured all the Commandos.

The sequel to this was that the Governor of the Island next day received a complaint from the civilians who had been in the train and were terrified. Things looked awkward for a short time, but the Staff Officer who had sent out the S.O.S. took all responsibility, and said that the Regiment had done a first class job.

All this time the war on the African mainland had been surging forward. January saw Tripoli taken and early in February the Eighth Army crossed the Tunisian frontier. This meant that they now came under the command of General Eisenhower, with, however, General Alexander in executive command.

The Germans were unlucky that spring. Not only were they retreating in Africa but all along the Russian front as well, suffering there tremendous losses. In Tunisia on February 14th, Rommel made a desperate effort to regain some of the ground he had lost, but, although he gained temporary possession of Kasserine, Feriana and Sbeitla, in a fortnight the ground he had won was back in our hands.

General Montgomery meanwhile, in the south, arranged his three divisions, the 7th Armoured, the 51st and the 2nd New Zealand, near Medenine, rightly supposing that when Rommel had been dealt with north at Kasserine he would concentrate on the British threat to the Mareth Line. On March 6th, Rommel did attack in strength, four times, employing his three Panzer Divisions, and was beaten off each time with heavy loss. This was his last action in Africa as soon afterwards he was invalided home and the Afrika Korps was taken over by General von Arnim.

On March 21st, Montgomery's attack of the Mareth Line began and, after a week of desperate fighting, this whole twenty-mile-long line of defence was captured. By April 18th, the Eighth Army was up to Enfidaville and, after very heavy fighting, the 7th Armoured Division entered Tunis on May 7th and joined up with the Americans at Bizerta. Six days later the Tunisian campaign was over, and there was to be no more fighting in Africa. As well as the quantities of enemy killed there were a quarter of a million prisoners taken. It was indeed a great victory. The Regiment, far away amongst the hills and flowers of Cyprus, did not feel too much 'out of it'. They had given towards that victory all that was humanly possible and had only been pulled out of the last triumphal march because they had nothing left with which to fight. However, before they reached the paved streets of Berlin they were to take their place in the van once more.

While in Africa plans were being made for the invasion first of Sicily and then of Italy, the weather in Cyprus was becoming increasingly hot. As a result the malarial mosquitoes throve on the plain by Kondea, and in May the Regiment moved to a new camp, at Milestone II on the Nicosia-Morphou road. Here, also, they would be better placed to deal with an enemy landing in Morphou Bay to the west, which was considered a likely place.

Although it was a mostly tented camp it was reasonably comfortable as floor boards were supplied. Their old friends, the 4th Queen's Own Hussars were only about two miles away and co-operated in every way. During this period training was re-commenced and one of the highlights of it was to see the Commanding Officer and the second-in-command, both old Cavalry soldiers, supervising training on motor-bicycles and both riding in the correct Cavalry manner.

On June 6th, Lieut.-Colonel Goulburn attended a conference at 25 Corps and was warned that the Regiment was under orders to leave the Island any time after June 9th. All war equipment was handed in during the next few days, and every kind of rumour started as to what event they were being sent back in time for.

Regimental T.E.W.T.s helped to pass the last few days, as they were without their armoured cars, and on June 12th, the G.O.C. paid an informal visit to say good-bye to Lieut.-Colonel Goulburn and the Squadron Leaders.

On June 20th, orders were received from 25 Corps to leave the next day for Fama-gusta and embark that same night. Accordingly, the next day the Regiment marched two miles to the station where they boarded the miniature train for the seaport. After a slow journey across the island they arrived at Famagusta and found H.M. Minelaying Cruiser *Abdville* waiting for them. The Navy, as usual, had everything well organised and it was not long before they had embarked, in pitch darkness, and at about midnight they sailed.

II. CYRENAICA

June-November 1943

THE REGIMENT remained for the night of June 23rd in the Transit Camp at Beirut which was crowded with troops of every colour and nationality. Next evening, they left by train for Egypt and arrived at Giza on the 25th. On their journey they were escort to thirty Greek officers under arrest for political crimes on their way to Egypt for Court Martial. Later that day Lieut.-Colonel Goulburn went to General Headquarters where he was told that the Regiment was to go to Cyrenaica for anti-paratroop duties at the airfields there.

By the middle of July the Regiment had been issued with fifty-eight Marmion Harrington Mk. III Armoured Cars. Twelve of these were without turrets and there was a great shortage of wireless sets. On July 8th Major-General C. Norman, M.G., A.F.V.'s, G.H.Q., inspected the Regiment at Beni Yusef Camp, near Cairo, and Lieut.-Colonel Goulburn took the opportunity of protesting against the Regiment's future static rôle in a back area.

On July 16th the Regiment arrived at Barce and the District Commander, Major-General Collier, described their rôle, which was to be that of district mobile reserve, ready to be sent anywhere in the district. Their most probable task would be to deal with any paratroop landings in the Benghasi area, from where large numbers of U.S. bombers were operating, carrying out raids on Italy and the Balkans.

Lieut.-Colonel Goulburn had particularly asked that the Regiment might be kept together and Kilo 18 on the Benghasi-Agedabia road was allotted as a camp site. Squadron Leaders were warned to keep their men on the alert in case of attacks by low-flying enemy planes searching for the big United States bomber bases.

In Italy, Mussolini had fallen from power, to be succeeded by Marshal Badoglio, and it seemed likely that at any moment the Italians would capitulate or even join the Allies. By August 17th, the invasion of Sicily was over and the gate was opened on to the road to Rome.

August saw the Regiment still at Kilo 18, continuing their training, with an occasional expedition as bullion guard to Derna and Tripoli. On August 4th, there was a flutter of excitement, when at 3 p.m., local Arabs brought the information that some Italians were lying up in the area between the camp and the sea to the north-west. The Commanding Officer of H.Q. Squadron to whom the Arab had reported this information, was ordered to despatch two armoured cars from his troop at once, and 'C' Squadron was ordered to send out two troops, all taking Arabs as guides. Nothing had been heard from higher up of enemy landings or paratroop activities, and it was therefore thought advisable to warn 4 A.A. Practice Camp that Italian troops were in their vicinity. The enemy was quickly discovered in a ruined house to the north-east of el Abiou, where they were being besieged by local Arabs armed with rifles. Unluckily, the leading car, commanded by Lieutenant R. P. G. Dill, ran into a soft patch in a salt-marsh and the crew had to dismount and go forward on foot. However, before they could reach the house the patrol sent out by 4 A.A. Practice Camp had already arrived and to whom the Italians, one officer and three men of the San Marco Marine, surrendered. A similar party of Italians had also landed at Suani et Terra, and were captured by a patrol of the Sudan Frontier Force. These Italians had landed during the night of August 3rd/4th from a submarine with the purpose of sabotaging U.S. bombers. They were handed over to a troop of 'C' Squadron, who escorted them to Headquarters, 93 Sub Area.

Later in the month, on the 16th August, an unfortunate accident took place when on the journey by 'A' Squadron to field firing at Sceleidima, an armoured car ran on to a minefield, resulting in the death of Lance-Corporal Kyle and Trooper Low, and with serious injuries to Sergeant Smith, the car commander.

At the end of September the Regiment was re-equipped with modern Humber Mk. IV. armoured cars with 37-mm. guns co-axily mounted with a 7.92-mm. Besa.

For the Eighth Army in Italy, however, September was full of incident. On the 3rd, the first landings were made on the toe across the Straits of Messina from Sicily, and by the 8th, Italy had surrendered. This, however, was not as advantageous as it sounded. The Germans were in possession and there they were determined to stay. They captured Mussolini on September 12th in a daring raid on his prison in the Abruzzi and flew him off to meet Hitler in Munich. They fought grimly round Salerno where the main Allied landings had taken place. On September 19th Sardinia became ours, quickly followed by Corsica. By the 21st the Salerno battle was over and the Allies were pushing on towards Naples. This they reached on October 1st, and on the 13th, Italy declared war on Germany. All this led to confusion, and fierce fighting continued all the autumn until in December when winter temporarily clamped down on both armies and left them facing each other along a line between Cassino and Ortona.

On October 22nd the Regiment received orders to move to Mena Camp on the outskirts of Cairo, under the shadow of the Pyramids. Before leaving Benghasi they had received a very favourable report on their standard of training. News also came through that they would be leaving for home about the middle of November. Much had to be done before then. Vehicles had to be handed in and baggage packed, including the Regimental furniture and pictures that had been stored in Cairo since the beginning of the war. Certain postings were ordered too, including that of the padre, the Rev. F. Hone, who had been with the Regiment throughout all the Desert campaigns. Though the Commanding Officer did all he could to alter this decision it was some months before their padre finally returned to the Regiment.

On November 8th, General Sir Maitland Wilson came to say good-bye and congratulated the Regiment on its fine record during nine years and eleven months in the Middle East. There were still some officers and men present who had served continually during this time, namely Lieut.-Colonel Goulburn, Majors Phillips, Dunne and Threlfall, Captain Firth and Lieutenant (Q.M.) O'Malley and R.S.M. McMaster, T.Q.M.S. Day, Sergeants O'Callaghan and Williams and Trooper Huggan.

On November 10th, 'B' and 'C' Squadrons and L.A.D. attached under the command of Major Phillips left for the Transit Camp at Suez, and embarked on H.M.T. *Duchess of Richmond* on November 12th. Regimental Headquarters and 'A' Squadron left for Amiriya on the 12th and stayed in a Ship's Camp at Ikingi Maryut until the 16th when they embarked in H.M.T. *Almanzora* at Alexandria.

One can imagine with what mixed feelings those 8th Hussars who had fought through the Desert Campaigns must have watched the shores of North Africa fading behind them. In spite of the obstinate British pride that allows no expression of any sort of emotion, there must have been a feeling of relief at going home, thankfulness at having got through so far unscathed, trepidation as to what was next in store, an odd sort of sorrow at knowing the grim and yet glorious days of desert fighting were over forever, sadness that so many were left behind in the sand round Sidi Rezegh and many other places, and pride at having been through it all and having earned, as had few others, the right to the title of Desert Rats.

III. ENGLAND

December 1943-May 1944

On December 8th, after three weeks on board ship, and very nearly ten years to the day since they left for Egypt, the Eighth Hussars were sailing into the cold winter sea round England. The half of the Regiment in the *Duchess of Richmond* went to Liverpool, while the other half disembarked at Gourock.

Both Lieut.-General Sir Oliver Leese, commanding 30 Corps and Major-General G. W. E. J. Erskine of the 7th Armoured Division came on board at Gourock to welcome them home. They also brought the news that the Regiment was to become the Armoured Recce Regiment of the 7th Armoured Division.

After the usual frustrating delay in disembarking, the whole Regiment proceeded to a dispersal camp at Woodlands Park, Great Missenden, where excellent arrangements had been made for them. On December 14th, the Colonel, Brigadier J. Van der Byl, D.S.O., paid them a visit. After lunch he inspected the Regiment on parade and afterwards addressed them in a formal welcome home after their ten years continuous service in the Middle East.

The next day the whole Regiment went off on leave for four weeks, with the exception of a small party of officers and men who returned after a fortnight to move the heavy luggage to West Tofts Camp, near Thetford, and who acted as an advance party until the remainder of the Regiment returned. They then went off to finish their own interrupted leave.

All that spring elsewhere tremendous preparations went ahead for the long-awaited invasion of Europe. These involved not only new and secret inventions such as 'Mulberry', the pre-fabricated harbours, and 'Pluto', the submarine petrol pipe lines from the Isle of Wight to Normandy, but the difficulty of keeping concealed from the Germans the whereabouts of the embarkation ports and the destination of the invading armies. This created an immense amount of planning and, eventually, great secrecy in troop movements, censorship and general deception.

The whole of the 7th Armoured Division was concentrated in Norfolk. It now consisted of the 22nd Armoured Brigade, 1st and 5th Royal Tanks, 4th County of London Yeomanry; the 131st (Queen's) Brigade; Divisional Troops which were the 8th and 11th Hussars and Divisional Signals as well as regiments of artillery, engineers and others. The Division came under General G. W. E. J. Erskine, the Brigades under Brigadiers W. R. N. Hinde and M. S. Ekins.

The Eighth Hussars at West Tofts found themselves in desolate sandy pine-woods, housed in a Nissen hut camp, and the first tasks to be tackled were the long-forgotten mysteries of home documentation, food and coal rationing and war-time travel.

The theoretical rôle of an Armoured Reconnaissance Regiment in an Armoured Division equipped to fight in a European theatre was that of close tactical reconnaissance in front of the other units of the Division. On the other hand, the rôle of the Armoured Car Regiment was deep reconnaissance in mobile operations. It was recognised that, for cross country movement in a European terrain, tracked vehicles would be necessary, since armoured cars would be confined to the roads. The Regiment, therefore, was equipped with tanks, four Cromwells in Regimental Headquarters and nineteen in each of the three sabre squadrons (Squadron Headquarters four tanks and five troops each of three tanks). In addition, the Regiment had a Reconnaissance Troop in Headquarters Squadron comprising about ten Light tanks and twelve Daimler Scout Cars which was intended to operate directly under Regimental Headquarters. All the Cromwell tanks were equipped with the 75-mm. A.P./H.E. guns except two in each Squadron Headquarters. These were armed with the 95-mm. H.E. guns. A Besa machine-gun was mounted co-axially with the main armament of each tank.

The chief difference between the Regiment's establishment, as the Armoured Recce Regiment, and that of the Armoured Regiments in the Division was that the former had no gun heavier than the 75-mm. whereas the latter had one Sherman tank in each troop armed with a 17-pounder gun. This tank was known as a 'Firefly'. There was no Reconnaissance Troop in the Armoured Regiment.

As events turned out later in the fighting terrain of Normandy, it was seldom possible to carry out close tactical reconnaissance. Very soon the Regiment became a fourth Armoured Regiment in the Division, and fire power was strengthened by the issue of one Cromwell type tank with a 17-pounder gun on the scale of one per troop. This tank was known as a 'Challenger'.

An excellent training area existed literally at the Regiment's back door. This was the Stanford Battle Area. The land had been requisitioned by the War Department from Lord Walsingham and other local landowners. The civilian population had been evacuated and there were a number of deserted hamlets. Although small (about 4 miles long from north to south by 2 miles wide) the area enabled good troop and squadron schemes to be carried out with live ammunition. In addition, there were large tracts of land outside the battle area where tanks had limited use of the country if they wished to leave the roads.

On February 24th His Majesty King George VI honoured the Regiment with a visit. This was an historic occasion, considering the Regiment had not been visited by a King or Queen of England since the 12th May 1856 when Queen Victoria visited them at Portsmouth on their return from the Crimea. His Majesty, on this occasion at West Tofts, requested that no special parade or inspection should be ordered for him but that he would see the Regiment at its normal work in camp. The Commanding Officer therefore ordered a maintenance parade of all four squadrons; and His Majesty was taken round to see the officers and men at work on their tanks and 'B' vehicles. He showed great interest, stopping and talking informally to a number of individuals. On asking one man the name of a certain tool, he was informed that it was a 'bleeder' (for bleeding the hydraulic brake system of the tank). His Majesty was somewhat taken aback and nonplussed, but laughed heartily when it was explained to him that this was not intended as a joke!

Men who were employed in offices, stores and cook-houses were permitted to leave their job and stand in orderly groups outside their places of work. In this way, every officer and man had a chance of seeing His Majesty.

On February 17th, a day of bitter snow, General Montgomery addressed all ranks of the 7th Armoured Division at Divisional Headquarters, including, of course, the Regiment. Another interesting visitor was General Skliaron, the Russian Military Attaché, who dined with the Regiment on April 21st. Sitting down to dinner on the right of the Commanding Officer, General Skliaron at once noticed the battle honours of the Crimean War woven into the fine linen tablecloth. "Hullo, what is this?" he said. "Alma, Balaclava, Inkerman, Sevastopol?" "Oh," replied the Commanding Officer somewhat embarrassed, "those are our battle honours gained for fighting against your country. An unfortunate event which will never happen again, of course. But we are very proud of our cavalry charge at Balaclava, and we commemorate the day, 25th October 1854, with a Regimental holiday every year on that date."

"Oh do you," said the Russian General, "so do we!"

This caused great laughter, and the ice was broken.

On the following day when the Russian mission visited the Regiment, one of their Generals was very suspicious and kept on asking where the big tanks were kept, larger ones than were being shown to him.

During its four months at West Tofts the Regiment worked very hard to make itself battle worthy for the coming invasion of Europe. A large number of reinforcements, young officers as well as other ranks, were posted to the Regiment, none of whom had had battle experience. The Cromwell tank, too, was new to all ranks, and drivers, wireless operators and gunners had to become accustomed to the new equipment. Many officers and other ranks too, were sent on courses of instruction in driving and maintenance, wireless, gunnery, mine-lifting and gas-warfare. Troop, Squadron and Regimental Training was carried out as well as many T.E.W.T.s. On one occasion an exercise between two squadrons fighting each other with live ammunition (Besa) was arranged; and on another occasion one squadron co-operated in an exercise with the 1st Grenadier Guards commanded by Lieut.-Colonel E. H. Goulburn, the brother of the Regiment's Commanding Officer.

No nearby tank ranges were available at West Tofts so, during this period, squadrons were sent to Bawdsey in East Suffolk, Brancaster in North Norfolk, and Kirkcudbright in South Scotland.

During this time Major Threlfall and Lieutenant Peglar attended the investiture at Buckingham Palace, being awarded the M.C. and D.C.M. and M.M. respectively.

On April 24th Brigadier Van der Byl, D.S.O., paid a visit to his Regiment, and on the 27th the long-awaited move to Bognor began. This was carried out by road, and the tanks passed through the middle of London in the early morning of Sunday when no traffic was about. Once there, they found billets in a school and several private hotels while the tanks were parked in a recreation ground.

The whole of May was taken up with 'waterproofing' vehicles, and experiments were carried out in the sea to prove that it was effective in four feet of water. Some wireless exercises on the downs above Bognor, making use of Scout Cars, were held. During a 'Flag March' by 'C' Squadron through the streets of Bognor one day, the streets were torn up at certain corners and the curbs chipped. This resulted in a visit by an angry Borough Surveyor, but the bill for damages was waived as an act of patriotism by the Mayor. Mention must also be made of the great hospitality shown by Mrs. Rank at her home of Aldwich Park to all the officers at this time.

On May 11th there was an inspection by Major-General Erskine. The Regiment was paraded at full strength, and after the inspection General Erskine expressed his pleasure at the good turn-out, and then went on to speak of the coming operations and the part the Division and the Regiment would play in them. He wound up by wishing them good luck and good hunting. Brigadier Van der Byl, D.S.O., also inspected his Regiment on May 24th, and by the 28th, as from 9 a.m., they were at six hours notice to move.

In Italy, May had been a month of bitter fighting, culminating at last in the capture of Rome on June 4th. In Russia all Spring the war had been going well, and by April the Germans were pushed back into Roumania and Poland, while the Russians planned a new offensive to coincide with the Allied one in France.

In Burma, the Japanese had been held at Kohima on the Assam Valley, and on the northern front the airfield at Myetkyina was recaptured with the assistance of the

Chindits. But it was impossible to send more troops to the Far East; every one was needed for the coming operations in Europe. There, the time for training was over. Everywhere was a feeling of tension, of time running out, of anticipation, and above all of determination that at last, with the weapons given them and their own skill, they would defeat this enemy once and for all.

PART FOUR

1944-1945

I. NORMANDY

June-August 1944

(a) Across to France, June 1944

IT is as well, before the actual landings were made, to describe briefly what manner of country and defences awaited the 7th Armoured Division, and what was to be the general plan of attack.

The coast chosen for the invasion was a stretch between the rivers Orne and Vire, and the first task of the invading armies was to gain a bridge-head that included Caen and Bayeux. The plan was to land on a front of some thirty miles, protected by the air-borne troops who would have already landed and established themselves. The American 1st Army, under Lieut.-General Bradley, would make for the crossings over the Vire and push on to Cherbourg, while the British 2nd Army on the left, consisting of two corps under Lieut.-General Sir Miles Dempsey, would secure the crossings over the Orne and the roads to Bayeux and Caen. On the right hand of this assault was to be Lieut.-General G. C. Bucknall's 30 Corps, coming in over the Arromanche and Le Hamel beaches with the 50th Division in the van, followed by the 7th Armoured and 49th Divisions in that order.

After landing, the attackers were to find two entirely different types of country awaiting them. After a strip of open marshy ground, that stretched inland for some few hundred yards from the beaches, the 'bocage' started. From the air this looked like one continuous wood but it was in reality small fields surrounded by high-banked hedges of pollarded trees, orchards and a network of narrow muddy tracks, so over-hung with gorse and broom and hazel that they were almost tunnels. This extended west and south of Bayeux and was hopeless for tanks or even artillery. Chief landmark here was Mont Pinçon, some ten miles south of Villers Bocage, the highest feature of a range of wooded hills. To the south and south-east of Caen the country was quite different, the 'campagne', open rolling plain, all arable, broken by wooded valleys.

The enemy forces in this area were the 7th and 15th Armies, commanded by the Desert Rats' old opponent, Field-Marshal Rommel. The coast line, protected by an immense amount of wire, mines, concrete blocks and other obstacles, was held by a second-grade infantry division, and behind them, south-west of Bayeux, the 352nd Infantry Division. At Falaise and Bernay were the 12th S.S. and 21st Panzer Divisions, with two more, the 17th S.S. and 2nd Panzer within easy reach. These four divisions were equipped with Panther and Tiger Tanks, both heavier armed and more heavily armoured than our tanks, and which, although less manoeuvrable, were well suited for the defensive fighting ahead.

By May 28th, in Bognor, all plans were completed. Officers were briefed and camps were sealed. There was now no more to do but wait, as all armadas have done, for favourable winds and tides. On June 3rd, came orders to move next day to their Marshalling Area. Lieut.-Colonel Goulburn spoke to each squadron in turn, and told them the points stressed by General Montgomery in his final address to Unit Commanders. The move was postponed for a day, but on June 5th the Regiment, less 'C'

Squadron, moved off at 2.30 p.m. It was a necessarily slow journey, all the roads in the south were a-crawl with transport heading for the coast, and it was not until 9.45 that night that they arrived at Havant. All tanks and 'B' vehicles were parked by craft-loads in roadside standings. Eleven L.C.T.'s had been allotted to the Regiment on the scale of one per nine tanks or twelve 'B' vehicles.

Next day was D-Day. June 6th. Maps were drawn and issued, and orders were received to move on the morning of the 7th. Lieut.-Colonel Goulburn gave a final briefing to officers and tank commanders. Last letters were written home. The feeling of unreality deepened. They watched the Airborne troops going over, and knew that it could not be long now.

There was, however, one more delay, but on June 8th, the first craft-load rumbled out of the Marshalling Area at 1.30 in the morning, followed at five minute intervals by the remaining parties. Having arrived at Gosport they parked by the sides of various roads leading to the hards, and everyone appeared to be happy, singing and shouting and waving.

Embarkation began at about 2 p.m. and as each L.C.T. was loaded, so it moved out into the stream to await sailing orders.

At one o'clock in the morning of June 9th, the convoy moved out to sea. It was an uneventful voyage, if any voyage at that date and in that vicinity could be called uneventful. There were ships of every shape and size spread across the Channel, and for some people there was the sight of their first dead body afloat upon the water. All round, as they neared the shore, were sunken ships. The Regiment, less 'C' Squadron, landed about 7 p.m. at Le Hamel and moved off to Sommervieu. They leaguered that night, their first in France, in an orchard and round the hedges of a hayfield.

Meanwhile, 30 Corps had already made good progress. Bayeux was occupied, but the advance was held on the left short of Tilly-sur-Seulles and Caen, with enemy pockets north at Sully and Port-en-Bessin. Caen was to be a scene of much bitter fighting with the Germans hanging grimly on. The day of the 10th was spent by the Regiment in de-waterproofing and maintenance. Major Dunne and 'B' Squadron came under command of the 22nd Armoured Brigade, while Major Huth and 'C' Squadron had still not yet sailed.

(b) Operations in the Bocage, June 1944

AT 5.15 a.m. on June 11th, Regimental Headquarters and 'B' Squadron moved up through Bayeux to another orchard. There had been a small advance the day before by such of the 7th Armoured Division as had arrived, and the 5th Royal Tanks had pushed on as far as Ellon where they were held. In order to make clear the bigger picture it should perhaps be explained that this advance by the 7th Armoured was part of a southern pincer movement carried out by 30 Corps, while 1 Corps maintained steady pressure on the town of Caen itself. On the morning of the 11th, an attempt was made by the 7th Armoured Division to reach Bernieres-Bocage. The reconnaissance troop, a mile beyond the village, had a Honey destroyed by a self-propelled gun. 'B' Squadron were carrying out reconnaissance on the right flank of the advance, which continued through Ellon and Folliot until open cornfields were reached on the east of the road to Bernieres-

Bocage. Here several British tanks were knocked out, but the ground was held and the 5th Royal Tanks, the 8th Hussars and the 2nd Essex remained in position to cover the right flank while the advance on the left was held at Bucéels. Meanwhile, Regimental Headquarters and 'A' Squadron had to move from their orchard as spent armour-piercing shells were landing uncomfortably close.

Next morning, the Regiment was still in position watching the right flank of the Division. Whilst here, a 'B' Squadron tank was knocked out by a gun-in 7.5-cm. Pak 40 at about twenty yards. Four of the crew were killed and one managed to escape out of the burning tank, though wounded, and was rescued by Trooper Raynsford who was in a following tank. Meanwhile, the advance on Tilly from the north and west was not being successful and several tanks were lost. The enemy, the Panzer Lehr Division, now started working back round Bucéels, and, hearing that the Americans to the west were meeting little opposition and advancing on Caumont, General Erskne received orders to disengage and attack south-south-east through Briguessard and St. Germain to Villers Bocage.

The Eighth Hussars were to lead this attack, followed by the 4th County of London Yeomanry with a company of the 1st Rifle Brigade. The remainder of 22nd Brigade consisted of the 5th Royal Horse Artillery, 1/7th Queen's Royal Regiment, 5th Royal Tanks, two companies of the Rifle Brigade and the 4th Field Squadron, Royal Engineers.

At about 1 p.m. the Regiment moved out, 'A' Squadron in the lead. It was a hot afternoon and they drove down steep and narrow country roads in a cloud of choking white dust by way of Trungy, St. Paul du Vernay, Ste. Honorine de Duchy, La Miverie, and not until they reached Livry did they meet any enemy opposition. Here, Lieutenant D. Rampf of Two Troop, 'A' Squadron, had his tank knocked out by an infantryman with a 'Raketen Panzerbuchse 43' the German answer to the 'Bazooka'. Two of the crew were killed and Rampf and the remainder were wounded. At this moment the 4th County of London Yeomanry appeared on the scene, and Lieut.-Colonel Goulburn asked them to put the company of the 1st Rifle Brigade, which was under their command, into Livry to clear the village. This they were able to do, but as it was by then about 8 p.m. it was decided to advance no further that night.

Meanwhile, 'A' Squadron was ordered to recce down the main road from Caumont to Caen as far as the Granville crossroads. Lieutenant Talbot-Hervey and Three Troop, 'A' Squadron, approached the crossroads and as they did so the two leading tanks were knocked out at point blank range. Only one survivor out of the two crews made his way back to Squadron Headquarters to tell the tale. Two years after this action the grave of Talbot-Hervey and his comrades was found under a pear tree, near where their tanks had been destroyed.

The Regiment leaguered near Livry that night and over on their right they could see the Americans fighting for the burning Caumont, which they occupied early the next morning.

The plan for the 13th was to advance on through Briquessard and Amayé-sur-Seulles to Villers Bocage. 'A' Squadron came under command of 131st Brigade and gave protection to the left flank of the advance. The rest of the Regiment, less 'C' Squadron, advanced as right flank guard to 22nd Brigade, which was moving along the main road. The track the Regiment was ordered to take proved to be non-existent so instead they made for Cahagnes. On their way there the leading Troop of 'B' Squadron met a patrol of the 11th Hussars who warned them that Cahagnes was held by the enemy. To this 'B' Squadron paid no attention and, regardless of a few shots fired, pushed on through Cahagnes to Tracy Bocage only a mile short and to the west of Villers

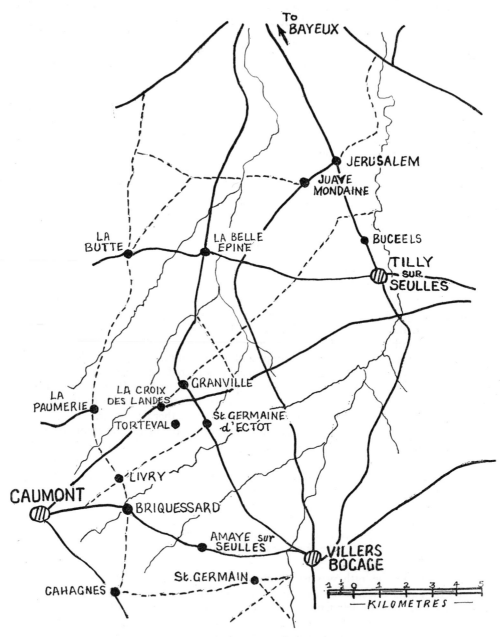

To BAYEUX

JERUSALEM

JUAVE MONDAINE

LA BUTTE

LA BELLE EPINE

BUCEELS

TILLY SUR SEULLES

GRANVILLE

LA PAUMERIE

LA CROIX DES LANDES

TORTEVAL

St. GERMAINE d'ECTOT

LIVRY

CAUMONT

BRIQUESSARD

AMAYE sur SEULLES

VILLERS BOCAGE

St. GERMAIN

CAHAGNES

1 ½ 0 1 2 3 4 5
— KILOMETRES —

Map A. Operations in the Bocage.
Villers Bocage 12th-14th June, 1944.
Briquessard 15th-17th June, 1944.

Bocage, where they were ordered to take up a line of observation north of the village.

Meanwhile, the main advance of 22nd Brigade had met with disaster. They had entered Villers Bocage, meeting no opposition, but on arrival had met the 2nd Panzer Division on its way to attack them, and this unexpected encounter resulted in the leading units of the 4th County of London Yeomanry and the Rifle Brigade being cut off and overpowered. Extremely close quarter fighting then took place in the streets and houses of Villers Bocage, soon to be flattened by close-support bombing out of recognition. However, holding it meant there was a risk of the entire force being cut off, so it was decided to withdraw to the east of Amayé-sur-Seulles until the 50th Division on the left, could come up into line.

During the afternoon 'B' Squadron in their position at Tracy Bocage were attacked by infantry supported by a Tiger tank. They beat off the attack, losing three tanks in the process but suffering no fatal casualties. By the evening, the 22nd Armoured Brigade Group had formed a defensive 'box' in the area north and south of the road through St. Germain, on the high ground east of Amayé, with the enemy attacking from every point of the compass. The line back to the Division was cut and as night fell the Group was surrounded.

This was fighting country very different from the open expanses of the desert. Here a Tiger tank could remain concealed until its target was at point blank range. Here banks and tall hedges gave ample cover to guns and infantry. Here a brewed-up tank could block the road effectively for hours. It was perfect defensive country, but the Regiment had not fought all the way from el Alamein to be held up only a few miles inland from the French coast.

After a moderately calm night the 14th dawned, and at 5.30 a.m. 'B' Squadron moved out on patrol, while 'A' remained with 131st Brigade. Throughout the morning it became increasingly clear that the enemy infantry were closing in all round the Brigade area, particularly from the south. Panzer Lehr in the north were patrolling towards them too but were being kept too busy by 50th Division in the north, to be capable of mounting a very heavy attack. In the south, as was later discovered, 2nd Panzer Division were on their way across to the American part to counter attack at the junction of the British and American armies, when they suddenly found themselves mixed up on their own centre line in the 7th Armoured Division's attack on Villers Bocage. By 11 o'clock the enemy renewed their shelling and put in an attack. This was driven off by the 1/7th Queen's but the mortar fire continued. 'A' Squadron, in the Livry area, managed to work their way down to Point 198, a commanding hill two thousand yards south of the road to Villers Bocage, during which manoeuvre they lost three tanks, while Amayé was occupied by the 1st Royal Tanks and the 1/6th Queen's.

The enemy continued to try to break through the defences from the Villers Bocage direction, but when he found himself unsuccessful there he turned his attention to the road behind it, and at 4 p.m. German infantry were seen a few hundred yards from the southern approaches to Amayé. 'A' Squadron had by now been withdrawn from Point 198, and an enemy tank was seen making for the ground they had occupied. Although it was stopped, the infantry with it kept going until they were halted by Besa fire from the British tanks. That day Lieutenant M. M. Browne of 'A' Squadron was killed.

'B' Squadron was also engaged during the afternoon and knocked out two Mk. VI Tiger tanks.

The left flank of the Division in its 'box' position was uncomfortably exposed, and the attack by the 50th Division in an attempt to straighten out the line was making very little progress against the Panzer Lehr. In spite of the thrust that had carried the 7th Armoured to Villers Bocage, far ahead of the rest of the line, it was regretfully decided to abandon the position as it was too difficult to hold without sufficient infantry support. The 22nd Armoured Brigade were to withdraw behind a firm base formed by the 131st Brigade in the Briquessard area, where they would be in contact with the Americans on the right and be able to send patrols across the lightly-held enemy salient between their left and the 50th Division.

As evening approached a general feeling of expectancy was in the air and occasional glimpses were caught of infantry and tanks forming up to attack. At 8 p.m. the Adjutant issued a warning to both Squadrons to prepare for an attack. Half an hour later heavy mortaring started all along the southern and eastern edge of the position. One battalion the 5th Royal Horse Artillery were in the box and were firing at extremely short range. Defensive fire was coming from both the 50th Division and the Americans in Caumont and further back. Shortly after this an attack in Battalion strength came in against 'B' Squadron, supported by two Tigers and an armoured car and proceeded by a heavy mortar barrage. The British infantry suffered considerable casualties, but Four Troop and the Norfolk Yeomanry together brewed up the armoured car and one Tiger and caused very heavy casualties to their supporting infantry. Several more company attacks were delivered all along the line but were also repulsed. The 5th Royal Horse Artillery had an exciting moment as at one time they were firing over open sights at infantry at five hundred yards, aided at a distance by the Americans and even the Royal Navy. Until last light the enemy continued these attacks on a smaller scale, but against such a concentration of tanks in so small an area could achieve no success. During these attacks 'B' Squadron suffered several casualties including Lieutenant P. F. de May killed and the Squadron Leader, Major Dunne, wounded, and Captain Robertson took over command of the Squadron temporarily. During the height of the attack a German sniper, who had crept into the Regimental Headquarters orchard, was seen peeping through a window of a farm building fifty yards from the Commanding Officer's tank. Heavy Besa fire was directed from the latter into the building until a message from Brigade Headquarters, over the next hedge, complained that flying tiles were causing them some discomfort!

The attacks petered out as darkness fell and there was an uneasy silence. At half-past midnight, in the dark and dust, the tired troops began pulling out. In order to divert the enemies' attention an attack was made at about midnight by heavy bombers on Villers Bocage, and at the same time the withdrawal started, ambulances, infantry, trucks, half-tracks, carriers, anti-tank guns, self-propelled guns, artillery and tanks all streaming down one small road. The noise sounded tremendous, and it seemed impossible that the enemy should not know what was happening. To those inside the box the noise was greatly exaggerated as up until then all conversation had been carried on in a whisper. The anxiety of those last moments in the box was well nigh unbearable. 'B' Squadron was to hold the now tiny perimeter until the last. Each troop had a platoon of Queens under command and were stationed on one of the lanes leading out of St. Germain. It was pitch dark and enemy infantry could very well have infiltrated between the troops. To the men of that rearguard, both Queens and 8th Hussars, the strain was greater than any during the last two days' fighting. Not a man had had more than three hours' sleep a night for over a week of continuous action. Everyone would have preferred an attack to waiting and expecting one at any moment. The lines of vehicles moving out were endless. Everyone was dead tired and time and again drivers ran into the vehicles in front of them causing frequent hold-ups in the line. By one o'clock the diversionary aerial attack on Villers Bocage was in full swing, tremendous flashes lighting up the whole horizon, and the southern sky was full of parachute flares and the bursts of ack-ack shells. The first vehicles of the Brigade had pulled out at midnight, and it was not until 4 a.m. when it was growing light that the first of the 'B' Squadron tanks left the village with the Queens riding out on the back of the tanks. Even then it seemed certain that the enemy would cut the centre line as they could easily have done. Indeed when 'B' Squadron saw a burning Bren-gun carrier it was thought that this was what had happened. But it was only one which had broken down and had been set on fire by its crew. At last after what seemed an endless journey but which was in fact about two miles, the Squadron reached the outposts of the main line, and such was the relief that more than one tank Commander promptly fell asleep in his turret.

Of the men taken prisoner during the two days' action, several eventually managed to escape.

By now 'C' Squadron had appeared in France. They had left Gosport on June 12th, the day before the flying-bomb menace started, and sailed that night, arriving on the beaches at Arromanche next afternoon. On the 14th Major Huth, went to report to the Headquarters, 7th Armoured Division near La Butte. By now there was the heartening sight of many prisoners on the roads, and the Squadron leaguered that night in an orchard near Deraye.

(c) Further Operations in the Bocage, June 1944

ON the 15th, 'C' Squadron came under command of the 131st Brigade and was attached to the 1/6th Queens, commanded by Lieut.-Colonel Forrester, at Briquessard where they were reunited with the rest of the Regiment. Already members of 'A' and 'B' Squadrons looked like veterans, hung round with egg-grenades and with tired faces and stories to tell of casualties suffered already in the few days they had been in France. However, 'C' Squadron were very shortly going to make up for having missed the Villers Bocage action.

After the withdrawal from Villers Bocage there was a three mile gap left between the Rifle Brigade on the 7th Armoured Division's left and the 50th Division. This gap was covered by the Regiment who did much excellent patrolling, a difficult task for a tank as the noise and dust made movement impossible to conceal, and the ground too was to their disadvantage.

While the rest of the Regiment remained in a cornfield south of La Butte, in reserve and doing some much needed maintenance, Huth of 'C' Squadron left his second-in-command, Captain Firth, to bring the Squadron to Briquessard in the afternoon while he and Lieutenants H. R. D. Peglar, Scott and Young went ahead to do a recce of the area they were to occupy. He was ordered to carry out a recce immediately as far as Amayé to find out, firstly, if that area was occupied by the Germans and, secondly, to confirm the number of enemy vehicles destroyed during the withdrawal of the 22nd Armoured Brigade from Villers Bocage.

Before leaving, Huth placed troops out to forestall any imminent attack, Lieutenant Peglar and One Troop, with 'B' Company, 1/6th Queens, in the area immediately south, and Lieutenant Scott and Two Troop, with 'A' Company south-east of Briquessard. Then, having collected his troop leaders he made a careful recce of the area concerned from the top of a small hill to the north-east. However, whilst giving orders to advance on down the road, a report came in from One Troop of an infantry attack starting up near Le Quesnay, south of Briquessard, and also of fourteen Tigers about four miles east.

By 5 p.m. Lieutenant Scott and Two Troop began to advance up the road with Three and Four Troop in support. Lieutenant Peglar and his Troop were still holding the attack round Le Quesnay, and Lieutenant G. Atkinson-Willes and Five Troop moved two miles east to try and find out more about the previously reported Tigers. Meanwhile, Captain Firth and the Sergeant Major, with an observer from the 3rd Royal Horse Artillery, moved to a good viewpoint just north-east of Briquessard to be able to support the troops should they run into trouble.

Scott's Troop reached Amayé and reported it held by about a hundred infantry. They fired some high explosive into them, and a house which must have been storing petrol, went up in flames. Meanwhile, Sergeant Hunter's tank, Cyclonic, had become ditched and Lieutenant M. S. Payne and Four Troop stood by to give protection as sniping was continuous. Lance-Corporal French got out to stalk a sniper, but was shot, but Trooper Stack promptly shot the sniper. Payne made a gallant attempt to reach Lance-Corporal French, but the sniping was too accurate. The Armoured Recovery Vehicle under Corporal Swetman, R.E.M.E., was sent out and that also became ditched. The situation threatened to become critical on account of the snipers.

By now Atkinson-Willes, seeing and hearing nothing of the fourteen Tigers, had been ordered to make a small detour to the east and come in behind Two Troop, which they did having found nothing to report.

At about 9.30 p.m. the order to withdraw into the Briquessard box was given out, and all troops returned complete, except that it had been found impossible to salvage 'Cyclonic' which had to be abandoned. The crew rode in on the back of the Armoured Recovery Vehicle which was then hit by the German equivalent of the Piat from close range. Sergeant Hunter was killed and the vehicle itself slightly damaged. All troops returned to leaguer for the night except Scott and Two who remained with 'A' Company, and Peglar and One with 'B' Company.

During the day Peglar had gone forward with an infantry patrol to locate the enemy, and had become involved in a hand to hand fight with a German patrol. He had been hit over the head with a rifle, but apart from that returned unhurt and with some very useful information. However, during the early hours of next morning, June 16th, this gallant officer went out again with a patrol, was wounded and subsequently died of his wounds.

All that day, the 16th, the enemy made three separate attacks to capture Briquessard and each one was driven back by the 1/6th Queen's and 'C' Squadron. The village was shelled intensely and things were not made easier when R.A.F. Typhoons put the fear of God into everyone by shooting up Briquessard with rockets, causing some casualties among the infantry. They had mistaken the village for Cahagnes from which place the enemy was shelling. (Our own troops were partly to blame as we had failed to put out ground/air recognition strips.)

During the morning, One Troop, 'C' Squadron, now commanded by Sergeant Langmead, with the help of the infantry and a 17-pounder, had knocked out one Mk. VI Tiger, damaged one Mk. IV and caused casualties to the enemy infantry. They were, however, forced to withdraw and in doing so took the wrong track. Sergeant Langmead in 'Cresta Run' became bogged and all the crew returned except Langmead who was reported missing. Lance-Sergeant Pilkington's tank was last seen moving east, and both tank and crew became missing, and were believed to have run into an enemy patrol and anti-tank gun known to be in that area. Lance-Corporal Gibbins in 'Captain Cuttle' also became bogged, having previously been hit, but the crew of three returned safely.

During this time three separate attacks were being put in against 'A', 'B' and 'C' Company sectors. Young and Three Troop took over from Sergeant Langmead with 'B' Company. Payne and Two Troop with 'A' Company had helped to knock out a German armoured car, whilst Squadron Headquarters with 'D' Company had assisted in beating off the attack.

Corporal Smith's tank, belonging to Two Troop who were watching the west side of the village, developed engine trouble and while the crew were repairing this, Smith, the tank commander, was wounded in the leg by a splinter from a mortar shell, the same shell killing Trooper Stark, the hull gunner.

During the night, Scott's Troop was left out in the 'A' Company Sector, Young's in 'B' Company's and Atkinson-Willes' in 'C' Company's, west of Briquessard, watching the Caumont road. Sergeant Langmead's Troop came back to Squadron Headquarters in the 'D' Company area.

On the first day at Briquessard, Major Huth's own tank had been damaged by going over "some of our own mines which should not have been down and had no sentry over them." The result was a damaged track and clutch and a cut over his eye. Next day, his Humber scout-car had also been hit by an anti-personnel shell about 6 inches below his feet, but no great damage done. During the night his jeep was hit by shelling.

'C' Squadron stood to all that night expecting an infantry attack, and by the morning of the 17th were very tired, having been in their tanks for three days and two nights. After a night of continuous sniping and shelling a bigger attack developed at about 4.30 a.m., involving two battalions of Panzer Grenadiers, supported by tanks, but this attack was held although Squadron Headquarters had to move its position.

During the morning, Sergeant Major Cole spotted a Mk. VI Tiger in a narrow lane about 1,500 yards from Squadron Headquarters. After manhandling a 17-pounder anti-tank gun from the Norfolk Yeomanry into position, the Tiger was hit with the fifth shot and brewed up, amidst great shouts of glee. The Commanding Officer, Major Huth, and the Yeomanry Troop Commander were debating the widsom of satisfying their natural curiosity by going forward to examine the tank, when an enemy patrol of three men started to walk towards them. The British party slipped behind the hedge, a click was the only sound as the cocking handle of the Bren gun was drawn back, to be followed a few seconds later by a staccato burst of fire. Death was as sudden to the enemy as it was unexpected.

As evening drew on the 1/6th Queen's and 'C' Squadron were ordered to withdraw from the village, 'C' Squadron to join the Regiment at Cahagnolles and the Queen's to go to Briquessard wood, some 500 yards to the north. The withdrawal was timed to start at 11.15 p.m., but by 10.30 heavy shelling began which continued up to the time of the 'get out', and was directed principally on the exit from the village. At the same time enemy artillery made an extremely accurate and unpleasant stonk on the western side of the 'box', which held Squadron Headquarters, a description of which was written at the time by Lieut.-Colonel Goulburn and is quoted: "Brigadier Ekins, Tony Case and I ran for the nearest slit trench and jumped in. Although a long one, it had six men packed in it already. I succeeded in getting my feet on the ground but the best I could do for shelter was to lie over the top of a young Queen's soldier who was blubbering with fear and fatigue. Shells were bursting so close that earth and stones were coming in on top of us. Something heavier landed on top of us, however, in the shape of Trooper

Smith, my scout car driver. He had been sheltering in my car until a shell burst under it when he decided to bale-out and run for a slit trench. Whenever there was a break in the shelling we all came up for air, if thick dust, smoke and cordite could be called air, only to crouch down again a moment later as a fresh stonk fell upon us. After fifteen minutes the shelling ceased, and this seemed the moment to get mounted and on the move. I had a quick look at my scout car which appeared towable. We fixed the tow rope to the fitter's half-track, Case jumped aboard the latter and I into Henry Huth's tank, and we pulled out of the orchard on to the road. Thank goodness the traffic was on the move even if only crawling, and very soon all four troops of the Squadron reported themselves clear of the village. On reaching the village of Livry, which was being shelled, we met our first traffic check. While waiting to get through, a shell burst against a house close behind our tank, and a shell splinter penetrated Huth's silver flask in his breast pocket. By 1 a.m. the Squadron was back safely in the Regimental Headquarters leaguer."

In spite of a certain amount of confusion, the withdrawal was carried out with no casualties to 'C' Squadron. They even managed to take with them two 17-pounders that would otherwise have been left to the enemy.

During the three days and two nights in Briquessard, 'C' Squadron had lost five tanks, Lieutenant Peglar, Sergeant Hunter, Lance-Corporals French and Stark killed, Sergeant Langmead, Lance-Sergeants Pilkington, Wade, Bennett, Sherriff and Lance-Corporal Shirley missing. On the other hand they had supported the 1/6th Queen's to such good effect that largely due to them the position was held. They had a half-share in knocking out two Tigers and one Mk. IV damaged, as well as approximately fifty Germans killed and they rejoined the Regiment more than ready for a well-earned sleep.

All three Squadrons remained in reserve during the 18th, and on the 19th orders came through that the Regiment was to move back to a new area near La Butte in case of an enemy thrust from the south-east. Accordingly, Lieut.-Colonel Goulburn ordered the Squadrons to carry out a reconnaissance of battle areas south-east of St. Paul du Vernay, and to be prepared, if necessary, to hold them. The Regiment spent the night at the La Butte cross-roads with 'C' Squadron which had received five new tanks to replace those knocked out during the fighting, at St. Paul du Vernay.

For the fighting between the 12th and 19th June in the thick bocage country, the Regiment was granted the major battle honour of Villers Bocage.

The 20th and 21st June were spent in reconnaissance of battle positions and in maintenance. As a result of what they had experienced in their first engagements, a hundred Sten guns were issued to tanks and scout cars.

Apart from a certain amount of shelling the rest of the month passed fairly quietly. The three battalions of the Queen's Regiment were holding a ridge now, just north of Briquessard, with the Rifle Brigade on their left around Le Pont Mulot. The five thousand yards between the Riflemen and the 50th Division east of St. Paul du Vernay were covered only by the 8th Hussars. The enemy-held villages opposite Anctoville, St. Germain, Granville and Longraye, were strongly held by infantry with tanks well back. The ground in between was held by a thin screen of machine-gun posts which changed their positions frequently, and were reinforced by night. It was a wearying time of short nights and little sleep. The enemy was constantly on patrol, and the country was ideal for mines and trip wires and booby traps.

On June 24th, Lance-Corporal Balcombe of 'B' Squadron was killed when the Squadron area was shelled. On the 25th, the Regiment was ordered to relieve the 4th County of London Yeomanry near Quesnay Guesnon. 'A' Squadron was to be forward, with 'C' in reserve in front of Regimental Headquarters. The positions were recced and 'A' Squadron moved forward, ready to send out patrols at first light.

On the 26th, the Regiment came under command of the 22nd Armoured Brigade. The Squadrons took up their positions, 'C' Squadron camouflaged in an orchard. 'A' Squadron moved on to the La Butte crossroads, facing south towards Granville and St. Germain d'Ectot. "Two Humber armoured cars streak past my position and one is knocked out by an anti-tank gun 300 yards forward round the corner," reads the diary of a newly-arrived 'A' Squadron subaltern. "Report of Tigers in area. Standing-to. I wonder if I will knock out a Tiger? Two bloody survivors return from armoured cars. Bill Bellamy, very brave, rescues a third. At night moved back to village and slept in a deserted priest's house."

For the next two days slight enemy activity was reported by 'A' Squadron, and the usual shooting at night kept everyone on their toes. On June 29th, the Regiment came under command of the 56th Infantry Brigade of the 50th Division, and were visited by both General Erskine and Brigadier Pepper. The 2nd Battalion the Essex Regiment moved in ahead of them that evening so that they then had protection in front of them. For the Regiment June ended quietly, and they remained with the 56th Brigade. At the end of the month the 7th Armoured Division handed their sector of the front over to the American 2nd Armoured Division and withdrew to rest and refit near Jerusalem. They had lost some 1,149 officers and men during their three weeks in Normandy, as 'bocage' was horrible country from an armoured point of view, and it could only be hoped that the open fields east of Caen would give the tanks a better chance.

(d) Operations South-east of Caen, July 1944

THE REGIMENT stayed near La Butte sending out patrols and being intermittently shelled until July 4th. Trooper Cameron was killed in this way while having breakfast outside his tank on July 1st. On the 2nd, Major Gwyn, M.C., and the residue party landed in France. They were eagerly awaited as the men were needed to replace casualties, and almost more important was the electric welding plant which they were bringing with them. They arrived the next day together with Major Dunne and Lieutenant Rampf who had been wounded and were returning from hospitals in England.

The weather was wet and beastly, and when the order came through on July 4th to leave the mud they were in and move to some more near Jerusalem, the news was more than welcome. The Regiment came back under command of 131st Brigade and their rôle, should the Germans counter-attack, was to be prepared to take up defensive positions just north of Tilly-sur-Seulles, while 131st Brigade established itself in a firm position, and then to withdraw to protect the Brigade flanks.

They had left the 'bocage' country now and were in the dust or mud of the 'campagne', according to the weather. Operation 'Goodwood', for which they were now preparing, was to be an attempt to enlarge the small Allied bridgehead over the River Orne, while the Canadians broke out from Caen itself. The bridgehead was only about ten thousand yards long and three thousand deep. There was one bridge across the river and three Baileys that had been built. Through this small area three armoured Divisions of 8 Corps were to pass, the 11th leading and making south-west across the main Caen-

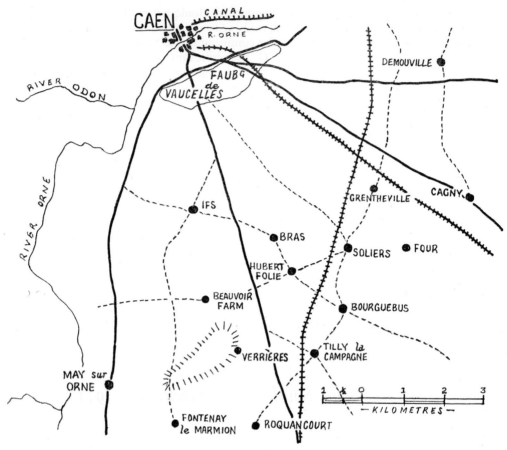

Map B. Efforts to break out South and South-east of Caen.
19th-29th June, 1944.

Falaise road towards Bretteville, then the newly-arrived Guards turning south-east towards Vimont and lastly the 7th making straight for Falaise. The 3rd Infantry Division on the left was to go east to Troarn, while the Canadians grappled with the factory area and suburbs of Caen, the whole operation to be preceded by a tremendous air assault. As the British advanced from the north, the Americans were to drive forward from the west and south and it was hoped that a large number of Germans would be trapped between them in the 'bocage'.

The days until Operation 'Goodwood' were spent in intensive training. On 5th July the Commanding Officer wrote: "During the day a troop of 5.5-inch medium artillery came into action in the field behind the Regimental Headquarter leaguer. They fired in a harassing rôle all that night and their blast was deafening. I laid a wooden table on its edge alongside my camp-bed to try and check the blast, and I stuffed some four-by-two into my ears which had quite helpful results. The next morning, accompanied by Captain Ladenburg (Adjutant) and Lieutenant Hepburn, I motored all round the district searching for an alternative leaguer position. Every field and hedgerow was occupied for a radius of two miles. We were utterly beaten. In addition to the inconvenience of the noise, we stand a good chance of being shelled by the enemy should they start any counter-battery fire." There was time too, to go into Bayeux to shop and have baths, but most of the days were spent in perfecting the co-operation between the Regiment and the infantry to whom they were attached. Parties from the Queen's came over to inspect the tanks they were to work with. "Very impressed but say they prefer to be on their 'bloody feet'."

As the day drew nearer, Lieut.-Colonel Goulburn accompanied Brigadier Pepper, commanding the 131st Brigade, on a recce east of the Orne as it was known that the Regiment might operate there. On July 17th, they moved to a concentration area near Brécy. Major Dunne of 'B' Squadron, whose wound received at Villers Bocage had not properly healed, had to be evacuated. Captain Robertson took over the Squadron again. Elsewhere on that day, Rommel was wounded when low-flying fighters attacked his car. He did not die of his wounds, but his command was taken by General von Kluge.

On July 18th, the Regiment moved out on the approach march to the Orne bridgehead. As can be imagined, with three Armoured Divisions on the move in so small a space, the traffic congestion was tremendous. The river was not reached until about ten o'clock that night and had to be crossed while the bridge was in the process of being bombed. One Troop Leader wrote: "Flares and bombs all over the place. My crew sing and smoke inside closed-down turret, trying to ignore the terrible bangs whilst waiting to cross. How much longer will I enjoy life? Flies are biting terribly."

Although they only leaguered just east of the crossing in the early hours of the morning they moved off again at 8 a.m., after a bomb-ridden night, to Demouville where the 131st Brigade were establishing a firm base at Cuverville with the Regiment in reserve behind them. Quite a few dead Germans were lying about and also there were attacks by German planes using rocket projectiles.

The whole of July 19th the Regiment spent at the village of Demouville in a big field of standing wheat. All three Squadrons were spread out in 'desert formation' to lessen casualties from enemy shelling. The fields were pock-marked with bomb craters and shell holes, the whole place a mass of noisy vehicles, dust-flattened crops and upturned soil. And larks singing even so. Every village was in ruins with the trees stunted or snapped off.

On July 20th, orders came through for the Regiment to support the 1/7th Queen's in Bourguebus, Fours and Soliers. Major Huth and 'C' Squadron were despatched on this task and took over from the 5th Royal Tanks in Bourguebus that evening. 'A' Squadron sent a troop to Fours which was held by the 1/6th Queen's, while 'B' Squadron remained in reserve, in observation of Hubert Folie and Bras.

Regimental Headquarters moved to Grentheville where they remained for five days between the road and the railway embankment. Lieut.-Colonel Goulburn had time to jot in his diary the things above all others that would remind him of this time. "Mosquitoes that tormented us at night; the heavy rain; the difficulty of getting my boots off and into bed in the pit shared by Captain Ladenburg and the remainder of my tank crew without filling the bed with mud. The tot of rum and piece of plum cake from Cheltenham, given me by Corporal Lloyd who had just received it from his mother; the heavy enemy bombing attack and the feeling of nakedness as the parachute flares slowly descended on us; the low-flying attack of nine Messerschmits which caught me unprepared, in the open with my trousers down one morning!"

Elsewhere, the advance had gone slowly but successfully. The Germans fought bitterly for every inch of ground, but by the 20th the Canadians were into Cormelles and

Vaucelles, on the southern outskirts of Caen, the Guards had reached Cagny and Fremouville, and the 11th Armoured Division, although greatly reduced in strength, had taken Bras and Hubert Folies. Then the rain came down, in such torrential floods that tanks started becoming bogged and thus the armour had to come temporarily to a standstill.

July 21st, saw the Regiment still at Grentheville with 'A' Squadron at Fours and 'C' at Bourguebus. Both Squadrons came under heavy and accurate shell-fire all day. Later, enemy patrols from La Hogue and Tilly-la-Campagne were seen trying to approach the village, but were routed by 'C' Squadron.

Lieutenant D. S. Scott was killed that evening by a shell splinter. He was the second 'C' Squadron Troop Leader to be killed in France, and had been with the Squadron since May '42.

In the evening, the North Shore Regiment, 8th Canadian Brigade, relieved the 1/7th Queen's at Bourguebus. 'C' Squadron also was to have been relieved but plans were altered and they stayed on, and the Regiment returned once more to the 7th Armoured Division.

There was less shelling at Bourguebus on July 22nd, though the Nebelwerfers or 'whistling Minnies' were unpleasant. Squadrons changed places, 'B' taking over from 'C' and 'A' from 'B'.

July 23rd started quietly, but in the evening Lieutenant A. B. Brodie of 'A' Squadron was killed, another great loss, and two men were wounded from shelling.

In the evening, Lieut.-Colonel Goulburn issued orders for Operation 'Spring', and visited 'B' Squadron to tell them they were being relieved by a Canadian armoured unit the next day.

The attack known as Operation 'Spring' was launched by the 2 Canadian Corps with the object of advancing in the general line of the Caen and Falaise road, and also taking the attention of the Germans from the American break-through at St. Lo. The 7th Armoured, with the 22nd Armoured Brigade leading, was to go on to the La Bruyere feature, in support of the 2nd and 3rd Canadian Divisions, who were to attack May-sur-Orne and Tilly-la-Campagne respectively. However, the enemy had had plenty of time to dig himself in and prepare for what might be coming.

(e) Further attempts to break out south of Caen, July 1944

July 24th was spent in preparation for the advance next day. 'B' Squadron returned from Bourguebus, exhausted after being forced to remain in their tanks for forty-eight hours owing to the very heavy shelling. The Regiment at Grentheville was shelled too, as they had been ever since they had been there, and would continue to be until the end of the month. It was an exhausting time for everyone, as unpleasant as any the troops were to encounter during the whole campaign, confined as they were by day to tanks and by night to slit trenches, strafed by air and shelled and mortared ceaselessly. One cheering sight was the R.A.F. Tyhpoons who could blow up even a large German tank with their rockets, cheering, that is, as long as they did not come too close.

After a night of heavy bombing, July 25th dawned. This was the day the Americans began their great drive south to St. Lo. At 6 a.m. the Regiment formed up, ready to follow the 1/7th Queen's. The first part of the battle went well, although things slowed down later. Verrières was taken, but was isolated as the Canadians were unable to hold May and the attack on Tilly was only completed after dark.

During the evening, the Regiment suffered a great loss when Major G. W. G. Threlfall, M.C., commanding 'A' Squadron, was killed by a shell-burst as he sat smoking behind his tank. Threlfall was the only officer left in the Regiment who had been in every battle since 1940, and after having had six or seven tanks shot from under him, to be killed in such a way seemed particularly tragic.

Captain R. H. Ames took over the Squadron, and the Regiment leaguered near Ifs, three miles south of Caen, ready to support the 131st Brigade if a counter-attack developed. It was here the 8th Hussars really learnt to dig, and how hard the ground was!

The night was spent inside the tanks as there was heavy bombing and shelling throughout. On the 26th, the 131st Brigade with the Regiment in support were ordered to take over from the 22nd Armoured Brigade and form a firm base east and west of Beauvoir Farm by 6 p.m.

In the afternoon the Regiment moved up into position and took over from a Squadron of 4th County of London Yeomanry, and 17-pounders and M10's of the Norfolk Yeomanry were brought up. 'C' Squadron was in immediate support of the 1/5th and 1/6th Queen's and had some of their tanks dug in by an armoured bulldozer. The whole area was under shell-fire and the day was spent either in tanks or in slit-trenches.

After a night of shelling and mortaring, 'A' and 'C' Squadrons moved their troops into position by first light. The shelling continued all day, and the Squadrons were able to send back plenty of information as to where the firing was coming from. In the evening, the South Saskatchewan Regiment took over from the 1/6th Queen's.

July 28th was a day very much the same as its predecessor. Shelling continued, less heavily in the morning, but in the afternoon it intensified. "One big fellow in particular kept plastering the area and making life most uncomfortable, but we stay inside our tanks and nothing short of a direct hit into the open turret will do us any harm."

Lieutenant P. G. Hartwright and One Troop of 'C' Squadron were up in the forward position by Beauvoir Farm, bulldozed into pits with two big Mayflies, Sherman's with 17-pounders, with them. One Troop engaged an enemy observer post in a factory south of Verrières, but apart from that nothing was seen but dust-clouds moving along the roads.

'A' and 'C' Squadrons were out again at first light on July 29th. The morning was quieter than usual, but during the afternoon and evening the shell and mortar fire grew stronger. The Canadians on their right seemed to get the worst of it, but the Squadrons had their fair share too. R.A.F. Typhoons were very busy during the day. They must have been giving the enemy hell, and several 'brews' were noticed after their attacks.

Then the welcome news came through that the 7th Armoured Division was handing over this very unpleasant sector of the front to the Canadians and moving across to join 30 Corps at Caumont. They were badly in need of a rest but there was to be no time for that. For nearly a fortnight they had been fighting hard and suffering heavy casualties to hold an advance of only about six hundred yards. However the Americans had now broken out of the Cherbourg Peninsula and were advancing on the Vire, and the whole German line from Caumont to the sea was in danger of being turned. Although the Canadian thrust had been unsuccessful it had succeeded in keeping occupied five Panzer Divisions which would otherwise have been used against the Americans.

In order to assist the Americans, who were having more trouble round St. Lo than had been expected, Operation 'Bluecoat' had been planned. This was an assault by 30 Corps south-east of Caumont to clear Mont Pinçon and sweep on towards Condé-sur-Noireau and Flérs. 8 Corps would meanwhile be advancing on the right, while 12 Corps secured a bridgehead over the Orne at Thury Harcourt, and the Canadians drove on from Caen. 30 Corps was made up of the 43rd and 50th Divisions who were already in position, and the 7th Armoured who would not be needed at first. The 7th Armoured, when it did move, had to cross 8 Corps centre line and became entangled with the 50th Division who were moving in the same direction.

At last light on the 29th, the Regiment handed over to the Royal Scots Greys. 'B' Squadron and part of Recce Troop went on ahead and the others followed at 1 a.m. They marched by night for about 35 kilometres to Juaye-Mondaye just south of Bayeux. They were returning to the 'bocage' and it was to be hoped that the hated woods and banks would, after all, be preferable to the loathed dust and mud of the Caen plain.

They drove into Caen and then alongside the Caen–Bayeux road by the tank track. It was not an easy march, with choking dust and narrow bridges, equally narrow streets in the ruined and devastated Caen, and no lights allowed, which consequently made driving very difficult. Although two tanks collided they all arrived at their destination which showed what a high standard of driving and maintenance had been reached. Lack of sleep was another hindrance.

"I have never been so tired," wrote one Squadron Leader. "For the last five days I have averaged three hours sleep per night and that inside a tank. During this night march I kept falling down in my turret and at last handed over to my Lance-Corporal and slept on the back of the tank."

The Regiment arrived at about 7.30 a.m., and, as they did so, were told that they might have to move later on a new advance. Immediate maintenance followed by rest was the order of the day, but by the evening they were told there would be no move before next day. Squadrons and Echelons were all harboured in neighbouring fields and the day ended with a fitting comment from the same diary. "Had a grand night's sleep, and by Jove, we needed it."

(f) The break-out from the Bocage, August 1944

THERE was, after all, no move until August 1st. The last day of July was spent sorting out administrative problems, a pay parade and so on. A day was not long enough for everything that had to be done, but nevertheless by first light on August 1st the Regiment was ready to move. However, the order did not come through until 9.30 a.m., when they moved off slowly towards Cahagnes, going by La Belle Epine, Granville and Caumont. It was a slow journey and they did not arrive until eleven that night. It had been a nightmare of moving two hundred yards and then stopping. Roads were choc-a-bloc with traffic, a wonderful chance for a German air attack but there were no enemy planes to be seen at all, and the Regiment leaguered just north of Cahagnes at last light.

That night several men in 'B' Echelon were wounded by bombing, but otherwise it was quiet. The advance had gone steadily but very slowly during the day against fierce opposition and a profusion of mines.

Lieut. A. Newman, Intelligence Officer, 'Ici on parle Francais', June, 1944.

A 'brew-up' at Bourgebus, July 21st, 1944.

The 8th Hussars moving up to the battle area near Caen, July, 1944.

Cromwell tanks advancing through the ruins of Flers, July, 1944.

Capt. Best, R.E.M.E., Major Huth, M.C., Sergeant McNab and L. Cpl. Jacoby after pulling out from Bricquessard, June 17th, 1944 (page 154).

'Grif' Talk. The Commanding Officer, Lieut.-Colonel C. Goulburn, D.S.O., explaining to the Regiment the plan for Operation 'Goodwood', July 18-20th, 1944 (page 156).

An 8th Hussars Cromwell crossing the Seine at St. Pierre du Vanvray, August 30th, 1944 (page 170).

Dongen. 8th Hussars tank crossing the canal by a Bailey bridge, October 30th, 1944 (page 183).

On the 2nd, the 1st Royal Tanks led the advance on Aunay-sur-Odon, four miles south of Villers Bocage, with 'B' Squadron as left flank protection. They moved out at 6 a.m. advancing with one troop up, and the first difficulty was to get clear of 50th Division. Once this was accomplished they made good progress until the leading tank was knocked out by a well-sited anti-tank gun and that route was abandoned in favour of the one to La Vallée. However, just east of La Vallée again the leading tank was knocked out and the troop leader, Lieutenant Tisdall, withdrew in the sole remaining tank, having been able to report that the village was still held by the enemy. He was complimented on his enterprise by the Brigade Commander. The Squadron advanced no further, but remained in observation of the road junction and leaguered that night short of Aunay. The 1st Royal Tanks were at the cross-roads at Robin with the Inniskillings who had replaced the 4th County of London Yeomanry in the Division the day before, and the Queen's behind them, but the advance was held up by mines and infantry. The enemy here was the 326th Division, disorganised but determined, fighting on in small pockets after they had been surrounded. They were firmly dug-in, with tanks and anti-tank guns, in the triangle between Villers Bocage, Aunay and the Robin cross-roads, and fully resolved to stay there. The country all round was in a frightful mess having been fought over two days before. Dead cows were lying everywhere and the smell was ghastly.

On August 3rd the Regiment came under command of the 131st Brigade instead of the 22nd Armoured. By 4 a.m. the 1/6th Queen's had, after a night attack, secured the high ground round Sauques, two miles from Aunay. North of them the 1/7th Queen's were clearing the woods of the enemy, supported by 'A' Squadron, 8th Hussars. This was successfully done by 5 o'clock, ten minutes later a message came through from the 1/6th Queen's at St. George d'Aunay to say that they were being attacked and wanted tank support. Although it seemed as though infantry rather than tanks were needed, 'C' Squadron moved off to their rescue.

It appeared that the 1/6th Queen's had been attacked and had two companies overrun by shouting and screaming S.S. infantry supported by twelve tanks and mortar and artillery fire. Six 17-pounders of the Norfolk Yeomanry had also been knocked out during the afternoon.

Major Huth brought 'C' Squadron up at speed, but with their arrival the enemy counter-attack disappeared. However, the mortar, shell and small-arms fire continued, and to begin with it was 'a very hot spot'. Ten deserters from the 3/276 Feld Ersatz Battalion surrendered to Captain Hepburn shortly after the Squadron arrived.

The plan was to withdraw after dark to the high ground to the north-west. This they did, starting at midnight, the last two troops leaving at 1.30 in the morning, bringing with them a section of infantry who had remained with them for their local protection.

Meanwhile to the north the Inniskillings had reached Tracy Bocage which was strongly held by the enemy. Not much progress anywhere was made on August 4th although the 11th Hussars reached the outskirts of Villers Bocage. 'A' and 'C' Squadrons, 8th Hussars, remained in firm bases with the 1/5th and 1/7th Queen's, with 'B' Squadron in reserve. 'C' Squadron's Four Troop, under Lieutenant J. G. M. Young, forward with an infantry patrol, came in contact with the enemy and Young with Three Troop advanced right into St. George d'Aunay village in the evening and found it clear. There was every indication that the enemy was withdrawing southwards. The Squadron also acted successfully as O.P.'s for the Artillery who put down 'stonks' with great effect on the targets, including a large enemy transport column withdrawing south.

L

It was on this day that Major-General Erskine who had commanded the Division since Tripoli, left them, and was replaced by Major-General Verney of the 6th Guards Tank Brigade. With him went Brigadier Hinde of the 22nd Armoured Brigade whose command was taken over by Brigadier Mackeson and Lieut.-General Bucknell of 30 Corps who was replaced by Lieut.-General Horrocks.

Progress east of Aunay was so slow that it was decided to push the 22nd Armoured Brigade up to La Poste and, moving across country under cover of darkness, they by-passed Aunay to the north, and gained the high ground by Mont Pinçon. Villers Bocage was by now impassable owing to mines and rubble.

At first light on the 5th, 'C' Squadron went out in thick mist to the position they had evacuated the night before, but there was nothing to be seen. The enemy withdrew, laying mines on the roads behind them, to take up new positions on and around Mont Pinçon. Meanwhile, the 131st Brigade was advancing east, 'B' Squadron as left flank protection, followed by the remainder of the Regiment. These passed through 'C' Squadron at 7 a.m. but were held up by mines at the railway bridge. Huth went down into the village of St. George d'Aunay. It was a frightful mess, looted by the Huns and shelled to hell by us. There was a dead German in practically every house. They found a German tracked lorry from which they got some useful stuff. After a day of moving and halting for mines and moving on again the Regiment eventually joined 'B' Squadron who had reached a point about 4 kilometres north of Aunay and leaguered there for the night.

Meanwhile, the 22nd Armoured Brigade had reached Bonnemaison and were just north of Hamar, which gave a good view of Mont Pinçon, and its surrounding hills, while a company of the 1/7th Queen's, operating with the 22nd Armoured Brigade, had reached La Vallée. For all of the 6th the Regiment remained in their leaguer north of Aunay at Maisoncelles Pelvey. In fact for most of the Division it was a day of rest and maintenance. All the roads they could have used, except country lanes which were too small, led to Aunay and Aunay was a horror of desolation unlike anything that had yet been seen. There was nothing standing except the church and one building, and they were both shells. Until the Royal Engineers could clear a way through, the only way south was through La Vallée, insecurely held by a company of 1/7th Queen's. Meanwhile the enemy on the slopes of Mont Pinçon could observe every move below him. On the night of August 6th the 1/7th Queen's were ordered to attack the small village of Les Trois Maries south of La Vallée and at the top of a high hill.

Accordingly, that night the 1/7th Queen's put in what has since been called a 'model attack', and by daylight on the 7th they held the roads south of Vallée. There was good news coming in from all directions. The 43rd Division was up to Ondefontaine, and the 50th had advanced to Le Plessis to clear Mont Pinçon. Further afield the Americans had broken out of the Cherbourg Peninsula and were pouring into the centre of France.

The Regiment after a busy morning of maintenance, moved off at 9 p.m. to a corn-field near Noire Nuit where they lay up awaiting the advance next day. The plan was to by-pass Mont Pinçon to the east and so reach Condé-sur-Noireau which would close the trap on the German Divisions retreating from the Americans at Mortain. The Division was to move in two columns, one along the Aunay-Condé road and the other from La Vallée. The left-hand column consisted of the 22nd Armoured Brigade made up of the 1st Royal Tanks and the 1/7th Queen's, with 'A' Squadron, 8th Hussars doing recce, while the right-hand was the 131st Brigade consisting of the Inniskillings, the 5th Royal Tanks and the 1/5th and 1/6th Queen's, with 'B' Squadron, 8th Hussars, doing recce with 'C' in reserve. Much of the movement would be under constant observation from enemy troops on the slopes of Mont Pinçon.

By 10 a.m. on August 8th 'A' Squadron was north of Cauville where the advance was held up by anti-tank fire. The Squadron remained in observation while artillery fire was brought down. The enemy in this sector was the Battle Group Landsky and the country was almost impassable to tanks. Infantry and bazookas, supported by anti-tank guns, were plentiful and the Germans were resisting every foot of ground.

At the end of the day's action 'A' Squadron had had three tanks knocked-out and 'B' Squadron one. Lieutenant R. G. Anstey was shot through the shoulder, Lieutenant M. J. E. Jephson was wounded, Sergeant Webber and six men were killed, three were wounded and six were missing. In return one German anti-tank gun was knocked out, one Panther and one self-propelled gun were also believed to be destroyed, about ten prisoners were taken and approximately twenty or more Germans were killed. Troopers Frost and Freeman of 'A' Squadron were captured by some Germans they were about to shoot. However Anstey went up in his tank and, by throwing hand-grenades into the Jerry fox-holes, enabled them both to escape, though he was wounded.

The Squadrons were still in the same rôles on August 9th, and a troop from 'A' Squadron south of L'Aceard passed back valuable information, the gist of which showed that the enemy had withdrawn most of his forces. An attack was therefore put in at 1 p.m., the advance covered by an intense artillery barrage, and was most successful. That night 'B' Squadron came back under command, having taken over from the 5th Royal Tanks.

After the successful attack on August 9th 'C' Squadron put out two troops facing east near La Vallée on the morning of the 10th, in case of an enemy counter-attack. But they saw nothing and the locals said that the Germans had withdrawn in the early hours of the morning.

In the evening of the 9th came the news that for the Regiment their present rôle was over and that they were to 'rest and refit with no commitments at all.' They moved back to join 'C' Squadron, and Sergeant Wyatt was killed by a stray shell.

At first light on August 10th in thick mist, Major Ames ordered one troop of 'A' Squadron and the platoon of the 1st Rifle Brigade to advance to the top of Point 281. This was unopposed as it was found that the enemy had withdrawn during the night. Five enemy deserters, who had remained on the hill, surrendered to the troop. At midday both 'A' and 'B' Squadrons withdrew from their positions and joined the Regiment in the valley to the north, down which ran the road from Aunay-sur-Odon to Thury Harcourt. And here they were to stay for the next six days.

August 10th was the last in this particular operation for the Regiment, and for the whole 7th Armoured Division. There had been such heavy losses, especially in the infantry, that there were no longer the reserves with which to fill the gaps. Since July 18th the Division had been in constant close contact with the enemy, never free for a moment from continuous shelling. All ranks were more than ready for a rest, and it was for this fortnight's hard fighting that the Regiment was awarded the battle honour of Mont Pinçon.

During the first week of August the Germans launched their ill-fated counter-offensive through Mortain and on towards Avranches. This was intended to cut off the Americans who had broken out of the Cherbourg Peninsula and were pouring into France. This attack, however, did not check the Americans for long, and, while the Canadians broke out of Caen and attacked south to Falaise, they cut the Germans' escape routes between Orleans and Paris and pushed on to Arjentan, thus forming what was to become the 'Falaise Gap', graveyard of so much of the German Army. 30 Corps, too, on the north and west of the pocket, encountered desperate resistance as the enemy tried to keep open their one remaining corridor of escape.

(g) Advance to the Seine. Crossing the River Vie at Livarot, August 1944

ON the first day of their brief period of rest, all officers and N.C.O.'s of the Regiment were addressed by the new Commander of 30 Corps, Lieut.-General Horrocks. He painted a very rosy picture of the progress of the war and spoke of his pleasure at having the Division under his command.

This short pause in operations was used by 'C' Squadron to try and trace the graves of those who had died at Briquessard. Major Huth, with some of his officers and N.C.O.'s, found the bodies of Sergeant Hunter and Lance-Corporal French lying near their tanks, and Sergeant Langmead's and Lance-Corporal Gibbins' tanks were also found, burnt out. There was no sign of those belonging to Sergeant Walsh and Lance-Sergeant Pilkington. It was during this short rest period that the Regiment received their first three Challenger tanks, which though the chassis was the ordinary Cromwell, the gun mounted was a 17-pounder, a weapon far superior to the 75-mm. with which the other Cromwells of the Regiment were armed.

The Germans were now in full retreat as the jaws of the trap closed on them at Falaise and Argentan, and more allied soldiers landed in the south of France. However, on the afternoon of the 15th orders came through that the 7th Armoured Division was to move east of the Orne, operating under command of the 1st Canadian Army near St. Pierre-sur-Dives and to drive on towards Livarot and Lisieux. As far as St. Pierre the country was the familiar rolling Caen plain but beyond there it rose into wooded plateaux cut by steep valleys. It was rather like the 'bocage', but the enemy were retreating and were in nothing like such great numbers as before. However there were four rivers ahead, the Vie, Touques, Orbec and Risle whose bridges would all have been destroyed, and along the roads on the high ground every corner would conceal a Tiger, Panther or anti-tank gun manned by a determined rear-guard.

The Regiment was ready to move at dawn on August 16th, but their start was delayed by other units. At about 9 a.m. they took their position in the column. Movement was almost non-existent during the morning as the Division crept through clouds of dust across the battle-scarred Normandy countryside. Their route lay by Hamars, Amayé-sur-Orne, Clinchamp-sur-Orne, Laize-la-Ville, Roquancourt and thence by tank track to Cintheaux. By 6 o'clock that evening they had arrived in their leaguer area at St. Aignau de Cramesuil, south of Bourgebus.

At first light on August 17th the Regiment advanced east, with the object of securing a crossing over the River Vie at Livarot. They were to work with the Queens, 'C' Squadron with the 1/6th, 'B' Squadron with the 1/7th and 'A' in reserve with the 1/5th.

At 9.30 a.m. 'C' Squadron joined the 1/6th Queen's at Poussy-la-Campagne and the Commanding Officer, Lieut.-Colonel J. H. Mason, gave out his orders. The Brigade, with the 8th Hussars under command, were to lead the advance of the 7th Armoured Division. They reached Magny-la-Campagne and here owing to unexpectedly strong enemy resistance, fresh orders were given. The plan had changed and the intention now was to capture Livarot. Major Huth was put in command of the forward body which consisted of, in addition to 'A' Company 1/6th Queen's, a troop of Norfolk Yeomanry, one section of the Royal Engineers and two carrier Sections of two O.P.'s belonging to the 3rd Royal Horse Artillery. They left the main body at 3.30 p.m., crossed the river at St. Pierre-sur-Dives and passed through the outposts of the 51st Highland Division which were about three thousand yards east of the town. Atkinson-Willes and Five Troop were leading, followed by Payne and Four Troop and finally Young and Three Troop, who had one platoon of infantry with them.

Atkinson-Willes passed through the village of Boissy and was some five hundred yards east of it when the leading tank of Four Troop was hit by a Bazooka at short range. The driver, Trooper Golding, gallantly managed to bring the tank back in spite of the fact that the commander, Lance-Corporal Mitchell had been killed, Lance-Corporal Chitty had had his arm blown off and Trooper Sinner was wounded.

Shortly afterwards the leading tank of Five Troop, Lance-Sergeant Kay, was hit by an anti-tank shell on the front, killing Trooper Lowe the gunner, instantly, while Trooper Jones died shortly afterwards from wounds. Lance-Sergeant Kay, Richards and Thompson had all to be evacuated as wounded.

While all this was going on Young's troop were successfully engaging small parties of enemy infantry on the west side of the village, and at last light the village and some high ground to the north-east were firm based by the 1/6th.

'B' Squadron had also met stiff opposition and one tank of Lieutenant Lombard's troop was knocked out. But at nightfall they had reached Miltois, about three miles over the river.

Next day the plan was for the 1/6th Queen's and 'C' Squadron to take the northern route and make for Livarot by Boissy and La Saminière while 'B' Squadron and the 1/7th were to go by Miltois, Quevrue and join the others at La Saminière.

At 9.30 a.m. 'C' Squadron renewed their advance. They made fairly good headway although they were hindered by a good many unreliable but well-meant civilian reports. 'A' Company, 1/6th Queen's, with Sergeant Wilson and Two Troop in support, secured some high ground and were able to engage and knock-out a self-propelled gun near Ste. Marguerite des Viette and scatter some German infantry. Meanwhile, 'B' Company with Hartwright and One Troop worked their way on to some high ground on the south side of the road near Les Gens and captured two 20-mm. anti-tank guns intact, the crews having abandoned them. 'C' Company with Payne and Four Troop were then pushed on through Ste. Marguerite des Loges and succeeded in establishing themselves at Point 177. Squadron and Battalion Headquarters moved up into Ste. Marguerite and received a terrific reception from the inhabitants. Flowers, eggs, cider and kisses were showered on them all.

'B' Company and Hartwright's troop were then switched from Les Gens to an area 1 kilometre east of the village, while Young's troop and a section and a half of carriers carried out a recce towards Livarot down the main road. "I did not like this task," wrote Huth, "but was told to get on with it!" Before they had gone far a carrier was brewed up, while Young engaged and knocked out a 88-mm. at the bend of the road at La Saminière. However, this brought down a barrage from other anti-tank guns and both he and Corporal Anderson were knocked out themselves. Hepburn and the Carrier Commander, Captain Docton, who were close by at a farm, tried to reach the tanks that had been hit. However when they had gone about half-way they met Lance-Corporal Bell and Troopers Walker and Smith, all of whom were slightly wounded crawling back along the ditch. They brought the sad news that Young had been killed. Meanwhile the carrier sections were making their way through the fields on each side of the road towards La Saminière, when firing was heard from behind them and it was decided to give up the attempt to reach Three Troop.

On returning to the farm buildings some enemy were seen to the north of the road. One of them threw a sticky bomb at Hepburn's tank but it did little harm beyond damaging a wheel. Hepburn and Lance-Corporal Perston then took up hull-down positions on the bend of the road and remained there until ordered to withdraw into the defended Ste. Marguerite.

While all this was going on 'B' Company and Hartwright's Troop were west of Cour Livet and reported the enemy coming in from the east and south. Enemy were also seen on the high ground east of Mont Viette, a mile south-west of Livarot, in front of 'B' Squadron and the 1/7th Queen's.

'B' Squadron itself had been having a difficult time, as Mont Viette was strongly held. The country there was definitely unsuited to tanks, and the infantry led, closely supported by 'B' Squadron. They cleared the Bois de Quennie but the leading company found the enemy holding a more or less organised line on the high ground commanding a stream about a mile further on. And there they stopped and dug in as no one could tell how many Germans were hiding in the thick woods.

Many casualties were caused that day when several times low-flying Spitfires mistook the leading troops for Germans. Troopers Watkinson, Schofield and Patching from 'C' Squadron were wounded and Sergeants Steptoe and Porteus and Lance-Corporal Aidulis from the Echelon. Captain Newman, the Intelligence Officer, was severely wounded in the stomach and arm while driving Lieut.-Colonel Goulburn in his jeep, and he too was badly shaken as a result of the smash. There was damage done to guns of the Norfolk Yeomanry and other vehicles also.

At last light 'C' Squadron Headquarters and Five Troop went into leaguer north of Ste. Marguerite des Loges whilst One, Two and Four Troops remained in support of their respective companies for the night. 'A' Squadron with the 1/5th Queen's moved across the river to Ste. Marguerite des Viettes close behind the 1/6th.

On August 19th at first light, 'A' Squadron and the 1/5th Queen's relieved 'C' and the 1/6th who came into reserve some two miles east of St. Pierre-sur-Dives. As opposition was considerable on the main road to Livarot, 'A' Squadron with one company 1/5th Queen's was brought forward to investigate the approaches to the river Vie further north. They met no opposition and eventually at 4 p.m. found a rickety bridge that had missed being blown up by the Germans. This good news was wirelessed back to Divisional Headquarters, while the 1/5th Queen's and 'A' Squadron crossed and formed a bridgehead astride the main Livarot-Lisieux road. In the evening patrols were sent on into Livarot and reported the town clear.

That night the forward areas were raided by about fifteen enemy planes, and from 'C' Squadron Troopers Moffat, Jones and Commerford were killed.

(h) The Seine reached. Chateau St. Hilaire, August 1944

ON August 20th the Regiment moved to Boissy to spend a few days in Divisional reserve, less 'A' Squadron who were to come under command of the 22nd Armoured Brigade that night. Meanwhile 'A' was still operating with the 1/5th Queen's. They left their leaguer area at 7.30 a.m. and pushed on down the main road to Livarot. There was no opposition and by midday they had secured a second bridgehead over the Vie, one and a half miles north-east of Livarot on the Lisieux road. This had been blown but was soon repaired and by 3 p.m. the 1/6th were into the town. This was the first town of any size to be liberated undamaged, and the welcome was terrific, as were the welcomes all across France. Here for the first time local members of the Maquis were of great service in producing information and interfering with enemy movements by Fifth Column activities.

In the afternoon of the 20th 'C' Squadron moved up to an area east of Boissy where they leaguered for the night. Squadron Headquarters was a small farmhouse where they made themselves very comfortable. After they were settled in Major Huth took a party forward to where Young's and Corporal Anderson's tanks had been brewed up. There they found Young and Corporal Porter dead in the ditch by the side of their tanks. Anderson they found too about twenty yards from his tank shot through the back. They questioned some French locals who said that the other four from Anderson's tank had been taken prisoner, three having been wounded.

They then went on with Captain Henri Belmont, the French Liaison officer attached to the Squadron, to the farm near where Hartwright had been with his troop on the 18th. It appeared that when Hartwright's troop arrived they were the first British troops to be seen and that they were greeted with cries of, "Vive les Anglais!" and given eggs and butter and flowers. Some Germans had been watching this, and when the troop withdrew in the evening four Germans went into the house and shot the farmer, his wife and two daughters and wounded another daughter and a boy of ten. "We had this story from the daughter who had been wounded. The Germans believing her dead had left her. This only goes to show what foul creatures we are up against. The culprits were either 12 S.S. or 272 Fusilier Division." Even so there was no lack of French civilian assistance.

For the next five days the bulk of the Regiment remained in Divisional reserve, catching up on all-important maintenance and rest. On the 21st 'A' Squadron was patrolling the main Livarot-Lisieux road while 'C' Squadron was called out at about 9 a.m. to move up at once to support the 1/6th Queen's guarding Livarot. They had had one of their companies attacked by a German tank followed by infantry who had overrun a platoon. However when the three troops were sent out into Company areas, the infantry retired and all was quiet.

That evening 'C' Squadron handed over to a squadron of Northants Yeomanry. Urgently needed reinforcements arrived too in the shape of four complete troops of Northants Yeomanry with their tanks. Lieutenants Venner, Ryde, Davies and Saxby and the seventy-two other ranks were all to become loyal and efficient 8th Hussars.

By the 22nd the Division was almost up to Lisieux, and having gained Fervaques, and found advance from the east impracticable, were coming in on it from the west. Lisieux was strongly defended as it was essential to the Germans' line of retreat. 'A'

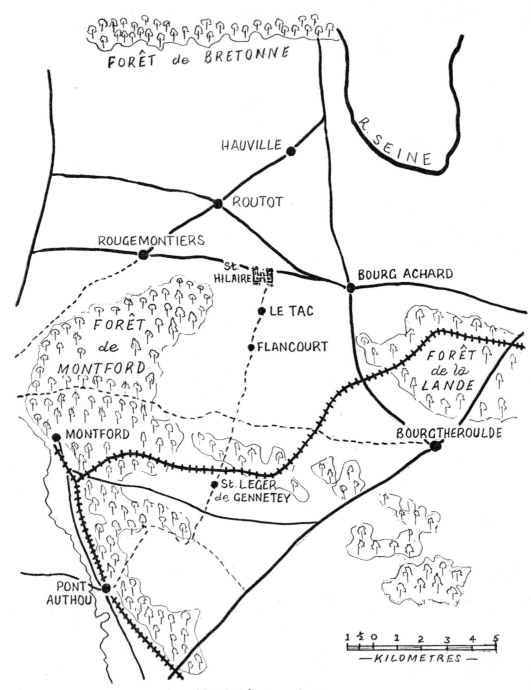

FORÊT de BRETONNE

R. SEINE

HAUVILLE

ROUTOT

ROUGEMONTIERS

St. HILAIRE

BOURG ACHARD

LE TAC

FORÊT de MONTFORD

FLANCOURT

FORÊT de la LANDE

MONTFORD

BOURGTHEROULDE

St. LEGER de GENNETEY

PONT AUTHOU

1 ½ 0 1 2 3 4 5
— KILOMETRES —

Map C. Advance to the Seine.
26th-27th August, 1944.

Company of the 1/7th Queen's, with 'A' Squadron, reached Orbec but found the country there heavily defended and the going too soft for tanks. However by the middle of the afternoon the 1st Royal Tanks and the 1/5th Queen's were into both the town and St. Jacques on the outskirts to the east.

The Regiment, less 'A' Squadron, moved to a new leaguer area north of Livarot in the afternoon, after some had "had a real bath in the Chateau in the morning!" 'C' Squadron established the Squadron office and officers' mess in a pig sty. "There had been no pigs in here for quite a while and we have had it cleared out. It makes a very good office and mess, but rather a come-down from the chateau!" So strange a thing is war when a pig-sty can be deemed comfortable.

Early on the morning of the 24th the armoured cars were through Lisieux and on down the main road beyond, heading for Pont Authou on the River Risle. The Regiment, complete with 'A' Squadron, moved in the afternoon of the 24th to La Grieurie, eleven kilometres east of Lisieux, where they leaguered in a small peaceful orchard. There was cheering and flags were out all the way. From all parts the news was good. The 2nd French Armoured Division was on the outskirts of Paris and the Americans had reached Sens and Elboef between Rouen and Paris. Although the 7th Armoured Division might be held up on the Risle this was very different fighting from Caen and the bocage where advances were only a matter of yards.

By the 25th rumours reached the Regiment that patrols had reached the Seine. They themselves were still held up while the engineers threw bridges over the Risle. But by the 26th the river had been crossed and the enemy's next line of defence was the railway line running east and west of the Forêt de Montfort. By this time the Canadians were in Bernay to the south-west and the 49th Division up to Pont Audemer, five miles to the north, while between the two the 7th Armoured Division drove the Germans east on to the Seine. All that remained to be done was the mopping up of stragglers and enemy rearguards, of which there were plenty in the Forêts de Montfort and Bretonne.

On the 26th the Regiment crossed the Risle at Pont Authou and came under command of the 131st Brigade. In the evening 'C' Squadron took over the task of protecting the right flank of the 22nd Armoured Brigade, and the Regiment leaguered that night near Bonneville Appetot. They continued in the same rôle on the 27th, although this time with two squadrons up. 'B' Squadron on the left encountered strong opposition in the shape of infantry and anti-tank guns at St. Hilaire, a beautiful chateau surrounded by a beechwood. These knocked out two tanks and caused nine casualties of which one was the Troop leader, Lieutenant S. E. Apthorpe.

Meanwhile 'C' Squadron had cut the main road between Bourg Achard and Routot and the 51st Highland Division passed through them to secure the area. At last light the Regiment withdrew to leaguer 3 kilometres south of Bonquetot.

There was no task for the Regiment on the morning of the 28th, so the Commanding Officer, accompanied by Captain Belmont, took the opportunity of inspecting Lieutenant Apthorpe's two tanks. No customary sign of a body consumed in a brewed tank was found, and a search through the potatoes, the haulms of which were very high, produced a negative result. During the night our artillery had shelled the chateau and the Germans had abandoned it before the proposed attack by the 7th Argylls was launched. The magnificent tall beech trees had protected the chateau from damage and only one shell had penetrated the roof. The other shells had struck the top of the trees all of which were decapitated. The farm and stables, however, which were just outside the area of the trees, were utterly wrecked. The Commanding Officer called upon the owners, the Count and Countess du Chastel, who were in residence, and were informed that five English soldiers had been brought in by the Germans on the previous evening. As the Germans possessed no medical facilities, the Countess had done what she could for one of our men who was badly wounded. She was unable to say whether the group included an officer. She and the Chateau staff had spent a very uncomfortable night in the cellars during our bombardment which included medium as well as field artillery, and she agreed that it was a miracle that the chateau was so little damaged.

In the evening the whole Division was pulled back a few miles for some ever-welcome rest and maintenance. The news came through that the British were into Rouen and that the Americans were up to the Marne. It did seem at last as though the backbone of the German resistance was broken and indeed in the next phase, apart from stubborn rearguard actions and the demolishing of bridges they were withdrawing at speed to the Vosges and the Meuse, the next natural line of defence with the Eifel and Siegfried lines behind them.

On the 29th orders were given out for next advance, to Ghent, the immediate objectives being the seizure of the Seine crossings between Amiens and Abbéville, the main task being to secure the Low Countries and capture the Channel ports to ease the supply question.

For the very active part the Regiment had played in the operations since August 16th they were awarded the battle honour of the Dives Crossing. Casualties had been considerable but morale was very high.

(i) Across the Seine and Somme. St. Pol, September 1944

On August 30th the Division came under command of 12 Corps, Lieut.-General N. M. Ritchie, with whom they were to stay almost continuously until they reached Hamburg eight months later. By now the 22nd Armoured Brigade were very low in Cromwell Tanks, and in 131st Brigade each Battalion of the Queen's was two companies short. In spite of this, however, they were not replaced, as during the last few weeks' fighting, the co-operation between this armour and infantry had attained a very high standard indeed. The 4th Armoured Brigade now joined the Division together with the Royals, an armoured car regiment, and both of these were already across the Seine.

The plan was for a general advance, the American 1st Army to make for the country between Brussels and Namur, the 2nd Army for the vital port of Antwerp, and the 1st Canadian Army for the Channel ports. The 2nd Army was to advance, 30 Corps on the right led by the 11th Armoured Division heading for Antwerp and the Guards Armoured Division for Brussels, while 12 Corps on the left, led by the 7th Armoured Division, made for Ghent.

At 2 a.m. on August 30th in the cold and dark and rain the Regiment formed up and the advance began. They went by Louviers to the Seine, stopping and starting in the worst traffic congestion they had yet encountered. When at last they did reach the river at St. Pierre du Vauvray the bridge was being repaired which entailed yet more waiting. But at last they were over, and sweeping on through cheers and ringing bells through Les Andelys, Morgny and Gournay-en-Bras. There they met a column of German Prisoners of War being marched away by the triumphant Maquis.

Having covered some forty miles the Regiment leaguered for the night at Grumes.

Just as the Commanding Officer and Lieutenant Craven arrived, seven Germans were seen leaving the leaguer area and who promptly made themselves scarce.

The advance recommenced at first light on August 31st, 'A' Squadron in the lead again with orders to secure the crossing over the river Somme at Hangest-sur-Somme. The Squadron Leader got his whip out and his Cromwell tanks responded to such good effect that the Commanding Officer travelling in a scout car immediately behind was barely able to keep up. The column roared along country roads, through endless villages, wet bunches of chrysanthemums and unripe apples thrown by cheering Frenchmen as the vehicles rushed by being the only danger.

At Montagne-Fayel, seven miles short of the river, two of 'A' Squadron troops ran out of petrol. But the remainder pushed on to Hangest to find the bridge already blown. They had covered a distance of eighty miles in seven hours. A reconnaisance up and down stream confirmed that all other bridges had also been blown, which was a great disappointment. However this was somewhat offset by the satisfaction gained in beating the 22nd Armoured Brigade to the river. They had been on a shorter and a better road. The Regiment was complimented by Brigadier Pepper of the 131st Brigade on the speed of their advance.

At 9 p.m. the Regiment received orders to move at once eastward to Amiens, some fourteen miles away, by Molliens Vidame and to cross the river by a small bridge over a lock which had been discovered intact in the western outskirts of the town. Lights were not permitted, but a clear sky and a half moon aided their progress. By 1 a.m. the Regiment was in leaguer four miles north of the river at Vaux-en-Amienois. The 131st Brigade followed them over the bridge, which, having served its purpose, quietly subsided into the water. Lieutenant Mossop having arrived with the next days' maps, all ranks lay down exhausted for three hours' sleep.

Next morning, September 1st, came the orders that they were to advance and capture St. Pol and secure the high ground to the north. They made good speed to Frevent, some eighteen miles from St. Pol, where they were greeted with champagne and Calvados, which as it happened was rather like the port and plumcake at a meet before the actual hunting begins. In fact they had not long to wait before they found, and, in the early afternoon, 'C' Squadron ran into the enemy at Herlin-le-Sec on the outskirts of St. Pol. The town was still strongly held with an anti-tank gun out on the Frevent road. Atkinson-Willes and Two Troop were leading and at once Corporal Gibbins' tank was brewed up and he was killed. Troopers Willis, Fraser and Lance-Corporal Arthur were seen to get out and of these Arthur was hit and fell while Fraser was subsequently reported missing. Willis shammed dead, and although the Germans went through his pockets and turned him over he managed to deceive them and, during a heavy 'stonk', was able to get away, although terribly burnt and nearly blinded. Squadron Sergeant-Major Fleming went up later in his tank with the medical half-track to try and fetch back a wounded man but was himself hit by a 75-mm. He climbed out of his tank all right but went back to fetch Lance-Corporal Jacoby, the driver, and was shot dead. Jacoby, too, had been killed when the tank was hit.

Meanwhile Major Huth had managed to push Lieutenant G. J. Davies and Four Troop round to the west of the town while Sergeant Head and Three Troop were north-west and Hartwright and One watched the road to the east. St. Pol was thus surrounded by 'C' Squadron on three sides and by the Inniskillings to the north. Three and Four Troops between them brewed-up a convoy of three lorries, a staff car and a motor-cycle, entering St. Pol. Three Troop also bagged a staff car and altogether they must have accounted for about twenty Germans killed and eight prisoners. From a

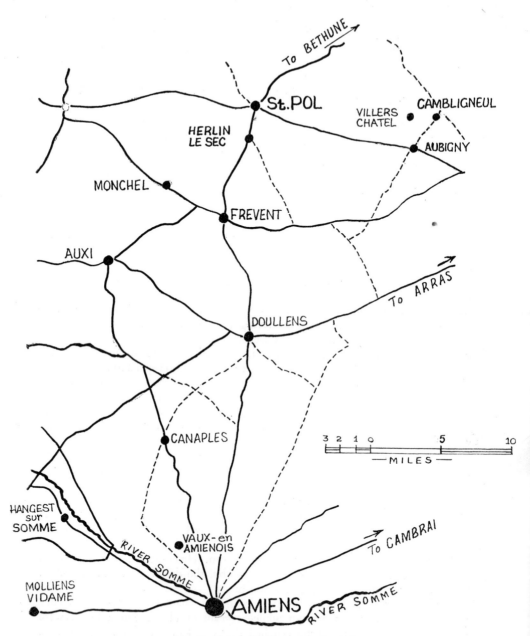

Map D. Across the Somme to St. Pol.
30th August–2nd September, 1944.

prisoner they discovered that one of the lorries had been carrying the pay of the garrison, about £250.

Although 'C' Squadron had encircled the town it was much too strongly held to be taken by such a small force. Neither was it worth wasting time in clearing it as elsewhere the advance was hurrying on. General Verney decided to by-pass St. Pol and sent for the 22nd Armoured Brigade who would pick up 'A' Squadron and 1/7th Queen's and try to find a way round both to the east and west. The 131st Brigade would keep 1/5th and the remainder of the Regiment masking the town, while 1/6th were to watch Auxi le Chateau to the west which was strongly held. The enemy had a line of fairly stout defence from Auxi, through St. Pol to Lilliers and along the canal to La Bassée. That evening, while Three and Four Troops of 'C' Squadron kept the roads out of St. Pol cut, the 1st Royal Tanks and the 1st Rifle Brigade broke across the Hesdin road and pushed on to Cauchy.

On the 2nd at midday, two companies of 1/7th Queen's supported by One and Two Troops, 'C' Squadron, put in an attack on St. Pol from the south-west. During this Atkinson-Willes was severely wounded in the leg and had to be evacuated. His troop was taken over by Sergeant Wakefield and, under the guidance of a French gendarme, the leading Company and One Troop pushed right on to the town, while two anti-tank guns were knocked out by mortar-fire. They were also able to witness the extra-ordinary sight of the Maquis shaving the heads of certain French girls who had been co-habiting with German soldiers.

In spite of the fact that the French had given them the exact position of all the German anti-tank guns, thus enabling accurate shelling to take place, it was decided that the town was too stubbornly held. Lieut.-Colonel Goulburn had drawn up a plan of attack but the 131st Brigade ordered its postponement and the Regiment was warned to prepare to disengage and to by-pass St. Pol to the east. At midday 'A' Squadron came under command of the 22nd Armoured Brigade who were to lead the advance.

Meanwhile the Regiment had been collecting a considerable bag of both prisoners and transport round St. Pol and west of Frevent. Frevent had been re-occupied by the Germans, and 'B' Squadron at Monchel carried out a number of successful skirmishes against an enemy struggling to withdraw through the British line of advance, and Lieutenant Tisdall reported knocking out two anti-tank guns.

In the evening the Regiment was relieved by a Battalion of the Welch Regiment and at about 8.30 p.m. they moved out to join the 131st Brigade which was already pas-sing up the new axis. They went by Aubigny and leaguered for the night at Villers Chatel at the edge of a large wood. 'B' Squadron was called out at midnight to protect the 131st Brigade Headquarters who were leaguered on the Servins-Hersin road and had been rudely awakened in the middle of the night by a horde of excited Frenchmen who reported two thousand German tanks approaching. Nothing, however, materialised, but at 2 a.m. the Regiment was ordered to stand to. They moved away from the wood and into a large field where they adopted the old desert 'close-leaguer' in three columns. No further alarms were raised and all ranks turned in after an exhausting twenty-two hours fighting and moving.

The Regiment, who had been in the forefront of the fighting since they landed in France, were now to sustain a bitter disappointment. There were orders to move at first light on the 3rd, and they stood by in readiness to lead the advance on Ghent once more. Then came a change of plan, and in a cold wind they stood-to all morning. The Germans were still holding out on the La Bassée Canal between La Bassée and Bethune, and the only way through appeared to be by routes south and east of Lille. However it was decided that a small force was all that could make this last desperate rush as petrol was so scarce, and the Regiment had to hand their stocks of fuel to 30 Corps and watch 'Ghent Force' rumble away.

Communications with the 7th Armoured Division soon became impossible and it was evident that the Regiment was dropping far behind the main advance. By the 6th the forward part of the Division was well into Belgium and that night the German garrison in Ghent surrendered.

The country in which the Regiment spent these six days of rest was full of names that were household words on most people's lips, Arras, Vimy, Ypres and Menin, a few miles of France that had had its share of bloodshed in the 1914-18 war.

Then on the 11th the Polish Armoured Division took over and the whole 7th Armoured Division was pulled out for a few days rest at Mâlines where the Regiment was to join them. For the moment the advance had come to a standstill, partly because the Albert Canal was fairly strongly held, but mostly because all supplies, ammunition and petrol for both the American and British Armies had to come from Cherbourg and Arromanches, four hundred miles away. While Antwerp was already ours we could not use it as a port until we held both sides of the Scheldt. As it was, there were bands of enemy stragglers there to be dealt with and the Channel Ports were still holding out. The advance had been so rapid that quite often troops had to turn round and fight an enemy behind them.

On September 11th the Regiment crossed the Belgian frontier and spent the night at Vlierzele on the main road from Alost to Ghent. They received a tremendous welcome as they drove into Belgium and all along the route there were flags and fruit and shouting. At Impe they were the first British troops to be seen and the people swarmed round them, very interested in everything, and most friendly. At one moment there were about fifty little children watching them eat, and next day, which the Regiment spent in the same leaguer, there were literally thousands. When Ghent was visited in the evening there was still shelling going on in the northern outskirts. It was not the first time 8th Hussars had been to Ghent. In April 1794 they had landed at Ostend to fight in Flanders with the Austrians against the French. At the end of June they had been forced eastwards and had had to retire to Ghent, losing everything on the way, Regimental baggage, stores and papers. By November they had withdrawn to the River Vaal and in December, when the frosts began, they fell back slowly all through that terrible winter across the frozen heathland east of Arnhem until they crossed the Ems in March, occupying the villages as they went. They were now retracing those hundred and fifty year old footsteps, but this time instead of retreating they were advancing into Germany.

II. THE LOW COUNTRIES

September 1944-January 1945

(a) Canal Warfare, September 1944

ON the 13th the Regiment joined the Division near Mâlines, their vehicles gay with Belgian flags, for a short period of rest, and a leave party was immediately sent to Brussels. However, forty-eight hours later they were ordered to take over a stretch of the Junction Canal that ran between Oeleghem and Herenthals, here parallel to but south-west of the Albert Canal. The Germans were dug in on the north bank in fair strength and came over to the south from time to time, chiefly raiding for food. 'A' and 'B' Squadrons were on the Canal bank, with 'C' in reserve, and each squadron had a Company of 1/5th Queen's under command. A certain amount of enemy activity was seen south of Herenthals where all the bridges across the waterway were found to be blown.

Mention should here be made of Captain Gaston Serruys who joined the Regiment on the 13th. He proved of great value as liaison officer and interpreter in Flemish, while his wife became the mother to any 8th Hussar officer who subsequently went to Brussels on leave.

On September 16th the Regiment came under command of 131st Brigade and moved to a new sector of the Junction Canal. This stretch reached from the eastern outskirts of Antwerp to the bridge at Grobbendonck and there were Germans dug in all along the north bank of the canal and in the factory area in the north-east outskirts of the town, and all bridges had been blown.

The main feature they had to guard were the sluice gates opposite the Eenhorn factory, as if the Germans had destroyed these much of the Antwerp area would have been flooded. 'C' Squadron took over the left of the new line, making their Headquarters in one of the old Antwerp forts, 'B' had a sector from Oeleghem to Grobbendonck, while 'A' came into reserve.

Next day there was spasmodic shelling. Lieutenant Davies of 'C' Squadron set up an observer post on the top floor of the deserted Eenhorn factory on the bank of the Canal overlooking the sluice gates, and kept in touch with their tank further down. However later in the day the Germans spotted this and Troopers Jevon and Beddingfield were wounded by shellfire. Sergeant Wilson, also of 'C', put up a very gallant show by going across the canal in a boat with some Belgian patriots and bringing back a Belgian family who gave valuable information. Acting on this 'C' Squadron shot up a house and café, one containing twenty Germans and the other an officer and thirty men. Major Huth scored a direct hit on the first house which went up in flames, while Captain Hepburn engaged the second successfully with his 95-mm. That was the first day of the famous battle of Arnhem, and from their position the Regiment was able to see shoal upon shoal of gliders being towed north towards their battle areas.

The 11th Hussars took over from the Regiment at first light on the 18th, and they moved over to the Gheel bridgehead in support of the infantry of the 131st Brigade, the scene of much bitter fighting.

But it was at Arnhem to the north-east of Gheel that the really desperate fighting was going on. Faced with two alternatives, that of a slow slogging advance over the Dutch waterways with winter drawing on in country unsuitable for tanks and with the port of Antwerp still unusable, or the bold but dangerous airborne operations which would skirt the Siegfried Line and secure for us the all-important bridges, General Eisenhower chose the latter. Its success could end the war by Christmas.

Accordingly it was planned to drop a 'carpet' of airborne troops, the British 1st Airborne Division furthest ahead at Arnhem, the U.S. 82nd Airborne near the bridge over the River Waal at Nijmegen and the U.S. 101st Airborne on the canals north of Eindhoven. Meanwhile 30 Corps headed by the Guards Armoured Division would form a spear-head with Arnhem as its objective, regardless of the opposition on its flanks. This advance was to be protected by 12 Corps on the left and 8 Corps on the right, and as it happened the enemy resistance here was far stronger than had been expected. The drop was to go in on September 17th, and on the 18th the 7th Armoured Division were relieved by the Canadians of their positions in and east of Antwerp and moved out to the flank of 30 Corps between Herenthals and Gheel. However, when the time for the advance into Holland came, it was found necessary to leave the Division behind to watch the canal crossings at Herenthals and Antwerp until the Canadians could finish clearing Antwerp and work east to join them.

The 19th was, for the Regiment, an uneventful day. They remained watching their sector of the Junction Canal and also watching the gliders going over, east and north-east, towards Arnhem, Nijmegen and Eindhoven. They were still there on the 20th, putting in some valuable maintenance while they waited. On this day the Guards Armoured Division reached Eindhoven, and, fighting desperately, managed to secure the vital bridges over the Waal at Nijmegen. At Arnhem, things were not going well. The enemy had a strong screen of anti-tank guns south-west of the town and bad weather had prevented drops of reinforcements and supplies to the beleaguered parachutists. As well as that, the lines of communication for the whole spear-head force stretched back down a single road for forty miles and thence for several hundred miles more, and all of it most dangerously exposed. On the 22nd this road was cut by an enemy force at the village of Veghel and, although driven off next day by the Guards and the 50th Division, it was cut again by a much stronger force with tanks and artillery on the 24th.

On the 21st the Regiment moved up past the bridgehead at Gheel; which had been evacuated on the 19th as the resistance there had been so strong and the losses so heavy, to take up a line of observation along a further section of the Meuse-Eseort-Junction Canal at Donck, relieving the 44th Brigade, 15th Scottish Division. The take-over was uneventful, but there was a big wood in the middle of their domain where the Germans were lying up. They were also all along the north bank of the canal, and although all the bridges over the canal appeared to be blown, the Germans crossed on the damaged bridges and on barges.

Later in the day the Regiment, with the 1/6th Queen's under command, extended eastward and took over a further section of the Albert and Junction Canals.

There was not much opposition apart from spasmodic enemy machine-gun fire and mortaring. Tanks could do little in a country of marsh and scrub intersected by canals and huge drainage ditches. For the most part, too, the roads were raised above the surrounding countryside and any movement along them was immediately noticed. It was a depressing landscape as well, made more so by the thought of approaching winter.

The Regiment enlisted the help of the Armée Blanche and on the 23rd, from these and their own patrols' reports, it seemed as though the Germans had pulled out under cover of darkness. They were soon able to confirm this as, although all the bridges

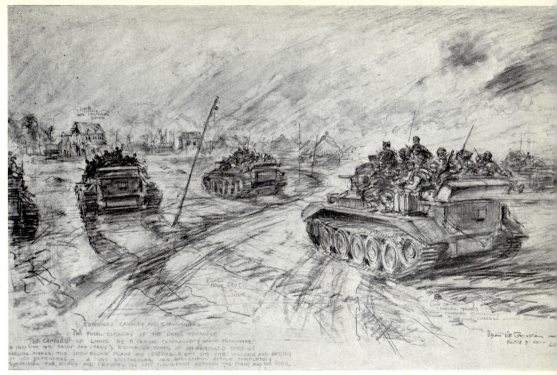

'C' Squadron supporting the Commandos at Linne. 'Each tank, with ten Commandos on the back, dashed across the open and through the smoke-screen into the outskirts of Linne.' January 25th, 1945 (page 199).

A 'Crocodile' of the Buffs, supported by 'B' Squadron, 8th Hussars, firing into the back of the houses of St. Joost, January 21st, 1945.

8th Hussars tanks and infantry moving up to attack St. Joost, January, 1945 (pages 193-198).

The village of St. Joost during the battle.

Start at dawn. Germany, March, 1945.
Drawn by Edward Ardizzone. Capt. Ardizzone served during the war as an official War Artist. He was attached to the Regiment during the final advance to the Elbe, and soon became a friend and companion to many. He had the unusual faculty of being on the spot when wanted, especially when it was a question of mending a track!

Sergeant Wilson receiving the Military Medal from Field-Marshal Montgomery, November, 1944 (page 188).

The devastation of war. The advance through Waldfeucht, February, 1945.

Crew of a Recce Troop scout car keeping watch on a woodland road. Germany, March, 1945.
A drawing by Edward Ardizzone.

The liberation of Stalag IIB, April 16th, 1945. Drawn by Capt. Bryan de Grineau (page 213).

Tanks massed at Brunen awaiting orders to continue the chase, March, 1945 (page 202).

Hamburg and the end of 3,000 miles of fighting, May 4th, 1945. The Regiment crossing the Kiel Canal (page 227).

'B' Squadron tanks at Hamburg Railway Station, May, 1945.

'B' Squadron, 8th Hussars, forming a Guard of Honour for the Investiture of Marshal Zhukov and Marshal Rokossovsky by Field-Marshal Montgomery, Brandenburger Tor, Berlin, July 12th, 1945 (page 230).

Victory Parade, Berlin, July 21st, 1945. Hycilla, an 8th Hussar Cromwell tank, passing Mr. Winston Churchill at the Saluting Base (page 230).

Major-General L. O. Lyne, Commander 7th Armoured Division, inspecting the 8th Hussars, who formed part of the Division, Berlin, 1945.

across the canal were blown and tanks could not cross, a Rifle Brigade patrol crossed by a footbridge and reported Rethy clear, and many villages beyond.

That evening the Regiment received orders to concentrate at Moll, preparatory to a move forward into Holland.

(b) Keeping open the 'Corridor', Nederrijn, September 1944

In the pouring rain early on September 24th the Regiment moved northwards through Lommel and over the Dutch frontier. At Heers, five miles short of Eindhoven, they leaguered for the day but it was far too wet to do any maintenance. Later that night the news came through that the enemy had cut 30 Corps centre-line between St. Oedenrode and Veghel and that on the following day the 8th Hussars, with 1/5th Queen's and one company of 1/7th Queen's under command, would simultaneously clear the centre-line between St. Oedenrode and the Canal, and attack and capture Schijndel. 'A' Squadron and 1/7th Queen's would have the task of clearing the centre-line from St. Oedenrode to Veghel while 'C' Squadron, supported by 1/5th Queen's, would advance on Schijndel with 'B' as left flank protection on the road towards Olland.

At first light on the 25th the Regiment moved out. They passed through Eindhoven, meeting the terrible traffic block of the supply columns of the forward Divisions, which had been there already for a day and a night. Before they reached St. Oedenrode, 'A' Squadron was told that their job had been taken over already by the Americans and the 5th Dragoon Guards, so they came into reserve.

However, 'C' Squadron advanced up to the outposts of an American glider-borne Battalion about 1 kilometre north of St. Oedenrode, and another kilometre further on came under heavy spandau fire from the enemy in a monastery. 'C' Squadron were ordered to by-pass this, while the 1/5th Queen's put in a successful attack. By last light they had pushed on about 2 kilometres, captured forty prisoners and killed approximately twenty enemy, while clearing the woods on the way to Schijndel with the 1/5th Queen's. They also reckoned that had brewed up two lorries and two 88-mm. anti-tank guns, with no casualties to themselves.

It then became evident that the enemy was holding the line of the railway east of Schijndel in some strength and 'C' Squadron was ordered not to advance any further. They had been shelled a good deal during the day and had also encountered a certain amount of spandau fire and sniping, but no anti-tank guns. Several were seen in the area but they all seemed deserted or derelict.

September 25th, further north, was a day of great disappointment, for that night the gallant Arnhem garrison was withdrawn, and with it gone there would be no chance of crossing the Rhine until the spring of 1945.

The task of the 7th Armoured Division, as part of 12 Corps, was therefore to be the clearing of south-west Holland from Grave west towards s'Hertogenbosch and Tilburg so that the great port of Antwerp might be freed for the use of the Allies.

'C' Squadron patrols moved up to their positions of the previous day near the monastery an hour before first light on September 26th, while 'A' Squadron took over 'B' Squadron's rôle of blocking the Olland road. Progress by 'C' Squadron during the morning was slow. The country was made up of open grass fields cut up by dykes, quite

M

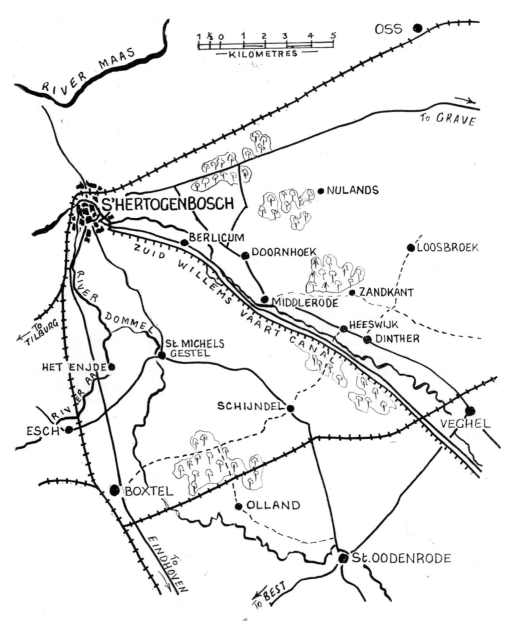

Map. E. Nederrijn.
Keeping open the corridor, 25th-30th September, 1944.
The Lower Maas, 22nd-25th October, 1944.

flat and with no hedges. But by hopping from one small farm to the next they made some progress towards Schijndel, supported by the 3rd and 5th Royal Horse Artillery. By 3 p.m. they had crossed the open country, advanced about a mile and secured a bridgehead over a wide and deep dyke, hastily vacated by the enemy. The Squadron, each tank of which had fired about fifty rounds of high explosive during the day, had been under intermittent fire from enemy guns in the wood along the railway, some eight hundred yards away. It had punished the enemy severely, captured a number of prisoners, and adopting the principles of fire and movement, had destroyed every farm house within sight. It was a credit to Major Huth that up until now he had not lost a tank.

The 1/5th Queen's were then ordered to establish two companies in the dyke, an operation which was carried out successfully by moving them forward behind the screen of tanks. When this was completed 'C' Squadron made a further attempt to advance but lost Corporal Richard's tank immediately to an anti-tank gun concealed near the railway. Troopers Parfitt and Sutherland were killed as they baled out, Corporal Richards missings, believed burnt inside his tank, and Troopers Field and Gardiner wounded, the latter losing his leg.

The Commanding Officer, who had been with Major Huth at his Headquarters, a farmhouse christened 'dead man's farm' on account of the seven Germans lying in a row killed by Besa fire from the tanks, then withdrew in his scout car. The driver, however, soon got it bogged, and Lieutenant Walker, in a Squadron Headquarters' tank had to pull him out in full view of the enemy who opened fire with 20-mm. anti-aircraft fire. The Commanding Officer and his wireless operator were dodging backwards and forwards between the scout car and a small ditch, fixing and unfixing the towrope, and the former made no further visits to Squadron Headquarters that evening!

While all this was going on 'A' Squadron had been active on the Olland road and had suffered some casualties, including Lieutenant Venner, one of their best troop leaders, who was killed by shell fire. Orders for the next day were to consolidate the position gained by 'C' Squadron and the 1/5th Queen's, but to be as offensive as possible with fire. 'B' Squadron took over from 'A' on the Olland road.

At first light on the 27th 'A' Squadron took over from 'C' who remained in their leaguer north of St. Oedenrode where, in spite of a certain amount of shelling and heavy rain, they were comfortably installed in a small house.

Meanwhile, during the morning the Regiment less 'A' and 'B' Squadrons were ordered to move to a new area south of Veghel, 'A' Squadron to remain where they were until the 131st Brigade was relieved by the 158th Brigade of the 53rd Welsh Division. 'B' Squadron was to come under command of the 158th Brigade on its arrival and then act as a mobile reserve. During the night the enemy counter-attacked on the Regiment's right flank but 'A' and 'B' Squadrons reported all quiet.

The Recce Troop had been in trouble that day. They had started by patrolling south of Schijndel with the 5th Dragoon Guards who lost three tanks to a Bazooka just in front of the Recce position. The 5th Dragoon Guards then retired, leaving the Recce Honeys holding an extended line. Meanwhile Sergeant Pickin's tank dropped through a stone slab by a cottage into a cellar and had to be abandoned. They tried to recover it with the L.A.D. at night, covered by the 1st Rifle Brigade, but had to leave it as the tank was on open heathland and they were under enemy fire.

For the next few days the Regiment stayed in their position near St. Oedenrode and took on the rôle of a counter-attack force to deal with any enemy threat to the centre-line between St. Oedenrode and Veghel from the north-west. They were spread out, each Squadron in their own area with a company of 1/7th Queen's. There was time at last for maintenance and even things like hot baths and cinema shows in Eindhoven.

On September 30th the Regiment came under command of the 15th (Scottish) Division. 'B' Squadron, at St. Oedenrode and still in support of the 158th Brigade, carried out an exemplary action when Lieutenant Martin-Smith's troop destroyed, without loss to themselves, a house believed to contain enemy company headquarters. On October 6th the 44th Tank Battalion (King's Own Liverpool Regiment), part of the 46th Independent Armoured Brigade, arrived to take over. The Regiment then came under command of the 131st Brigade and were responsible for the defence of Veghel, whence they moved in the morning to take over from the 5th Royal Tanks, and went into comfortable billets.

The enemy was holding the west bank of the Zuid Willemsvaart Canal, and patrols from Recce Troop were sent out to counter possible enemy crossings. They stayed out until last light but had nothing to report.

'B' Squadron moved in the morning to Loosbroek towards s'Hertogenbosch, and 'A' Squadron took over from them on the 10th. In the early days of October the weather began to grow cold and wet and wintry, and day succeeded day in a monotony of patrols and shelling and standing-to. At this time the Division held a fourteen mile line from Veghel to the Maas north of Oss, and here they remained for nearly a month. The enemy's policy seemed to be simply an attempt to gain time until the winter should make a crossing of the rivers guarding Germany's frontiers an impossibility. Although Antwerp itself was in Allied hands it could not be used as a port as the north and south banks of the Scheldt Estuary were still held by the Germans. Their salient ran in from s'Hertogenbosch in the south through Tilburg and Breda to Bergen op Zoom where a road linked it with the South Beveland peninsula and Walcheren Island. Until the approaches to Antwerp were clear there could be no full-scale advance, so during October all efforts were directed in clearing the country round the port.

For their part in the operations to widen the corridor in the area of St. Oedenrode, Schijndel and Olland, the Regiment was awarded the major battle honour 'The Neder-rijn' and the minor battle honour 'Best'.

(c) Clearing South-west Holland, The Lower Maas, October 1944

THE next operation, code name 'Alan', was to be an advance by the 1st Canadian Army to drive back the Germans from the Estuary, Walcheren Islands and the South Beveland peninsula, while the 2nd British Army cleared both south-west Holland up to the line of the River Mass and the Scheldt estuary. They were to attack from east to west with 12 Corps and from south to north with 1 Corps, from the Antwerp bridgehead on to Breda, thus cutting the enemies' land line of communication over the Moerdijk bridge near the mouth of the Maas. The enemy held a line Oss-Schijndel-Best.

The plan for 12 Corps was for the 15th (Scottish) Division to take Tilburg while the 51st (Highland) Division advanced north-west from the Veghel-St. Oedenrode road towards Schijndel. The 53rd (Welsh) Division, which had been brought up with great secrecy, was, with the 5th Dragoon Guards, to capture s'Hertogenbosch, while the 7th Armoured was to advance to within two miles of s'Hertogenbosch and then pass between the 15th and the 51st and establish themselves at Geertruidenburg near the mouth of the Maas, thirty miles away. The 52nd (Lowland) Division, who were specially trained in mountain warfare, carried out their first operation by landing on Walcheren Island, a large part of which is below sea level.[1]

The detailed plan of attack was as follows. The 53rd Division would go in on the right and the 7th Armoured on the left. The first objective was a line running north and south through Berlicum, three miles east of s'Hertogenbosch. The attack by the 7th Armoured Division was to be carried out in three phases, firstly the 1/5th Queen's supported by 'A' Squadron was to capture Doornhoek, secondly the 1/7th Queen's supported by 'B' Squadron was to make for Middelrode and thirdly the 1/6th and 1/5th Queen's were to secure the final objective, Berlicum. 'C' Squadron was to take over the area just west of Loosbroek from the 1/6th Queen's, and provide right flank cover to the 131st Brigade.

The country they were to fight over was typical of Brabant. From the River Dommel westwards it was mainly thick woods interspersed with stretches of pine-covered sand-dunes. Further south it was more cultivated but still thickly wooded. The roads over the whole area were few and poor, for the most part raised above the surrounding fields and liable to collapse under the weight of a tank. It was nearly always wet and often very cold.

At 2 o'clock on the morning of October 22nd the battle for s'Hertogenbosch began with a tremendous softening-up barrage from the 15th (Scottish) Division. The attack itself was held up slightly by bad visibility but by 7.30 a.m. 'B' Squadron was across the start line and advancing up the sandy tracks towards Middelrode. The right-hand troop suffered an early casualty when one tank was lost on a mine, and the remainder of the troop were then held up by an enemy strong point. The left-hand troop reached the main Dinther-Middelrode road and then turned west. Here the troop leader's tank was mined and almost immediately engaged by a medium calibre anti-tank gun. Another troop, sent down to assist, had two tanks bogged and the troop leader, Lieutenant A. L. Preston shortly afterwards was wounded by a sniper.

The right-hand troop, together with the reserve troop, brought heavy fire to bear on some houses and knocked out a 75-mm. anti-tank gun. A simultaneous attack by both these troops overran the area and the two troops were able to fire on the enemy retreating along the road to Berlicum. During this engagement 'B' Squadron second-in-command, Captain MacGillycuddy, was wounded by shrapnel.

Meanwhile on the right 'A' Squadron, with the 1/5th Queen's, had similar difficulties with boggy ground and mines, losing two tanks to the latter. However, they made steady progress in bitter fighting against dug-in infantry, a few prisoners being taken and many enemy killed. By last light the forward troop of 'A' Squadron was in Doornhoek, with 1/5th Queen's established between the village and the river, while 1/7th Queen's with 'B' Squadron, took Middelrode during the night, finding the enemy had withdrawn under cover of darkness. The 131st Brigade had reached its objective, 3 kilometres east of s'Hertogenbosch, and the 53rd (Welsh) Division had made a similar advance to the right, north of 'C' Squadron who had been watching the woods to the west all day.

The second part of the attack went smoothly on October 23rd, and on the 24th the Regiment, which had now been placed under command of the 22nd Armoured Brigade, was ordered to move to Schijndel. They crossed the Zuid Willems Vaart Canal at Heeswijk by a Bailey bridge built the previous night, and arrived in leaguer at 4 p.m. The plan for next day was for the 22nd Armoured Brigade to cross the River Dommel at

[1] See Map E page 178.

St. Michels Gestel and then advance in two groups. This all depended on how successful the 51st (Highland) Division was in securing bridgeheads over the river Aa that night.

They did not, however, manage to capture the bridge at Het Ende, as planned, but secured one at Esch, where the Regiment, as part of the 22nd Armoured Brigade, crossed on the 26th. In the evening they moved up to Udenhout, to assist in its defence during the night, along roads lined with burning houses, past homeless farmers and their families who stood round the gutted remains of their farms. They reached Udenhout in the dark and found the town in flames. 'B' Squadron took over responsibility for the north-south road up which, it was expected, the enemy rear-guards would withdraw.

The enemy had by now established a second line, the left flank resting on Waaspijk and thence running to Loon-op-Zand and the surrounding woods and sandhills. The right was well dug-in in the woods surrounding Dongen. South-east of this, resistance below the Wilhelmina Canal had practically ceased and the 15th (Scottish) Division had no difficulty in entering Tilburg on the 27th. However, the enemy north of Tilburg was a different proposition, and orders were given that night, read by the light from burning houses, that the Regiment was to capture Loon-op-Zand next day. 'C' Squadron was to lead by two parallel routes, north by the road from Udenhout to Loon-op-Zand, and south from Udenhout to the main Tilburg-Loon road, while the Inniskillings and the 1st Rifle Brigade secured Dongen.

(d) South-west Holland cleared, Loon-op-Zand, October 1944

AFTER a delayed start, owing to the mist, 'C' Squadron first made contact on the 27th with infantry who had dug themselves in by the side of the road. The road itself was covered by anti-tank fire. Here Lieutenant Davies and Four Troop were held up, but the advance continued westwards, and One, Two and Three Troops cut the Tilburg-Loon-op-Zand road two miles south of their objective at about 2 p.m. Here they too were held up by dug-in infantry and artillery and could go no further as Loon-op-Zand itself appeared to be held by approximately a Battalion with anti-tank guns.

Meanwhile Four Troop, trying to clear the road for the main advance, had successfully dealt with the infantry but had had two tanks knocked-out by anti-tank guns north of the main road. Sergeant Kennedy's tank was brewed up and Sergeant Sprigg's penetrated by an anti-tank shell, and Trooper Morfin, the gunner, killed. The only other casualties were five men slightly wounded. Davies's tank was attacked by a German with a hand-grenade and Davies, in anger, got out and chased him with a pistol and shot him dead.

In the evening the 1/7th Queen's made an attack on the town from the south, supported by 'A' Squadron, while 'C', with the troops already in position, provided left flank guard. They managed to advance as far as the castle but the enemy here were ready for them and put up such a determined defence that they could get no further.

The battle for Loon-op-Zand went on all next day. The fog had by now cleared and the sun was shining, and the attack was due to commence at 7.30 a.m., but just before this time the area where the infantry and tanks were forming up prior to the attack was so heavily shelled that it prevented them from going in when planned. 'A' Squadron was going to support the 1/7th Queen's to enable 'C' Squadron to have a rest, and at 8.15

a.m. the attack went in. They immediately encountered very heavy machine-gun and mortar fire, but the leading company, supported by Lieutenants Bellamy and Saxby reached successive objectives until they captured the castle. A second company was passed through and become involved in fighting in the south of the village, while a third company joined up with 'B' Squadron, west of the road, and attacked the village from the west. They however were unable to gain the open fields from the woods, so a company of the 1/5th Queen's swept further out to the west, with 'C' Squadron in support. Thus all three Squadrons of the Regiment were engaged. However, just as the original company of the 1/7th Queen's was making good progress into the village they were ordered to withdraw to let the 1st Gordons from the 51st (Highland) Division attack from west to east. This was a bitter disappointment as the Regiment and the Queen's had fought doggedly and now, when the plum was to be had for the picking, it was snatched away from them.

Loon-op-Zand was taken on the morning of the 29th, with very little opposition and the Regiment came into the 131st Brigade reserve, except for 'C' Squadron, who continued, with the 1/5th Queen's, battling with the Germans west of Loon-op-Zand. Their immediate objective was to clear the western road from the town and the sand-dunes where they had tried and failed the night before, and then push on to Moer. 'D' Company advanced across the road before first light and took up positions north-west of Loon. Lieutenant Ryde and One Troop went up to join them at first light while 'B' Company supported by Two Troop cleared the sand-dunes. Major Huth followed up this attack closely with the Battery Commander, Major Tyroll. They bagged about a dozen prisoners, one of which Huth took personally. While jumping out of one foxhole into another he landed on a German hiding there and with great presence of mind took him prisoner by the simple expedient of jumping on his stomach. He turned out to be a German artillery officer, a lieutenant acting as an O.P. "Anyway I got a pair of binoculars from him!"

The woods to the west were heavily 'stonked' before 'B' Company and Two Troop pushed forward. During this advance Corporal Hillditch fired at a German half-track. He missed the half-track but hit an ammunition dump which blew up, killing fifteen Germans. Meanwhile One Troop, in support of 'A' Company, passed through Two and reached Moer, while Three, to the north of the road and in support of 'D' Company, advanced to a position north of Moer, where they all leaguered for the night. And where they got heavily 'stonked' by German long-range guns. However it had been a successful day, no casualties and many Germans killed and wounded. Lieutenant Gadsby, who had been sent to investigate Sergeant Sprigg's tank, was blown up on a mine. Although the dingo was ruined neither Gadsby nor the driver, Trooper Hardy, were hurt.

At first light on the 30th three troops of 'B' Squadron drove in to Dongen to take up positions at the canal and river bridges. They got a really tremendous welcome from the Dutch townspeople, usually so reserved. They were showered with apples, oranges, plums and flowers, flags were out everywhere and the town rang with cheers. The rest of the Regiment arrived at about 11.30 and went into comfortable billets, where they expected to stay for a few days. The town had been very little damaged and everyone was under cover, for which, as there was a snow warning, they were very thankful.

Later that day the 1st Royal Tanks and 1/7th Queen's took Oosterhout, and the Rifle Brigade were up to a village short of Geertruidenburg. The whole area south of the Maas was now cleared, except for the country between the Aftwaterings Canal and the Maas, known as 'The Island'.

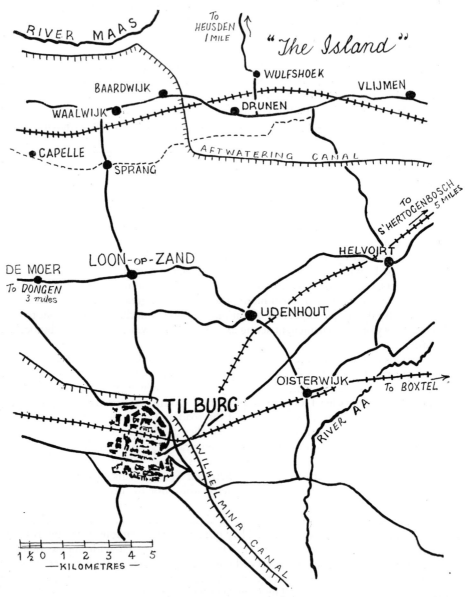

Map F. Loon-op-Zand.
26th-28th October, 1944.

However on October 31st the Regiment was ordered in to the 131st Brigade reserve and moved to Sprang to relieve the 51st (Highland) Division along the Maas. Again for a few days the Regiment was to have time to rest and put themselves straight.

To gain this strip of Western Brabant the Division had, in ten days, lost twenty-two tanks and many killed and wounded. These figures help to show why the advance was so slow. The country was totally unsuited to Cromwells which were at their best where there was plenty of space in which to manoeuvre. Here they had been tackling woods and dykes and embanked roads and had had to fight an infantry battle. However they now had some ten days in which to prepare for their next advance, none too pleasant a prospect either in the cold damp lowland winter.

From the 1st to the 11th of November the 8th Hussars stayed at Sprang, north of Loon-op-op-Zand. It was a small agricultural village, most of it damaged by shell-fire but enough houses still standing for all the men to find billets. The village was shelled by the Germans as the Regiment arrived, but never afterwards, and so they settled down to a period of rest and maintenance, interspersed with patrolling duties and firing on to certain targets. In fact on the evening of 3rd November the Burgomaster and Corporation of Tilburg gave an evening party with dancing in honour of the 'liberators' in the town hall. Three officers from each of the Regiments and battalions of the 15th (Scottish) Division and 7th Armoured Division were invited; and the Commanding Officer, Major Huth and Lieutenant Dill attended. This was the first time since the war began four and a half years before that they had seen ladies in evening dresses and gentlemen in white ties, and they found it a strange sight.

On November 4th the Regiment was called upon to assist the 51st (Highland) Division in clearing the 'Island'. Their task was to engage the villages of Drunen and Wolfshoeck, and in the evening they put in an attack with all the fire power they possessed. It was a great success and the villages were soon blazing. There was surprisingly little counter-battery fire, none at all landing in the Regimental area. Meanwhile the 51st put in their attack across the canal and captured all their objectives, helped by the Regiment's 'extremely effective' fire, as the Commander of the 152nd Brigade said afterwards.

The 'Island' was cleared, and for the next four days the Regiment remained at Sprang, all, that is, except 'C' Squadron who, on November 6th, moved across the Aftwaterings Canal to Vlijmen in support of the 1/5th Queen's.

The 131st Brigade was taking over from the 51st and 'C' Squadron was in reserve as a counter-attack force at two hours notice. During this period the Commanding Officer and Major Huth visited Heusden, an interesting old 17th century fortress town on the banks of the Maas. The inhabitants were digging out their dead from the ruined town hall. It seemed that the Germans, when they withdrew, advised the townsfolk to take cover in the town hall against the attack of 51 (Highland) Division, since that building was the strongest in the town. Shortly afterwards a time bomb, placed by the Germans in the cellar, exploded killing 120 people.

The task of clearing the south bank of the Maas was now over, and it was for this autumn battle, which involved the clearing of the country east of Antwerp, therefore opening up the port, that the Regiment was awarded the major battle honour of 'The Lower Maas'.

(e) The Panheel Lock,[1] November 1944

As soon as the Scheldt and south-west Holland operations were over, the 2nd Army set about regrouping and facing east for a drive to the line of the Meuse. The Germans held a bridgehead over the river and one front ran along the Wessem Canal from about five miles north of Maeseyck, across the front of Weert, Meijel, Venrai to Maashees. The plan was to to attack towards Venlo with 8 Corps in the north and 12 Corps in the south. The 7th Armoured Division was still part of 12 Corps, and the concentration of the Division near Maeseyck was all part of this plan.

The Americans now held the frontiers of Germany from Switzerland to Aachen; France, Belgium and Luxemburg were free and the British 2nd Army had cleared Holland up to the Maas and held a salient jutting out towards Arnhem. All the same the 2nd Army was not in such a favourable position for an invasion of Germany as were the Americans. For one thing they were on the wrong side of the Maas and on a hundred mile front and for another they had only just finished operations in which they had had to drive west to free the Scheldt Estuary and now wanted to push both north and east. General Montgomery's plan was to use the Canadians, as soon as they had finished with the Scheldt, to clear the south bank of the Maas, and to use the 2nd Army to secure the crossings below Maastricht.

On November 11th the Regiment moved out to Maeseyck, a town in Belgium on the west bank of the Meuse, where the 7th Armoured Division had been ordered to concentrate. Their route took them by Tilburg and Lichtaert to the well-remembered country round Gheel and Moll and Lommel where they had fought in September. Then on by Lille St. Hubert, Guirtrode and Neeroeteran to Maesyck on the Dutch frontier. They had a good trip down, driving all day for over 100 miles and arriving just as it was getting dark. Regimental Headquarters and 'C' Squadron were in the old Belgian barracks while 'A' and 'B' Squadrons were billetted in the town, having been warned that there were large numbers of spies there. 'B' Squadron was not too well organised. "We are living in extremely uncomfortable coal merchant's house," wrote one member, "where Richard Dill unfortunately smashes a Diety. Richard searches for better accommodation and returns with joyous news of marble-inlaid schloss in town centre. We move into new mansion next day. Amateur jockey and wife. More convenient and very comfortable, and," as an afterthought, "near to Squadron lines."

To get back to more professional matters, the Regiment came under command of the 131st Brigade that evening. The 1/7th Queen's were at Kessenich, the 1/6th forward round Thorn and the 1/5th facing north at Ittervoort. The Germans were two miles away at Wessem on the west of the river and the approaches to the village were lit up by searchlights.

On November 12th the Commanding Officer was called to a conference at the 131st Brigade Headquarters where a plan to attack the Panheel Lock was discussed. This lock on the Wessem Canal was five miles north of Maeseyck and controlled the level of water in the Canal. In the event of the Germans opening or blowing it, the water from the Meuse would flood some of the country across which 12 Corps proposed to attack, and if the water level fell in the canals it would disorganise the attacks going in the north, which depended on pontoon bridges. These would be put in by the 53rd Division,

[1] See Map G page 190.

attacking across the Western Canal, and it was hoped to draw the enemies attention from them by the Panheel operation. The capture of the Canal was, therefore, a preliminary phase in the main operation, and it was in fact the only task given to the 7th Armoured Division in the operation of eliminating the German bridgehead west of the Meuse. The 1/7th Queen's and the 8th Hussars were ordered to seize the lock, and on the 13th the Regiment sent out a recce party. The country here was very unattractive; wooded, sodden with water and abounding in mines. There was an undulating plateau of high ground between Thorn and the canal, although the right flank from the lock to the south was flat and marshy. The enemy was dug in along both sides of the raised canal bank and had a good field of fire to his front. One sunken track running through a copse provided the only approach and forming-up place, and this meant that the attack would have to go in on a one company front. Five hundred yards from the lock was a cottage, already in use by forward patrols of the 1/7th Queen's, and from it considerable enemy earthworks around the lock could be seen. From the cottage to the lock ran a narrow strip of ground broken by trees and ditches. The going was obviously very boggy and impassable to tanks; but it was across this ground that the assaulting infantry proposed to advance. On the right of this was another tank obstacle in the shape of a poplar plantation, but on the left, however, was an open ploughed field which seemed the obvious approach for tanks.

'C' Squadron was ordered to give direct support to the Company from the area of the cottage and from the ploughed field across which they could move, keeping pace with the advancing infantry. A diversion was to be created by 'A' Squadron engaging any targets on the canal bank to the west of 'C', while 'B' fired into Wessem from the east.

At midday on November 14th, 'A' Squadron left Maeseyck and moved forward to some concrete works between Thorn and Wessem. It was hoped that the noise of the tanks in that direction would give the enemy the impression that an attack on Wessem was imminent. At 4 p.m. they put down a smoke barrage on Wessem and at 4.15 (when the attack was due to go in) they engaged targets on the Wessem Canal. At the same time 'C' and 'B' Squadrons left to take up their battle positions. This they had purposely left until the last moment so that the enemy would not guess where the attack was coming from.

As soon as the leading company of the 1/7th Queen's, closely supported by 'C' Squadron, crossed the start line they were met by an intensely and unexpectedly heavy barrage of machine-gun and artillery fire, and in a short time the Queen's had suffered serious casualties. Furthermore the strong earthwork on the Canal bank near the lock held up the attack for some time, and 'C' Squadron found that the smoke which was hanging about made it very difficult to distinguish friend from foe. After about forty-five minutes and when a second company had passed through the leading one, the left-hand platoon and One Troop with Lieutenant Hartwright reached the canal bank across the ploughed field; then, turning right, they attacked along the bank of the canal and success-fully assaulted the lock buildings. Panheel Lock was captured undamaged, and, as was later found out from prisoners, the attack had been a complete surprise.

The casualties to the Queen's had been very high and included two Company Commanders, two Platoon Commanders, the adjutant and the intelligence officer, but 'C' Squadron had lost only one man, Sergeant Spriggs, although five tanks had been bogged. Lieutenant Hartwright and his troop had done particularly well.

After the infantry had finally established themselves at the lock, 'C' Squadron moved back into leaguer in the pitch dark. The rest of the Regiment withdrew to Maeseyck for the night, including 'B' Squadron who had fired continuously during the action, with all four troops up.

At first light on November 15th One and Two Troops from 'C' Squadron moved forward again to the Lock to support the Queen's should a counter-attack develop. They were 'stonked' heavily during the day by two troops of 88-mm. who were somewhere in the vicinity of Panheel, but received no casualties, and there was no attempt at a counter-attack. The enemy was fully occupied with the successful advance south and east by the 53rd (Welsh) Division.

Meanwhile 'B' Squadron was making efforts to recover the five bogged tanks, one of which had run down a steep bank and nearly buried itself in mud. This provided an occupation which lasted most of the day. Lieutenant McClurg and Sergeant Sayers fixed towropes to them under spasmodic fire from the far side of the canal which made life rather uncomfortable. Lieutenant Jephson, newly returned after his wound received in the Mont Pinçon action, brought two more tanks up to help recover the others, one of which promptly bogged down, as did the three recovery vehicles. However Sergeant Sayers with half a bottle of whiskey and the remaining tank managed to extricate four of the others and at nightfall they all returned to Maeseyck.

The remaining two tanks were recovered on the 16th. Shelling at Panheel had ceased and it became apparent that the enemy had departed and moved the guns back, although there was still a certain amount of sniping round the lock in the morning. By the afternoon that too had ceased, and 'C' Squadron returned to Maeseyck.

The attacks by the 53rd and 51st Divisions had been entirely successful. Wessem was cleared and by the end of the month the banks of the Meuse beyond, the enemy retaining a small bridgehead in Bell Island, formed by a canal and a loop in the river. This section was now lightly held by infantry while the tanks remained concentrated to the rear. For the 8th Hussars, and indeed for the whole Division, the rest of November was uneventful. Courses were embarked upon and lectures given. The Regiment played the 11th Hussars at football in full view of the Germans and beat them 3-0. There was a performance in the local cinema of a Belgian resistance film and before the show Lieut.-Colonel Goulburn was presented with a bouquet of flowers in token of the gratitude of the people of Maesyck. The town was still shelled from time to time, most of the damage being done to civilian property, although on the 27th the L.A.D. lost several vehicles when shells landed on the Square. On the 28th there was an Investiture at Brée when Field-Marshal Montgomery presented the bar to his M.C. to Major Huth and the M.M. to Sergeant Wilson.

In the Division many changes were taking place. On November 22nd Major-General Verney left for Italy, his command being taken over by Major-General L. O. Lyne, D.S.O., who came from the 50th Division which was to be disbanded. Shortly after this 131st Queen's Brigade, which had fought with the 8th Hussars since landing in France, had to be broken up owing to their very heavy casualties. One battalion, the 1/5th, remained in the Division, the other two going home, and their places being taken by the 2nd Devons and the 9th Durham Light Infantry, both from the 50th Division. Brigadier Cox, commanding 131st Brigade, also left and his place was taken by Brigadier J. M. K. Spurling, from the 50th. With the Division now up to strength it was possible to form a Divisional Battle School near Brussels.

(f) Holding the line in Limburg, December 1944-January 1945

ON December 2nd, the Regiment moved on once more. They were to go ahead of the 22nd Brigade and take over a stretch of the line from Roosteren to Buchten from the 2nd Battalion, Irish Guards. The Regiment therefore joined the 5th Guards Armoured Brigade for four days until the 22nd Brigade moved over the Maas and took over. The Regiment left Maeseyck at 1 in the morning and arrived at Grevenbicht at 6 a.m. 'A' and 'B' Squadrons went straight to their leaguer areas, after a fifty mile journey via Maastrict and no sleep all night. 'A' was to take over Buchten and Gebroek, four hundred yards from the German lines the wrong side of the Juliana Canal, one troop mounted with tanks and three, so scarce were the infantry, dismounted in slit trenches. 'B' was to do the same thing at Roosteren, while 'C' was in reserve with Regimental Headquarters at Papenhoven.

While the Regiment had been at Maeseyck the Americans had pushed through the German town of Geilenkirchen and on to the Roer. Now the line ran from Linnich on the east through Gangelt to Sittard where the British took over and held the ground east of the Maas to Roosteren. There remained a cold, waterlogged, unattractive triangle of ground to be cleared, stretching up to Roermund, and this task was given to General Horrock's 30 Corps, with whom the 7th Armoured Division was to operate.

Almost before 'A' Squadron had settled down an officer from the Rifle Brigade arrived to lecture them on dismounted patrols, and by 6 p.m. the first patrol of this nature had been sent out. Siting Bren guns in trenches and fortifying houses with only two or three tanks per Squadron was a new experience for the 8th Hussars. Luckily there was to be a week's training in infantry defence at Grevenbicht and the 1st Rifle Brigade ran courses on patrolling.

At Gebroek 'A' Squadron found themselves in still and deserted surroundings. "It could hardly be styled a village," the 11th Hussars, who took over from 'A' Squadron, were to write. "It was just a knot of ruined and semi-ruined houses and farms, knocked about by shell-fire and without a sign of human habitation. Even in the daytime there was an eerie feeling about Gebroek; nothing was alive here, all crumbling and rotting away as the wind and the rain did their destructive work. Even the vegetables in the little plots were frozen hard, and it was a relief when the snow came to carpet everything in white, smoothing over the ugliness and roughness of the place, lessening the sense of desolation. Even so there remained that inexplicable feeling of foreboding which so many people felt at Gebroek." They were facing a formidable enemy too, a parachute regiment, and had nothing between themselves and the Germans five hundred yards away at Bakenhoven but a couple of mine-filled orchards. These were something of a problem as the line had been held by both sides since September and no one had kept any record of where the mines had been laid.

'B' Squadron at Roosteren were in slightly different circumstances. They had the Juliana Canal between themselves and the enemy at Oud Roosteren, a frail barrier indeed as it was almost always frozen over. Here four troops were covering a thousand yards front, and night reconnaissance patrols were sent out frequently. Many men became familiar with the art of silent movement, lying up in positions of observation, probing for trip mines, with being soaked to the skin and with frozen hands and feet. They learnt

RIVER MAAS

ROERMOND

R. ROER

PANHEEL

HOLLAND

WESSEM

WEERT

LINNE

MAASBRACHT

BRACHTERBEEK

BELGIUM

MONTFORD

JULIANA CANAL

ECHT

St. JOOST

HINGEN

SCHILBERG

MAESEYCK

ROOSTEREN

GEBROEK

SUSTEREN

HOLTUM

PAPENHOVEN

BUCHTEN

GREVENBICHT

BORN

NIEUWSTADT

GERMANY

BERG

SITTARD

—KILOMETRES—

1½0 1 2 3 4 5

Map G. Holding the line in Limburg.
2nd December, 1944–10th January, 1945.

not to look up at the enemy flares which periodically lit the darkness, as well as to memorise during the daytime every hedge and fold in the ground that was to be covered that night.

Another great inconvenience at this time to unfortunate tank crews training to work as infantry was the continual problem of preventing machine-guns and vehicle engines from freezing solid. This necessitated the constant starting up of vehicles and the stripping and assembling of machine-guns all with numbed and frozen fingers.

Daily the Germans became more active, and they seemed to have more ammunition and artillery available than at any time since Normandy. On the 5th 'C' Squadron went up in support of the 1st Rifle Brigade with Headquarters at Buchten and a troop forward at Nieustadt. The enemy's principle line of defence here was the Vloed Beek, a small stream running from the south-east to the north-west. 'C' Squadron stayed at Buchten for ten days, when they were relieved by 'A' Squadron.

From December 7th, when the 11th Hussars finally took over from 'B' Squadron, the Regiment came into Brigade reserve at Grevenbicht. They had, with the exception of 'C' Squadron, successfully completed four days in a dismounted rôle, had suffered no casualties and, by keen patrolling, had gained a great deal of knowledge of the enemy. They now restarted their courses and on the 16th sent a party of officers and men to the new Divisional Training School near Brussels.

On the 16th, the famous Ardennes offensive began, with the Germans attacking with ten Panzer Divisions and fourteen divisions of infantry, on a forty mile front held by the Americans. The enemy were considerably aided during the offensive by bad weather conditions which made aerial reconnaissance and the use of the superior allied air power virtually impossible. The right of the enemy attack was at Monschau, thirty miles east of Liège, not immensely far from Sittard, and its purpose was to drive a wedge between the two Armies and secure crossings over the Maas between Liège and Sedan. They pushed back General Hodges' 1st American Army about 50 kilometres and advanced through Malmedy towards Liège. Field-Marshal Montgomery postponed his intended offensive, the purpose of which was to clear the country up to Roermond, and instead sent 30 Corps to the north-west of Liège. However, the 7th Armoured Division was not affected and by the 21st the German advance, after very heavy losses on both sides, was checked.

The effect of this operation was felt in the boggy district held by the 8th Hussars. Guards were doubled and reports came in of parachutists and saboteurs and of renewed activity in the enemy lines across the Vloed Beek, but, as it turned out, it all came to nothing.

On the 19th 'B' Squadron moved out to Holtum and were back in the trenches once more with frozen feet and numb fingers as they crawled over canal and dyke banks in search of information. The Squadron strength was made up with Echelon personnel to almost Company numbers, but no one liked this rôle, they would rather be in their tanks. Typical was a patrol of three men out one night of driving rain, with visibility down to almost zero, and who found on their way along the canal bank a small barge tied up that could have held half a dozen men. They untied the rope and let it drift noiselessly away and continued their advance towards their objective, the bridge over the Vloed Beek between Susteren and Nieustadt. Flares went up on the other side of the canal and from some way behind them came a burst of spandau fire. The rain stopped and the clouds parted, revealing a nearly full moon that glittered on the water. Then suddenly and most unexpectedly two figures were seen approaching from the opposite direction. As one man the two parties sank to the ground and lay watching one another, neither liking to be the first to move. The two Germans were joined by two more. Five minutes passed and then the 'B' Squadron patrol slid noiselessly away to the left. When all seemed clear they made for the canal once more and advanced more cautiously along the bank to the bridge. The moon was covered again by dark rain clouds but it was not too dark to see the bridge when they reached it nor to see that it was unoccupied and too badly damaged for any vehicle to cross. On the bank slit trenches had been dug and the faint smell of cosmetics with which the Germans scented their louse powder showed they had been recently occupied. It began to rain again heavily, and having accomplished what they had set out to do, the patrol returned to Holtum.

Again on the 20th 'B' Squadron had another sort of encounter. At 9 a.m. there was a thick fog and when it lifted an enemy patrol of about fifteen men was revealed. These were immediately engaged by the outpost and they soon retired with casualties.

On the 11th Hussar front a similar incident occurred and eight enemy were reported just north of Gebroek. They proved troublesome and a troop of 'A' Squadron, 8th Hussars, was sent out to deal with them. At least one of the enemy was killed and it was evident that they were probing the defences strongly, with what intentions it was not yet clear. Later that afternoon 'B' Squadron Headquarters was heavily shelled and some direct hits scored, causing a number of men to be cut by splintered glass.

On another occasion a stray German patrol of at least two platoon strength attacked the most isolated troop position shortly after dark and did not withdraw until just before first light. All this time the weather was bitterly cold and the snow made life in a slit trench anything but comfortable.

Enough of patrols. On the morning of the 20th Lieut.-Colonel Goulburn left for England on compassionate leave and Major J. W. Phillips took over, with Major Huth as second-in-command while Captain Hepburn took charge of 'C' Squadron.

On the 22nd 'B' Squadron returned to the fold and the Regiment was together again, until 'C' Squadron was sent off to Holtum on Christmas Day. The Germans in the Vloed Beek sector were showing signs of increasing preparation for a large-scale attack, and Intelligence identified two Divisions on the Regiment's immediate front.

Christmas Day was celebrated by the 8th Hussars in traditional manner with a Carol Service in Papenhaven drill hall, followed by enormous Christmas dinners and the usual festivities. The Germans across the canal were quiet all day and the singing heard from their lines that night showed that they too were celebrating.

However, they showed their claws on Boxing Day when a patrol attacked Gebroek, held by the 11th Hussars, at 5.30 in the morning, captured it and brewed-up the Observation Post tank and several armoured cars. The rest of the vehicles could not be started or moved owing to the frost. As soon as the 11th Hussars were clear, the artillery brought down a tremendous barrage on the village, followed by an attack by a troop from 'A' Squadron, 8th Hussars, who went in and recaptured the village about midday. Six Germans were killed in this engagement and the twelve rifles left behind indicated that more had been wounded. However, 'A' Squadron had one man wounded and lost a tank and two dingoes.

The last few days of 1944 were uneventful. It really did seem at last that there would not be another year of war and the toasts that were drunk that frost-bound New Year's Eve were to a speedy deliverance from the cold and sodden country. Lieut.-Colonel Goulburn returned to the Regiment on December 30th.

The Regiment continued to be responsible for Gebroek and Buchten until Janaury 9th, on which date they were relieved of all responsibilities in the forward area.

Next day, the 10th, when the Inniskillings had taken over, the Regiment moved to Munster-geleen and two days later to Krawinkel. The whole district was in the grip of a

The Prime Minister, The Rt. Hon. Clement Attlee, riding in an 'A' Squadron jeep at a demonstration at Warminster, 1946.

St. Patrick's Day Rugger Match, Leicester East Airfield, March 17th, 1949.

The Officers at Itzehoe, 1945.

Back row, left to right: Lieut. G. P. R. Bowlby, M.C., Lieut. P. D. Mott, Lieut. S. Bates, Lieut. J. S. Greaves, Lieut. R. E. Beckett, Lieut. W. C. Brookfield, Lieut. D. W. Davies, Lieut. J. R. Malseed, Lieut. J. A. G. Worledge.

Middle row: Capt. W. St. C. Tisdall, M.C., Lieut. A. L. Preston, Capt. (Q.M.) E. G. Nias, Capt. D. L. Astley-Cooper, Capt. G. V. Vickers, Capt. R. S. Sunderland, R.A.M.C., Capt. M. B. Marwood, Capt. F. G. Turner, Capt. H. T. Pierson, Lieut. F. D. C. Barnes, Lieut. G. W. Gould, M.C.

Front row: Capt. A. J. Hind, Capt. C. J. G. Meade, Major W. G. Lowther, Major P. H. V. de Clermont, Lieut.-Col. G. R. D. Fitzpatrick, D.S.O., M.B.E., M.C., Major H. H. Firth, Capt. A. V. Case (Adjutant), Capt. J. N. Lombard, Capt. G. J. Davies (Technical Officer).

Not present: Major D. R. W. G. Charlton, Major W. V. H. Nelson, Major J. A. Comyn, Capt. L. T. Ford, Capt. J. F. Weston-Simons, M.C., Capt. R. P. G. Dill, Capt. L. G. Bellamy, M.C., Lieut. G. L. Atkinson-Willes, Lieut. P. G. Hartwright (I.O.), Lieut. B. V. Hinson, Lieut. P. W. Pierrepoint, Lieut. S. K. B. McClurg, Lieut. D. F. Craven, Lieut. C. P. R. Anstey, 2nd Lieut. E. N. Norris, Capt. D. W. J. Harriwell, R.E.M.E.

The Sergeants Mess at Itzehoe, 1945.

Back row, left to right: Sgt. C. Lawrence, Sgt. R. Stanbury, L./Sgt. R. David, Sgt. W. Robinson, Sgt. W. Teasdale, Sgt. N. Thomas, Sgt. P. Morley, Sgt. G. Davies, Sgt. N. Blair, L./Sgt. J. Goldsmith, Sig./Sgt. Bond, Sgt. R. Lofthouse.
Third row: L./Sgt. F. Shufflebottom, Sgt. A. Scott, A./Sgt. R. Hey, Sgt. E. Payne, Sgt. R. Davis, L./Sgt. D. Hunter, Sgt. A. Hadley, Sgt. N. Wrigley, Sgt. J. Blyth, L./Sgt. G. Everett, S./Sgt. T. Walters, M.M., S./Sgt. S. Blythe, Sgt. A. Schofield.
Second row: Sgt. D. Williams, Sgt. R. Dean, Sgt. J. Connor, Sgt. T. Flynn, Sgt. W. Field, Sgt. A. Wright, Sgt. G. Bennett, Sgt. E. Whittaker, L./Sgt. D. E. Glass, L./Sgt. R. Palmer, Sgt. G. Jeffreys, Sgt. D. Palmer, L./Sgt. J. Copley, Sgt. B. Smithy, L./Sgt. E. Blackhall.
Sitting: Sgt. G. Dennison, S.Q.M.S. L. Barnett, M.M., S.S.-M. J. Knill, S.S.-M. L. V. Harrold, M.M., Capt. R. P. G. Dill, Lieut.-Col. G. R. D. Fitzpatrick, D.S.O., M.B.E., M.C., R.S.M. T. W. Hegarty, M.Q.M.S. D. Friel, S.S.M. J. Taylor, M.M., S.Q.M.S. J. Marshall, Sgt. Russell, M.M.

Winner of the Grand Military Gold Cup, 1949.

Major J. W. Phillips (8th Hussars) on his 'Demon Vine', 7 years old, 11-st. 2-lbs. (carried 11-st. 6-lbs.); bay gelding by 'Scarlet Tiger' out of 'Cellerette'.

hard frost. To add to the difficulties of discovering mines the ground was deep in snow, and on the 14th all tanks and scout cars were whitewashed, in preparation for the coming attack, the clearing of the country north-east up to the river Roer. Major Huth returned to 'C' Squadron from his temporary post as second-in-command, a job which he decided was no better than being "a glorified N.A.A.F.I. manager."

By this time the Ardennes offensive had been repulsed and the Allies were advancing once more. On January 14th the plan that had been postponed in December for clearing the Roer-Maas triangle was revived. It was to be called Operation 'Blackcock' and 12 Corps was to carry it out, having under command the 7th Armoured, 52nd (Lowland) and 43rd Infantry Divisions and the 6th Guards Tank Brigade. The 7th Armoured Division was to play the leading part, and had under command to start with the 8th Armoured and the 155th Brigades, from the 52nd Division, and later the 1st Commando Brigade. Their first objective was to be the main road from Sittard to Schilberg, an attack to be carried out simultaneously by two separate forces, the left hand one by the 9th Durham Light Infantry who would capture Dieteren and go on to Echt, Schilberg and Hingen, while on the right the 1/5th Queen's would make for Susteren. Having captured that, forces would drive on east to meet the 52nd (Lowland) Division making for Waldfeucht. Meanwhile the 43rd Infantry and 6th Guards Armoured Divisions would advance up the Worm valley to the Roer. After the 7th Armoured had captured Echt they were to clear the triangle between the Maas and the Roer with the assistance of the 1st Commando Brigade. The opposing force on this last stretch before the Siegfried Line were believed to be two German Infantry Divisions, the 176th and the 183rd, supported by self-propelled guns and probably by parachutists holding the Maas to the north. The whole operation depended upon the ground remaining frostbound, otherwise the tanks could not move across country, and what roads there were (mostly built up on embankments, and only single-track at that) would disintegrate under the heavy traffic. On January 15th orders were given to the 8th Hussars as to the part they were to play in Operation 'Blackcock'. They were to lead the 22nd Armoured Brigade and were to advance from Echt, when it was taken, to secure Montford. They would have under command 'K' Battery, 5th Royal Horse Artillery, 'I' Company, 1st Rifle Brigade and a half squadron of the Buffs with flame-throwing Crocodiles, Churchill 'I' tanks adapted for flame-throwing. On the 16th the initial dual attack by the 131st Brigade on Susteren and Dieteren, postponed a day owing to a smokescreen that froze into a dense fog, went in at first light. The fighting was very bitter and casualties high and, in spite of the frost, vehicles almost immediately became bogged. However, by the 19th the 1st Royal Tanks and the 2nd Devons were through Echt and into Hingen, while the remainder of the 1st Royal Tanks had secured Schilberg. The 8th Armoured Brigade were up to Kloster Lilbosh and had joined up with the 52nd (Lowland) Division near Waldfeucht.

(g) Advance to the River Roer, St. Joost, January 1945

ON the 20th, after heavy fighting by the 131st Brigade, supported by the 8th Armoured Brigade, the 22nd Armoured Brigade was able to begin its task of driving on towards Montford, four and a half miles beyond Schilberg. The first obstacle on that road was the village of St. Joost.

N

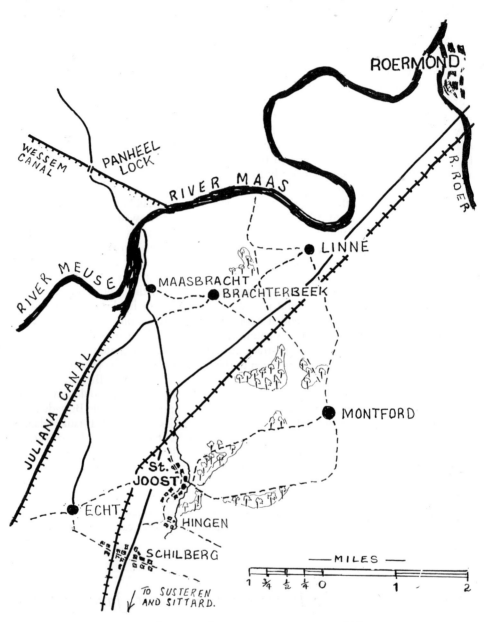

Map H. Advance to the River Roer, St. Joost and Linne.
20th–21st January, 1945.

At first light on the 20th in bitter cold weather, Lieut.-Colonel Goulburn, Major Gwyn of 'A' Squadron and Major Huth of 'C' went on a recce up to Hingen where they met Lieut.-Colonel Brind of the 2nd Devons. In front was the village of St. Joost which the enemy was holding in some strength, but it was hoped that they were disorganised and would not put up much resistance. However, it did seem as if the outskirts of the village had been fairly heavily mined. A road running through the Devon's forward position approached the village from the south, crossing a completely open space of half a mile. Parallel with the road and village on the right ran a stream, the Krom Beek, too wide for tanks to cross. St. Joost itself was a long straggling village some thousand yards from north to south; and the road to Montford forked off in the centre, to cross the Krom Beek by a bridge.

As the task of the 8th Hussar Group was to break-out and exploit eastwards to Montford, Lieut.-Colonel Goulburn ordered 'I' Company, 1st Rifle Brigade under Major Luke, supported by 'C' Squadron and the Buffs' Crocodiles, first to clear the village. 'A' Squadron was to protect the east flank by crossing the Krom Beek east of Hingen and then moving north to the area of some fir woods which were believed to harbour enemy self-propelled guns. The opposing strength was estimated to be one company.

H-Hour for the attack was half-past two, and the plan was for two platoons of Major Luke's Green Jackets to advance, one on each side of the road, closely supported by Payne and Two Troop of 'C' Squadron moving up the road, while two other tank troops gave fire support from well forward on the left flank. The Buffs' Crocodiles were to follow up through the back gardens on the western outskirts and flame any of the houses as the necessity arose. 'K' Battery were to fire concentrations on the north end of the village, and Lieutenant Ryde with Three Troop was sent north-west of the village to try and catch any bolting rabbits.

The attack went in on time and was met by furious opposition. Gone were all thoughts of a walk-over and the Roer reached in twenty-four hours. 'B' Squadron could hear a terrific din coming from St. Joost where the infantry were fighting up through the houses on either side of the road. They reached a grass-covered square about 300 yards into the village but their casualties were very severe, the left hand platoon being more or less wiped out. The leading tank of Two Troop had been knocked out and the second tank also hit, while so exposed was the right flank that the enemy were able to knock out two tanks in the reserve troop on the Hingen-Schilberg road. In exceptionally hard and close fighting, however, they managed to clear half the village and capture about sixty prisoners. These were not the riff-raff with no stomach for a fight that had been expected, but men from the notorious Hubner Parachute Regiment, who unquestioningly obeyed the order of their Colonel, "You will not retreat".

Meanwhile two sections of Recce Troop with a troop from 'A' Squadron had crossed the Krom Beek at Hingen, making for the main road to the north-east. However enemy self-propelled guns in the woods prevented this, and one Honey was knocked out.

Brigade ordered a change of plan. The Durhams were to clear the village during the first part of the night, until the road junction had been secured, and the 8th Hussars Group was then to break-out and go for Montford in the early hours of the morning, with searchlights providing artificial moonlight. It was obvious to those who knew him well that Lieut.-Colonel Goulburn did not think much of this idea, but he made it sound very convincing. However St. Joost had to fall first. Lieut.-Colonel Mogg of the Durhams, realising that the enemy would expect the advance to continue up the village street, decided upon a right flanking move by one company, which was to cross the Krom Beek, then re-cross it somewhere in the neighbourhood of the bridge, reach the road junction and establish themselves there. The second company was to pass through the Green Jackets and clear the remaining three hundred yards of houses between 'I' Company and the junction. H-Hour was to be 9 p.m. It started to snow again.

For those listening in at the joint Regimental and Durham Headquarters the time seemed to pass interminably. At 10 p.m. the Krom Beek company went off the air, and at midnight fourteen survivors returned, with the news that the remainder of the company had been killed or captured in the village near the road junction. The second company then went out but fared no better. They were counter-attacked and forced back to the very edge of the village. The enemy reinforcements were identified as a second parachute battalion. Payne's troop stayed out until 3 a.m., and Lieutenant G. Gould's until 6, supporting the Green Jackets who had also had very heavy casualties. Gould's tank was hit by a bazooka which killed Lance-Corporal Flatt and Trooper Partoon. 'C' Squadron casualties so far had been Trooper Eccles killed, Lance-Corporals Conner and Brown and Trooper Brindle wounded and Corporal Fountain, who lost a leg. From 'B' Squadron Lieutenant G. Milner had been wounded in the ankle.

During the night another company of Durhams was sent up to reinforce the one holding the few houses on the edge of the village. The waiting squadrons tried to snatch a few hours' sleep, knowing their turn was coming. They crowded into the one sound room left in the house at Hingen which had a stove. It was very warm and overcrowded. Lieutenant S. Pott, who could sleep anywhere, snored lustily, oblivious of the fact that his gunner and co-driver lay wakefully beneath him. Shelling was intermittent, and it was snowing again.

Things were becoming critical. Major McCartney with 'A', the only remaining company of the Durhams, was ordered to retake the village, supported by Major D. R. W. G. Charlton and 'B' Squadron. Time to cross the start-line was 8 a.m. on, by now, the 21st. Between them they decided there was nothing for it but to slog through the houses on either side of the road, in much the same way as the Green Jackets had attacked the previous afternoon. 'K' Battery was to fire concentrations. One Troop was to get close in on the right, another troop to move up the gardens behind the houses on the left of the road, two troops forward on the left flank to pour shells into the village, Squadron Headquarters to move up the road behind the infantry, the Crocodiles to move up the road or through the gardens on the left according to the situation.

A thick fog now descended which reduced visibility to seventy-five yards. During this time an enemy 75-mm. self-propelled gun advanced down the village street and was knocked out by Lieutenant Ryde's troop at close range. Unfortunately at about the same time, Lieutenant Anstey's troop of 'A' Squadron, east of the Krom Beek, was stalked by another enemy 75-mm. self-propelled gun and had two of its tanks destroyed, and a second 'A' Squadron troop lost its Sherman 17-pounder tank (a Firefly) a few minutes later from the same cause. Both troops were surprised just as the fog was clearing. Credit had to be given to the enemy who was employing his self-propelled guns with great skill.

Shortly after eight the attack went in. Soon the right flank troop reported they were having difficulty with mines and could not get in as close as had been hoped, and the troop moving up the gardens on the left of the street reported similar trouble and that they had lost a tank. By 10.30 a.m. they had only recaptured four houses on either side of the street which was slow going. The troop in the gardens with the infantry had further trouble with mines, losing a second tank. It was established later that the enemy troops had been reinforced during the night.

Progress seemed to be slowing down and word came over the air that Division were not too pleased. Also the best use did not seem to be being made of the Crocodiles. Once they had squirted their flame they had to withdraw for refuelling and by this time, too, three had been knocked out by panzer fausts. 'C' Squadron on the left flank could locate exactly where the infantry had got to as they hung bedding out of the windows of the captured houses. There were now only two Crocodiles left as the rest had been sent back to refuel. The flank troops were ordered to bring their fire closer. Over the air came the news that Two Troop was being shot up by self-propelled guns and that Lieutenant Jephson and his operator had been wounded seriously and the gunner slightly. One of the tanks brought back the wounded and then rejoined, bringing up some more ammunition on the back of the tank, a rather chancy undertaking. Sergeant James now took over command of Two Troop who, in spite of their exposed position, were able to remain in position.

By 12.30 the remaining Crocodiles were withdrawn and 'B' Squadron was given their close support rôle. Progress then quickened, thanks to the initiative of Major Charlton, who acted as a spearhead up the village street. It was now possible to see across the green and up to the built-up area surrounding the cross roads, for on the right of the road there were fewer houses with larger gardens than the semi-detached buildings on the left. They were remarkably well-built houses too and refused to ignite easily. Back down the road was one of 'C' Squadron tanks, still burning. The first few houses were alight too and the flames made a sharp contrast with the clear whiteness of the snow.

The rest of the operation can be told in extracts from Major Charlton's diary.

"Meanwhile Major Macartney of the Durhams was magnificent. During this very tough advance he had led the left-hand platoon at one moment and its forward section the next. The only way to advance at all was by knocking a hole in the wall between adjoining houses, and Macartney had been wielding a pick himself. In the last house as soon as they got a brick out of the wall a German had poked a Smeiser through from the other side and sprayed the room. The next house was a solid stone building, standing back in its own garden. The flank's troop had made little impression on it, the troop working up the gardens on the left of the road had lost two tanks and was some way behind; the Crocodiles were refuelling. Macartney asked me if I would do a sharp left turn with my tank and fire shells into the front door and windows of the stone house at ten yards range to clear it. This was damn foolishness and it annoyed me, a Troop had no business on the narrow road, let alone Squadron Headquarters, however neither had Macartney any business to be wielding a pick with the leading Section, and as Division and Brigade were a bit sour with our progress, I agreed. As we turned to the left an incredible scene presented itself. The Square was honeycombed with slit-trenches, packed extraordinarily close together, and there seemed to be Germans popping out of the ground and running about everywhere. I put two shells through the front door and then a couple through each of the ground floor windows, and was greeted with a stream of spandau and two bazookas which came too close for comfort. As we pulled back, Macartney, in front of the remnants of his platoon, dashed through the door into the house.

"By now the left flanking troops were running short of ammunition. The armoured recovery vehicle was ordered to take more up to them, a somewhat unpleasant task which the game R.E.M.E. lance-corporal undertook with alacrity.

"Lieut.-Colonel Goulburn suddenly arrived on the scene and, on stepping into the road, was greeted with a burst of spandau and a heavy 'stonk' of mortars. 'What the bloody hell was Squadron Headquarters doing so far up, get back at once.' My tank had just been fired at by a panzer faust and I had a bullet through my beret. I explained that as the Durhams' Company Commander, Major Macartney, was leading his Company himself I was determined to do likewise. The mortaring continued and we retired into a convenient space between the tank and a house. The Colonel wondered if we wouldn't be better off inside the house, but as it had no roof and was on fire we decided to remain where we were. The mortaring continued. The Colonel looked bored and Lieutenant D. J. Mossop, like the good Intelligence Officer he was, pretended to study his map.

"After two or three minutes things became quieter, although it looked as if the enemy were still in possession of the stone house, and that Macartney's gallant dash with his platoon had been unsuccessful. Lieut.-Colonel Goulburn decided we must now wait until the Crocodiles were refuelled and had pressure up and that they must then be used collectively. Our gun tanks were then to engage each of the first six houses in turn for two minutes, starting with the stone house, followed by the Crocodiles, each of which were to be launched at one house. The Colonel then left, accompanied by more mortar bombs. I then pulled back Squadron Headquarters into a small yard where Lieutenant Dill ran over a mine which luckily did no more than give the crew a shaking and blacken one side of the whitewashed tank. The enemy mortars continued to be unpleasantly attentive. However a flash and loud explosion in the vicinity of the cross roads announced the fact that an enemy ammunition dump had gone up, claimed by Lieutenant Meade with his 95-mm. gun.

"Nothing was heard from the infantry so I went in through the holes in the smouldering houses to contact Macartney. I found only the Company second-in-command and the Company Sergeant-Major who said the Germans had counter-attacked and that Macartney was on ahead and they had lost touch with him.

"At 3 o'clock in the afternoon the left-hand tank troops moved forward and in closer, and for twelve minutes fired systematically at each house in turn. Twelve minutes later the Crocodiles went in, each flaming their allotted house and wheeling away. It worked like a charm. The remnants of the Durhams dashed forward and the tanks closed up. Over the air came a congratulatory message from the Divisional Commander. Division at Headquarters had been listening in on the enemy wavelength and had heard the Commander report that it was no longer possible to exist in the flaming houses and that the roofs and floors were collapsing on his men as they fought. The left-hand flank troops crept in even closer and Squadron headquarters moved up to the cross roads. By 4 all was quiet except for intermittent shelling.

"In the candle-lit cellar at the cross roads I found the company second-in-command. Macartney had been killed and he was the only surviving officer of the Company. I was given tea and biscuits. The air smelt of brick dust, cordite and burnt-out masonry. I heard the roar of engines and came up to see the 5th Royal Tanks speeding over the bridge eastwards, presumably the fighting had been so intense that no one had had time to blow it.

"It began to snow again, great soft thick flakes. As we drew back to Hingen past the bloody shambles of the stone house where Macartney and his Durhams lay, surrounded by German dead, St. Joost burnt fiercely, the flames eerie in the winter night, and the snow continued to cover the village like a shroud."

(h) The Roer Reached. Linne, January 1945

NEXT day, the 22nd, the Regimental Reconnaissance troop patrolled forward on both roads leading to Montford, to report whether the bridges over the stream on the near side of the town were intact. Air photographs showed that this stream was a considerable obstacle, and early information on the bridges was important. Lieutenant H. T. Pierson commanding the troop, showed considerable initiative, reaching the bridges early in the morning. Both were blown, but he reported that it was not too wide for a scissors bridge. The Regiment received a congratulatory message from the Brigade Commander on this information, and shortly afterwards the 5th Dragoon Guards with bridge-laying tanks passed through. The Regiment was then left to re-organise after its twenty-nine hour battle, and with 'C' Company, 1st Rifle Brigade, mopped up round the still-smouldering St. Joost. The final score was sixty prisoners and a number of self-propelled guns, but according to Hubner, the commander of the parachutists, one company had been annihilated while the other had received very heavy casualties indeed.

On the 24th 'C' Squadron moved up to Brachterbeek to support a battalion of the 1st Commando Brigade. They had captured Brachterbeek that afternoon, but had been driven out of the railway station by an enemy counter-attack, leaving behind six wounded men. These men were found the following day, stripped of their clothing and dead from cold and wounds. The remainder of the Regiment concentrated at Schilberg and came into Divisional Reserve.

The Division was now pushing forward three attacks. On the right the 131st Brigade, with the 1st Royal Tanks and the 1/5th Queen's, advanced on Posterholt; in the centre the 22nd Armoured Brigade, with the 2nd Devons and the Inniskillings, were to clear St. Odilienberg, and on the left were the Commandos and 'C' Squadron, 8th Hussars.

On January 24th 'C' Squadron and the Commandos captured Weerd after only slight enemy resistance, but were held up at Linne by self-propelled guns. The Commandos consolidated for the night along a stream between Linne and Brachterbeek, 'C' Squadron leaguered in Maasbracht, clearing one tank ditched out in front of the forward defence posts.

Early next morning, the 25th, Two, Three and Four Troops of 'C' Squadron crossed the Montforterbeek by a scissors bridge and spread out over about 500 yards. While this was being done a smoke-screen blanketed off Linne and the mediums fired into the town. Just after 8 a.m. the three troops, each with ten commandos on the back of every tank, dashed across the open and through the smoke screen into the outskirts of Linne. This was a real cavalry charge and great credit was due to Major Huth for his dash. The Commandos immediately dismounted and rushed into the town to clear it. On returning from visiting the Squadron, the Commanding Officer stopped at the beck, where the Commando forward posts had been the previous night, to search the bodies of some fifteen dead Germans, no doubt a fighting patrol, which had been caught by Bren-gun fire at close range. These bodies were frozen stiff, and while extracting a map from one of their pockets, they were surprised by the angry voice of a Commando Major from behind: "Ha, looting my dead!"

Next morning 'C' Squadron withdrew, having been relieved by the 5th Royal Tanks. This was the first time the 8th Hussars had worked with Commando troops, and 'C' Squadron was commended for its co-operation by the Commando Brigadier.

'C' Squadron then withdrew to Schilberg on January 26th and went on to Roosteren where so many hours had already been spent patrolling the frozen waterways. Operation 'Blackcock' was completed and the whole triangle south of the River Roer had been cleared.

That night a farewell party was held in the Officers' Mess at Schilberg. It was a very sad occasion as Lieut.-Colonel Goulburn was leaving the Regiment after having been in command since the latter part of the Desert campaigns, through Cyprus and on from the Normandy beacheads. The party was attended by Brigadier-General Wingfield of the 22nd Armoured Brigade and Lieut.-Colonel The Earl of Lewis representing the 7th Armoured Division. Lieut.-Colonel Goulburn was handing the Regiment over to Lieut.-Colonel Desmond Fitzpatrick, O.B.E., M.C., of the Royals, who was to stay with them until the end of the campaign. For his leadership at St. Joost Lieut.-Colonel Goulburn received the immediate award of the D.S.O.

The rest of the month was spent in Divisional reserve and it was there decided that the Squadrons should consist of four fighting troops, each troop to be made up of two Cromwells and two Challengers, when the latter should become available in sufficient numbers.

III. GERMANY

February–July 1945

(a) Over the Rhine, February 1945

FEBRUARY opened with orders for the Regiment to go to Koningbosch to relieve the 13/18th Hussars and to come under command of the 52nd (Lowland) Division as Armoured reserve. They moved on the 2nd, sending 'B' Squadron to Waldfeucht with a troop at Bruggelchen under the 52nd Recce Regiment. Thus 'B' Squadron, when they crossed the frontier at 10 a.m. were the first of the 8th Hussars to enter Germany during the Second World War. They found Waldfeucht almost deserted by civilians, but all the same it was a step nearer Berlin. On the 5th the 52nd (Lowland) Division was relieved by the 25th United States Division, the Regiment coming under command of the Americans for the first time in their history. However, they were not called upon to operate in any form as the thaw had started. The roads were disintegrating rapidly and movement was becoming so difficult that it was doubtful if the Regiment could have fought even if it had been asked to. When they moved to Grevenbicht on the 7th every 'B' vehicle had to be towed some three miles out of Konigsbosch. The Regiment was now in Divisional reserve and they spent the next few weeks round Maesyck, their second stay in this area.

On the 11th Major-General Lyne attended the 8th Hussars church service and read the lessons. Afterwards he inspected all officers and N.C.O.'s and then lectured them on the part the Regiment had played in clearing the enemy out of the Roer-Maas triangle and complimenting them on their fighting at St. Joost and Linne. It was for that period, January 16th to 25th, that the Regiment received the major battle honour, 'Roer'.

This interval of rest and re-organisation lasted until mid-March. At the end of February Major P. H. V. de Clermont rejoined the Regiment as Adjutant after his adventures as an escaped prisoner-of-war in Italy. On the 5th March Field-Marshal Montgomery held an Investiture at Veert and from the Regiment Lieutenant L. G. Bellamy was awarded the M.C., S.Q.M.S. Winch the M.M. and Sergeant Taylor, a bar to his M.M.

The Regiment moved from Grevenbicht to Maesyck and from Maesyck to Zomeren. All the time the shooting on the Lommel ranges continued and was extremely successful. The new Challengers were tried and found, after a few teething troubles, most satisfactory, and the last two weeks were spent in co-operative training with the 1/5th Queen's. As March wore on so also did the time when the Regiment would move out once more, on, perhaps, this time, the final march to Victory. In the fine clear weather of March 22nd the Regiment watched hordes of aircraft passing overhead on their way to soften-up the Reich. The time was very near for them to move themselves, and everyone was on tip-toe.

During these last three weeks the whole 7th Armoured Division had been resting and training round Weert and Bree; flat, depressing countryside, overcrowded with troops and a long way from Brussels. During this time there had been much fighting elsewhere to prepare the ground for the final crossing of the Rhine. Early in February the clearing of the west bank of the Rhine had begun. The 1st Canadian Army came down from the north while the 9th American Army worked up from the south. The country was favourable to the defenders, waterlogged, flooded in places, heavily mined and including the great forest of the Reichswald. Thus the fighting was extremely hard and progress slow. However, by March, the two armies had joined up at Geldern and the whole west bank of the Rhine was clear to the Moselle at Coblenz, while a good bridge at Remagen south of Cologne had been seized intact by the Americans. In the east the Russians were up to the Oder. Operation 'Plunder' was ready to be put into force.

This plan was for General Montgomery to open the offensive with his three armies, Canadian, British and American. His aim was to encircle the Ruhr, first seizing Wesel, on the east bank, held by fanatical parachutists. The British 2nd Army, which included the 7th Armoured Division in General Ritchie's 12 Corps, was to be in the centre of the line and it fell to them to make the most important move in the first stage of the offensive. That was to be the crossing of the Rhine at Xanten and Rees and the capture of Wesel. 30 Corps was to be directed on Rees and 12 on Xanten and Wesel. The 6th British and 17th U.S. Airborne Divisions were to land on the other side of the river and seize crossings over the Lippe and Ijessel, while south-east the 9th American Army would cross at Dinslaken.

On the evening of the 23rd all was ready. On the west of the Rhine the 52nd (Lowland), 15th (Scottish), 53rd (Welsh) Divisions and the 4th Armoured Brigade were holding the line, with a mass of bridging equipment behind them, while on the opposite side was part of the 2nd Parachute Division, north of Bislich, and the Grenadiers of the 84th Infantry Division up to Wesel.

All went according to plan. After a tremendous barrage by the R.A.F. and the artillery the Commandos captured Wesel; on March 24th the 15th (Scottish) had a foothold at Bislich, although the 51st (Highland) were meeting very stiff opposition round Rees. The 6th Airborne had suffered heavy casualties but had captured the bridge at Hamminkiln and the Americans at Dinslaken had joined up with the airborne troops at the Lippe bridges. In spite of shelling and bombing the 12 Corps bridges made progress and by the 27th a tank bridge was in position between Xanten and Bislich. Over this it was General Ritchie's intention to push his armour north, and the divisional centre line was aimed at Bremen by way of Borken, Stadtlohn, Ahaus and Rheine.

On March 24th the 8th Hussars waiting at Zomeren, at last received their orders to move. They watched that morning the Airborne Divisions passing over en route for the bridgehead and knew that it would not be long before they too were across the Rhine. On the 25th they and the whole Division moved east towards Geldern. After a slow start due to the bottleneck on the Bailey bridge at Needeweert they had a good run to Venlo where they met a further traffic-jam on the Meuse crossing. They reached their leaguer that evening, at Studt Struden, east of Venlo, in Germany at last.

There was a day of waiting on the 26th while bridges were being thrown across the Rhine. Major Huth crossed to find a harbour area near Bislich, and saw Mr. Winston Churchill on his very game adventure to the front with Field-Marshal Montgomery. The Regiment heard that they were to lead the 131st Brigade the next day. The night was very noisy with enemy planes bombing the bridge and our small-arms fire at the German mines floating down the river.

On the 27th the progress to the bridge at Xanten was very much slower than that laid down by formation staffs, as for once traffic control seemed to have been neglected, with the result that the congestion due to at least one Corps converging on three bridges, only one of which could carry armour, was unbelievable. The start point which should have been passed in the early morning was not reached until 5 p.m., when another long halt took place. However, by moving in the dark better progress was made and with 'C' Squadron in the lead the Regiment crossed the bridge at Xanten in brilliant moonlight at 11 p.m. "All my crew have a nip of rum," wrote a troop leader in 'B' Squadron. "The feeling of victory is running through the Troop. I believe we could do anything."

The orders next morning were to move to Brunen, and the final advance, for which the Regiment received the major battle honour 'Rhine', had begun. The roads were still jammed with traffic and lay through the main dropping and landing area of the 6th Airborne Division. The countryside was littered with crashed gliders and equipment, and it was obvious that the operation, although successful, had been very costly.

The escarpment running north and south through Brunen had not been held and orders were given to advance to Raesfield and firm base there. The 22nd Armoured Brigade had already cleared the town and had turned north towards Borken. On reaching Raesfield the Recce Troop spotted a self-propelled gun on to which they directed the gunners, with successful results.

In the evening 'A' Squadron was ordered north to Borken, to assist the 2nd Devons as the 5th Dragoon Guards who had taken the town in the morning had pushed north. The rest of the Regiment leaguered that night in the pouring rain on the north-west outskirts of Raesfield, which by that time, had been occupied by the 1/5th Queen's. During the day Sergeant Russell, 'B' Squadron, was wounded.

(b) Weseke and Oding, March 1945

THE REGIMENT came under command of the 22nd Armoured Brigade on the 29th, and started the day "by moving up the centre line in fits and starts in the pouring rain towards Borken." At about 11 a.m. 'C' Squadron was ordered to the north to give flank protection to the main Borken-Weseke road. They moved off, considerably hampered by the heavy going which had resulted from the rains of the last few days. A certain amount of opposition was encountered from odd parties of the enemy and a few self-propelled guns that were lurking in the background.

The Brigade was held up by strong enemy opposition at Weseke and Ramsdorf. The 5th Dragoon Guards tried to by-pass to the west but were held up. The main bridges across the stream to the south-west of Gemen had been blown and it was therefore considered unlikely that there would be any strong enemy opposition to the north. At about 1 p.m. the 8th Hussars were ordered to attempt to outflank Weseke by moving north through Borken to Gemen and then north-west to Gr. Burlo and on to Oding. The Regiment had under their command 'I' Company, 1st Rifle Brigade and 'G' Battery, Royal Horse Artillery.

'C' Squadron led the advance and pushed off towards Borkenwirthe. Two or three self-propelled guns continued to cause trouble and more were known to be south of Borkenwirthe. It was hoped that it might be possible to cut them off. 'C' Squadron met some opposition near the railway crossing but this was satisfactorily dealt with and

Lieutenant Gould's troop was soon in Borkenwirthe. During this time however part of 'C' Squadron was bogged further south, and a self-propelled gun drove practically into Regimental Headquarters, causing some consternation for a few minutes. Altogether 'C' Squadron brewed up two staff cars and a half-track, captured an ambulance with an M.O. in it and five Germans, and advanced up to Borkenwirthe.

The Regiment meanwhile was still south of Borkenwirthe. It was intended that 'B' Squadron with one Motor Platoon under command, should pass through 'C' Squadron who was established at Borkenwirthe as southern flank-guard, and go on to capture Gr. Burlo and Oding. 'B' Squadron's leading troop, however, met some opposition at Burlo railway station, and their leading troop, commanded by Lieutenant Ryde, came under fire from a self-propelled gun concealed in the edge of a wood. A Challenger received a direct hit but it never penetrated the mantles although the 17-pounder gun was put out of action. Ryde immediately closed with the self-propelled gun and knocked it out at close range. A number of German infantrymen then withdrew from the Station area, but by this time it was getting dark.

'B' Squadron was ordered to send a patrol into Gr. Burlo to see if it was held, but its defenders were found to be gone. However it was decided to be too late to continue the advance and 'B' Squadron was ordered to leaguer astride the road about 1,500 yards south of the station. The remainder of the Group leaguered for the night in the distillery at Borkenwirthe, a night which was uneventful except, as the War Diary put it, "for the capture of one German dispatch rider who was not in the picture."

The 30th started with a dawn move towards Oding through Gr. Burlo in an effort to outflank Weseke where the 22nd Armoured Brigade was still being held up. 'A' Squadron was in the lead and, on reaching the road and railway crossing, came under heavy mortar fire and sniping from the north. The leading troop, which was first into the woods, was also attacked by men armed with bazookas, and two tanks were quickly knocked out. It was soon clear that it would be impossible to open this road through the woods to Oding without methodically clearing the area with infantry supported by tanks. The going off the roads was very boggy, the woods were thick and came right down to the road, which it was impossible to leave, and were full of determined bazooka men and snipers in an ideal defensive position. These troops were chiefly from Battle Group Primus of the Hermann Goering Division and from the 7th Paratroop Division, more of the fanatical parachutists that had been met before. It appeared that they were their Division's east flank guard covering Winterswijk.

By now the leading troop of 'A' Squadron was virtually written off by Bazooka fire, the troop leader, Lieutenant R. H. Anstey being killed. However two tanks had advanced as far as the stream on the southern outskirts of Oding. One had been knocked out and the other had been ordered to withdraw when its commander, Sergeant Constable, had been badly wounded in the head. Constable had, however, with the utmost gallantry, continued to fight with what remained of Anstey's troop (despite the fact that due to his serious wound he was eventually blinded), until ordered finally to withdraw when his was the only tank remaining in action.

The company of Green Jackets under command went in and cleared the woods on the west of the road and although they killed a few Germans, the greater number escaped across the road where they remained strongly entrenched and fought on with great determination.

In the meantime Recce Troop had the task of finding a route by which an approach from the south-east might be made on Oding from Burlo station. Here they met at once the difficulty of muddy lanes with deep ditches on either side into which two of their Honeys and a Jalopy[1] slid in quick succession, their rubber tracks giving them little purchase on the slippery mud. These unfortunately blocked two approaches, and incidentally, were inordinately difficult to recover. By the time the troop had found a route by which 'B' Squadron could attack Oding, the parachutists on the east of the road had moved forward. Nevertheless 'B' Squadron was ordered to proceed this way, to wipe out the enemy in Sternbush and, if possible, to outflank the wood and rejoin the main road higher up.

'B' Squadron was now to encounter some of the stiffest opposition they had yet come up against since crossing the Rhine. What with this and the bad going their progress was extremely slow. Lieut.-Colonel Fitzpatrick requested that more infantry be sent up to him and accordingly one company of 2nd Devons was dispatched. However owing to the circuitous route they had to take they did not arrive until nearly 5 p.m. The plan for clearing the road was that the Devons were to attack the woods to the east while the Green Jackets once more cleared those to the west, supported by 'A' Squadron and the artillery. It was hoped that additional artillery might be forthcoming but this was not certain.

Whilst this attack was being organised 'B' Squadron had been fighting persistently, and after brewing up several farmhouses they managed to obliterate the parachutists in the woods up to a small circular wood to the north. Here, after a tough fight, Sergeant Taylor, who was subsequently wounded, captured fifty German paratroopers. Probably as a result of this action the enemy in the woods astride the road withdrew. Certainly there were very few to be found when the attack went in at 6.30 p.m.

Lieutenant Pott, commanding a troop of 'B' Squadron, advanced up to the bridge on the southern edge of Oding and removed the explosive charge. Oding was definitely held at this time and Major Charlton of 'B' Squadron was ordered not to attempt to enter the village until the road had been cleared and it was possible to bring reinforcements and infantry up to his leading troop.

It was now growing dark and 'B' Squadron was ordered to harbour near the road junction with a platoon of Devons as protection. The rest of the company remained with 'A' Squadron, about 800 yards to the south-west. The rest of the 8th Hussars Group leaguered near Burlo station.

As a result of the day's fighting 'A' Squadron had lost four tanks destroyed and one damaged, Lieutenant R. H. Anstey, Sergeant Scott and Troopers Saunders, Morton, Collinson and Laurie killed, Sergeant Constable blinded and Lance-Corporal Coles and Trooper Southall wounded. Corporal Bunner and Troopers Coombe, Weldon, Elden and Hollins were missing believed prisoner and Trooper Patten missing. 'B' Squadron had Sergeants Taylor and Cliff, Corporal Hills and Trooper Stebbings wounded. Altogether one hundred and six enemy were captured, including fifteen Italians, two Greeks, two of Tito's men who had escaped from a prisoner-of-war camp, a postman and a German officer in civilian clothes, mostly from the Hermann Goering Division. There were about fifty Germans killed and 'A' Squadron had brewed up a lorry and an anti-tank gun and 'B' two lorries, some ammunition dumps and a civilian lorry carrying soldiers.

That evening Recce Troop was joined by 2nd Lieutenant Robin Anstey whose brother Richard had been killed that morning.

Next day, the Regiment moved into Oding and reverted to command of the 131st

[1] This was Recce Troop's own name for a turretless Stuart tank. They had removed the turrets of half the Recce Troop Stuarts at Maeseyck in Holland. This made a very fast and useful vehicle, carrying three or four men who could get out quickly to reconnoitre if necessary.

Lorried Infantry Brigade. 'A' Squadron, who was first into the town, found road blocks and the bridge to the east blown and enemy in the woods to the north. These were engaged, with casualties to the Germans, and the Regiment moved on to Stadtlohn, which was nothing but a heap of rubble with only the church left standing. 'B' and 'C' Squadrons were put astride the roads coming in from Vreden and Ottenstein respectively to prevent any attack on the centre line, and the Regiment leaguered between the two Squadrons on some high ground to the west.

(An interesting sideline on the troops that were being brought in to supplement the parachutists was found in Oberst Primus, Commander of the 4th Parachute Training Regiment, who was captured on the 31st. This nice clueless old body clocked in with the forward squadron having been out of touch with higher formations for two days. His last order had been to report to Winterswijk, but bearing in mind the reception given to stragglers by the 2nd Parachute Army's Forward Court Martial, and that it was probably an invitation to be shot, he sent his adjutant instead and walked over to the nearest British troops. The Oberst was a handsome, dignified, if slightly vague old buffer. His Regiment, which he insisted was a Training Regiment and not intended for active service, was brought down from Holland and put under command of the 15th Panzer Grenadier Division. On March 29th he was ordered to hold a sector from Rhede to Burlo, but he did not bother to find out the location of the 15th Panzer Grenadier Divisional Head-quarters as he considered them ugly common people who never took any trouble to look after him.

When warned to conceal his nice new leather dispatch case from the covetous eyes of the British Liberation troops, the Oberst replied mournfully: "I've lost my house and all I possess already, so I don't really care who has my dispatch case and shaving kit." He carried in his pocket the summary of a long and involved Court Martial, the highlight of the evidence therein being the N.A.A.F.I. ration drawn by 5 Company Primus on February 27th.

> 24 bottles Champagne
> 24 bottles Liqueur
> 10 bottles Cognac
> 27 bottles Wine

Thirsty work, training.)

By April 1st the Regiment was four miles south-west of Rheine, in sandy country sparsely covered with hazel bushes and fir trees.

Away on the right the 11th Armoured Division, who had crossed the Rhine on the 29th, were, with their new Comet tanks, making good progress. Further still to the right the 6th Guards Tank Brigade, carrying men of the 6th Airborne Division on their Churchills, swept on even further. On the left, progress was slow which meant that gradually the 7th Armoured Division had a longer and longer open left flank. To help cover this the 155th Brigade of the 52nd Division came under command.

The Division had now reached the next big river line, that of the Ems, having covered in a week a hundred and twenty miles, and hardly one of them unopposed. They had caused severe casualties to the Germans and taken many prisoners. However, although the opposition, except by the parachutists on the long left flank, had been disorganised, some groups of fifty and a hundred men had fought on desperately, and the bazooka men hidden in the woods were a never-failing menace.

(c) Ibbenburen, April 1945

A REGIMENTAL GROUP, consisting of the 8th Hussars, 'G' Battery, Royal Horse Artillery and one company 1st Rifle Brigade, stood by all April 2nd waiting for orders to move. The 11th Armoured Division had secured a bridgehead over the Ems and the canals to the north, just south of Ibbenburen. The road leading north to Ibbenburen, however, passed through a defile flanked by the steep wooded Tecklenburg Hills. This admirable defensive position was occupied by several thousand enemy officer cadets and N.C.O.'s, as Ibbenburen housed the Hanover Cadets School and its inmates had sworn to die in its defence. As they knew these wooded hills backwards they were a tough and formidable opponent, exceptionally highly trained and quite indifferent to death. It was intended that the 11th Armoured Division should clear the road to Ibbenburen and then swing east, followed by the 7th Armoured, with 131st Brigade in the lead. The use of the same bridges would slow things up but it could not be helped. They would then advance north-easterly over the Dortmund-Ems Canal and secure the ridge of the Tecklenburg Hills while the 11th Armoured pushed on east to Osnabruck. The resistence at Rheine was proving much tougher than had been expected and after savage fighting the 9th Durhams gave way to the 52nd Division.

An original order to move at 3 a.m. on the 3rd was mercifully cancelled as Rheine was still proving troublesome. However at 4 a.m. a Liaison Officer from the 7th Armoured Division came round to inform the Regiment that they were now under command of Divisional Headquarters for the push forward and that there would be no move before 10 a.m. Accordingly a recce was made near Riesenbeck to choose a leaguer area, but when they returned they were told there was to be no move after all. The Intelligence Officer, Lieutenant Tisdall, involved himself in a motor smash and had to be removed with a suspected fractured leg.

On the 4th the Regiment moved up to Riesenbeck to join the rest of the Division. The 131st Brigade had meanwhile taken over the operation south of Ibbenburen from the 11th Armoured Division and were having considerable success in clearing the woods on either side of the pass. The plan was for the 8th Hussars and the 1/5th Queen's to capture Ibbenburen as soon as the 155th Brigade from the 52nd (Lowland) Division had cleared the pass. A group under Major Charlton consisting of 'B' Squadron, Recce Troop and one company the 1st Rifle Brigade, was to establish itself south of the town and carry out a detailed reconnaissance of all the approaches and flanking routes. Recce Troop was given the task of reconnoitering three bridges south-west of the town, lying off the main road leading to it. From the map they appeared to be situated in flat open country, overlooked by houses on the outskirts, not a very pleasant job to contemplate.

The force moved north of the Canal and harboured between the Canal and the southern entrance of the pass in readiness, while Recce Troop covered the steep-sided defile through which passed the road to the town.

Meanwhile opposition continued to be so strong at Ibbenburen that it was decided, by 4 p.m., to waste no more time there with mobile troops but to hand it over to the 53rd (Welsh) Division which was available with all its artillery. The 22nd Armoured Brigade would pass along part of the 11th Armoured Division's centre line and thence out on to the road to Westecapallen, Halen and Bramsche.

It was by now late afternoon and this move developed into a most unpleasant night march. A composite advance guard was in the lead consisting of 'C' Squadron and 'B' Company, 1/5th Queen's in Kangaroos, under the command of Major Firth. The advance started at 7 p.m. along a road heavily congested with traffic and progress was very slow. A winding road, up and roundabout on a pitch black night is no fun to travel on without lights.

However all went well until about 10.30 p.m. when the leading troop of 'C' Squadron reached the railway bridge at Landenbeck. Here the enemy was holding a line along the north side of the railway and opened up with infantry and bazooka fire. Lieutenant J. Pim's tank was hit and he was severely wounded but the driver and gunner continued and drove on over the bridge and disappeared into the darkness beyond. The Queen's started to clear the houses on the south side of the railway and when this had been completed one platoon was sent on to try and contact Pim's tank which had become bogged. They were immediately heavily engaged by the enemy and lost seven casualties in as many minutes. The situation had become confused and, after much firing and the capture of two prisoners, it was decided to break the action off until first light on the following morning. To add to the difficulty the road was so tortuous and narrow that it was not possible to pass vehicles along the column.

Regimental Headquarters, Recce Troop and 'B' Squadron closed up and leaguered on the high ground to the south of Landenbeck. 'A' Squadron remained at Ledde for what was left of the night and Major Lilley, M.C., of the Queen's, crawled forward and disposed the remainder of his Battalion on the high ground near Landenbeck. This was not a satisfactory operation and it was considered that a night advance against unreconnoitred positions on a narrow front is not a sound manoeuvre of war. The casualties that night were one tank and two Kangaroos resulting in about twelve wounded, eight of whom were Queen's, and Lieutenant Pim and two men missing.

No sleep that night, but no further trouble either. At first light on the 5th, 'C' Squadron and the Queen's successfully cleared the houses in the north of the village of Landenbeck and pushed forward Lieutenant Gould and Four Troop to the cross roads where they engaged the enemy for several hours. As at Ibbenburen this area was held by the officer cadets, 'real tough thugs'. Pim's tank was recovered but there was no trace of him or the other two members of the crew. From a prisoner they learnt that he had lost a leg and had been sent to a civilian hospital somewhere in the north. Later they heard that he had died in hospital at Ibbenburen on April 8th.

At about midday the Regiment broke off contact with the enemy and moved east to Halen in support of the 1/5th Queen's who were acting as flank guard to the Brigade centre line.

During the evening Three Troop of 'C' Squadron, which was in support of a carrier platoon of the Queen's, was attacked and Sergeant Manning, the Troop Leader, was killed in the action that followed.

After a much needed night's sleep the Regiment moved off early on the 6th. It was a quiet day for them as they were under command of the 22nd Armoured Brigade and in reserve. The Brigade went forward on two centre lines, the 1st Royal Tanks on the right and the 5th Royal Tanks, whom the Regiment followed, on the left. They went through Engter, Venne, Hunterburg and Deillingen, passing south of Bramsche and north of Osnabruck. Here 'B' Squadron was sent on ahead to firm base Diepholz, and the Regiment then passed through them to Rehden, finally arriving after a long wait in the dark at Gr. Lessen near Sulingen.

During the day the Luftwaffe made its first offensive appearance when four Messerschmidts strafed the tail of the column, fortunately without damage to anything but the bedding and a captured wireless set on the back of Major Huth's tank which were riddled with bullets. On the road they met many Russian, Polish, French and Belgian prisoners who had escaped as the Germans withdrew. Major G. Armitage and 'K' Battery, Royal Horse Artillery, joined the Regiment here, replacing 'G' Battery.

On the 6th the Divisional centre-line was switched to run north-east to secure the crossings over the Weser at Hoya and Verden before they were blown.

(d) Up to the Weser, April 1945

THIS race for the Weser bridges was taken up by the 8th Hussars and 1/5th Queen's on the 7th. They were away at first light with 'A' Squadron in the lead and, so fast had their progress been that they were running short of maps. Already they were on to the 1 : 100,000 Bremen sheet and had visions of being in that great port before long. At first they met no opposition other than sniping, until they reached a cross roads where one of 'A' Squadron's tanks was put out of action by a hit from a light anti-tank gun, fortunately causing only one casualty when Trooper Goossens was wounded. Altogether one hundred prisoners and six 22-mm. anti-aircraft guns were captured here. Wasting no time the Regiment pushed on through sandy tracks and woods to be held up again at Vilsen. Here more fighting took place, 'K' Battery firing a number of rounds into the village. However, whilst plans were being made to attack and clear the village, its citizens telephoned to the house on the cross roads saying they were most anxious to surrender. 'A' Company, 1/5th Queen's and two tank sections from Recce Troop were ordered to clear the village, and while doing so Lieutenant Gadsby was wounded.

By midday the village was clear and Brigadier Wingfield of the 22nd Brigade visited Regimental Headquarters and ordered the 8th Hussars Group to capture intact the bridge over the Weser at Achim. 'C' Squadron was to take the lead, with a company of 1/5th Queen's, and to advance by Susdedt, Heiligenfelde, Godestorf, Eminghausen and Thedinghausen, while 'B' Squadron was to go direct to Heilingenfelde by way of the main road and then to follow 'C'. The advance started early in the afternoon and minor opposition was encountered at Godestorf. This was dealt with and they pushed on to Eminghausen where more fighting took place. When 'B' Squadron arrived they were ordered to picket the flanks to the north-west and south-east, and met with more enemy fire in the north-west.

In the meantime, 'C' Squadron was grappling with determined bazooka fire, during which Lieutenant Jephson was wounded for the third time in the campaign and two tanks were knocked-out. However Eminghausen was clear about three-quarters of an hour before last light and 'C' Squadron, with their company of 1/5th Queen's, was ordered to push north to Thedinghausen as a last desperate attempt to reach the bridge while it was still intact. Once again they were held up, this time 5 kilometres south-west of the river, and the surprise attack by the Queen's in Kangaroos that had been planned became impossible. Darkness fell while they were still fighting, and 'C' Squadron was ordered to remain where they were for the night. The rest of the Group closed up on Eminghausen. Recce Troop had earlier found some wounded and starving Russian prisoners in a windmill.

Again on the 8th the task of the Regiment was to push forward to the bridge, only 5 kilometres to the north-east. At first light 'C' Squadron and one company, 1/5th Queen's, cleared Thedinghausen without difficulty, but, on attempting to emerge in the required direction, were held up by four self-propelled guns and a Panther, who fought a rearguard action for the bridge. Recce Troop was given orders to move south-east and reach a point from which it could observe the movements of these guns, which were employing their usual tactics and firing a few shots from one position, then rapidly moving to take up another. 'C' Squadron was unable to get forward without incurring very heavy losses and 'B' Squadron, who had been moved up to Eissel, was unable to close with the guns and could not cross the canal east of Eissel.

Corporal Spencer of Recce Troop managed to instal himself in the roof of a house from where he could see the bridge across the Weser and also one of the guns. Acting on his information the artillery put in a 'stonk' which resulted in the departure of all four guns, not before, however, the enemy had time to blow the last and only bridge.

At this setback the Brigade plan was altered and the Regimental Group was ordered to turn west and advance through Brinkum to Delmenhorst. At 4 p.m. the 8th Hussars and 1/5th Queen's were ordered to about turn and advance east. They laid on an attack with artillery support on to the village of Westerwisch and captured it with only slight opposition.

At midnight Major Huth, second-in-command, and Captain F. G. Turner, Intelligence Officer, went to see the Burgomaster of Riede and arranged to send him forward into the next village to ask them to surrender.

By now everyone was getting desperately tired with never more than four or five hours' sleep each night, and on the 9th they were off again at first light. In this respect, to advance to victory in modern highly mobile war is equally physically as exhausting as defence or withdrawal. The objectives this time, to start with, were the villages of Sudweyhe and Kirchweyhe which were reported held by S.S. troops. The Regiment advanced by two routes, 'A' Squadron to the cross roads and thence north to Sudweyhe, while 'B' Squadron pushed on to the same target by way of Ahausen. At the latter place 'B' Squadron was engaged by some determined men with bazookas. One German soldier leapt on to Corporal Commons's tank and engaged him in a hand to hand fight, wounding him in the hand. Corporal Commons however was not the type of N.C.O. with whom such liberties should be taken. He overpowered the German and took him prisoner. Lieutenant F. W. Saxby, commanding the leading troop of 'A' Squadron, was nearly through Sudweyhe and had reached the stream crossing, when his Challenger was hit by a bazooka. Although the front was penetrated there were no casualties and Lieutenant Saxby found himself involved in a fight with a number of S.S. troops. The leading company of Queen's was rushed up and quickly had the situation in hand, and a large number of the enemy were killed and many more captured. In a short while the southern part of the town was cleared.

A further plan was made for clearing Kirchweyhe but in the meanwhile the citizens very sensibly claimed they would surrender the town. This they did, but not until one platoon of 1/5th Queen's and Lieutenant Saxby had been involved in some stiff fighting in the cemetery between Sudweyhe and Kirchweyhe. 'B' Squadron had in the meanwhile been firing into both these villages and had also engaged the enemy in the village of Dreye. On these sort of occasions Lieut.-Colonel Fitzpatrick often used the reserve squadron to provide indirect supporting fire, using his tanks as artillery, thereby supplementing the artillery and giving an impression of greater strength. In order to avoid delay 'C' Squadron was ordered to pass through Sudweyhe and continue the advance on Leeste and Brinkum.

On reaching a bend in the road, 'C' Squadron and 'C' Company, 1/5th Queen's in Kangaroos, met strong opposition from the same troops who had caused trouble earlier in the day. They came from the 12th S.S. Ersatz Battalion, which itself was almost at Divisional strength, its companies consisting of between 300 and 500 men. They were established in villas on the side of the road and almost immediately killed Sergeant Wakefield of 'C' Squadron and the leading platoon commander.

The ground on either side of the road was too soft for tanks except along tracks, and Lieut.-Colonel Freeland of the Queen's ordered 'B' Company, supported by a troop of 'A' Squadron, to advance east along the railway that ran east and west. Here they met very heavy opposition and, the tanks being unable to advance, the infantry went on alone.

Meanwhile Recce Troop was employed in trying to find a way round to the north in the general direction of Brinkum. The first section met trouble in the shape of boggy ground at the foot of the railway embankment, but profiting by this experience, Lieutenant C. R. P. Anstey's and Corporal Spencer's sections made use of the railway line itself and forged rapidly ahead. They soon found themselves, without having seen any of the expected S.S. troops, on the aerodrome which lay to the east of Brinkum. And this in fact was the nearest point to Bremen reached by troops of the Division. From a vantage point on one of the mounds surrounding a searchlight post there was an excellent view of the road leading north through Brinkum to Bremen, and on this road could be clearly seen an intermittent column of enemy transport and self-propelled guns pulling back towards the last remaining bridge over the Weser.

Just before last light the northern company, 'B', of the Queen's, got right into Leeste and became heavily involved, and at about 5 p.m. an anti-tank gun appeared at the cross roads and hit and penetrated one of the 'C' Squadron tanks. The gun was promptly knocked out by 'K' Battery. By evening the fighting had become very sticky and it was obvious from the quantity of snipers and bazooka men, that it was not going to be possible to clear Leeste and Brinkum without the assistance of at least one infantry battalion as the country was too built up for the use of tanks alone.

The Regiment together with the Queen's leaguered that night near Kirchweyhe and later the orders came through that the advance was not to be continued but that the Group was to remain where they were, sending one squadron, 8th Hussars, to support the 5th Dragoon Guards to the west of Syke.

The 10th was a day of comparative quiet. 'B' Squadron left at 7 in the morning to join the 5th Dragoon Guards and had the task of protection to the west where there were still a great many enemy troops, and 'C', following a route Recce Troop had found as far as Hagen, probed forward to the outskirts of Leeste. However the village was still held by the Germans and they did not attempt to push into it. One tank was unfortunately blown up on a mine and the hull gunner, Trooper Mason, killed.

And there at Kirchweyhe the Regiment came to the end of the first phase of their part in the Battle of Germany, a phase which had taken them from the Rhine at Xanten to the Weser and nearly, but not quite, to Bremen in twelve non-stop days. There followed what might be described as a 'Half time' pause. For the next day, April 11th, the Regiment handed over their sector to a Brigade of the 52nd (Lowland) Division, and moved south to a concentration area near Nieuburg higher up the Weser, where they were told there was a prospect of forty-eight hours' rest.

Meanwhile Captain Pierson and Recce Troop had a somewhat nerve-racking night recovering one of their tanks which was bogged down in a ditch some way in front of the forward positions. This, however, they achieved, and rejoined the Regiment next morning.

Edward Ardizone, the well known war artist, was attached to the Regiment at Kirchweyhe and remained with them until the Elbe was reached. His charming and intelligent personality was greatly appreciated by all and especially his friends at Regimental Headquarters.

The 7th Armoured Division in their drive for Bremen had met exceedingly tough resistance and even strong counter-attacks. It was clear that the First Parachute Army was prepared to fight hard to keep the city and their only lines of withdrawal which ran through it. As the 7th Armoured was spread over a forty mile front the chance of a quick success was small, so it was decided to switch the Division south to where the 11th Armoured and 6th Airborne were making rapid headway. So they handed over their section of the front to the 3rd British Infantry Division from 30 Corps and moved to a concentration area near Nieuburg to wait, while the 53rd (Welsh) Division, who had crossed the Weser unapposed, were struggling round Rethem to secure a bridgehead over the Aller. This they did on the 14th, as did the 11th Armoured fifteen miles to the south-east, and on the 15th the 22nd Armoured Brigade was across, ultimate goal, Hamburg.

For the 8th Hussars, after their arrival at Nieuburg on the 11th, there followed three of the pleasantest days they had spent during this part of the campaign. While the 53rd Division were fighting for the Aller crossing, they rested amongst delightfully peaceful and fragrant pine forests to the west of the Weser. In the cool woods when darkness had fallen and they were full of that sense of well-being brought about by a full stomach and a sense of achievement, the troop guitars made their appearance, and for the last hour before turning in there was quiet melody filling the darkness. The old and much-travelled tunes floated through the trees and hung momentarily on the air before drifting away, leaving an unaccustomed and exquisite peacefulness.

The Regiment crossed the Weser on April 13th, which the superstitious, remembering the fate of the Pied Piper's rats in this same river, took as a bad omen. But all crossed without so much as a splash, and before going on paused two nights between the rivers. The B.B.C. news was excellent and the Americans were only fifty miles from Berlin. But it was sad to hear that President Roosevelt had died, so near to the moment of victory. The 4th Armoured Brigade, who had crossed the Aller, were having a struggle to expand their bridgehead and delay, although irritating, was inevitable.

(e) Walsrode, April 1945

AFTER a couple of days' rest the Regiment packed up and moved off across the Aller at Rethem on the morning of the 15th. With them, under command, went 'A' Company, 1st Rifle Brigade, 'K' Battery and a detachment of Royal Engineers, and they themselves were under command of the 22nd Armoured Brigade. Their task was to advance through Walsrode to Soltau and on north-east to Hamburg. The 4th Armoured Brigade, who had crossed the day before, were having considerable trouble at Elstorf where the German 6th Marine Regiment was holding out very stubbornly. Eventually with the help of flame-throwers the village was reduced to a burning mess and they pushed on to

Kirchboitzen, seven miles along the main road to Soltau. The Division, led by the 8th Hussars, followed, but progress was slow owing to the many bomb craters in Rethem, and to the fact that beyond it the road had to be improvised across country by the Royal Engineers, the main road having been blown to pieces. Finally at Kirchboitzen the road was completely blocked and the 8th Hussars were sent to find a way across country by the sandy tracks to the south. Accordingly the 8th Hussars Group made a detour to the south, rejoining the centre line between Kirchboitzen and Walsrode. As they did this 'B' Squadron ran into enemy infantry fire from the houses along the road and Lieutenant Mossop was wounded. These Germans shot at Regimental Headquarters, narrowly missing the war artist, and were hunted away by the Green Jackets. 'B' Squadron rapidly cleared up the situation and knocked out three 20-mm. guns to the north of the road. They then moved north-east and established themselves on the high ground astride the road overlooking Walsrode.

Recce Troop meanwhile had been sent south-east of the Walsrode-Soltau road with the dual task of giving flank protection and recceing an alternative route in case the Regiment was held up. This included examining four bridges over the river Bohme. While doing this Lieutenant Anstey's section was fired on three times by panzer-fausts, none of which scored a hit. Small bands of enemy lurking in the woods were also successfully dealt with and others, firing from some farms were engaged, the farms brewing satisfactorily after a few rounds of 37-mm.

Civilian reports informed the Troop that all the bridges in which they were interested had been blown. This was soon confirmed in the case of the first, similarly in the case of the second, approaching which Sergeant Spencer got his Jalopy into what might have been a disastrous position. The road up to the bridge crossed a small stream by a rickety wooden contraption, which collapsed immediately the Jalopy reached terra firma on the other side. Sergeant Spencer found himself faced with a blown bridge in front, a collapsed one behind, and on each side of the road that joined them nothing but marshes. To rebuild the wooden bridge with the aid of some telegraph poles, which the section's Honey pushed down, and some sleepers found alongside a nearby railway line took a couple of hours, during which he was lucky to be left unmolested.

Meanwhile Sergeant Hearn had found that the third bridge had followed the fate of the others (while Corporal Judge found a German N.A.A.F.I. wagon containing enough cigarette lighters to supply the whole Regiment) but not only was the fourth, a fairly substantial wooden one, still intact, but in the event of it not standing up to the weight of a Cromwell, less than a hundred yards away stood a massive stone and concrete railway bridge. Sergeant Hearn's section daintily crossed the wooden one, and, breasting a small wooded rise the other side, narrowly missed colliding with a crowded German staff car that flashed past flat out along the broad concrete road making its escape from Walsrode.

Some Sappers were sent down to pass professional judgement on the wooden bridge and they thought it might take a Cromwell. The troop leader of the leading troop of 'C' Squadron, who had by now joined in the party, was the guinea pig. Recce Troop watched fascinated as the timbers creaked and sagged, but he and his troop all made it. The whole Squadron followed, and with Recce Troop pushed on up the other side.

While this had been going on 'B' Squadron and 'A' Company had set about clearing Walsrode. The south-western entrance to the town had been heavily cratered and was held by a company of Marines with bazookas. These were soon disposed of and a road to the south was found, and though the bridge was mined and ready for demolition, it was captured intact before the Germans had time to blow it.

That evening Walsrode was occupied by the 1/5th Queen's, who found it crammed with civilians as well as eight Britons in the three hospitals full of German wounded. The Regiment, having covered twenty-two miles that day, leaguered on the high ground near the town, while 'C' Squadron and Recce Troop, having failed to get through Duishorn to rejoin the Regiment, had to leaguer south of the centre line, which they did in the largest patch of open ground they could find, a field of roots. They massed the vehicles in a tight bunch in the middle and, although they had not eaten since their very early breakfast that morning, dared not light any kind of fire. The only thing to do was to sleep.

Late that night, after dark, about forty enemy approached the Regimental leaguer, who promptly opened up on them and they soon cleared off. The Regimental bag that day was two 20-mm. guns, two staff cars, about half a dozen spandau positions as well as many buildings brewed which contained enemy strong points.

(f) Fallingbostal, April 1945

THE DIVISION was directed on the 16th on Soltau. The 22nd Armoured Brigade took the lead with two columns, one led by the 8th Hussars along the main road and another further north by the 1st Royal Tanks. The event that overshadowed all others for the Regiment, and Recce Troop in particular, and what has been called "the greatest achievement of the operations of that day" was the discovery and liberation of the great prison camps in the woods south-west of Fallingbostal.

It was a 5 o'clock in the morning start, in the dark and cold, and a hurried breakfast of a fried egg between two pieces of bread and a mug of tea beside the tanks. Some were parked near a small garden in which were two cherry trees in blossom, and through the branches could be seen the other tanks in the meadow below, their brew fires flickering in the half light. It was an oddly beautiful scene, and a fine dawn which promised an even finer day.

'B' Squadron, with one motor platoon under command, was ordered to move east to Fallingbostal. 'C' Squadron was to advance from its night leaguer among the turnips through Duishorn also to Fallingbostal. 'A' Squadron, with a section of carriers was to try to cross the River Bohme and establish itself on the high ground to the north of Fallingbostal. Recce Troop, who had spent the night with 'C' Squadron, were ordered to find the two prison camps that were in the vicinity. They lay somewhere to the east and the map showed a large expanse of ground covered with regularly grouped blocks of buildings, any of which might have been the camps. It also showed part of an Autobahn, which with the mental picture it gave of broad concrete roadways, fly overs and bridges, should have proved an unmistakable landmark.

'C' Squadron reached the railway bridge without incident and 'B' arrived at the western outskirts of the town where they were held up by enemy infantry in the town itself. 'A' Squadron reported that the bridge, by which they had been ordered to cross, had been blown and that they were unable to cross the river anywhere else.

Recce Troop, meanwhile, succeeded in locating and liberating the two large prison camps at Fallingbostal, and the story is best told by Captain Pierson.

"Nosing its way cautiously along sandy tracks that skirted or went through the many pine-woods that were the main feature of this country, the leading section of Honeys started off slowly. Though there was no sign of any enemy, similar woods had produced quite a few the day before, and the leading tank occasionally raked the edges of the trees and suspicious hollows or clumps of grass to discourage any panzerfaust expert that might be waiting hopefully for us to get within range of his very useful weapon. The afternoon before, when he had been missed three times, Lieutenant Anstey, the leading tank commander, confessed to feeling like a goalkeeper in a football match, but this particular sunny morning there was, much to our relief, no sign of them.

"A wide clearing confronted us, obviously man-made, cut at right angles through the woods, its sandy surface covered with tufts of grass, stretching dead straight to the right as far as we could see, and to the left turning out of sight through two small mountains of earth. This must be the autobahn, though scarcely what we had expected, the maps have given no hint of this rudimentary stage in its construction.

"We turned left, came to the huge heaps of earth and halted while the leading commander, Corporal Spencer, dismounted to have a look at what lay round them out of sight. No more woods, but a flat open expanse of grass bounded, some thousand yards away, by a long uneven line of low buildings, out of which, further to our left, rose what looked like half a dozen tall warehouses. Binoculars showed that the main mass of low buildings lay behind a high wire fence—and people, at first we saw one or two moving about, then made out groups of a dozen, and finally realised that the thickening of the bottom half of the fence was in fact a solid mass of them. At this moment the leading tanks of 'C' Squadron, approaching on a different route, came up behind us, and without waiting to see any more we jumped into our tanks and shot out into the open. In high spirits we crossed the grass as quickly as the ground would allow, but as the distance between us and the fence grew less we noticed that the predominant colour of the mass that was now streaming out of the gates towards us was grey, dark grey. And at the same moment saw a French flag—or was it Dutch—which in our excitement we had not noticed before, fluttering behind the main gate. Our hopes sank; these were not British prisoners, but another of the camps full of all nationalities of Europe that we had come across so many times before. Perhaps there were some British amongst them, then again perhaps there was no British camp at all, and the Germans have moved XIB as they had moved so many others out of the way of the Armies advancing from East to West.

"The leading tank came to a stop as the first of the breathless, shouting stream of humanity surrounded it, and Corporal Spencer, still clinging to a faint hope, lent down and yelled, 'English soldaten?' He repeated himself in a moment's hush, and then a hundred hands pointed to his left, and the clamour of the excited crowd broke out with increased intensity. As he looked round for someone out of whom he could get some sense it seemed that every nation was represented, women as well as men, the majority in civilian clothes, with but two things in common; they were all happy, and all indescribably dirty.

"Noticing one persistent man who seemed to have a smattering of English he hauled him up on to the tank and asked which way. The fellow pointed, and as the tank moved slowly forward the crowd melted away in front. He glanced over his shoulder and noticed that he was still leading, the Cromwells of 'C' Squadron were as uncertain as he had been as to the route, but were now following hot on his heels. It was going to be a close thing who reached the Camp first.

"Parallel to the fence, which he had now reached, ran a concrete road, and turning left along this, to the accompaniment of cheers from the waving smiling crowd of prisoners and D.P.'s that thronged its entire length, he soon passed the tall warehouses that had first been noticed in the distance.

"The fellow in the turret pointed excitedly forward, but Corporal Spencer could see nothing, except a road, tree-lined on both sides, that met ours at right angles. We halted at the junction; to our left the road went under a stone bridge built to carry the autobahn, but with no autobahn to carry looking comically like a piece from a child's set of toy bricks. A quick glance to the right revealed nothing more than an empty road. But the guide was tugging at Spencer's sleeve and jabbering away—and following with our eyes the direction of his pointing arm we saw across the road through a gap between two trees a khaki-clad figure wearing a maroon-coloured beret, clinging to a wire fence beyond and jumping up and down, obviously shouting his head off, though not a word reached us over the noise of the engines and earphones.

"And then all the way down to the right we could see between the tree-trunks more figures racing along the wire. We'd got there, and before the Cromwells, which came up behind just as we moved off down the road giving the glad news over the air. Three or four hundred yards down the road was the main gate to the camp and as we approached the sound of welcome from the crowd that lined the wire and covered the roofs of the camp buildings grew to a roar that penetrated our earphones above the noise of our engines. Inside the main gates was an open space packed with British Prisoners, and, beyond another wire fence, what looked like an inner enclosure was black with figures. This was Stalag XIB.

"Quite staggering was the contrast between this scene and that which we had seen at other camps containing prisoners of the Allied nations. Despite the enthusiasm of the men inside you could see at a glance that here was order and discipline. The remarkable R.S.M. Lord, Grenadier Guards, of the 1st Airborne Division had already taken charge and was busily engaged in his office giving peace-time orders to his Orderly Warrant Officers. Camp M.P.'s, each with a red armband, policed the gates, and as the crowd came out to meet us there was no ugly rush but a steady controlled stream that surrounded each tank as it stopped, a stream wearing the headgear of what looked like every unit in the Army. The Airborne beret predominated—men of D-Day, Arnhem, even the Rhine crossing who had only been inside for a few weeks—but you could pick out the hats, caps, berets and bonnets of a score of others. And under each one was such a look of happiness and thankfulness that made us as happy to be the cause of it. It was a quiet crowd that thronged round us; they had had their cheer, and now when the moment came for words, few words came. Mostly they were too moved to speak, men who could only grin broadly and clasp your hand as the tears ran down their cheeks. You couldn't speak yourself, only shake as many as possible of the hands that stretched towards you, and grin back, trying to take it all in, and marvel. For these men didn't look like prisoners; their battle-dresses were pressed and clean, here and there web belts and gaiters were scrubbed white and the brasses gleaming, they might have been off duty in a town at home instead of just walking out of prison wire behind which they had been for anything from five weeks to five years.

"Memories of that scene leaves a picture of a healthy and, if not overfed, certainly not starving crowd; of apologetic requests for cigarettes and one man turning green with his first puff, having given up the habit for his three years inside; of the creases in the tartan trews and the shining buttons on the jacket of a C.S.M. in the 51st Highland Division, who admitted having marched five or six hundred kilometres from East Prussia, and who didn't look as if he had been more than five or six hundred yards from his own front door; of the Camp M.O. indignantly denying any cases of Typhus; of the German Commandant and a few of the camp guards standing apart in a small group watching unmoved the reversal of his rôle, and handing over his automatic with an offer to show us over the nearby storehouses; scraps of conversation 'I've been waiting five years for this day'—'Three days ago we expected you' and in contrast, 'You've come too soon, my jacket's still wet,' this from one who had washed his battledress specially for the occasion; and from one as impressed by our appearance (we hadn't washed or shaved for nearly forty-eight hours) as were we by theirs, 'You look like real soldiers.' There were several requests to see a Jeep, which we could not unfortunately produce at that moment; much signing of autographs on both sides and nearly always the first question 'What's your mob?' and finding several members of the Regiment in the camp, taken at Sidi Rezegh in 1941; and finally, on asking news of their erstwhile captors, being told that they were not long gone and were carrying panzerfausts. This was more serious, with all these fellows about, and on asking the police to clear the road we got the most startling proof of the state of the camp discipline. For at a word from a tall figure wearing the Airborne beret, R.S.M. Lord, the Camp M.P.'s went round, and in a very few moments and without a murmur these scores of men, some of whom were tasting freedom for the first time in more than five years, made their way back behind that same barbed wire and netting that to them must have been the symbol of all that was hateful and depressing in this life.

"We left as the vanguard of visitors was arriving, the V.I.P.'s and the not so V.I.P.'s, the Press and the frankly-curious, all wishing to get a first-hand glimpse of the first large predominantly British camp to find itself in the path of the British Army of Liberation. And we left taking with us an impression that will never fade; of men whose courage and hope had been kept alive through long years of boredom and privation by their faith in their comrades and their country; and whose behaviour in their moment of triumph when faith had been rewarded was an example of the highest traditions of the Army to which they belonged.

"And that might have been the end of our part in the proceedings of what was for all of us a great occasion. But later on that day we happened to pass that way again when things were more normal; erstwhile prisoners were strolling about in groups, or sitting in the sun enjoying a smoke and waving contentedly at the passing traffic. But all was not quite normal, for as we came up to the main gates where we had received such a reception a few hours earlier, we saw a troop of Armoured Cars obliging some movie-cameramen by driving slowly past a group of wildly waving and shouting ex-prisoners; and, for a brief moment, as we beheld the scene as spectators and not actors, we felt again all the emotions of that most memorable day."

But at the other camp, Stalag 357, it was a different state of affairs. Major Huth took with him Captain Edward Ardizzone, who recalled: "Here we were the first troops to arrive and when we halted in the wire approach to the camp we were surrounded by a great crowd of men almost hysterical with joy. They nearly overwhelmed us, climbing over our cars, patting us on the back, shaking our hands, bombarding us with questions, shouting, laughing, some even crying.

"Here, unlike the other camp, was none of that air of discipline and smartness. The clothes most of the men wore were nondescript. Many wore gym-shoes and few had either hats or caps.

"I am not for a moment suggesting that morale and discipline had gone, far from it. But these men, unlike the others, had been prisoners for a long time, some for as much as four or five years, and even their faces showed it.

"It was a very moving and wonderful experience. As I have said, some men were crying, and I do not think we ourselves were very far from tears; but perhaps the saddest and most moving sight of all was when, after disentangling ourselves from the crowd and having been given a parting cheer as we drove away, we looked back and saw so many hundreds still clinging to the wire as if by habit, a habit caused by long imprisonment. They could not realise that they were free."

In these camps liberated by the Regiment there were, in Stalag XIB, 6,500 British and Americans, of which 550 were in hospital, and 8,000 assorted Allied nationals of which 2,600 were French. At Stalag 357 there were 3,500 British and Americans and the same amount of Allied nationals. Captain Bonham-Carter was the British Commandant of the latter and there were also in the camp Greek, Czech and Russian colonels, all of whom greeted Major Huth in a tremendous way and kissed him on both cheeks.

'B' Squadron at 11 a.m., decided that Fallingbostal town was too large to be cleared by one motor company. Although considerable fire power was available the riflemen quickly became absorbed in the streets and houses. The task therefore was handed over to the 1/5th Queen's with 'B' Squadron in support. When this was done eventually, it was to find that the vital bridge at the end of the main street, which was burning well, had been blown. 'A' Squadron was by now on the south of the town on the high ground and able to give fire support.

In the meanwhile 'C' Squadron, having left the prison camps, were ordered to work north to try and find an unblown bridge across the Bohme to the north-east of Fallingbostal. By 3 p.m. they had reached the southern outskirts of Dorfmark but had found all the bridges there blown. From what they could gather from local inhabitants and various displaced persons, the bridges in the town were blown as well, but some slight opposition prevented this from being checked at once. Regimental Headquarters moved up and a plan for clearing Dorfmark was made. The autobahn had not yet been completed, the alignment had been graded only and there was no soling or surfacing. It was therefore impassable to all but tracked vehicles. Recce Troop were ordered once again to make a sweep to the south and east and find a route to link up with the centre-line beyond the town, with a view to taking Dorfmark along that axis. One company 1/5th Queen's, came under command for this purpose.

During this day Recce Troop destroyed two staff cars, captured and subsequently brewed-up three armoured tracked mortar carriers and took nearly 40 prisoners.

Meanwhile the leading troop of 'C' Squadron reported that it considered that Dorfmark was clear and the Troop Leader was ordered to move up to the bridge which was in fact blown. Back at Fallingbostal the town had been occupied, but as the bridge had been blown, 'B' Squadron was sent west to Walsrode, thence in a wide circle north and east to Dorfmark.

The Regiment finally leaguered in the village, with 'B' Squadron by now west of the river, which separated it from the rest of the Regiment. The bag for the day in exchange for six wounded was unusual to say the least, three mortar carriers, three 81-mm. mortars, four cars, two 20-mm. guns, 80 plus prisoners and two Stalags liberated.

At dusk the 1st Royal Tanks were two miles west of Soltau, which was very strongly held, the 8th Hussars were at Dorfmark four miles to the south-west, and the 131st Brigade, less the Queen's, were at Walsrode. The 4th Armoured Brigade had pushed north-west of Soltau and the 11th Armoured Division were level, twelve miles to the east. There would obviously be a considerable delay as it would take at least an infantry bridgade to capture Soltau, so it was decided to by-pass the town to the west by way of Neuenkirchen and Schneverdingen with the 22nd Armoured Brigade, and to reduce Soltau with the 155th Brigade who were taking over Walsrode from the 131st. The 8th Hussars and a squadron of the 11th Hussars were to try and find a way round to the east.

(g) Heber, April 1945

DURING the night a bridge was built at Fallingbostal and at first light on the 17th the Regiment crossed the Bohme by it and rejoined 'B' Squadron in the western part of Dorfmark. The 8th Hussars Group, having been ordered to by-pass Soltau, moved fast by Kroge intending to rejoin the main road north of the town.

'B' Squadron was in the lead and made good progress through country reminiscent of Aldershot until they reached an 11th Hussar troop who were held up while trying to rejoin the main road, and had had an armoured car destroyed by what they took to be a party of bazooka men. 'B' Squadron was ordered to fight its way on to the road and moved into the attack, led by One and Four Troops. After leaving the small wood where the 11th Hussar troop had taken shelter they advanced successfully, and Two and Three Troops had a good shoot at German vehicles moving up and down the road. However as they approached the Hamburg road they came under heavy fire, not only from anti-tank guns but from a Panther tank that had been lurking in the trees. The Panther received a direct hit and the crew baled-out and ran into the woods. 'K' Battery knocked-out a self-propelled gun to the east of the main road and an 88-mm. was also destroyed.

Lieutenant P. D. Moll and Three Troop were now ordered to make for the road. However he at once became bogged in the soft grey earth, so Lieutenant Pott and Two Troop took over, only to be held up again, short of the main road. There was much less enemy movement now and things seemed to be quietening down when without warning Squadron Headquarters and Three Troop were heavily shelled by Nebelwerfers, which 'K' Battery at once did its best to neutralise, although in the meantime Trooper Bodle was killed and two men wounded.

Meanwhile 'A' Squadron was ordered to advance on Heber, and at the same time Pott reported all quiet and managed to gain and turn north up the main road, but suddenly reported that the wood on the other side of the road was strongly held by enemy infantry. Immediately after this report the air went dead, and some minutes later Sergeant Taylor reported that the leading tank of Two Troop had been set on fire by a large mine. Taylor's tank brought back the wounded, Pott terribly burnt. It was obvious that the woods astride the road just here were full of enemy infantry and 'B' Squadron was ordered to fall back. By now the rest of the Regimental Group had followed 'A' Squadron who had reached Heber, dealing satisfactorily with the resistance they met there.

Recce Troop meanwhile, who were protecting the right flank of 'A' Squadron and were followed by 'C' Squadron, were given the task of finding an alternative route in a loop to the west that might reach Hillern, south of Heber up the centre line. This was successfully accomplished and a suitable crossing place was found, after two bridges were discovered blown, for 'C' Squadron to pass through and on to Hillern.

Heber was cleared by about 5 p.m. and one troop of 'A' Squadron was ordered to push north along the main road as far as possible. They found no German soldiers in the village, only civilians. Brigade ordered the 8th Hussars Group to establish themselves that night along the road from Hillern to Heber.

Much later a 'C' Squadron patrol on the road near Hillern was approached by a party of Germans. These however were quickly routed, two being killed and six captured. But the Regiment had suffered heavily itself that day, with Troopers Jones (or Gough) and Bodle killed, Lieutenant Pott and four men wounded and suffering from burns from 'B' Squadron, and Corporal Scott and Troopers Brogden, Bunn and Meadows missing believed killed, all from 'A' Squadron. 'A' Squadron had been in the rear on the move from Dorfmark. One of their tanks was a straggler and missed the turning off the road leading north-west from Soltau. It must have motored down the road into Soltau and been knocked out on the edge of the town, because it was never heard of again. Two tanks were lost that day, but to make up for that the Regiment had added to their score one Panther, two 88-mms., two half-track vehicles, a staff car, two horse-drawn wagons, about twenty-five prisoners and twenty enemy killed.

That evening the 1st Royal Tanks reached Welle, seven miles north of Heber and the same night the 155th Brigade's attack on Soltau went in. At dawn the entire town, most of which was in flames, had been captured. Patrols pushed on and joined up with the 8th Hussars to the north. The next task was to press forward as fast as possible in the hopes of capturing the bridges over the Elbe at Harburg before they could be destroyed, and also to keep clear the centre line which would have to run through Lüneburg Heath which was known to be full of the enemy. Bremen had by now been captured but there was plenty of opposition still in the west, and the remnants of the First Parachute Army, squeezed between Hamburg and Bremen, were trying to escape by way of Bremer-vörde and on over the Elbe.

(h) Hollenstedt, April 1945

A VIOLENT thunderstorm during the night of the 18th brought a balmy spring morning in its wake. At first light the 8th Hussars Group moved on north in the wake of the 1st Royal Tanks who were held up south of Welle. There were many halts on the way, and on each occasion Recce Troops were sent out to watch the flanks, returning each time with an odd straggler or two. Eventually Lieut.-Colonel Fitzpatrick visited the Colonel of the 1st Royal Tanks and learnt from him that his Regiment had run into strong opposition in the Forest of Langeloh and could not advance any further with the force they had. The Colonel hoped he might be able to by-pass the forest and already had one Squadron at the Railway bridge. Just after midday the 8th Hussars were ordered to try and cross the railway, capture Tostedt and make for the high ground overlooking the Elbe at Elstorf. This would open a route for the 5th Guards Armoured Brigade who were having trouble at Rotenburg.

The first problem was the crossing of the railway in order to reach Tostedt as the bridge over it at the village had been blown. 'C' Squadron was ordered through Otter, which had already been cleared by the 1st Royal Tanks, and thence to the high ground to try and probe round to the west and find a crossing there. 'A' Squadron meanwhile was to advance along the main road from Welle to Tostedt and to try to cross the railway west of the bridge that had been blown, while Recce Troop had various tasks, that of contacting the armoured cars of the Guards Armoured Division which were known to be somewhere on the western flank and the searching of the small villages west of Otter.

Presently 'C' Squadron reported having found a bridge under the railway that was undefended but the approaches were so bad that it made their route impassable. However they presently found one, still intact, over which the Squadron proceeded to cross. After the first two tanks were over it the bridge collapsed, but luckily they had with them, as well as a motor platoon, a Royal Engineers Recce officer who was able to supervise its reconstruction.

'A' Squadron also found a way over the railway but when two troops had crossed they were fired upon by a self-propelled gun which was thought to be situated at Todtglusingen. As this village had been cleared already by the 1st Royal Tanks and the 11th Hussars, the firing probably came from a roving Tiger and some light anti-tank guns at a cross roads nearby. 'A' Squadron eventually pushed north into Tostedt which they occupied just before dark. Here the Royal Engineers started work on a Bailey bridge to carry the centre line across the railway, protected by Recce Troop.

In the meantime 'C' Squadron had concentrated on the right side of the bridge and set about clearing Wistedt. Here the leading troop ran into snipers and bazookas who were not dealt with until last light and after most of the village had been set on fire. However 'C' Squadron established themselves there satisfactorily and the rest of the motor company came up to join them for the night. At last light the 1/5th Queen's took over Tostedt and organised the town for the night, with 'A' and 'B' Squadrons in support.

The plan for the 19th was to advance north to Hollenstedt, then east along the autobahn for 6 kilometres, then north again to Elstorf. The 8th Hussars Group lost no time and was off at first light, hotly pursued by Recce Troop. 'B' Squadron, who were in the lead, managed to snatch breakfast before they left as there seemed little chance of another proper meal before nightfall. In spite of that, morale was very high as final victory at last seemed near, but everyone was desperately tired.

Lieutenant Ryde and Three Troop led, with Squadron Headquarters following. It had been arranged to give Dohren, the first village on the route, a short artillery concentration, as it was suspected that it was occupied. However the Regiment sailed through the burning village with no trouble, and roared on down a small country road leading northwards at thirty miles an hour. With the sun shining on the new green leaves of the trees the advance seemed something in the nature of a joy ride. It was at Dohren that Recce Troop caught them up and were allowed to stop and have breakfast. Taking advantage of the surrounding holocaust, in a very few moments every crew had its brew-can and frying pan balanced precariously on the flaming woodwork of one house or another, while simultaneously the owners were trying to recover their property or putting the blaze out with fire hoses.

'B' Squadron meanwhile, going at full speed, had reached the autobahn and turned east. As Four Troop who were following Squadron Headquarters, turned on to the broad road, 88-mms. opened up on them from Hollenstedt. As troops were now only two tanks strong each the whole Squadron took up a hull down position on the autobahn, facing north, and returned fire, knocking out two 88-mms. Sergeant Winch, commanding Four Troop, reported a Tiger moving in the small wood to the left of Hollenstedt. Shells were now coming over thick and fast, but as the autobahn was slightly below ground level it afforded good protection. Charlton was anxious to push on with 'B' Squadron but was told to stay where he was. Regimental Headquarters halted on the side road above the dip on which the autobahn ran and did not fare so well. The Brigade Commander, Brigadier Wingfield, and Lieut.-Colonel Fitzpatrick had to take cover in a convenient ditch.

'A' Squadron was ordered to take Hollenstedt and the leading troop, advancing on to the bridge over the autobahn, came under fire from anti-tank guns. One tank was knocked out and Trooper Edwards killed and Corporal Logan wounded. Meanwhile the 1/5th Queen's came up to assist in the capture of Hollenstedt. They were supported in the attack by Typhoons of the R.A.F., and 'B' Squadron, further down the road to the east, had a fine view of the aircraft diving and beating up the village. The Queen's and 'A' Squadron then put in a set-piece attack, but when they entered Hollenstedt it was to find it empty and the Germans fled, leaving a dozen prisoners and a destroyed 88-mm. battery behind. The Group was now astride the communications of the enemy who were holding up the 5th Guards Armoured Brigade at Rotenburg.

By now 'B' Squadron had reached the next cross roads eastwards along the autobahn, and at the village they ran into an enemy strong point and, taking it by surprise, rapidly knocked out four 88-mm. guns and continued advancing northwards towards Rade.

Meanwhile Recce Troop sent patrols north to Oldendorf and south to Wennersdorf and Wenzendorf. At the first of these places, Sergeant Dickinson and Corporal Cohen captured a party of Hamburg policemen who had been sent out to protect the autobahn, and subsequently cleared the village. At Wennersdorf, Lieutenant Anstey's section knocked-out an 88-mm. gun, but unfortunately the crew managed to escape, while near Wenzendorf Sergeant Hearn's section knocked-out another 88-mm., wounding some, and this time capturing all the crew. This was a great achievement, and the statement that the guns were manned was at first received rather sceptically on the air. Admittedly the crews were not very determined, nor highly trained, but in each case were seen trying frantically to traverse their guns in the required direction. Each village produced some additions to the bag of prisoners, amongst them some more of the Hamburg police force. One group of these confessed to having been invited to dinner a few nights previously by the Burgomaster of the village they were sent to defend. After a few bottles of wine he had explained to them that defending his village meant its inevitable destruction, and that would be an awful shame, didn't they agree? Furthermore some of them might get hurt, and by now they were such good friends of his that he couldn't bear to see that happen. As a result of this 'cri de coeur' they agreed to hand over to him their arms, which included a goodly number of panzerfausts, and lie low until a suitable moment came to give themselves up. This they did to Recce Troop, who considerably shook the village and its inhabitants by detonating their store of grenades and panzerfausts in a deep slit trench.

This was a great day for the Recce Troop. Sergeant Hearn, who was doing a recce of a small aerodrome nearby, reported an Allied Prisoner of War Camp. On investigation this proved to be Stalag XB, containing some 800 assorted Russians, Poles, Czechs, French and 20 Italian officers. All the Russians, who were practically starving, looked as if they had come from west of the Urals and took no notice of orders to stay put until someone arrived to look after them. They just set out in groups of two or three in every direction of the compass, obviously determined not to stay in that place a moment longer than they need. This was by far the dirtiest camp yet encountered, and it gave some indication of the love the Germans bore their erstwhile allies, the Italians, by putting their officers in such a place. The camp guard added to the Troops' bag of prisoners, which at the end of the day totalled 120.

By now 'A' Squadron had been brought up to the cross roads south of Rade and

'B' Squadron continued on northwards. With the Rifle Brigade company and supported by 'K' Battery, they cleared Rade by 2 p.m., after some opposition, and, leaving behind them a smoking ruin, turned north on to a side road, making for Elstorf. However, on reaching a bend in the road they came under very heavy artillery fire from the north-east and accurate armour-piercing fire from the villages of Elstorf and Schwiederstorf. There were high trees on either side of this road and high explosive shells bursting in the top of them were particularly unpleasant. The ground too was either wooded or boggy and any attempt at leaving the road would have been fatal. A mile short of Elstorf the country changed, the woods ending and a rolling open plain taking their place. The moment One Troop, now in the lead, left the woods they were heavily engaged by enemy guns in Elstorf. Their shooting was accurate and Squadron Headquarters were sniped at by 88-mms. Movement forward became very difficult because of the exposed nature of the countryside.

Lieut.-Colonel Fitzpatrick now arrived on a visit to 'B' Squadron in a scout car, and the moment he left the woods an 88-mm. opened up on him. This experience encouraged him to give some very firm orders over the air to make the Squadron push on, but this was difficult as every movement on this open plain brought instant and unwelcome attention. Eventually they moved very wide to the left (west) flank and got round to due west of Elstorf. It was now after 4 p.m. and Lieut.-Colonel Fitzpatrick ordered them to return for the night to the Regimental leaguer in the woods. However, having come so far Major Charlton, commanding 'B' Squadron, suggested that they tried to rush Elstorf from the west on the chance of the enemy having pulled out. They started to move towards the village with three troops up, well spread out, but had only advanced a few hundred yards before 88's opened up, luckily firing wildly.

It was beginning to grow dark and as it was now obvious that the village was still held and that there was no chance of a surprise rush in, Major Charlton decided to abandon the 'arm blanche' form of attack and they leaguered where they were for the night, about a kilometre south of the village, with the comforting knowledge that their advance that day was a useful achievement. The rest of the Regiment leaguered at Rade, with 'A' Squadron at the cross roads to the south. The night itself was not entirely uneventful and the place must have been surrounded by Germans as there were exchanges of fire all round during the night. Corporal Cohen of Recce Troop in the guard tank about midnight heard a rustling in the undergrowth and, dismounting to investigate, had three grenades thrown at him, which luckily failed to hit him. However, they spent the remainder of the night standing-to. Another incident that livened up the hours of dark-ness was when a large white bus and trailer full of strayed Germans motoring south from Elstorf, blew itself up on Hawkins mines.

The bag that day included eight 88-mms. and over 140 prisoners for the loss of one tank and one man killed.

(i) Race for the Elbe, April 1945

THE 20th brought the Regiment to the last scene of the final act. Those who were still resisting round Hamburg did so with renewed ferocity, but for the British troops there was a feeling that it could not be long now. The morning was dull and misty but everybody, although desperately tired, was in tremendous form as they were hoping to reach the Supreme Commander's objective that day, the River Elbe, and everything was set for what might well be, and in fact was, the Regiment's last real engagement.

After a hasty breakfast, in the knowledge that there would probably be no chance until nightfall of having anything else to eat, 'B' Squadron moved out at first light to continue their attack against Elstorf. Artillery support was supposed to be provided but the Artillery later admitted having attacked Ardesdorf by mistake. Luckily this mistake was soon rectified and after a short sharp fight, the town was cleared and an 88-mm. gun, which was found abandoned in a garage, was destroyed by Sergeant Winch. 'A' Company, 1st Rifle Brigade, less two platoons, was ordered forward immediately to clear Schwiederstorf and as their leading men and the leading troop, Three, of 'B' Squadron, met on the cross roads a small party of determined enemy was encountered. Lieutenant Ryde's tank was bazookad and he jumped out into the cover of a slit-trench. As he did this a German from an adjacent slit-trench shot him through the chest, killing him instantly. There never was a better leader, and he had commanded his troop with consistent gallantry since he joined the Regiment from the Northamptonshire Yeomanry in June 1944. That very morning, though his troop was only two tanks strong, he had begged to be allowed to lead the Squadron in the attack on Elstorf, but Charlton had refused, feeling Ryde had done enough and had had more than his fair share in the preceding weeks. He was therefore virtually in reserve, moving behind Squadron Headquarters, when his tank was hit. More pathos was added to this bitter blow by the fact that only a few hours after his death a message was received at Squadron Headquarters recalling him for a Lulworth Gunnery Course.

'A' Company, Rifle Brigade, and Two Troop of 'B' Squadron, were next ordered to clear Schwiederstorf, the adjacent village. But though the outskirts were reached, the attack was held off by the enemy.

Lieut.-Colonel Fitzpatrick then decided to outflank the position to the east with 'C' Squadron under Major Firth, and they, in the morning mist, entered the village of Schwiederstorf which is just east of Elstorf, without meeting any opposition. Meanwhile 'B' Squadron had completed the capture of Elstorf and were ordered to make a firm base there while 'C' Squadron continued the attack. Carrier patrols in the north had reported Daerstorf held and 'C' Squadron was ordered to advance on it, two troops up, Lieutenant C. C. Kennedy's on the right and Lieutenant G. R. A. C. Kirkham's on the left, followed by Squadron Headquarters and two troops in reserve. A patrol of the Rifle Brigade carrier platoon had already reached a small wood to the east of Daerstorf and were well placed to observe the road running north from Daerstorf as soon as the mist cleared.

As 'C' Squadron advanced, Kennedy's troop on the right was fired on by Panzer-fausts from the southern end of the village and Sergeant Bennet's tank was hit. As they dashed for cover an anti-tank gun hit Kennedy's tank and the troop were ordered to take up positions in a little orchard about 700 yards south of the village. Neither tank was immobilised although Troopers Parker, Wilson and Little were wounded and evacuated. Lieutenant Kennedy, although wounded, stayed with his troop. Parker was a most cheerful soldier and although seriously wounded continued to crack jokes while being put into the ambulance half-track.

Meanwhile the left hand troop under Lieutenant Kirkham had reached some high ground and were in a good position from which they could observe and fire into Daerstorf. The Squadron already knew of one anti-tank gun on the eastern side of the village and further reconnaissance discovered one and perhaps two on the western side and also the fact that the village was very strongly held with a large number of infantry. Obviously Daerstorf and Wulmstorf were considered to be important places tactically, because whoever held them overlooked Hamburg and the Elbe.

The Squadron was ordered to capture these places as soon as possible and given another platoon of the Motor Battalion and any gunner help they needed. The plan briefly was as follows: concentrations were to be fired on Daerstorf and Wulmstorf and under cover of smoke two troops of tanks, with men of the Rifle Brigade riding on their backs, were to dash for the eastern end of the village and assault it from that flank, supported by all available tanks in the Squadron.

Lieutenant Gould and Sergeant Robinson were commanding these troops, and as the smoke screen developed both troops with their riflemen drove flat out across country for their objective. By this time, with the concentrated fire coming down on Daerstorf, the village was burning merrily, which added to the general chaos.

Perhaps fortunately, Gould slightly lost direction in the smoke and came on to the precincts of the village from the south-east instead of the east, thus enabling that very gallant N.C.O., Sergeant Pass, M.M., to enter the outskirts and, in the smoke, drive straight over a 75-mm. anti-tank gun, killing its crew. This good news came over the air interrupted by very amusing instructions given by Sergeant Pass to his crew when he was on the 'A' set and not as he thought, on the inter-com. Even the exasperated Squadron Leader was forced to laugh out loud in spite of the fact that he was waiting to give important orders to the rest of the Squadron. While overrunning the gun, Pass had been wounded in the head but remained in command of his troop until ordered out of action later. At about this time Gould too was wounded in the head by a sniper. As soon as his crew had evacuated him his place was taken by Sergeant Spriggs, who had been riding in a Scout Car, and he and the tank went back into battle. During this attack the Squadron came under heavy shell-fire and, as Squadron Headquarters joined Kirkham's troop, his tank received a direct hit, fortunately incurring no serious damage.

At this stage the village was blazing well but the enemy resisted every inch of the way. The two troops and the riflemen were now clearing house by house towards the centre of the village and Kirkham's troop and Squadron Headquarters had a good shoot at some of the enemy, trying to escape to the west.

Due to the smoke from the burning buildings it was impossible to see exactly where people were, and the Squadron was ordered to clear up the village towards the north and to rendezvous on the northern edge. By this time another anti-tank gun had been knocked-out on the western side of the village, large numbers of the enemy had been killed while many others surrendered. A very gallant figure was Major Milner of the Rifle Brigade, who led his men through burning houses that fell all around him, whilst being shelled and sniped at the whole time.

By about 3 p.m. Daerstorf had been captured. It contained three anti-tank guns and about two hundred infantry, of which some had succeeded in escaping to the north and north-west. 'B' Squadron had meanwhile killed and captured a number of Germans at a searchlight site.

A rapid appreciation was made and it was decided to attack Wulmstorf, 1000 yards to the north, immediately, before the enemy had time to recover. The troops and two platoons of riflemen, plus what carriers were available, were to advance on a broad front supported by the remaining tanks and artillery. Concentrated fire was brought to bear on the village and the attack went in. At this moment Lieut.-Colonel Fitzpatrick arrived in his tank out of the flames behind 'C' Squadron, to send them on their way.

Wulmstorf fell with little opposition and this brought 'C' Squadron on to the high ground overlooking Hamburg and the Elbe. This brisk and extremely successful action

P

had resulted in 'C' Squadron securing the Supreme Commander's furthest objective, the first troops of the 7th Armoured Division to do so, and they were truly proud and happy as they signalled the information back.

Enemy shelling continued for some time after Wulmstorf fell but eventually the gunners of 'K' Battery silenced them. In the meantime a company of 1/5th Queen's commanded by Major Lilley, M.C., arrived and firm based in Daerstorf and Wulmstorf for the night, where they were joined by 'C' Squadron at last light, while 'A' Squadron occupied Schweiderstorf and Regimental Headquarters, 'B' Squadron and Recce Troop, Elstorf.

The bag that night was most satisfactory. One 88-mm. gun, two 75's, two 50-mms., three half-tracked vehicles, one gun tractor, a motor-bus and trailer and various assorted small fry, while over 200 prisoners had been taken. Against this was the loss of Lieutenant Ryde, the last 8th Hussar to lose his life in the field, and four men wounded.

(j) In sight of Hamburg, April 1945

EVERYTHING was quiet on the 21st, and orders were to sit tight and to watch the enemy's defensive perimeter round Hamburg. The 7th Armoured Division itself was now occupied in clearing up the salient towards Hamburg that had been overrun during the last few days, and to strengthen the bound reached, the high ground overlooking the Elbe. This was a role that fell principally to the Infantry, and the 131st Brigade took over the front between Hittfield and Vahrendorf. East the 5th Royal Tanks stretched towards Winsen, where the 11th Armoured Division took over, and west were the 22nd Armoured Brigade. There was much mopping up to be done as the forest was full of armed enemy troops, and in fact some villages had been by-passed altogether in the race for the Elbe. Then followed a most curious phase, a kind of second 'phoney war'. Everyone realised that the conflict was almost over, yet there was an obvious need for constant watchfulness and there were frequent incidents to remind the Regiment that they had not completely finished the job.

Of the 22nd Brigade the 8th Hussars were the right-hand Regiment and held the sector of the front from the woods north-east of Neu Wiedenthal to Buxtehude where the 5th Dragoon Guards took over. They kept their dispositions of the 19th and, during the day, sent out a number of patrols but little was seen of the enemy. 'K' Battery from their forward observation post found plenty of targets to shoot at, mostly on the road to Fishbeck. At last light a Medium Battery settled itself all round Regimental Headquarters, much to the consternation of the latter since it was feared that their activities would attract enemy attention.

On the morning of the 22nd, Regimental Headquarters was moved to the north-east end of Elstorf to elude this battery of Medium guns that were by then sitting on their doorstep. During the afternoon a train appeared, moving from west to east across 'C' Squadron's front, on the railway line running from Buxtehude, obviously making for Harburg along the valley, about 3000 yards below their heights. 'K' Battery immediately opened up and hit a truck which at once burst into flames and exploded, whereupon the engine unhooked itself and steamed off to Harburg. This was too much for the 'C' Squadron tanks, and they at once started to destroy the trucks one by one, a most satisfactory target as it was an ammunition train. In the meantime the engine driver had been ordered back to his train (one could imagine the caustic comments of the Harburg stationmaster when he arrived without it). He bravely backed up to the leading truck which had not yet been blown up, and, as he was about to attach himself the engine received a round through the boiler. It exploded in a cloud of steam, to the intense delight of a large number of distinguished spectators, including the C.R.A., Brigadier T. Lyon-Smith.

During the day about twenty German soldiers gave themselves up, and many more escaped Allied prisoners arrived. At last light, four enemy aircraft attacked Elstorf, two of their four bombs falling within thirty yards of the Orderly Room.

'A' Squadron relieved 'C' in Daerstorf on the 23rd and the latter returned to Schwiederstorf. 'A' Squadron sent a patrol to investigate a Belgian Offlag at Fishbeck and found that while the fit prisoners had been marched away a week previously the camp still held about a hundred and twenty sick and aged Belgian officers. They took the German guard prisoner, two officers and eighty odd men, but did not move the Belgians as they were better off where they were and finding means to move them was difficult.

Major Huth, the second-in-command, started running a sort of transit repatriation camp for escaped prisoners and forced labourers of every nationality. They were fed on food that had been taken from the Germans and then transported to near Soltau, where there was a reception camp for those sort of people. On the 23rd the Regiment dealt with about a hundred and fifty, mostly Russian and French.

Patrolling continued to the end of the month with nothing of outstanding excitement to report. On the 27th, Field-Marshal Montgomery held an investiture at Divisional Headquarters and yet another 8th Hussar was decorated when Lieutenant Payne of 'B' Squadron received his M.C. Even though the end was near everyone still had to keep on the alert. The 2nd Devons had a patrol overrun at Vahrendorf on the 26th and only after heavy fighting did they regain the ground they had lost. On the 28th Major Huth left the Regiment for a Staff College Course at Quetta having served continuously since December 1941, and Major de Clermont was promoted Acting Major and took over the duties of second-in-command. During the day Captain Hantz, the Belgian Liaison Officer from 12 Corps, came to thank the Regiment for rescuing his compatriots and to say there were still another fifteen in Fishbeck. These apparently were in another camp and were rescued by 'B' Squadron that night in a raid similar to the one carried out by 'A'. After a church service in the village church on the 29th the G.O.C. (General Lyne) visited the Regiment.

All this time rumours of surrender had been circulating to an increasing degree. It became known that high German officials from Hamburg had been received in the British lines; that the Divisional Commander had granted them interviews; and that surrender was imminent. To lend tone to these stories the Divisional Intelligence Staff published a report to the effect that visiting enemy negotiators had been heard to comment most favourably upon the intellectual abilities and personal appearance of the 'I' staff, which depressed some people's spirits and did much to discredit the rumours of surrender. On the 29th 8 Corps and the Americans on the right were over the Elbe and the 11th Armoured and 6th Airborne Divisions had reached the Baltic at Wismar and Lubeck. Holland had been overrun by the Canadians and the Russians had broken through the defences of Berlin. The Americans in Czechoslovakia and Bavaria had the whip hand there and in Italy the Germans surrendered to Field-Marshal Alexander on May 2nd.

The 7th Armoured Division was still confronted by the last citadel of German defence, the mantelet of Harburg in front of the Hamburg fortifications, and in fact they were never to have to fight to cross the Elbe. Sooner than endure another night of bombing, Hamburg surrendered, a move that led eventually to the final surrender of the whole of Germany, Holland, Denmark and Norway. On May 1st came the news that Hitler had met his tardy end in his Command Post or 'Bunker' in Berlin and the next night, after a certain amount of shilly-shallying, Major-General Wolz, the Kommandant of Hamburg, brought his famous message to the 7th Armoured Division: "The principal point is the actual time General Lyne wishes to enter Hamburg." Although all details of the final surrender were not yet complete, on May 3rd the Division moved over the Elbe and occupied the city.

(k) The End of the War, May 1945

For this coup-de-grâce the Regiment was to be under command of the 131st Infantry Brigade and was to form part of the force that entered Hamburg on May 3rd. However there was a delay and on the 3rd the Regiment with 'A' Company, 1st Rifle Brigade, was sent to secure the high ground at Marmstorf, with instructions to move forward when ordered and to take over from the 11th Hussars who were guarding the north-east and west approaches to the town. The Regiment leaguered that night at Marmstorf and were off again at 5.15 a.m. on the morning of May 4th to march through Harburg and into the city of Hamburg itself. Descriptions of the devastation of that city have become commonplace. No one expected to find it untouched but it was doubtful if anyone had anticipated the magnitude and extent of the damage. The city was completely ruined and over everywhere hung the sweet haylike smell of death. There must have been thousands and thousands of bodies buried beneath the rubble. The leading troop had difficulty in map-reading along streets which no longer existed.

By 7.30 a.m. the Regiment had taken over guarding the east, north and western approaches to the city from the 11th Hussars, but shortly after this 'B' Squadron handed over the eastern approaches to the 53rd Division and came into reserve, sending three troops to act as heavy support to three squadrons of 11th Hussars who were ordered to 'stop' the main roads into Hamburg from Quickborn, Pinneburg and Wedel. The scenes on these roads were amazing, a steady stream of all kinds of troops, the utterly disorganised rabble that the mighty German Army had become, all ambling hopelessly towards a prison-camp where they might lay down their arms.

It was Lieutenant Moll and Three Troop of 'B' Squadron at Quickborn with 'D' Squadron, 11th Hussars, who had a hand in the most sensational event that day. At almost 3 in the afternoon they stopped a German staff car inside which was General-Admiral von Friedeburg carrying a message from Admiral Doenitz, the new Fuhrer, stating that he was prepared to talk about the surrender of the German Armies. This momentous message was reported back and shortly afterwards General Dempsey himself arrived and rode for a short way on Moll's tank. An hour later the Commander-in-Chief of the German Army North arrived and the whole cortège set off towards Hamburg.

Meanwhile the other Squadrons had been ordered to establish themselves fan-wise from the centre of the city, whilst a charming site had been reconnoitred for Regimental Headquarters by the second-in-command who had instinctively selected a stretch of lake shore opposite the Atlantic Hotel, Hamburg's Ritz. They had barely finished breakfast there before they were moved away from the precincts of the Atlantic, which had become an Infantry Division Headquarters.

They then tried the other side of the lake. This time an unerring intuition selected the Gauleiter's residence. This sumptuous building (now an Officer's Club) contained a Nazi shrine, the centre of which was a very fine bronze head of A. Hitler, which is now in a museum. Once again they were moved and this time they found a delightful piece of park by the lake, which was like Kensington Gardens. The end of that epic day is best summed up by Lieut.-Colonel Fitzpatrick himself.

"That evening we listened to the wireless and heard our English broadcast from Radio Hamburg. The speaker gave us more news of the forthcoming surrender, and said that he was at that moment using Joyce's microphone and desk. Although there were yet three days to go before the official cease-fire, it was there, I think, that we realised fully that it was in fact all over. There was no rejoicing amongst the crowd of men round the wireless set, just silence. I believe that the first reaction was a sensation of uncomprehending relief.

"It started to rain."

(*l*) *The Beginning of Peace, May-June 1945*

IT was an odd end to the war, with the official VE-Day postponed until the 8th May, four days later. After the rumour of a move to the Danish frontier on the 5th the Regiment eventually went to a concentration area nearby where they remained until the 7th. Lieut.-Colonel Fitzpatrick went to Brigade Headquarters that day for orders and returned with the news that Germany was signing a treaty of unconditional surrender with the three Allies, which would come into effect from May 9th, and also that the Regiment was to move later that day to the Keil area.

They travelled by way of Hasloh, Pinneburg and Itzehoe to Wachen which they reached at 9 p.m. This was the first of many villages that they searched for arms and S.S. men in hiding. Here also they spent VE-Day, which started for them with a thanksgiving service held in the village church and was followed by the flying of a Union Jack from the tallest wireless aerial available and, in the evening when the victory spirit had spread through the whole Division, the night sky was lit up for miles around by Very lights and tracer ammunition, while what moonlight there was was hidden by thick clouds of smoke from 2-in. mortar bombs. Then the Regiment, having expended all their ammunition, sang songs around a bonfire until the early hours of the morning.

Later on that same morning the Regiment moved to Schwabstedt near Friedrichstadt, about 30 miles to the north-west. 'A' Squadron was billeted in a former S.S. Headquarters, where they dug-up a quantity of arms; 'B' Squadron supported the 1/5th Queen's at the small village of Lunden, through which long columns of marching German troops passed on their way down from Denmark to concentration areas along the coast; and 'C' Squadron was in support of the 2nd Devons nearby with the task also of providing a check post at the level crossing with the purpose of disarming troop trains and directing stragglers. The Brigade's rôle here was to marshal, disarm and to a large extent organise the movement of German military personnel into the Tonning Peninsula. The intention then was to seal off the Pensinsula when it was full to capacity with German troops.

So until the end of the month the Regiment stayed in Schleswig-Holstein, sending out daily patrols to search the surrounding villages, collecting and destroying many thousands of rifles and machine-guns, blowing up ammunition dumps, with an occasional bumper haul in the shape of a bicycling civilian who on interrogation proved to be a Lieut.-Colonel of the S.S., or parties of German soldiers who were captured trying to cross the River Eider by ferry. For the most part maintenance and interior economy were the order of the day, with, on May 14th, the revival of ceremonial guard mounting, while on the 15th the Regimental flag was flown in Germany for the first time since the Regiment was engaged in the Occupation of the Rhineland after the First World War.

On May 26th came the news that the 131st Brigade was handing over its present duties to the 11th Armoured Division and would then concentrate south of the Kiel Canal, and on the 28th the Regiment moved to Schenefeld. Here they were dispersed, 'A' Squadron at Huje, 'B' at Kaaks and 'C' at Vaale, and came under command of the 22nd Armoured Brigade whose rôle was to guard the Kiel Canal from a bridge to the south-west up to the River Elbe.

The Regiment remained here throughout June, chiefly employed in training, maintenance and recreation. Also the painting of all the vehicles in the Regiment was embarked upon and the news came through that they had been chosen to go to Berlin to take part in the Victory Parade in July. The efforts at painting were redoubled at this news, and on the 20th when the Commanding Officer inspected their labour he was highly satisfied with the results. By this time the Regiment had six Comet Tanks and two were allotted to each Sabre Squadron. Men were already away on instructor's courses at the Divisional School, and although the move to Berlin would delay the instruction of the men on Comets, the Commanding Officer stressed the importance of getting as many as possible trained so that the change-over, when it came, could be more easily effected. However, this was not to be for some time, and June ended peacefully for the Regiment near Itzehoe.

On July 1st the advance party, commanded by Major Charlton, left for Brunswick where they were to join up with parties from the 131st Brigade. Lieut-Colonel Fitzpatrick left that day for England and the Regiment in his absence was commanded by Major de Clermont. On the 2nd a signal came back from two officers of the advance party, who had by now reached Berlin, saying that "everything was flat and filthy."

The Regiment itself was ordered to move in two batches, the tank party under Major Firth on transporters as far as Brunswick on the 4th and the rest of the Regiment a day later. The move was successfully completed and the Regiment stayed in billets north of Brunswick until the 6th, carrying out even more maintenance and cleaning, which latter reached new heights when the commanding officer of 'C' Squadron found some varnish with which he proceeded to varnish the tanks in his squadron. This manoeuvre resulted in the whole Regiment having to do the same in order to look alike. News came through too, while they were here, from Major Charlton in Berlin that although accommodation had been found there for the Regiment, owing to damage by bombs and Russian attacks it was more than doubtful if it could be made habitable before they arrived.

However on the 7th the Regiment moved off by road and drove the last two hundred miles to Berlin on their tracks. It was a most remarkable sight to see a complete armoured regiment on the march at a steady thirty miles an hour, but the route was along the autobahn and the tanks made the most of it, only one failing to complete the course.

Their new quarters were luckily not nearly so bad as had been expected, chiefly owing to tremendous efforts of cleaning on the part of the advance party. They could have been ideal as they were the barracks built to house the Olympic Games in 1936, but they now had to depend on only two water hydrants for the whole Regiment, supplemented by water-carts.

They were met on arrival by Brigadier Spurling, commanding the 131st Brigade, and under whose command they now came, and the whole Regiment parked their tanks in the Olypischer Platz area. This was the first time they had been able to live centrally since the winter of 1944 at West Tofts.

For the next few days the cleaning of tanks was redoubled, taking an even higher priority than the clearing of the new quarters, for which a bull-dozer had to be used and a bomb disposed of. However on the 10th and 11th there were trial runs at dawn from the Brandenburg Gate and down the Charlottenburger Chaussée.

On July 12th the Regiment had the task of sealing-off the north and south approaches of the Brandenburg Gate when Field-Marshal Sir Bernard Montgomery invested the Russian Marshals Zhukov and Rokossovsky with the G.C.B. and the K.C.B. The weather was brilliant and a small but impressive ceremony took place, when 24 gleaming Cromwells from the Regiment formed up round the dais, while 11th Hussar armoured cars lined the Tiergarten and the Grenadier Guards provided a Guard of Honour.

July seemed to everyone in the Regiment to be made up of one parade after another. On the 13th the first full-scale Divisional Parade took place, which was in fact only a rehearsal for the Victory Parade. This particular parade took place in ideal weather and in the lovely setting of the Charlottenburg Chaussée. Everything worked smoothly and Major-General Lyne motored down both sides of the Chaussée inspecting the parade. He then moved to the saluting base while tanks and other vehicles wheeled into position. Just before the base a press photographer was lying in the middle of the road facing Lieut.-Colonel Fitzpatrick's tank. This, without slackening speed, drove straight over him while he remained on the ground taking photographs. It could be said that never had the Regiment been photographed by so many different people from so many strange positions.

All this was, however, but a preliminary for the great day, which was eventually decided to be July 21st. Cleaning and polishing which had been feverish before now became frantic, but when the moment came it was a moment of immense and lasting triumph. At 10 a.m. all the distinguished visitors were present and the parade opened with a Salute from 17 guns of the 3rd Royal Horse Artillery. Then, led by the Prime Minister, Mr. Churchill, a procession of eight half-tracks carrying all the war leaders and many members of the Government, moved off down the Charlottenburg Chaussée to inspect this great parade of British Troops. Forty minutes later the Prime Minister returned to the saluting base, ready for the march past.

There has been much written of this parade, and perhaps the *Evening News* described it best:

"As the men swung by, their equipment polished and gaiters cleaned as they never were during battle, and, although feeling somewhat conscious of the occasion, they cannot help having thoughts of the events two or three years ago. Most of them are men who have seen more fighting than any soldiers in the last war. They are led by the 3rd Regiment of the Royal Horse Artillery. Also in the parade are the 5th Royal Horse Artillery who defended the last road to Dunkirk. Behind the Artillery came the 8th

Hussars, who being in Egypt in 1933 are entitled to describe themselves as the oldest Desert Rats. They, too, had been in the ebb and tide of battle in this war. Their tanks, named after horses and hounds (in what other army would you find this?), have the spit and polish of peace time and not the dust of Normandy to-day. The first of them, named 'Hurry On', now rumbling past the parade dais, has travelled more than 3,000 miles. It has come all the way from the beach-head of Normandy, and is now being driven by Corporal Morris, who has had seven tanks shot from under him during the long trek to Victory."

It had indeed been a long trek, and a hard one, through heat and thirst and sand, through bitter cold and mud, through fear and boredom, elation and despair. Many were left behind, none were forgotten, and the great words of the Prime Minister's speech set a seal for all time upon men's thoughts and turned them towards peace.

PART FIVE

1945–1950

I. ARMY OF OCCUPATION

(a) Moll and Itzehoe, July 1945-July 1946

AFTER the Victory Parade on July 21st the tempo of life in post-war Berlin slowed down. Courses and training were the order of the day with an occasional guard duty like that of the Potsdam Guard in the British Delegation Area. The living conditions for the unfortunate troops detailed for this were far from satisfactory, and after a visit by Lieut.-Colonel Fitzpatrick, men from each squadron were put on a cleaning fatigue of the barracks to remove some of the traces of German rout and Russian occupation. There was also a guard put on a wood-alcohol store in a bombed-out building in the city. This duty was taken over from the 1/5th Queens' whose sentries had found out that the Russians offered bribes to the guard in an effort to obtain the spirit, which they both drank and used to fill the petrol tanks of their cars with a fine impartiality. Otherwise July and early August were chiefly occupied with sport which, as the Regiment was billeted in the Olympic Games Stadium, gave them every opportunity for all sorts of events.

However on August 13th the Regiment sent the squadrons to Itzehoe to hand in their Cromwells, 'C' Squadron being the first to go and followed by 'B' on the 17th and 'A' on the 22nd. On the 15th came the news of the unconditional surrender of Japan, so that, at last, the war was truly over, and on the 30th the Regiment moved to Moll in Belgium where they were to convert to Comet tanks, while a rear party went to Itzehoe.

At Moll the Regiment went into civilian billets in the town, an unwelcome change from the barracks in Berlin. However, training started almost at once and continued throughout September. On the 14th Lieutenant D. Astley Cooper rejoined the Regiment. He had been captured at Sidi Rezegh in November 1941. R.S.M. Hegarty and Sergeant Ferridge also rejoined that day.

The Regiment returned from Moll to Itzehoe with their new tanks on October 17th, their training finished, and arrived on the 21st. Here they were to stay until next July, settling in as an army of occupation and organising themselves as comfortably as possible. Their immediate duty was to provide a guard at the S.S. Hospital at Itzehoe and so prevent the inmates from escaping or from mixing with and polluting the civilians.

October passed with men being posted home and replacements arriving from the 1st and 2nd Fife and Forfar Yeomanry and the 23rd Hussars, 107th R.A.C., 49th A.P.C.R. and the 9th Royal Tank Regiment. Throughout November and December there was an enormous turnover of personnel, all those under 30 Group being drafted out and replaced by higher age groups. It was a quiet time for everyone with a certain amount of training and many changes, not only in the Regiment but outside as well. During December Major-General L. O. Lyne, G.O.C. 7th Armoured Division, left for England and was replaced by Major-General G. P. B. Roberts, late of the 11th Armoured Division. December also saw the opening meet of the Regimental Beagles, organised and brought over from England by Major Charlton. The country round the barracks was perfect and abounded with hares. Another most popular form of sport at this time was the Motor Cycle Club which scored a great success at most of the meetings it attended. At the end of the month Lieutenant F. W. Saxby was killed in a jeep smash, just a month before his award of the M.C. came through at the end of January. Also decorated at that time were Sergeants Carsley and Harris who were given the M.M.

The first six months of 1946 slid by leaving hardly any trace. Apart from Regimental training there was, on March 24th, the Divisional Motor Cycle trial at which 1st, 3rd and 6th places were won by the Regimental Teams. On the 22nd April the 22nd Armoured Brigade held a Horse Show at which there were many entries from the Regiment and where R.S.M. Hegarty won the other ranks Scurry. Training was still in full swing throughout May, when, on the 28th Lieut.-Colonel G. R. D. Fitzpatrick was posted to England, command of the Regiment being taken over temporarily by Major Charlton. June started with the 1st Kings Own Yorkshire Light Infantry Horse Show, at which Captain H. T. Pierson and Lieutenant J. R. Malseed both won their events, followed on the 8th by a Victory Parade through Itzehoe. Later that day command of the Regiment was taken over by Lieut.-Colonel C. Goulburn, after an absence of eighteen months.

(b) Lingen, July-October 1946

AT the end of June the Regiment received orders to move to Lingen on July 22nd. This move was part of a general move of the 7th Armoured Division from Schleswig-Holstein in the north of the British Zone, to an area of responsibility as big as Wales in the west of the occupied zone. The town of Lingen, a small market town in a flat, sandy and poor agricultural district, was a bad exchange for Itzehoe where they had enjoyed the benefits of Divisional welfare on their doorstep. And the barracks, which had been occupied since the end of the war by 4,000 Polish Displaced Persons were nothing like the clean, well-conditioned ones they had left behind. There was no cookhouse or mess room for the men, no officers' mess, no hard standing for truck stands, and few windows or electric light fittings in the barrack blocks. However, everyone set to work to provide welfare and improve living conditions, and though the speed at which Royal Engineers works services were carried out was adversely affected by the shortage of materials and labour, much was done during the autumn to provide the essentials. The previous occupants were not the cleanest of people, and tins, rubbish and bones worked their way to the surface of the sand in the barrack area for many months to come.

At the end of July the 7th Armoured Division held its small arms meeting at Bielefeld. As a result of the Regimental rifle meeting at Itzehoe a fortnight earlier, the team won the three-day Divisional meeting by a narrow margin from the 11th Hussars.

Early in the summer there had been a rumour that the Regiment would have to find one squadron as a demonstration squadron at the School of Infantry, Warminster in the early autumn, and, after a brief rumour that the whole Regiment would be leaving for England after September, it was again fined down to one squadron. After a major reshuffle of personnel, 'A' Squadron was selected, and on the 6th September they left. For some time the War Office had been negotiating with Headquarters Rhine

Army for a squadron of tanks both to carry out demonstrations at the School of Infantry in England and to tour Commands with the object of showing the flag. It was a great compliment to the Regiment when the 8th Hussars were selected as the first Regiment to provide this squadron. Individual feelings were mixed when the men left the Regiment and Germany for an unknown period estimated at one year. But the pleasures of the week-end habit in England, when every soldier buys his ticket on the railway from after duty Friday to 9 a.m. Monday, quickly made up for the loss of cheap and plentiful cigarettes.

The officers who accompanied 'A' Squadron were:

> Major W. G. Lowther
> Captain H. T. Pierson
> Captain D. L. Astley Cooper
> Lieutenant P. D. Moll
> Lieutenant R. N. C. Scrimgeour
> 2nd Lieutenant C. J. Massy
> 2nd Lieutenant C. de V. Wellesley.

Once established in Warminster the Squadron Leader, Major Lowther, was faced with the mammoth task of building up a fully equipped Squadron, trained ready to commence demonstrations within six weeks. It was therefore apparent from the start that normal channels were to be short-circuited and within a few days 'A' Squadron was enjoying top priority with everyone from the War Office down to Ordnance Stores.

The demonstrations were many and varied, the most important as far as the Squadron was concerned being the fire power show. This was carried out by a Crocodile, Cromwell (95- and 75-mm.) and by two troops of Comets, one of which fired direct and the other indirect.

In their nine months stay the Squadron had many experiences. They advanced at night in pitch darkness through exploding sapper mines and mortars and under heavy cross fire. They drove the Prime Minister, Mr. Attlee, during his visit, in an 'A' Squadron jeep; they covered hundreds of miles of country and Major Lowther, after setting the pace, handed over to Captain Ford, who in turn handed over to Major Weston-Simons.

One of the greatest difficulties encountered during this time at Lingen was the enormous distances between the Regiment and the nearest supply services. In most cases there were over fifty miles to be covered three times a week to draw rations and over a hundred miles from time to time to draw technical spares. All of which entailed a waste of petrol and time and, later, accidents on the icy roads.

On October 3rd a composite squadron, after some preliminary troop training during August and September in an area some twenty miles west of Lingen and near to the German-Dutch frontier, proceeded to Vogelsang to carry out joint training with various battalions of the 53rd (Welsh) Division. Vogelsang, west of the Rhine and half-way between Bonn and Malmedy on the German-Belgian frontier, was situated in lovely surroundings. The barracks, built in the grand style by Adolf Hitler for the union of fine young specimens of the German Army with German girls specially selected for their bone and stamina, were most interesting despite the damage they had suffered in the heavy bombardment by the Americans south-east of Aachen. Although accommodation provided in the barracks lacked sanitation, heating arrangements, electric light, water, cookhouse and canteen, all these were provided under squadron arrangements, the men were by no means uncomfortable and valuable training was carried out. They left as the weather broke and a snow storm pursued them as they drove away.

The beagles had moved with the Regiment to Lingen and there was much specula-
tion as to what sort of country it would be. It turned out to be similar to that round
Itzehoe, although poorer, sandier and with fewer hares. The pack caused considerable
interest amongst the local farmers and it took a long time to persuade them that they
really hunted hares for sport. Some of the questions were naive in the extreme and not
without their humour, the classic example being perhaps when a farm hand politely and
in all seriousness enquired when the circus was due to open. The pack was hunted jointly
by Captains Dill and Davies while Captains Bellamy, Weir and Bromiley, did sterling
work as whips.

(c) Lingen, December 1946-January 1947

THAT winter will remain in everyone's memory on account of the exceptionally cold
weather. For three months from the 15th December there was a continuous spell of
frost which was broken only for one short period around Christmas. One point in
favour of this extreme cold was that it made it possible to play some violent games of
ice hockey. Players turned up in a gay assortment of clothes. The Commanding Officer
was properly dressed as for parade, though later, heated by the fury of the sport, he
removed his battle dress tunic and revealed a striking pair of red braces. The Adjutant
wore navy blue skiing trousers, and Major Nelson's head was swathed in an ample
Balaclava helmet. However in spite of several players having to give up half-way
owing to excessive battering and bleeding, no one was seriously injured.

Before the cold weather made outdoor training impossible, three regimental exercises were held. As a result of the autumn policy of putting about half the tanks into
heavy preservation, these operations were reduced to signal exercises, Regimental
Headquarters, 'B' and 'C' Squadrons turning out in skeleton. For the remainder of the
winter the manpower shortage, which was making itself increasingly felt, allowed
individual training for a few specialists only to be carried out. Demobilisation without a
corresponding intake of reinforcements, accentuated by the absence of 140 men of 'A'
Squadron, made the problem of unit administration, let alone training, a difficult
one. Administration commitments remained the same, regardless of the number of
men present with the Regiment. The life of a transport driver who had to travel long
distances over indifferent roads in bad weather conditions was a hard one. To be precise,
135 men were released during the first three months of the year, and 29 reinforcements
were posted. Barrack administration, however, was considerably eased by the 120-odd
Germans, male and female, which the Regiment was allowed to employ. They varied
considerably in their capacity for work, but the free midshift meal was an inducement
for them to retain their job. Incidents during the winter that will be remembered were
the German children's Christmas party, the training of Yugoslav ex-prisoners of war,
the arrival of the first families under Operation 'Union', and the complete cessation of
all outdoor sport due to the hard weather.

Two days before Christmas 500 German and 100 Polish Displaced Persons children
were entertained with a cinema show, conjuror and tea party. A vast number of buns and
cakes, which had been made from rations saved by all ranks over a long period, were
consumed to the last one. And the kindly interest and assistance provided by the many

soldiers on that afternoon did more towards the re-education of German youth than a year's instruction in a classroom on the benefits of British democracy.

In December and again in February two batches of 75 Yugoslav ex-prisoners of war were received. All had belonged to the Royal Yugo-Slav Army, and for political reasons, dared not return to their country. The task was to train them, over a period of six weeks, in guard duties for the civil mixed Watchman's Corps, an organisation formed to look after installations in the British Zone thereby releasing British man-power. Despite five years of agricultural and other work performed for the Germans, these men won the admiration of all for their keenness, good discipline and efforts to regain that military bearing for which the old Serbian infantry were famous.

In January it was announced that the Yorkshire Hussars were to be an affiliated Territorial unit, that they were to be organised and equipped as for an Armoured Regiment and that the 8th Hussars were to provide a permanent staff of an Adjutant and eight other ranks, including the Regimental Sergeant Major. Subsequently the North-amptonshire Yeomanry, a Divisional Regiment, R.A.C., was also affiliated, though the 8th Hussars were not called on to find so many of the permanent staff.

(d) Lingen, January-June 1947

THE spring was notable for the sudden return to life of the countryside. The rapid thaw of snow lying on top of ground which was frozen feet thick, gave considerable anxiety in Emsland in general, and Lingen in particular. Emergency plans were made for being in a barracks cut off by water on all sides. But the banks of the river held and the danger was averted.

This spring found the Regiment in Germany in a worse state for man-power than ever before. Tanks, guns and, in particular, 'B' vehicles, became even more difficult to maintain satisfactorily. The lowest level reached was on May 31st, when the posted strength of the Regiment, less 'A' Squadron in England, was 244 other ranks. If one subtracts 25 per cent from this figure for men away on leave and courses, some idea can be gained of the difficulties undergone at this time. However from May onwards a trickle of reinforcements began to arrive.

On April 27th a half-squadron, under Major M. B. Marwood, composed of officers and other ranks from both 'B' and 'C' Squadrons, proceeded to the training area of Lopshorn. Here for three weeks they trained with battalions of the 4th Infantry Brigade (3rd Division). Cold, wind, rain and mud for the first few days made conditions in a tented camp somewhat unpleasant. But a sudden change and a hot sun provided what was required for an enjoyable and valuable fortnight with the 2nd Battalion Grenadier Guards, Royal Welsh Fusiliers and East Lancs.

At about this period, with the posting of a number of semi-trained reinforcements from the Training Regiments, the Commanding Officer decided to reorganise the Regiment and form a 'Training' Squadron. 'B' Squadron was selected and its task was to take in hand all reinforcements on their arrival, continue their individual training, both technical and general, until they had obtained a trade, and pass them out to an 'Opera-tional' Squadron.

Mid-March saw sport recommence with the first round of the Cavalry Cup, when their old rivals, the 11th Hussars, defeated them, 2–1. On May 30th the Regimental sports were held on the airfield at Rheine, but with little time and facilities for practise, a considerable amount of keenness though little athletic prowess was shown.

On June 24th 'A' Squadron rejoined the Regiment from England. For nine months the Squadron had been in the public eye as the representative of the R.A.C. in general and of the 8th Hussars in particular. If the kind words spoken by the School of Infantry and elsewhere can be taken as a guide, 'A' Squadron set a fine example of efficiency and discipline. Their demonstrations at the School not only provided considerable value to the spectators, infantry, Officers and N.C.O.'s from all units of the British and Allied Armies, but also, from the training aspect, to the Squadron itself. Their troop 'Circus' which toured the J.T.C.'s of Eton and Winchester, and P.T.C.'s, Training Battalions and Basic O.C.T.U.'s in Southern Command, proved of excellent propaganda value for the R.A.C. Exercises for Russian Marshals and film-making for future training in combined operations, were other activities of the Squadron. Out of the 140 men who left the Regiment in September, 85 had been demobilised and 65 retained. The other 52 men returning with the Squadron were all reinforcements received during the last three months. The addition of 117 men to the Regiment in Germany was a nett gain in the badly needed man-power problem. For ten months the Regiment in Germany had been weaker by approximately 130 men, than any other armoured regiment in the country. And as the Regiment became weaker month by month so was the absence or departure of every man increasingly felt, and this unfortunate difference in man-power with other units had its effect both in work and sport.

(e) Lingen, June-September 1947

WITH the return of 'A' Squadron from Warminster the Commanding Officer chose this moment to once more reorganise the Regiment. 'C' Squadron was put into suspended animation, its personnel being distributed among the other Squadrons. 'H.Q.' Squadron took over all transport commitments, 'A' became responsible for the individual training of all reinforcements, who, after some weeks of training in 'B' Squadron, were then trade tested and posted to 'A' Squadron to carry out their collective training. This system proved both simple and satisfactory and was found to be economic in the man-power overheads.

As regards the lighter side of life, every week-end horses were sent off either racing or show jumping, sometimes both. Racing took place at Hanover, Hamburg, Dortmund and Dusseldorf, where the courses had luckily escaped any serious bomb damage. As they were almost all shaped in a figure of eight it required something of a map-reader as well as a rider to complete the course. It was not uncommon for a jockey to go the wrong way, but that fortunately never happened to any riders from the Regiment, which was lucky for them whilst Major Dunne was running the stables.

Throughout the long season keenness was shown by everyone. Training the horses was hard work as they had to be out every morning before breakfast. Some of the jockeys were hard to wake but nobody was ever actually left behind. Officers who took part in the racing were Majors Dunne and Nelson, Captains Dill, Pierson, Bromiley and Willman and Lieutenants Preston and Malseed, while among the other ranks were

R.S.M. Hegarty and Lance Corporal Dickinson. Trooper Monro was in charge of the stables which consisted of four thoroughbred and four half-bred horses, plus six show jumpers and six hacks. The show jumping members were Lieut.-Colonel Goulburn, Majors Dunne, Nelson and Firth, Captains Dill and Pierson, Lieutenant Malseed and R.S.M. Hegarty. At the end of the season there were eleven firsts in show jumping and ten winners racing.

This fine hot summer in Germany was enjoyed by all. Major Firth took 'B' Squadron to the southern shore of the Mohnsee where they lived for a week under bivouac conditions. This holiday camp was in sight of the dam which was smashed by Squadron Leader Gibson, V.C., thereby destroying the supply of electric power of many Ruhr factories. During July Major Marwood with 'A' Squadron carried out training with the Norwegian Brigade on the Lopshorn training area and on their large-scale exercise Hedmark in the country to the south of Hanover. In May, two months earlier, the Squadron had already been training at Lopshorn with the 4th Guards Brigade so the one troop which was sent knew their way around. Two surprises however were in store for them. Firstly the quality of the food of which they partook in the Norwegian dining tents; and secondly the remarkable keenness and enthusiasm shown by our allies during their training. The 'A' Squadron men appreciated the latter more than the former! As for Hedmark, a number of valuable man-days were lost en-route to and from the exercise by the tanks travelling on transporters. Owing to the poor condition of these much-flogged transporters and to the lack of spare tyres, a four-day journey to the exercise developed for some of the tanks into a fourteen-day return journey. However as this was the first occasion in history in which Norwegian troops had co-operated with tanks, the political value in producing tanks for their battle probably outweighed the cost to the British public. Certainly the Norwegian Commander's letter of appreciation to the Commanding Officer showed that the efforts of allied co-operation were fully recognised.

'A' Squadron carried out further training throughout the month of September in conjunction with a number of Infantry Battalions of the 7th Armoured and 2nd Division at Vogelsang, west of the Rhine in the German Eifel, a country very different from the flat, ugly country of Emsland where Lingen was situated. The civilian population had been evicted from the surrounding country to provide a battle area for the occupation troops.

On September 5th an important event occurred in Regimental history. The Colonel of the Regiment, Brigadier J. Van der Byl, D.S.O. visited his Regiment and inspected it for the last time prior to his retirement at the end of the year. Having taken the salute he addressed all ranks in most moving and inspiring terms. After two days in Lingen he motored to Vogelsang to spend two days with 'A' Squadron. En route, accompanied by the Commanding Officer, he visited Krupps armament factory in Essen to view the work of Bomber Command. From the top of the only remaining building for miles around they surveyed the largest single factory in the world. For two miles in every direction could be seen ton upon ton of twisted girders, mountains of rubble and innumerable smashed machines in the hundreds of worshops which comprised the factory area. After a brief spell with 'A' Squadron which included further sightseeing of the Siegfried Line, only ten miles to the west, the Colonel departed. His physical and mental activity and his charm was an inspiration to all, and as on so many previous occasions when he visited the Regiment he so dearly loved, he left no doubt that the 'Buff' was a great Eighth Hussar.

Throughout the summer, swimming, cricket and rowing were enjoyed by a large

Q

number of men. And the regular week-ends to the leave centre at the Friesian Island of Nordeney where the Regiment had a standing order for twenty vacancies every week-end for three months provided a change from the dull social amenities of Lingen.

Musketry proved a full-time job during the summer for certain men in the Regiment. They were all rewarded by successes at Brigade, Divisional and Army Meetings where their shooting was superior to all the Armoured Regiments and a large number of infantry battalions. The Shooting VIII were much inspired by the keenness and personal instruction of the Commanding Officer himself.

First light on almost any September morning at Lingen presented a very sporting sight with hounds going out in one direction and the race horse string in the other. Hounds continued under the joint mastership of Captains Davies and Dill with Major Nelson and Captain Ormrod assisting. By mid-September early morning and evening meets were being held. Scenting conditions were poor and there was a scarcity of horses, but all the same some entertaining sport was enjoyed. In February the bulk of the pack left for England in their new and very smart trailer, and their new country was to be that formerly hunted by the Thorpe Satchville in Leicestershire.

The autumn terminated with a series of Physical Training tests for all personnel of the Regiment. One final test of walking and running for ten miles in full marching order, carrying a rifle and shooting on the range on completion was carried out with determination and good humour by the majority. Some good times were recorded, one of the oldest members clocking in in one hour, twenty-five minutes, while the Officers' Mess Cook clocked in the next day.

(f) Lingen, October 1947-February 1948

PESSIMISTS who forecast another freeze-up were happily proved wrong. The man-power shortage, however, continued to cause much concern. Individual training included tank driving which was carried on at full blast in 'B' Squadron. 'A' Squadron was fully occupied maintaining vehicles and equipment and carrying out innumerable fatigues such as unloading coal trains and so on. Headquarters Squadron was mainly concerned with the very heavy transport commitment which the administration of the Regiment demanded. The daily trip of 'B' vehicles drawing rations or stores was seldom less than 150 miles. To enable repair to keep pace with the wear and tear of vehicles the fitter staff was divided into a day and night shift.

On the departure of their neighbours, the 1st Royal Leicesters, increased work fell on the Quartermaster and his staff. For example at one time he was rationing 150 families and minor units of various nationalities which necessitated intricate bulk breaking of supplies. The Regiment, too, had to take over the security patrols previously carried out over a wide area by the 1st Royal Leicesters. With the departure of the 1st Polish Armoured Division, however, crime had decreased and any which did occur was attributed to Displaced Persons or Germans coming up from the Rhur on black market expeditions. A further commitment, namely the administration and discipline of four detachments of that delightfully-named organisation, the 'Civil Mixed Watchman's Service' (Ex-prisoners of war of the Yugoslav Royal Army) fell on the Regiment. Efforts by the Commanding Officer to improve the standard of cleanliness of their rifles by carrying out an arms inspection nearly met with disaster. For the future guidance of others they are advised to stand well clear of any C.M.W.S. on giving the order "Ease Springs".

Throughout the Regiment's stay at Lingen they were responsible for the Internal Security of the Lingen-Ems District of the Hanover Province. In those days Great Britain had no enemies, all countries thought of nothing but peace and the enemy was still considered to be the defeated Germany. Looking back one realises that it was quite impossible for the German nation to give any trouble with an enormous occupation force in their midst even if they had wished to do so, but out in Germany in 1947 Werewolves and disguised Nazis or S.S. Officers were visualised amongst every group of villagers or townspeople. The situation in the Regiment's district was especially aggravated by smuggling across the Dutch Border and by the many Displaced Persons of various nationalities left in Germany after the war whose morals were sometimes as low as their morale. A number of deserters of all the allied armies had gone native and lived with their German girl friends, and these men were a great source of trouble. The fraternisation ban was lifted in 1947 and this alleviated the desertion problem.

Initially the German Civil Police were weak in numbers and disorganised due to the denazification of their force. Backed by the Regiment they gradually brought effective law and order to the district so that when they left it was not considered necessary to send another Regiment to Lingen to take over their duties.

The Internal Security Role was largely administered by the Regimental Intelligence Officer, Captain Atkinson-Willes a stepson of Brigadier Van de Byl, and the Recce Troop in Scout Cars under a series of enthusiastic Cornets were his offensive weapon. He derived much of his intelligence from a rather attractive blonde who was on strength as an Interpreter, and his main personal weapon of offensive defence was his tin leg which he could swing with accuracy and effect at the shins of anyone who got in his way. If his opponent could by then retaliate he found that tin legs make an unsatisfactory target.

This organisation during the two years at Lingen, unearthed several caches of ammunition, illicit stills, and stocks of food, discouraged smuggling across the Border, except when Captain Dill brought his girl friend from Paris to the Regimental Dance, and encouraged the inhabitants of lonely villages who were the target for raids by Displaced Persons and the like.

The '12 hour day' was introduced at the end of November when all ranks worked from 5.15 p.m. to 7 p.m. on four days a week. For some months past a number of officers and men in responsible, administrative positions had already been working in the evenings. For the majority however this was a new departure. The increased hours however were well spent in lecture, discussions, miniature range, boxing and 'all in' football in the Riding School.

Christmas week was filled with a succession of parties, dances and festivities. The Regiment gave one party for the German employees who worked in the barracks and one for the German children who lived in Lingen. The German party was attended by 250 men and women who were given a 'square meal' supplemented by beer and cigarettes. The 16 wild geese shot in one day by Lieut.-Colonel Goulburn came in handy for this repast.

The German children's party, consisting of a cinema, tea, conjuror and Father Christmas, gave great happiness to hosts as well as guests. Handling 700 German children between the ages of 4 and 12 is not such a problem as it sounds. Discipline and obedience are bred in Germans. The party only became a riot when Major Sir Edward Malet tried to pack 700 children into a room large enough for only 500.

Another feature of winter at Lingen was the shooting on the wild fowling marshes at Aschendorf. In October came mallard and teal, although not in such quantities as in the winter before owing to the mild weather. But later great flocks of geese spread themselves over the flooded meadows. One day in January yielded 66 to 6 guns and the total bag of wild fowl throughout the shoot was 596. Early in January the Regiment sent a team to Ehrwald in Austria to compete in the B.A.O.R. Skiing Championships.

For over a year the Officers had anxiously watched the building of a very fine Officers' Mess, and anxiety increased as rumour spread that the Regiment was due for a move. Soon after Christmas all was finished and a Regimental Ball was held, long to be remembered by all who attended and those who helped. Sergeant Pavitt and an efficient staff made everything run smoothly, so much so that as the last guests left for their beds the first guests were coming back for breakfast.

At the begining of the winter it was announced that the Regiment was due for the United Kingdom in February or March. The British taxpayer was finding the cost of maintaining a large Army of Occupation in Germany more than he could stomach. For instance, each time a soldier went home on leave it cost £14. Some job however had to be found for the six Regiments recalled to England, and the one allocated to the 8th Hussars was that of Territorial Army assistance to the Midland Brigade (T.A.). Their new station was to be Leicester East Airfield, a Nissen-hutted camp occupied during the war by the Royal Air Force, and now about to be inhabited by squatters.

The opinion of the men, who were to find themselves in a particularly arctic February living in huts that leaked and rattled and were practically without heating, was that no self-respecting squatter would have been seen dead in any of them. However, luckily memories of wartime conditions were not too distant and the 8th Hussars managed eventually to snug themselves down in their scattered draughty quarters, keeping their Commanding Officer's opinion that this was a strictly temporary abode firmly in their minds.

An advance party commanded by Major Phillips went on ahead on February 4th. A 'B' vehicle party under Captain Davies travelled by train with the 100 odd 'B' vehicles to Hamburg, shipped the vehicles and met them again at Tilbury. The baggage officer, Captain Bromiley, and his party saw the unaccompanied baggage of 2,300 boxes, the heaviest 4½ tons, safely into the freight train bound for Hamburg.

At 5 p.m. on February 14th the main body, headed by the Commanding Officer, marched out of barracks and was played down to the station by the band of the 5th Royal Inniskilling Dragoon Guards. The Brigade Commander, Brigadier P. Harding, and the Colonels of other Regiments of his Brigade, came to bid them farewell to Germany and to the 7th Armoured Division (Desert Rats) in which they had served and fought since the far distant Desert Battles. To the tune of the Regimental March the train pulled out of the station. Thus for the second time in its history the Regiment left Lingen, they had been stationed there before in 1795. An old chapter was closed and a new one opened.

After a journey well organised by Movement Control and a smooth though somewhat hard crossing on S.S. Manxman, they arrived at Harwich at 11 o'clock on Sunday morning, February 15th. A lovely day greeted the Regiment's return to England after its tour of foreign service which had lasted, with the exception of the first five months of 1944, for sixteen years. On the quayside to meet them was their new Colonel, Air Marshal Sir John Baldwin, K.B.E., C.B., D.S.O., and the band of the 4th Hussars. Having received the usual attention from the Customs the Colonel addressed the Regiment in terms of appreciation and welcome. A somewhat delayed railway journey on British Railways finally brought the Regiment to its destination by 11 p.m. that night.

II. ENGLAND

(a) Leicester East Airfield, February-July 1948

AFTER fourteen days disembarkation leave taken in three parties, and the arrival of all baggage and vehicles, the Regiment began to settle down and become organised. The camp proved to be a large and very dispersed Royal Air Force war-time station, the entire accommodation being in Nissen huts. The comforts of the latter were quickly tested by a very cold snap and heavy snow. Many began to wish they were back in the modern German barracks of Lingen with central heating and German employees to do the chores. But with the arrival of warmer weather the camp became more comfortable, though the walk of one and a half miles to and from work twice daily was very expensive on men's time and shoe leather, so the pedal cycle soon came into its own.

Work on tanks and 'B' vehicles started in earnest. The former, all in heavy preservation, had to be prepared for summer training; the latter had to be brought into a fit condition for handing in once again to Ordnance Depots.

The Regiment found themselves, on arrival in England, in the 9th Independent Armoured Brigade (Territorial Army) as the one regular Regiment whose rôle was to assist the training of the four other Armoured Regiments in the Brigade, namely the Leicester Yeomanry, the Warwickshire Yeomanry, the Nottinghamshire Yeomanry (Sherwood Rangers) and the 43rd Royal Tanks from Newcastle.

It soon became apparent that Leicester East Airfield was not the best place for outdoor training. The runways were put 'out of bounds' to tanks by the Air Ministry, who, thinking in terms of the next war, did not wish to have them cut up by tracked vehicles. And the ground inside the perimeter fence was equally prized by the Ministry of Agriculture, by virtue of the fact that the War Agricultural Committee had ploughed and sown the land right up to the edge of the runways. With their tanks 'hangar bound' the future training of the Regiment itself, or the Territorial units they were to sponsor, did not look too bright. However, by the goodwill of the local agriculturist, the Regiment was able to provide some tank driving for the Leicestershire Yeomanry during a successful week-end visit that they paid the 8th Hussars in the middle of April. Dealing with the bureaucrats of a Socialist State proved itself somewhat frustrating to those members of the Regiment who had been soldiering overseas for some years and were not accustomed to such delay or method of 'passing the buck' when any decision had to be taken.

Whilst in Germany a few officers and other ranks had been keen gliding enthusiasts. Now that they had a huge aerodrome at their disposal several graduated to flying. Nearby at Rearsby was the Auster factory whom, as a side line, gave flying lessons and amongst those to avail themselves of the chance of taking out an 'A' licence were Page, Dill, Goldsworthy and Whitfield who proved to be the star pilot. With the chance of keeping an Auster of their own at Leicester East the possibilities that opened up were tremendous, but bank managers frustrated this idea. The chief air activity was the arrival of a debutante and her father who said they were lost in the fog and had to land. The deb later proved to be a great asset to the Cornets as she lived quite near to the Airfield.

News filtered through from Yorkshire that the Yorkshire Hussars, reformed in March 1947, had become firmly established with squadrons at York, Leeds and Middlesbrough. At the end of their first year Regimental strength reached over a hundred all ranks, and preparations were started for the first annual camp at Great Cowden.

Captain Astley-Cooper was Adjutant and Captain Pelling the Quartermaster, and they were responsible for all the early organisation from the Regimental Headquarters in York. Nearby was the Yorkshire Club where Lieut.-Colonel Jones, an old commanding officer of the 8th Hussars, could be found ever ready to welcome any of the present members of the Regiment.

The man-power situation with the 8th Hussars was as critical as ever. The task of administering Territorial Camps and providing all equipment including tanks for each regiment while in camp employed to the limit every officer and man. In common with other units on a Territorial Army assistance rôle they were kept on an 'under posted' establishment. Man-power figures permitted only two squadrons to be kept in being; 'Headquarters' to administer the Regiment and 'A' to maintain equipment. (In December 1948 there were only 196 men in the Regiment, the lowest figure since 1740. From December numbers rose steadily with the arrival of reinforcements regularly every four months in batches of forty. In August 1949, it became possible to reform 'B' Squadron.)

The summer of 1948 will be remembered by many for a long time as the year they were at Birch Hall Camp. In lovely surroundings and only a few miles from the attractions of Scarborough, the camp site for the summer was on a bog. It was selected by Headquarters Northern Command for the Territorial Army. Furthermore, the training area on Fylingdale Moor, in many places a peat bog with a thin crust on top, confirmed for the second time the discovery made in the last war, that it was no place for armoured vehicles. Eight weeks of rain taught some people at any rate, the importance of selecting well-drained ground for a camp site which is to be occupied throughout an English summer. Efforts by the G.O.C. North Midland District, by his 'Q' staff and by the Services did a lot to better the initial disadvantages of rotten tentage, badly constructed field cookhouses and a poor scale of accommodation stores. Despite the appalling weather and personal discomfort suffered by all ranks, morale remained very high. Erecting and re-erecting tents, laying 150 tons of stone, and picking it up at the end of the camp, and doing all the chores kept the staff busy from dawn till dusk. All units of the 9th Independent Armoured Brigade attended camp each for a period of one week. Thanks to Major Dunne, Captain Dill and officers and men of his squadron, excellent value was obtained from the gunnery aspect. Efforts to carry out tactical training, however, resulted in whole days being spent in unditching tanks. At times it became impossible to move them out of the tank park and drive them up on to the moor.

On arrival in Camp the 43rd Royal Tank Regiment laid a magnificent carpet in the Officers' Mess. After the first evening moisture was showing through and after fourteen days the carpet was completely under the mud. The 8th Hussars, being wise and poor Irishmen, wore gumboots in their section of the bog.

Not until the final week of the period, when all four battalions of the 147th Brigade, came to camp as a Brigade, did the sun come out and shirt sleeves became the order of the day. The success of this Brigade camp was the one bright spot of Birch Hall 1948.

At the end of July the Bisley team, which had been training hard at Leicester under the guidance of Lieutenant Page, came near to winning the Cambridge Shield at the Army Rifle Meeting, being beaten into second place by the 4th Hussars.

(b) Leicester East Airfield, January-May 1949

Work during the winter consisted mainly of administration and maintenance of equipment, the former under the able guidance of Major Nelson, the latter first under Major Dunne and subsequently under Major Davies, commanding 'A' Squadron.

Not until January 1949 when the War Office policy was implemented by sending some National Servicemen to Territorial Army assistance Regiments did they have enough men to start some individual training in driving, maintenance, wireless and gunnery. The man-power shortage was further aggravated by the Regiment being made responsible for finding anti-squatter guards in three widely separated War Department camps. Necessary though this may have been, no worse deployment of soldiers can exist. Despite these difficulties the Regiment was able to assist the Army Cadet Force in various ways; to hold unit cadre courses; to run one officers' day a fortnight throughout the winter and to send officers and men away on courses.

An open winter enabled sport to be carried out without a break. Many officers kept horses in converted Nissen huts and hunted with the Fernie and the Quorn. Hay had been made by the Regiment on the airfield which solved some feeding problems. The beagles came out of quarantine where some had died and others had been born. They were hunted two days a week under the joint masters, Major Davies and Captain Ormrod, the latter who managed to break his nose by falling off a fence on to his hunting horn. Otherwise apart from a surplus of hares and a somewhat wild pack it was a successful season. Hounds were looked after in kennel by Trooper Munro reputed to be the oldest serving trooper in the British Army. Paddy Munro very much enjoyed his bottle of Christmas Port given by the Masters, so much so that the story in the Band Boys Hut was that Boxing Day dawned to find him asleep on the benches with Mariner lying across his chest. However the highlight of the sporting season was the victory of Major Phillips in the Grand Military at Sandown on his horse Demon Vino, with Major Dunne in third place on Closure which was a very fine effort on the part of all four.

During the winter the Quartermaster, Lieutenant Evans, retired and the Regiment was both surprised and delighted to welcome back Captain Hedley who had not been with them since he was taken prisoner in 1942.

The spring of '49 found the Regiment assisting the Territorial Army again by providing some tanks and men over a period of six weeks to units of the 8th and 9th Armoured Brigades, T.A., at the A.F.V. Range at Warcop, Westmorland. While busy at Leicester preparing tanks for the coming Territorial camp in Norfolk and training new men to man them, they were ordered to provide a guard of honour of three officers and a hundred other ranks for H.R.H. The Duke of Gloucester who was due to open the Leicester Industries Fair in May. Thanks to the admirable keenness shown by Captain Ormrod, the Adjutant, R.S.M. T. Hegarty and all ranks, who paraded every morning before breakfast for three weeks, a really high standard of drill was attained and was commented on very favourably by His Royal Highness.

(c) Leicester East Airfield, May 1949-June 1950

To meet the summer Territorial Army commitments, a reorganization of the Regiment from two Squadrons (Headquarters and 'A') to four smaller ones (Headquarters, 'A', 'B' and 'C') became necessary. On 20th May, Regimental Headquarters, 'A' Squadron less two troops and 'B' Squadron moved to Bodney Camp, Norfolk. On the same date 'C' Squadron, under Major W. G. O. Butler, moved to Marske Camp, Yorkshire, while Headquarters Squadron remained as a holding party on Leicester East Airfield. Shortly afterwards one troop 'A' Squadron under command of Captain Hartwright, who had handed over the Adjutancy of the Northamptonshire Yeomanry to Captain Ford, moved to Yorkshire as a demonstration troop on tour of all 50th Infantry Division, Territorial Army camps during June, July and August. A further troop under Sergeant Hyndman moved to Fylingdales for use of R.E.M.E. in recovery work. It can be seen, therefore, that though the major effort of the Regiment was at the Territorial camp at Bodney, the other unit was deployed simultaneously at four other places.

In spite of the very heavy Territorial Army commitments at Bodney, the Regiment found time to train the Bisley team on the local rifle range, send it to the Army Rifle meeting and win the Cambridge Shield for the first time since 1908. This gave great personal pleasure to the Commanding Officer, and also credit must go to Lieutenant Norris, Cornet Aykroyd and Sergeant Pavitt who led the team.

By September 10th the whole Regiment was back again at Leicester preparing firstly for the Part II inspection which was to be carried out by Major-General Cooke, G.O.C. North Midland District and secondly for the departure of 'B' Squadron under Major Nelson to the School of Infantry, Warminster. Just before the Part II inspection 'A' Squadron under Major Davies was dispatched to the Yorkshire Moors to put out fires on the Ranges that had been raging for several months, and so their return just before the Inspection was a severe test upon all members of the Squadron. The other Squadrons displayed an exceptionally high standard of drill and turn out, their administration proved to be in excellent trim and the Regiment therefore secured an exceptionally good report.

Once again one of the Squadrons was demonstrating at the School of Infantry. This was indeed an honour and, in addition, a great advantage as it was not possible to carry out much worth while outdoor training at Leicester East Airfield. 'B' Squadron was up to full strength in personnel and vehicles, under command of Major W. H. Nelson, Captain P. Bollard as second in command, Captain de Las Casas as second Captain and S.S.M. Vallance.

The Beagles spent part of the winter at Warminster, being hunted by Lieutenant R. H. Cooke, the first hare being killed in a gateway by an ex-Parachutist member of the field who fielded her like a rugger ball.

As a result of a strong 'B' Squadron at Warminster the rest of the Regiment was at low strength in Leicester. Major Huth took over 'C' Squadron from Major Dunne who went to the Northamptonshire Yeomanry as second in command. Sir W. G. Lowther, Bart. commanded Headquarters Squadron and Major Collins-Charlton 'A' Squadron. During this period they were indebted to Major Sir Edward Malet who looked after the welfare and P.R.I., but it could hardly be thanks to him that so many members of the Regiment married Leicester girls in 1949.

The Officers enjoyed the best hunting they were ever likely to experience in their lives, and there were fourteen horses in the stable.

Early in 1950 the Regiment was placed in the 29th Independent Infantry Brigade, which was the strategic reserve, and warned that they would move to Mooltan Barracks, Tidworth in the Spring.

A large party of volunteer painters went ahead under Captain Astley-Cooper, worked like blacks (or whites) and very much improved the sub-standard Barrack Rooms before the Regiment moved in.

In June Lieut.-Colonel Goulburn, D.S.O., handed over to Major J. W. Phillips, who incidentally was Master of the Taunton Vale Foxhounds at this time. The Regiment welcomed him and his charming wife as much as they deeply regretted the departure of Lieut.-Colonel Goulburn. The latter had been a tower of strength to the Regiment since 1942 and was known widely throughout the Army, afraid of no one and prepared to fight for the Regiment on every occasion. This was a time of general post, Captain Bellamy took over from Captain Ormrod as Adjutant; R.S.M. Hegarty, a brilliant rider of young horses, retired from the Army to be replaced by R.S.M. Leckie (ex Irish Guards); Major Collins-Charlton moved to the War Office together with Captain Dill, and Major de Clermont returned to take over 'A' Squadron.

PART SIX

1950-1951

KOREA

(a) The Retreat, October-December 1950

BEFORE embarking on the War in Korea, it is perhaps as well to give a very short history of the events that brought it about.

After the unconditional surrender of Japan in August, 1945, the Russians, who had only declared war on the Japanese shortly before, occupied the whole of Korea north of the 38th Parallel four days after the Americans had moved in to the southern part of the country. They then immediately established an Iron Curtain along the Parallel, beyond which no one from the south was allowed to pass.

During the next eighteen months all efforts by the United Nations to unite Korea failed, the Russians refusing even to discuss the matter and saying it had nothing to do with the United Nations.

At the same time the United States started a peaceful civil reconstruction programme in the south of Korea, while Russia, in her zone, set about creating a North Korean Army, obviously to be used to conquer the south, and turn the whole peninsula into a Communist satellite. In 1948 the United Nations authorised a general election in Korea, and in due course this took place, but in South Korea only, and resulted in the creation of a new Republic of Korea, headed by Mr. Syngman Rhee as President. The Russians then announced they had held their own elections and had formed a Korean People's Democratic Republic, which they said was the rightful government of Korea.

This, as can be imagined, led to a series of border incidents along the 38th Parallel. At dawn on the 25th June, 1950, North Korean armed forces crossed the Parallel and began advancing into South Korea, and thus the War in Korea began.

At the time of the invasion, Korea was almost an unknown country to the western world, and the full significance of this sudden incident was hardly realised until the Security Council of the United Nations met, passed a resolution condemning the North Koreans as aggressors, and called upon all member nations to give every possible assistance to the South Koreans. Thus started the first major war to be fought voluntarily by many nations allied together, not for personal advantage or because of individual interests, but to stop an act of aggression that threatened world peace.

By the 30th June the first American troops reached Korea, but by then the small Republic of Korean (R.O.K.) Army was being pushed back, and by the time the United Nations Forces, under General MacArthur, were organised, all that remained of free South Korea was a small perimeter in the south-eastern corner of the peninsula, round Pusan.

What might be called the second phase of the war in Korea began on the 15th September, when 10 U.S. Corps made a daring amphibious landing near Inchon on the west coast, some twenty miles from Seoul. The landing was a complete success, Suwon was captured; followed by Kimpo airfield, the largest in Korea; and finally, after a furious battle, Seoul was liberated. In co-ordination with the landing at Inchon, on the 16th September the Eighth U.S. Army launched an all-out offensive to break out of the

Pusan perimeter. This also was a success, and once under way it began to sweep forward with sensational speed, and by the 15th October units of 1 U.S. Corps had penetrated more than fifteen miles into North Korea and were moving rapidly towards the enemy capital of Pyongyang. As a result of this rapid dash forward six North Korean divisions were trapped in South Korea and the main strength of the enemy army was cut to pieces.

Pyongyang was captured on the 19th October and on the following day 10 U.S. Corps made unopposed amphibious landings at Wonsan on the east coast. They then moved up to Hungnam, passed the Chosan reservoir and reached the Yalu River.

Hopes for a peace before Christmas ran high, and General MacArthur called upon the North Koreans to end the war. But he was doomed to be disappointed, for no answer was ever received. Although the North Koreans knew that their initial gamble had failed they also knew that other plans were ready which still offered a chance of victory.

A vast Chinese Communist Army lay close at hand behind the Yalu River, only waiting the order to launch their attack.

As a result of the appeal in the United Nations Assembly, Britain decided to send two brigades to Korea, the 28th Infantry Brigade from Hong Kong and the 29th Independent Infantry Brigade from the United Kingdom. Carefully-laid plans for summer leave and training were halted, mobilisation plans transformed the 8th Hussars in a day. Many old friends rejoined as reservists were recalled, men who had fought in the Western Desert and North-West Europe. Some officers and N.C.O.'s were attached from other County regiments, and as we shall see later everyone took up the spirit of the 'fighting Eighth' and enabled another fine period of the Regiment's history to be written.

On October 11th 1950 the Regiment left Tidworth for Southampton. There they were to board H.M.T. *Empire Fowey* and sail for Korea to become part of the 29th British Infantry Brigade, which in itself was part of the Eighth United States Army. Lieut.-Colonel J. W. Phillips was in command, with 'A', 'B' and 'C' Squadrons commanded by Majors P. V. de Clermont, W. V. H. Nelson and P. H. Huth.

They were to be the first Regiment to try out the new 52-ton Centurion tanks, vast immensely powerful vehicles, still on the Secret list.

If it is asked, as it has been and will be asked again, why they ever went there, one out of many answers may be offered. The British, in their championship of the United Nations, that fallible but industrious body of human beings, have done something that nobody in history has done before. They sailed to a foreign war in the name of Decency and nothing else. Courageous, peaceable men of a dozen nations, with no other bond to bring them together, met and fought as comrades, each under his own flag, on the field of honour, with an undivided purpose. They were to fight over a malodorous, nearly unheard-of peninsula, for many of them as far away across the globe as a man could travel. They were to fight defiantly, in a loathsome climate, against numerical and strategic odds that appeared to mock their weapons and military science.

It was a thoughtful decision that took them there, accepting such conditions as they may never, in war, be called upon to support again. That they did accept them, open-eyed (growling complaints but always purposeful in the face of the enemy) gave their grim antagonist new and serious problems to ponder.

The voyage lasted just over a month, and on November 14th they dropped anchor in Pusan. They had already been joined at Singapore by Captain Strachan and Captain Astley-Cooper who had flown out ahead of the Regiment with the Brigade Advance party. The tale is now best told by Captain The Hon. Roland Winn whose account, with elaborations here and there, cannot be bettered.

"The chronicle of the 8th Hussars in Korea appeared likely to end before it began, and the certainty of seeing action, against our officially moribund foe, was not clear for some time even after landing, to those who, understandably, paid attention to the words of our grandiloquent and dressy Commander-in-Chief. But unreliably-numbered throngs of Chinamen began to stream over the Yalu river into North Korea and when we landed on Pusan quayside, among posies and prettily gathered local *Bambine* (to the stirring notes of a dark-complexioned transpacific band), it was to hear the famous promise—that we would be 'Home by Christmas'.

Even more heartening to us on the docks, than a brassy rendering of 'St. Louis Blues', was the gay and reassuring presence of Major Medley, who boarded without delay, and with a piquancy of humour entirely his own, gave an account of his journey and activities in command of the advance party: an account which strove, without full effect, to conceal the hard and exasperating work which had occupied that period.

The fruits of his patience and enterprise were not, when we came to taste them, so succulent as could be wished, but they were still a good deal richer in quality than any other Quartermaster in the Army would have obtained, under such circumstances. Jap Camp (or Q.M.6 by its official title) was an assortment of ill-favoured barrack buildings, set on a refuse-ridden slope, and pierced by the knifing November wind, so mild and kindly compared to the climate which was waiting for us in the weeks to come. But all the buildings had roofs, some had windows, American 'cots' and sleeping-bags were waiting for issue, the cookhouse was installed and steaming. No other British unit so far landed on this forbidding coast, had even a pretence of such preparations. Moreover, on looking about us, we found that our dwellings were set to look down upon a small bay, whose contours and colourings were a satisfaction, even a pleasure, to the eye. There was hardly a member who, shivering under canvas or between clapboards, beneath the frown of those hills did not give thanks for the genial energy and achievement, against odds, of Major Hedley.

The next days were taken up in tracing the marine course of certain cargo-ships, meeting them, and unloading our massive vehicles and equipment on to the disordered quays of Pusan Port. Progress at sea, and the assignment of port facilities, were unpredictable. The Order of March northward to the battle front was dependent upon which Squadron's tanks and echelon vehicles could be landed and made ready first. It grew evident that nothing like an even 'starter's gate' would be seen. Among the Sabre Squadrons, first one runner, then another, appeared likely to break away in the lead. Rivalry in this respect, with not always the *lightest* of badinage, became the order of the week. Such hitherto undistinguished vessels as the *Pine Hill, Maple Hill, London Statesman, Berralbanach*, became the course of suspense and triumph among the Light Cavalry.

Finally 'A' Squadron's tanks led the way north, to join an advance party already at Pyongyang under Major Lowther. With them travelled one troop of 'C' Squadron under Lieutenant Moore and four Regimental Headquarters tanks under Lieutenant Hurst. The Squadron travelled on flat cars from Pusan and spent an intensely uncomfortable seven days and seven nights as they rumbled north in extreme cold and dirt and discomfort. The only person who could bring himself to show any interest in the journey was the Squadron Leader, Major de Clermont, who noticed the number of pheasants close to the line with considerable interest.

On December 1st the new 29th British Brigade, consisting of the Gloucesters, the Royal Ulster Rifles and the Northumberland Fusiliers, moved up to the front line for a last ditch stand. If that line, Suchon, did not hold, it was certain that Pyongyang would fall.

Up to this date, American communiqués had continued carelessly exultant. But on Saturday, December 2nd, with 'A' Squadron still on the rails, came the first news of a heavy defeat, north of Pyongyang. Hard on the heels of this report, came physical signs of a movement south. Lieut.-Colonel Phillips, who had reached Seoul with most of his Headquarters, estimated that in a general retreat, which now appeared imminent if not afoot, fifty Centurion tanks, with a purely nominal load of ammunition and no reserves, would be a grave liability in the forward area. He took measures to halt what tanks he could at Kaesong, forty miles northwest of Seoul. By the time action could be taken, 'A' was already unloading in Pyongyang, and 'B' Squadron slipped through Kaesong station in darkness, a matter of minutes before Major Dunne reached the platform with orders to halt. Only 'C' Squadron was halted and detained at Suwon.

'A' Squadron finally concentrated itself on the morning of December 2nd in some barracks on the western outskirts of Pyongyang. The 'C' Squadron troop was placed under command for a while but then reverted to 'Lowther Force' on being given a special rôle guarding the crossing in the town on the north bank of the river Taedong.

At midday on the 3rd, Major de Clermont accompanied Major Lowther to Brigade Headquarters, where orders were received for 'A' Squadron to move in to support the Royal Ulster Rifles. As considerable preparation was still required to make the Squadron operational, it had had to leave Pusan without being fully 'bombed up', permission was given to move the following day. The news of the Chinese intervention had been heard by the Squadron in Kaesong on the way up and from then on columns of transport nose to tail heading south had been visible for two days. Only, however, in Pyongyang did the enormity of the 'flap' become apparent. It was their first experience of an American withdrawal, and very instructive too. One learns at school that this phase of warfare is either organised or a shambles. This was neither except a very dangerous race.

High-level communiqués, and the rich rumour which festooned them, were now as contradictory to their earlier opulent promise as the mind could imagine. But even an untutored Korean peasant, tenderly spreading the new-gotten Allied ordure over his plot of paddy, was left in little doubt that the fortunes of war had switched. Glancing up from that creative task, he saw the great convoys go swinging and rocking south or dammed impatiently in cluttered queues of traffic. As the wild words of alien profanity, high-pitched or fruity, floated over his ancestral acres from the main highway, he can have pondered little as to their meaning.

Throughout the day at Pyongyang explosions rent the air as dump after dump went up, and by night the sky was lit with fires of burning petrol. Unfortunately 'A' Squadron was without its full complement of transport and was responsible for the maintenance of 'Lowther Force', across the river. However certain acquisitions were made quickly by the fitters in the form of three American lorries and a jeep, which greatly eased the situation. Unhappily the expected imminence of a battle necessitated these being loaded with ammunition as opposed to the more 'attractive items' which could have been had by the load without even asking before they were committed to the flames.

On the afternoon of Sunday 4th December, 'A' Squadron moved with all its transport to a bombed-out school. The weather was bitterly cold and the ground like rock. The continuous demolitions ensured a disturbed night, and a tremendous detonation in the early hours, which subsequently transpired to be the second line ammunition blown by accident at the station, shook the building to its foundations.

The Squadron stood to at 6.30 on the morning of the 5th and all engines were warmed up. After breakfast Major de Clermont went to an 'O' Group with the Ulsters, where he received a request to place one troop in support of the company holding the road fork

Winner of the Grand Military Gold Cup, 1957.
Major R. P. G. Dill's 'Easter Breeze' (owner up) takes the last fence to win (page 312).

Centurion tanks of the 8th Hussars move north while the refugees stream south, January, 1953.

Centurion tanks of the 8th Hussars arriving at Suwan for the Korean Campaign,
December, 1950 (page 259).

Sunday morning in Korea, 1950.

A Centurion tank of 'C' Squadron firing on enemy positions on top of Hill 327 during the assault by the Glosters (page 268).

'C' Squadron and the Glosters moving up to the F.U.P. before the attack on Hill 327, February, 1951 (page 268).

and one in support of the platoon at the crossing. These tasks were allotted to Three and Four Troops commanded by Lieutenants Butler and Norris. The rest of the Squadron in reserve joined the Ulster Battalion's Headquarters, while 'Lowther Force' were in support of the Gloucesters.

Throughout the day withdrawing forces streamed back through the positions. News was of the scantiest, and there had been no contact for four days. It was obvious by now that there was no intention to hold the Taedong line, in spite of its being an almost perfect position. Towards evening orders, or rather information, filtered through that the withdrawal would commence after the whole of 1 and 9 Corps were south of the river.

About 6 p.m. Lieutenant Norris reported that one of his tanks had thrown a track when coming out of the river bed to concentrate at dusk. The fitters were immediately dispatched and reported that they could do nothing about it without an oxyacetylene welding equipment with which to burn the track through, as the tension was such that it could not be broken normally. Due to the hurried departure from Pusan the Squadron's gas bottles had not even been unloaded off the ship and American bottles did not fit British equipment. An appeal was made through 'Lowther Force' for some help from the workshop section, which was well south of the river, but there was a long delay before it arrived and it was then needed to attend to a 'Lowther Force' tank in the same predicament. At about 8 p.m. information was received that the withdrawal would probably begin about an hour later and Major de Clermont therefore asked for instructions about what to do with the tank if it had not been repaired in time.

The matter was referred to the Brigade Commander who decided that the tank must be prepared for demolition. Orders were given for the removal of the breech block, the sighting gear, certain secret equipment, and any other parts that could be carried away. The tank was loaded with high-explosive shells, eighteen were put in the engine compartment and fifty inside round the stabilizer and through into the driver's hatch, and finally the petrol leads were cut which flooded the tank with over one hundred gallons of petrol. The camouflage net was then trailed out from the engine compartment, soaked in petrol and a fifty yard trail made to ignite it. When it was touched off, the shells actually started to explode before Lieutenant Clode had reached his dingo fifty yards away. It blazed and blitzed for an hour and a half and little could have remained beyond an overcooked carcase. Later, in case the Communists should discover its secrets it was blown up by American jet planes, directed by 8th Hussars in spotter planes. At 1.30 on the morning of December 6th orders were received that the withdrawal was about to begin. The order of march was the Northumberland Fusiliers followed by the Ulsters and 'A' Squadron, with the Gloucesters and 'Lowther Force' last over the bridges. Again there were delays and it was 2.30 a.m. before the Gloucesters, led by the Centurions and Cromwells of the 8th Hussars fell back through Pyongyang under a pale quarter moon. Flames leapt hundreds of feet from petrol dumps and equipment set alight by the retreating army. Civilians, including women and children, left their homes in the biting cold and, as the fires cast a huge lurid glow over the city, joined the troops heading south.

The very smell of panic was in the air. To 'B' Squadron still jolting northward, grimed with smoke and filth and frozen snow, it was an odd experience. For stretches of many miles the railway ran beside the road, and as the great sheeted Centurions and their crews steamed on, drawn by one protesting engine against the turn of the military tide, a slow, staunch proudness grew out of men's hearts, to find expression on their lips and faces. Within a stone's throw of them, along the roadside, they could observe

R

the acts of men who behaved—as they would not behave. Down that detestable train there crept a spirit that had not been apparent on the ship or in Pusan; needless, indeed impossible, to name it or describe it. But still it was more tangible than the other signs it overcame.

'B' Squadron moved north, but came to rest one station south of Pyongyang. The train, its locomotive removed, lay there immobile through the day, and into dusk. No contact had been available with the Regiment since departure from Pusan. Repeated promises were made by the station staff, that an engine was coming. It never came. Earlier, on the swaying flatcars, in wind growing still more bitter with every mile, vehicle-cooking, gun-cleaning, and normal maintenance had been carried out en route. The tanks were fit to go forward in a fighting rôle on descent from the flats. Darkness fell, and the headlamps marked the route of retreat, throughout the night. 'B' Squadron slept.

At 2 o'clock, Major Nelson passed the word along, "Get operational!", waking the sleepers from uneasy dreams. The night sky to the north was ablaze; rising and sinking crescendos of gunfire and musketry indicated what might be a battle, beyond the river. By the beams of their own spotlights the Centurions were driven off the flats. There was no loading ramp and each had to swing on its tracks; then inch forward to make its drop on to the platform as gently as possible. By 4.30 the whole Squadron was in close leaguer in the goods yard area, awaiting the dawn. The 'battle' had died away within an hour of its opening, and with the first light came information, from an American whose truck broke down close by, that it had been the demolition of an ammunition dump inside the city.

In the morning Major Nelson sent one officer forward into Pyongyang to make contact with Regimental Headquarters and return. This was done, and later, orders were given to move forward. But after a few miles advance fresh orders came through, that these tanks would join the road retreat of the Allied Forces.

Of the long trek south, as scattered sections of the mass retreat, memories still remain to those who took part; but they are not memories that one eagerly summons back. The Eighth Hussars had taken part in other retreats, in fighting retreats, from which a final victory was later secured. But this was not a fighting retreat, and it did not seem that anything would be secured but shame and disaster. That such was not eventually the fate of this Army was owed, a fortnight later, to a change of leadership more dramatic than could be foreseen or hoped for, at that sorry stage.

In the grip of cold, and a disillusion that was harsher than cold, the British units, with the Regiment among them, rolled down the roads and over the frozen passes of North Korea, unwilling and out of place in the great wheelborne retreat across the Parallel. The troops were furious at having come 10,000 miles to fight and then to withdraw without having even seen the enemy. Millions of dollars worth of valuable equipment had been destroyed without a shot being fired or an attempt made to evacuate it. No contact had been made with the enemy for four days, yet no attempt had been made to stand and see what effort could be produced in order to save the equipment. Seldom has a more demoralizing picture been witnessed than the abandonment of this American forward base before an unknown threat of Chinese soldiers who were, as it transpired, ill-armed and on their feet or on horses.

The 29th Brigade had received orders to withdraw to Sinmak, about eighty miles south of Pyangyong. Nobody had considered whether it was feasible to move Centurions that were hardly run in, eighty miles in a day and it was doubtful if anyone in the Squadrons had appreciated exactly how far it was. Once out of the town the pace was increased to a steady twenty to twenty-five m.p.h. The dust was appalling and after the first few hours running, petrol stoppages began to occur, though these may have been as much due to the newness of the tanks as the dust. The cold too, was terrible, there was solid ice on the outside of the tanks and the crews did not think they would ever get warm again. The fitters though were marvellous and worked all hours of the day and night despite the bitter weather.

All night long to the dawn they fumbled southwards in the freezing cold, past burning villages and long columns of South Korean troops, half asleep on their feet. In the first light they stopped to breakfast in a snow-filled ditch at Hwanju, and shortly after moving off the first and only accident occurred while descending a steep diversion into a river bed, the lid of the cupola of Lieutenant Butler's tank, which was not secured, swung over, pinning his head against the bracket of the X10 binoculars. Butler was slightly concussed and had to have five stitches in his forehead. It was not the first accident that had happened due to the cupola not being secured, it was too heavy to open and close easily and liable to cause grave injury if left in the free position.

Later that afternoon there was another incident. Lieutenant Cooke's tank knocked down a South Korean soldier and ran over his leg, breaking it. Cooke stopped and jumped down to assist the unfortunate man, but before he could do anything the South Korean platoon officer pulled Cooke's ·38 pistol from its holster and shot the man dead. Life in Korea was nothing if not rugged and in a withdrawal a wounded man was a liability. "Autre pays, autre meours."

Apart from one 'C' Squadron tank, commanded by Lieutenant Moore, which was having petrol stoppages and was a considerable way behind, the journey, though hideously uncomfortable was uneventful. From Sariwan good speed was made for the first ten miles through a rolling plain, but the road then started to climb into the hills with difficult bends that reduced speed to walking pace and placed a great strain on both drivers and tracks.

A line had been formed to the north of Seoul, protecting the capital and Brigade was given positions athwart the main highway. 'A' Squadron finally rolled into Sinmak as darkness was falling on the evening of December 6th. No one had had any sleep for over thiry-six hours and the cold had at times been such as to prevent coherent thought.

All Centurions, by order of the Army Commander, were, for the present, to be stationed south of the Han. The Regiment therefore moved back to Suwon, where billets awaited them of comparative comfort, 'B' Squadron arriving on the 8th and 'A' on the 9th, and a breathing space was granted for maintenance needs. The 'running in' period of two whole Squadrons had been taken up by a reluctant night and day race to the rear. The tanks had stood the test remarkably. The damage suffered was more sadly measured in terms of morale. The conduct of the campaign, within their experience, had so far been uninspiring.

'C' Squadron, commanded by Major Huth, now moved forward from Suwon, where they had been held, to Yongdungpo, on the south bank of the River Han. The other two Sabre Squadrons and Headquarter Squadron prepared for Christmas, outside the ancient walls of Suwon.

But one element of the Regiment had not come back across the Han.

Captain Astley-Cooper's Recce Troop, in its Cromwells, had remained, built up into 'Cooper Force' by the reinforcement of six other Cromwells, the tanks of the Gunner OPs, all pooled under one command. This force was to support 29th Brigade, north of Seoul. From the 8th Hussars Captain Astley-Cooper had three officers, Lieutenant D. Probyn, Lieutenant G. Alexander, and Lieutenant B. Dowling in charge of the echelon. From the Gunners came Major R. Howe, Captain Holman and Captain Gibbons and their crews. It was this modest force which was to fight a valiant and, for us, a tragic battle, in the Regiment's first Korean encounter with the enemy.

For a moment all was still. The Communists seemed amazed, suspicious of this truant army, and its headlong strategy. Contact was so completely broken, that the only ground information of the enemy came from the stammering tongues of refugees, such remnants of these straggling, famished files of men and women that were not destroyed; who had started on foot from northernmost Korea; strewn dead and dying over the snow, by the Allied airforce on patrol.

The year 1950 drew to its close. The weather sharpened with each week. Squadrons prepared for Christmas, with all the ingenuity of the British at war. The sumptuous table set by Major de Clermont, and 'A' Squadron Mess, was a matter of wonder to many guests from a wealthier nation.

On December 18th 'C' Squadron, under Major Huth, had taken up defensive positions on a featureless snow-bound island in the Han; the twenty-pounders pointing over the river at the city. In case of a general pull-back they were there to give additional fire power to 29th Brigade, who would defend Seoul while the 25th (U.S.) Infantry Division and the 1st R.O.K. withdrew through them, the tanks giving fire support while the infantry crossed the remaining bridges. The tanks on the island were harboured in a wrecked hangar while the men went under canvas. Thick snow made the picking of 'tankable' ground unduly hazardous. In one instance, a tank drove unsuspectingly into an ice and snow-covered pool, and lay half submerged during most of the day, while recovery was organised.

Shortly before Christmas the Army Commander, General Walker, was killed in a jeep accident and his place was taken by Lieut.-General Mathew Ridgeway. Plans were already afoot to send the Regiment down to Kure and out of the danger zone, and on the 27th December Lieutenant C. Coldrey went to Taegu to arrange for the move of Regimental baggage.

(b) The Battle of Happy Valley,
December 1950-January 1951

IN the days between Christmas and the New Year, there was a stir of activity at the front. Regimental Headquarters were established at a leather-factory at Yongdungpo. 'B' Squadron was summoned forward to new positions supporting the Turkish Brigade on the Kimpo Peninsula, west of Seoul. Apart from the rolling sea-board near Pyongyang, this was the only promising country for tanks they had as yet prospected. The new Army Commander had decided to stand and fight north of the city and new dispositions were being made.

The line of the Imjin River was to be held from left to right by the 25th United States Division, and the 1st and 6th R.O.K. Divisions. The 29th Brigade was to hold an 8,000 yard sector of a bridgehead round Seoul (with 'Cooper Force' in support and 'C' Squadron and the 7th Royal Tanks in reserve) with the task of either counter-attacking should the enemy gain ground in the 1st R.O.K. Division area, or to withdraw to the Seoul

bridgehead, with the Gloucesters and the Royal Ulster Rifles holding the Seoul perimeter, while the Allied troops withdrew south of the Han River and the Northumberland Fusiliers held the bridges and blew them when the Brigade had passed through. The
29th Brigade was also to dig positions along a line of hills running west and east to the
north of a valley ten miles northwest of Seoul. They were to be occupied by the troops
holding the Imjin River line and were to be dug by local labour under the supervision of
the 29th Brigade, with a possibility that they themselves might have to occupy them.
This order was only given on December 29th, and the 30th and 31st were occupied in
digging.

On the last day of December came the news that the South Koreans were being
attacked in strength across the Imjin. The front was alert and New Year's night was
observed under 'stand to' conditions. Sporadic action was joined with a clearly numerous
and offensively-minded enemy, later to be estimated at between one and two battalions,
supported by artillery. As New Year's Eve came to an end and the New Year was seen
in it became evident that the enemy had gained a lot of ground on the 1st R.O.K.
Division front, and as a result the 29th Brigade was ordered to counter-attack. However
it rapidly became apparent, even before the recce parties arrived at Tonggori that it would
be an operation of the first magnitude to find the enemy, let alone to counter-attack
him, so this order was countermanded. Those units of the Brigade that were already en
route, the Royal Ulster Rifles, 'C' Squadron 7th Royal Tanks, 'Cooper Force' and others
had to be halted, turned round and redirected. They were now supposed to take up the
positions they had been digging for the last two days, initially for the South Koreans,
and now had to dig new, more suitable ones, which were eventually finished on January
2nd.

At midday on the 2nd the 21st Infantry Regiment, from Thailand, came under
command and were ordered to take up defensive positions. An attack seemed imminent
and in the evening another South Korean Regiment was sent to help, but before they
could take up their positions it was already too late.

During the night of the 2nd/3rd, the battle opened. Before first light, both the
Ulsters (with 'Cooper Force' under command) and the Northumberlands were attacked
and forced to give ground. Enemy broke into the Battalion Headquarters building of
the Fusiliers, and were driven out in a hand-to-hand tussle. One Support Company
Commander was killed. This was the first occasion that the Regiment, in any form, had
come into contact with the clever way the Chinese Infantry used cover. They could crawl
and infiltrate up whole hillsides through the undergrowth. This was opposed to their
other method of advance, blowing bugles and horns and beating drums and gongs. The
Brigade found itself situated astride the boundary between two separate attacking
armies, which could account for the unco-ordinated attacks that were made on either
flank. On the right, that is eastwards, was a village held by the Gloucesters supported
by the Northumberland Fusiliers. This was quickly overrun and the resulting chaos was
increased by the fact that the telephone exchange was captured and the signallers killed
during the first onslaught. From the sniping coming from a hill behind the Gloucester
position it was obvious that the Chinese had crawled through under cover of darkness.

Meanwhile on the left flank the Ulsters were preparing to counter-attack and regain
the ground lost earlier in the morning. This they were able to do with the aid of 'Cooper
Force' and the Churchills of the 7th Royal Tanks, who were hotly and successfully
in action with the enemy during the morning. The Cromwells fired every round of
ammunition, enabling the Riflemen to regain their lost positions. By mid-afternoon
both infantry battalions, with armoured support, had restored their line, the tanks were

replenished, and the enemy had a 'bloody nose', with little to show for it. There was a lull in the evening, and spirits were high.

Before six o'clock a Corps Order was delivered to Brigade for a general withdrawal across the Han. By seven o'clock, the method laid down at the Ulster 'O' group was also known. The tanks would move out last, in darkness, behind the Ulster Battle Patrol, with a platoon of infantry for local protection. Captain Astley-Cooper asked permission for the tanks to leave before dark but was refused as it was thought that the noise of the tanks would give too much away.

The Infantry Companies began withdrawing soon after 9 p.m., at ten minute intervals, but came immediately under fire from the flanking hills. The withdrawal lay down a valley, along a track barely wide enough to carry tanks. The last element of the Ulsters was the Support Company, largely carrier-mounted. They crammed the track, and drew heavy fire from the guns above them on the west side of the valley. It is now apparent that when the enemy hit the Ulsters during the day they made an effort to infiltrate round the west flank of the Battalion and, when the Company established on the hill there withdrew, the Chinese took their place. They had also come through the gap left on the eastern flank when the 25th United States Division holding that ground withdrew four hours too early, thus leaving the flank wide open.

At ten that night the last company of the Ulsters was about to move off when they came under heavy fire from the hills to the west. During this time the Cromwells under Captain Astley-Cooper had been holding off all attack from the north; but now the hills to their west and rear were dense with enemy. He observed that the village on his line of withdrawal was ablaze. He ordered Lieutenant Alexander to reconnoitre a detour to the right, by a frozen river-bed. The fighting was at closer quarters. The platoon of infantry allocated to the tanks was scattered among them, out of touch with their own Commander. They were shot off the backs of the tanks, as these slowly picked their way, in line ahead, along the track. This was continually being blocked by carriers and other vehicles which kept slipping off it on the ice and in the darkness. The Chinese were firing the whole time with intense but luckily inaccurate fire. Twice parties of Chinese cut the road and twice they were driven off. As the column moved on more and more carriers became bogged and had to be abandoned, and although the enemy were suffering heavy casualties they were also inflicting many. The remaining tanks were called up and, with what was left of the infantry, charged the burning village that was held by the Chinese and cleared the route. But unfortunately the leading tank became bogged and so the road was blocked for good.

Lieutenant Alexander then left the road and moved over the paddy towards the river-bed, under the fire of mortars and machine-guns, to which he was replying with H.E. and Besa. He felt his way in the darkness up the ice-covered river-bed, but the mortar concentration increased. The enemy were much closer and appeared to have been ready for the likelihood of the track being blocked and were carrying pole-charges and sticky bombs and had also arranged little heaps of sticks and straw which, when lit, gave a silhouette effect.

After travelling some distance down the river-bed Alexander rejoined the track. He forced his way through the burning village, which was also the scene of a brisk battle. As he emerged from it, a mortar exploded on the cupola of the tank. He drew in his head as another bomb landed on the tank. At this moment the tank lurched off the track, and came to a stop. Alexander put his head out of the turret to give instructions. He gave two orders, and as he spoke the second time, another bomb landed directly on the turret-ring. Alexander made no movement; when his gunner pulled him down inside the tank he was dead. Shortly after that another tank tried to pass and ran off the track on the opposite side, effectively blocking it. The surviving crew-members took to the hills.

Meanwhile Captain Astley-Cooper had also moved in the direction of the river-bed, and along it for some distance. He was engaging targets almost continuously while on the move. Suddenly he gave the order to leave the river-bed and they took to the paddy fields, going at a tremendous speed, lurching over the bunds, and still firing. Finally they shuddered to a stop, having shed a track. They all baled out and split up, Astley-Cooper, his gunner Trooper Farmer, and another man going to the left, Corporal Livett and Trooper Fawcett right. As Astley-Cooper's party crossed a paddy field, about twenty enemy infantry approached from their front. These infantry had been firing at them as they baled out of their tank. Farmer fell on his face in the middle of the paddy and lay still while Astley-Cooper and his companion ran on, bent double, towards the ditch. That was the last that was seen of him. Trooper Farmer meanwhile was able to evade the enemy infantry and join a Cromwell belonging to the Artillery, where he eventually met up with Livett and Fawcett. They all crammed into the Cromwell and blasted a way through the burning village and out the other side, until they were held up by two Cromwells, both with their tracks off. They baled out once more and took to the hills with a party led by Major Shaw of the Ulsters. After travelling for about ten miles they eventually reached the American lines.

All units of the Brigade had by now broken off engagement with the enemy, and troops fell back, without further serious fighting, across the Han. The last bridge was blown up and the river left as a momentary check to the Chinese pursuit.

Of the 8th Hussars who had taken part in the action, ten miles to the north, two officers were killed and Lieutenant Probyn captured. Among the Other Ranks, twenty were posted killed or missing. Lieutenant Dowling, by cool and intelligent management, saved his Echelon intact, for which he was mentioned in dispatches. The Gunners had twenty men missing.

The Ulster Battalion suffered a loss of two hundred and thirty, in the battle which is now, austerely, known as 'Happy Valley.' Had it not been for Captain Astley-Cooper and his tanks, the final reckoning might have been closer to annihilation.

The Brigade moved back to Suwon, the Regiment leaguering on the airfield. At noon on Friday, January 5th, all units again took the road south. 'C' Squadron stopped with the Infantry at Pyongtaek. The rest of the Regiment continued towards Taejon.

Little or nothing was known of the circumstances of the capture of Lieutenant Probyn, but the following account by his gunner, C. Christopher, serves to show some of the hazards of this particular form of warfare. There was a certain amount of feeling, too, that in the last action it was lack of experience on the part of the Allies that caused so many casualties. "The Americans have no idea how to carry out a fighting withdrawal" wrote one who had been there. "The Chinks fight on the hills, they don't come down the main roads as they don't like our tanks. Until we get Infantry that will get up the hills and forget about their tents, space-heaters and trucks we will never do any good."

A STATEMENT BY GUNNER C. CHRISTOPHER (R.A.)

"I was hull gunner on Lieutenant Probyn's tank. On 3rd January 1951 at about 2210 hours fire was opened with Bren Guns on the 'B' vehicles of 'Cooper Force' as they withdrew. As the tanks were about to leave a message was received over the wireless that the enemy had caused a road block in front of the tanks. Another message was received asking if the tanks could get through. Shortly after this the first tank moved off and the others followed at short intervals. All the tanks stopped shortly after they had started. All the tanks were firing both 75-mm. and Besa and the Infantry on the backs were firing their own arms. I could see enemy infantry on the right hand side of the road and to our rear about 20 yards away. They were then closing in steadily. We moved on about 50 yards almost up to the broken bridge. Captain Holman came up to our tank and called me by name. I opened my door and called to Lieutenant Probyn. I started to get out when Captain Holman cried out "Oh dear, Oh dear" and sank down on to the ground. Lieutenant Probyn and I got out. We got down beside him. I lifted his head up and he regained consciousness and said "Where am I?" We put him on to the top of the turret. We asked him if he was all right. He said, "I have had my lot," and lost consciousness. Lieutenant Probyn got back into the turret. I was getting to the ground when I was hit through the thigh by a burst of machine-gun fire at about 5 yards range, and fell to the ground. There was a great number of enemy infantry all round and heavy casualties were being caused to them by our own tanks and infantry. I fired off all my revolver ammunition, standing beside Lieutenant Probyn who had climbed out of the tank again. The tank in front of ours had slipped off the track and the crew abandoned it, and transferred themselves to ours. Lieutenant Probyn said, "This is a bad show, we had better get out of it." The other crew had climbed on the tank and Lieutenant Probyn and I were about to follow suit when the tank started to pull away. I saw Gunner England sitting on the front track guard. He cried out "I've got it," and pitched forward on to the ground. I was holding on to the wire round the ration boxes. The Chinese were throwing hand grenades in to the tracks and I felt pieces of shrapnel hitting my legs and face. I thought it better to let go. As I rolled clear of the tank which was travelling quite fast, I dropped into the ditch on the left-hand side of the road. I last saw Lieutenant Probyn standing beside me as the tank moved off. He had his revolver levelled and cried out to a Chinese about a yard from him "Drop that gun or I'll shoot." He did not drop into the ditch with me and I never saw him again. As I fell the Chinese infantry stepped over me and made for the tank firing as they went. I could hear them shouting the whole time, "Don't shoot," "Don't shoot we are friends," and "Don't shoot I'm an American" and "Give us a lift" and many other remarks in English.

"The tank went off about 200 yards and then the engine started labouring and stalled as if it was bellied. I heard a great deal of firing where it had stopped and five minutes later everything was quiet. Chinese bugles were blowing all the time and about 200 infantry came past me going south. I lay in the ditch for about an hour. While I was there I heard two English soldiers coming along. One sounded like a Scotsman. He said to the other, "Throw your gun down, Jimmy, we will give ourselves up. We have no chance behind their lines." I was about to get up and go over to them when the same men called out "We are giving ourselves up, we are English." I heard a burst of machine-gun fire and another voice said "What did you do that for?" There was another shot and I looked over the top. The two men were on the ground and I saw about six Chinese walking away laughing. I thought I had better go. When the road was empty I started to crawl on the way the tanks had been going. I had not gone far when about twenty Chinese started to come along. They were between me and the tank. I then started crawling away from the tank and towards the hills. I crawled over two Paddy Fields and found the track. There I found our two Scout Cars and a Bren Carrier which was overturned beside the track. I looked around for some weapons. I found a Bren Gun but no ammunition. Beside the Scout Car were an Officer and two men. They were all dead. It appeared to me that the three had been tipped out of one of the Scout Cars which was on its side in the ditch. I presumed the two men to be the 8th Hussars crew of the Scout Car although I could not be absolutely certain. The Officer I am almost certain was Captain Fleming. He was wearing a camouflage windproof suit and he had a scarf round the lower part of his face. His glasses were hanging from one ear. I could not see anyone round the other Scout Car. I started walking across the paddy fields towards the hills. The Chinese began to come back from the south and I could hear a different call being blown on the bugles. I lay down in the middle of the field and they passed within a few yards of me. They appeared to congregate round the first tank which had been put out of action. I heard a great deal of chatter and one vehicle start up. I carried on to the south and climbed into a ditch because I could still hear enemy infantry at the bottom of the hills. I decided to go to the right and this ditch seemed to veer that way and in the direction of the road. As I reached the end of the ditch and almost to the road I stood up to look around. As I stood up I saw five North Koreans about four yards from me. As soon as they saw me they opened fire with sub-machine-guns. They missed with the first bursts so I threw myself to the ground making out that I had been hit. They kept firing. I felt my arm move and knew that I had been hit. I lay still and they walked over to me and looked at me. They then walked on. I lay there for some time not daring to move. When I did look over the top of the ditch I saw two more enemy soldiers coming towards me. As they came they searched all the dead both Chinese and British. It was too late to move so I lay there quite still. When they reached me they lifted my arms up and I imagine they were looking for watches and rings. Finding none they kicked me in the ribs and left me. They went on up the road. I got up again and found that I could not move my leg. I found a stick which enabled me to walk. Just then I heard a whistle. My first instinct was to drop to the ground. However I saw a man waving a stick at the back of one of the tanks. Taking him to be British I hobbled towards him. When I reached him I found him to be a Scotsman from the Royal Ulster Rifles. He told me he had been shot that morning. He had a broken leg and he asked me if I could help him to his feet. I found that I was too weak to do so. He told me that his friend was round the other side of the tank. There I found another Scotsman of the Ulsters with a broken leg and a bullet wound through his chest. I helped him round to his friend leaving him leaning against the tank. I broke open a tin of milk for them to drink. They told me that there were two more men of the Ulsters at the top of the hill. I said I would go up to them and also look for more men round the tanks. I walked on and when I reached the second tank I saw a dead gunner on the back of the tank whom I knew to be Gunner Yates. He had been shot through the head. In the front compartment of the second tank were a dead driver and hull gunner. I knew the hull gunner to be Gunner Slade and the driver Gunner Clinton. There were about twenty British dead around their four tanks. I thought that I recognised Bombardier Morgan but I could not be certain.

"It was now about 0830 hours on 4th January 1951. An American spotter plane circled round followed by six jet planes. We waved as we thought that they might be intending to bomb the tanks. The spotter plane circled very low and the pilot waved and went off. I walked up to the two other Ulster men on the hill. I found there two more men of the Ulsters. One was Rifleman Thompson who was wounded in the neck, arm and both knees. He could walk. The other was an Irishman of the Ulsters who had a broken thigh. I could do nothing for him.

"The plane came back and dropped a sheet of paper which I retrieved. On it was written:—"Go west to SEOUL river bed." I called out to the men at the foot of the hill that Thompson and I would go off and get help. We walked about a mile and a half when two helicopters came over. We waved to them and they both started circling round us. We pointed North towards where the others were and one of them went off in that direction. The other came down two fields away. We went up to him and he told us that we were being sniped. By this time we were both very exhausted and had already decided that we could not go any further. We told them about the other three and he told us not to worry as the other helicopter would look after them. He was very calm. When we were in the air he told us to look down just past where we had been picked up. There were apparently a large number of Chinese at the bottom of the hills."

(c) The Attack on Hill 327, January-March 1951

FROM here and for the next five weeks, the story of the 8th Hussars in Korea is the story of 'C' Squadron. Due to strategic indecision, above their heads, the order was issued for all Centurions to move out of Korea. The order was countermanded within a week. But by that time, most of the personnel of 'A' and 'B' and Regimental Headquarters Squadron had arrived in Kure. The shipping of the tanks was then officially frozen, and so they remained, the crews divided from their tanks by the hundred miles of the Sea of Japan.

'C' Squadron remained in the Brigade sector, and on January 6th it was split into two half-squadrons: one under Major Huth in support of the Northumerlands, and a troop with the Gloucesters, the other under Captain Strachan in support of the Ulsters. An attack was expected at three o'clock the following morning, and an all-night stand-to was maintained in a temperature 20 degrees below freezing. The Northumberlands were supposed to have picked up a refugee who had given them the information. No attack came in, although the enemy was known to be in Suwan, and the Brigade was watchful. Needless to say on asking the Northumberlands the next day what the alarm was about they knew nothing about it, and had spent a quiet night. The 10th was a night of still more intense cold and fog (a temperature of 38 degrees below freezing was recorded), through which armies of refugees poured into the lines, and were passed back.

Further days of indescribable cold followed. The Squadron Leader put a flask to his lips, and the skin came away on the metal. It was dangerous to touch the side of a tank with the bare hand. To shave in the morning, a metal razor had to be tipped out of its case, into warm water, before it could be safely handled. Beer arrived frozen solid in its bottles. The Squadron worked under the continual strain and handicap of mechanism freezing fast overnight: the fluid of brakes, bearings and other essential parts of the tank, had to be individually melted each morning, before movement was possible. Extensive use was made of straw, both in lining foxholes, and spreading over the tanks, but on especially cold nights this was insufficient. On January 12th, 48 degrees of frost was recorded. The next day the Fusiliers moved south to a village, and for the first time troops were living in houses and could find shelter from the biting wind. Up till then they had had to blanket off the sides of their vehicles with corrugated iron or some such wind-resisting material, and cover them with straw, as their only shelter against the cold.

Enemy pressure had shifted east, and the active front was now around Wonju. In the Brigade sector, American task forces began probing up the road, into and beyond Suwon. The Brigade's first-line mission was now provisionally over. 'C' Squadron moved back some miles to another village for maintenance.

Slowly the United Nations Forces took the offensive again, all along the line. On January 15th three columns, supported by tanks, struck on the western front. One advanced twelve miles to Kumyangjangni, twenty-three miles south-east of Seoul, against only small-arms opposition. The others met none at all. One recaptured the town of Osan, thirty miles south of Seoul, and the other moved west of the main Seoul-Osan road. The Squadron, as part of a Battalion Group under the Ulsters, made a sweep forward through the country west of the centre-line, encountering nothing. For the next fortnight training was carried out with the Infantry. In early February Lieut.-Colonel Sir W. G. Lowther, now commanding the Regiment, who had taken over from Lieut.-Colonel Phillips who was sick and later evacuated to the United Kingdom, joined the Squadron with his Tactical Headquarters, and 'A' Squadron reappeared in the sector, with 'B' to follow.

At Osan on February 11th, Captain Strachan and Lieutenant Radford took their tanks up the road to Yongdungpo, and searched the opposite bank of the river for enemy. A tank was observed in the mouth of a tunnel, near the far bank. It was engaged and, at a range of 3,800 yards, the second shot struck and disabled the target, which had been firing 75 H.E. It was identified as a Cromwell tank, presumably captured and repaired after the 'Cooper Force' battle. This was the first, and therefore historic, occasion that a Centurion had engaged an enemy tank with fire. A subsequent round went into the tunnel and started a fire (suspected as a POL dump) behind the Cromwell. The tanks remained firing for two hours, during which they assisted an American foot patrol on the north of the river, knocking out machine-guns and other weapon positions, by whose fire they had been pinned.

On the evening of this action, while 'A' Squadron remained at Suwon and 'B' was still at Pusan, the whole of 'C' Squadron moved to Kyongan-ni, to the north-east of Suwon. The journey was a strain on Commanders and drivers, as ice made the roads treacherous, and it took one and a half hours to negotiate one saddle. The Brigade had taken over the right boundary of 1 Corps from the 8th U.S. Cavalry Brigade. A patrol of two Troops, Infantry from the Gloucesters and some Sappers, went out the next morning. Nothing more serious than sniper-fire was encountered but they had to keep to the main road and supplies were brought up to them by porters.

It was obvious that the Chinese were not resisting west of the road but had taken up a series of positions on high ground which commanded the road from the east. The following day, February 13th, 'C' Squadron moved forward, with one Gloucester Company under command, but was held up by the enemy firmly dug in on the highest feature of the surrounding countryside, Hill 327. It was not possible to dislodge them and a battalion attack was laid on for the following day to co-ordinate with an American attack on 89. While observing the Infantry's attempt, Major Huth's tank was struck by an enemy shell at about 1200 yards, and the idler wheel damaged. The Americans secured the ground to the right of 107, but a strong counter-attack pushed them off it during the night and the plans for the attack on Hill 327 had to be cancelled.

The attack was eventually made on February 16th, and became known, by virtue of its outcome, as 'Operation Copy Book'. The 2nd Battalion, the 24th Brigade were to go in and capture features 189 south and north while the 3rd Battalion, the 24th Brigade captured feature 131 known as Cheltenham. Then two companies of the Gloucesters were to go in and capture 327. All three attacks were to be supported by 'C' Squadron.

Captain P. C. Ormrod moved off on foot with the leading Company of Gloucesters, and Lieutenant S. Portal with the Americans, each taking a man-pack 62 wireless set. The idea of a tank forward observation officer among the forward infantry, calling down fire on individual targets, was an entirely new one to the Americans, and one which had not been developed in action even by themselves. The tanks were deployed to train their guns on the hilltops. The attack went in at 9.30 a.m. and the Americans were almost at once held up by machine-gun fire from a knoll, north of the saddle. Number Two Troop engaged this position. The first slope of the Gloucester objective was taken with comparative ease. On the second slope, however, more opposition was met, and Captain Ormrod called on the tanks for fire support, indicating the targets bunker by bunker, and confirming their destruction as it occurred. From Squadron Headquarters the fight was being watched with stage-box convenience. Through the 'times ten' periscopes of their tanks, the Colonel, Major Huth and Captain Strachan studied the Infantry tussle on the hillside, while enjoying a bacon-and-egg breakfast.

The final objective offered yet tougher resistance, and Captain Ormrod laid out a recognition panel in front of the leading section, and requested a 'stonk' on the hilltop. Seventeen tanks opened up with H.E. and Besa. At the end of a ten-minute concentration, the word was passed over the air to Captain Ormrod, "All finished—go ahead". The Infantry worked their way up and gained the summit. Thirty-three Chinese dead and five prisoners were picked up. The action had taken approximately two hours from start to finish.

"The 20-pounder used as a close support gun for Infantry made its name, both with the Gloucesters and the 24th Brigade and from that point of view the attack was a great success," wrote the Commanding Officer. "Our Tank Observation Officer, Peter Ormrod, with the Gloucesters, was quite outstanding and led their advance, and it was chiefly through him that they had only nine killed as he directed the fire of the tanks most accurately. It was the first time any of us had supported an Infantry attack up a mountain, but thanks to our Tank Observation Officers who told us the whole time where the leading sections were, and to florescent panels which were put down by the Infantry when they stopped to get their wind, we could keep the Chinks quiet."

On February 17th Numbers One, Three and Four Troops went out to support the Gloucesters in capturing the final hill, Bursley, where they were still winkling out the enemy. Thanks to the Squadron's Bridge-Layer this enabled the tanks to cross a large crater in the road and push on down the main road to Seoul. The Infantry reached their objective by midday and phase three of the Operation then took place. The Squadron pressed on up the road towards the Han but no Infantry were forthcoming for local protection. As darkness was falling and as it had begun to snow very heavily the Squadron withdrew back to the river-bed for the night, having gone some five miles north up the road.

The next morning found the roads five inches deep in snow which made them treacherous going. A fighting patrol consisting of One and Two Troops went out with a Company of Gloucesters to try and reach the Han River, which they did without meeting any resistance. A foot patrol, covered by One Troop, went up to Hill 94 to see if it was occupied by the enemy and were fired on by a machine-gun, so withdrew without any casualties, back to their former positions.

Again on the 19th Three and Four Troops went up to the Han River to make sure that the road was still secure, while the Infantry Battalions moved up. The Ulsters endeavoured to take Hill 94, but they also did not succeed, so a stronger attack was planned for the next day.

On the 20th One and Two Troops, under Captain G. Murray, were to support the Ulsters during their attack on the range of hills running down to the Han. This was to be done by One Troop giving support at 90 degrees to the advance, while the Infantry straddled it and advanced towards the Han with a Company either side of the feature. In the meanwhile Two Troop and a Battle Patrol would do a left flank movement down to the river's edge and take up a position at an angle of 120 degrees to the line of advance, so as to cut off the enemy as they withdrew.

Accurate mortar fire was brought down on the force by mortars on the far side of the Han, wounding the Patrol Commander and three others, who were brought out on the back of one of the tanks. The Infantry had so much difficulty in reaching the top of the ridge, owing to machine-gun fire, that an Air-strike was called for. However American Infantry managed to gain the highest part and the strike was diverted to another knoll. The three highest knolls were secured, but the whole range could not be cleared before the light failed so Captain Murray's force withdrew to the Northumberland's leaguer area for the night.

On the following day another tank-supported reconnaisance to the river discovered that the enemy had decamped. At midday the Squadron returned to the river-bed once more. It started to rain for the first time and by nightfall the roads had turned into rivers of mud, while in the once-dry river-beds waves were lapping through Regimental Headquarters.

On the 22nd Three and Four Troops under Captain Strachan, together with the Ulsters, recced the island and village north-west of the hills. Captain Strachan met and questioned a Korean 'agent', and passed back information that there were three hundred Chinese in a hill village ahead. An air-strike was put in, and a number of enemy killed.

And that was the end of serious fighting south of the Han. The Brigade was transferred to Corps Reserve. 'A' Squadron moved with Regimental Headquarters to the Brigade Area at Ichon. 'C' Squadron went back, first to Anyang for a week and then to Suwan, where 'B' Squadron was arriving after its refreshing sea trip from Pusan to Ichon. A period of training and demonstration followed; the demonstrations mainly undertaken by 'A' Squadron, in co-operation with the Infantry Battalions round Ichon.

After this, their first brief action, the Regiment were delighted with their Centurions. They at last had a tank that mounted a gun capable of tackling on equal terms any opponent.

The Commanding Officer wrote home: "Everyone is in top form. The young and newly-joined officers are now seasoned soldiers and good troop-leaders. Everyone is settling down. Henry Huth is absolutely convinced that his 'C' Squadron and the tanks are going to win this war! So I have my suspicions already where he will be when he should be waiting patiently in reserve somewhere."

Training was emphatically, if briefly, interrupted by Paddy's Day. This was celebrated by Squadrons. In view of conditions, an almost phenomenal amount of liquid refreshment was obtained. The best that can be said is that the tempo of festivities rose to an accustomed frenzy to the astonishment of some wide-eyed and wide-eared American 'cousins', singing and kindred sounds continued round bonfires; while the worst that can be said is that they lost their football match against the Ulsters to the tune of 4-1.

(d) The Ulster Crossing, March-April 1951

AT the end of a month the Brigade went forward from Suwon to Yongdongpo, preparatory to moving over the Han and taking a place once more in the line. 'C' Squadron moved on March 23rd to their old haunt on Seoul airfield where they had been for Christmas. Life became very tedious with nothing of interest to report save the discovery of a minefield some five hundred yards from their leaguer area. "This never-ending period of inactivity is really too depressing," reads an entry in the 'C' Squadron diary. "We begin to wonder whether we shall ever fire our guns in anger again." They also had a company of R.O.K. soldiers attached to them for training and found them alert and very bold. Their Commanding Officer had been in the Japanese Army for seven years and they were glad to be fighting with and not against him. During exercises with tanks giving supporting fire they did not mind when the shells fell close in front of their feet.

There was a good deal of inter-squadron rivalry too as 'A' Squadron demonstrated to 'C' various trials they had undergone with their Centurions, and they would have had to have been pretty near perfect to have escaped the pungent comments made by the onlookers. Of the demonstration of how to retrieve a bogged tank from a paddy field, all 'C' Squadron noted was that it took so long and appeared to be so impossible to bog it down that the watching Infantrymen would be firmly convinced that Centurions could go anywhere. When 'A' Squadron demonstrated hill-climbing the best that could be said about them by 'C' was that if it was true that one learns from other people's mistakes, then the morning was certainly not wasted. And that when 'A' Squadron supported the South Koreans assaulting a hill, at least the South Koreans were extremely good. However, really these demonstrations were a great success from the point of view of the high-ups and proved that the Centurions were a first class tank.

The rumours, however, that kept coming in were not so reassuring. There were reports of huge enemy forces massing on the 38th Parallel and prisoners said they would attack on April 11th with a thousand planes in support. There were also rumours of giant Russian tanks, the sixty-ton Josef Stalin, which mounted 90- or 105-mm. guns.

At this time the North Korean troops were almost entirely supplied by coolies who used 'Jikkays', an 'A' frame wooden carrier that enabled these men to carry up to five hundred pounds weight normally, and about two hundredweight across country by night at about one and a half miles per hour.

Also their most favoured method of attack was by night with infiltration behind our defended positions. Bodies of troops would find a soft spot in the defences and creep through at night, lying up behind the lines until the main attack started, usually an hour before dawn when they put in a determined attack from the rear, overrunning gun positions and Headquarters, and also building road-blocks behind the lines to cut off reinforcements.

On March 21st United Nations Forces entered and occupied, without firing a shot, Chunchou the former Chinese base, about eight miles south of the Parallel. It had been subjected to very heavy aerial bombardment. At the same time South Korean troops were reported to have advanced to within about the same distance of the Parallel on the eastern sector. On the western side, north of Seoul, however, the enemy were putting up a stiff resistance a little south of the Parallel, while in Washington Mr. Acheson stated that to cross it United Nations Troops would need fresh permission.

It was in March that the 8th Hussars were detailed to guard the British Legation in Seoul, which stands next door to the Anglican Cathedral of Seoul. In their off-duty moments the guard tidied up the damaged cathedral and the looted house of the Bishop, who himself was a prisoner-of-war. In the Bishop's garden one trooper discovered a damaged crucifix, bearing on its mother-of-pearl face the date 1641. The Commanding Officer decided to have it repaired and eventually restored to the Cathedral as a Regimental token memorial of those killed with the Regiment in Korea.

On March 23rd American paratroops dropped in the area Munsan-ni. The Regimental Bridge Laying Troop had been lent to their support column for this action, Lieutenant Hurst was in command of the Troop and during the operation he was blown clean out of his scout car when it struck a mine. Returning as a 'walking-wounded' case, he called on 'C' Squadron for a glass of brandy and was assured that the delayed reaction to a mine explosion was similar to that of an atomic bomb. The same day a 'B' Squadron Carrier ran over a mine in the main street of Seoul and Troopers Costello and Wilmott were killed.

There was, on March 24th, a rather grisly task to be performed, when a volunteer party was sent north to search the area where 'Cooper Force' had fought, to find and bury the bodies of those killed in the Battle of Happy Valley. Major Nelson, Captain Roffey and the Regimental Sergeant Major were the prime movers behind this grim task in which they found and buried some fifty-three bodies. One of the few they were able to identify was that of Captain Astley-Cooper, the first knowledge they had that he had been killed and not taken prisoner. Of Lieutenant Alexander there was no sign, only some old letters of his lying in a paddy field near his tank. Sergeant Rowley was another one identified, the rest were Ulsters and Artillerymen. They were all buried in a big grave on the hill overlooking the battlefield, and the Regiment ordered a stone memorial to be made, in conjunction with the other Regiments, to be put up near the grave. As always the men were simply splendid, and carried out this grim task in true Regimental style.

Easter Sunday saw the squadrons still well scattered, Regimental Headquarters and 'A' at Yongdungpo, 'B' at Suwon, 'C' on the island in the Han river and 'B' Echelon back at Pusan. However things were warming up. Orders placing the 29th Brigade under command of the 3rd American Division were received in the last week in March, and the move was complete by April 5th. 'B' Squadron alone took part in this, as higher policy only permitted one squadron of Centurions at a time, north of the Han. They crossed the river on March 31st and went into reserve on the northern outskirts of Seoul in the Forestry station.

The new sector, in which a memorable piece of history was to be written, lay to the west of the main Seoul-Uijongbu-northward highway. Brigade held the left wing of the Division, and on the Regiment's own left was the 1st R.O.K. Corps, who had the best name for steadiness among the South Korean formations. The sector was, at first glance, a promising one for defence, but in fact required a minimum of three Brigades instead of one. The basic topography gave them an area of steep hills, looking down over the strip of comparatively flat country which lay between their forward positions and the Imjin river, looping across the front from east to west at a distance of three to six miles. At the centre of this area, the giant peak of Kamak San rose and glowered down on the lesser ridges and intervening valleys which composed the territory. Well might it glower, for it was to occupy an ominous place in their lives in the none too distant future.

But basic topography does not go far towards explaining the position and problems of the 29th Brigade in its new rôle. The country was almost untouched by civilisation, and its recent introduction to the tanks and transport of a modern army had destroyed what so-called roads existed beforehand. Recent heavy rains had turned the valley floors into quagmire country, through which lay narrow tracks that would disgrace a Sussex farm in February. Even jeeps were hard put to negotiate the deep ruts and crumbling shoulders which conditioned every yard of progress, while heavier vehicles pitched inextricably into the flooded paddy on either side.

Into this district, then, moved the 29th British Independent Brigade Group under Brigadier Brodie. At the beginning, the Sappers had a more active and significant mission than the Infantry. They toiled manfully and effectively to improve supply routes to the front line units. Two main valleys twisted northwards through the hills; at the top of the western and narrower valley the Gloucesters took up their positions. Their route was only a jeep-track, not wide enough for trucks and later to prove impassable to tanks. The Gloucesters were usually supplied by passing trucks up the Ulster route, and across the front of the Brigade. At the top of the eastern and slightly broader valley, were the Ulsters. The Northumberland Fusiliers held some heights to right of the Gloucesters, and these could also only be reached up the Ulster's supply route.

The ordeal and glory that lay ahead for the Gloucester Battalion can hardly begin to be understood by those who have not stood where they stood and battled, facing to every compass point, or followed each yard of the road that lay behind them. Here it must suffice to say that their road climbed and fell through a valley which, along most of its length, was a gorge, in which only jeeps could move, crossed at frequent intervals by weakly-embridged torrents of mountain water, and over-hung at every turn by frowning, naked crags and precipices.

It was believed that the strip of low-lying country south of the Imjin was clear of enemy. Probing patrols confirmed this, and Battalions moved Companies on to features overlooking the river, and incidently over the 38th Parallel just beyond the river. Patrols crossing the river proved that enemy *were* in position there. With what determination they held their ground was still in doubt, and tanks were essential for the next development.

So far 'B' Squadron, commanded by Major W. G. O. Butler, had been held back in the Han river area, since the roads were in no state to bear Centurions, and the Infantry had no task for them. But as the roads improved with the better weather and the work of 35th Field Squadron, the importance of armour came to the fore.

There was one road which, though of no service to the Infantry, could be used by tanks. It was the road which led from Munsan-ni on the Seoul-Kaesong highway (far over to the west, in the R.O.K. sector), extended along the Imjin, and crossed the whole Brigade front, well forward of the main Battalion positions. For much of its course the route lay close to the river, and therefore in sight and under the fire of the enemy on the north bank. It was believed that the enemy would have no weapon capable of quickly engaging and knocking out a Centurion, and so, on April 3rd, Lieutenant Benson's and Lieutenant Wolfe's troops, under command of Major Butler, ran the gauntlet from Munsan-ni, coming under mortar and machine-gun fire along the exposed section of the route. This was replied to with 20-pounders and by gun-fire from the 45th Field Regiment, one of whose observer tanks accompanied them. The tanks took hull-down positions in the Northumberland sector and fired for two hours at targets across the river. They then returned to Munsan-ni, having been under fire for the first time, "good battle inoculation", the Commanding Officer said. Lieutenant

Major George Strachan's tank firing from Yongdungpo across the River Han at enemy tanks in Seoul, February, 1951 (page 267).

The result of the above action. A direct hit by Major George Strachan at 3,500 yards (page 267).

'C' Squadron firing upon the enemy who were entrenched on small hills to their immediate front. During this action Major Huth's tank was hit by an anti-tank gun (page 267).

'B' Squadron carrying men of the Royal Northumberland Fusiliers over the River Imjin during the advance of Lowther Force, April, 1951 (page 274).

'C' Squadron Day Harbour in the River Imjin area on April 22nd, 1951. The enemy were on the hills over-looking the harbour by first light the following morning (page 275).

The first day—moving out as the POL goes up, April 23rd, 1951. The enemy were firmly ensconced on the hill partly concealed by the smoke (page 276).

An 'O' Group on the third day of the Battle of the Imjin. Major Huth ('C' Squadron), C.O. and I.O. of the Belgian Bn., Capt. P. Hartwright (Regt L.O. at Brigade H.Q.) (page 280).

Sergt. Cole's and Sergt. Holberton's tanks after being knocked out by Chinese anti-tank grenades and sticky bombs in the same battle (page 282).

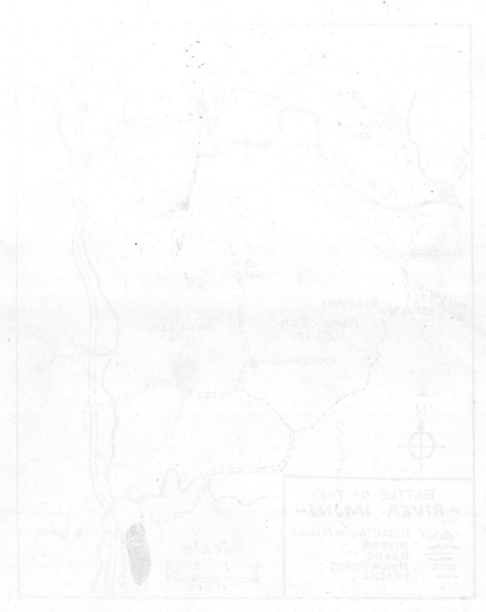

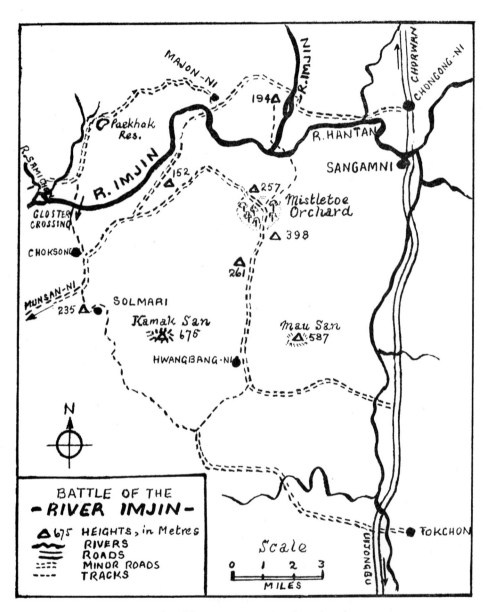

MAJON-NI

194△

R. IMJIN

Paekhak Res.

R. SAMICH

R. IMJIN

R. HANTAN

CHONGONG-NI

CHORWAN

SANGAMNI

GLOSTER CROSSING

152

△257

Mistletoe Orchard

△398

CHOKSONG

261

MUNSAN-NI

235 △

SOLMARI

Kamak San
△ 675

Mau San
△ 587

HWANGBANG-NI

N

UIJONGBU

FOKCHON

BATTLE OF THE
RIVER IMJIN

△675 HEIGHTS, in Metres
RIVERS
ROADS
MINOR ROADS
TRACKS

Scale

0   1   2   3
MILES

Map 8. Battle of the River Imjin, April 22nd–25th, 1951.

Benson's troop was delayed by the bogging of one tank, which had to be pulled back on to the road by an Armoured Recovery Vehicle from the 73rd U.S. Tank Battalion, kindly sent from Munsan-ni.

The following day it was agreed that the Squadron would take up permanent 'residence' with the Brigade. Consequently on April 5th the half-Squadron in Munsan-ni, led by Major Butler, ran the gauntlet once again, with no thought of returning by that route. This time they fared less fortunately, as one of Lieutenant Wolfe's tanks slipped off the road and shed a track in plain view of the enemy. The disabled tank came under mortar and artillery fire from across the Imjin. Wolfe, after initial recovery efforts had failed, brought back his crew under cover and then returned and cleared a jammed track but had to leave the tank still exposed until further help arrived. For his handling of this difficulty he was Mentioned in Despatches. Efforts were resumed in the evening under the direction of Captain Whitfield and later the Squadron Leader, but only next morning, no further fire being received, was the tank finally towed into safety and repaired.

Meanwhile the Squadron's second-in-command, Captain B. C. de las Casa, took the other half of the Squadron to a leaguer behind the hill of Kamak San, in between the now-famous Gloucester and Ulster roads. Here, the Ulster route to the rear having been made passable to tanks, the other half-Squadron joined him on April 6th. The Squadron then took up permanent leaguer well forward, in a grove of leafless trees at the top of the Ulster valley. This leaguer area was used hereafter by 'B' Squadron and subsequently by 'C' and 'A' in turn. It lay at the junction of the Ulster valley and the western river-road. Immediately forward of this, between the leaguer and the river, was some close, hilly country where an Ulster Company was established. The Belgian Battalion, which had just joined the Brigade, and to which Captain the Hon. Roland Winn was attached as British Liaison Officer, was at the time in reserve, and provided a platoon for local protection of the tanks.

The impending operation was to be a crossing of the Imjin by the 1st Royal Ulster Rifles in order to bring the Brigade front level with the American Brigade on the right. 'B' Squadron's task was to give fire support to the infantry during this operation. It was virtually impossible for the tanks to move off the tracks except near to the Imjin and on the drier paddy fields in the larger valleys running into the hills. On the Brigade front the banks of the Imjin were formed of cliffs about fifty feet high. The Sappers promised to construct approaches to the river so the next problem was the depth, and this could only be solved in the old-fashioned way. First Major Butler and later Captains Whitfield and de las Casas rolled up their trousers and waded through the icy, swift-flowing water, delighted to find many fordable places and a firm bottom.

Lieutenants Wolfe, Troughton and Scott each in turn took their troops across the river to support the infantry, but it was largely the terrain and not the enemy which gave trouble. During this time the Regiment became most proficient in close support work with the infantry of all nations. Thanks to the greater mobility and a superior wireless network they were able to co-ordinate the work of other supporting arms as well, such as the U.S. Air Force with their Sabre jets, the U.S. Medium Artillery and our own Gunners with 25-pounders and 4.2-inch mortars. Many of our officers actually fought with the Infantry as mobile fire controllers, an A.P. shot into a dug-out at long range immediately fixed the occupants so that tanks were much in demand.

The rough terrain limited the penetration of the infantry fighting patrols, so armoured columns with infantry riding on the rear tanks probed northward up the wider valleys. It was an odd sight to see the rearmost tanks completely covered with infantry, the

S

occasional man falling off as the tanks bounced over each bund between the paddy fields.

On several occasions the Regiment received a particular thrill when, in calling for air support, flights of Australian Meteors from far-off Japan, or Royal Naval aircraft from the carrier lying off Inchon gave them their personal attention.

A crossing was made on April 12th by a half-squadron of Centurions, under command of Captain Whitfield, who carried over two companies of Gloucesters, unopposed. Probes were carried out up two valleys, and no enemy showed their heads. The only casualties were the Squadron-Leader's feet after a punishing day spent in the peripatetic company of the Gloucester Colonel. The next day another, slightly deeper patrol, was also unopposed. On the 14th a larger patrol was made by half the Squadron with the Belgian battalion, who kept one company on the north bank of the bridgehead and worked four miles into enemy country with two others. There was some skirmishing, a brace of Chinamen were killed and one prisoner taken. This was the first time the Squadron had worked with the Belgians, and the result was pleasing for both parties. Co-operation had been excellent: the Infantry were impressed by our gunnery and the tank crews by the Infantry's quickness on to their objectives. Lieutenant Coldrey was especially remarked upon for his energetic and competent work as Forward Observation officer. On the same day Captain de las Casas went over with the Ulsters, when one of his tanks ran on to a mine and blew off a track. Recovery was speedily effected.

At this time it was learned with some surprise that General MacArthur had been relieved of his post and that General Ridgeway had taken his place.

On the 16th, a more comprehensive 'Armoured Thrust' was planned. The entire Northumberland Battalion passed through a Belgian bridgehead, established overnight, and penetrated nine miles, with no more excitement than a little light firing back and forth. The suspicion now grew firmer, that the Chinese were prepared to oppose the infiltration of unaccompanied Infantry patrols, but when the metal monsters appeared, they stood not upon the order of their going, but went at once. They slipped away into the dead ground behind their hill positions. Infantry winkling out silent bunkers discovered signs of recent occupation but never a tenant in residence. Thus the Squadron had to count for information upon the villagers, and although these were by no means bashful or reticent, their evidence was generally inconclusive. The merry waving of United Nations flags outlined their moral and political principles, but on statistical appreciation they were poor. In a language which required eight minutes to say "perhaps", battleground interviews of this nature were often more exasperating than instructive.

The Northumberland Fusiliers had by now been moved to fill part of the wide gap between Gloucesters and Ulsters. The heights they had previously held had been taken over by a widening of the R.O.K. sector's right boundary. But still in the Squadron's own sector, the scowling Kamak San remained unoccupied by any element of friendly troops. A Belgian reconnaissance party had reported that this feature alone had ample room for a Brigade position. The sides were steep, cover plentiful, and there was a spring of water within a hundred yards of the summit.

On the 20th April, a small 'Army' labelled 'Lowther Force' set out to sweep a system of valleys reaching eighteen miles into hostile territory. It consisted of the complete 'B' Squadron, the first half of 'C' Squadron under Captain Ormrod (which had just arrived in the sector to take over from 'B'), three armoured O.P.s (Cromwells), a section of Sappers and two companies of Gloucesters, the whole under the command of Lieut.-Colonel Sir William Lowther. At the main valley junction the 'Army' split in two; 'Basil Force' and 'Neil Force' thrusting respectively north and north-west. 'Basil Force' met no enemy. 'Neil Force' had a brush with some Chinese on a hill in which forty enemy were estimated killed or wounded. This operation was marked by the same characteristics as the earlier and smaller scale patrols: enemy elements were discovered, engaged and dislodged, chased along trenches and over the hills by Besa and 20-pounder fire. To all appearance and expectation, the country opposite their sector was held by no more than a flexible screen of observation posts.

On the morning of April 22nd, 'B' Squadron left the sector for the south and was replaced by 'C' Squadron.

At nine o'clock of that night, the Battle began.

At that time Captain Ormrod was speaking to the Adjutant of the Gloucesters concerning an armoured patrol that would cross the river next day. Distant firing was then heard from the direction of the Gloucester crossing, and the telephone line went dead. This was possibly the last telephone contact between the Gloucesters and the rest of the Brigade.

(e) The Battle of the Imjin, April 1951

THE 'Battle of the Imjin' has now been woven into the great tapestry of the Regiment's military past. It has confirmed the standards by which British soldiers in battle have been recognised through ringing centuries. The hard-fought fame of the Gloucester Battalion stands out, and has been justly honoured, above the rest. But our pride in them has been made warmer by the certainty that not only the Gloucesters, but any unit among us, would have stood fast and won the same high recognition, had the lot fallen otherwise. It was a time when each soldier, behind his more immediate thoughts and reactions, remembered how men had fought before in British ranks, and felt the stronger sense of purpose from it. And it must also be remembered that, in the first night and day of conflict, the Belgian Battalion, by their lonely and unfaltering action beyond the river, became more truly and integrally a part of our Brigade, than even those who knew and valued them most could anticipate.

Throughout the warp and woof of that epic encounter, the colours of the 8th Hussars shine with traditional brilliance.

The Centurions fought in terrain for which they were never built. 'C' Squadron, commanded at first by Captain Ormrod and then by Major Huth on returning from leave, took extravagant toll of the swarming enemy. Troops were committed to missions which entailed a certain cost of sacrifice, but missions that saved the existence of a whole Brigade.

The enemy attacked, as usual, by the full moon's light. During the first hours of battle, the tanks lay silent and immobile in their leaguer, lapped by the furious rolling of gun-fire in the hills about them. To their front, the road wound forward to the Ulster crossing, and the Belgians beyond. Before midnight the Battle Patrol of the Ulster Rifles had driven through from the rear, to occupy and hold their old crossing-place. When they arrived, a Chinese force had already secured it, strong in numbers and well dug-in. Some of the Battle Patrol were driven off, and some made captive. From that hour the Belgians were fighting with the bridge behind them in enemy hands.

At first light on the 23rd, the gun positions of the 45th Field Regiment, on the flat ground to the left of 'C' Squadron, were under rifle fire. The enemy had crossed the River in great force. All the forward Battalions, Belgians, Northumberlands and Gloucesters, had been fighting throughout the night, and one Northumberland company had been forced off a hill, which immediately dominated their Battalion Headquarters and the three batteries of field guns. The guns were firing over open sights at enemy on the hill, and Lieut.-Colonel Foster of the Fusiliers, rudely driven from his foxhole, had come back to Squadron Headquarters at 4 a.m. to ask for tank support.

At a quarter past five, with barely light to steer by, three troops of tanks left leaguer under Captain G. Murray, with the two tasks, one, of supporting the Fusiliers counter-attack to recapture the hill dominating the gun lines, and, two, of extricating 'Y' Company of the Fusiliers from their position in a northward loop of the river, which was now well forward of the precariously-held line, but had so far been more or less ignored by the enveloping enemy force. Captain Murray, leaving one troop to assist in the counter-attack, himself led the way into the threatened loop.

Meanwhile Captain Ormrod, who was in the centre of the valley and had heard from Murray that the Recce carriers were in the village and in sight of 'Y' Company, heard heavy firing from the leaguer area. He dashed back in his scout-car to find Sir William Lowther, on his feet, shooting the Northumberland Fusiliers on to the hills overlooking the leaguer with four tanks and some bren guns. The Fusiliers had hardly gained these hills when a Regiment of Allied gunners, who were just pulling out of the Gun Area, opened fire on to the hilltops with some machine-guns, causing the Fusiliers to withdraw quickly with losses. This tragic affair caused the valley to be untenable through the loss of the hills and also severely lowered the morale of the Fusiliers.

One of the Carriers, clearing mines, had been brewed up near the village and it was reported that the crew of four were pinned down under small-arms fire. Two Troop tanks moved around, searching in the ditches, and soon all four men were inside the turrets. Lieutenant D. Boyall was instrumental in their rescue as he had spotted where they had gone to ground. Lieutenant J. Venner, commanding the Carrier Troop, then reported by W/T that he and Sergeant Rowan would first evacuate the wounded and that a troop of tanks must be sent north of the 'Y' Company position to cover their withdrawal. Captain Ormrod called forward Three Troop to pass through One and Two Troops and then to climb over the 'Y' Company hill. While they were doing this the rest of the force thoroughly smoked the sides of the valley with two-inch smoke and some 20-pounder smoke to cover the transportation of the wounded to safety.

Everything then went quiet and whilst Lieutenant M. Radford of Three Troop shepherded 'Y' Company, Captain Ormrod looked for a route to the Gloucesters, still fighting hard some miles to the west of his position, but found a deep ravine cutting the flat ground between the river and the hills, an impassable tank obstacle.

By now Three Troop had alarmingly disappeared completely out of sight behind a hill, and soon 'Y' Company came streaming back, a very relieved body of men. They threw themselves and their equipment on the back of the tanks for a taxi service to safety. There was a little small-arms fire and considerable ill-aimed mortar fire from the thwarted enemy but the tanks soon had 'Y' Company out of it.

With 'Y' Company now in safety, Two Troop was left plugging off the end of the valley from the western approach of the enemy, and covering the withdrawal of the 45th Field Regiment with their 25-pounders. One Troop covered the northern hills now strongly held by the enemy who were in the rear of the Belgians. Frequent and good-natured calls for help were heard from Captain Winn, anxiety creeping into his voice as the day wore on.

The Ulsters had meanwhile been brought up to take over the east side of this north-south valley, and fresh tasks were to be assigned to the tanks: one of them being to race up the westward arm of the valley, moving behind part of the enemy's force and reaching the Gloucesters along the river-road. This, however, was far too difficult to attempt without Infantry support or with less than a full Squadron, which could not be spared, and Captain Ormrod therefore asked the Commanding Officer to see they were not ordered to undertake this task.

The Chinese had by this time forced a wide passage between the Northumberland and Gloucester positions, were in full possession of the hills on either side of the westward valley and, worst of all, had established themselves on Kamak San, the dominant mountain. Desultory firing continued, but in general the enemy were content to hold their present gains in this sector without provoking the armour; they were clearly not aware of our weakness in every arm. The main attack was still being pressed against the Belgians to the north and the Gloucesters in the west, both out of reach of our support. All efforts to take the much-battered Northumberland Hill had failed, and the tanks, together with the O.P. Troop of the Gunners under Major Howe, were now lying in the valley between the Northumberland and Ulster forward localities. There was a rumour that at about 3 p.m. an American Force was to try to force the pass and go on to rescue the Belgians, who were being now supplied by helicopter and beating off all attacks with great fortitude, but there was no sign of them.

However at about 6 p.m. the Yanks swept up, their Commanding Officer with a very clear idea of what he wanted. There were the silent ridges, the Centurions would cover them with fire and smoke for ten minutes, then his own medium tanks would seize and hold the actual pass whilst the infantry shinned up the hill-sides. All would be over in a brace of shakes. Captain Gorman, Royal Australian Armoured Corps, as Liaison officer would keep the two forces tied up.

'C' Squadron understood this refreshing language and they set every hill-top ablaze. The American tanks thrust boldly forward. But where were the infantry? The Liaison officer said: "Pinned down by enemy fire," but from where nobody knew. Things slowed down, it was after 7 p.m., the pass was dark and uninviting. Last light was in ten minutes time. Captain Ormrod apologised to the Colonel commanding the American tanks and asked to withdraw his support. The Colonel also thought better of it and withdrew his force.

The Belgians, at about the time the Centurions withdrew, had fought their own way out in a miraculous fashion to the east, and were in action again two days later. The Squadron prepared to pull back to a new night leaguer area when Captain D. Holmes of the Sappers came up the road, with orders to destroy some bridging equipment near the old Northumberland Headquarters, overrun early that morning. Two tanks accompanied him up the darkening valley, and stood by while the destruction was carried out. It was with some relief that Captain Ormrod saw four bonfires blaze up and heard the tanks returning.

'C' Squadron then withdrew south down the valley to their new leaguer, two miles behind the forward positions, where they found Major Huth who had flown back to his Squadron from Tokyo.

By the next day the increasingly desperate plight of the Gloucesters dictated that all possible effort should be made on their account, and Major Huth led half his Squadron into the southern end of their tortuous valley. The Gloucesters were now completely surrounded, and their position dominated by fire from the lofty Kamak San to their east and rear. Airstrikes throughout the morning had failed to dislodge the enemy from there, and a party of Gloucester prisoners who escaped their guards during one of these napalm attacks, brought back evidence of the numerous Chinese force now in possession. With the Centurions, a Philippino Force was to attempt to clear the hills flanking both sides of the valley behind the Gloucesters. Major Huth's tanks were to break through on the road itself while Philippino Infantry kept level on the hills and re-established the Battalion supply route. The first part of the operation went well, against light opposition, but the Infantry made slower and slower progress on either side. The narrow, twisting road presented extreme difficulty to the Centurions, and the whole advance was brought to a halt when the foremost of three Philippino light tanks, which were leading the column, was knocked out, blocking the road to all vehicles behind it. The second Philippino tank failed to push it off the road, and the armoured column of about ten tanks then reversed over one mile before they could clear the defile and turn off the road. The Infantry also abandoned the undertaking.

Captain Ormrod remained in command of the other half-Squadron operating in the same area as the previous day. At six o'clock in the morning an early call for help was received from the Northumberlands at the northern end of the valley. Throughout that day and the next, tanks were in perpetual demand, invoked like guardian angels, at every point of threat and crisis.

Captain Ormrod led his half-Squadron up to the Northumberland Headquarters, where Lieut.-Colonel Kingsley Foster explained the situation as it stood. His Battalion, holding the left side of the valley, had been forced off their former feature during the night, and wished to retake it, as fire from it was embarrasing one of the Companies on another feature. On the east of the road, opposite the newly-captured Northumberland hills, Ulsters were strongly defending another high feature. Captain Ormrod's plan was in two phases. First, he would move his tanks well forward into the open, beyond the mouth of the valley, and fire back on to the new enemy position, kill as many as possible on the north face, set the hill on fire, and force the Chinese to congregate on the reverse slope, where they could be engaged from the Fusiliers' positions and by a 25-pounder concentration, brought down by the Gunner Observer Tank. On the success of this, the second phase would be an Infantry attack on the shaken enemy still holding the position, supported by the guns of One Troop, while the remaining tanks took the enemy in the rear. The first phase achieved its full object, but when it came to the assault the Infantry were too tired and too shaken themselves to undertake it. All enemy fire from the captured hill had, however, been silenced, and remained so throughout the day, until dusk. Captain Murray was in immediate command of this operation, in which the tanks had to expose themselves in open ground, without Infantry protection, for two hours.

By mid-morning a strong enemy force in possession of Kamak San, which was bringing fire to bear on the Gloucesters in the west, was also menacing the supply route down the valley behind Northumberlands and Ulsters. The enemy now dominated all and occupied much of the high ground between the two main valleys, and with all his forces committed Brigadier Brodie had no means of counter-attack.

A re-disposition of the Centurion Troop in the east valley was therefore necessary. Captain Murray was left holding the north of the valley with four Centurions and a Gunner Observer tank. The remaining troops were posted at tactical points down the road to keep it open at all costs. Cornet Venner and his Recce Patrol moved up and down the road between these points.

In the early afternoon enemy movement was increasing on the western ridges, and sniping at transport began at a point two miles back from the Battalion positions. This was dealt with effectively by a fighting patrol from the Reserve Company of the Ulsters, supported by the tanks of Three Troop. As light was fading, fire opened again from the former Northumberland Hill, which had been plastered by both tanks and artillery in the early morning. Captain Murray picked out on the hill-side what appeared to be some fresh bushes. He fired, and as many bushes as were able ran over the crest!

Captain Ormrod, who was back at Brigade Headquarters by now, reporting on the seriousness of the situation in the Pass, was told that at daylight the next morning an American Brigade would be pushing through them, one Battalion to the east of the valley where there had been some infiltration, the other two Battalions just over the hills south-west of the old Northumberland Hill and then westward to the Gloucesters. A Regiment of medium tanks would sweep down the valley after the Centurions, then on to the Imjin and turn westwards, so trapping all the enemy. This sounded fine in tired mens' ears and the Squadron left their infantry with confidence to what would obviously be a nasty night on lonely hilltops.

All tanks of the Squadron returned to night leaguer near Brigade Headquarters, the Troops having been in almost continuous action throughout the day. Owing to the difficulty of making arrangements there was no hot meal nor a wash for anyone, nor had there been for forty-eight hours. It is to be doubted if even the oldest soldier slept with much tranquility. But sleep was an essential, since everything indicated that the day to come would be the most gruelling of all.

It had been assumed that the Ulsters and Northumberlands, at the top of their valley, would be cut off during the night, and with daylight, the Centurions would have to break a way through to them up the road. Activity, in fact, began earlier than was expected. At half-past two in the morning, firing was heard not far north of Brigade Headquarters and the Squadron Leaguer. The Reserve Company of the Ulsters was under heavy attack by Chinese who had come down from the Kamak San. The attack was held off, but the Company remained under scattered fire with the tanks in earshot but immobilized by darkness. At five o'clock they moved out of harbour under Captain Ormrod, but were held up by a thick ground mist blanketing the roads and ridges. As the mist melted, they passed on up the road through fire directed at the Ulster Company. They were carrying a Troop of Sappers under Captain Holmes, acting as Infantry for the day, and they were to play a noble and effective part in the day's engagement. They and Lieutenant Boyle's troop were dropped off to remain with the rearmost Ulster Company and to keep the road open at that important point. The rest of the tanks, comprising Three Troop under Lieutenant Radford, two carriers, Four Troop under Lieutenant Hurst and the command tanks of Captain Ormrod and Captain Murray, continued north. Radford in the leading troop, came under very heavy, accurate mortar fire. The column was ordered to close down hatches and press on, but due to the lingering fog all periscopes were misted, and two tanks of Three Troop went off the road into the paddy. The first stopped, sensibly, and awaited a slackening of the fire. But the second plunged into further difficulty by throwing both tracks. In the steep, rocky country, with no accompanying Infantry, the tanks were open to close range attack and there were perhaps two hundred enemy in the area of this steep bend. One Chinaman leapt out from a ditch and threw a sticky bomb against the side of Radford's tank. It exploded, blowing a hole through the skirting plate, but leaving the suspension undamaged. Chinamen were now swarming among the rocks and bushes beside the road, but the closed-down tanks managed, by alert inter-support Besa fire, to shoot them off each other's backs and turrets. The enemy had clearly chosen this place as our death-trap, and stationed a determined unit to effect the Centurion's downfall. Captain Ormrod and Sergeant Reekie turned to offence so vigorously that they had the Chinese on the run, dodging apprehensively from cover to cover. A group of them took shelter in a nearby house, and two high explosive shells at fifty yards range accounted for the four in it. Lieutenant Radford meanwhile pushed on to the Northumberland Headquarters, where all were in ignorance of what the savage outburst of firing behind them signified.

The fight in the trap continued, where the biter was being bitten with some enthusiasm. Some M.T. drivers from the Northumberlands had arrived and lent ground-support to the clearing operation. The tanks of Ormrod and Murray and four others, aided by Cornet Venner in his scout-car, stood round, 'thrashing' the area with fire. Chinamen were crawling and scuttling for cover, and those who were able made their way into an irrigation ditch running down from the hills, and in this way placed themselves out of reach.

Lieutenant Hurst, who had been sent up the road, had run into more trouble and there was a brisk action, in which Sergeant Napier placed his tank in a spot from which he could blast the enemy, and here he created great slaughter. Captain Ormrod coming up behind, having quietened the trap area and posted tanks to maintain the status quo, dealt with some remnants of the new opposition. One Chinaman who dashed at him with a sticky bomb, he crushed under his tracks.

At about this time decisions were being made at Brigade Headquarters. None of the British Infantry Commanders were there, as they were all hotly involved with the enemy, and in fact each of their battalions had been cut off from Brigade during the night. The Gloucesters were now six miles away, out of touch and being pressed into an ever-decreasing perimeter. Brigadier Brodie, who, in the course of the campaign, had won the affection and loyalty of all under his command, was faced with the bitter prospect of losing almost certainly one Battalion, and possibly a great deal more of his Brigade, before the day's end. In a few words he outlined the situation, the main weight of the enemy's general offensive had been thrown against the Brigade front, passages had been forced between the Gloucesters and the R.O.K.'s on the extreme left, and between the Gloucesters and Northumberlands; in both places the enemy had penetrated deeply, and numbers of hostile soldiers were known to be on the hills behind the present Brigade Headquarters location. Major Huth was present at the conference, as was the Belgian Colonel, who had brought his Battalion round after their close escape, and placed it on a high feature to the south-west side of Brigade Headquarters, warding off attack from that direction. His troops had been in light contact during the night and reported growing activity. Firing could be heard from that quarter as the 'O' Group was in progress. The 65th American Brigade, with two Battalions and a powerful tank force, had formed up the previous night beside the Belgians, with the intention of counter-attacking at first light, clearing the ground ahead, freeing the Gloucesters and re-establishing the position. The counter-attack was launched, two hours later than planned, but after a short advance the architects thought better of it, and before long those units were somewhere to the rear, and largely ineffective.

This laid Brigade Headquarters itself open to attack, and the Belgian Battalion was heavily outnumbered in its protective task. Major Huth placed his one remaining Troop under command of Colonel Crahay, who had been ordered to pull in his Companies from the high feature, into the closer proximity of Brigade Headquarters. He would also be guarding the road junction through which the Ulsters and Northumberlands would pull out, before turning east towards the main supply route to Uijongbu.

The Brigadier had received and passed on orders for the Brigade to withdraw. Some American tanks were to attempt a new break-through to reach the Gloucesters, but not with any sanguine prospect of success. The Centurions were all fully engaged in the east valley, keeping it open for the Ulsters and Northumberlands.

At the top of this valley, Lieut.-Colonel Kingsley Foster, of the Fusiliers, had been placed in command of the withdrawal, and had formed a plan in consultation with Captain Ormrod. One of the hill features of his perimeter had been partially occupied by the Chinese during the night, and in order to evacuate his wounded and the forward Company, this opposition must be cleared. Tanks were to assist the Reserve Company in this task. The Companies would then withdraw in turn, followed by the Battalion Headquarters of both Ulsters and Northumberlands, followed by the Ulster Battalion. The tanks would withdraw last. Little local protection could be promised to them as the Infantry, after seventy-two hours of fighting, were in no state to do more than walk out on their own feet.

Despite the tremendous activity since dawn, it was by now only a quarter to nine in the morning. Captain Ormrod described the danger spots on the road, which were now 'covered' by tanks, but under continuous threat. Lieutenant Boyall, with the Reserve Company of the Ulsters two miles back, had perched his tank on a startling eminence and obtained an admirable field of fire. He and his Troop were in lively action against the Chinese visible on the foothills of the Kamak San, and so far had kept them at bay, and the valley open at this point. But now they had reason to believe the road had been cut behind them. Just forward of this position and protected by the Sapper Troop one of the bogged tanks was being recovered, under a fluctuating volume of fire, with Captain Murray superintending. This effort, thanks to Murray's sangfroid and determination, was crowned with success. He was wounded several times in the course of the morning, but was not evacuated until the afternoon, when the last elements were pulling out.

The withdrawal began smoothly, but presently interruption increased from the hills on the west of the road, which were teeming with Chinese. Pressure was experienced at various points on the road, tanks had to be strung out to meet it, instead of fighting in troops, and therefore became more vulnerable themselves as they could not protect each other.

There was then a very serious development. An identification panel was observed on a hillside immediately above and to the west of the Ulster Reserve Company and Lieutenant Boyall's troop, with considerable activity round it. This was taken to be the advance of the American Brigade, which might reasonably have been expected in that location, and a natural relief was felt. In fact the Brigade had given up their effort a full hour before. The panel and activity were being displayed by Chinese troops. This misunderstanding allowed them to approach dangerously close, without hindrance, until they could be properly identified and fire opened. They had gained valuable ground, from which it proved impossible to eject them.

Most of the Northumberlands had already withdrawn, Lieut.-Colonel Kingsley Foster following in his jeep. At the pass he was strongly advised by Captain Miller, commanding the Ulster Reserve Company, against going further down the road in a vehicle, but he felt confident and pressed on. He was killed a matter of minutes later by mortar fire.

The rest of the Fusiliers and the Ulsters were falling back towards the pass, the tanks covering them with continuous counter-fire against the enemy-populated hillsides, alas their ammunition was now threateningly low. Sergeant Rowan, with what remained of his carrier troop, was intensively engaged near the bogged tank, where the cauldron had come to a boil.

This was the critical hour, when the withdrawal, as planned, became confused, and decisions had to be taken rapidly, at many places, by the officer on the spot. A co-ordinated wave of Chinese swept down the hills all along the west of the valley. The closeness of the enemy enforced periscope-direction upon the tank commanders, and yet they must contrive to fight off the Chinese at every point. This attack was clearly due to be followed up by others, and there was a very realistic danger of all the tanks being cut off irrecoverably, by Chinese straddling the southern end of the valley. The Ulsters were now cutting over the hills to the west, making no attempt to follow the road. Captain Murray was ordered to destroy the second tank he had been trying to recover, and replied, "Much against the grain, I obey your order." He laid and completed the demolition, sheltering behind the Armoured Recovery Vehicle, which had moved into place for the purpose. From then on, minutes counted, to be carefully measured against yards. Lieutenant Radford, from the north, reported the enemy were all over the valley floor. Part of the Ulster Reserve Company, with the Sapper Troop, made off across the hills, and some mounted tanks for the dash down the now hostile valley to their rear. The rearguard to the British force was a troop of tanks under Lieutenant Radford. The road to the pass here being blocked by Chinese anti-tank teams, Captain Ormrod ordered the troop to work down across country, despite the danger of bogging down in the paddy. This they did, reaching the head of the pass and withdrawing through the position held by Lieutenant Boyall's troop and three Squadron Headquarters tanks commanded by Captains Ormrod and Murray. Unfortunately the Troop Sergeant, Sergeant Holberton, was lost when his tank went head-first into a deep dyke and spiked its gun into the ground.

Few of the latter survived. The tanks ran the gauntlet of treacherous ground and bomb-throwing Chinese. Two tanks were knocked out by sticky bombs. Infantrymen, packed thickly on the tanks, were falling off like swatted flies under the close-quarters fire. As the last tanks came through the Ulster Reserve Company position, Lieutenant Boyall was still poised like a mountain goat on his hilltop, and he and his troop were effectively picking off Communists on the slopes above the road, so that an area of relative calm existed on this stretch of the road itself. Captain Miller withdrew his Company rapidly and led the way east, though many of his riflemen chose to mount tanks. Captain Holmes rushed out to recall an outlying section of Sappers. From further back along the valley, the doctor, Captain Patchett, who had been working with great courage all day, treating and clearing the wounded in his half-track, was heard over the air to say, "I am about to be captured . . ." and a moment later, "I have been captured!" This was alarming as it was the first news of how bad the situation was further down the valley near Brigade Headquarters position.

At this point the voice of the 8th Hussars officer with the Belgians, Captain The Hon. Roland Winn, was heard, on behalf of their Colonel, requesting permission to withdraw immediately. The Battalion, which all day had held unfavourable ground, with enemy firing from the tall hills above them, were now in acute danger from being cut-off themselves. They had been engaged with the Chinese to the south and south-west throughout, but as the valley they were protecting filled with enemy from another direction, they came under fire from the north-west as well. Two Companies were lying along a low ridge, with two of Lieutenant Paul's tanks among them and a third slightly behind. They held their own until heavy mortar fire, the bombs well grouped and accurately observed, began falling on and behind the ridge. At the same time an attack by about a Battalion was put in from the hill opposite, where the enemy were seen scrambling down the flank, and were heavily punished by the Centurions and Infantry. But the mortars thickened their fire, while the new elements on the ridge behind became more active. It was clear that in five minutes it would be too late to withdraw. But the Battalion's orders had been to remain until the last Ulster Infantry had come out of the valley behind them, when the Ulster Adjutant would inform the Belgians of this on the air. It was not known to anyone that the Ulster wireless had been lost over a precipice, and no possible contact now existed.

With little more than seconds to spare Winn learned through Major Huth that the Ulsters had changed direction and cut over the hills, and at the same time he observed Ormrod's tanks emerging from the bottom of the valley. The Brigadier gave permission to withdraw, and the Belgians and Two Troop pulled out, firing 'over their shoulders' at the oncoming Communists. One of the tanks stuck in reverse gear and crawled backwards at considerably less than walking pace. Major Huth, when informed, gave permission for it to be destroyed, but the Belgian Colonel said, "No, no—we must look after it as long as we can!" The rate of withdrawal was slowed to keep pace with the lame tank. In another eight hundred yards the column from the valley and the Belgians had reached the tanks' night leaguer, where Major Huth had been waiting, and all tanks came under his direct orders.

Ormrod's tanks had forced their way down the last lap of the valley through milling masses of Chinese. They could see what was estimated at 2,000 or more, swarming down the western hillsides, from the heights where they had been held back all day. The Centurions came through, crushing enemy under their tracks. Sergeant Cadman found one battering at his turret to get in, and directed the tank straight through the wall of a house, to brush him off, and then ran over a machine-gun post beside the road. Cornet Venner, who had behaved with great gallantry at every stage of the three days of fighting, lost his scout-car, but guided one Centurion out of trouble, and escaped, wounded, himself. Ormrod was wounded in the head by a grenade. Three platoons of enemy infantry suddenly appeared, in parade ground order, out of the river bed, and were blown to confusion with some of the last ammunition the tanks carried. Some tanks took to the paddy fields and were ploughing-in Communists, crouched under every bank. The firing was a continuous iron rain on the outside of the tanks, and only a small proportion of the Infantry on the top survived this death-ride. Ormrod went round the wet paddy-field where Murray was stuck, paused to pick up Murray and his turret crew, and hurried on through a small village and over two enormous dykes where a tank would normally have stuck. A little more than a year before these officers were learning the way to cross country with the Fernie. It was during this dash that Captain Miller of the Ulsters was killed. The tanks came out of the valley to see the Belgians leaving their ridge, that all day had guarded this southern opening.

Momentarily, contact with the enemy had been broken, but no more than a short breathing space was to be vouchsafed. The Ulsters and a few Northumberlands who had cut across out of the valley, were now scrambling across the hills to the main supply route. Most of the Centurions, loaded with dead and wounded infantry, with their ammunition exhausted, were ordered to drive straight on past the place where the tanks of the Squadron Leader and Lieutenant J. Lidsey, of Regimental Headquarters, were posted.

The full importance of Ormrod's force had not been foreseen in the morning's planning. Their mission had proved vital, and without their presence in the valley, their skilful management, and the courage of the crews, the whole of the Northumberland

and Ulster Battalions might well have been overrun. But the most distinguished single action of the day still lay ahead.

It began with disaster. When the tanks of Paul's troop came in, behind the others, to the area of the night leaguer, they were halted, and an effort was made to tow the lame tank, so as to accelerate the speed of withdrawal. As this was being done, bullets began to sweep through the trees and enemy appeared on the nearby hills. A stray bullet hit the phosphorus grenade in one of the open dischargers on the front tank, and ignited it. The burning phosphorus foamed out, and the turret was so traversed at the time that it flowed into the engine setting the whole tank on fire. The Belgian Colonel, who was standing beside this tank, was also badly burned and evacuated. With one blazing tank and one lame, Major Huth ordered that both should be abandoned, and moved his own up to put an armour-piercing shell through the turret of each, at fifty yards range.

He then traversed his turret left and engaged the Chinese at a distance of only seventy yards. As he engaged them over the back of his tank, he was aware that scarcely that distance behind him, the last Belgian soldiers were making their way through the trees. For three deliberate minutes he did not budge, but swinging his turret this way and that, firing long bursts of Besa while bullets smacked against his armour, he held down the advance; then, when only absolutely necessary, he ordered the driver to advance, *fast*. A hundred yards back, outside the grove where the leaguer lay, Lidsey was waiting, and the two tanks joined, and continued the delaying action as the Chinese came out from among the trees. Then, seeing over his shoulder that the Infantry had placed an acceptable distance between themselves and the enemy, they pulled back more rapidly along the road.

Within half a mile they came upon a new crisis. The Royal Ulster Rifles who had cut across the hills were coming down on the reverse side of them, to meet the road along which the tanks and Belgians were now withdrawing. They could be seen on the mountain crest, in a long, tired line, creeping downward and across the paddy, to the road. Some were carrying, some were supporting wounded friends, all had reached a state of desperate exhaustion. They wound down a rough track, and along a narrow bund over the paddy towards the road. At the point where it met the road, among a huddle of shacks, the space was crowded, for elements of an American unit were also grouped there.

Taking in this scene and situation, Major Huth ordered those tanks which had halted in the vicinity, to load first wounded and then unwounded men to capacity, take them to the main supply route, unload, and such of them as had ammunition left, to return to fight again.

A spotter plane flew low over the gathering and dropped a message, which was handed to an 8th Hussar officer. It said that a force of 2,000 enemy was approaching from the west, and could be expected to overtake these tired troops within ten minutes. In fact scattered fire had already been opened, and to protect the Infantry who had not yet reached the road, Major Huth and Lieutenant Lidsey, in the only tanks now available, had to move forward to meet it, and force back the leading enemy. This they accomplished, but only for a few minutes, before the enemy thickened and widened their advancing line. The paddy-country gave them admirable concealment for a close approach, and even the most intense alertness was hardly sufficient to watch every foot of cover and gauge the activity behind it. Slowly, in turn, the two tanks gave ground. Some straggling bands of Infantry were making for a point on the road further removed from the shooting and closer to the main supply route. On the road itself, the nearest Infantry were a hundred and fifty yards beyond the tanks and moving as fast as they could. The enemy came forward at a remarkable pace, taking up fire positions behind the banks, ignoring losses inflicted on them at every bound. From the turrets of the two tanks it was easy to observe, at a distance seldom greater than a hundred yards, and frequently no more than fifty, the losses suffered in the enemy's line. Major Huth so accurately measured his own fire-power against the fire and speed of advance of the enemy, that he imposed the minimum rate of advance upon them, allowing the Infantry precious minutes of extra safety. He was hampered by the presence of personnel on the outside of his own tank, but in the whole action, none of these was seriously wounded, and so far as is known not a single casualty was caused among the weary Infantry on the stretch of road in his rear. More American Infantry joined the column en route, and came under the protection of his two tanks. Two other tanks then returned to join him and strengthened the escort.

Before the withdrawing Infantry had reached safety, the power traverse of Major Huth's tank failed and it became impossible to bring fire to bear speedily where required, from the co-axial machine-gun. Fire was continued by Brens and other automatic weapons from his tank, and the enemy were still kept at a distance without the speed of retirement being increased. In many instances it was necessary to engage at right-angles to the axis of withdrawal. Not until the last Infantryman was seen to have reached the main supply route, where more powerful friendly gun-power was available to them, did Major Huth give orders to draw out of the enemy's reach.

Lidsey, whose tank was closer to the enemy throughout, showed an admirable coolness and bravery vital to the operation, in carrying out Major Huth's instructions. His humour and clarity of judgement must have set an inspiring example to his crew. But it was Major Huth's own example of skill and determination which made all those present in the action proud to obey his orders to the best of their ability.

The last shot fired by Major Huth ended the Battle of the Imjin.

The final day of the battle had caused the loss to 'C' Squadron of six Centurion tanks, one Cromwell tank, two Bren Carriers, one scout-car and one half-track. It is difficult to understand how the Korean Campaign can go down in history as a police action after such a battle."

(f) Pause to Gain Breath, April-September 1951

BRITISH losses had been grievous by any standard. Over a thousand men were lost in the course of only three days fighting. Nothing had served to save the Gloucesters, so at the end they were told to break out in individual parties. Four officers and thirty men came back a few days later. The night after the withdrawal, the battered, exhausted balance of the Brigade held defence positions north of Uijongbu, but were relieved before daylight, without further contact with the enemy.

They moved back to Yongdungpo, south of Seoul.

A new defence area was then assigned, on the Kimpo peninsula, the wide, flat wedge of land to the west of the capital, cut off from the mainland by the broadest stretch of the river Han. This was where, four months before, 'B' Squadron had prepared to support the Turks. Its main interest lay in the fact that it was the only piece of South Korea suitable to heavy tanks. And although the sadly-reduced Brigade could not expect to cope with a large-scale attack from the hostile territory across the river, those who came would have suffered great havoc and slaughter, once they arrived in the Regiment's 'killing-ground'. 'A' and 'B' Squadrons were in position there, carrying out recces to determine which sections of the peninsula were generally good going, and which had to be more carefully negotiated. The chief complications were large irrigation dykes, some filled with water, and built as if on the plan of deliberate anti-tank obstacles. Some of them were bridged, and a few largely unsuccessful controls were imposed, through the Civil Affairs Commission, to prevent farmers flooding their paddy in harmony with the season. This was one of the richest rice-growing areas in Korea, and some equation had to be made between military and agricultural necessity.

At about this time, news was received that the following awards had been made to the Regiment for gallantry during the Battle of the Imjin:

Distinguished Service Order	Major P. H. Huth, M.C.
Military Cross	Captain P. C. Ormrod
	Captain G. S. Murray
	Cornet J. Venner
Military Medal	Sergeant F. Rowan
	Trooper H. L. Bomber
Mention in Despatches	Lieutenant M. A. Radford
	Lieutenant Wolfe

On May 23rd Captain N. Whitfield was wounded when 'A' Squadron went across to an island in the mouth of the Han river.

Before very long the Regiment was on the move again. The Communist offensive, damaged irreparably by the fierce resistance of United Nations troops, among which the British had met the greatest wave and won the highest fame, had hardly advanced beyond the line where they broke contact. Now the enemy was giving ground again. After a few days of great comfort on the north-west edge of Seoul, the Brigade went forward to the identical section of the Imjin they had held before. But not quite identical, for this time two British Brigades were given what one had occupied before. The newly-arrived 28th Brigade, which had fought gallantly in its first action some weeks before, were their neighbours to the east, occupying the valley in which the fight had raged five weeks before. And into reserve behind them moved the Canadian Brigade. The 29th Brigade occupied the old Gloucester position and the country behind it, the Sappers with bulldozers very soon opened up a wide track through the fateful defile that had stopped Major Huth's relief column.

For the first time the three Commonwealth Brigades were geographically placed together. It was a fortifying feeling to them all. 'C' Squadron spent several days here searching their old battle area for casualties lost in April. Of war-like activity there was comparatively little in June. 'A' Squadron worked with the Australians and Canadians in crossing the Imjin at a new point, and led patrols out from the former Belgian position, against small opposition.

This time the Belgian Battalion was in the old Gloucester area, and some patrols were made over the Gloucester crossing, supported by 'B' Squadron. But the water at the ford had risen almost to the wading limit of the tanks, besides which several were damaged by anti-tank mines. 'A' and 'B' Squadrons also worked with the Northumberlands, Ulsters and the Kings Own Scottish Borderers and the Kings Shropshire Light Infantry. All the tanks lost by enemy action on the 22nd to 25th April were recovered except for one Cromwell and one Centurion which were total wrecks.

July saw the Regiment still in the same positions, 'A' Squadron with a troop with the Shropshires, 'B' with the Belgians and 'C' back at Kimpo. On the 3rd a memorial stone was unveiled in Happy Valley, where 'Cooper Force' was in action on the 3rd and 4th January, to the memory of the 8th Hussars and the men of the 45th Field Regiment, Royal Artillery, the 170th Mortar Battery, Royal Artillery and the 1st Royal Ulster Rifles who were killed in action there. A few days later 'C' Squadron took over from 'A' and still there was little or no enemy activity on any front.

In the middle of the month an operation that was more of a reconnaissance than anything else was carried out by 'B' Squadron and half of 'C'. The troops crossed the river at the Gloucester crossing but owing to a certain amount of enemy fire the objective, Hill 187, was not reached. The whole operation was across country as there was no road on either Battalion axis. Although the going was soft and difficult, the tanks did particularly well in climbing the hills and positioning themselves on the tops of important features.

Truce talks were going on at this moment and orders were given from Brigade Headquarters that only further advances that would not mean unnecessary casualties would be considered. As it was, one of 'C' Squadron tank commanders was wounded, as were some Belgians. Lieut.-Colonel Sir W. G. Lowther flew three sorties over the battle area in a light spotter plane, and had the recce been of a more forceful nature the information he sent back and the direction of units on to the best going would have been invaluable.

On July 28th the 1st British Commonwealth Division was formed and the Regiment left the 29th Independent Infantry Brigade Group to come under command. The occasion was marked by a church parade and march-past. The Regiment now came directly under the inspiring leadership of Major-General A. J. H. Cassells and instead of being part of a small force, to be used at the whim of a Corps Commander, a reliable stop-gap in time of emergency, and small enough to be forgotten during an offensive, they would be the armoured regiment in a Division which was to become the finest in the United Nations forces, and to prove that the forces of the Commonwealth could fight as one nation.

And still it rained and rained. It had done so now almost continuously for a month. The ground was completely waterlogged and the level of the Imjin rose from its normal four feet six inches to a raging torrent, twenty feet deep. Some infantry were cut off on the north bank. A building scheme was started, whereby 'bashas' were to be built over every tank and as living quarters for the crews. At this time the Regiment was still split up, 'A' Squadron in that old favourite 'Mistletoe Orchard', 'B' waiting to overhaul its vehicles in Seoul and 'C' at the bottom of the old 29th Brigade Axis.

In May, Lieutenants J. Browning and D. Martin went on an Air Attachment Course with the United States Air Force, to be relieved in August by Lieutenant Randle Cooke. They were sent to K-6 Airbase, situated outside Pyongtaek on the west coast, and twenty miles south of Suwan. All the pilots were American and the observers were drawn from the British Commonwealth and American Divisions, and, after brief training, on the observers part, were attached to two special operational squadrons, who between them covered the whole front. Their primary job was to direct fighters on to targets, and secondly to recce up to the bomb line. On September 15th Lieutenant Cooke and his pilot were shot down north-west of Chorwan. He could have been rescued by helicopter if the clouds had not been so low, but, just before the Regiment sailed in December, came the news that he was prisoner of war.

The advance across the Imjin from line Kansas to line Wyoming was in early September. The 28th Brigade, supported by 'A' Squadron, secured a bridgehead across the river and the 29th Brigade moved in on the left flank while the Canadians took over the right from the 28th Brigade. The only incidents of interest concerned Three Troop when, after a humorous buoyancy test on the Sappers' ferry, two tanks were blown up by mines within a few yards of each other on the landing beach. 'C' Squadron then came up to support the 29th Brigade, while 'A' moved across under the old Northumberland positions of April.

On September 14th half 'C' Squadron under Lieutenant Boyall took up positions so as to cover the advance of a Company of Northumberlands who had the task of occupying a hill feature. The Infantry reported seeing and hearing enemy tanks. 'C' Squadron was at a fever pitch of excitement. It seemed that a tank engagement might take place at last and they were wonderfully situated astride the key hilltops and ridges. From these positions they commanded all the lines of approach which could be used by enemy armour. Tank Commanders were suddenly gifted with second sight and were able to change bushes into T34's and shadows into well-camouflaged Josef Stalin tanks. One troop leader sighted a self-propelled gun but when engaged it miraculously changed into an ox-drawn honey cart at full gallop. The maximum number of enemy armoured vehicles reported at any one time amounted to eleven, this was gradually decreased to five, and lack of evidence of track marks finally dissolved the hopes and fears of 'C' Squadron and the Infantry respectively. The next day two tanks of Four Troop moved over the ford of the River Samichon to be with the Northumberlands, while the other two remained behind with the Gloucesters.

(g) The Battle of Kowang San, September-October 1951

By this time the Division was firmly established on line Wyoming. Patrols by day and night met opposition which varied in proportion to the size of the patrol and the depths of attempted penetration. As at all full moons everyone was alert and waiting for the Chinese sixth offensive. The crystal gazers were sure that unless it came by September 22nd it would not come at all. The reason for this assertion was that by this date the Air Force would have effectively sealed off the Chinese from their supplies. From that date onwards they would have to use those stock-piled for either offensive or long defensive action.

It would be helpful here to give a short description of the ground over which the next engagement was to be fought. Dominating the ground north of the Imjin is Hill 355, Kowang San, which in exactly the way that Kamak San is the key to the ground lying south of the river, so Kowang San is the key to the area north of the Imjin. The line Wyoming was overlooked by Kowang San, along whose southern slope ran a very important lateral road. This road joins Kunwahri with the main north-south axis running from Yonchon through Uijongbu to Seoul. It was down this axis that the North Koreans launched their main drive towards the capital in June 1950. The United States 70th Tank Battalion had some time previously patrolled in a westerly direction down this road. They had lost several tanks on mines, and more bogged in the paddy on either side. Little of any value was known about this area.

It was planned that 1 Corps should move forward and establish itself on Line James-

The 8th Hussars Fire Control Team during an action between American and R.O.K. Forces and North Koreans, April, 1951. Captain Gorman (Royal Australian Armoured Corps.) Lieut. Lydsey, Major Huth, and an R.O.K. Infantryman.

The back-door route to the position held by the Glosters during the Imjin Battle. It will be appreciated that the nature of the country made the task of the relief force, led by Major Huth, a near impossibility, April, 1951 (page 286).

Major Huth's tank hit by an enemy gun at 1,200 yards, February, 1957 (page 267).

Sergt. Reekie's tank and the R.N. Fusiliers' carriers at the corner where the Chinese laid a trap. Captain Patchett was captured here. You can see the marks of the 'C' Squadron tanks where they broke across the fields on the right (page 282).

In the Summer the paddy fields were nearly impassable to tanks. Tank Commanders and drivers had to display great skill. Room for manoeuvre in the valleys was limited.

Lieut.-Col. Sir W. G. Lowther, Bt., Commanding the Regiment, T.Q.M.S. Alfie Day and Major-General A. J. H. Cassels, C.B., D.S.O., Commanding 1st Commonwealth Division, July, 1951 (page 287).

Capt. Niel Whitfield's Recce of the Inchon peninsular ends in becoming well and truly bogged, May, 1951.

A Daimler armoured car of the Recce Troop damaged by a Chinese box-mine. A typical Korean main road.

town. In doing this they would deny to the enemy, positions prepared for either winter defences or offensive action. At this time 1 Corps was comprised of the 1st R.O.K. Division on the west, the 1st Commonwealth Division, the 1st United States Cavalry Division and the United States 3rd Division on the Corps' eastern flank. The 9th R.O.K. Division was held in Corps reserve. The Divisional plan was revealed early enough to allow time for thorough and exhaustive recces. Squadron Leaders together with Company Commanders toiled up hills, and Troop Leaders were invariably embarrassed by their infantry counterparts who always reached the top first. The very difficult nature of the ground necessitated all this foot work.

The big attack, Operation 'Commando', was to be in three phases. In phase one, the 29th Brigade, with 'C' Squadron and half 'B' in support, would feint on the west, prior to D-Day. In phase two, the 28th Brigade with the Regiment in support less 'C' Squadron, would attack on the right flank to secure Kowang San and Maryang San. Phase three would see the 25th Canadian Brigade, with 'C' Squadron, Lord Strathcona's Horse, moving up to Point 159 and forward on to the ground to the south, completing the new line. However, phase one was subsequently cancelled and the Regiment concentrated in support of the 28th Brigade.

The Brigade plan itself was divided into two phases. First, 'A' Squadron, under Major P. V. C. de Clermont, would support the King's Shropshire Light Infantry along the ridge from Point 208 to Point 210, and then push north to Point 227. The King's Own Scottish Borderers would capture Kowang San by working along the ridge from Hill 238. 'B' Squadron, under Major Butler, would support the Australians who were to capture Point 199. The second phase was the capture of Maryang San by the Australians, and Point 217 by the Northumberlands. 'B' Squadron would again support both these attacks.

Briefly, the armoured plan was as follows: 'A' Squadron, with the Shropshires, would attempt to go down the Infantry axis, while 'B' Squadron with the Australians would get tanks on to the top of the highest features, enabling them to shoot the Infantry on to their objectives. The ground here was too rocky for much manoeuvring with the tanks, and also so wooded that unless they were on a pinnacle it was impossible to see or to have any field of fire. Luckily they had plenty of time in which to prepare for this action and could make a detailed reconnaissance of the ground they were going to have to fight over, which as always, paid off.

'A' SQUADRON

October 3rd was fixed as D-Day. Heavy rain had fallen during the week before, the valley running between Points 238 and 199 was known to be almost bottomless, as was shown by the Americans who had left six Shermans bogged down there seven weeks previously. On D-2 the Regiment, less 'C' Squadron, concentrated east of the Imjin. This was done in the late afternoon, and fir trees from a wood a hundred yards away were cut down and replanted to conceal the approach of the tanks from the enemy on Point 213 and the hills to the north. It was very necessary that they should be kept unaware of forty Centurions on their side doorstep. At last light the next day half 'A' Squadron and half 'B' moved west across the river and leaguered under the final ridge. Divisional artillery, directed by the gunner observer in his Cromwell, brought down a stonk on Points 208 and 355 and kept up the noise as the tanks whined their way uphill. It is now best to split up and follow the fortunes of 'A' Squadron.

T

On D-Day the whole countryside was cloaked in a thick mist which lasted until 9.30 a.m. According to plan, by first light the Shropshires had gained Point 208, and at 6 a.m., still in heavy mist, 'A' Squadron moved to their support. Unluckily the leading tank of Two Troop, under Lieutenant J. Butler, was blown up on a mine as it was turning off the road, and the second was bogged while attempting another route. In case 'A' Company, who had reached Point 208 in the dark, should be counter-attacked, Three Troop, under Lieutenant W. Clode, was sent to try another route further to the south. They went some way along the ridge and then three tanks bogged down in impossible going, two with tracks off.

Meanwhile Butler, commanding Two Troop, did a foot reconnaissance over the paddy, and managed to get his other two tanks up a one in two climb to Point 208, six hundred and fifty feet high, and on down the ridge to the Kidney. Four Troop, under Lieutenant Hart, who had been supporting from a distant hill, were now ordered up to Point 208 and to work their way to the Pimple. This troop successfully made the hill, but the last two tanks threw tracks on a narrow defile over the path and blocked the way, while another tank broke its final drive.

By now, midday, 'C' Company of the Shropshires was meeting considerable enemy resistance in their attempt to take the high ground south of the Pimple, but Two Troop, with one tank perched on Point 208 and one half-way to the Pimple were able to give accurate and successful fire despite heavy enemy mortar and shell fire.

As the route by Point 208 was now out, One Troop, under Lieutenant Paul, was ordered to go down the road to the pass and try and work up to the top, west of the track. Paul, having done a foot recce up to the top himself under heavy shell-fire, succeeded in bringing his own tank to the summit. The second tank lost its tracks turning on the crest and the third bogged down in the paddy, attempting another route. Paul was then ordered to push on alone, and finally reached 'B' Company at the Pimple at half-past three.

By four o'clock the tank situation, to put it mildly, was discouraging. One Troop had one runner, Two Troop had two, Three Troop had one and so had Four Troop. Ten tanks were bogged, had tracks off or were mechanically broken, and in places where no lessons learnt at Bovington would be of any use. At the same time the Chinese on Point 355 were giving each and every one all they had.

All this time the Infantry were making progress, closely supported by the two tanks of Two Troop and by that of Hart of Four Troop who had got up by the pass. The Chinese were holding the ridge along its full length with deep emplacements, but on the whole the situation was in hand.

At this stage Lieut.-Colonel Barlow, commanding the Shropshires, decided that it was too late to attempt to take Point 210 that day. As every tank was carrying a carefully thought-out scale of supplies for the Infantry, Major de Clermont told Butler that he must reach the leading company at all costs. Among the normal things, such as ammunition and rations, water and batteries, there were twelve rolls of barbed wire and a stretcher on each tank. Butler reached his objective and the infantry were much elated.

There were now four runners on the top. There was no question of replenishment, or of bringing them down, they would never have got back again, so they were ordered to bomb up from the bogged tanks and draw into the nearest company locality. The crews of the bogged tanks were ordered to disarm their tanks, lock up and dig in with their Bren guns with the nearest infantry. By last light all were in, ready for any counter-attack, with the defensive fire tasks all tied up.

The British now held three of the intermediate objectives and, as the Squadron

Leader said: "Point 210 was on the menu for first light." At nine that night Colonel Barlow issued orders for 'D' Company to attack and capture Point 210 at dawn. All Divisional Artillery was to be made available from six in the morning to half-past seven. Butler was given command of the four runners on the ridge, and ordered to reach Point 210 "Come hell or high water as soon as he could see to drive." Clode, the sole runner from Three Troop, was to push down the road to secure the right flank, followed by the four tanks of Squadron Headquarters.

During that morning Captain G. Beith, the Medical Officer was killed by shell-fire near the Regimental Aid Post.

The night was quiet, no counter-attack materialising on any part of the front. At half-past four 'D' Company started to edge forward in the dark. At six, as soon as it was light enough to drive, Butler and the three remaining tanks moved west towards Point 210. It was a knife-edge drive, and misfortune came early when Corporal Hawkins in the last tank bogged and threw a track. It then became the Story of the Three Musketeers. Out of sixteen tanks the three troop leaders alone, Butler, Hart and Paul, were left in the hunt. With great determination and no mean skill on the part of both commanders and drivers, 'Allenby', 'Artist's Pride' and 'Abbotts Dream' crashed and cleft their way through heavily-wooded ridges of virgin pine, parting the trees like Wagnerian monsters, and pausing only for a foot reconnaissance or to pour death and destruction on to Point 210.

Finally they burst into the open, two hundred yards short of the objective, to crash high explosive into the bunkered hill top. The Infantry, who had been creeping along with them, descended into the dip for the final assault. The murderous effect of high explosive bursting in the trees just over the heads of the enemy at point blank range was soon apparent, but still the Chinese in their holes shot on. Then as the Infantry worked to within forty yards of the top, they called for the change from high explosive to Besa.

Immediately the roar changed to the crackle of machine-guns, and under an umbrella of tracered lead, 'D' Company, with bayonets fixed, swept up on to the hill. Within five minutes all three tanks were on the objective, eliminating the possibility of an immediate counter-attack. Fifty dead and dying Chinese lay on the top, and another fifteen gave themselves up. The Shropshires had only suffered fifteen casualties.

Meanwhile Squadron Headquarters and Clode of Three Troop had moved through the pass and down the road in the valley to the north of the ridge, with the task of securing the right flank and supporting the exploitation when the forces on Point 210 turned north. The time was now about 10 a.m. All objectives to the south of the road were clear and by 11 the King's Own Scottish Borderers had captured Point 355 to the north.

Pending the arrival of the Canadians to take over, Colonel Barlow was now faced with the somewhat unusual manoeuvre of firming-up Point 210, turning his battalion 90 degrees and exploiting north across his front with his objective, Point 227. Clode, down in the valley, was sent up a spur as far as he could get, while Squadron Headquarters, who could not afford to be bogged, supported from the road. At four o'clock Clode moved up the spur and was immediately engaged by a recoilless gun from the lower slopes of Point 227. Clode then 'went to town' and by close co-operation was able to direct his fire as called and successfully reduced the opposition. Fierce defence was again met however, as the top was reached, and the leading infantry had to be asked to pull back fifty yards so that a final stonking could be administered before the assault. Squadron Headquarters tanks were able to help in this, from the 'stage box' down on the road. The hill was finally carried in the failing light, and some dead and wounded were taken. The majority must have slipped off the back through the trees as dusk was falling. We had virtually to share the hill with the Chinese that night, and considerable shell and mortar fire was put down as it grew dark. Captain Meade reported himself engaging a tank or self-propelled gun, and his fire order was not repeatable. A steady and increasing crackle of small arms fire approached down the wooded slopes of the south side of the valley, but however no counter-attack materialised and the noise could only be attributed to some lost Canadians having a late night shoot into the enemy bunkers on the wooded hills above the valley.

(h) The Battle of Maryang San, October 1951

To revert now to D-Day, October 3rd, and 'B' Squadron. The night before, the Squadron Leader and Captain Wolfe joined the Tactical Headquarters of the Australians across the Imjin, while One Troop also crossed the river. On D-Day, as soon as the Australians had reached their first objective, Point 199, Four Troop, under Lieutenant Coldrey, moved up to join them. From here the tanks were able to shoot on to the northern slopes of Kowang San, Point 217, and round on to the main Australian objective of Maryang San, and also on to Chinese positions further north. Two Squadron Headquarters tanks on Hill 238 brought effective crossfire down on these same targets.

At first light Lieutenant Lidsey brought One Troop up into position on Finger and then tried to move forward to find a good position on Tongue. However the valleys running parallel north and south to Finger were extremely boggy, and Lidsey brought his troop back to his original position where he was able to do some excellent fighting.

Meanwhile on the left the King's Own Scottish Borderers were encountering fierce opposition on Long. Lidsey's and Coldrey's Troops were able to give good support by shooting up Kowang San in order to help them forward. Four Troop at one time caught the Chinese coming off the back of the hill and did great damage there.

Lieutenant Wood was put in command of a force named after him, comprising his own Three Troop, two American Light tanks, an American reconnaissance platoon and the anti-tank platoon of the 3rd Australians. Just after five on D-Day morning, 'Task Force Wood' moved up a tributary of the Imjin into a position from where they were able to protect the left flank of the 1st Cavalry Division. They were also able to shoot out the high ground north of Point 199. At night the Task Force leaguered where it was, with Squadron Headquarters on Hill 238, Four Troop at Point 199 and One Troop back at the F.U.P., defended by the Northumberland Mortar Platoon.

October 4th was not a busy day for 'B' Squadron, and the tanks which had remained east of the river, moved up to join the rest. One and Four Troops again gave help to the Borderers on Kowang San and Three Troop killed many Chinese in the same area. Major Butler and the Australian Command Post moved up on to the top of Point 199 for the night.

There was a thick mist on the morning of October 5th, and the position was that the Borderers were in possession of Kowang San, but the ridge from Point 217 running north through United to Maryang San was held by the Chinese. The Australians were given the task of taking this position, while the Northumberlands had to capture Point

217. They started off without any tank support as tanks could neither see to move or shoot in the heavy mist. This was in some ways compensated for by the concealment the mist provided for the advancing Infantry, and both attacks went well to begin with. The Northumberlands made the southern end of their objective, but could not take United, the feature dominating Point 217, owing to sustained and accurate machine-gun fire. This attack was not too well 'tied-up' as the tanks did not know the Northumberlands plan, and no officer had been to their briefing. The main effort that day was concentrated on helping the Australians, who, when the mist lifted, found themselves at the east end of the ridge running up to Maryang San via Baldy.

The Australians, to begin with, were slightly suspicious of 'B' Squadron fire, but with each shoot they gained more and more confidence, walking almost in to the concentrations at the end of the day. Keeping close behind the shells they moved up the ridge running from Maryang San. Baldy caused a certain amount of trouble, but on reaching it the Australians reported finding sixty dead. They stated they had killed about ten so the rest may well have been from the Squadron's fire.

The concentrations were then switched on to Maryang San, and at about five that evening the Australians assaulted and captured the peak. The only word that described them was 'magnificent'. They simply walked up the front, tossing grenades into holes, and seemingly immune from the enemy fire and mortars which were raining down on them. Once on Maryang San they were there to stay, and gradually collected the feature to the west as part of their perimeter. 'B' Squadron then brought down fire on United, from where the enemy were firing at the Northumberlands on Point 217, as well as the Australians on Maryang San.

During this time, on the left, a Company assault by the Northumberlands had failed to hold Point 217, which they had actually taken. But they were by then out of ammunition and eventually driven off by a Chinese counter-attack. They had suffered a good many casualties and so the attack was called off for the night. The Northumberlands withdrew towards Tongue, while Lidsey and One Troop evacuated the serious casualties on the backs of their tanks.

There was a fair amount of shelling that night, and most crews spent an uncomfortable time in their tanks.

Full tank support was given to the Northumberlands when they set off again next morning to capture Point 217. Again all went well to the south edge, and then the trouble started. From this point they were dominated by the enemy, dug in on United, and were subjected to a very intense mortar and artillery barrage. Despite 'B' Squadron's accurate and lightning fire and the full weight of the Divisional artillery, the ferocity of the Chinese fire in no way diminished. Twice the Squadrons blasted the top of Point 217 and the bunker just behind it, and United was stonked regularly but they were unable to quieten the Chinese.

It must have been at this stage that Lieutenant Walker, the tank observation officer who had been invaluable during the Northumberland attack on the previous day, was killed. Although 'B' Squadron were able to hear the Northumberlands on the wireless they could get no reply from them.

Twice, with great gallantry, they attacked Point 217 and got within twenty yards of the top, only to be driven back by pitiless small arms and mortar fire. The tanks were firing as close as they dared to the Northumberlands, and then accurate and sustained fire broke up two Chinese counter-attacks while they were in the process of forming up.

The Northumberlands suffered heavy casualties, and decided to call the attack off for the day. They had made a splendid effort, and it was through no fault of theirs that the attack failed. No one could have advanced through the merciless hail of artillery and mortar fire which fell on them.

They returned to their previous night's location, under cover of tank fire, and the tanks did likewise. It was another night of heavy shelling, and it was estimated that about six hundred shells fell in their positions.

It was decided the next morning that the Australians should try and capture Point 217 by attacking down the ridge from the north. This was to be done in three phases: first capture Pimple, then United, then 217. All these attacks were to be done under a tank barrage on the objectives. The Australians were to move right up to the edge of the barrage, and, as soon as the shooting ceased, assault the objective. Timed programmes were considered inadequate, and Major Butler took a wireless set up to the top of Mary-ang San where the Australian Colonel Hasselt was directing operations. The Squadron second-in-command Captain G. Strachan, was to control all fire from his position on the top of Hill 238. The scheme worked beautifully, although communications were often interrupted by the very heavy shellfire which was falling. Maryang San was a centre for their fire all day, and about three hundred shells must have fallen there.

The battle started at eight in the morning, and for ten minutes the Squadron fired intermittently from its position of the previous day. Then came two minutes of intense fire. The intensity of the fire may be judged by the fact that at times there were five shells from one gun in the air at the same time. All this time the Australians were edging forward to the front of the barrage. The 'Cease Fire' was given, and they went straight in. The leading two Platoons took Pimple without a casualty and began to consolidate. They found about fifty dead Chinese. As the reserve platoon moved up, the Chinese counter-attacked from the north, and hit the reserve platoon heavily, inflicting many casualties.

The tank fire then switched to United and plastered that feature. However the Australians decided they could hold Maryang San and Pimple but could not attempt the capture of United and Point 217. So the attack was called off, and a full scale one was planned by the Borderers for October 9th.

The tanks returned that night to their leaguer. The anti-tank platoon which was with Three Troop was called up to reinforce the Company on the Pimple, and Lieutenant Wood was slightly dubious when a section of the Brigade Defence Platoon under a Sergeant, turned up for his local protection with no water and no rations. However all went well, and no attack developed.

One amusing incident occurred with Three Troop, when during the day a Chinese turned up in their position complete with kitbag and bag of rice. He was most surprised to see Three Troop and thought it a poor end to his leave.

During the night the Chinese counter-attacked heavily on Pimple, but the Australians held firm, and in the morning they counted three hundred dead round the position.

That was really the last effort the Chinese made for the time being in that area. October 8th was a quiet day, and there was a great absence of shelling. The Borderers, who were taking over Maryang San from the Australians, sent a battle patrol over on to United and met no opposition. The Northumberlands put in a silent attack on Point 217 and took it without any trouble. As they reached the top they saw the Chinese gunnery observer, who had caused so many casualties and so much trouble during the previous days, scuttling down the far side with his wireless set, and put paid to his activities. This then was the end of the battle of Kowang San and Maryang San.

Although perhaps not a major engagement, it had been interesting from the point that the two Squadrons fought, in one small area, two totally different battles. 'A' Squadron went with the Infantry, in very close support. The country was terrible, but at least one tank arrived at the right place, although perhaps there were too many starters. None of 'A' Squadron's objectives were less than six hundred and fifty feet high, all were heavily wooded and bounded by snipe bogs at the base and the average ascent was one in two. The sight of a big tank lumbering along over ground which is thought impassable has a very sobering effect on the enemy.

'B' Squadron, on the other hand, sat back and shot the Infantry into their positions. They suffered in this battle from not having enough ammunition stacked on the backs of their tanks, as it takes many more rounds to support successfully an attack by sitting back than by going with the Infantry. Again was seen the importance of tanks remaining at night with the Infantry, and not drawing back to leaguer. Even one tank lifted the morale, especially when the Bovington-trained N.C.O.'s were able to get the football results on their wirelesses.

Although the 1st Commonwealth Division was now established on the Jamestown line, the United States 1st Cavalry Division on the right, had been less fortunate, and against stubborn enemy defence had suffered heavy casualties. Major-General A. J. H. Cassels, commanding the Commonwealth troops, received a letter from Major-General W. O'Daniel, the Corps Commander, expressing his admiration of the way in which Operation 'Commando' had been carried out and of the courage and skill of the men who fought in it.

On the completion of 'Commando', the 28th Brigade, with the 8th Hussars in support, were holding the general line, which included the road, Point 227, Point 217, United, Hinge, thence along the ridge to Maryang San, Baldy and on to the river.

The Regiment was sorry to see its friends, the 1st Battalion Royal Northumberland Fusiliers depart for Hong Kong. They had fought together in several stiff engagements and it was sad to see so many casualties only a few days before the Battalion left Korea.

(i) The Battle of Point 227, October-December 1951

FOR those who now expected a period of relaxation there was a rude and inconvenient awakening in store. The shelling which had commenced on October 7th maintained its monotonous accuracy and increased in intensity. In the Korean campaign shelling of this order was a new and unpleasant experience; the infantry had to build firmer bunkers and the tank crews found themselves doing much unwelcome digging.

The front was comparatively quiet from October 8th to the end of the month. The Infantry put down about thirty feet of wire in front of their positions and a minefield was laid across the whole front. 'A' and 'B' Squadrons prepared their vehicles for winter, while 'C' Squadron had the tedious task of training the new battalions of the 29th Brigade in co-operation between tanks and infantry. It had been found that the old Churchill A.R.V. was not powerful enough to pull Centurions out of bogs, so certain tanks had their turrets removed in base workshops and were known as 'tugs'.

During this period 'A' Squadron supported Shropshire patrols on the ground in front of Jamestown, and 'B' Squadron worked closely with the Australians, who by now had formed the habit of using the Centurion tugs to carry their defence stores up the hills. It was quite some time before it was discovered that packed under a thin layer of wire and trip flares was a solid layer of crates of 'Asahi' beer. The Australians insisted that this was an integral part of their defensive plan.

On Balaclava Day, October 25th, Regimental celebrations were much the same as always, China notwithstanding. At 10 p.m. the New Zealand Gunners fired a five-round salute to commemorate the ninth anniversary of el Alamein.

Earlier in the afternoon the Divisional Artillery had fired an 'Uncle' target in memory of the Charge of the Light Brigade. At a cocktail party given in the evening the Commanding Officer entertained, amongst others, Major-General O'Daniel, the Corps Commander, who arrived by helicopter. The Divisional Commander and Commander Royal Artillery were also present; Colonel McFalls, commanding their friends the U.S. 70th Tank Battalion, presented to Lieut.-Colonel Lowther, on behalf of his battalion, an American tanker's helmet and Armoured Branch scarf, and Lieut.-Colonel Lowther was made an honorary member of the 70th Tank Battalion, thus sealing the bond of friendship. A few days later the announcement was made of the immediate awards of the Military Cross to Captain R. W. Piper and Lieutenant J. Butler, the former for constantly endangering himself under accurate fire in his work of recovering broken-down tanks.

On November 1st a draft of ninety-two men from the 5th King's Dragoon Guards joined 'C' Squadron back at 29th Brigade Headquarters. The Skins were eventually to relieve the Regiment and these forerunners were welcomed with open arms and it did everyone a power of good to see their badge in evidence for the first time.

All was comparatively quiet until half-past three in the afternoon of November 4th, when, with the moon in its first quarter, the Chinese in Brigade strength attacked the Borderers on Hinge and Maryang San. It was a fine, warm afternoon, and most of the officers and the Commanding Officer were shooting the local 'A' Squadron coverts. The now famous attack was accompanied by the most concentrated artillery barrage so far experienced in Korea, and it was estimated that during four hours, sixteen thousand rounds fell on the Borderers positions. The last drive of the afternoon held more shells than pheasants, and the Commanding Officer's post-venal drink was shattered by a salvo landing in the campus.

The main attack came in on the Borderers from the west. A subsidiary attack on the Australians on Baldy and on the Shropshires on Point 227 came both from the west and north in greater-than-battalion strength at 5 p.m., with the object, according to a wounded prisoner taken the next day, of capturing Point 227 and then on to Kowang San.

As all communications to the Battalion Control Post were cut and Brigade Headquarters was not aware of the situation until 4 p.m., there was a disastrous delay in artillery defensive fire on selected points. Owing to the very intensive shelling on this sector and the presence of some elusive snipers, the defensive wire and mine-fields were not as thick in front of the Borderers positions as in other battalion locations. The mine-fields were soon exploded by the barrage, and the very little wire which remained was crossed at the expense of only the first wave of Chinese. They were killed or maimed on the wire by fire from their own side as much as ours, and the succeeding waves then availed themselves of the 'human bridge'.

By six that night, through sheer weight of numbers, the Borderers had been forced off Hinge, Maryang San, United and Point 217. It was during this defensive fighting that Private Speakman gained his Victoria Cross. By seven the situation was very serious, and the Shropshires on Point 227 reported that they were surrounded but holding out. Lieutenant Paul with One Troop, 'A' Squadron, on the Spur to the south-east, covered their targets with defensive fire and by midnight the attack was beaten off. The Australians were ordered to withdraw their left hand company off Baldy and link up with the Borderers. 'B' Squadron tanks on Points 238 and 199 fired over a hundred rounds per gun until it was too dark to shoot. Two Squadron Headquarters' tanks had moved up Hill 238 on to an ideal position from which to control the Squadron, and Lieutenant C. Troughton moved his troop down the road in front of Hill 238 in case the Chinese came on down the valley. Divisional Headquarters ordered the 1st Leicesters, who had been training with 'C' Squadron, to move from the 29th Brigade to the general area of Point 238.

At first light on the 5th an 'O' Group was held on Point 238 and it was decided that the Leicesters should counter-attack and regain Point 217, Hinge, and Maryang San. The original plan had been rehearsed by the Norfolks, supported by 'B' Squadron; but the Eighth Hussars were now faced with the task of trying to support a battalion which had only just arrived in Korea, which had never before seen the ground, the Chinese, or more important still, 'B' Squadron. This battalion was invited to attempt an attack which had proved too much for the Northumberlands a month before when we held the initiative.

Fourteen 'B' Squadron tanks gave the attack direct fire support, and in addition a troop was to work its way up Italy towards United, but the going was known to be pretty near impassable as there had previously been four tanks bogged near here during Operation 'Commando' a month beforehand. The Infantry were to attack Point 217 and United simultaneously, with one Company going along Crete and attacking Point 217 from the south, and another advancing up Italy towards United. An officer in a scout-car would stay at their Battalion Control Post to control tank fire. Alas, little did anyone appreciate how much the war had changed in the last twelve hours.

Although it was planned to cross the start line at midday it was not in fact crossed until one-thirty, which did not give sufficient time for the attack to achieve success.

On the right 'A' Company of the Leicesters managed to reach a point more than half-way up Italy towards United, and two tanks got to within about two hundred yards of United right into the Chinese forward positions, where they sat, coolly firing for two hours waiting for the Infantry to join them for the final assault. But that proved impossible against the terrific hail of enemy mortar and Artillery fire. On the left a Company of the Leicesters managed to reach Point 217, only to be shelled off it. The Chinese were holding the reverse slope and they counter-attacked down the ridge. Luckily these were seen coming in by the two tanks still on Italy awaiting the Infantry, and they had a real field day at close range.

It was now half-past four and the Leicesters were ordered to withdraw. Seeing this the Chinese charged down from United after them, and on three separate occasions, the charges were broken by very telling fire from the tanks on Italy. By seven that evening the troop of tanks was back in the valley, and the two that had played such a conspicuous part had managed to bring out the wounded infantry from the forward positions. However while doing this three members of one crew were seriously wounded.

The Australians offset some of the misfortunes of the day by retaking Baldy after a magnificently co-operated shoot with 'B' Squadron. The intensity of fire before the final assault raised such a blinding dust in the enemy positions that the Australians suffered no casualties in the assault. Because the lost ground could not be re-taken immediately without heavy casualties, the line was adjusted. On November 11th an immediate award of the D.S.O. was made to Major W. G. O. Butler, M.C., commanding 'B' Squadron.

Until November 17th the Commonwealth troops held the initiative during the daytime, and any sign of enemy movement was immediately engaged either by Divisional Artillery or by tanks who kept a continuous watch for the Chinese. But at night it was the turn of the Chinese, who probed continually at all points along the Divisional front. Chinese Artillery was active during the late afternoons and evenings, and was always well-directed and accurate.

On the left the Shropshires considered the two 'A' Squadron tanks, on the spur to the south-east of Point 227, so important to their defence that the G.O.C.'s authority was obtained to dig them in permanently for the winter, and in addition a further two were to be dug in on Point 227. It was necessary to prepare permanent winter quarters for the tanks, as later on frosts would render the road and hill tracks impassable.

The administration problems of Troops out on the hills was constant and critical. Strings of Korean bearers were organised to get ammunition up to the tanks, who if they came down might not be able to return. It was an odd sight to see these bearers plodding in long files, carrying shells. Sledges were also improvised to tow behind the tanks to carry supplies where the lorries could not follow.

Saturday, November 17th, dawned like any other day. The usual afternoon harassing had for some days been starting earlier, and Point 227 had recently been receiving a mild dusting in the mornings as well. November 4th had, however, taught that the enemy could concentrate his artillery apparently at will, and a Polish-born trooper in the Regiment, after listening in to the enemy wireless net, reported that artillery orders were now being given in Russian. At half-past four in the afternoon an intense barrage opened on Point 227. Within a few minutes the top of the hill was shrouded in dust and smoke, and all communications with 'A' Company of the 1st Shropshires had gone. At quarter to five a gunner observer reported no less than twenty-nine enemy batteries firing at once. Seldom can such a concentration of artillery fire on such a small area have been seen.

The position had been covered by three double apron fences, fifty yards of low 'spider' wiring and a minefield. The following day no piece of wire more than three feet long could be found. The defenders, blinded by dust and smoke, and in many cases buried in their bunkers, their weapons blown sky-high, were overrun in a matter of minutes. Some of the few survivors reported the Chinese walked into their own barrage, and that the first waves were led by a woman in black. Within an hour, when the smoke and dust began to clear, what had been a thickly wooded hill top was now a bald and sandy pate.

The tank troop below had been powerless to give much support as visibility was nil and it was impossible, in the dust and half-light, to distinguish friend from foe. One tank was rendered ineffective as the crew had been caught outside the tank when the barrage started and both commander and operator seriously wounded.

By ten that night it was obvious that Point 227 had fallen, and Colonel Barlow was ordered to put in an immediate counter-attack, supported by 'A' Squadron. In fact the only support that the Squadron could give was from the two tanks on Spur, firing on its fixed lines and switches already laid. The inadvisability of moving tanks down a very narrow road in that particular country, albeit moonlight, was only too obvious, and after a good deal of argument the attack was postponed until next morning. At first light a patrol reported the Chinese had gone.

Two tanks were now sent up on to the ridge, four hundred yards west of Point 227, while 'D' Company took possession of the hill and swept the valley to the west. They also promised to leave a patrol with the tanks. As there were now only two places left where tanks could climb up the hill, this operation was fraught with hazard. However the track was still not mined, and they reached the top safely. Little movement was seen anywhere, but as the afternoon passed, shelling and mortaring increased. Just before five, the protecting Infantry having disappeared, Lieutenant Paul and the tanks were ordered to withdraw. By the time they had backed off, turned and reached the bottom of the hill twenty minutes later, the Infantry on Point 227 were again being heavily attacked from the west and north. History will never relate how close to being overrun were those two tanks. The Infantry maintained that the enemy waited for the Centurions to withdraw before attacking, but the game of committing tanks unattended in close country can be played once too often and in this particular case it was considered that they were only saved by an expedient and fortunately-timed withdrawal.

By seven that night 'D' Company on Point 227 were again surrounded. Lieutenant Clode's troop on the Spur below had been hotly engaged for a short while, but the light was failing as the attack came in, and they soon had to revert to fixed lines. The situation on Point 227 was now confused, and it later transpired that the Company Commander and fourteen men had managed to break out and reach 'B' Company locality. The remaining survivors shared the hill that night with the enemy and the Divisional Artillery.

As before, by dawn the Chinese had departed, and it was decided on the 19th that Point 227 was untenable by either side. The same day a Shropshire patrol counted four hundred dead Chinese on the west of the hill.

That night the enemy attacked Kowang San from the north, approaching down from Point 217. This time they came up against the Leicesters on Crete, and the Borderer's on Kowang San, who had taken over from the Norfolks. It was now 'B' Squadron's turn, and for the first time gun flashes were seen on Point 217. These were hotly engaged and successfully silenced, and the attack was beaten off.

On November 20th, at the request of Colonel Barlow of the Shropshires, two tanks were sent to the ridge to the west of Point 227. Full Sapper support was given, as it was probable that mines would have been laid on the tracks. Five were lifted, but one, or two probably, were missed, and the troop leader's tank was blown up as it manoeuvred into the firing position. No worse place could have been chosen as the tanks were in full view of the enemy. There had been tanks at that particular place many times in the last six weeks and the site was accurately ranged by enemy guns. A Centurion tug towed the tank back to safety, and in spite of considerable mortaring there were luckily no casualties, except for a Churchill recovery vehicle which broke down and had to be left as a Christmas present for the Chinese.

The night of the 20th/21st November was quiet, but on the 21st a lot of fresh diggings were observed on Point 217 and engaged all day. It was assumed the enemy had dug self-propelled guns into the hill, and two of the bunkers were seen to 'brew-up'. By half-past three it was clear that the enemy were preparing to attack. Points 238 and 199 were under heavy shell-fire, and the attack and accompanying artillery barrage came down on the Leicesters on Crete and the Australians to the east. Tanks on Point 238 were sniped at by Self-propelled guns on Point 217, but the only damage was a grooved gun band. Armour piercing shells were fired at the flashes and after that there was a marked silence from that quarter. The Chinese attack then fizzled out in the face of a barrage put down by the Divisional Artillery.

On November 22nd the 7th Brigade of the 3rd United States Infantry Division began to move up to relieve the 28th Brigade, which were by now, not only extremely tired but also very thin on the ground. Casualties had been high and the strain was beginning to tell. The tanks of 'A' and 'B' Squadrons stayed on in their positions so as not to give the show away. But the Chinese seemed to have realised that a re-disposition of some kind was going on, and that night shelled Points 238 and 199 as hard as they could. But as the American companies who were to take over these two features were driven up in vehicles with blazing headlights, it was hardly surprising that the Chinese reacted. A ripple of rockets, straddling Point 238, inflicted casualties on the Americans. When the bearing and the range of six thousand and twenty-five yards was sent back to the Gunners by the 5th Dragoon Guard Troop Leader, who had taken over Point 238 from the 8th Hussars, it was received with scorn. But when however they were taunted into putting down an 'Uncle' target they could next day claim one Rocket Launching Lorry destroyed.

As soon as it was light on the 23rd, and as the first snow of winter began to fall, the Centurions came lumbering down the hills, which by now were covered in 20-pounder shell cases. The snow could not have come at a worse time. Mixed with rain, thaw and freeze it played havoc with roads, hillsides and the Divisional Staff who were planning the move. Everybody was very tired, so by the time the 'World's Best Tank', the Patton, discovered it could not get up the slopes, the Regiment were well on their way to a new home.

Up to the final handover to the 5th Dragoon Guards on December 6th, 'A' and 'B' Squadrons were busy getting their tanks and soft vehicles up to standard. 'C' Squadron alone remained with the 29th Brigade, with 'Boyall Force' on the west side of the Sami-chon. There was little activity as they had been ordered not to fire unless the enemy opened first or moved about too blatantly in the open.

Festivity during the last few days was rife. News that the Skins had been delayed for twenty-four hours was received with horror, whereas a month before one day either way would have meant little. Yet being so near to sailing time it seemed like five years.

By stages, during the 5th and 6th of December, the Regiment moved down to Britannia Camp. At midday on December 6th at Regimental Headquarters the Regimental Flag was lowered and that of the 5th Dragoon Guards was raised in its place. By seven that evening the entire Regiment was together for the first time since landing in Korea thirteen months before. On the 7th the Divisional Commander came to bid them farewell and made an excellent speech which was very well received. On the morning of the 8th they entrained at Uijongbu for their journey to Pusan, and compared with previous rail journeys in Korea, was most luxurious. Having left at 1 p.m. they arrived at Pusan, to their surprise, at nine the following morning, as the journey used to take two days. By lunchtime the whole Regiment was in Seaforth Camp, where they learned their sailing date had been put back to December 16th.

On the morning of December 10th the whole Regiment assembled in the United Nations Cemetery at Pusan in order to pay tribute to their comrades who had given their lives in the Korean war. It was a most moving ceremony that started with a Piper of the Princess Patricia's Canadian Light Infantry playing the 'Flowers of the Forest', and followed by the sounding of the Last Post and Reveillé by the buglers of the Shropshires. Then the names of all the Regimental casualties were read out, both killed, missing, or prisoner of war.

The last few days before embarkation were eagerly seized by quartermasters and their staffs of tailors. Reluctant parka-clad queues disappeared into numerous stores and emerged in gaily-be-ribboned battle-dress; it was very often difficult to recognise these men as the winterised, stained crews who had disgorged from the train only a few days previously.

At nine in the morning on December 15th the Regiment marched out of Seaforth Camp, and by midday was embarked on M. V. *Georgic*, leaving behind them a war that was to drag on for another eighteen months. And as they sailed, in everyone's mind was the thought: "At last, thank God! And the best of luck to the Skins!"

PART SEVEN

1952–1958

'A' Squadron supporting the King's Own Scottish Borderers during our "advance to contact" north of the River Imjin, August, 1951 (page 288).

A wounded Canadian soldier being evacuated during the attack on Hill 88. 'C' Squadron tank provides covering fire, September, 1951 (page 288).

'A' Squadron tanks support the King's Shropshire Light Infantry during Operation 'Commando' and the attack on Point 355. The tanks moved from hill-top to hill-top to obtain good fire positions. October, 1951 (page 291).

Major de Clermont, with map, commanding 'A' Squadron during Operation 'Commando' (page 290).

First visit of H.R.H. Prince Philip to Luneberg, September 30th, 1953. H.R.H. inspecting the Quarter guard (page 307).

Dinner in the Sergeants' Mess.
Facing: S.S.M. Peart, Lieut.-Col. Huth, R.S.M. Vallance, His Royal Highness, R.Q.M.S. Pavitt and S.S.M. Burrough (page 307).

H.M. Queen Elizabeth II arriving at the Balaclava Centenary Ball at the Hyde Park Hotel, escorted by Sir John Baldwin, November 26th, 1954 (page 308).

LUNEBURG

(a) British Army of the Rhine, December 1951- January 1952

THE REGIMENT arrived at Liverpool on January 14th 1952, where they were met on board ship by their Colonel, Air Marshal Sir John Baldwin, K.B.E., C.B., D.S.O., Brigadier Hackett, and a number of friends and serving officers of the Regiment. They arrived at Tidworth the same evening, and, due to some extremely hard work put in by their advance party, they were all able to go on leave for six weeks the following morning. When they returned from leave, the move to the British Army of the Rhine started, where they were to take over from the Greys.

At the same time fifteen officers and men toured the factories in some of the towns where the Centurions were made, sometimes visiting as many as twelve factories in a week, to boost production and to say thank you personally to those who made them.

Lieut.-Colonel Sir W. G. Lowther, during the tour, horrified the Ministry of Supply officials who arranged the visits by expressing his opinion of the Centurion in no uncertain terms. In his opinion it was the best tank in the world, with the best gun, turret and sighting gear.Nothing could stop it except roads that were too narrow, deep paddy or almost sheer loose rock. The Regiment had had twenty six tanks blown up, and everyone of these was afterwards driven home under its own power, some after being abandoned for five weeks. The Communists had swarmed over them like monkeys, stealing pin-up pictures and everything that took their fancy, but showing no interest in the more secret parts.

Another advantage of the Centurion was its extraordinary capacity for carrying infantry. Lieut.-Colonel Lowther could recall carrying fifty-six men on his, while on the American Patton ten made a crowd. Also maintenance was extremely simple, and after those thirteen strenuous months, all the tanks passed the searching R.E.M.E. tests before being handed over to the Skins. The American tanks were thought to be good only for Hollywood, and the rate of exchange in Korea was one Centurion for two Pattons. Of course the great regret was that there had been no tank versus tank battle.

All this was far too outspoken for the Ministry officials, and questions were asked in Parliament, but what did emerge was the fact that the Centurion was a first class tank.

The main party of the Regiment arrived in Lüneburg on March 22nd and in spite of snow, found it an extremely nice old town, with excellent barracks, good cinemas, canteens and a Y.M.C.A., and lastly, and perhaps the most important, very good married quarters. The next few weeks were spent unpacking and the settling in of the wives.

On May 14th the Regiment went out to camp for a month on the Soltan Training Area, which was only twenty miles from the barracks. They soon discovered that peacetime schemes in B.A.O.R. bore no resemblance to any other form of warfare, so they were slightly out of their depths at the start. They returned to barracks on June 14th and

V

went out again on the 28th to take part in a Corps exercise down on the Rhine. In this exercise the 7th Armoured Division had to defend a long stretch of the river and the Regiment was in Divisional Reserve, where they had a busy and successful time, moving during most nights and counter-attacking at dawn. It was good fun and renewed their confidence in their own ability.

No sooner were they back off the exercise, than most officers and all light vehicles were off on August 9th to umpire a battle between the 6th and 11th Armoured Divisions. This was hard work but very interesting, and the work done by the Canadian Brigade came in for much admiration.

On September 15th they packed up and left for Command Manoeuvres down in the south. Exercise 'Holdfast' was most enjoyable, for 7th Armoured Division were enemy to the rest of the forces of the Northern Army Group. The Regiment was particularly lucky as they fought with the 1st Battalion, The Royal Hampshire Regiment most of the time, and as they shared the barracks at Lüneberg with them they were firm friends before they started. Their first training season ended with their return to barracks on September 23rd. It had been hard work but they had made some good new friends.

Of the officers that returned with the Regiment from Korea, Major de Clermont, had gone to the Yorkshire Hussars, Captain Tisdall, to the Driving and Maintenance School at Bovington as an instructor and Captain Ormrod, to the Mons O.C.T.U. Major Huth, left for Kenya to grapple with the Mau-Mau.

The winter was spent in individual training and firing at the Hohne Tank Ranges for a week in December, January and February, and it was cold. At Christmas they enjoyed the usual celebrations, and gave an excellent party for the hundred and eight children on Regimental Charge. The carpenters did exceptionally well, making most of the toys for this very large family.

(b) March-November 1953

THE first excitement of the New Year was on March 12th, when, during an Officer's Day, a Lincoln bomber was shot down by a MIG right over their heads. As they were practising the new wireless procedure and had all the jeeps and scout cars out, they were not only able to report quickly details of this cold-blooded attack, but also to search the country at once and with some success.

A few days later the Regiment went out to the training area for Troop Training. The weather was kind, and His Royal Highness the Duke of Edinburgh paid them a flying visit, and later they put on a demonstration for the Army Commander, General Sir Richard Gale. They returned to barracks at the end of the month, and were faced with the huge problem of the run out of a hundred and fifty crew men, from April to September. As no drafts were forecast they had to re-train as drivers a high percentage of the remaining crewmen as this was the trade hardest hit. The next few months were spent in individual training and preparing ten tanks for the Coronation of Queen Elizabeth II Parade in Hamburg.

To represent the Regiment in the parade in London, a party consisting of Major W. G. O. Butler, Sergeant Vallance, Sergeant Scrugham, and five others stayed at

Bovington for two weeks and took part in the parade through London on June 2nd. The Coronation Parade at Hamburg was also an impressive sight and General Jones, the Divisional Commander, led the Armoured march past. But by far the most impressive thing for the Regiment on Coronation day was the fact that Her Majesty, the Queen, appointed His Royal Highness, The Duke of Edinburgh, to be their Colonel in Chief, and by so doing most graciously bestowed on the Regiment the greatest honour and distinction, and one to which they had long aspired.

During July the Regiment went out on six weeks training, spending a fortnight with the 2nd Royal Welch Fusiliers and another on the ranges at Hohne, firing the 20-pounder. While they were there they gave a demonstration to General Gruenther, the Allied Commander. The last two weeks consisted of Brigade and Divisional training and as there were so many new Troop Leaders and Tank Commanders they had to hasten slowly.

On September 30th, a memorable day, the new Colonel-in-Chief, flying his own aeroplane, landed at Lüneburg to inspect his Regiment. In more moments than minutes Prince Philip was 'One of the Regiment' as he inspected every rank of each Squadron. His quick questions and gay laugh endeared himself to everybody honoured to be on that historic parade.

After this great day, individual training continued as a draft of about seventy men had just arrived. Perhaps, apart from military matters the next important concern of the Regiment was its stables. These housed about twenty-four horses, and also consisted of one large and one small indoor riding school. Racing played a prominent part and, including point-to-point horses, there were fourteen in training at one moment. Major Dill trained these, and also rode with some success, as did Captain Randall and Corporal Tovey, while Captain Coldrey became a promising show jumper. Lieut.-Colonel Lowther himself was the biggest owner and gave his full support to racing.

It was with many regrets that the Regiment said good-bye to Lieut-Colonel Lowther in November when he handed over command to Lieutenant-Colonel de Clermont, D.S.O. Another who retired from the Regiment at about the same time was Major (QM) C. F. Hedley, M.B.E., who had served for thirty-two years and was greatly missed by everyone. With their leaving, the Regiment lost from its ranks two stalwart Hussars, who both had spent a considerable period of their lives putting the Regiment first in their thoughts and actions, and, but for the misfortune of having been captured in the Desert, would have featured more prominently in this History. However their absence was compensated for by their activities over their last ten years. They were both sometimes unconventional and always bubbling-over with confidence and cheerfulness. These characteristics gave to other members of the Regiment the lead required to keep the name of the 8th Hussars second to none. In August, 1953, came the sad news of the death of Brigadier John Van der Byl, D.S.O., who joined the Regiment in 1898. He was Honorary Colonel from 1930 to 1948, when he retired, and during the whole of his career he remained in close touch with the Regiment and followed all its doings with the utmost personal interest until the end. Many a serving officer will recall a happy and encouraging visit to Elsenwood, near Camberley.

(c) December 1953-November 1954

HAVING already endured one year of training at Lüneburg, the succeeding ones followed with monotonous similarity. There was always the endless stream of reservists to be broken in, trained and released, and then it started all over again. Much the same pattern of training took place. Rheinsehelen Camp—the Soltan Training Area—Kreuz B—Timmerloh—the river Luhe—familiar names to those who left and trebly familiar to those who remained. When it was not raining, there was the dust, which tasted much the same.

The highlights of the year were perhaps the Regiment's own Indoor Horse Show held in the large Riding School just before Christmas.

In June the Regiment was well represented at Hamburg in the Parade in honour of Her Majesty the Queen's Birthday, and at the end of June they were honoured by another visit from their Colonel-in-Chief. On this occasion they were able to share the day with their friends and neighbours The Cameron Highlanders, who also have the honour to have Prince Philip as their Colonel. The Regiment laid on a small demonstration of Infantry-Tank co-operation on Victory Hill.

July saw the Light Brigade Musical Ride at the Rhine Army Horse Show. That it took place at all, let alone was a success, was largely the result of some very hard work by Major Bob Duncan, who was the Regiment's last Squadron Sergeant Major Riding Instructor, and now in the Royal Pioneer Corps.

In September the Regiment took part in an exercise called 'Battle Royal'. It was said to be the biggest Army Manoeuvre that had ever taken place in peace time. It took eighteen months to lay on and was all over in five days, but all the same a great deal was learnt, and if the Regiment's part was finally less glamorous than the opening moves promised, what was required was done cheerfully, quickly and effectively.

In the field of sport they had successes and disappointments. The Regiment won the Brigade Boxing Shield and were only beaten by one point in the Semi-Final of the Divisional contest. In the field of equitation they also continued to show the flag, but on the whole it was an unlucky racing season.

On October 25th was celebrated the centenary of the Charge of the Light Brigade which included a good deal of revelry of one kind and another, and a full Regimental Parade at which were present both the Brigade Commander, Brigadier Hobson, and the Garrison Commander, Brigadier MacDonald.

The final high-light of these celebrations was the unforgettable Light Brigade Ball at the Hyde Park Hotel in London on November 26th. The Ball was honoured by the presence of Her Majesty the Queen, His Royal Highness the Duke of Edinburgh, in the uniform of the Colonel-in-Chief of the 8th Hussars, and Queen Elizabeth the Queen Mother. All five Regiments were well represented and the total company numbered over six hundred and fifty. Probably not since 1914 has such a colourful spectacle unfolded itself in a London ballroom. Full dress of all five Regiments was in ample evidence, and, mingled with them, many others from affiliated Yeomanry Regiments gave reminder of a more gracious age. And although they were wearing superb jewellery just for once the ladies did not dominate the scene.

At a quarter-past ten the Royal Party arrived and were received in an ante-room by Sir John and Lady Baldwin, who presented the Colonels of the other Regiments and their wives. Meanwhile a Guard of Honour of four Other Ranks in full dress from each Regiment had formed up in front of the Band. Her Majesty the Queen, escorted by the Air Marshal, then entered the Ballroom. She was followed by the Colonel-in-Chief, The Queen Mother and the rest of the Royal party. To those who saw it, the scene will never fade from their memory.

At half-past eleven the Royal party came to see a representative collection of silver and relics from the five Regiments. The dog collar of Colonel de Salis' 'Jimmy' was a source of particular interest.

The Ball went on in all its elegance until a late hour, but there was no need to dance that night, it was far more satisfying to watch others, some in uniforms that had been worn at the time of the Crimean war, every person a blaze of colour, of orders, of chain epaulettes, cloaks and clinking spurs that echoed a far distant age. The sad part was that their like will not be seen again.

(d) December 1954-December 1955

THE year 1955 was a year of much change, and the Regiment said goodbye to a number of old friends. Chief among these was the Rev. B. A. Howarth, C.E., who had been with them since Tidworth 1950, when they had sailed for Korea. He was with them throughout that campaign and the whole Regiment felt a sense of loss when he left. R.S.M. Leckie also left for promotion to Quartermaster's rank, he too had joined at Tidworth, and had ever since ruled with a rod of iron. Major J. F. Weston-Simons went as an instructor to the Pakistanis in Quetta, Major M. B. Marwood joined the Yorkshire Hussars and Major Pierson went to the War Office.

Once again the Regiment was honoured by a visit from the Colonel-in-Chief, and on this occasion His Royal Highness stayed the night, and for the first time his personal Standard flew over the Mess. There was no facet of Regimental life in which he was not deeply interested, and he graciously undertook to have the Regimental kettle-drums restored at his own expense.

A major contribution to Regimental prestige throughout B.A.O.R. was made by the band which performed at many different gatherings, the Trumpeters being in themselves a show piece. At sport the Regiment achieved no outstanding success, although they acquitted themselves creditably in the final of the Brigade Shield. The football team was made up mostly of very young players, National Service men, who although they tried hard never quite made the grade, and cricket was no longer played at all as the Regiment was out on the Training Area when they should have been practising.

Already there were rumours as to the uncertainty of the future. Experimental organisations were being tried out, and it was not yet known whether the Armoured Division would continue in its present form, and if it did not whether it would mean a change of station for the Regiment. However morale was high and whatever the future held in store it would be undertaken cheerfully and effectively in the same spirit as of old.

(e) January 1956-March 1957

IN fact 1956 found the Regiment still at Lüneburg and with yet more changes in store for them. In the spring they passed from under command the 7th Armoured Division to under command the newly reconstituted 4th Infantry Division. They became an integral part of the 10th Infantry Brigade, whom they already knew well as the 31st Lorried Infantry Brigade. The emphasis in training was therefore mainly in the direction of Armoured-Infantry co-operation. With the 8th Hussars the only Armoured Regiment available for three infantry battalions, this placed a great strain on the officers and senior other ranks. The success that was achieved was in large measure due to the untiring energy and enthusiasm of the Squadron Leaders and the second-in-command.

In the realm of sport the Regiment had some notable successes. The winning of the 7th Armoured Divisional Boxing Championship was outstanding enough, as was the winning, in October, by the Regimental team, of the Army and Open Hunter Trials. But far more creditable was the winning of the B.A.O.R. Soccer Cup. The Regiment had fought their way to the finals, where they were playing the 3rd Royal Tank Regiment. After a tremendously exciting game at Hanover on March 9th, 1957, the Regiment were victorious, four goals to one, and were presented with the cup by General Sir Dudley Ward, the Army Commander.

The Regiment had two visitors in 1956 from their affiliated regiments. In July by Captain Ian Hendry of the 8/13 Victorian Mounted Rifles, and in September by Captain John Harrison of the 6th Duke of Connaught's Royal Canadian Hussars. The importance, apart from the pleasure, of these visits was considerable, and a warm welcome awaits any 8th Hussar who visits Melbourne or Montreal.

However already the threat of amalgamation was in the air. 1956 saw the end of the Yorkshire Hussars, who were now made part of the Yorkshire Yeomanry together with the Yorkshire Dragoons and the East Riding Yeomanry, and also of the Northamptonshire Yeomanry who were now to form an additional squadron in the Inns of Court Regiment. It was more than sad to see the end of two Regiments with such fine and long records of service but it was certain that all who stayed on, albeit in a Regiment of another name, would carry the splendid traditions of these two Yeomanry Regiments with them, and weld together a new Regiment made of the finest qualities of the old. The 8th Hussars thus had no affiliated yeomanry regiments.

(f) April 1957-October 1958

THE year of 1957 brought a shock to all those who had ever been connected with the Regiment. Mechanization in 1935 had seemed at the time to be a death-blow, and there were some who felt it would kill the spirit of the 8th Hussars. There could have been no greater misapprehension, as the list of battle honours won in the Second World War will show. This time however the Regiment was to lose its name and its entirety. In July Lieut.-Colonel Huth was informed by the Colonel, Sir John Baldwin, that the

Regiment was one of the unlucky six cavalry regiments chosen for amalgamation. Sir John Baldwin and the Commanding Officer had fought tooth and nail to preserve their identity, but the dice were too heavily loaded against them. However if it had to be, there could be no happier choice of a partner than their sister regiment, the 4th Queen's Own Hussars. They had charged together at Balaclava, fought at el Alamein as 4th/8th Hussars and were neighbours at that time in Germany. On the day the news came through, Lieut-Colonel Kennard, who commanded the 4th Hussars, sent a telegram, "Deepest sympathy. Congratulations. Long live the 4th/8th Hussars."

It was in that spirit that plans went forward and final details were arranged. In October a round table conference was held at the 4th Hussars Officers' Mess at Hohne. The 8th Hussars advisers, known as 'The Three Wise Men', consisted of Sir John Baldwin, Colonel D. Pope and Colonel P. H. V. de Clermont, while the 4th Hussars had a similar though rather larger team. Field officers attended, and advised by the ex-officers, plans were discussed throughout the morning, and in the afternoon the two Colonels and Commanding Officers recorded firm proposals and forwarded them to the War Office. They were also approved by His Royal Highness, Prince Philip the 8th Hussars Colonel-in-Chief, and Sir Winston Churchill, Colonel of the 4th Hussars.

The formation of the Queen's Royal Irish Hussars, as the new Regiment would be known, was also decided. The second-in-command, the 8th Hussars, Major W. G. O. Butler, D.S.O., M.C., was to be Commanding Officer. The new second-in-command would be a 4th Hussar. By and large all officers and members of the Sergeants Mess would go over to the new Regiment, with the exception of those who were leaving the Regiment under the new 'accelerated retirement' plan. These were Majors Marwood, Roffey, Ford, Bromiley, Dill and Hartwright; Captains Hurst, Coldrey and Browning and Lieutenant Harvey-Kelly. No more National Service recruits were to be posted after June, so that by the time of amalgamation in October 1958, regimental strength would be approximately three hundred other ranks. All the officers, warrant officers and most of the rank and file would be regular soldiers.

The Queen's Royal Irish Hussars had all the makings of a strong and efficient Regiment, and had also the added honour of having His Royal Highness, Prince Philip, as Colonel-in-Chief and Sir Winston Churchill as Colonel, with Sir John Baldwin as Deputy Colonel. The whole amalgamation went forward in the most friendly manner possible, the best distinctions of the dress of both Regiments being chosen, and the new badge being the 4th Hussars' circle with the 8th Hussars' harp in the centre, the Queen's crown and lion at the top and their motto 'Mente et Manu' below. The same integration applied to the new uniform, to the Regimental Marches and the Regimental Flag.

And so, after two hundred and fifty-five years, the last year of the Regiment as the 8th Hussars passed only too fast. They remained part of the 10th Independent Infantry Brigade Group, but in August the Brigade ceased to be part of the 4th Infantry Division and became part of the 7th Armoured Division, the Desert Rats of which the Regiment were founder members. There were two deaths to be recorded, namely that of Lieut.-Colonel James Blakiston-Houston who had joined the Regiment in 1903 and had commanded in 1927 and 1928, and that of Major E. G. Weldon who had joined the same year. The Battle Honours for the Second World War and Korea came through, a truly honourable list and of which almost all were to be incorporated in the Queen's Royal Irish Hussars Battle Honours.

Troop, squadron and group training went off satisfactorily, although much of the ground in the Soltau area had been afforested and was therefore useless as a training ground. In September the Regiment took part in a most interesting N.A.T.O. Exercise,

'Brown Jug'. The aim of this exercise was to test Danish mobilization plans and their mobility to repulse an invasion. As part of Orange Force the Regiment simulated a landing on the east coast of Zealand, the island on which Copenhagen stands. The tanks had to be prepositioned to cut damage to a minimum, but the Highland Light Infantry landed on the beaches and the British and American parachutists were dropped with all their heavy equipment. The actual exercise only lasted three days, but many of the Regiment were in Denmark for two or three weeks and learnt the true meaning of Danish hospitality—it was tremendous.

As usual there was a good deal of sport undertaken in one way and another. Apart from the more orthodox kinds, there was sailing in the Baltic, ski-ing up in the Hartz Mountains, while the Wessex hounds were kept at Fallingbostal. As well there was great interest and enthusiasm taken with all forms of equitation; a team was entered for the Army Pentathlon, under Lieutenant Webster. However by far the greatest achievement for the Regiment in the racing world was Major R. P. G. Dill's splendid win in the Grand Military Race at Sandown in 1957 on 'Easter Breeze', the second 8th Hussar to win this race since the war.

In October and November the Regiment was busy preparing for their yearly Administration Inspection, which took place on December 10th. General Hackett, himself an 8th Hussar and who was at that time commanding the 7th Armoured Division, carried out the inspection.

In March 1958 His Royal Highness, The Duke of Edinburgh, paid his third and sadly but inevitably his last visit to the Regiment. A few days earlier it had been announced that he had consented to become the Colonel-in-Chief of the amalgamated Regiment, which was the cause of deep pride and satisfaction. But there was no one who was not conscious that this was the first of many 'lasts'.

This visit was the most informal so far, and in many ways the most intimate. Prince Philip had asked that there be no formal parade and had dropped in, almost casually, piloting a helicopter of the Royal Navy, which landed on the barrack square shortly after a snowstorm had blown itself out. Amongst all the other things that he managed to cram in to one short day was to drive a Centurion back from Victory Hill and to fire its machine-guns.

One last incident must be mentioned. The 8th Hussars, being a Cavalry Regiment, had no depot in the same way as County Regiments, and up until 1922 all the memorials to their dead were put in St. Patrick's Cathedral in Dublin, a practice which became neither practical nor logical. Therefore it was thought that what was most needed, and indeed the 4th Hussars already had one, was a portable Memorial that could move with the Regiment and be a permanent reminder to serving generations of the glories of the past. A beautiful bronze triptitch was therefore designed, about seven feet high and with closing doors, surmounted by the Regimental crest. On the front of the doors were the battle honours of the two world wars and of Korea and inside the names of those who gave their lives. On July 18th, in a simple and moving service at the Royal Military Chapel at Wellington Barracks, the Memorial was unveiled by the Colonel, Sir John Baldwin, and dedicated by the Reverend J. Good, Chaplain to the Household Brigade.

And so, on, to the last and final incident, the dropping of the curtain on the 8th Kings Royal Irish Hussars.

This ceremony was to take place at Hohne on the 24th October 1958, and was to combine not only the amalgamation of the 4th and 8th Hussars but also the presentation of the Guidon by His Royal Highness, Prince Philip. For six weeks the Regiment had been perfecting their drill, while the band rehearsed endlessly. Equal care and trouble

Brigadier J. Van der Byl, D.S.O.,
Colonel of the 8th King's Royal Irish Hussars, 1930–1948.

Air Marshal Sir John Baldwin, K.B.E., C.B.E., O.B.E., D.S.O.,
Colonel of the 8th King's Royal Irish Hussars, 1948–1958.

The final slow march past of 'C' Squadron, 8th Hussars, October 24th, 1958 (page 313).

Lieut.-Col. P. H. Huth, D.S.O., reporting the parade present and correct to the two Colonels—
H.R.H. Prince Philip and Sir John Baldwin, October 24th, 1958 (page 313).

H.R.H. Prince Philip, Duke of Edinburgh, Colonel-in-Chief, presents the Guidon to the
Queens Royal Irish Hussars, October 24th, 1958 (page 313).

In Memoriam

(11th November, 1953)

To us it seems that only yesterday
We knew you happy in the task of living.
Now you have gone; flowers fallen by the way,
Your total selves too freely set on giving.
And as you crossed the last and great divide,
We like to think a trumpeter did sound,
While we in spirit travelled at your side.
Oh valiant friends, you proudly stood your ground
And met unflinchingly whatever came.
So may your great example all inspire
To keep undimmed the Regimental name,
You passed unblemished through the burning fire.
We, who are left, still groping for the stars,
Proudly remember fallen Eighth Hussars.

D.R.W.G.C.–C.

was taken with the arrangements for the many guests and old friends who were to spend a week-end with the Regiment and who would have every possible comfort planned for them. A special aeroplane flew them out, they were lodged in their own mess and on the evening of the 24th a spectacular ball was planned.

October 24th dawned cold and grey. There was to be no blaze of glorious sunshine nor high wind to send the flags billowing. This was to be a day of very ordinary weather, the sort of day on which victories are won and Queens crowned. By half past nine the stands were crammed with both foreign and British visitors, huddling into mackintoshes and fur coats as the light rain fell. Then the combined bands marched on, followed by the two Regiments. It was a solemn and moving moment, the climax of so much hard work and efficiency. But it was not just the hard work of the last six weeks that led to such an impeccable parade, that effort was but the end of a long thread of many strands; strands of duty, valour, loyalty and pride, that stretched back for over two hundred and fifty years. As proof that no one man nor generation had fashioned the 8th Hussars into what they were, so were the Regimental guests not the only people watching silent round the parade ground. There too, as the flag was lowered for the last time, and, for the last time, the Regiment marched past to its own slow march, stood another silent host.

There were the earliest of all: Conyngham's Dragoons, in scarlet coats and yellow breeches, at ease upon their chargers, armed with long swords and muskets; Pepper's Dragoons, the first to win and wear the Spanish Crossbelts; St. George's Dragoons, the Redcoats, who marched against the Young Pretender, also in scarlet and with scarlet cloaks; the King's Royal Irish Dragoons who campaigned in the Low Countries against Napoleon, and who were the first of the Regiment to know the bitter cold and mud of a Flanders winter; the Hussars who fell at Balaclava, and, falling, reached immortality; the Hussars who sweated and died under the blazing Indian skies during the Mutiny, and there won four Victoria Crosses in one action; Hussars in dusty khaki who fought gallantly in South Africa against a worthy foe, a foe who knew that wild country like the palms of their hands; mud-caked veterans of the First World War, riding for the last time their troop horses into action; and finally all those who lost their lives in the Desert and in France, and the gallant few who rest in the far hills of Korea. Of all these men it might be truly said, that they were men of valour, who never stopped to count the cost but made sure, in their own superb way, that the name of the 8th King's Royal Irish Hussars was known as the counterpart of honour.

APPENDICES

APPENDIX I

Roll of Honour

1939-1945

OFFICERS

Lieut. R. H. ANSTEY
2nd.-Lieut. S. E. APTHORP
Capt. J. N. A. BALDWIN
Lieut. A. B. BRODIE
Lieut. M. M. M. BROWNE
2nd.-Lieut. L. F. CARTER
Lieut. F. R. CHARLES
2nd.-Lieut. F. L. COLEMAN
Lieut. P. F. DEMAY
Major C. E. R. DUFF
2nd.-Lieut. J. D. de la C. ELLIOTT
Lieut. N. A. ST. G. GIBBES
Major J. D. HARBORD

2nd.-Lieut. E. McC. HECTOR
Lieut.-Col. G. P. KILKELLY
Lieut. R. E. McDONNELL
Lieut. H. R. D. PEGLER, D.C.M., M.M.
Lieut. J. P. S. PIM
Lieut. L. PRESTON
Lieut. F. W. RYDE
Major P. D. SANDBACH
Lieut. D. S. SCOTT
Lieut. H. L. TALBOT-HARVEY
Major G. W. G. THRELFALL, M.C.
Lieut. A. B. VENNER
Lieut. J. G. M. YOUNG

WARRANT OFFICERS

W.O.11 R. FLEMING

W.O.11 D. W. JORDON

SERGEANTS

Sgt. F. E. AVERY
Sgt. C. J. CHAPMAN
Sgt. J. W. CLOUGH
Sgt. A. E. CRAWLEY
Sgt. G. W. DESALVO
L.-Sgt. W. DONNELLY
Sgt. H. HAYLOCK
Sgt. W. H. HUNTER
Sgt. L. R. R. INNES
Sgt. F. J. JONES

Sgt. J. S. MANNING
Sgt. R. C. PICKIN
L.-Sgt. H. R. G. SCOTT
Sgt. D. S. A. SHAW
Sgt. F. SMITH
Sgt. H. K. STEWART
Sgt. E. G. WAKEFIELD
Sgt. H. E. WEBBER
Sgt. J. WELCH
L.-Sgt. H. WYATT

CORPORALS

Cpl. I. ALDRIDGE
Cpl. A. L. ANDERSON
Cpl. V. A. BALCOMBE
Cpl. L. E. BLACKMUR

Cpl. E. C. F. COOK
Cpl. J. R. FAIRLESS
Cpl. J. FORRISTER
Cpl. F. J. GIBBIN

317

Cpl. A. W. Heath
Cpl. D. S. Heath
Cpl. E. F. Newell
Cpl. A. C. Perry
Cpl. G. P. Porter

Cpl. W. H. Richards
Cpl. A. S. Russell
Cpl. R. A. Sidwell
Cpl. J. Wylie

LANCE-CORPORALS

L.-Cpl. J. H. Amos, M.M.
L.-Cpl. W. L. Angel
L.-Cpl. W. C. Burbidge
L.-Cpl. F. J. Coates
L.-Cpl. J. H. Colman
L.-Cpl. W. Flatt
L.-Cpl. J. French

L.-Cpl. A. R. Hope
L.-Cpl. W. L. Howe
L.-Cpl. E. T. Kyle
L.-Cpl. A. A. Mackay
L.-Cpl. D. Mitchell
L.-Cpl. A. Whitehouse

TROOPERS

Tpr. J. F. Allen
Tpr. J. R. Andrews
Tpr. R. F. Arthur
Tpr. G. W. Attwood
Tpr. N. G. Austing
Tpr. E. Ballantyne
Tpr. J. M. Barrass
Tpr. A. S. M. Barter
Tpr. A. P. Bartley
Tpr. G. C. Bell
Tpr. J. E. Bergin
Tpr. W. F. B. Bishop
Tpr. W. Bodle
Tpr. W. Boyett
Tpr. A. W. Brogden
Tpr. F. F. Bunn
Tpr. J. Burns
Tpr. A. Calvert
Tpr. G. R. Cameron
Tpr. C. P. L. Carpenter
Tpr. H. Cashmore
Tpr. B. Clerk
Tpr. K. P. Clay
Tpr. G. Clifton
Tpr. J. K. H. Collins
Tpr. W. E. Collison
Tpr. T. Commerford
Tpr. A. F. Connor
Tpr. B. E. Coppin
Tpr. C. S. Cox
Tpr. J. Crossley

Tpr. H. W. Davies
Tpr. L. R. Dixon
Tpr. A. R. Drakeford
Tpr. H. J. Edwards
Tpr. E. Edwards
Tpr. N. R. Edwards
Tpr. E. T. Eeles
Tpr. C. W. Emblem
Tpr. F. F. Esdale
Tpr. W. J. Esdale
Tpr. J. A. Gardner
Tpr. J. C. George
Tpr. G. R. Gitsham
Tpr. F. Goodyear
Tpr. T. St. J. C. Halford
Tpr. N. Hampson
Tpr. L. Harley
Tpr. O. J. Hewlett
Tpr. F. A. Hibbart
Tpr. A. R. Hicks
Tpr. S. R. Hoare
Tpr. J. P. Holland
Tpr. S. J. W. How
Tpr. W. F. Howard
Tpr. H. W. Howard
Tpr. H. N. J. Howlett
Tpr. W. L. Hutchings
Tpr. E. H. Jacoby
Tpr. P. L. Janney
Tpr. H. P. Jones
Tpr. E. Jones

Tpr. R. J. Jones
Tpr. A. C. J. King
Tpr. G. S. Kirkham
Tpr. O. Lancaster
Tpr. J. F. Lawrie
Tpr. W. R. Lawson
Tpr. J. Low
Tpr. H. V. Lowe
Tpr. C. E. Lyne
Tpr. F. Maddocks
Tpr. L. Mason
Tpr. K. Meadows
Tpr. F. P. Melville
Tpr. J. Moffatt
Tpr. G. A. Morfin
Tpr. D. Morton
Tpr. G. Offley
Tpr. R. Packer
Tpr. R. Painter
Tpr. A. J. Parfitt
Tpr. J. I. Partoon
Tpr. H. Pickering
Tpr. T. J. Powell
Tpr. J. C. Powick
Tpr. J. Prescott
Tpr. J. W. Quick

Tpr. M. Rainbow
Tpr. H. F. Redfern
Tpr. J. I. M. Rees
Tpr. L. Saunders
Tpr. F. Sharp
Tpr. J. Shaw
Tpr. A. R. Sisman
Tpr. C. G. Smith
Tpr. E. R. Smitherman
Tpr. J. Sowray
Tpr. W. G. Sparey
Tpr. C. H. Spilbey
Tpr. L. H. Spiller
Tpr. W. N. Stark
Tpr. J. B. L. Sutherland
Tpr. C. Taylor
Tpr. W. G. Thompson
Tpr. C. A. Thorne
Tpr. A. T. W. Tout
Tpr. G. W. Varney
Tpr. A. K. Vinicombe
Tpr. A. J. Walton
Tpr. E. D. Wescott
Tpr. R. Williams
Tpr. F. Williams

Officers	25
Warrant Officers	2
Sergeants	20
Corporals and Lance-Corporals	30
Troopers	113

Korean War

1950-1957

OFFICERS

Lieut. C. G. Alexander
Capt. D. L. Astley-Cooper
Capt. G. H. F. Beith (R.A.M.C. attached)

Lieut. D. F. P. C. Probyn (3 H. attached)
Lieut. J. C. F. Walker

SERGEANTS

Sgt. E. R. Collins

CORPORALS

Cpl. F. C. H. CAMERON   Cpl. E. STONE
Cpl. J. S. LIVETT

TROOPERS

Tpr. C. ADAMS   Tpr. A. R. SMITH
Tpr. J. COLLISON   Tpr. W. E. THOMAS
Tpr. G. C. COSTELLO   Tpr. M. L. WALTON
Tpr. S. J. O'CONNOR   Tpr. A. G. WILLMOTT
Tpr. C. A. SADLER

APPENDIX II

HONOURS AND AWARDS
(Other Ranks)★

Owing to the length of time that has elapsed since the actions described in this History took place it has been impossible to trace the names of all those who received awards while serving with the Regiment. To these N.C.O.'s and other ranks whose names have been omitted from this list the author offers her sincere apologies.

D.C.M.
W.O.1 R. Vallance
Sergeant R. P. Pitchforth
Trooper R. Weir

M.M.
Captain (then Sergeant) Winch
W.O.1 L. V. Harold
W.O.1 J. McMaster
W.O.1 O'Shaunessy
W.O.2 L. T. Barnett
W.O.2 J. Taylor (and bar)
W.O.2 F. Rowan
W.O.2 A. J. Russell
W.O.2 R. Scrugham
Staff Sergeant Walters—R.E.M.E. attached
Sergeant Wilson
Sergeant Harris
Sergeant Jennings
Sergeant Pass
Corporal A. Vollans
Corporal F. Daniel
Lance-Corporal French
Lance-Corporal Amos
Lance-Corporal Bamber

M.B.E.
T.Q.M.S. Day
A.Q.M.S. Friel

★ For Officers' Honours and Awards see Alphabetical List of Officers, Appendix III.

B.E.M.

Sergeant J. S. WILLIAMS
S.Q.M.S. J. HINDMAN

MENTIONED IN DISPATCHES

W.O.2 HILLS
Staff-Sergeant R. ADAMS
Staff-Sergeant J. MOOR
Corporal CHILDS
Lance-Corporal CHEESEMAN
Lance-Corporal MELLOR
Trooper REMBLANCE

APPENDIX III

ALPHABETICAL LIST OF THE OFFICERS OF THE VIII KING'S ROYAL IRISH HUSSARS

and those permanently attached

1928–1958

1. In the column showing Period commissioned in the Regiment, the dates given will normally be those during which Officers were 'badged' as 8th Hussars, and will not necessarily denote their actual period of service with the Regiment.
2. No distinction is made between regular, short service or national service commissions. Highest rank shown includes acting and temporary ranks, whether with the Regiment, on the staff or extra-regimentally employed.
3. While every effort has been made to achieve complete accuracy, mistakes will have occurred inevitably owing to omissions and discrepancies in official records, and to the passage of time.
4. Decorations without brackets denote those awarded while serving with the Regiment.

Name	Period commissioned in the Regiment	Highest rank reached while commissioned in the Regiment	Notes
ACWORTH H. J.	Feb. 53–Amalgamation	Captain	
ADAMS F. E.	Feb. 42–Sep. 43	Lieutenant	From 2 Royal Gloucester Hussars
AGNEW R. I. J.	Dec. 53–Aug. 56	Lieutenant	
AKEROYD M. H.	Aug. 48–Sep. 49	Lieutenant	
	Sep. 50–Dec. 51		Recalled from reserve, served with the Regt. Korea.
ALCOCK A. S.	July 41–May 42	Captain	R.A.O.C. attchd.
ALEXANDER C. G.	Oct. 48–Jan. 51	Lieutenant	Killed in action Korea.
AMES R. H.	May 40–Dec. 45	Major	
ANSTEY C. R. P.	Mar. 45–Sep. 47	Lieutenant	
ANSTEY R. H.	Apr. 42–Mar. 45	Lieutenant	Killed in action N.W. Europe
APTHORP S. E.	Apr. 44–Aug. 44	2nd Lieutenant	Killed in action N.W. Europe
ARKELL R. J. O.	July 47–June 48	2nd Lieutenant	
ARMSTRONG J. R. B.	Jan. 15–Aug. 20	Captain	
	Aug. 39–Aug. 45		Recalled from reserve, service not with Regt.

ASTLEY-COOPER D. L.	May 40–Jan. 51	Captain	Killed in action Korea.
ATKINS D. H.	June 53–June 55	2nd Lieutenant	
ATKINSON-WILLES G. L.	Feb. 44–Jan. 48	Captain	
ATTENBOROUGH B. T.	May 40–Jan. 46	Captain	
BAGSHAWE P. P.	July 47–May 48 Aug. 50–July 51		Recalled from reserve, service with the Regt. Korea.
BALDWIN Sir John E. A. K.B.E. C.B. D.S.O.	Sept. 11–June 20 Jan. 48–Amalgama- tion	Colonel	Seconded to R.F.C. 1916, transferred to R.A.F. 1920. Air Marshal. Col. 8th Hussars 1948. Order of the Crown and Croix de Guerre (Bel- gium) Air Medal U.S.A.
BALDWIN J. N. A.	Jan. 37–May 42	Captain	Killed in action, N. Africa.
BALLANTYNE H. R.	Mar. 55–May 55	2nd Lieutenant	
BARLOW R.	Mar. 48–Feb. 53	Captain	From Para. Regt.
BARNES F. D. C.	Apr. 44–June 48	Captain	
BATES Sir Geoffrey V. Bt., M.C.	Mar. 42–June 45	Captain	
BATES S.	Oct. 45–Sept. 46	Lieutenant	From 23 Hussars. Men- tioned in Despatches.
BECKETT R. E.	Nov. 45–Dec. 46	Lieutenant	
BECKINSALE S. E.	Nov. 39–June 40	2nd Lieutenant	To Royal Tanks.
BEITH G. H. F.	Apr. 51–Oct. 51	Captain	R.A.M.C. attchd. Killed in action, Korea.
BELLAMY L. G. M.C.	Nov. 43–Aug. 50	Captain	
BELMONT H. J.	Sept. 40–Nov. 41	Captain	From French Army (Spahis). To Free French Forces.
BENNETT F. B.	Apr. 44–June 44	2nd Lieutenant	
BENNIE D. G. R.	July 43–Oct 43	Lieutenant	Seconded from Union Defence Forces, South Africa.
BENSON J. A.	Dec. 50–Jan. 52	Captain	11 Hussars attchd. Korea.
BERESFORD M.G. de la P.	Dec. 47–June 48	2nd Lieutenant	
BERRINGER G. S. J.	Mar. 41–Feb. 42	2nd Lieutenant	To 4 County of London Yeomanry.
BEST W. B. P.	July 43–Nov. 45	Captain	R.E.M.E. attchd.

BLAKE H.	July 52–Apr. 54	Captain	R.E.M.E. attchd.
BLAKISTON HOUSTON J. E.	Sept. 02–Apr. 28	Lieut.-Colonel	
BLYTH E. C.	Nov. 15–May 30	Major	
	Aug. 39–June 49		Recalled from reserve, service not with Regt.
BOLLARD P. F.	Mar. 46–Amalgamation	Major	From Royal Tanks.
BOWERS B. A.	Nov. 45–Mar. 46	Lieutenant	From 23 Hussars.
BOWLBY C. P. R. M.C.	Nov. 45–July 46	Lieutenant	From Fife and Forfar Yeomanry.
BOWLER G. P.	Dec. 47–Aug. 48	2nd Lieutenant	
BOYALL D. C.	Sept. 50–Dec. 51	Captain	15/19 Hussars attchd., Korea.
BRACEY-GIBBON J. J. R.	July 52–Sept. 53	2nd Lieutenant	
BRADISH-ELLAMES J. E. M.	Dec. 14–Apr. 25	Major	
	Oct. 40–Feb. 41		Recalled from reserve, served with the Regt.
BRINSON W. L. H.	Sept. 50–Jan. 52	Captain	3 Hussars attchd., Korea.
BRODIE A. B.	Aug. 43–July 44	Lieutenant	From 11 Hussars. Killed in action, N.W. Europe.
BRODIE C. A.	Mar. 49–Mar. 50	2nd Lieutenant	
BROMILEY N. P.	Nov. 46–June 58	Major	From Indian Army (7 Lt. Cav.)
BROOKFIELD W. C.	May 45–Dec. 46	Lieutenant	
BROOKS A. D. B.	Dec. 56–Amalgamation	2nd Lieutenant	
BROWNE M. M. M.	Aug. 43–June 44	Lieutenant	Killed in action N.W. Europe.
BROWNE W. M.	Feb. 53–Oct. 54	Captain	R.A.M.C. attchd.
BROWNING J. E. P.	Dec. 48–Mar. 58	Captain	Air Medal (U.S.A.)
BUIST V. A.	Mar. 41–May 46	Lieutenant	
BUNTING M. B.	Jan. 53–May 54	2nd Lieutenant	
BURNETT H.	Jan. 47–Oct. 54	Captain	To R.A.O.C.
BUTTERELL T. K.	Feb. 48–Apr. 48	2nd Lieutenant	
BUTLER J. C., M.C.	Oct. 48–Aug. 52	Lieutenant	
BUTLER J. W.	Sept. 12–Mar. 19	Captain	
	June 41–Apr. 42		Recalled from reserve, service not with Regt.
BUTLER W. G. O. D.S.O. M.C.	May 48–Amalgamation	Lieut.-Colonel	From Indian Army (Guides Cav.)
CAIRNES J. R.	Jan. 31–Jan. 35	Lieutenant	
CAMERON E. J. F.	May 53–Aug. 54	2nd Lieutenant	
CAMPBELL J.	Apr. 54–Aug. 55	Captain	R.E.M.E. attchd.

CARROLL H. E. Y.	Dec. 17–July 26 Aug. 39–Mar. 43	Lieutenant	Previous O.R. Service with Regt. Recalled from reserve, service not with Regt.
CARTER L. F.	Mar. 41–June 42	Lieutenant	Killed in action N. Africa.
CARVER H. C.	Oct. 39–Sept. 45	Captain	
CARY L. E. W. P.	Oct. 54–Nov. 55	2nd Lieutenant	
CASE A. U.	July 42–May 46	Captain	Mentioned in Despatches.
CAVENDISH C. F. A. C.	Jan. 39–Feb. 40	2nd Lieutenant	
CHAPMAN C. A. J.	Sept. 50–Jan. 52	Lieutenant	Bays, attchd., Korea.
CHAPMAN J. E.	July 42–Feb. 46	Major	Previous O.R. Service in the Regt.
CHARLES F. R.	July 39–Nov. 41	Lieutenant	Killed in action N. Africa.
CHARLTON D. R. W. G. see COLLINS-CHARLTON			
CHILDS J. M.	Nov. 45–Mar. 46	Captain	R.A.M.C. attchd.
CHIRNSIDE P. E. F.	Oct. 15–Apr. 38 Aug. 39–Dec. 46	Major	Recalled from reserve, service not with Regt.
CLARK N. C.	June 55–Apr. 58	Lieutenant	
CLIFFORD G. C. J.	Feb. 13–Feb. 28 Aug. 39–May 40	Captain	Recalled from reserve, service not with Regt. Killed in action with Pioneer Corps.
CLODE W. A.	Sept. 50–Jan. 52	Lieutenant	10 Hussars attchd., Korea.
COLDREY C. A.	July 48–Aug. 58	Captain	
COLDREY W. G.	Nov. 51–Sept. 52	2nd Lieutenant	
COLE T. H.	Feb. 54–Amalgamation	Captain (Q.M.)	Previous O.R. service in the Regt. C.-in-C.'s Certificate.
COLEMAN F. L.	Mar. 41–May 42	2nd Lieutenant	Killed in action N. Africa.
COLLINS-CHARLTON D. R. W. G.	Aug. 33–Amalgamation	Lieut.-Colonel	D.S.C. (U.S.A.)
COMINS J. F. I.	Apr. 58–Amalgamation	2nd Lieutenant	
COMYN J. A.	Aug. 35–Jan. 51	Major	
COOKE R. H.	Feb. 49–Amalgamation	Captain	
COOPER B. A.	Mar. 54–Aug. 55	2nd Lieutenant	
COOPER D. L. A.	See ASTLEY-COOPER.		
CORMACK D. G.	Aug. 54–Amalgamation	Captain	
COVELL D. C.	May 54–Aug. 55	2nd Lieutenant	
COVILL A. P.	June 57–Sept. 58	2nd Lieutenant	
COVILL R. V.	June 53–Sept. 54	2nd Lieutenant	
CRAIG G. L.	Oct. 44–Dec. 44	Lieut.-Colonel	From 4/7 Dragoon Guards. Did not serve with the Regt. Colonel.

Craven D. F.	Apr. 44–May 47	Lieutenant	
Crawshay W. S. C.	Nov. 21–Mar. 32	Major	From 5 Lancers.
Cripps D. S., D.S.O.	July 20–Mar. 39	Lieut.-Colonel	
	Sept. 39–July 45		Recalled from reserve, served with the Regt. Mentioned in despatches.
Critchley D. W.	Mar. 55–Nov. 55	2nd Lieutenant	R.E.M.E. attchd.
Crossley L. H.	Jan. 40–Oct. 45	Captain	
Cullinan P. J. F.	July 57–Oct. 58	2nd Lieutenant	
Currell A.	Aug. 00–June 28	Lieut.-Colonel	
Curtis E. P. S.	July 57–June 58	2nd Lieutenant	
Cuthbert J. C. M.	Jan. 50–Aug. 50	2nd Lieutenant	
Dale Smith P.	Oct. 42–Dec. 42	Lieutenant	
Daly D. W., O.B.E.	Nov. 14–Jan. 32	Lieut.-Colonel	
	Aug. 39–Oct. 45		Recalled from reserve, service not with Regt.
Dansey-Browning G. C.			R.A.M.C. attchd.
Daunt T. L. A.	Feb. 55–May 56	2nd Lieutenant	
Davidson	Aug. 45–Oct. 45	Lieutenant	
Davies D. W.	Nov. 45–Sept. 46	Lieutenant	From 2 Fife and Forfar Yeomanry
Davies G. J.	Aug. 44–Dec. 51	Major	From 2 Northants Yeomanry.
Davies S. J., O.B.E.	Apr. 57–Aug. 58	Captain	R.A.Ch.D. attchd.
Davy J. T.	Sept. 48–Jan. 50	2nd Lieutenant	
Day A. N., M.B.E.	Nov. 53–Amalgamation	Captain (Q.M.)	Previous O.R. service in the Regt.
Day R. F.	Apr. 50–Aug. 50	2nd Lieutenant	
Dear A. A.	Mar. 41–Sept. 41	2nd Lieutenant	To Royal Tanks.
Dearden R. R.	Nov. 54–Apr. 56	2nd Lieutenant	
Deas G. N.	Dec. 18–May 29	Lieutenant	
	Jan. 40–Jan. 44	Major	Recalled from reserve, service not with Regt.
de Blank I. P. M.	Aug. 52–Sept. 53	2nd Lieutenant	
de Clermont P. H. V. D.S.O.	Jan. 32–Mar. 37 Oct. 39–Dec. 56	Lieut.-Colonel	Recalled from reserve, served with Regt. Mentioned in Despatches.
de Courpalay C. R. H.	Aug. 39–May 49	Lieut.-Colonel	Recalled from reserve, from Indian Army served with the Regt.
de Las Casas B. C.	Mar. 47–Mar. 52	Captain	From Irish Guards.
de Lavison D. J.	Mar. 52–Oct. 52	2nd Lieutenant	
de May P. F.	Nov. 43–June 44	Lieutenant	Killed in action, N.W. Europe.

de Morgan B. W.	July 53–Amalgamation	Captain	
Derouet J. D.	Mar. 41–Mar. 46	Lieutenant	
de Salis R. J.	Oct. 55–May 56	2nd Lieutenant	
Dickinson J. L.	Jan. 44–Dec. 45	Lieutenant	
Dill R. P. G.	Apr. 42–Amalgamation	Major	Adopted surname of Murray 54–56. Mentioned in Despatches.
Donadio C. A.	Aug. 48–Sept. 49	2nd Lieutenant	
Dowling B. L.	Sept. 50–Oct. 53	Captain	Recalled from reserve, Royal Tanks, served with the Regt., Korea. To Royal Australian Armoured Corps. Mentioned in Despatches.
Duff C. E. R.	Feb. 27–Nov. 41	Major	Killed in action N. Africa.
Dunlop M. L. G.	Dec. 51–Nov. 52	Lieutenant	
Dunne N. G. F.	Jan. 30–July 52	Major	
Dunning-White J. M.	May 40–July 46	Lieut.-Colonel	Served with Commandos.
Earle P. K.	Jan. 40–July 50	Major	
Easun M. J.	Oct. 49–Sept. 50	2nd Lieutenant	
Edinburgh Prince Philip Duke of (K.G. P.C. K.T.)	June 53–Amalgamation	Colonel-in-Chief	
Elliott J. D. de la C.	July 41–May 42	2nd Lieutenant	Killed in action N. Africa.
Elton H. C.	Apr. 39–Dec. 40	Major	From R.A. Returned to R.A.
Enderby J. S. G.	July 49–Feb. 50	2nd Lieutenant	
Enfield E. R.	Mar. 53–Sept. 54	2nd Lieutenant	
Evans D. L.	Apr. 44–Sept. 44	2nd Lieutenant	
Evans W. H., M.B.E.	Oct. 46–Mar. 49	Lieutenant (Q.M.)	From 1 Fife and Forfar Yeomanry
Evans-Lombe T. B. A. (O.B.E.)	Oct. 16–Jan. 40	Major	Commanded 3 Hussars.
Fernie K. G.	Dec. 17–Oct. 28	Lieutenant	
Firth H. H.	June 40–Mar. 50	Major	Mentioned in Despatches.
Fitzherbert G. E.	Apr. 57–Mar. 58	2nd Lieutenant	
Fitzherbert Y. L. M.	Mar. 40–July 42	Captain	To Transjordan Frontier Force
Fitzpatrick G. R. D. D.S.O. (M.B.E. M.C.)	Jan. 45–June 46	Lieut.-Colonel	From Royals. Major-General. Mentioned in Despatches.

FORBES-ADAM N. C.	Oct. 49–Oct. 50	2nd Lieutenant	
FORD L. T., E.R.D.	Apr. 46–June 58	Major	From Recce Corps.
FRANK P. M.	Aug. 47–Mar. 48	2nd Lieutenant	
FRANCE S. R. B.	May 55–Sept. 56	2nd Lieutenant	
FULLER-GOOD M. R.	Apr. 54–Aug. 55	2nd Lieutenant	
GADSBY R. T.	Mar. 44–Apr. 46	Lieutenant	
GIBBES M. H. A.	May 55–Sept. 56	2nd Lieutenant	
GIBBES N. A. St. G.	May 40–May 42	Captain	Killed in action N. Africa.
GILBEY S. R.	Dec. 49–Nov. 54	Captain	
GIMBLETT D.	May 41–Dec. 45	Lieutenant	
GOLDSWORTHY D. E.	Dec. 47–July 48	2nd Lieutenant	
GOODSON D. F. J.	Aug. 39– 41	Lieutenant	Recalled from reserve, served with the Regt.
GOULBURN C., D.S.O.	Mar. 27–Jan. 58	Lieut.-Colonel	Brigadier. Mentioned in Despatches.
GOULD G. W., M.C.	Nov. 44–July 47	Lieutenant	
GRAHAM J. J.	Dec. 51–Amalgamation	Captain	
GRATTAN-BELLEW B. A. H.	June 56–June 57	2nd Lieutenant	
GREAVES J. S.	Mar. 46–Oct. 46	Lieutenant	
GREENSTREET W. M.C.	May 17–July 33	Major (Q.M.)	Previous O.R. service in the Regt.
GREGORY M. K.	Aug. 52–Sept. 53	2nd Lieutenant	
GREGORY R. E.	Mar. 41–Oct. 41	2nd Lieutenant	To Greys.
GROSVENOR G. H. (D.S.O.)	Sept. 40–Nov. 40	Major	From 9 Lancers, did not serve with the Regt.
GWYN J. W., M.C.	Sept. 36–May 45	Major	
HACKETT J. W. (C.B. C.B.E.) D.S.O.(2 bars) M.C.	Jan. 31–Nov. 51	Lieut.-Colonel	Major-General. Mentioned in Despatches thrice.
HALL N. D. A.	May 40–Mar. 46	Major	
HALL-GARDINER A. M.	Oct. 52–Feb. 53	Captain	R.A.M.C. attchd.
HANNAY D. H. A.	May 55–Aug. 56	2nd Lieutenant	
HANSEN B. B.	Nov. 45–Oct. 46	Lieutenant	
HARARI M. E.	Nov. 39–May 43	Major	
HARARI P. V.	Mar. 55–May 56	2nd Lieutenant	
HARBORD J. D.	Aug. 29–Nov. 42	Major	Killed in action N. Africa. Mentioned in Despatches four times.
HARBORD S. J. F.	Dec. 52–Dec. 53	2nd Lieutenant	
HARROWELL D. W. T.	46– 47	Captain	R.E.M.E. attchd.

Hart K. I. G.	Sept. 50–Jan. 52	Lieutenant	7 Hussars attchd., Korea.
Hartwright P. G.	Jan. 44–Aug. 58	Major	Mentioned in Despatches.
Harvey-Kelly H. D.	Feb. 53–July 58	Lieutenant	
Hector E. McC.	Mar. 41–Aug. 41	2nd Lieutenant	Died on active service N. Africa.
Hedley C. F., M.B.E.	June 40–Apr. 47	Major (Q.M.)	Previous O.R. service in the Regt. Mentioned in Despatches twice.
Hepburn J. A. S.	Oct. 42–Mar. 46	Captain	From Royal Tanks.
Heycock J. B., M.C.	Aug. 40–Nov. 45	Captain	R.A.M.C. attchd.
Hilliard D. G. M.	Oct. 52–Dec. 53	Lieutenant	
Hilliard J.	Sept. 56–Nov. 57	2nd Lieutenant	
Hilltout A. J.	Nov. 39–Nov. 40	2nd Lieutenant	From Royal Tanks. To Royal Tanks.
Hind A. J.	Jan. 43–Apr. 48	Captain	Mentioned in Despatches.
Hone F. L.	Aug. 41–Aug. 45	Captain	R.A.Ch.D. attchd.
Hooper J. G.	Jan. 40–Nov. 45	Lieut.-Colonel	
Hope-Murray H. C.	Aug. 18–July 37	Captain	
	Aug. 39–Sept. 45	Major	Recalled from reserve, service not with Regt.
Hornby R. F.	Sept. 10–May 29	Captain	
How F. R. W.	July 19–Aug. 36	Major	
	Aug. 39–Sept. 45		Recalled from reserve, served with the Regt.
Howard G. F.	Apr. 58–Amalgamation	2nd Lieutenant	
Howard M. C.	May 54–Sept. 55	2nd Lieutenant	
Howarth B. W.	Sept. 50–Apr. 55	Captain	R.A.Ch.D. attchd.
Howell J.	July 49–May 50	2nd Lieutenant	
Huntington	Mar. 41–Nov. 41	2nd Lieutenant	
Hurst F. J. E.	Oct. 42–June 44	Lieutenant	
Hurst J. G.	Aug. 50–June 58	Captain	
Husband J. S.	May 51–July 52	Captain	R.E.M.E. attchd.
Hutchings R. N.	July 52–Sept. 53	2nd Lieutenant	
Hutchinson I. M. O.	Aug. 43–Mar. 44	Captain	From Fife and Forfar Yeomanry.
Huth P. H., D.S.O. M.C. and bar.	Aug. 35–Amalgamation	Lieut.-Colonel	
James P. C. R.	Dec. 52–Apr. 54	2nd Lieutenant	
Jarvis A. G.	July 57–Sept. 58	2nd Lieutenant	
Jenkins J. C.	Feb. 48–Sept. 48	2nd Lieutenant	
Jephson M. J. E.	Jan. 44–Feb. 46	Lieutenant	
Jermyn Scott G. W.	Feb. 40–July 41	Captain	
Jones B. R.	Apr. 46–June 48	Captain	
Jones F. T. D.	Jan. 47–Jan. 48	Lieutenant	
Jones H. L., D.S.O.	June 28–Apr. 32	Lieut.-Colonel	From 13/18 Hussars.
Justham	Aug. 45–Dec. 45	Lieutenant	

KELLY B. N. D. G. T.	Feb. 49–Aug. 49	2nd Lieutenant	
KENNEDY C. C.	Mar. 45–Mar. 46	Lieutenant	
KESSEL	Oct. 52–Sept. 53	2nd Lieutenant	R.E.M.E. attchd.
KILKELLY G. P.	Dec. 19–Aug. 44	Lieut.-Colonel	Killed in air raid P.O.W. Camp, Germany.
KIRKHAM G. R. C. A.	July 43–Mar. 46	Captain	Previous O.R. service in the Regt.
KNIGHT R. A. W.	Dec. 14–Mar. 33	Captain	
KNOWLES R. G.	June 47–Mar. 48	2nd Lieutenant	
KUNZER T. H. S.	Feb. 54–Amalgamation	Lieutenant	
LADENBURG J. A. G.	Mar. 42–Mar. 46	Captain	Mentioned in Despatches.
LEATHAM C. W. B.	Feb. 48–Dec. 48	2nd Lieutenant	
LE MARCHANT M.	Dec. 56–Mar. 58	2nd Lieutenant	
LIDSEY J. H.	Aug. 50–Jan. 52	Captain	K.D.G. attchd., Korea. Mentioned in Despatches.
LINDSAY-REA R. D.	May 55–Aug. 56	2nd Lieutenant	
LOCKHART W. G.	Aug. 41–July 45	Lieutenant	
LOMBARD J. N.	July 42–May 46	Captain	
LORD C. A.	May 54–Sept. 55	2nd Lieutenant	
LOUGHLAN K. F. M.	Feb. 45–Apr. 48	Lieutenant	
LOWTHER Sir William G. Bt., O.B.E.	Sept. 32–Feb. 54	Lieut.-Colonel	Mentioned in Despatches twice.
LYSAGHT D. E.	Jan. 55–May 56	2nd Lieutenant	
McCLINTOCK A. F.	Apr. 41–Jan. 46	Captain	From 7 Hussars.
McCLOGHRY C. E.	Nov. 39–Dec. 39	Captain	R.A.M.C. attchd.
McCLURG S. K. B.	Apr. 44–June 47	Captain	
McCORQUADALE E. N. J.	Oct. 49–Nov. 49	2nd Lieutenant	
McCULLOCH G.	Mar. 41–Nov. 41	2nd Lieutenant	
MACDONALD H. S.	Sept. 56–May 57	2nd Lieutenant	
McDONNELL R. E.	Jan. 35–Feb. 41	Lieutenant	Killed in action N. Africa.
the McGILLYCUDDY of the REEKS.	Aug. 44–Apr. 45	Captain	From 2 Northants Yeomanry.
McGILLYCUDDY J. P.	see above.		
McGOWAN J. G.	May 48 49	Major	From Indian Army (18 Cav.)
MACKWORTH J. D.	Mar. 57–Amalgamation	Captain	R.E.M.E. attchd.
MAHON Sir Bryan T. K.C.B., K.C.V.O., D.S.O.	Feb. 83–Apr. 04 Mar. 10–Sept. 30	General Colonel	

MALET Sir Edward W. St L., Bt. (O.B.E.)	Mar. 30–Apr. 55	Lieut.-Colonel	Mentioned in Despatches.
MALSEED J. R.	Nov. 45–June 47	Lieutenant	From 23 Hussars.
MARTIN A. C. N.	Mar. 47–Dec. 47	Lieutenant	From Inns of Court.
MARTIN D. W.	Dec. 49–Aug. 53	Lieutenant	Air Medal (U.S.A.).
MARWOOD M. B.	June 46–Feb. 58	Major	From 3 Dragoon Guards.
MASSY C. J.	June 46–Mar. 47	Lieutenant	
MEADE C. J. G.	May 41–Amalgamation	Major	From 2 Royal Gloucester Hussars. Mentioned in Despatches.
MIDDLETON J. P. (O.B.E.)	Jul. 33–Dec. 55	Lieut.-Colonel (Q.M.)	Previous O.R. service in the Regt.
MILLINER G. A. G.	Aug. 44–Jan. 45	Lieutenant	From 2 Northants Yeomanry.
MILLS T. M.	Nov. 40–Feb. 46	Captain	
MILNER T. J. L.	Aug. 48–Sept. 49	2nd Lieutenant	
MOLL P. D.	Nov. 44–Aug 47	Lieutenant	
MOLLO B.	Feb. 55–May 56	2nd Lieutenant	
MONTGOMERY S. M.	Oct. 16–Dec. 20		
	Aug. 39–Sept. 40	Captain	Recalled from reserve, service not with Regt.
MOORE H. M. (D.S.C.)	Oct. 47–Amalgamation	Major	From R.N.V.R.
MORGAN M. A.	Aug. 55–Mar. 57	Captain	R.E.M.E. attchd.
MORRIS R. J. W.	Nov. 55–Mar. 58	Lieutenant	
MORRIS-EYTON J. R.	Aug. 49–May 50	Lieutenant	
	Sept. 50–Oct. 51		Recalled from reserve, served with the Regt., Korea.
MOSS W.	Nov. 40–May 42	Captain	
MOSSOP D. L.	July 43–Oct. 45	Lieutenant	Seconded from Union Defence Forces, South Africa.
MULLINER A., M.C.	May 10–Sept. 33	Major	
MURRAY G. S., M.C.	Aug. 50–May 51	Captain	5 Inniskilling Dragoon Guards, attchd., Korea.
MURRAY R. P. G.	See DILL.		
NELSON Sir William V. H. Bt., O.B.E.	Feb. 34–Amalgamation	Major	Mentioned in Despatches.
NEWMAN A. R.	July 42–Aug. 48	Captain	Previous O.R. service in the Regt.
NEWMAN G. D. J.	July 49–Apr. 50	2nd Lieutenant	
NIAS E. G.	Nov. 45–Jan. 56	Major (Q.M.)	Previous O.R. service in the Regt.
NORRIS E. M.	May 46–Oct. 56	Captain	

Oakes H. O.	Sept. 47–June 48	Lieutenant	Did not serve with Regt. To R.A.E.C.
O'Connor F.	Nov. 54–July 57	Captain	R.A.M.C. attchd.
Oliver M. D.	Feb. 52–Amalgamation	Captain	
O'Malley E.	Aug. 42–Mar. 45	Lieut. (Q.M.)	Previous O.R. service with Regt.
O'Neill M. G.	Sept. 47–Feb. 53	Major	From Indian Army.
O'Neill The Lord	Aug. 26–Dec. 29	Lieutenant	
O'Neill S. E. R.	see above.		
Ormrod P. C., M.C.	May 47–Oct. 53	Captain	From Scots Guards.
O'Rorke B. R.	Feb. 52–Amalgamation	Captain	
O'Shaunessy (G.C., M.C., M.B.E.), M.M.	Dec. 39– 45	Major	Previous O.R. service with Regt. Served with Pioneer Corps.
Ottey, G. R.	Mar. 44–Amalgamation	Major	From Indian Army. (Guides Cav.)
Paine N. R. B.	July 50–Mar. 55	Lieutenant	
Page A. H. C.	May 46–Sept. 52	Captain	
Patchett D. R.	Aug. 50–Apr. 51	Captain	R.A.M.C. attchd.
Paton J. D.	Sept. 15–Nov. 28	Captain	
Paul C. E., M.C.	Sept. 50–Jan. 52	Lieutenant	14/20 Hussars, attchd., Korea.
Payne M. S., M.C.	Feb. 44–Oct. 47	Captain	From Para Regt. (Air Landing Recce).
Peacock G.	Aug. 57–Amalgamation	Captain	R.A.M.C. attchd.
Pegler H. R. D. (D.C.M., M.M.)	Oct. 42–June 44	Lieutenant	Killed in action N.W. Europe.
Pelling A. D. M.B.E.	May 49–Amalgamation	Major (Q.M.)	From Life Guards.
Pezzani R. R.	Nov. 52–Dec. 53	2nd Lieutenant	
Phillips J. W.	Sept. 27–Dec. 51	Lieut.-Colonel	Mentioned in Despatches.
Pickup E. S.	Nov. 45–Mar. 46	Captain	R.A.Ch.D. attchd.
Pierrepont P. W.	Oct. 44–Jan. 48	Captain	From 2 Northants Yeomanry.
Pierson H. T.	Aug. 44–Amalgamation	Major	From 2 Northants Yeomanry.
Pilsbury J. G.	Aug. 46–Oct. 46	Lieutenant	From 1 Fife and Forfar Yeomanry.
Pim J. P. S.	Mar. 45–Apr. 45	Lieutenant	From R.A. Killed in action N.W. Europe.
Piper R. W., M.C.	Sept. 50–Amalgamation	Major	From reserve Royal Tanks, served with the Regt., Korea.

Pope C. J. R.	Nov. 55–Nov. 57	Lieutenant	
Pope D., M.C.	Sept. 10–Apr. 36	Lieut.-Colonel	
	Aug. 39–Jan. 45		Recalled from reserve, service not with Regt.
Portal S. G. M.	Sept. 50–Jan. 52	Lieutenant	17/21 Lancers attchd., Korea.
Pott J. A.	Nov. 44–July 47	Lieutenant	
Powerscourt Viscount	Feb. 26–Nov. 29	Lieutenant	
Pratt J. L. C.	Aug. 53–Jan. 55	2nd Lieutenant	
Preston A. L.	Apr. 45–July 47	Lieutenant	
Preston L.	Jan. 43–Oct. 44	Lieutenant	From Westminster Dragoons. Killed in action N.W. Europe.
Pringle J.C., M.C. and Bar	Aug. 35–July 46	Captain	
Probyn D. F. P. C.	Sept. 50–Feb. 51	Lieutenant	3 Hussars attchd. Died while P.O.W. Korea.
Pullen J. A.	Oct. 46–Dec. 47	2nd Lieutenant	
Radford M. A.	Aug. 50–Amalgamation	Major	Recalled from reserve 3 Dragoon Guards, served with the Regt., Korea. Mentioned in Despatches.
Rae N. M. D.	Jan. 52–Oct. 52	2nd Lieutenant	
Ralphs H. R. P.	Nov. 38–Nov. 39	Captain	R.A.O.C. attchd.
Rampf D., M.C.	July 43–Oct. 45	Captain	Seconded from Union Defence Forces, South Africa.
Randall R. J. H.	Dec. 51–Amalgamation	Major	
Rea M. F.	Oct. 55–Amalgamation	Captain	From 5 Inniskilling Dragoon Guards.
Read C. W. M.	Sept. 49–Feb. 50	2nd Lieutenant	
Rhodes G. L. H.	Nov. 39–May 40	2nd Lieutenant	
Ricardo D. C.	May 40–June 43	Lieutenant	
Robertson J. R.	May 40–Jan. 46	Major	
Robertson J. R. L.	Nov. 47–Aug. 48	2nd Lieutenant	
Robinson F. E. S.	Apr. 48–Mar. 49	2nd Lieutenant	
Robinson J. P.	Oct. 20–July 21		
	Aug. 39–Feb. 46	Lieut.-Colonel	Recalled from reserve, service not with Regt. Mentioned in Despatches (twice).
Rodgers G. K. C.	Dec. 49–Dec. 50	2nd Lieutenant	
Roffey R. S.	Jan. 40–Amalgamation	Major	

Rothery R. H.	May 51–Oct. 51	Captain	Recalled from reserve, served with the Regt., Korea.
Rothwell M. J.	Sept. 54–Apr. 55	Lieutenant	Recalled from reserve 12 Lancers, served with the Regt.
Rowley G. G.	June 56–Amalgamation	Lieutenant	
Rowley G. S.	Dec. 11–Feb. 29	Major	
Ruddle K. A.	May 55–Apr. 58	Lieutenant	
Ryde W. F.	Aug. 44–Apr. 45	Lieutenant	From 2 Northants Yeomanry. Killed in action N.W. Europe.
St. Oswald, Lord, M.C.	Jan. 43–Feb. 46 Oct. 50–Jan. 52	Major	Recalled from reserve, served with Regt., Korea. Chevalier of the order of Leopold with palm, Croix de Guerre with palm (Belgium).
Salmon E. J. L.	Aug. 55–Aug. 56	2nd Lieutenant	
Sandbach P. D.	July 37–Dec. 41	Major	From 12 Lancers. Killed in action N. Africa. Mentioned in Despatches.
Saxby F. W., M.C.	Aug. 44–Dec. 45	Lieutenant	From 2 Northants Yeomanry. Killed on active service.
Scott A.	Aug. 50–	Lieutenant	7 Hussars attchd., Korea.
Scott D. A.	Sept. 49–Sept. 50	2nd Lieutenant	
Scott D. S.	Mar. 42–July 44	Lieutenant	Killed in action N.W. Europe.
Scott G. W. J.	see Jermyn Scott.		
Scrimgeour R. N. C.	July 46–Jan. 51	Captain	
Scrimgeour S. J.	Mar. 57–July 58	2nd Lieutenant	
Searle J. G.		Lieutenant	R.A.M.C. attchd.
Serruys G.	Sep. 44–Dec. 44	Captain	4 Belgian Lancers attchd.
Sibley N. T.	Dec. 56–Jan. 58	2nd Lieutenant	
Simons J. F.	see Weston-Simons.		
Smith M. H. C.	Aug. 44–Oct. 44	2nd Lieutenant	
Soper R. F., M.B.E.	June 55–July 58	Captain	R.A.P.C. attchd.
Southerton R. C.	Jan. 50–June 51	Captain	R.E.M.E. attchd.
Southwell P. A. J.	see below.		
Southwell, Viscount	Dec. 51–July 55	Captain	
Spiro R. M.	Feb. 57–June 58	2nd Lieutenant	
Stamper C. L.	Apr. 48–July 49	2nd Lieutenant	

STANILAND E. A.	Sept. 13–June 33 Aug. 39–Dec. 42	Major	Recalled from reserve, service not with Regt.
STEWART G. M., M.B.E.	June 58–Amalgama- tion	Major	R.A.P.C. attchd.
STOKES T. G. H.	Apr. 57–Aug. 58	2nd Lieutenant	
STRACHAN G. H. (M.C.)	Nov. 47–Amalgama- tion	Lieut.-Colonel	From King's Own Lancashire Regt.
STUBBS V. G.	Oct. 52–July 55	Major	R.A.P.C. attchd.
SUNDERLAND R. S.	Mar. 46–June 46	Captain	R.A.M.C. attchd.
TALBOT-HARVEY H. L.	Feb. 44–June 44	Lieutenant	Killed in action, N.W. Europe.
TAYLOR C.	Dec. 39–July 40		R.A.M.C. attchd.
TAYLOR G. D. T.	Jan. 42–Dec. 42	Lieutenant	From Warwickshire Yeomanry.
THORNTON F.	Apr. 36–Oct. 38	Lieut.-Colonel	From 16/5 Lancers. Mentioned in Despatches.
THRELFALL G. W. G. M.C.	Sept. 32–July 44	Major	Killed in action, N.W. Europe. Mentioned in Despatches.
TISDALL W. St. C. M.C.	Apr. 42–Amalgama- tion	Major	
TOLPUTT W. P. R.	Jan. 47–Dec. 48	Lieutenant	To R.A.
TOWNLEY D. A.	Dec. 47–June 48	2nd Lieutenant	
TRAVES A. R.	Apr. 52–Aug. 53	2nd Lieutenant	
TREVES M.	Apr. 49–Apr. 50	2nd Lieutenant	
TROUGHTON C. D. B. M.C.	July 49–Amalgama- tion	Captain	
TURNER F. G.	Mar. 45–May 46	Captain	
Van der BYL J., D.S.O.	May 98–Nov. 24 Sept. 30–Jan. 48	Colonel	Brigadier
VAUGHAN-ARBUCKLE D. K. T.	June 58–Amalgama- tion	2nd Lieutenant	
VENNER A. B.	Aug. 44–Sept. 44	Lieutenant	From 2 Northants Yeomanry. Killed in action N.W. Europe.
VENNER J., M.C.	Aug. 50–Jan. 52	Lieutenant	7 Hussars attchd., Korea.
VERNON S. H.	Jan. 31–Apr. 35	Lieutenant	
VERNON-MILLER J. C.	Oct. 26–Oct. 43	Major	Mentioned in Despatches.
VICKERS G. V.	Oct. 45–Nov. 46	Captain	From 23 Hussars.
VICKERY P. A.	Sept. 40–Feb. 42	Major	From French Army (8 Cuirassiers).
VOELCKER C. D.	May 52–Aug. 53	2nd Lieutenant	
VOS P. S.	Jan. 40–May 42	Lieutenant	

WAGG R. E. V.	Mar. 48–Mar. 49	2nd Lieutenant	
WAGSTAFFE P. H.	Jan. 40–Mar. 46	Major	
WALKER J. C. F.	Sept. 50–Oct. 51	Lieutenant	Recalled from reserve. Greys. Served with the Regt., killed in action, Korea.
WALKER M. C.	Jan. 42–Apr. 45	Captain	
WALLER C. J.	Sept. 54–Amalgamation	Captain	
WARR B. J.	Nov. 46–May 47	Lieutenant	From 1 Northants Yeomanry.
WATHEN H. J.	Aug. 54–Sept. 55	2nd Lieutenant	
WATHEN L. W. D.	Sept. 10–Dec. 33	Major	
	Aug. 39–Feb. 43		Recalled from reserve, service not with Regt.
WATSON T. G.	Dec. 14–May 41	Lieut.-Colonel	Colonel. Mentioned in Despatches.
WEBSTER R. S.	Feb. 55–Amalgamation	Captain	
WEIR J. H.	Sept. 46–June 47	Captain	From 1 Fife and Forfar Yeomanry.
WELLESLEY C. deV.	June 46–Jan. 48	Lieutenant	
WELLMAN M. R.	47– 48	Captain	R.E.M.E. attchd.
WESTON-SIMONS J. F. M.C.	July 39–Amalgamation	Lieut.-Colonel	
WHARTON J.	Jan. 43–June 46	Lieutenant	From 2 Royal Gloucester Hussars.
WHEATLEY D. P. F.	Dec. 46–Jan. 48	2nd Lieutenant.	
WHITE M. D.	Dec. 55–Amalgamation	Lieutenant	
WHITFIELD G. N. R. (M.C.)	Mar. 47–Nov. 51	Captain	From Irish Guards.
WILD C. A.	Feb. 48–July 48	2nd Lieutenant	
WINCH R. W., M.M.	May 45–Feb. 46	Captain	Previous O.R. service in the Regt.
WINDSOR W.	July 40–Oct. 40	Captain	R.A.M.C. attchd.
WINGFIELD the Hon. M. P.	see POWERSCOURT.		
WINN the Hon. R. D. G.	see St OSWALD		
WODEHOUSE A. G.	Aug. 24–Jan. 30	Lieutenant	
WOLFE G.	Sep. 50–Jan. 52	Captain	9 Lancers attchd., Korea. Mentioned in Despatches.
WOOD H. H.	Feb. 48–Amalgamation	Major	From K.D.G.
WOOD J. L.	June 54–Sept. 55	2nd Lieutenant	
WOOD R. O. G.	Mar. 50–Amalgamation	Captain	

x

WORLEDGE J. A. G.	Oct. 45–June 47	Lieutenant	
WRIGHT B. H. F.	June 53–Amalgama-tion	Captain	
WRIGHT J. T.	June 40–July 42	Captain	
WRIGHT M.	Mar. 57–Amalgama-tion	Major	From R.A.
WYATT C. E. N.	Apr. 40–May 41	Lieutenant	To 10 Hussars.
YOUNG J. G. M.	Feb. 42–Aug. 44	Lieutenant	Killed in action, N.W. Europe.

APPENDIX IV

COLONELS OF THE REGIMENT, LIEUT.-COLONELS IN COMMAND AND OTHER SENIOR OFFICERS

COLONEL IN CHIEF

H.R.H. the DUKE of EDINBURGH, K.G., K.T., G.B.E. ...	1953–Amalgamation

COLONELS

General Sir Bryon T. MAHON, P.C., K.C.B., K.C.V.O. D.S.O.	1911–1930
Brigadier J. Van der BYL, D.S.O.	1930–1948
Air Marshal Sir John E. A. BALDWIN, K.B.E., C.B., D.S.O....	1948–Amalgamation

COMMANDING OFFICERS

Lieut.-Colonel A. CURRELL	1924–1928
Lieut.-Colonel H. L. JONES, D.S.O.	1928–1932
Lieut.-Colonel D. POPE, M.C.	1932–1936
Lieut.-Colonel F. THORNTON	1936–1938
Lieut.-Colonel T. G. WATSON	1938–1941
Lieut.-Colonel D. S. CRIPPS, D.S.O.	1941–1941
Lieut.-Colonel E. KILKELLY	1941–1942
Lieut.-Colonel C. GOULBURN, D.S.O.	1942–1945
Lieut.-Colonel G. R. D. FITZPATRICK, D.S.O., M.B.E., M.C.	1945–1946
Lieut.-Colonel C. GOULBURN, D.S.O.	1946–1950
Lieut.-Colonel J. W. PHILLIPS	1950–1951
Lieut.-Colonel Sir W. G. LOWTHER, O.B.E.	1951–1953
Lieut.-Colonel P. H. V. de CLERMONT, D.S.O.	1953–1956
Lieut.-Colonel P. H. HUTH, D.S.O., M.C.	1956–Amalgamation

SECONDS-IN-COMMAND

Major J. E. BLAKISTON-HOUSTON	1927–1928
Major D. POPE, M.C.	1929–1930
Major L. W. D. WATHEN	1932–1933
Major T. G. WATSON	1933–1938
Major T. B. A. EVANS-LOMBE	1938–1940
Major G. KILKELLY	1940–1940
Major F. R. W. HOW	1940–1941
Major J. D. HARBORD	1941–1941
Major J. W. PHILLIPS	1941–1945
Major P. H. V. de CLERMONT	1945–1945
Major D. R. W. G. COLLINS-CHARLTON	1945–1946
Major N. G. F. DUNNE	1946–1948
Major J. W. PHILLIPS	1948–1950
Major Sir W. G. LOWTHER	1950–1951

Major W. V. H. Nelson 1951–1953
Major J. F. Weston-Simons, M.C. 1953–1956
Major G. H. Strachan, M.C. 1956–1957
Major W. G. O. Butler, D.S.O., M.C. 1957–1958
Major H. T. Pierson 1958–Amalgamation

ADJUTANTS

Captain T. G. Watson 1927–1929
Captain T. B. A. Evans-Lombe 1929–1930
Captain F. R. W. How 1933–1936
Captain C. E. R. Duff 1936–1938
Captain J. D. Harbord 1938–1940
Captain P. D. Sandbach 1940–1941
Captain J. N. A. Baldwin 1941–1942
Captain P. H. Wagstaffe 1942–1943
Captain J. A. G. Ladenburg 1943–1944
Captain A. V. Case 1944–1945
Captain P. H. V. de Clermont 1945–1945
Captain A. V. Case 1945–1946
Captain R. P. G. Dill 1946–1948
Captain P. C. Ormrod 1948–1950
Captain L. G. Bellamy, M.C. 1950–1950
Captain C. J. G. Meade 1950–1951
Captain W. St. C. Tisdall, M.C. 1951–1952
Major W. G. O. Butler, D.S.O., M.C. 1952–1953
Major R. P. G. Dill 1953–1953
Captain C. A. Coldrey 1953–1954
Major M. B. Marwood 1954–1955
Captain J. G. Hurst 1955–1957
Captain C. D. B. Troughton, M.C. 1957–1957
Captain R. H. Cooke 1957–Amalgamation

QUARTERMASTERS

Major (Q.M.) W. Greenstreet, M.C. 1917–1933
Captain (Q.M.) J. P. Middleton 1933–1940
Lieutenant (Q.M.) C. F. Hedley 1940–1942
Lieutenant (Q.M.) E. O'Malley 1942–1945
Captain (Q.M.) C. F. Hedley 1945–1945
Captain (Q.M.) E. G. Nias 1945–1946
Lieutenant (Q.M.) W. H. Evans, M.B.E. 1946–1948
Major (Q.M.) C. F. Hedley, M.B.E 1948–1953
Major (Q.M.) A. D. Pelling, M.B.E. ... ... 1953–Amalgamation (previously with Yeomanry)
Captain (Q.M.) A. N. Day, M.B.E. (Tech. Q.M.) ... ... 1957–Amalgamation (previously with Yeomanry)
Lieutenant (Q.M.) T. H. Cole ... ... 1954–Amalgamation (with Yeomanry)

REGIMENTAL SERGEANT MAJORS

R.S.M. T. Nicholson, M.M. ...	1927–1930
R.S.M. C. O'Shaughnessy, M.M.	1930–1939
R.S.M. C. F. Hedley ...	1939–1940
R.S.M. T. Hegarty ...	1940–1942
R.S.M. W. McMasters, M.M.	1942–1945
R.S.M. T. Hegarty ...	1945–1950
R.S.M. T. V. Leckie ...	1950–1955
R.S.M. R. I. Vallance, D.C.M.	1955–Amalgamation

REGIMENTAL MEDICAL OFFICERS

Captain C. E. McCloghry	1939–1939
Captain Taylor ...	1939–1940
Captain Windsor...	1940–1940
Captain Heycock, M.C.	1940–1945
Captain Childs ...	1945–1946
Captain Sunderland	1946–1946
Captain Patchett	1950–1951
Captain Beith ...	1951–1951
Captain Hall Gardiner ...	1952–1953
Captain Browne	1953–1954
Captain O'Connor	1954–1957
Captain Peacock ...	1957–Amalgamation

CHAPLAINS

Captain F. L. Hone	1941–1945
Captain E. S. Pickup	1945–1946
Captain B. W. Howarth	1950–1955
Captain S. J. Davies	1957–1958

PAYMASTERS

Major V. G. Stubbs	1952–1955
Major R. F. Soper, M.B.E.	1955–1958
Major G. M. Stewart ...	1958–Amalgamation

E.M.E.

Captain H. R. P. Ralphs...	1938–1939
Captain A. S. Alcock ...	1941–1942
Captain W. Best ...	1943–1945
Captain D. W. T. Harrowell	1946–1947
Captain M. R. Wellman	1947–1948
Captain R. C. Southerton	1950–1951

APPENDIX V

NOTES ON REGIMENTAL DRESS AND INSIGNIA
AS ILLUSTRATED

1. The King's crown pattern badge, worn in the No. 1 Dress Hat and the S.D. Cap, without backing cloth, by the Officers, the R.S.M. and the Bandmaster. The whole in gilt except for the angel harp which was silver plated. A similar design was worn upon the Beret by the Officers and the R.S.M. It was embroidered upon a black back-cloth.

2. The King's Crown Badge worn by all ranks below Bandmaster, without backing cloth, in the No. 1 Dress Hat, the S.D. Cap, the Beret and the coloured F.S. Cap. The whole in gilding metal except for the angel harp which was in white metal.

3. The King's Crown Collar Badges. Worn in pairs facing inwards, by all ranks (including Officers) in Battle Dress, and by the Bandmaster and all ranks below in S.D. and No. 1 Dress. The crown was of gilding metal and the angel harp of white metal. Similar designs in gilt and silver plate, and in bronze were worn by the Officers and the R.S.M., on No. 1 Dress and on S.D. respectively.

4. The Shoulder Title worn by the Officers, the R.S.M. and the Bandmaster on S.D. and No. 1 Dress, only. It was gilt. A white worsted Title, of similar design, on Khaki melton, was worn by these ranks on Battle Dress.

5. The Shoulder Title worn by all ranks below Bandmaster. It was of gilt metal and was worn upon S.D. and B.D. only.

6. The King's Crown pattern button worn by the Officers, the R.S.M. and the Bandmaster upon the fronts of S.D. and No. 1 Dress. A similar smaller button was worn by these ranks on the pockets and sleeves in these orders of dress, and on the S.D. Cap and No. 1 Dress Hat.

7. The Queen's Crown, without crimson caps or enamel, worn by Majors and above on S.D. and No. 1 Dress. This was worn as an alternative to the King's pattern Crown within the Regiment It was also worn alternatively surmounting the Officers pattern cap badge (Fig. 1), the Collar Badges (Fig. 3) and the cypher on the buttons (Fig. 6).

8. The gilt star without enamel, worn by officers upon S.D. and No. 1 Dress.

9. The gilt King's Crown worn alternative to the Queen's Crown (Fig. 7.) Similar badges of rank embroidered in buff and brown worsted upon a yellow cloth background were worn on B.D. Large gilt crowns and stars, about one inch in diameter, were worn by Officers on the great coat.

10. The button worn by the Officers and the R.S.M. on greatcoat fronts, full domed gilt. Similar buttons of gilded metal were worn by all ranks below the R.S.M. upon their greatcoat fronts, and smaller versions were worn on S.D. and No. 1 Dress. Full ball buttons were alternatively worn by O.Rs.

11. The Regimental pattern Spur, nickel plated, worn by the Officers with No. 1 Dress and Mess Dress. A lighter and more swan-necked version was worn by the R.S.M. and Bandmaster.

12. The white metal Arm Badge worn by all ranks below R.S.M. down to inclusive Full Corporal. The Badge worn by the R.S.M. which was of hall marked silver was slightly smaller and bore the Queen's Crown. It is claimed that this badge has been handed down since 1842. Arm Badges were worn without backing on No. 1 Dress, S.D. and B.D.

13. The collar badges as worn by Officers in Mess Dress. They were embroidered in gold wire and gold sequins upon a dark blue cloth background.

14. The gold lace Pouch Belt worn by all Officers, the R.S.M. and the Bandmaster, in No. 1 Dress over the left shoulder. The belt was of Regimental gold lace, of shamrock pattern mounted upon red cloth. Sword slings and the Bandmaster's Frock Coat Girdle were of a similar design. (Approx. quarter scale).

15. The 'Tent Hat' worn by the Officers in virtually any order of dress, at the Commanding Officer's discretion. It was of dark green cloth with Regimental braid as shown. The front of the cap faces to the right in the illustration. The left side of the cap did not bear the intersected 'V' of gold russia braid shown. It was worn with neither badge nor buttons. (Approx. quarter scale). A coloured F.S. Cap of universal pattern, in dark green with gold russia braid was available to all ranks below the R.S.M. for purchase at their own expense.

16. The gold lace cheveron as worn by all ranks between Lance-Corporal and Trumpet Major inclusive upon No. 1 Dress. The cheverons were of Regimental pattern gold lace and were stuffed so that they stood out from their red cloth backing to a depth of about half an inch. These cheverons were both broader and longer than the universal pattern. The cheverons worn on S.D., B.D. and on the greatcoat were of normal pattern drab worsted. Lance-Corporals however wore two cheverons on the right sleeve, only, of their greatcoats.

17. Full Dress Officers Pouch. This was of red cloth embroidered in gold wire, excepting the lettering, cypher and harp strings which were of silver wire and the caps to the crowns which were of crimson velvet. (Approx quarter scale.)

A Black patent leather pouch with gilt mountings, but with no badge or other decoration was worn by those not in possession of the full dress pouch. Pouches were worn with the pouch belt on occasions by those as stated.

A similar black patent leather pouch was worn with a white pipe-clayed belt by the Orderly W.O.

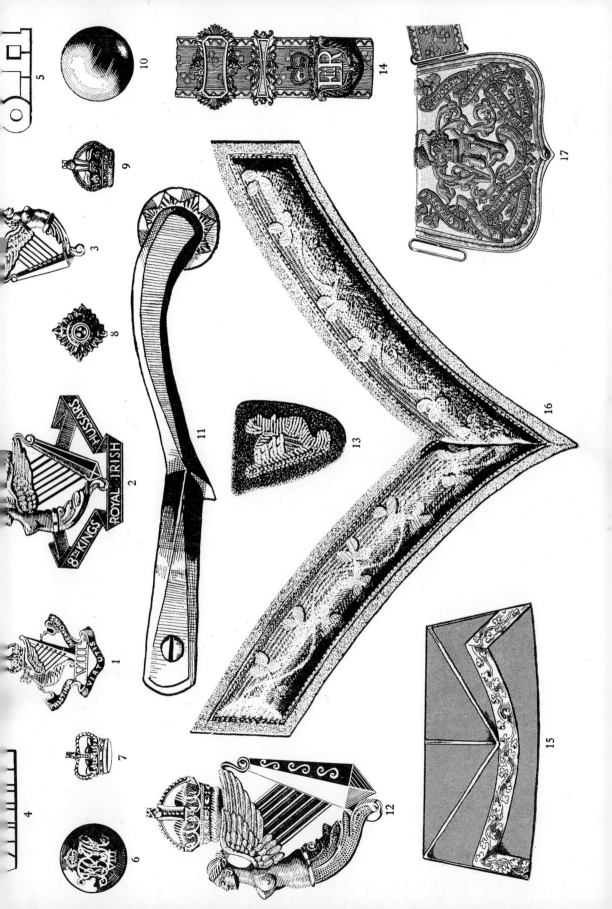

MISCELLANEOUS NOTES ON DRESS NOT ILLUSTRATED

The forage cap (No. 1 Dress hat) was of universal pattern, the whole in red cloth with black patent leather chinstrap and peak. Field officers wore the universal pattern gold braid on the peak.

The Green 'smoking' suit was worn optionally by the Officers in the evening. This was of green cloth, double breasted. It bore Officers Regimental pattern buttons but no badges of rank; and was worn with a white shirt and black evening tie.

The Stable belt was worn optionally by all ranks, in shirt sleeve order. It was of emerald green webbing and was fastened by a single large plain brass buckle in the case of officers, and by two small white metal buckles in the form of stirrup irons for other ranks.

A dark green lanyard was worn by all other ranks excepting the R.S.M. and the Bandmaster upon the right shoulder in S.D. and B.D.

Shoulder chains were worn by all ranks on No. 1 Dress.

Officers Greatcoats were embellished by narrow yellow piping on the shoulder straps, collar, and cuffs.

APPENDIX VI

MAIN FIGHTING EQUIPMENT OF THE VIII KING'S ROYAL IRISH HUSSARS

1928–1958

	Fighting Equipment	*Armament*	*Dates*	*Notes*
HORSED REGIMENT	Horses	Sword and rifle One troop: ·303 Vickers M.G.	1928–35	
RECONNAISSANCE	Ford 'pick-up' cars	·303 Vickers Berthier M.G.	1935–39	
LIGHT TANK REGIMENT	Vickers Mk. VIb. Light tanks	·5 Vickers H.M.G. ·303 Vickers M.M.G.	1939–41	
	One squadron Cruiser tanks	2-pdr. Gun 7·62-m.m. Besa M.G.	1939–41	For some of this period
	General Stuart tanks	37-mm. Gun ·30 Browning M.G.	1941	
MEDIUM TANK REGIMENT	General Grant tanks	75-mm. Gun 37-mm. Gun ·30 Browning M.G.	1942	
	One squadron General Stuart tanks			
ARMOURED CAR REGIMENT	Marmon Harrington Armoured Cars Daimler Armoured cars Humber Armoured cars	·05 Boys A/Tk. rifle ·303 Bren L.M.G. 2-pdr. Gun 7·62-mm. Besa M.G.	1943	Initially squadrons were equipped with Marmon Harringtons with one Daimler per troop. Later Humbers were substituted for the Marmon Harringtons.

MEDIUM TANK REGIMENT	Cromwell tanks	75-mm. Gun two 7·62-mm. Besa M.G.	1944–45	After Normandy one 17-pdr. tank per tp. was added. Later succeeded by Chaffee tanks with 75-mm. Gun
	Recce troop General Stuart tanks			
	Comet tanks	77-mm. Gun two 7·62-mm. Besa M.G.	1945–50	
	Centurion tanks	20-pdr. Gun 7·62-mm. Besa M.G.	1950–Amalgamation	
	Recce troop Cromwell tanks		1950–51	In Korea

MAIN FIGHTING EQUIPMENT, 1928-58.

Troop Horses, 1928-1935.

Ford Pick-up Car, 1935-1939.

Cruiser Tank, 1939-1941.

Mark IV Light Tanks
1939-1941.

Marmon Harrington
Armoured Cars, 1943.

'Honey' or 'General Stuart' Tank
1941–1945.

General Grant Tank
1942.

Humber Armoured Car
1943.

Cromwell Tank, 1944-45.

Centurion Tank. 1950-Amalgamation.

APPENDIX VII

EXTRACTS FROM THE
VIIIᴛʜ KING'S ROYAL IRISH HUSSARS WAGERS BOOK

1. (First recorded in Wager Book).
   'Clowes backed the telegraph versus Army Signalling to furnish the result of the Derby in 1895 from the Grand Stand, Epsom to Hounslow barracks.'
   Result:—Sandwitt with the Regimental signallers won.

2. '2nd Lieutenant Anderson backs himself for £2 to run against 2nd Lieutenant Broadhurst's pony Mercury 40 yards round a post and back, 1902.'
   Result:—Pony wins by 15 yards.

3. '2nd Lieutenant Charters bets 2nd Lieutenant Blackloch an even £5 that he (Blackloch) is summoned for excessive speed, and danger to the public, before he (Charters) is.'
   Result:—2nd Lieutenant Blackloch wins.
   2nd Lieutenant Charters fined at Greenwich 14.11.08.

4. 'Lieutenant Weldon challenges Lieutenant Ryder to a race from the mess to the Ipswich Arms public house, the former mounted, the latter driving his car, and having to wind his car up after the word go. Routes at choice of competitors.
   P.S. Race postponed in case of meeting a funeral or a policeman hoving in sight.'
   Result:—Undecided; Lieutenant Ryder held up by a locked gate.

5. 'Mussenden bets Alexander Rs 10 that he (Mussenden) shoots a tiger before Alexander does. (28.7.14).'
   Result:—Bet off. Both missed.

6. 'Captain Daly bets Lieutenant Paton £15 to £5 that Captain Straniland (nominated by Captain Daly) is married before 2nd Lieutenant Woodhouse (nominated by Lieutenant Paton). Death on the part of either of the runners cancels the bet.'
   Result:—Daly wins. Lieutenant Paton's nomination just surviving last condition of bet. Paid 1st September 1928.

7. 'At the Cavalry Barracks Wiesbaden on December 19th, 1926. Major Pope bets Major Regnart £5 that given two vessels of similar shape and capacity, one of copper, the other of marble, that if these vessels be filled with water of equal temperature and volume and the temperature taken at the same time, the temperature of the water in the marble vessel will be higher than that in the copper vessel. The temperature to be taken at the time the water is turned off.'
   Result:—Pope wins. Paid 29.9.27.

8. 'Lieutenant Wodehouse bets Captain Watson 20 marks to 10 marks that the copper bath is the hotter under conditions as above.'

   Result:—Wodehouse pays Watson.

   'Lieutenant Lowther bets Lieutenant de Clermont a level fiver (£5) that he (de Clermont) is married in a church before Lieutenant Lowther.

   In the event of de Clermont losing, and the lucky woman is a platinum blonde Lieutenant Lowther will forfeit £25.'

   Result:—'Lowther is the UNLUCKY looser' [sic!] Paid in Vestry, Holy Trinity, Brompton 18.7.39.

9. 'Major Watson bets C. Goulburn an even £1 that Gordon Richards is declared an undischarged bankrupt within five years of riding his two hundredth winner. 1933.'

   Result:—Unsettled. Watson died 1952. Gordon Richards still riding, still champion jockey and nigh a millionaire!

10. 'Major Bell bets Lieutenant Dunne fifty piastres that Captain (Bimbarlis) Kilkelly makes a century during his tour of duty in Egypt, with the Regiment. (The decision of the Men's Committee to be final).'

    Result:—Lieutenant Dunne loses as the Bimbarlis made a century against a team, elected by Bell, composed of the lame, the rich and the blind. Paid.

11. 'Cornet Bernard Kelly bets Cornet Anthony Donadio an even £2 that he (the party of the first part) will be demobilised before the party of the second part, notwithstanding the disparity between their release groups, and the vicissitudes of nature. By mutual agreement the "vicissitudes of nature" are to include any device, artifice or stratagem employed by either. Graft to be regarded as an Act of God. March 29th, 1939.'

    Result:—Cornet Kelly wins. Settled.

12. 'Hurst wagers Graham an even sovereign that he (Graham) will not eat the candle which is placed before him at dinner tonight during the course of the meal. 9.10.52.'

    Result:—Graham wins!! Having taken it with fish, meat and savoury.

13. "Captain Dill wagers Lieutenant Hurst an even five (5) pounds that he (Lieutenant Hurst) cannot drink all the port remaining in the three decanters (all practically full!) before midnight. The wager being laid at 2207 hours.'

    Result:—Hurst wins—3 pints of port in 63 minutes.

14. 'Lieutenant R. O. G. Wood wagers Cornet B. H. F. Wright the sum of three pounds that Cornet Wright will not eat either 20 Players Cigarettes, or the ash therefrom in 30 minutes, without the aforesaid Cornet vomiting.'

    Result:—Cornet Wright wins by 30 seconds.

15. 'Major Richard Dill wagers Cornet Mike Oliver £4.0.0 that he will not consume all the petals (chrysanthemums) in the two bowls in the ante-room within one hour. 5th November, 1958.'

    Result:—Dill wins. Oliver defeated by the smell after consuming three-quarters of the first bowl in 40 minutes.

16. 'Capt John Paley 4th Light Dragoons bets Major John Weston-Simons, Cunninghams Dragoons that Captain Noolan belonged to the 15th Hussars and not to the 16th Hussars.'

   Result:—Captain John Paley wins. Simons paid 3 June 1954.

17. 'Major Richard Dill wagered the assembled company on the Lavenbury Ferry, one sovereign to nil, that no one would push the doctor (Captain M. Browne) into the Elbe. June 1954.'

   Result:—Pierson pushed.
   Dill paid.
   The doctor got very wet.

18. 'Cooke wagers Webster that he, Cooke, can, with one leg in plaster walk faster forwards than Webster can backwards, the distance from the mess to the gate, and for half a sovereign.'

   Result:—Cooke wins.
   The doctor was on leave otherwise Cooke would have gone back to hospital accompanied by Webster with multiple hand injuries.

19. 'Lieutenant Waller wagers Cornet Scrimgeour an even 10/- that he can stand on one leg longer than him (the latter). 15.7.57.'

   Result:—Scrimgeour wins in an open push after no less than 31 minutes on one leg.

APPENDIX VIII

AFFILIATED REGIMENTS

(a) Brief History of the 6th Duke of Connaught's Royal Canadian Hussars

DURING the war of 1812-14 between Great Britain and the United States of America, the Montreal Cavalry was raised as a Volunteer unit for the defence of Canada under the command of a British Regular Officer, Colonel Baynes. No. 1 Troop of the Montreal Cavalry was raised by Captain George Platt, with George Gillespie as Lieutenant and John Molson as Cornet. No. 1 Troop was employed on patrols along the U.S.-Canada frontier and also carried despatches to Kingston, Ontario, whence the despatches were relayed to York, as Toronto was then known, by a York troop of Volunteer Cavalry which is now perpetuated by the Governor General's Horse Guards of Toronto. The Montreal Cavalry was thus one of the two oldest Volunteer cavalry units in Canada. Sir George Prevost, the British Commander-in-Chief in Canada, was so pleased with the work of the Montreal Cavalry that he authorized it to assume the title 'Royal Montreal Cavalry', which it continued to bear until absorbed into the newly formed Canadian Militia in 1855 as the 'Montreal Squadron' of Cavalry.

The Royal Montreal Cavalry saw service during the rebellion of 1837-38 and took part in operations at St. Charles, St. Eustache, Napierville and along the U.S. border.

In 1849 the passing of the Rebellion Losses Bill led to serious rioting in Montreal where Lord Elgin was pelted with stones while driving through the streets from 'Monklands', the Vice-Regal residence, to the Assembly meeting at the Chateau de Ramezay and back again. Lord Elgin was saved from death or serious injury by a Volunteer troop of the Queen's Light Dragoons, part of the Royal Montreal Cavalry.

The outbreak of the Crimean War in 1854 led to the withdrawal from Canada of a number of units of the British Regular Army forming part of the Canadian garrison. The Canadian Government hastily passed the Militia Act of 1855 by which existing Volunteer units were incorporated as Active Militia units. Sixteen independent troops of cavalry were authorized, including the Royal Montreal Cavalry which was redesignated the 'Montreal Cavalry', and consisted of No. 1 and No. 2 Troops and the Royal Guides Troop.

By 1865 the Montreal Cavalry was authorized to draw 16 days pay annually for men and horses who attended 32 parades of $2\frac{1}{2}$ hours each. All training pay was pooled and spent for the good of the units, and recruits were ballotted for admission, three black balls sufficing to disqualify a candidate. A system of officer training was set up by the 13th Hussars, a British Regular Cavalry regiment then stationed in Canada at Toronto and on St. Helen's Island opposite Montreal. The 13th Hussars also furnished instructors to the Montreal Cavalry who adopted Hussars dress 'as for 13th Hussars' as a tribute to the cordial relations which existed between the 13th Hussars and the Montreal Cavalry.

In 1866 the Montreal Squadron of Cavalry took part in an operation at Pigeon Hill against Fenian raiders from South of the U.S. border in which the Prince of Wales Rifles (now the Canadian Grenadier Guards), the Victoria Rifles and the 3rd Montreal Battery repulsed and defeated the Fenians, who fled with the Royal Guides troop of the Montreal Squadron in hot pursuit.

In 1867 No. 2 Troop and the Royal Guides Troop of the Montreal Squadron were disbanded, leaving No. 1 Troop, Montreal Cavalry as the sole Militia cavalry unit in Montreal. On the 24th May, 1867, while the Montreal Garrison were assembling on the Champ de Mars for a Queen's Birthday review, word came that the Fenians were gathering south of the U.S. border for another raid. The entire Montreal Garrison was entrained as rapidly as possible for St. Johns, Que. No. 1 Troop, Montreal Cavalry and the Victoria Rifles of Canada went on and detrained at Stanbridge East. Next day the Fenians attacked Eccles Hill and were repulsed by a company of the 60th Rifles, a British Regular rifle battalion, assisted by local home guard units. The Victoria Rifles, with No. 1 Troop covering their flank, joined the 60th Rifles and about 5 p.m. joined in an attack which drove the Fenians headlong from the field. For this operation the Victoria Rifles were awarded the battle honour 'Eccles Hill'. The Fenian raids were over.

In 1879 the Canadian Government decided to group together in regiments of cavalry the Independent troops of cavalry localized along the U.S. border. Some independent companies of infantry and batteries of artillery were converted into cavalry for this purpose. The 6th Hussars was the Quebec regiment of cavalry formed in this manner, with eight troops localized along the border from Hemmingford to Stanstead in the Eastern Townships. Five regiments were localized in Ontario.

The Montreal Cavalry were not included in the formation of the 6th Hussars in 1879 and No. 1 Troop remained as an independent Troop, the only one in Montreal. In 1891, No. 1 Troop, Montreal Cavalry furnished an escort to T.R.H. the Duke and Duchess of Connaught during their visit to Montreal.

In 1894 consideration was given to the formation of a regiment of Cavalry in and around Montreal. The Montreal Cavalry was redesignated the 'Duke of Connaught's Royal Canadian Hussars' and granted permission to wear as cap and collar badges the personal badge of the Duke of Connaught, a lion guardant on a royal ducal coronet. No. 1 Troop, Montreal Cavalry became 'No. 1 Troop, Duke of Connaught's Royal Canadian Hussars', under command of Captain A. F. Clerk.

In August 1896 the Duke of Connaught's Royal Canadian Hussars were amalgamated with the 6th Hussars. The amalgamated regiment was designated the '6th Duke of Connaught's Royal Canadian Hussars" and was permitted to wear the Duke of Connaught's personal badge. No. 1 Troop, Duke of Connaught's Royal Canadian Hussars became 'A' Squadron, 6th Duke of Connaught's Royal Canadian Hussars, under the command of Captain F. Whitley.

The union was not an enduring one, for in June 1897 'A' Squadron, 6th Duke of Connaught's Royal Canadian Hussars was detached from the regiment as an independent Squadron to be known thereafter as the 'Montreal Hussars'.

The 6th Duke of Connaught's Royal Canadian Hussars, with its squadrons localized along the U.S. border, continued to function actively and efficiently as a rural cavalry regiment. In 1904, owing to the formation of a new Eastern Townships cavalry regiment, the 13th Scottish Light Dragoons with squadrons from Stanbridge East to Stanstead, the 6th Duke of Connaught's Royal Canadian Hussars, now part of the 4th Mounted Brigade, was relocalized with squadrons at Covey Hill, Hemmingford, Huntingdon and Lacolle.

In 1920 the Canadian Militia was re-organized. The 6th Duke of Connaught's Royal Canadian Hussars became inactive and remained so for over a decade.

In 1936 the Canadian Militia was re-organized and to some extent streamlined. The 6th Duke of Connaught's Royal Canadian Hussars was reactivated and amalgamated with the 1st Canadian Motor Machine Gun Brigade to form an armoured car regiment. An alliance was approved between the 6th Duke of Connaught's Royal Canadian Hussars and the 8th King's Royal Irish Hussars which, like the 13th Hussars, took part in the celebrated charge of the Light Brigade at Balaclava. Permission was granted for the Regiment to wear as a cap badge the personal arms of the Duke of Connaught which are the old arms of the Kingdom of Connaught, which are, dexter, a demi eagle displayed, sinister, an arm holding a dagger, all borne upon two sabres crossed above a VI over a scroll 6th D.C.R.C.H.

Montreal thus possessed two city regiments of Militia cavalry, the 6th D.C.R.C. Hussars (armoured car) and the 17th D.Y.R.C. Hussars (horsed), comprising the 3rd Cavalry Brigade. Both Regiments could claim to stem from the Montreal Cavalry from which they derived their titles and badges.

The record of War service of the Montreal Cavalry is impressive. As Volunteer Cavalry it took an active part in the War of 1812-14 against the United States. During the rebellion of 1837-38 the Montreal Cavalry were actively engaged in repelling the Fenian Raids of 1866 and 1867.

To the South African War of 1899-1902 Canada sent a large contingent consisting of the Royal Canadian Dragoons, the newly raised Lord Strathcona's Horse, the Royal Canadian Regiment and several regiments of Canadian Mounted Rifles, to which both the 6th Duke of Connaught's Royal Canadian Hussars sent officers and other ranks. The success of mounted rifles in the South African campaigns led to a large increase in cavalry regiments in Canada before the Great War of 1914-18.

In the Great War of 1914-18 Canada followed the precedent established in the South African War of 1899-1902 and raised special units for overseas service instead of embodying or mobilizing Militia units as such. In many cases these special units were raised under the auspices of Militia units, in which case all officers were first posted to the Militia unit and all other ranks first signed a service roll of the Militia unit, thus establishing a claim for battle honours awarded to the special unit.

In addition, Militia units were required to provide details for protection of vulnerable points and internment camps. The 6th Duke of Connaught's Royal Canadian Hussars organized and administered the 1st Composite Regiment which handled Militia guard details and personnel called out for service other than with the Canadian Expeditionary Force. In 1917 the Composite Regiment became part of the C.E.F.

A first step in mechanization was the despatching of two mobile machine gun units. One of these, the 1st Canadian Motor Machine Gun Brigade was raised in Montreal and served with great distinction throughout the War. At the conclusion of hostilities the 1st Canadian Motor Machine Gun Brigade became a Militia Unit in the Montreal Garrison and in 1936 was almalgamated with the 6th Duke of Connaught's Royal Canadian Hussars.

In 1939, upon the outbreak of World War II, the Canadian Government proceeded to mobilize Active Militia units as such or to call upon them to furnish special components of the Canadian Army 'Active'. Protection of vulnerable points was provided by Militia units called out for service until special constables acting under the Royal Canadian Mounted Police relieved them in November 1939. The 6th Duke of Connaught's Royal Canadian Hussars furnished details for these duties.

In 1941 the 6th Duke of Connaught's Royal Canadian Hussars were called upon to furnish the Headquarters Squadron of 5th Canadian Armoured Division which landed in England later in that year. In November 1943, 5th Canadian Armoured Division landed in Italy as part of 2nd Canadian Corps and the Division went into action in mid-January 1944. In February 1945 the Canadian Corps started to move by sea from Italy to Belgium and by March 15th the 1st Canadian Army were reunited under one command.

The 15th Armoured Regiment (6H) R.F., as the 6th Duke of Connaught's Royal Canadian Hussars were designated until the end of the war, furnished large numbers of recruits and officer replacements for the Canadian Armoured Corps and units in need of replacements.

Shortly after the conclusion of hostilities, the war-time designation the 15th Armoured Regiment (6H) was discontinued and the peace-time unit, now re-organized, became known once more as the 6th Duke of Connaught's Royal Canadian Hussars, R.C.A.C., retaining their role of an Armoured Regiment.

On September 16th, 1958 the 6th Duke of Connaught's Royal Canadian Hussars, R.C.A.C. were amalgamated with the 17th Duke of York's Royal Canadian Hussars, R.C.A.C. to form The Royal Canadian Hussars (Montreal) R.C.A.C.

(b) Brief History of the 8th/13th Victorian Mounted Rifles

1885 to 1948

ON 2nd November, 1885 the Governor-in-Council approved of the formation of the Victorian Mounted Rifles which was to consist of such members of Rifles Clubs as elected to join the Mounted Branch of the Club and were approved by the Officer Commanding the Battalion.

The rank and file were armed with the Martini Henry Rifle and Sword Bayonet; equipment issued consisted of regulation bit, bridle, haversack, water bag, regulation cloak and cape, head rope, heel rope and peg, wallets with straps, cloak straps and nose bag.

Each mounted rifleman supplied his own saddle and received no pay, but a maintenance allowance was granted to the unit on the basis of 20/- per annum for each effective member.

The first Commanding Officer of the Victorian Mounted Rifles was Lieut.-Colonel Tom Price, who had previously served in India and in the 103rd Foot (Dublin Fusiliers). Lieut.-Colonel Price was considered an exceptional judge of man and horse. The Organization and Training given to the Regiment was to prove very valuable in later years when the Commanding Officer and many members of the Regiment served in the South African War.

During this War, Lieut.-Colonel Price was given Command of the 2nd Australian Contingent and battle honours of the South African War are emblazoned on the Regimental Guidon.

After the South African War and Federation, the organization of the whole of the Australian Defence Forces was changed and the Cavalry Units were styled Australian Light Horse.

This Regiment perpetuates the 8th Light Horse Regiment (Indi Light Horse) the 13th Light Horse (Gippsland Light Horse) and the 20th Light Horse (Victorian Mounted Rifles), and the title is a combination of the titles of those Regiments.

Y

354 APPENDIX VIII

Each of these units served with distinction during the Great War, and the following Battle Honours earned in this War show the wide area over which the Units served:

8th Light Horse Regiment

Defence of Anzac 'Sari Bair', Rumani, Maghdaka-Rafak, Gaza-Beersheba, Jerusalem, Jordan (Es Salt) Megiddo, Sahron, Damascus.

13th Light Horse Regiment

Somme 1916-19, Pazieres Bapaum 1917, Arras 1917, Ypres 1917, Albert 1918, France and Flanders 1916-18, Gallipoli 1915, Egypt 1915-16.

20th Light Horse Regiment

Anzac, Gallipoli 1915, Egypt 1915-17, Palestine 1917-18.

After the Great War, the Australian Defence organization remained comparatively unchanged although until 1929 service was compulsory and from 1930 until 1939 service was voluntary.

Each of the 8th, 13th and 20th Light Horse Regiments was organized on a Militia Regiment throughout this period and on the outbreak of war in 1939 formed part of the forces available for the Defence of Australia and a source of recruits for the 2nd Australian Imperial Force which was raised for service overseas.

Due to the many re-organizations of the Australian Army during the 1939-45 War it is difficult to trace clearly the history of the various Light Horse Regiments.

The 8th Light Horse Regiment remained a Commonwealth Military Force Unit until 1944, although it was renamed the 8th Recce Battalion in 1941 and again the 8th Cavalry Regiment in 1942 and disbanded in 1944, whilst its A.I.F. counterpart the 8th Armoured Regiment A.I.F., was raised in 1941 as a part of the original 1 Australian Armoured Division and later as the 2/8th Armoured Regiment, served in New Guinea and, still later, the personnel took to the sea and performed very valuable service in the 41st, 42nd, and 43rd Landing Craft Companies R.A.E.

The 13th Light Horse Regiment was linked with the 19th Light Horse Regiment as the 13th/19th Light Horse Regiment, and later became the 13th Motor Regiment, and then the 13th Armoured Regiment, and was disbanded to provide Infantry reinforcements in 1943.

The 20th Light Horse Regiment was re-designated 20th Motor Regiment and later was re-organized as the 20th Pioneer Battalion and saw service in Dutch New Guinea.

On April 1st 1948, the 8th/13th Victorian Mounted Rifles was organized as an Armoured Regiment under the command of Lieut.-Colonel T. Fogarty. The Regiment was equipped with M3M Grant tanks. It covered much of Victoria since R.H.Q. and H.Q. squadron were in Carlton, Melbourne, 'A' squadron was at Albury, 'B' squadron at Wangaratta and Benalla and 'C' squadron at Sale.

In December 1948 the unit strength was 12 officers and 142 O.R.'s; December 1949 saw it doubled and in December 1954 the unit reached its post war-peak in size at 28 officers and 1056 O.R.'s. Since then the strength has stabilized at between 300-500.

The Regiment held its first post war camp at Puckapunyal in March 1949.

On the 16th July 1952 a minor re-organization within the unit found 'C' Squadron moving from Sale to Albury.

The Regiment won the Hutton Trophy on the 27th January 1954. This was won in competition with all C.M.F. Armoured Regiments in Australia, for the best Tank Troop.

The Regiment had the honour on 28th February 1954, of being inspected by Field-Marshal His Royal Highness Prince Philip, The Duke of Edinburgh K.G., Colonel-in-Chief of the VIII King's Royal Irish Hussars.

On 30th June 1954, Lieut.-Colonel Hibberd succeeded Lieut-Colonel T. Fogarty as Commanding Officer.

In 1954 the unit became affiliated with Melbourne University Regiment. It was in this year too, that the unit changed over from Grant to Centurion tanks.

April 1955 saw R.H.Q. and H.Q. Squadron moved from Melbourne to Wangaratta. Lieut.-Colonel J. M. Allard took command in June 1958.

In June 1960 the Australian Army re-organization came into effect. The Victorian Mounted Rifles then took over its new role as an Armoured Personal Carrier Regiment.

(c) Brief History of the 3rd Royal Australian Regiment

IN 1945 the war in the Pacific came to an end with the unconditional surrender of Japan. In order to enforce the surrender terms, those Allies who had fought in the Pacific Campaign were asked to contribute occupation forces. Australia's main Army Contribution to the occupation force was a brigade group, the 34th Brigade Group.

The infantry element of the 34th Brigade Group consisted of three battalions designated 65th, 66th and in particular the 67th Infantry Battalion. Initially the 67th Infantry Battalion was at Wewak, Bouganville and Rabaul from volunteers drawn from the 3rd, 6th and 11th Australian Divisions. In November 1945 the Battalion moved to Moratai where the 34th Brigade Group was concentrated.

In February 1946 the Battalion sailed for Japan. On arrival the Battalion was stationed at Kaitaichi in the Hiroshima Prefecture. Initial duties given to the Battalion were the screening of returned Japanese Troops and the supervision of polling booths when Japan's first post-war election was held. Later troops were detached to various centres to supervise the destruction of Japanese ammunition and explosives.

Other duties given to the Battalion were guards on the Imperial Palace, Tokyo, patrolling duties North of Hiroshima, and guard associated with the Britcom Sub Area Kobe.

In 1947 the Battalion moved to Okyama and continued its occupation duties and training. During this period, the Battalion commenced competing annually against other Battalions for the Gloucester Cup. The Cup was won by the Battalion three years in succession.

Throughout 1948 and 1949 many British Commonwealth units left Japan including the 65th and 66th Infantry Battalions, and as a result the Battalion was moved from Okyama to Hiro.

In November 1948 the Battalion was re-designated the 3rd Battalion, The Australian Regiment. In April 1949 His Majesty the late King George VI approved the prefix 'Royal'. The 67th Battalion was now the 3rd Battalion, The Royal Australian Regiment.

The Battalion was preparing to return to Australia in 1950 when the Korean War broke out. Australia offered elements of all three services to the United Nations, which accepted. Australia's main Army commitment was to provide an Infantry Battalion. In August 1950 the 3rd R.A.R. was warned for service in Korea. Urgently needed reinforcements were flown in from Australia to bring the Battalion up to strength.

On the 27th September 1950 the Battalion disembarked at Pusan, Korea, and moved to Taegu joining the 27th Britcom Infantry Brigade. While settling down it was engaged in anti-guerilla patrolling. In October 1950 the Battalion was lifted by air to Kimpo to take part in the 8th Army Offensive. During this offensive the Battalion reached Yagadong, which at the time was the most northerly point reached by a United Nations unit. In November 1950, when the Chinese Communist Forces intervened in the war, the Battalion was only 50 miles south of the Yalu River.

During the 'Spring Offensive' of 1951 the Battalion captured a number of important features and had advanced as far as Kapyong when it was relieved by units of the 6th Republic of Korea Division. On the night of the 22nd/23rd April 1951 the C.C.F. launched an offensive and the 6th R.O.K. Division withdrew. The Battalion was encircled. Although suffering heavy casualties, successive counter attacks were launched until the position was restored. For this action the unit was singled out for distinction and was awarded the Distinguished Unit Citation by the President of the United States of America.

After the collapse of the C.C.F. offensive the Battalion joined the 28th Britcom Infantry Brigade, which formation became part of the 1st Commonwealth Division formed in July 1951.

In October 1951 the 1st Comwel Division launched its first major offensive north of the River Imjim. The Battalion played a major part in this offensive called 'Operation Commando'. The Battalion assisted in the capture of Point 355 and played the leading part in the capture of Point 317.

Peace talks were resumed in November 1951. As a result no major offensives were launched after this time. Instead patrolling and company-sized raids were carried out. The Battalion occupied various positions in what was called the Jamestown Line, with brief periods in Brigade and Corps reserve. The Battalion became known for the aggressiveness of its patrols, and the procedures largely evolved by the Battalion were accepted as the basis of the Divisional police for the organization and control of patrols.

After the Armistice on July 27th, 1953, the Battalion occupied positions on the new demarcation line and assisted in the enforcement of peace.

As a result of its service in Korea the Battalion was given the nickname 'Old Faithful'. On 9th November 1954 after more than four years in Korea the Battalion departed for Australia, arriving on the 20th November 1954. At this stage the Battalion had been in existence for nine years, but had never served in Australia.

Throughout 1955 and 1956 the Battalion was based at Ingleburn, New South Wales, and in May 1957 the Battalion moved to Gallipoli Barracks, Holsworthy, New South Wales.

The Battalion embarked at Sydney on the 25th September 1957 for service in Malaya. In Malaya, the unit was stationed in the area of Sungei Siput, Perak. In the campaign against the Communist Terrorists, the Battalion was responsible for fourteen eliminations.

The Battalion returned to Enoggera, Queensland on the 18th September 1959.

APPENDIX IX

OLD COMRADES ASSOCIATION

The 8th King's Royal Irish Hussars Association

PATRONS

General Rt. Hon. Sir Bryan T. Mahon, P.C., K.C.B., K.C.V.O., D.S.O.   1905–1930
Brigadier John Van der Byl, D.S.O.   1931–1946
Air Marshal Sir John E. A. Baldwin, K.B.E., C.B., D.S.O., D.L.   1947–1953
H.R.H. The Prince Philip, Duke of Edinburgh, K.G., P.C., K.T., etc.   1954–1958

VICE PATRON

Air Marshal Sir John E. A. Baldwin, K.B.E., C.B., D.S.O., D.L.   1954–1958

PRESIDENTS

Lieut.-Colonel H. N. M. Thoyts	1905–1918
Lieut.-Colonel F. W. Mussenden	1919–1931
Lieut.-Colonel H. N. Clegg	1931–1932
Major A. R. Mulliner, M.C.	1933–1945
Major R. H. Ames	1946–1947
Mr. A. V. Rogers	1948–1956
Major J. Robertson	1956–1958

HONORARY SECRETARIES

Mr. H. W. Pamplin	1905–1934
Mr. A. V. Rogers	1935–1946
Lieut.-Colonel J. Middleton, O.B.E.	1947–1958

In 1905 the Commanding Officer, Lieut.-Colonel H. N. M. Thoyts, formed 'The Old Comrades' Association', to bring and hold together past and present members of the Regiment, to foster and maintain its traditions.

From 1906 until the outbreak of war in 1914 a reunion dinner was held in the early summer each year, in London. An Irish branch was formed in Dublin in 1913. The renuions were always well supported, and after the end of the war in 1919 they were resumed. Three years later in October, a concert was held in London to commemorate the action of the Regiment in the charge at Balaclava. This too became an annual event and all three continued to flourish until the outbreak of the Second World War in 1939.

In May 1930 when the Regiment was stationed at Aldershot, a Rally of Old Comrades was held at Beaumont Barracks. The festivities lasted for a week and so great was the success that a similar Rally was held again in 1932. Regrettably these could not be resumed owing to the Regiment's posting, and its subsequent service overseas which was virtually continuous.

In 1939, through the good offices of Mrs. J. Van der Byl, the wives of past officers presented the Association with a banner. This portrayed the full crest, finely worked in gold, silver and coloured thread, on a field of crimson silk.

After the end of the Second World War the London reunions were resumed in 1946, and were attended by many of those who had served in its campaigns. A year later the title of the Association was changed to 'The 8th King's Royal Irish Hussars Association'.

In 1954, the centenary of Balaclava, H.R.H. The Duke of Edinburgh honoured the Association by consenting to become its Patron. On the 25th October a large reunion was held to commemorate the Charge of the Light Brigade, and in memory of this a special medallion was struck which was issued to all members who attended.

The news of the forthcoming amalgamation was announced in 1958. The circular ended with these words:—

"All serving personnel are determined that the amalgamation shall proceed smoothly and that the new Regiment will be a worthy successor and contain the best of both Regiments.

"This task will be considerably lightened if all we who love our Regiment approach the problem sympathetically and do everything in our power to foster and increase the respect and admiration that the 4th and 8th, as two famous cavalry regiments, have always had for each other."

INDEX

INDEX